D0119271

Sunset
Recipe Annual

2000 EDITION

Cream Puff Sundaes (page 53)

By the Editors of Sunset Magazine
and Sunset Books

Sunset Publishing Corporation ■ Menlo Park, California

SUNSET BOOKS

VP, General Manager
Richard A. Smeby

Editorial Director
Bob Doyle

Production Director
Lory Day

Art Director
Vasken Guiragossian

STAFF FOR THIS BOOK
Managing Editor
Cornelia Fogle

Production Coordinator
Patricia A. Williams

SUNSET PUBLISHING CORPORATION

President/Chief Executive Officer
Steve Seabolt

VP, Consumer Marketing Director
Robert I. Gursha

VP, Manufacturing Director
Lorinda Reichert

VP, Editor-in-Chief, Sunset Magazine
Rosalie Muller Wright

Managing Editor
Carol Hoffman

Art Director
James H. McCann

Senior Editor, Food & Entertaining
Jerry Anne Di Vecchio

Designer, Food & Entertaining
Dennis W. Leong

Chicken Cacciatore with noodles (page 241)

This year's edition of the *Sunset Recipe Annual* bids farewell to the familiar 1900s and welcomes a new century and new millenium.

You'll find bits of nostalgia in articles featuring recipes for meals on the farm, leisurely Sunday suppers, a neighborhood potluck, and a fiesta-style barbecue reminiscent of early California's hacienda hospitality.

Yet as we celebrate our past, we also look ahead. Take a look at some of the West's emerging wine regions, and investigate the resurgence of artisan cheesemaking. Learn what's new on the farm and in the markets. Try our ideas for easy entertaining, including parties inspired by the foods of India, Bali, and Spain.

Join us in a festive celebration as we move into an exciting new era, filled with stimulating ideas.

Cover: Fiesta barbecue tacos (page 148). Cover design: Vasken Guiragossian. Photographer: James Carrier.

Back cover photographers: (top) Leigh Beisch; (center) James Carrier; (bottom) Just Loomis/FRESHSTOCK.

First printing November 1999
Copyright © 1999 Sunset Publishing Corporation, Menlo Park, CA 94025. First edition.
All rights reserved, including the right of reproduction in whole or in part in any form.

ISBN 0-376-02705-3 (hardcover)
ISBN 0-376-02706-1 (softcover)
ISSN 0896-2170
Printed in the United States

Material in this book originally appeared in the 1999 issues of *Sunset Magazine*. All of the recipes were developed and tested in the *Sunset* test kitchens. If you have comments or suggestions, please let us hear from you. Write us at Sunset Books, Cookbook Editorial, 80 Willow Road, Menlo Park, CA 94025.

Contents

A Letter from Sunset

DEAR READER,

You may not think that events in today's news have much to do with tomorrow's dinner, but the way we cook and how we eat is influenced by new developments—sometimes significantly, sometimes subtly.

The timeliest example is the arrival of the year 2000. Turning the calendar page from one year to the next is always an occasion; moving from one century to another is all the more exciting. But entering a new millennium—well, that declares, "Party on!" (page 312)—a spirit of celebration to enjoy even when the year loses its youth.

As we approach an all-new era, there has been an upwelling of nostalgia for comfortingly familiar Sunday suppers, like those Lyle Davis and his wife, Sylvia Tawse, serve on their Colorado farm (page 48). Likewise with the not-quite-so "retro" roast chicken supper Rene Behnke presents to family and friends in her Seattle kitchen (page 52). Of similar sociability is the food lovers' picnic on page 220; this potluck, staged weekly during the summer, is the way Christina Ricci and friends weave together a friendly sense of neighborhood in busy Berkeley, California.

Enthusiasm for organic farming and sustainable agriculture has continued to gain steam. One outcome has been an explosion of lavishly stocked all-natural-foods supermarkets. Another has been improved selection in regular supermarkets, including organically grown produce and a steady supply of fresh herbs. Fresh bounty from our own gardens—or a farmers' market, or a produce-savvy supermarket—is cause for celebrations like Helene Henderson's spring garden party (page 70) in the Los Angeles area. In Noel Richardson's case, on Vancouver Island (page 152), fragrant home-grown herbs flavor the dishes she shares with friends for dinner.

Changing ethnic demographics have produced another kind of grocery store—the ethnic super. Be they Mexican, Chinese, Japanese, Southeast Asian, or even Indian, many stores that provide ingredients for dishes of specific cuisines are full-fledged, full-service supermarkets—with parking included. Ingredients introduced by these markets have become such everyday staples—from Asian fish sauce to dehydrated masa (tortilla flour)—that they can also be found in many supermarkets throughout the West. Shop a regular or ethnic super to produce Elena Cota's grand rancho-style San Diego fiesta barbecue (page 144), a Balinese party sparked with "Island sizzle" (page 122), or Laxmi Hiremath's intriguing sampler of Indian foods (page 32).

From my perspective, India's once-exotic cuisine is finally entering home cooking. More and more, talented specialists like Laxmi are translating the complexities of Indian foods into easy steps for Western kitchens. We have many more Indian food markets as resources, and a delicious plethora of Indian restaurants that serve very tasty dishes—especially vegetarian choices—relished by a big non-Indian following.

Food makes its own news, too. What's happening as artisan cheeses are revived and reinvented? See page 96. What are the new wine regions in the West, and how good are their wines? See page 170. What's new on the shelves? See "Amazing grapes" (page 230), "Fresh bean bounty" (page 196), "A passion for papayas" (page 104), and "A new dairy tale" (defining and using nondairy milks), page 85.

In Silicon Valley, where we're headquartered, technology is hot. So is how an oven heats. When *Sunset*'s test kitchen was updated last year, all the ovens installed were equipped with

THE FOOD WRITERS: (left to right, front) Elaine Johnson and Linda Lau Anusasananan, senior writers; Jerry Anne Di Vecchio, department editor; (back row) Andrew Baker, writer; Sara Schneider, senior editor.

THE SUPPORT GANG: (left to right, front) Bernadette Hart, editorial services and test kitchen manager; Angela Brassinga and Odette Morais, retesters; Eligio Hernandez, editorial services; (center) Dennis Leong, associate art director; Lisa Anusasananan, Linda Tebben, Bill Hickey, and Adele Di Giorgio, retesters; (rear) Keith Whitney, associate art director; James Carrier, staff photographer. On call but not pictured: Jacqeline John, associate photography editor, and Dorothy Decker, Allene Russell, Jean Strain, and Molly van Wagenen, retesters.

the option of convection heating. Now all oven recipes are tested using both regular and convection heat—similar to our barbecue recipes, which are all tested using both charcoal and gas as fuel.

Another extra mile we've gone for you is straight up. We've often given general directions for baking at high altitude. But in this book, all baking recipes have been tested at a mile high. When modifications are required, recipes include specifically tailored instructions.

Adding these services hasn't slowed down the flow of articles that highlight what's best in the West. As an example, we present a superb Thanksgiving picnic in a desert setting (page 278) and, for other territories, "Thanksgiving on the go" (page 260)—a grand collection of make-ahead dishes that journey well over the hills and through the woods, or just next door. An extra-easy party (page 54) and a delectable tapas menu (page 214) keep guests happily serving themselves. "Hooked on the grill" (page 184) takes the mystique out of barbecuing fish, and "Great catch!" (page 28) presents glorious fish stews that are perfect for easy dinner parties.

Quick, light, and healthy are the required qualities in "Single-pan suppers" (page 7), a collection that I, as a time-pressured cook, often make good use of at home. More recipes in the same vein appear in the regular features, *The Quick Cook* and *The Low-Fat Cook*. In my monthly *Food Guide*, I share my favorite recipes and news about foods, tools, and techniques. Our *Wine Guide*, by wine expert Karen MacNeil-Fife, provides extremely useful information and excellent wine choices; Karen's "monthly steal" tips are a great service to value-conscious oenophiles.

It takes quite a team to put together *Sunset*'s food section. In our annual "yearbook" pictures, you meet most of us—food writers and our invaluable behind-the-scenes crew. To learn more about the magazine and the rest of the team, visit us at our website (www.sunset.com). Click on "magazine" for excerpts of the current issue or click "subscribe" to become a regular reader or renew your subscription. If you are already a subscriber, enter your password and user i.d. (new each month in the *From the Editor* column) to access a two-year collection of articles. Either way, you can share your comments, ask a question or two, or submit recipes.

We love hearing from you. Your ideas and questions today help make our news for tomorrow.

Jerry Di Vecchio

Jerry Di Vecchio
Senior Editor, Food and Entertaining

For how to use our nutritional information, see page 336.

Prepared and cooked in a single pan, Salmon Fettuccine with Wasabi Sauce is ready to eat in just 15 minutes (recipe on page 16).

January

Mac and Cheese with Bacon and Peas

light *quick & healthy*

Single-pan suppers

On the stove or in the oven—27 self-contained meals in about half an hour

I can't resist a recipe for a one-pan meal—no stoveful of frying pans to tend, no sinkful of dirty utensils. On the other hand, I can't bear to reduce good ingredients to an indecipherable mess. But with a few simple tricks, I don't have to; one cooking container can produce sophisticated, flavorful meals.

Pastas, for instance, can be cooked in their sauces, casseroles assembled in their baking dishes. And for more complex presentations, I cook the ingredients in sequence in the same pan (a little heating in the microwave oven is a legitimate part of my plan).

These recipes are inspired by American classics, favorite flavors from south of the border, familiar Asian preparations, and old European traditions. Each dish belies its simplicity, tasting as if it required slow simmering or many steps. Our secrets are yours, unless someone else volunteers to wash up the pans—er, *pan*.

BY ANDREW BAKER • PHOTOGRAPHS BY JAMES CARRIER

AMERICAN STYLE

A NEW SPIN on an old classic. Macaroni cooks right in the sauce, a creamy blend of milk and broth. Add Canadian bacon and peas, then natural reduced-fat cheddar cheese, and stir until smooth. It's a one-pan operation—no draining, no fussing.

Mac and Cheese with Bacon and Peas

PREP AND COOK TIME: About 12 minutes

MAKES: 4 servings

- 2 cups fat-skimmed **chicken broth**
- 1 cup **nonfat milk**
- ½ pound **dried elbow macaroni**
- 1 tablespoon **cornstarch**
- 1 cup **frozen petite peas**
- ¼ pound **Canadian bacon,** cut into thin strips
- 1½ cups (6 oz.) **shredded reduced-fat sharp cheddar cheese**
  Fresh-ground **pepper**
  Fresh-grated **nutmeg**

1. In a 4- to 5-quart pan over high heat, bring broth, milk, and macaroni to a boil. Stir mixture often until the pasta is tender to bite, about 10 minutes.

2. Blend cornstarch and 3 tablespoons water until smooth. Stir into pan and continue stirring until mixture boils.

3. Add peas and Canadian bacon; mix well and remove from heat. Sprinkle cheese over pasta mixture and stir just until melted, 1 to 2 minutes.

4. Spoon into wide bowls or onto plates and sprinkle generously with pepper and nutmeg.

Per serving: 469 cal., 23% (108 cal.) from fat; 32 g protein; 12 g fat (6.9 g sat.); 53 g carbo (4.1 g fiber); 896 mg sodium; 45 mg chol.

Warm Spinach Salad

PREP AND COOK TIME: **About 30 minutes**

NOTES: To create a Cobb salad, put spinach in individual bowls and group each topping separately on leaves.

MAKES: 4 servings

- 1 package (10 oz.) **washed spinach leaves**
- 1/4 pound **turkey bacon,** chopped
- 1 cup finely chopped **red onion**
- 1 package (10 oz.) **frozen corn kernels**
- 1/2 cup **red wine vinegar**
- 4 teaspoons **sugar**
- 1/4 cup **crumbled blue cheese**
- 2 cups **purchased fat-free croutons**

1. If desired, stack spinach leaves and cut into 1/2-inch-wide strips. Mound spinach equally onto plates.

2. In a 10- to 12-inch nonstick frying pan over high heat, stir turkey bacon until browned and crisp, about 5 minutes. Spoon equal portions of the bacon over spinach.

3. To pan, add onion, corn, vinegar, and sugar. Stir mixture until onion is limp, 3 to 4 minutes. With a slotted spoon, transfer onion and corn onto spinach, then spoon cooking liquid over salads.

4. Arrange blue cheese equally on salads and add croutons.

Per serving: 265 cal., 28% (74 cal.) from fat; 12 g protein; 8.2 g fat (2.7 g sat.); 36 g carbo (3.4 g fiber); 721 mg sodium; 27 mg chol.

Buttermilk Crab Chowder

PREP AND COOK TIME: **About 30 minutes**

NOTES: Flo Braker of Palo Alto, baker and author of many cookbooks, created this delicately flavored, simple chowder. She adds crunchy green cucumber to each bowl for a burst of color and texture.

MAKES: 4 servings

- 1 pound **Yukon Gold potatoes**
- 1 cup chopped **carrots**
- 1 1/2 cups fat-skimmed **chicken broth**
- 1 pound **shelled cooked crab**
- 3 cups **low-fat buttermilk**
- 1 cup finely chopped **English cucumber**
  Salt
  Fresh-ground **pepper**

1. Scrub potatoes and cut into 1/2-inch chunks.

2. In a 4- to 5-quart pan over high heat, combine potatoes, carrots, and broth. Cover, bring to a boil, and cook until potatoes and carrots are tender when pierced, 10 to 12 minutes.

3. Meanwhile, remove any bits of shell from crab.

4. Add buttermilk to pan and stir until hot, 2 to 3 minutes.

5. Add crab, mix gently, and ladle soup into wide bowls. Add cucumber equally to portions. Season to taste with salt and pepper.

Per serving: 330 cal., 11% (37 cal.) from fat; 36 g protein; 4.1 g fat (1.4 g sat.); 35 g carbo (3.4 g fiber); 628 mg sodium; 125 mg chol.

Portabella Salad

PREP AND COOK TIME: **About 25 minutes**

MAKES: 4 servings

- 4 **portabella mushrooms** (5-in.-wide caps)
- 1/4 pound **cherry tomatoes,** rinsed
- 3/4 pound (14 cups, lightly packed) **arugula,** rinsed and crisped
- 1/2 cup **nonfat mayonnaise**
- 3 tablespoons **coarse-grain Dijon mustard**
- 1 1/2 tablespoons **red wine vinegar**
  Salt and **pepper**

1. Trim mushroom stems flush with caps; save stems for other uses. Quickly rinse mushroom caps and drain on towels, smooth side up.

2. Place caps, gills down, in a 10- by 15-inch pan. Broil about 4 inches from heat for 5 minutes (about 4 minutes in a convection oven), then turn over and broil until juice in caps bubbles and mushrooms are flexible, 6 to 7 minutes more (about 6 minutes more in convection oven).

3. Meanwhile, cut cherry tomatoes in half and discard tough arugula stems.

4. Mix mayonnaise, mustard, and vinegar.

5. Cut each mushroom cap into thin, slanting slices. Divide arugula among plates. Top arugula equally with mushroom slices (and any juices) and cherry tomatoes. Spoon mayonnaise mixture onto salads. Add salt and pepper to taste.

Per serving: 75 cal., 15% (11 cal.) from fat; 5.4 g protein; 1.2 g fat (0.2 g sat.); 11 g carbo (3.6 g fiber); 301 mg sodium; 0 mg chol.

Potato "Risotto" with Sausage and Broccoli

PREP AND COOK TIME: **About 30 minutes**

NOTES: While not made with rice, this dish achieves a surprisingly creamy, risotto-like texture with frozen shredded potatoes.

MAKES: 4 servings

Warm Spinach Salad

¾ pound **uncooked chicken-apple sausages**

3 cups (about ½ lb.) **broccoli florets**

5 cups **frozen hash-brown-cut** (shredded) **potatoes**

1 **onion** (about ½ lb.), peeled and finely chopped

1 tablespoon chopped **fresh sage** leaves

2½ cups **nonfat milk**

Salt

1. Discard sausage casings. In a 10- to 12-inch nonstick frying pan over high heat, stir sausages until broken up and no longer pink, about 5 minutes.

2. Add broccoli florets; stir until sausages are well browned and broccoli is tender-crisp to bite, 3 to 5 minutes more. Pour into a bowl; keep warm.

3. Add potatoes and onion to pan, reduce heat to medium-high, and stir until onion is limp, 2 to 3 minutes.

4. Add sage and milk to pan, and stir just until potatoes are tender to bite, 8 to 10 minutes more.

5. Pour potato mixture onto a platter; spoon sausage and broccoli mixture over it. Add salt to taste.

Per serving: 475 cal., 30% (144 cal.) from fat; 26 g protein; 16 g fat (4.4 g sat.); 62 g carbo (6.5 g fiber); 757 mg sodium; 79 mg chol.

SOUTH-OF-THE-BORDER FLAVORS

Mango-Shrimp Tostadas

PREP AND COOK TIME: About 35 minutes

MAKES: 4 servings

1 **firm-ripe mango** (about 1 lb.)

1 **firm-ripe avocado** (about 10 oz.)

6 tablespoons **lime juice**

¾ pound (26 to 30 per lb.) **shelled, deveined cooked shrimp,** rinsed and drained

1 teaspoon minced **fresh serrano chili**

⅓ cup chopped **green onions**

4 **flour tortillas** (8 in.)

1 can (16 oz.) **low-fat refried black beans**

¼ cup fat-skimmed **chicken broth**

3 cups shredded **iceberg lettuce**

½ cup **nonfat sour cream**

Salt

1. Cut pit and peel from mango and discard. Cut fruit into small pieces and put in a bowl.

2. Pit and peel avocado. Cut into small pieces and add to mango. Add lime juice, shrimp, chili, and green onions; mix gently.

3. Place tortillas side by side on a 14-by 17-inch baking sheet. Bake in a 400° oven until crisp and lightly browned, about 10 minutes (about 9 minutes in a convection oven), turning tortillas over once after 4 to 5 minutes. Let cool on pan 1 to 2 minutes.

4. Meanwhile, combine refried beans and broth in a microwave-safe bowl, cover, and heat in a microwave oven on full power (100%) until hot, about 1 minute.

5. Place tortillas on plates. Spread beans equally onto tortillas. Scatter lettuce equally over beans, then top lettuce with shrimp mixture and sour cream. Add salt to taste.

Per serving: 423 cal., 26% (108 cal.) from fat; 29 g protein; 12 g fat (1.9 g sat.); 53 g carbo (7.9 g fiber); 784 mg sodium; 166 mg chol.

Black and Gold Soup

PREP AND COOK TIME: About 20 minutes

NOTES: Donna Higgins of Halfway, Oregon, threw this soup together as a "desperation dinner." She used canned black beans and chicken broth from the pantry, and squash from her garden.

MAKES: 4 servings

Mango-Shrimp Tostadas

3 1/2 cups fat-skimmed **chicken broth**

2 packages (12 to 14 oz. each) **frozen puréed yellow squash**

2 cans (15 oz. each) **black beans**, rinsed and drained

2 cups shredded skinned **cooked chicken**

1/2 cup **tomato salsa**

About 1/4 cup **tequila** (optional)

About 1 tablespoon **lemon juice**

1/4 cup **fresh cilantro** leaves

1. Combine broth and squash in a 4- to 6-quart pan over high heat. Stir frequently until squash is thawed and mixture boils, 15 to 18 minutes.

2. Stir in beans, chicken, salsa, and tequila and lemon juice to taste; stir often just until hot, 1 to 2 minutes.

3. Ladle into wide bowls. Garnish with cilantro.

Per serving: 389 cal., 15% (57 cal.) from fat; 38 g protein; 6.3 g fat (1.5 g sat.); 46 g carbo (12 g fiber); 794 mg sodium; 62 mg chol.

Smoked Trout Enchiladas

PREP AND COOK TIME: **About 45 minutes**

NOTES: In his native Veracruz, Mexico, Eligio Hernandez of *Sunset's* editorial services department enjoyed the taste of trout wrapped in cornhusks and cooked on a *comal* over a fire. This cooking method gives the fish a firm texture and smoky flavor. He also likes meats cooked in *salsa verde*—green chili sauce. The two components combine well in his version of enchiladas. The tortillas must be fresh; otherwise they crack when rolled.

MAKES: **4 servings**

1 cup thin **red onion** slices

1/2 cup **lime juice**

3/4 pound **boned, skinned smoked trout**

1/2 cup (4 oz.) **nonfat cream cheese**

1 can (19 oz.) **green enchilada sauce**

1/2 cup fat-skimmed **chicken broth**

8 **corn tortillas** (6 in.)

3/4 cup chopped **green onions** (including tops)

1/2 cup shredded **reduced-fat jack cheese**

1. In a bowl, mix red onion slices and lime juice.

2. Break trout into flakes.

3. Cut cream cheese into 1/2-inch chunks.

4. Mix enchilada sauce and chicken broth and pour 1 cup of the mixture into a shallow 3-quart (9- by 13-in.) casserole.

5. Stack tortillas and put in a microwave-safe plastic bag but do not seal. Heat in a microwave oven on full power (100%) just until hot, 1 to 2 minutes.

6. Dip tortillas, 1 at a time, in sauce in casserole and turn over to coat. Stack at 1 end of the casserole. Scatter 1/8 of the trout, cream cheese, and green onions across center of 1 tortilla. Roll to enclose filling and set, seam down, in sauce. Repeat to fill remaining tortillas, pushing unfilled ones to the end of the casserole as you work.

7. Pour remaining enchilada sauce mixture over and around filled tortillas.

8. Bake in a 400° oven until sauce bubbles, 10 to 12 minutes (about 9 minutes in a convection oven). Sprinkle jack cheese over enchiladas and bake until melted, 2 to 3 minutes more.

9. With a slotted spoon, lift the red onion slices from bowl and scatter over the enchiladas. Serve with a wide spatula. Season to taste with lime juice from the bowl.

Per serving: 427 cal., 27% (117 cal.) from fat; 35 g protein; 13 g fat (4.4 g sat.); 45 g carbo (3.7 g fiber); 2,534 mg sodium; 35 mg chol.

White Chicken Chili

PREP AND COOK TIME: **About 20 minutes**

MAKES: **4 servings**

1 to 2 tablespoons minced **fresh serrano** or jalapeño **chilies**

1 teaspoon **ground cumin**

1 **onion** (about 1/2 lb.), peeled and chopped

1 pound **ground chicken**

1 can (15 oz.) **small white beans**, rinsed and drained

1 cup **nonfat milk**

2 cans (about 15 oz. each) **cream-style corn**

Ground California or New Mexico **chili**

Salt

Lime wedges

1. In a 4- to 5-quart nonstick pan over high heat, stir serrano chilies, cumin, onion, and chicken until meat is crumbled and onion is limp, about 8 minutes.

2. Add beans, milk, and corn. Stir just until hot, 1 to 2 minutes.

3. Ladle into wide bowls. Sprinkle with ground chili and season with salt to taste. Serve with lime wedges to squeeze over portions.

Per serving: 430 cal., 25% (108 cal.) from fat; 30 g protein; 12 g fat (2.8 g sat.); 56 g carbo (6.3 g fiber); 904 mg sodium; 95 mg chol.

Smoked Trout Enchiladas

Turkey Chipotle Masa Stew

PREP AND COOK TIME: About 40 minutes

MAKES: 4 servings

- 1 pound **boned, skinned turkey breast**
- 1½ quarts fat-skimmed **chicken broth**
- 1 **onion** (about ½ lb.), peeled and chopped
- 1 or 2 **canned chipotle chilies**
- ½ cup **dehydrated masa flour** (corn tortilla flour)
- 1 can (about 15 oz.) **diced tomatoes**

  Cilantro or parsley **sprigs**

1. In a 4- to 5-quart pan over high heat, bring turkey breast, broth, and onion to a boil. Cover, reduce heat, and simmer until turkey is no longer pink in center of thickest part (cut to test), 8 to 10 minutes.

2. With a slotted spoon, lift turkey from broth. When cool enough to touch, in 5 to 6 minutes, tear meat into fine shreds.

3. Meanwhile, wearing gloves, cut out and discard chili seeds and veins. Finely chop chilies.

4. Whisk masa into broth. Add tomatoes (with juice), then chilies to taste. Bring to a boil over high heat, stirring often. Reduce heat and simmer to blend flavors, about 5 minutes. Add turkey and stir just until hot, 1 to 2 minutes.

5. Ladle into wide bowls. Garnish with cilantro sprigs.

Per serving: 275 cal., 5.5% (15 cal.) from fat; 43 g protein; 1.7 g fat (0.4 g sat.); 21 g carbo (2.8 g fiber); 448 mg sodium; 70 mg chol.

Orange Carnitas

PREP AND COOK TIME: About 35 minutes

MAKES: 4 servings

- 1 pound **fat-trimmed boned pork shoulder** or butt
- 2 teaspoons grated **orange** peel
- 2 cups **orange juice**
- 1 **onion** (about ½ lb.), peeled and chopped
- 1½ teaspoons **ground cumin**
- 1 can (15 oz.) **black beans,** rinsed and drained
- 8 warm **flour tortillas** (10 in.)
- ⅓ cup thinly sliced **green onions** (including tops)
- ⅓ cup **nonfat sour cream**
- ⅓ cup **tomato salsa**

  Salt

Turkey Chipotle Masa Stew

1. Cut pork into ¼- to ½-inch cubes. Put a 10- to 12-inch nonstick frying pan over high heat, add pork, and stir often until meat is gray, 5 to 6 minutes.

2. Add orange peel, 1 cup orange juice, onion, and cumin to pan. Stir often over medium-high heat until liquid has evaporated and meat is lightly browned, about 20 minutes. Add ½ cup orange juice, scrape browned bits free, and stir until juice evaporates, about 5 minutes.

3. Add black beans and remaining ½ cup orange juice and stir just until beans are hot, about 2 minutes.

4. Serve pork mixture in warm tortillas, adding green onions, sour cream, salsa, and salt to taste. Roll to enclose filling.

Per serving: 703 cal., 23% (162 cal.) from fat; 38 g protein; 18 g fat (4.4 g sat.); 95 g carbo (7.6 g fiber); 1,017 mg sodium; 78 mg chol.

Tortilla Soup

PREP AND COOK TIME: About 20 minutes

MAKES: 4 servings

- 1 pound **boned, skinned chicken breasts**
- 2 **fresh poblano chilies** (also called pasillas; 5 to 6 oz. total)
- ½ cup chopped **onion**
- 8 cups fat-skimmed **chicken broth**
- 6 **corn tortillas** (6 in.)

  About ¼ cup **lime juice**

1. Rinse chicken; cut into 1-inch chunks.

2. Rinse chilies, then trim and discard stems, seeds, and veins. Cut chilies lengthwise into ⅛- to ¼-inch strips.

3. In a 4- to 5-quart pan over high heat, bring chilies, onion, and broth to a boil. Reduce heat, cover, and simmer 5 minutes. Add chicken, cover, and simmer until meat is no longer pink in center of thickest part (cut to test), about 4 minutes.

4. Meanwhile, cut tortillas into 1-inch squares. Divide squares equally among wide soup bowls.

5. Ladle soup over tortillas. Add lime juice to taste.

Per serving: 299 cal., 7.4% (22 cal.) from fat; 45 g protein; 2.4 g fat (0.5 g sat.); 23 g carbo (2.7 g fiber); 289 mg sodium; 66 mg chol.

Beggar's Bundle Soup

4. In a 5- to 6-quart nonstick pan over high heat, combine mushrooms, ham, ½ cup chopped onions, water chestnuts, cabbage, and ginger. Stir often until mixture is lightly browned, about 8 minutes. Spoon into a bowl.

5. Pour 1 cup water and enough of the broth into pan to make liquid 1 inch deep. Bring to a boil over high heat.

6. Immerse reserved green onion tops in liquid just until wilted, ½ to 1 minute. Turn heat to low and set a rack in pan above liquid.

7. Spoon ¼ of the mushroom mixture onto the center of each egg roll wrapper. Bring corners of wrapper together and tie with a green onion top to enclose filling.

8. Gently set bundles side by side on rack. Cover pan, turn heat to high, and steam until bundles are slightly translucent and egg roll wrappers are firm (cut a small piece from top to test), about 5 minutes.

9. With 2 large spoons, gently transfer 1 or 2 bundles to each of 2 soup bowls. Add remaining broth and green onions to pan, bring to a boil, then ladle into bowls. Sprinkle bundles with cilantro leaves.

Per serving: 253 cal., 20% (51 cal.) from fat; 26 g protein; 5.7 g fat (1.9 g sat.); 25 g carbo (4.9 g fiber); 1,043 mg sodium; 35 mg chol.

Egg Drop Soup with Mustard Greens

PREP AND COOK TIME: **About 45 minutes**

MAKES: **4 servings**

- ¼ pound **fat-trimmed boned pork loin**
- 2 stalks (about 2 oz. total) **fresh lemon grass** or 6 strips lemon peel (yellow part only; ½ by 3 in. each)
- 8 cups fat-skimmed **chicken broth**
- 1 pound **mustard greens**
- ¼ pound **rice noodles** (Chinese rice sticks, or *mai fun*)
- ¼ pound (26 to 30 per lb.) **shelled, deveined shrimp,** rinsed and drained
- 2 **large eggs**

   Asian fish sauce (*nuoc mam* or *nam pla*)

   Chopped **green onions**

   Asian red chili sauce or hot sauce

Beggar's Bundle Soup

PREP AND COOK TIME: **About 45 minutes**

NOTES: Egg roll wrappers are available in Asian markets and most supermarkets. They may also be labeled pasta wrappers.

MAKES: **2 servings**

- ¼ pound **fresh shiitake mushrooms**
- ¼ pound **sliced cooked ham**

   About 7 **green onions** (including tops)

- ½ cup (½ of an 8-oz. can) **sliced water chestnuts,** drained and chopped
- 3 cups chopped **napa cabbage**
- 1 tablespoon minced **fresh ginger**
- 2 cups fat-skimmed **chicken broth**
- 4 **egg roll wrappers** (6 in. square)
- ⅓ cup **fresh cilantro** leaves

1. Trim off and discard mushroom stems. Rinse caps, drain, and cut into ¼-inch slices.

2. Cut ham into thin slivers.

3. Trim off and discard root ends of green onions. Cut off 4 of the longest green spears from onion tops and set aside. Chop white parts of onions and enough of the remaining tops to make 1 cup. Discard remaining tops.

1. Cut pork into ¼-inch-thick slices; then cut slices into pieces about 2 inches long.

2. In a 4- to 5-quart nonstick pan over high heat, stir pork until most of the pink is gone, 2 to 3 minutes. Pour into a bowl.

3. Trim and discard root ends and coarse outer leaves from lemon grass. Crush lemon grass slightly.

4. Add lemon grass and broth to pan and bring to a boil over high heat. Reduce heat, cover, and simmer to blend flavors, about 15 minutes.

5. Meanwhile, rinse and drain mustard greens. Discard tough stems. Cut greens into 2- to 3-inch pieces.

6. Add mustard greens, noodles, and shrimp to broth mixture. Simmer just until noodles are tender to bite and shrimp are pink and opaque but still moist-looking in center of thickest part (cut to test), about 6 minutes. With a slotted spoon, lift out and discard lemon grass from broth. Return pork and juices to pan.

7. Break eggs into broth mixture and stir gently, breaking yolks, until eggs are set, about 1 minute.

8. Ladle soup into wide bowls. Add fish sauce, green onions, and red chili sauce to taste.

Per serving: 302 cal., 14% (43 cal.) from fat; 34 g protein; 4.8 g fat (1.4 g sat.); 30 g carbo (0.6 g fiber); 315 mg sodium; 166 mg chol.

Curried Lentils and Potatoes

PREP AND COOK TIME: **About 30 minutes**

NOTES: Hulled (decorticated) lentils, such as Red Chiefs, come from the Northwest. Smaller orange lentils are available in Indian markets. Both cook quickly.

MAKES: **4 servings**

- 1 pound **red thin-skinned potatoes**
- 2 **firm-ripe tomatoes** (½ lb. total)
- 1½ cups **hulled lentils** such as Red Chiefs
- 3 cups fat-skimmed **chicken broth**
- 1 tablespoon **curry powder**
- ¼ cup finely chopped **fresh mint** leaves
  Plain nonfat yogurt
  Salt

1. Scrub potatoes and cut them into ¼-inch slices.

2. Rinse tomatoes, core, and cut each into 6 wedges.

3. In a 12- to 14-inch frying pan, combine potatoes, tomatoes, lentils, broth, and curry powder. Bring to a boil over high heat, stirring occasionally.

4. Cover pan, reduce heat, and simmer until most of the liquid is absorbed and potatoes are tender to bite, about 20 minutes, stirring occasionally.

5. Spoon into wide bowls. Sprinkle with chopped mint and add yogurt and salt to taste.

Per serving: 381 cal., 3.1% (12 cal.) from fat; 29 g protein; 1.3 g fat (0.1 g sat.); 65 g carbo (12 g fiber); 80 mg sodium; 0 mg chol.

Lemon-Chicken Stir-Fry

PREP AND COOK TIME: **About 35 minutes**

MAKES: **4 servings**

- 1 **red bell pepper** (about ½ lb.)
- ¼ pound **edible pea pods**
- 2 cups **precooked dried white rice**
- 1 pound **boned, skinned chicken breasts**
- 3 cups fat-skimmed **chicken broth**
- 1 tablespoon minced **fresh serrano** or jalapeño **chilies**
- 1 tablespoon grated **lemon** peel
- 1 tablespoon **cornstarch**
- 2 tablespoons **lemon juice**
- ¼ cup chopped **green onions** (including tops)

1. Rinse, stem, and seed bell pepper, then cut into ¼-inch-wide strips.

2. Remove and discard stem ends and strings from pea pods. Rinse pods and cut in half crosswise.

3. Put rice in a wide 3- to 4-quart bowl.

4. Rinse chicken breasts and cut into 1-inch chunks.

5. In a 10- to 12-inch nonstick frying pan over high heat, bring 2 cups broth to a boil. Pour over rice, cover, and let stand until liquid is absorbed and rice is tender to bite, about 7 minutes. Fluff with a fork.

6. Meanwhile, return pan to heat. Add chicken and stir until surface is no longer pink, 1 to 2 minutes. Add bell pepper, pea pods, chilies, and lemon peel. Stir just until chicken is no longer pink in center of thickest part (cut to test), about 5 minutes.

7. Blend cornstarch and remaining broth until smooth. Stir into pan and continue stirring until mixture boils, about 1 minute. Add lemon juice.

8. Pour chicken over rice. Sprinkle with green onions.

Per serving: 379 cal., 4% (15 cal.) from fat; 37 g protein; 1.7 g fat (0.4 g sat.); 51 g carbo (2.6 g fiber); 138 mg sodium; 66 mg chol.

Pan-browned Udon Noodles

PREP AND COOK TIME: **About 15 minutes**

NOTES: Fresh udon noodles (¼ to ⅜ in. thick) can be found in many supermarkets and in Asian markets. You can also use similarly shaped fresh Shanghai-style noodles. Reserve any seasoning packets that come with the noodles for other uses.

MAKES: **4 servings**

- ½ cup fat-skimmed **chicken broth**
- 2 packages (7 oz. each) **fresh udon noodles**
- 1 teaspoon **Asian** (toasted) **sesame oil**
- 1 cup shredded skinned **cooked chicken**
- ¼ pound **shelled cooked tiny shrimp**, rinsed and drained
- 1 cup diagonally sliced **green onions** (including tops)
  About 2 teaspoons **reduced-sodium soy sauce**
  About 1 tablespoon **prepared sweet-hot mustard**

1. In a 10- to 12-inch nonstick frying pan over high heat, bring broth and noodles to a boil; stir gently to separate noodles. Boil until liquid is almost gone, about 4 minutes, then add oil.

2. Stir often until noodles are lightly browned, about 8 minutes. Add chicken, shrimp, and green onions, and stir until hot.

3. Spoon into wide bowls. Mix soy sauce and mustard and add to taste.

Per serving: 257 cal., 18% (46 cal.) from fat; 21 g protein; 5.1 g fat (1 g sat.); 31 g carbo (0.6 g fiber); 300 mg sodium; 86 mg chol.

Kung Pao Shrimp Risotto

PREP AND COOK TIME: **About 35 minutes**

MAKES: **4 servings**

- 1 pound (26 to 30 per lb.) **shelled, deveined shrimp,** rinsed and drained
- ½ cup diced **red bell pepper**
- 1 tablespoon minced **fresh ginger**
- 4 **dried hot chilies** (about 3 in.)
- 1 teaspoon **salad oil**
- 1 cup **white arborio** or pearl **rice**
- 1 cup **dry sherry**
- 3½ cups fat-skimmed **chicken broth**
- 1 teaspoon **Asian** (toasted) **sesame oil**
- ½ cup chopped or slivered **green** and/or red **bell pepper**
- 2 tablespoons chopped **salted roasted peanuts**
  Soy sauce

1. In a 10- to 12-inch nonstick frying pan over high heat, stir the shrimp until pink, about 2 minutes. Remove from pan.

2. Add diced red bell pepper, ginger, chilies, and salad oil to pan. Stir until vegetables are limp, about 3 minutes.

3. Add rice to pan and stir until opaque, 1 to 2 minutes. Add sherry and broth.

Kung Pao Shrimp Risotto

Bring to a boil and cook, stirring often, until rice is tender to bite, about 15 minutes.

4. Add shrimp and stir just until hot, 1 to 2 minutes. Stir in sesame oil.

5. Ladle risotto into wide bowls or mound on plates. Sprinkle portions with chopped bell pepper and peanuts. Add soy sauce to taste.

Per serving: 437 cal., 15% (66 cal.) from fat; 35 g protein; 7.3 g fat (1 g sat.); 40 g carbo (4.3 g fiber); 277 mg sodium; 173 mg chol.

Salmon Fettuccine with Wasabi Sauce

Salmon Fettuccine with Wasabi Sauce

PREP AND COOK TIME: **About 15 minutes**

NOTES: **Fresh salmon caviar (*ikura*),** available at Japanese grocery stores, has the most delicate flavor, but you can also use canned salmon caviar. Wasabi paste is also in Japanese markets and many supermarkets.

MAKES: **4 servings**

- 2 cups fat-skimmed **chicken broth**
- ½ pound **dried spinach fettuccine**
- ¼ cup **fresh salmon caviar**
- 1 tablespoon **cornstarch**
- ¾ cup **plain nonfat yogurt**
- 3 tablespoons **wasabi paste**
- ¾ pound **sliced smoked salmon,** cut into ½-inch strips

1. In a 5- to 6-quart pan over high heat, bring broth, 2 cups water, and fettuccine to a boil; cook, stirring often, until pasta is tender to bite, about 7 minutes.

2. Meanwhile, rinse caviar in cold water and drain well in a fine strainer.

3. Blend cornstarch with 3 tablespoons water until smooth.

4. Stir cornstarch mixture, yogurt, and wasabi with pasta, then stir until boiling again. Add salmon and stir gently just until hot, 1 to 2 minutes.

5. Serve pasta in bowls and garnish with salmon caviar.

Per serving: 402 cal., 17% (68 cal.) from fat; 34 g protein; 7.5 g fat (1 g sat.); 49 g carbo (6 g fiber); 2,033 mg sodium; 115 mg chol.

Chilean Seabass with Thai-spiced Mashed Yams

PREP AND COOK TIME: **About 35 minutes**
NOTES: **Buy the curry paste in a well-stocked supermarket or Asian market.**
MAKES: **2 servings**

- 1 pound **yams** or sweet potatoes
- 2 cups fat-skimmed **chicken broth**
- ½ teaspoon **Thai red curry paste**
- ½ pound **Chilean seabass,** cut into 4 equal pieces
- 2 tablespoons finely shredded **fresh basil** leaves

  Salt

1. Peel yams and cut into ½-inch chunks.

2. In a 10- to 12-inch nonstick frying pan over high heat, combine yams, broth, and curry paste. Bring to a boil, then stir often until yams are tender when mashed, 10 to 15 minutes. With a slotted spoon, transfer yams to a bowl. Pour broth into another bowl. Wipe pan dry.

3. Meanwhile, rinse fish and pat dry. Return pan to heat and add fish. Cook until well browned on each side and opaque but still moist-looking in center of thickest part (cut to test), about 10 minutes.

4. As fish cooks, mash yams with a mixer or potato masher. Add some of the reserved broth if you want softer yams. Save extra broth for other uses.

5. Spoon yams onto plates and top with fish. Scatter basil over portions and add salt to taste.

Per serving: 384 cal., 7.8% (30 cal.) from fat; 32 g protein; 3.3 g fat (0.6 g sat.); 55 g carbo (8.3 g fiber); 218 mg sodium; 47 mg chol.

Cambodian Steamed Mussels

PREP AND COOK TIME: **About 40 minutes**
MAKES: **4 servings**

Cambodian Steamed Mussels

- 4 pounds **mussels** (beards pulled off), scrubbed
- ½ teaspoon **salad oil**
- 1 to 2 tablespoons minced **fresh jalapeño chilies**
- 3 cups fat-skimmed **chicken broth**
- 1 can (14 oz.) **reduced-fat coconut milk**
- 1 teaspoon **ground dried turmeric**
- 1 tablespoon **rice vinegar**
- 1 cup **pineapple** chunks (about ½ in.; fresh or canned)
- 2 tablespoons chopped **fresh cilantro**

  Salt

- 1 loaf (1 lb.) **French bread,** sliced

1. Discard any gaping mussels that do not close when the shells are tapped.

2. In a 6- to 8-quart pan over high heat, stir oil and chilies until chilies are limp, 1 to 2 minutes.

3. Add chicken broth, canned coconut milk, ground turmeric, and rice vinegar. Bring mixture to a boil.

4. Add mussels, cover, and cook until shells open, 6 to 10 minutes.

5. Ladle the mussels and broth into wide bowls.

6. Spoon pineapple chunks equally over mussels and sprinkle portions with cilantro. Season to taste with salt.

7. Serve mussels with bread to dip into the broth as you eat.

Per serving: 540 cal., 20% (108 cal.) from fat; 32 g protein; 12 g fat (4.9 g sat.); 73 g carbo (3.6 g fiber); 1,151 mg sodium; 37 mg chol.

Sloppy Lasagna

PREP AND COOK TIME: **About 40 minutes**

MAKES: **4 servings**

1¼ pounds **uncooked mild** or hot **Italian turkey sausages**

1 **onion** (about ½ lb.), peeled and chopped

2 cloves **garlic,** minced or pressed

8 ounces **dried lasagna**

2 cups fat-skimmed **chicken broth**

1 can (about 15 oz.) **diced tomatoes**

1 can (about 8 oz.) **tomato sauce**

½ teaspoon **dried basil**

½ teaspoon **dried oregano**

1 cup (4 oz.) **shredded reduced-fat mozzarella cheese**

Chopped **parsley**

1. Remove and discard sausage casings.

2. In a 4- to 5-quart nonstick pan over high heat, combine sausages, onion, and garlic. With a spoon, break meat into small pieces and stir often until mixture is browned, about 15 minutes.

3. Meanwhile, break the lasagna into 2- to 3-inch pieces.

4. To pan, add broth, 2 cups water, tomatoes (with juice), tomato sauce, basil, oregano, and lasagna. Boil, stirring often, until pasta is tender to bite, about 15 minutes.

5. Ladle into wide bowls and sprinkle with cheese and parsley.

Per serving: 597 cal., 30% (180 cal.) from fat; 45 g protein; 20 g fat (6.4 g sat.); 60 g carbo (4 g fiber); 1,629 mg sodium; 86 mg chol.

Gnocchi with Sherried Shallots

PREP AND COOK TIME: **About 30 minutes**

MAKES: **4 servings**

2 cups thinly sliced **shallots** or onions

1 cup **dry sherry**

1½ cups **nonfat sour cream**

1 cup fat-skimmed **chicken broth**

1 package (about 18 oz.) **refrigerated gnocchi**

2 cups shredded skinned **cooked chicken**

⅓ cup chopped **parsley**

Fresh-grated **nutmeg**

Salt

1. In a 5- to 6-quart pan over high heat, stir shallots and sherry until shallots are limp, about 10 minutes.

2. Add sour cream, broth, gnocchi, chicken, and parsley. Stir until gnocchi are hot, about 5 minutes.

3. Spoon into bowls and season with nutmeg and salt to taste.

Per serving: 580 cal., 8.3% (48 cal.) from fat; 36 g protein; 5.3 g fat (1.4 g sat.); 79 g carbo (0.9 g fiber); 408 mg sodium; 71 mg chol.

Spaghetti and Meatballs

PREP AND COOK TIME: **About 40 minutes**

NOTES: If desired, omit veal and use a total of 1 pound ground lean beef.

MAKES: **4 servings**

½ pound **sliced mushrooms**

2½ cups fat-skimmed **chicken broth**

1 **large egg**

½ pound **ground lean** (7% fat) **beef**

½ pound **ground veal** or turkey

¼ cup **fine dried bread crumbs**

½ cup finely chopped **onion**

1 can (about 15 oz.) **diced tomatoes**

1 can (about 8 oz.) **tomato sauce**

1 teaspoon **Italian seasoning mix** or dried oregano

½ pound **dried spaghetti**

¼ cup slivered **fresh basil** leaves

¼ cup **shredded parmesan cheese**

1. In a 5- to 6-quart pan over high heat, frequently stir mushrooms and ¼ cup broth until liquid evaporates and mushrooms are lightly browned, about 5 minutes.

2. Meanwhile, in a bowl, beat egg to blend. Add beef, veal, bread crumbs, onion, and ¼ cup broth. Mix well.

3. To mushrooms, add remaining broth, 2 cups water, tomatoes (with juice), tomato sauce, and Italian seasoning. Drop rounded tablespoons of meat mixture into pan. Bring to a simmer, turn meatballs over gently, and cook until no longer pink in center of thickest part (cut to test), 5 to 7 minutes. With a slotted spoon, put meatballs in a bowl.

4. Turn heat to high and add spaghetti to pan. Boil, stirring often, until pasta is tender to bite, about 10 minutes.

5. Return meatballs and any juice to pan. Stir gently just until hot, about 2 minutes.

6. Spoon spaghetti and meatballs into wide bowls or onto plates. Sprinkle with basil and cheese.

Per serving: 595 cal., 30% (180 cal.) from fat; 41 g protein; 20 g fat (7.9 g sat.); 61 g carbo (4.6 g fiber); 827 mg sodium; 146 mg chol.

Poached Scallops with Dried-Tomato Orzo

PREP AND COOK TIME: **About 30 minutes**

MAKES: **4 servings**

2 cups fat-skimmed **chicken broth**

1 pound **scallops** (1½ to 2 in. wide), rinsed and drained

¼ cup (⅓ to ½ oz.) finely chopped **dried tomatoes**

½ pound **dried orzo pasta**

1 tablespoon **olive oil**

1½ teaspoons **honey**

1½ teaspoons **white wine vinegar**

1½ teaspoons **fresh thyme** leaves or dried thyme

Fresh-ground **pepper**

1. In a 10- to 12-inch nonstick frying pan over high heat, bring broth and 2 cups water to a boil. Add scallops and simmer just until opaque but still moist-looking in center of thickest part (cut to test), about 5 minutes. With a slotted spoon, transfer scallops to a bowl; keep warm.

2. Add tomatoes and orzo to pan. Stir often over high heat until most of the liquid is absorbed and orzo is tender to bite, 10 to 12 minutes.

3. Meanwhile, mix oil, honey, vinegar, and thyme.

4. Return scallops (and any juice) to pan and stir gently just until hot, 1 to 2 minutes.

Spaghetti and Meatballs

5. Spoon orzo and scallops onto plates. Drizzle scallops equally with honey mixture. Season with pepper to taste.

Per serving: 373 cal., 12% (46 cal.) from fat; 31 g protein; 5.1 g fat (0.7 g sat.); 49 g carbo (1.9 g fiber); 227 mg sodium; 37 mg chol.

Shepherd's Pie

PREP AND COOK TIME: About 35 minutes

MAKES: 4 servings

- 1 pound **ground lean (7% fat) beef**
- 1 cup **frozen pearl onions**
- 1 cup chopped **carrots**
- 2 tablespoons **red wine vinegar**
- 1¼ cups fat-skimmed **beef broth**
- 1 package (22 oz.) **frozen mashed potatoes**
- 2⅓ cups **nonfat milk**
- ⅓ cup **shredded reduced-fat sharp cheddar cheese**
- ¼ cup **prepared horseradish**
- 1 tablespoon **cornstarch**
- 1 cup **frozen petite peas**
- 1 teaspoon **dried marjoram**

1. In a 10- to 12-inch ovenproof non-stick frying pan over high heat, combine ground beef, onions, carrots, vinegar, and ½ cup broth. Stir often until meat is crumbled and carrots are tender when pierced, about 15 minutes. Spoon out and discard any fat.

2. Meanwhile, in a 2-quart microwave-safe bowl, combine potatoes and milk. Cook in a microwave oven at full power (100%) until hot and smoothly blended, 8 to 10 minutes, stirring every 2 to 3 minutes. Stir cheese and horseradish into potatoes.

3. Blend remaining broth and the cornstarch until smooth. Add broth mixture, peas, and marjoram to frying pan. Stir until mixture boils. Remove from heat.

4. Spoon mashed potatoes in dollops around edge of pan over beef mixture, leaving center exposed.

5. Broil 6 to 8 inches from heat until potatoes are lightly browned, about 8 minutes. Spoon onto plates.

Per serving: 536 cal., 27% (144 cal.) from fat; 35 g protein; 16 g fat (6.8 g sat.); 59 g carbo (5.9 g fiber); 597 mg sodium; 82 mg chol.

Polenta with Vegetable Ragout

Polenta with Vegetable Ragout

PREP AND COOK TIME: About 30 minutes

MAKES: 4 servings

- 2 **zucchini** (about 10 oz. total)
- ½ pound **mushrooms**
- 1 **onion** (about ½ lb.), peeled
- 2 cloves **garlic**, minced or pressed
- 5½ cups fat-skimmed **chicken broth**
- ½ pound **cherry tomatoes**, cut in half
- 1½ cups **instant polenta**
- 2 cans (about 15 oz. each) **cream-style corn**
- 2 tablespoons **grated parmesan cheese**
- ¼ cup diagonally sliced **green onions**

1. Rinse zucchini; trim off and discard ends. Cut zucchini into ½-inch slices. Trim off and discard stem ends of mushrooms. Rinse mushrooms, drain, and cut into quarters. Cut onion crosswise into ¼-inch slices.

2. In a 5- to 6-quart nonstick pan over high heat, frequently stir zucchini, mushrooms, onion, garlic, and ½ cup broth until broth has evaporated and vegetables are lightly browned, 12 to 15 minutes. Add ½ cup more broth and stir to release browned bits. Stir in tomatoes and pour vegetables into a bowl; keep warm.

3. To pan, add remaining broth, polenta, and corn. Stir over high heat until boiling, 3 to 4 minutes.

4. Spoon polenta into wide bowls. Top equally with vegetable mixture. Sprinkle cheese and green onions over portions.

Per serving: 645 cal., 5% (32 cal.) from fat; 18 g protein; 3.5 g fat (0.7 g sat.); 142 g carbo (16 g fiber); 763 mg sodium; 2 mg chol. ◆

EASY COMPLEMENTS

Here are a few starters, salads, and desserts that echo the point of a one-pan entrée: Less is more. Each takes 10 minutes or less to prepare, and serves four.

STARTERS

• **Salsa tidbits.** Mix ½ cup **green salsa**, ¼ cup minced **red onion**, and 2 tablespoons minced **fresh cilantro**. Serve as a dip with ¼ pound *each* **baby-cut carrots**, sliced **cucumbers**, and peeled, sliced **jicama**.

Per serving: 41 cal., 2.2% (0.9 cal.) from fat; 0.8 g protein; 0.1 g fat (0 g sat.); 9.1 g carbo (2.8 g fiber); 193 mg sodium; 0 mg chol.

• **Cheese-chutney crisps.** Mix ½ cup **chutney** and ¼ cup chopped **green onions**. Spread on 12 lahvosh crackers (about 2 by 4 in.). Top with slivers of **parmesan cheese** (1 oz. total).

Per serving: 289 cal., 11% (32 cal.) from fat; 7.3 g protein; 3.6 g fat (1.4 g sat.); 55 g carbo (0.9 g fiber); 650 mg sodium; 5.6 mg chol.

SALADS

• **Apple slaw.** Combine 4 cups **coleslaw mix**, 1 cup chopped **apple**, ⅓ cup **nonfat mayonnaise**, 1 teaspoon **cider vinegar**, and **hot sauce** to taste.

Per serving: 75 cal., 6% (4.5 cal.) from fat; 2.4 g protein; 0.5 g fat (0.1 g sat.); 17 g carbo (1.1 g fiber); 172 mg sodium; 0 mg chol.

• **Red and green salad.** Mix 4 cups bite-size pieces rinsed, crisped **butter lettuce leaves** with ¼ cup thinly sliced **red radishes**, 2 tablespoons minced **fresh chives**, and **seasoned rice vinegar** to taste.

Per serving: 15 cal., 12% (1.8 cal.) from fat; 0.8 g protein; 0.2 g fat (0 g sat.); 3.1 g carbo (0.7 g fiber); 153 mg sodium; 0 mg chol.

DESSERTS

• **Chocolate and strawberry pavlovas.** Fill each of 4 purchased **baked meringues** (3¼ oz. total) with ½ cup **chocolate frozen nonfat yogurt** and top each portion with ¼ cup sliced **strawberries** and 1 tablespoon **nonfat chocolate syrup**.

Per serving: 251 cal., 8.4% (21 cal.) from fat; 5.3 g protein; 2.3 g fat (0.1 g sat.); 56 g carbo (1 g fiber); 97 mg sodium; 5 mg chol.

• **Papaya splits.** Cut a 1-pound **ripe papaya** lengthwise into quarters and scoop out seeds. Whisk together ¼ cup **hot red pepper jelly** and 1½ tablespoons **lime juice**. Top each papaya wedge with ½ cup **mango sorbet** and pour jelly mixture equally over servings.

Per serving: 111 cal., 0.8% (0.9 cal.) from fat; 0.5 g protein; 0.1 g fat (0 g sat.); 27 g carbo (0.7 g fiber); 8.2 mg sodium; 0 mg chol.

The Wine Guide

BY KAREN MacNEIL-FIFE

RICK MARIANI

Washington's sipping scene

■ On a recent trip to Washington state, I sat in Starbucks and had an epiphany about wine. Let me explain.

As we all know, Starbucks has slipped into the fabric of American life. Here, college students, cappuccinos and computers at hand, surf the Net; latte-sipping women and men sit and talk for hours. Starbucks is America's psychological equivalent of the Parisian brasserie—a place where you can sit as long as you like and enjoy drinking a single delicious something.

I have three hypotheses about this phenomenon:
1. There's a reason Starbucks began in Washington state.
2. Starbucks could change the way we drink wine in America.
3. What Starbucks is to coffee, Washington wines could be to wine in general.

Young in spirit and happily detached from the cultural mainstream, Washington exudes a comfortable "otherness." And the same European sensibility that created Starbucks's "cafe society" has spawned a unique wine culture in the state. Like enjoying good coffee, enjoying good wine is a natural, easy part of the Washington lifestyle. With Star-

bucks as a model, why couldn't wine drinking throughout the country become as simple and convivial as meeting friends for coffee?

As for Washington wines, they are not "like California wines, only less famous," as I had imagined. There's a whole different aura up here. Perhaps it begins with the winemakers themselves, many of whom are completely self-taught and seem more like craftspeople than scientists. That makes a difference to the flavor of the wines in precisely the same way a dish made by a grandmother would taste, well, different from the same dish made by a professional chef.

There's another commonality at work here, too: most Washington vintners lack money. In California, it's virtually impossible to begin a winery without a small fortune behind you, but Washington has winery owners who not too long ago were waiters. The wines seem to capture this humbleness.

The wines also capture extremely concentrated flavors. The state's northern latitude translates into many hours of sunshine, cool nights, and a generally long growing season. During this slow dance toward ripeness, the flavor of the grapes grows ever more concentrated and nuanced.

You might imagine that, this being Washington, the grapes have all the water they could possibly need. Not so. The vineyards are located not in the wet western part of the state but in the arid eastern half, beyond the giant Cascade Mountains. Here the dry, sandy plains give rise to vineyards, orchards, and cornfields as far as the eye can see—but only because of irrigation.

Surprisingly enough, irrigation seems to be a contributing "secret" to the flavor and texture of the wines. By precisely controlling the amount of water vines get and when, winemakers can literally sculpt the vines and their grape clusters. This, in turn, impacts the character of the final wines. More than one winemaker I spoke with attributed the

WASHINGTON WINES TO KNOW

Washington state has 102 wineries, which make countless terrific wines. Some (*) are stellar. A few of my favorites:

■ CHARDONNAY: **Canoe Ridge 1996**, $14; **Caterina 1997**, $12; **Chinook 1996**, $20; **Columbia Crest Semillon Chardonnay 1997**, $8; **Covey Run 1996**, $9; **Hedges Fumé-Chardonnay 1997**, $9; **Kiona 1997**, $18; **Waterbrook 1997**, $11.

■ RIESLING: **Columbia Cellarmaster's Reserve 1997**, $7; **Paul Thomas Johannisberg 1997**, $6.

■ MERLOT: **Andrew Will 1995**, $27*; **Chinook 1995**, $24; **Covey Run 1995**, $10.

■ CABERNET SAUVIGNON AND CABERNET BLENDS: **Chateau Ste. Michelle "Horse Heaven Vineyard" 1995**, $25; **DeLille Chaleur Estate 1995**, $34; **Hogue 1995**, $15; **Kiona Estate Bottled Reserve 1995**, $30; **Leonetti 1995**, $45*; **Matthews Yakima Valley 1996**, $35; **Woodward Canyon "Canoe Ridge Vineyard" 1996**, $28.

often incredibly soft texture of Washington wines to the fact that water here is in man's control.

Softness. It's a very compelling attribute for any wine to have—especially if it's red. And indeed, over the last several years, Washington has become known for silky Merlots and Cabernets. But its Chardonnays can be pretty amazing too, particularly if you like Chardonnays that are elegant and structured rather than fleshy and fat.

In the end, it won't surprise me if all Westerners learn to appreciate the attributes of Washington's wines as quickly as they did the spirit of its coffee. ◆

SUNSET'S MONTHLY STEAL
■ **Hogue Johannisberg Riesling 1997 (Columbia Valley)**, $7. Fresh and lovely, with a fabulous exotic aroma.

... AND A SURPRISE
■ **Razz by Paul Thomas (WA)**, $14 for 375 ml. An outrageously delicious raspberry wine; begs for chocolate cake.
— *KAREN MACNEIL-FIFE*

food guide

BY JERRY ANNE DI VECCHIO

A TASTE OF THE WEST

For a winter's eve

Lyon's salad: A meal worth roaring about

CONVECTION CONNECTION
Most of the new ovens in *Sunset's* remodeled test kitchen convert to convection cooking with the flick of a switch. So beginning this month, we're passing convection times and temperatures along to you when they differ from those for a regular oven.

A HOT EGG, cooked as softly as you like, straight up or over easy, tops crisp sprigs of curly endive laced with bacon.

■ On my first serious eating trip to Paris, I made a mini culinary tour of the whole country by hitting the best of the city's regional restaurants. I had read in *Larousse Gastronomique* that Lyon was the culinary capital of France—famous for the poultry of Bresse and lots of pigs. So Aux Lyonnaise represented rich turf. One of those Lyonnaise porkers had, no doubt, given all for the bacon (*lardon*) in the time-honored salad I ordered—a meal well suited to a chilling night.

Salad Lyonnaise

PREP AND COOK TIME: About 30 minutes
NOTES: If side bacon is not available, cut sliced bacon crosswise into $\frac{1}{4}$-inch pieces.
MAKES: 3 or 4 servings

8 cups (8 oz.) **frisée** or tender inner curly endive **leaves,** rinsed and crisped

About $\frac{1}{4}$ pound **French bread,** sliced and toasted

$\frac{1}{2}$ pound **side bacon,** cut into $\frac{1}{4}$-inch dice

3 or 4 **large eggs**

$\frac{1}{4}$ cup **white wine vinegar**

1 tablespoon **Dijon mustard**

Salt and **pepper**

(Continued on page 22)

Stylish stops that snugly fit

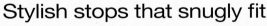

There's a handsome alternative to clamps and corks for keeping bubbles in opened champagne bottles and air out of leftover wine. These weighty metal (stainless steel, silver plate) stoppers are tapered to fit bottle necks of various sizes. Flexible gaskets keep the seals tight. The models with translucent, gemlike finials catch the light so prettily, I also use them in bottles of vinegars, oils, and miscellaneous seasonings that sit out for ready use in the kitchen. The stoppers are sold in some cookware stores and in well-stocked wine shops. To order the models at left (top, $19.95; bottom, $22.95) from Sur La Table, call (800) 243-0852. For the stopper at right ($30), call JMB Imports; (800) 201-8382.

JAMES CARRIER (4)

1. Tear frisée into bite-size pieces and place in a wide salad bowl.

2. Tear bread into ¹⁄₂-inch chunks and scatter over the greens.

3. Put bacon in a 10- to 12-inch nonstick frying pan over medium heat and stir often until browned and crisp, 10 to 12 minutes. With a slotted spoon, transfer to towels to drain.

4. Break eggs into drippings in pan, and when whites are firm on the bottom, slide a spatula under each egg and, if desired, carefully turn over. Cook until whites are no longer clear, about 1 minute total. With spatula, transfer eggs to a plate (place side by side); keep warm.

5. Quickly discard all but 2 tablespoons fat from pan. Turn heat to high, add vinegar and mustard, and whisk until mixture boils.

6. Pour hot dressing over frisée and bread, add bacon, and mix. Spoon into wide bowls and top each serving with a hot egg. Season to taste with salt and pepper.

Per serving: 483 cal., 73% (351 cal.) from fat; 14 g protein; 39 g fat (14 g sat.); 18 g carbo (2 g fiber); 727 mg sodium; 251 mg chol.

FLIPPED OUT of a frying pan, tender cake reveals candied fresh orange slices.

SEASONAL NOTE

Oranges are tops

■ Citrus is so ubiquitous in the market these days, the peak seasons of the various fruits tend to be forgotten. Right now, oranges and grapefruit offer prime quality and value. Take a fresh approach to oranges with an old dessert most often associated with pineapples: an upside-down cake.

Orange Upside-down Cake

PREP AND COOK TIME: About 1 hour and 15 minutes (1 hour if using a convection oven)

MAKES: 8 to 10 servings

1. Rinse 4 **oranges** (each about 3 in. wide). Cut off and discard ends from 1 orange, then cut fruit crosswise into slices about ¹⁄₄ inch thick. Put in a 10-inch ovenproof nonstick frying pan (with curved sides).

2. To frying pan, add ¹⁄₄ cup **water** and ¹⁄₄ cup **sugar** and boil over high heat, shaking to mix fruit, until liquid is almost gone and oranges are slightly caramelized, 6 to 8 minutes. With a fork, push slices into a neat pattern in bottom of pan.

3. Meanwhile, grate 1¹⁄₂ teaspoons peel from another orange. In a food processor, combine grated peel, ³⁄₄ cup (³⁄₈ lb.) **butter** or margarine, 1 cup **sugar,** 2 cups **all-purpose flour,** and 2 teaspoons **baking powder.** Whirl to mix, then add 2 **large eggs** and 1 teaspoon **vanilla.** Whirl until smoothly blended. Spoon thick batter in dollops over orange slices in pan.

4. Bake in a 350° oven until top is well browned and cake begins to pull away from pan sides, about 45 minutes (about 30 minutes in a convection oven). Remove from oven and let stand about 10 minutes.

5. As cake bakes, cut peel and white membrane from all 3 of the remaining oranges and slice fruit crosswise; put fruit in a bowl.

6. Run a thin knife between pan sides and cake. Hold a flat plate over pan and invert to release cake. Serve warm or cool in wedges with reserved peeled orange slices.

Per serving: 356 cal., 38% (135 cal.) from fat; 4.4 g protein; 15 g fat (9.1 g sat.); 52 g carbo (2.1 g fiber); 254 mg sodium; 80 mg chol.

Playing chicken
The Great Seal of Kiev

■ Up and down the West Coast—in Seattle, San Francisco, and Los Angeles—recent immigrants are reviving the old Russian neighborhoods with new restaurants, bakeries, and food stores. And an old classic, chicken Kiev, is making a comeback on Russian restaurant menus. Capturing a heart of melted butter in a slab of chicken breast was once considered a test of culinary skill—getting a good seal is the secret. Finishing the dish in the oven, rather than frying it in deep fat, is a healthy step forward. One caveat: Chicken Kiev spurts when cut, so warn your guests.

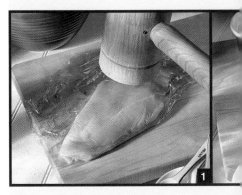

PREP AND COOK TIME: About 45 minutes

NOTES: Up to 4 hours ahead, shape and coat the chicken breasts with egg and crumbs; lay them slightly apart in a single layer on waxed paper, cover, and chill.

MAKES: 4 servings

1. With a flat mallet, gently pound 4 **boned, skinned chicken breast halves** (1¹⁄₂ lb. total) between sheets of plastic wrap until they're about ¹⁄₄ inch thick in center and ¹⁄₈ inch thick around the edges.

2. Mix ¹⁄₂ cup (¹⁄₄ lb.) **butter** or margarine with 2 tablespoons minced **parsley** and 1 teaspoon *each* grated **lemon** peel, **dried tarragon, dried thyme,** and **dried basil.** (Or make

Thermometer tactics

Is your cooking thermometer accurate? Checking it is simple if you know the boiling temperature at your altitude. At sea level, water boils at 212°; for every 500 feet of elevation gain, the boiling point drops about 0.9°. At 5,000 feet (Denver), for example, water boils at about 203°.

Immerse the stem of a thermometer that can take the heat (that is, register above 212°) in boiling water and take a reading. If it's off and can't be adjusted—but you don't want to toss it—simply compensate by the difference between its reading and the boiling point where you live. For example, if you're at sea level and it reads 205° at boiling, subtract 7°; if the pork needs to be cooked to 150°, remove it from the heat when the thermometer reads 143°.

To check thermometers that don't register at boiling or above, first check one that does, then let the water cool to the range of the others and stick them in. Compare their readings with that of the test thermometer, and calculate the differences. ◆

half this mixture for a dish that's less rich but not quite as impressive.) Peel plastic from chicken and mound equal portions of butter mixture in the centers of breast halves. To shape each breast half, lap a long side of chicken over the butter mixture. Fold narrow ends of chicken toward the center, slightly over butter, making the bundle about 5½ inches long. Lap remaining long side of breast over the first to completely enclose butter. If any butter is exposed, pull a thin edge of breast over it, or tear a bit of chicken from the edge and press it over the opening.

3. Break 1 **large egg** into a shallow pan and beat with a fork to blend. Put ½ cup **fine dried bread crumbs** in another shallow pan. Roll each breast half in egg, then in crumbs; place breasts slightly apart on a sheet of waxed paper.

4. Set a 10- to 12-inch ovenproof frying pan over high heat. Add 1 tablespoon **butter** or margarine. When butter sizzles, carefully lay crumb-coated chicken breasts side by side in pan. Brown, turning once with a wide spatula, 2 to 3 minutes total. Put in a 400° oven and bake until chicken is an even golden brown, 6 to 8 minutes (about 10 minutes if chilled). *Note: You can't cut to test without creating a leak.*

5. Transfer chicken to plates. Season to taste with **salt.** Serve with steamed diced **potatoes** (about 2 lb. total) to share butter filling.

Per serving with potatoes: 687 cal., 39% (270 cal.) from fat; 47 g protein; 30 g fat (17 g sat.); 56 g carbo (4 g fiber); 519 mg sodium; 222 mg chol.

Kitchen Cabinet

READERS' RECIPES TESTED IN SUNSET'S KITCHENS

BY LINDA LAU ANUSASANANAN

Hungarian Mushroom Pâté

Elizabeth Farquhar, Randle, Washington

This spreadable pâté reminds Elizabeth Farquhar of picking mushrooms for her Hungarian grandmother's mushroom soup. Use a food processor if you want a fine-textured, dense pâté; hand-chopping produces a looser, coarser texture.

PREP AND COOK TIME: About 35 minutes

MAKES: 10 to 12 servings

- 8 **dried shiitake mushrooms** (about 1 cup; $\frac{1}{2}$ oz. total)
- 1 **onion** (about $\frac{1}{2}$ lb.)
- 1 **shallot** (about 2 oz.)
- 2 cloves **garlic**
- 2 tablespoons **olive oil**
- 1 tablespoon **paprika**
- 1 pound **common mushrooms,** rinsed
- 2 tablespoons minced **fresh thyme** leaves or 2 tablespoons dried thyme

  About $\frac{1}{2}$ cup **plain nonfat yogurt** (optional)

  Salt and **pepper**

  Chopped **parsley**

  Crackers or toasted baguette slices

1. In a bowl, combine shiitakes and 1 cup hot water; let stand until shiitakes are soft, 7 to 10 minutes.

2. As shiitakes soak, peel onion, shallot, and garlic. Finely chop in a food processor or with a knife.

3. In a 10- to 12-inch frying pan over medium-high heat, frequently stir onion, shallot, garlic, olive oil, and paprika until vegetables begin to brown, 5 to 7 minutes.

4. Meanwhile, trim off and discard discolored stem ends of common mushrooms. Finely chop mushrooms in a food processor or with a knife.

5. When shiitakes are soft, squeeze in soaking water to release grit, lift out, and squeeze dry; reserve water. Trim off and discard stems; finely chop shiitakes in a food processor or with a knife.

6. Add common mushrooms, shiitakes, and thyme to onion mixture. Slowly pour reserved soaking water into pan, leaving sediment behind. Stir often over high heat until mushrooms begin to brown, 8 to 10 minutes. Remove from heat and let cool, about 10 minutes.

7. Add yogurt, salt, and pepper to taste. Spoon into a bowl and sprinkle with parsley. Serve warm or cool. Spread on crackers to eat.

Per serving: 46 cal., 50% (23 cal.) from fat; 1.4 g protein; 2.5 g fat (0.3 g sat.); 5.6 g carbo (1.1 g fiber); 3.1 mg sodium; 0 mg chol.

REFRESHING: Sweet orange slices on romaine.

Italian Orange Salad

Joanne Santoianni, Whittier, California

Like her mom from Italy, Joanne Santoianni makes the most of sweet, juicy oranges—navels this time of year—in this ultrasimple salad. Sometimes she even omits the lettuce.

PREP TIME: About 10 minutes

MAKES: 4 servings

- 4 **oranges** (10 to 12 oz. each)
- 8 to 12 **romaine lettuce** leaves (6 to 8 in. long), rinsed and crisped

  Sugar

- 1 to 2 tablespoons **extra-virgin olive oil**

  Salt and fresh-ground **pepper**

1. Cut peel and white membrane from oranges and discard. Thinly slice fruit crosswise.

2. Line salad plates with lettuce leaves and arrange orange slices on top.

3. Sprinkle fruit with sugar. Drizzle olive oil over salads. Add salt and pepper to taste.

Per serving: 126 cal., 28% (35 cal.) from fat; 1.5 g protein; 3.9 g fat (0.6 g sat.); 24 g carbo (5 g fiber); 0 mg sodium; 0 mg chol.

Delta Pear Cake

Vicki Vermeer, Tuolumne, California

Chunks of fresh pear make this dessert as moist as applesauce cake. It's a favorite of Vicki Vermeer, who acquired the recipe from Sarah Simpson of Simpson Ranch, a pear farm in the Sacramento Delta.

PREP AND COOK TIME: About 1 hour and 15 minutes (about 1 hour if using a convection oven)

MAKES: 12 servings

- 2 cups **sugar**
- 2 **large eggs**

  About $\frac{1}{2}$ cup **salad oil**

- 2 cups **all-purpose flour**
- 2 teaspoons **baking soda**
- 1 teaspoon **ground cinnamon**
- 1 teaspoon **ground nutmeg**
- $\frac{1}{2}$ teaspoon **salt**
- $\frac{1}{4}$ teaspoon **ground cloves**
- 3 cups diced ($\frac{1}{2}$ in.) peeled **firm-ripe pears**
- 1 cup chopped **walnuts**
- 1 cup **raisins**

1. In a large bowl with a mixer, beat sugar, eggs, and $\frac{1}{2}$ cup oil until well blended, about 2 minutes.

2. In another bowl, mix flour, baking soda, cinnamon, nutmeg, salt, and cloves. Stir in pears, walnuts, and raisins.

3. Add flour mixture to egg mixture and stir just until evenly moistened. Spread batter in an oiled and floured 9- by 13-inch pan.

4. Bake in a 350° oven until top of cake springs back when lightly touched in the center, about 1 hour (about 45 minutes in a convection oven). Cool on a rack. Serve warm or cool; cut into rectangles and lift out with a spatula.

Per serving: 430 cal., 36% (153 cal.) from fat; 5.2 g protein; 17 g fat (2.1 g sat.); 68 g carbo (2.7 g fiber); 321 mg sodium; 35 mg chol.

Penne with Dried Tomatoes

Rose Bellanca, Henderson, Nevada

Impressed by a restaurant's pasta with tomatoes and prosciutto, Rose Bellanca aimed to duplicate its summer-fresh taste—even in winter. She succeeded with a combination of dried and canned tomatoes.

PREP AND COOK TIME: About 25 minutes
MAKES: 4 servings

- ⅓ cup **cider vinegar**
- ¾ cup (1½ oz.) **dried tomatoes**, cut into ½-inch-wide strips
- ¾ pound **dried penne pasta**
- 2 to 3 ounces **thin-sliced prosciutto**, cut into thin slivers
- 1 can (about 15 oz.) **Italian-style stewed tomatoes**
- 2 cloves **garlic**, pressed or minced
- ½ cup chopped **parsley**
- 2 tablespoons **olive oil** (optional)

  About ¼ cup **grated romano** or parmesan **cheese**

  Salt and **pepper**

1. In a microwave-safe bowl, combine vinegar, ⅓ cup water, and dried tomatoes. Heat, covered, in a microwave oven at full power (100%) until steaming, about 45 seconds. Let stand, stirring occasionally, until tomatoes are soft, about 20 minutes.

2. Meanwhile, in a 5- to 6-quart pan over high heat, bring about 3 quarts water to a boil. Add the penne pasta and cook until it's barely tender to bite, 10 to 12 minutes. Drain.

3. As pasta cooks, lay prosciutto strips on a microwave-safe plate and heat in a microwave oven at full power (100%), stirring once, just until hot, 15 to 20 seconds.

4. Also, pour canned tomatoes into a strainer over a large bowl, then chop the tomatoes and add to juices in bowl. Add dried tomatoes and soaking liquid, garlic, parsley, pasta, and olive oil. Mix, and add prosciutto and ¼ cup cheese. Mix again, and add salt, pepper, and more cheese to taste.

Per serving: 431 cal., 9.7% (42 cal.) from fat; 20 g protein; 4.7 g fat (1.5 g sat.); 79 g carbo (6.1 g fiber); 792 mg sodium; 17 mg chol.

Sweet-Crunch Muffins

Marilyn Gill, Lewistown, Montana

In an inspired attempt to dress up plain oatmeal muffins, Marilyn Gill produced these sweet, crunchy snacks.

PREP AND COOK TIME: About 50 minutes (about 45 minutes if using a convection oven)

MAKES: 12 to 15 muffins

BITS OF SWEET DATES and mellow pecans speckle wholesome oatmeal muffins.

- 1 cup **regular rolled oats**
- 1 cup **buttermilk**
- ½ cup firmly packed **brown sugar**

  About ½ cup **salad oil**
- 2 **large egg** whites
- 1 cup **whole-wheat flour**
- 2 teaspoons **baking powder**
- ½ teaspoon **baking soda**
- ½ cup **pitted dates**, chopped
- ½ cup chopped **pecans**

1. In a large bowl, mix oats, buttermilk, sugar, ½ cup salad oil, and egg whites.

2. In another bowl, mix flour, baking powder, baking soda, dates, and pecans.

3. Add flour mixture to buttermilk mixture; stir just until evenly moistened.

4. Equally fill 12 to 15 oiled or paper-lined muffin cups (2¾ in. wide) with batter. Bake in a 375° oven until well browned, 20 to 25 minutes (15 to 20 minutes in a convection oven).

5. Cool in pans for 5 minutes. Invert to remove muffins. Serve warm or cool.

Per muffin: 197 cal., 50% (99 cal.) from fat; 3.3 g protein; 11 g fat (1.4 g sat.); 23 g carbo (2.1 g fiber); 135 mg sodium; 0.7 mg chol. ◆

Dried soup mix and a bottle of beer transform lean beef rump into tender Oxtail Soup Mix Pot Roast (recipe on page 39).

February

SPLIT LOBSTER TAIL arches over a
lavish blend of seafood in a classic
Italian cioppino with a citrus twist.

Great catch!

Shellfish soups around the world, from Veracruz to Saigon

BY LINDA LAU ANUSASANANAN • PHOTOGRAPHS BY JAMES CARRIER
FOOD STYLING BY VALERIE AIKMAN-SMITH

■ Wild Dungeness crab captured as they scuttle offshore anywhere from Alaska to Mexico, blue-black mussels hauled from cold waters along the coast of Spain, and giant shrimp gathered from the sea around Vietnam: in tide-splashed cuisines worldwide, exquisitely packaged creatures from the deep cook up into cauldrons of signature shellfish soups.

Add a salad and a loaf of crusty bread for a simply sensational supper, with any international accent you choose. These soups are definitely hands-on affairs, so provide big napkins, dump buckets for discarded shells, and wet towels or finger bowls for cleanup.

Orange-Fennel Cioppino

PREP AND COOK TIME: About 2 hours
NOTES: You can complete soup through step 4 up to 1 day ahead, then cover and chill. Reheat to continue. For a less costly version, omit the lobster tails and increase the shrimp to $1\frac{1}{2}$ pounds.
MAKES: 6 servings

- 1 head **fennel** (about $3\frac{1}{2}$ in. wide) with feathery green tops
- 1 pound **leeks**
- 3 cloves **garlic,** minced
- 2 tablespoons **olive oil**
- 2 cans (28 oz. each) **diced tomatoes**
- 3 cups fat-skimmed **chicken broth**
- 2 cups **bottled clam juice**
- 2 cups **dry white wine**
- 2 **dried bay leaves**
- 1 tablespoon minced **fresh thyme** leaves or dried thyme
- 1 tablespoon grated **orange** peel
- $\frac{1}{8}$ teaspoon **powdered saffron** (optional)
- 3 **spiny** or rock **lobster tails** ($\frac{1}{2}$ lb. each), thawed if frozen
- 1 pound **boned, skinned halibut** or swordfish, cut into 6 equal pieces
- $\frac{3}{4}$ pound (30 to 35 per lb.) **shrimp,** shelled and deveined
- $\frac{1}{2}$ pound **bay scallops**
- 12 **clams in shells,** suitable for steaming, scrubbed
- 12 **mussels** (about 3 in. each), beards pulled off, scrubbed

1. Trim off feathery fennel tops; rinse, drain, wrap airtight, and chill. Trim off and discard base of fennel head, any bruises, and tough stalks. Rinse and thinly slice fennel head.

2. Trim tough tops and roots from leeks; pull off coarse outer layers. Cut tender sections of leeks in half lengthwise, rinse well, and thinly slice.

3. In an 8- to 10-quart pan, combine fennel, leeks, garlic, and oil. Stir often over medium-high heat until vegetables are lightly browned, 8 to 10 minutes.

4. Add tomatoes with juice, broth, clam juice, wine, bay leaves, thyme, orange peel, and saffron. Cover and bring to a boil over high heat.

5. Meanwhile, with scissors, cut fins and sharp spines from lobster tails. Also cut through top shells lengthwise down the center. Set each tail, underside down, on a board. With a heavy knife, slice tails in half lengthwise through cuts in shells. Rinse lobster tails, halibut, shrimp, and scallops.

6. Add lobster, halibut, and shrimp to tomato mixture. Discard any clams or mussels that do not close when shells are tapped. Add clams and mussels to pan; cover and cook 5 minutes. Add scallops. Cover and simmer until mussels and clams pop open, 3 to 5 more minutes.

7. Transfer cioppino to a tureen or ladle

into wide bowls. Garnish with green fennel tops.

Per serving: 442 cal., 18% (79 cal.) from fat; 55 g protein; 8.8 g fat (1.2 g sat.); 22 g carbo (3.1 g fiber); 1,149 mg sodium; 158 mg chol.

Basque Steamed Mussels

PREP AND COOK TIME: About 45 minutes

NOTES: Chef Scott A. Barton, at Plouf in San Francisco, steams blue-black mussels in a vivid red broth of roasted peppers, then adds homemade habanero vinegar for a zing to match the color.

MAKES: 5 or 6 servings

- 5 **red bell peppers** (2½ lb. total)
- 1 **green bell pepper** (½ lb.)
  About 1 tablespoon **extra-virgin olive oil**
- 2 teaspoons minced **garlic**
- 1 cup chopped **onion**
- 2 cups **bottled clam juice** or fat-skimmed chicken broth
- 1 cup **dry white wine**
  About 2 teaspoons **habanero vinegar** (recipe follows) or hot sauce
- 6 dozen **mussels** (about 3 in. each), beards pulled off, scrubbed
- 2 tablespoons chopped **parsley**
  Salt

1. Place red and green peppers in a 10-by 15-inch pan. Broil about 4 inches from heat until pepper skins are charred and blistered all over, turning as needed, 15 to 20 minutes. Cool. Pull off and discard skins, stems, and seeds. Chop red and green peppers separately.

2. In a food processor or blender, purée ¾ of the red peppers until smooth.

3. In a 6- to 8-quart pan over high heat, combine 1 teaspoon olive oil and the garlic. Stir often until garlic is limp,

RED BELL PEPPER sauce sets off mussels in traditional Basque style.

about 1 minute. Add onion, clam juice, wine, 1 teaspoon habanero vinegar, and red pepper purée. Cover and bring to a boil.

4. Discard any gaping mussels that do not close when shells are tapped. Add mussels to pan, cover, and cook until shells pop open, 5 to 10 minutes. With a slotted spoon, transfer mussels to wide bowls.

5. Add chopped green and red peppers to broth; bring to a boil. Add parsley and season mixture to taste with salt and more habanero vinegar. Ladle over mussels. Drizzle each serving with olive oil to taste.

Per serving: 168 cal., 23% (38 cal.) from fat; 10 g protein; 4.2 g fat (0.6 g sat.); 18 g carbo (3.5 g fiber); 367 mg sodium; 18 mg chol.

Habanero Vinegar

PREP TIME: 5 minutes

NOTES: If making ahead, cover and chill vinegar up to 1 month.

MAKES: About 1 cup

In a blender, whirl 1 cup **champagne vinegar** or white wine vinegar and 1 rinsed and stemmed **fresh habanero chili** (½ oz.) until chili is puréed.

Per teaspoon: 0.8 cal., 0% (0 cal.) from fat; 0 g protein; 0 g fat; 0.2 g carbo (0 g fiber); 0 mg sodium; 0 mg chol.

Mexican Crab and Corn Soup

PREP AND COOK TIME: About 1 hour

NOTES: For best flavor, start with un-cooked crabs but have your fishmonger kill, clean, and crack them. Ask him or her to save the golden crab butter to enrich the broth. Keep crab cold and cook within 6 hours. Strong, resin-scented epazote, with mint and anise overtones, is sometimes found fresh,

and often dried, in Latino markets.

MAKES: 4 servings

- 1 pound **Roma tomatoes**
- 1 **onion** (½ lb.), peeled and cut into 1-inch wedges
- 4 cloves **garlic,** unpeeled
- 2 or 3 **fresh jalapeño chilies** (1 to 1½ oz. total)
- 1 tablespoon **olive oil**
- ⅓ cup **dehydrated masa flour** (corn tortilla flour)
- 3 cups fat-skimmed **chicken broth**
- 4 bottles (8 oz. each) **clam juice**
- 2 live or cooked **Dungeness crabs** (about 4 lb. total), cleaned and cracked; reserve golden crab butter (optional)
- 2 **ears corn** (6 to 8 in.) or 1 package (10 oz.) frozen corn kernels
- 3 or 4 **epazote sprigs** (4 in.) or 1 tablespoon crushed dried epazote (optional)
  Salt
- 2 **limes,** cut in half

1. In a 10- by 15-inch pan, arrange tomatoes, onion, garlic, and chilies in a single layer. Broil about 4 inches from heat until charred, turning as needed, 13 to 15 minutes. Remove vegetables as they char. Cool. Peel onion and garlic; pull off and discard chili skin, seeds, and stems. In a blender or food processor, purée vegetables.

2. Pour purée and oil into a 5- to 6-quart pan over high heat. Stir often until mixture is slightly darker, 5 to 7 minutes.

3. Mix masa flour and broth. Stir into pan along with clam juice.

4. For added flavor, if desired, rub crab butter through a fine strainer into pan.

5. Bring mixture to a boil, stirring; oc-

SWEET CRAB with corn is emboldened by the Mexican herb epazote.

BOWL FROM SUMMER HOUSE, MILL VALLEY, CA (415/383-6695)

HEADS-ON SHRIMP are an authentic option in Vietnamese sweet-sour soup.

casionally; cover and simmer gently for 5 minutes.

6. Meanwhile, remove husks and silk from corn. With a heavy knife, cut corn crosswise into 1-inch-wide wheels; if needed, pound back of knife gently with mallet to force blade through cob.

7. Add epazote (if dried, tie in cheese-cloth), corn, and crab pieces to pan. Cover and simmer until crab is hot, 5 minutes (if cooked) to 10 minutes (if raw). Remove and discard epazote.

8. Ladle soup into bowls. Season to taste with salt and juice squeezed from limes.

Per serving: 302 cal., 18% (55 cal.) from fat; 31 g protein; 6.1 g fat (0.8 g sat.); 34 g carbo (5.3 g fiber); 916 mg sodium; 64 mg chol.

Vietnamese Sweet-Sour Shrimp Soup

PREP AND COOK TIME: About 1 hour

NOTES: Sacramento-based Mai Pham, author of *The Best of Vietnamese & Thai Cooking* and owner of Lemon Grass Restaurant and Cafe, poaches shrimp in this spicy, sweet-sour soup base. For a striking presentation, use shrimp with heads; they are sold in Asian fish markets and some seafood markets. Buy 1½ pounds (21 to 30 per lb.) shrimp and devein in the shells: slide a thin metal skewer through each shell, under and perpendicular to vein, then pull skewer up through shell to draw out vein; repeat in several places along shell back. Rinse shrimp and cook in shells. Tamarind pulp is found in Asian and Latino markets. Purple-tinged Thai or anise basil and the tiny sprigs of cumin-scented rice-paddy herb can be found in Vietnamese markets.

MAKES: 4 servings

2 tablespoons **tamarind pulp** (optional)

¼ cup thinly sliced **shallots**

1 tablespoon **salad oil**

½ teaspoon minced **garlic**

½ teaspoon **Asian chili paste** or hot chili flakes

5 cups fat-skimmed **chicken broth**

1 pound (30 to 35 per lb.) **shrimp,** peeled, deveined, and rinsed

1 cup **pineapple** chunks (¾ in.)

2 tablespoons **Asian fish sauce** (*nuoc mam* or *nam pla*) or reduced-sodium soy sauce

3 tablespoons **sugar**

¼ cup **lime juice** (6 tablespoons if you don't use tamarind pulp)

2 **Roma tomatoes** (6 oz. total), rinsed, cored, and cut into ½-inch wedges

2 cups (6 oz.) **bean sprouts,** rinsed and drained

2 tablespoons chopped **fresh Thai** or anise **basil** (*rau hung que*) or regular basil leaves

2 tablespoons chopped **rice-paddy herb** (*ngo om*) or fresh cilantro

About 2 teaspoons finely chopped **fresh Thai** (*hang prik*) or serrano **chilies**

1. In a bowl, combine tamarind pulp and ⅓ cup hot water. Let cool, rub pulp

off seeds, and press mixture through a fine strainer into another small bowl; discard seeds.

2. In a 5- to 6-quart pan over medium heat, stir shallots with oil until golden and crisp, 3 to 6 minutes. Lift out with a slotted spoon and drain on towels.

3. Add garlic and chili paste to pan and stir until garlic is fragrant, about 10 seconds. Add broth, cover, and bring to a boil over high heat.

4. Add shrimp, pineapple, fish sauce, sugar, lime juice, and reserved tamarind pulp. Cook, uncovered, just until shrimp turns pink, 2 to 3 minutes.

5. With a slotted spoon, transfer shrimp and pineapple to wide soup bowls. Stir tomatoes, bean sprouts, basil, and rice-paddy herb into hot broth.

6. Ladle soup mixture into bowls and sprinkle with fried shallots. Add chopped chilies to taste.

Per serving: 281 cal., 20% (57 cal.) from fat; 32 g protein; 6.3 g fat (1 g sat.); 24 g carbo (1.6 g fiber); 556 mg sodium; 140 mg chol.

Portuguese Clam and Cilantro Soup

PREP AND COOK TIME: About 35 minutes

NOTES: The Portuguese add a coarse-textured bread to soak up the soup. If you prefer, serve bread alongside.

MAKES: 4 or 5 servings

1 **onion** (½ lb.), peeled and chopped

2 tablespoons **olive oil**

2 bottles (8 oz. each) **clam juice**

1 cup **dry white wine**

6 dozen **clams in shells,** suitable for steaming, scrubbed

1 tablespoon minced **garlic**

¼ teaspoon **pepper**

1 cup chopped **fresh cilantro**

2 cups 1-inch cubes **crusty bread**

1. In a 5- to 6-quart pan over high heat, stir onion in oil until limp, about 3 minutes. Add clam juice, wine, and 2 cups water. Bring to a boil. Add clams, garlic, and pepper.

2. Cover and cook until clams pop open, 5 to 10 minutes. Sprinkle with cilantro.

3. Distribute bread cubes equally among wide soup bowls. Spoon clams and broth into bowls.

Per serving: 200 cal., 31% (61 cal.) from fat; 13 g protein; 6.8 g fat (0.9 g sat.); 14 g carbo (1.3 g fiber); 339 mg sodium; 28 mg chol. ◆

CLAMS PORTUGUESE-STYLE pop open in a bath of wine and cilantro.

BOWL FROM SUMMER HOUSE

A taste of India

Familiar foods glorified, spices simplified, step by flavorful step

BY LINDA LAU ANUSASANANAN   PHOTOGRAPHS BY ROBERT OLDING

■ The enticing fragrance of mingling spices and the soothing sounds of Ravi Shankar's sitar heighten anticipation for a special dinner at Laxmi Hiremath's home. A self-taught cook and writer from Pune, India, Hiremath prefers to offer many small tastes—each with different hues, textures, and spices—to entice newcomers to her cuisine.

Even novice cooks will find this menu easy to prepare, because much of it can be completed far ahead of time (see Stepping Ahead, page 36). You will find all the basic elements at a supermarket, but for authentic details—black cumin, curry leaves, pickles, and flatbreads—shop at an Indian market.

Tandoori Quail

PREP AND COOK TIME: About 1 hour

MAKES: 6 to 8 servings

- ½ cup **plain nonfat** or low-fat **yogurt**
- ¼ cup minced **fresh ginger**
- 2 tablespoons minced **garlic**
- 4 teaspoons **tandoori masala** (recipe follows)

  About ½ teaspoon **salt**

- 6 to 8 **quail** (about ¼ lb. each)

1. In a large bowl, mix the yogurt, ginger, garlic, tandoori masala, and ½ teaspoon salt.

2. Rinse quail and pat dry. Using poultry shears or a sharp knife, cut out the backbone of each quail. Turn birds skin side up and press with the palm of your

hand to flatten; a few bones will crack.

3. Turn birds in yogurt mixture to coat. Cover and chill at least 30 minutes or up to 1 day.

4. To barbecue, place quail on an oiled grill over medium-hot coals or over medium-high heat on a gas grill (you can hold your hand at grill level only 3

Laxmi's Indian Sampler Supper for 6 to 8

Tandoori Quail (*Tandoori Panchi*) or Cornish Hens (*Murgh*)

Tandoori Roasted Vegetables (*Tandoori Sabji*)

Chopped Tomatoes and Cucumbers with Yogurt (*Tamatar Raita*)*

Creamed Kidney Beans (*Shahi Rajmah*)

Savory Rice with Peas and Cashews (*Chitranna*)

Toasted Lentil Wafers (*Pappadums*)

Flatbreads: *Nan, Paratha,* and *Chapati* or Whole-Wheat Tortillas*

Pineapple-Walnut Chutney (*Ananas Chatni*)

Sweet Lime Pickles (*Meetha Achaar*)*

Frozen Mango Cream (*Aam Kulfi*)

Chardonnay • Merlot

Hot or Iced Aromatic Ginger Tea (*Masala Chai*)

purchased

HOSTESS LAXMI HIREMATH (top left) brings the flavors of India to California.

CRISP, SPICY PAPPADUMS (bottom left) are an addictive accompaniment to tandoori-spiced grilled quail and roasted vegetables (right). Yogurt with cucumbers cools the mix.

COOL AND SPICY flavors together (top) provide contrast and balance.

GOLDEN RICE scented with turmeric and curry leaves (right) offsets spicy dishes.

to 4 seconds). Close lid of gas grill. Cook quail, turning as needed, until skin is well browned and meat at breastbone is still pink (cut to test), 12 to 14 minutes total. Season to taste with salt.

Per serving: Approx. 211 cal., 51% (108 cal.) from fat; 21 g protein; 12 g fat (3.4 g sat.); 3 g carbo (0.2 g fiber); 211 mg sodium; 77 mg chol.

Tandoori Masala

PREP AND COOK TIME: About 12 minutes
MAKES: About ⅓ cup

1. Remove seed from 6 **green** or white **cardamom pods** (or use ⅛ teaspoon cardamom seed).

2. In an 8- to 10-inch frying pan over medium heat, combine cardamom seed, 1 tablespoon **coriander seed**, 1½ teaspoons **black** or regular **cumin seed,** 1½ teaspoons **whole cloves,** ¾ teaspoon **black peppercorns,** and 1 **cinnamon stick** (1 in.). Stir often until the mixture is aromatic and the seeds are lightly browned, 4 to 5 minutes.

3. Pour the spice mixture into a blender or spice grinder and whirl or grind to a fine powder.

4. Add 2½ tablespoons **paprika** and ½ teaspoon **ground ginger;** whirl to mix. Season to taste with **cayenne** (about ¼ teaspoon for moderately hot). If making tandoori masala up to 1 week ahead, store airtight.

Per tablespoon: 20 cal., 41% (8.1 cal.) from fat; 0.8 g protein; 0.9 g fat (0.1 g sat.); 3.7 g carbo (0.6 g fiber); 4.4 mg sodium; 0 mg chol.

Tandoori Cornish Hens

PREP AND COOK TIME: About 1¼ hours
MAKES: 6 or 8 servings

1. Follow directions for **Tandoori Quail** (preceding), but instead of quail, use 3 or 4 **Cornish hens** (1½ lb. each). Cut hens in half through breastbones and backbones.

2. *To barbecue over charcoal,* ignite 60 briquets on firegrate in a barbecue with a lid. When coals are spotted with gray ash, in 20 to 30 minutes, bank about half the coals on each side of the firegrate. Place a drip pan in the center. Set grill above coals.

To barbecue over gas, turn gas barbecue to high heat and cover for 10 minutes. Adjust for indirect heat.

3. Set hen halves about ½ inch apart on center of grill, not over heat. Cover and cook until meat is no longer pink at thigh bone (cut to test), 30 to 35 minutes total.

Per serving: 389 cal., 60% (234 cal.) from fat; 33 g protein; 26 g fat (7.3 g sat.); 3 g carbo (0.2 g fiber); 249 mg sodium; 188 mg chol.

Tandoori Roasted Vegetables

PREP AND COOK TIME: About 50 minutes
NOTES: Use a mixture of these vegetables in proportions desired, changing for variety each time you prepare dish: 1-inch bell pepper squares, ¼-inch-thick diagonal carrot and asparagus slices, whole cherry tomatoes, and ½-inch turnip or zucchini chunks. Serve as a first course or with roasted meats.
MAKES: 6 to 8 servings

12 cups bite-size **vegetables** (see notes)

3 tablespoons **olive oil**

1½ tablespoons **tandoori masala** (recipe at left)

Salt and **pepper**

1. In an 11- by 17-inch roasting pan, mix vegetables, oil, and tandoori masala.

2. Bake in a 400° oven, stirring occasionally, until vegetables are browned and tender when pierced, 40 to 45 minutes (30 to 35 minutes in a convection oven).

3. Transfer to serving dish. Serve hot or cool. Cover and chill up to 1 day. Add salt and pepper to taste.

Per serving: 101 cal., 50% (50 cal.) from fat; 3.1 g protein; 5.6 g fat (0.7 g sat.); 12 g carbo (3.4 g fiber); 45 mg sodium; 0 mg chol.

Creamed Kidney Beans

PREP AND COOK TIME: About 35 minutes
NOTES: You can use pinto beans instead of kidney beans.
MAKES: 6 to 8 servings

1½ teaspoons **coriander seed**

1 teaspoon **black peppercorns**

¾ teaspoon **cumin seed**

1 tablespoon **butter** or margarine

1 cup minced **onion**

3 or 4 **fresh jalapeño chilies** (1½ to 2 oz. total), stemmed and minced

1 tablespoon minced **fresh ginger**

1½ teaspoons minced **garlic**

½ cup **tomato paste**

3 cans (15 oz. each) **kidney beans,** rinsed and drained

½ cup **milk**

½ cup **half-and-half** (light cream)

Salt

3 tablespoons minced **fresh cilantro**

1. In a 3- to 4-quart pan over medium heat, combine coriander seed, peppercorns, and cumin seed. Shake pan often until mixture is aromatic and seeds are slightly browner, about 6 minutes.

2. In a blender or spice grinder, whirl or grind spice mixture to a fine powder.

3. In a 3- to 4-quart pan over medium-high heat, melt butter. Add onion, chilies, ginger, and garlic; stir often until onion is lightly browned, 5 to 7 minutes.

4. Add tomato paste and ground spices. Stir until spices are fragrant, 1 to 2 minutes.

5. Add beans, 1 cup water, and milk. Bring to a boil, stirring often. Reduce heat, cover, and simmer until beans are hot and sauce coats spoon thickly, 6 to 8 minutes.

6. Stir in half-and-half. Add salt to taste. If making up to 1 day ahead, cover and chill; to warm, stir in pan over medium heat until steaming. Pour into a bowl and garnish with cilantro.

Per serving: 181 cal., 24% (43 cal.) from fat; 10 g protein; 4.8 g fat (2.3 g sat.); 25 g carbo (7.7 g fiber); 357 mg sodium; 12 mg chol.

Savory Rice with Peas and Cashews

PREP AND COOK TIME: About 25 minutes
NOTES: At least 3 hours or up to 2 days ahead, in a 3- to 4-quart pan, combine 2½ cups rinsed and drained basmati or long-grain white rice and 4½ cups water. Bring to a boil over high heat. Reduce heat and simmer, uncovered, until most of the water is absorbed, 6 to 8 minutes. Cover and cook over low heat until rice is tender to bite, 8 to 10 minutes more. Pour rice onto a tray and let cool, then cover and chill until cold. To use, break grains apart with your fingers.
MAKES: 6 to 8 servings

3 tablespoons **salad oil**

1 teaspoon **mustard seed**

1 teaspoon **cumin seed**

1 **onion** (about ¾ lb.), peeled and finely chopped

3 or 4 **fresh jalapeño chilies** (1½ to 2 oz. total), stemmed and chopped

½ teaspoon **ground turmeric**

12 **fresh curry leaves** (optional)

9 cups cold cooked **basmati** or long-grain white **rice** (see notes)

¼ cup **frozen peas**

About ½ teaspoon **salt**

1½ teaspoons **sugar**

2 tablespoons **lime** juice

⅓ cup **unsalted** or salted **roasted cashews**

2 tablespoons chopped **fresh cilantro**

1. Set a 5- to 6-quart pan or 14-inch wok over medium-high heat. Add oil, mustard seed, and cumin seed.

2. When the seeds begin to pop, in 2 to 3 minutes, stir in the onion, chilies, turmeric, and curry leaves. Stir often until the onion is limp, about 4 minutes.

3. Reduce heat to low. Add rice, peas, ½ teaspoon salt, and sugar. Stir until rice is evenly colored yellow. Sprinkle with lime juice and mix well. Cover and stir occasionally until rice is hot, 6 to 10 minutes. Add salt to taste. Transfer to a platter.

4. Sprinkle rice mixture with cashews and cilantro. Serve hot, warm, or at room temperature.

Per serving: 317 cal., 24% (76 cal.) from fat; 6.1 g protein; 8.4 g fat (1.3 g sat.); 53 g carbo (1.7 g fiber); 155 mg sodium; 0 mg chol.

A timetable for convenience

• Up to 1 week before the party: Make tandoori masala; store airtight. Toast lentil wafers; store airtight. Make chutney; cover and chill. Freeze mango cream.

• Up to 2 days ahead: Cook rice; cover and chill.

• Up to 1 day ahead: Marinate quail or Cornish hens, roast tandoori vegetables, cook beans, brew tea (to serve iced). Cover each separately and chill.

• The last hour: Grill the quail or Cornish hens. Bring the tandoori vegetables to room temperature or reheat. Season and heat the rice. Reheat the beans. Make tea to serve hot.

DIAMONDS OF FROZEN MANGO CREAM, dusted with chopped pistachios, are a cool, satisfying end to the meal.

Toasted Lentil Wafers

PREP AND COOK TIME: About 5 minutes

Lay **pappadum wafers** (5 in.) slightly apart on a baking sheet. Broil 4 to 6 inches from heat until wafers begin to buckle, 15 to 25 seconds; watch closely—they scorch easily. Turn wafers over and broil until surface is blistered, 8 to 12 seconds. Transfer toasted wafers to a rack. Repeat to prepare at least 2 wafers per serving. When cool, store airtight up to 1 week.

Per wafer: 27 cal., 6.7% (1.8 cal.) from fat; 2 g protein; 0.2 g fat (0 g sat.); 4.7 g carbo (1 g fiber); 260 mg sodium; 0 mg chol.

Pineapple-Walnut Chutney

PREP AND COOK TIME: About 50 minutes

MAKES: About 1²/₃ cups

2 **dried red chilies** (2 to 3 in. each), stemmed

1½ teaspoons **mustard seed**

1 tablespoon minced **fresh ginger**

4 cloves **garlic**, minced

1 can (20 oz.) **pineapple chunks in unsweetened juice**

⅓ cup **distilled white vinegar**

½ cup **sugar**

½ teaspoon **salt**

½ cup coarsely chopped **walnuts**

1. Coarsely crush chilies and mustard seed using a mortar and pestle, or seal spices in a heavy plastic food bag and roughly crush with a rolling pin.

2. In a 2- to 3-quart pan, combine the chili mixture, ginger, garlic, pineapple with juice, vinegar, sugar, and salt. Bring to a boil over high heat, then lower heat to medium and simmer, uncovered, stirring occasionally, until most of the liquid has evaporated, 35 to 40 minutes.

3. Stir in walnuts. Serve warm or cool. Cover and chill up to 1 week.

Per tablespoon: 44 cal., 32% (14 cal.) from fat; 0.5 g protein; 1.5 g fat (0.1 g sat.); 7.9 g carbo (0.3 g fiber); 44 mg sodium; 0 mg chol.

Frozen Mango Cream

PREP TIME: 10 minutes, plus at least 3 hours to freeze

NOTES: Look for canned Alphonso mango pulp in Indian markets, valued for its overtones of rose, pineapple, and nectarine. Or purée 3 cans (about 1 lb. each) mango, drained, or about 3½ pounds pitted, peeled, diced fresh ripe mangoes. If using fresh mangoes, add more sugar to taste. In India, servings are often adorned with edible gold or silver leaf.

MAKES: 12 to 16 servings

1 package (8 oz.) **cream cheese**

¾ cup **sugar**

1 carton (8 oz.) **frozen whipped topping**, thawed

1 can (30 oz.) **Alphonso mango pulp** or 3½ cups mango purée (see notes)

Fresh mango slices (optional)

Finely chopped **pistachios** (optional)

1. In a large bowl with a mixer, beat cheese and sugar until well blended. Add whipped topping, in dollops, beating to combine. Gently whisk in mango until blended.

2. Pour mango mixture into a 10- by 15-inch rimmed pan. Freeze until firm, at least 3 hours or overnight. When frozen, serve or wrap airtight and freeze up to 1 week.

3. To serve, cut into diamonds or rectangles and lift out with a wide spatula. Garnish with mango slices and pistachios.

Per serving: 175 cal., 45% (78 cal.) from fat; 1.6 g protein; 8.7 g fat (6.2 g sat.); 25 g carbo (0.7 g fiber); 47 mg sodium; 16 mg chol.

Aromatic Ginger Tea

PREP AND COOK TIME: About 15 minutes

NOTES: To crush the cardamom seed, smash it with a flat-bottomed glass. For iced tea, brew up to 1 day ahead, replacing the whole milk with water and substituting Darjeeling tea for the Assam; to serve, pour the tea into ice-filled glasses.

MAKES: About 8 cups; 8 servings

1 quart **milk**

⅓ cup **sugar**

1 teaspoon **ground ginger**

8 **cardamom pods,** hulled and seed crushed (see notes), or ¼ teaspoon ground cardamom

8 **Assam** or orange pekoe **tea bags** or 3 tablespoons tea leaves

1. In a 3- to 4-quart pan over medium-high heat, combine milk, 1 quart water, sugar, ginger, and cardamom seed. Bring to a boil, stirring occasionally.

2. Add tea and simmer, stirring gently, 1 to 2 minutes.

3. Remove pan from heat, cover, and let stand until tea is a dark reddish brown color, about 1 minute.

4. Pour through a fine strainer into a hot teapot.

Per serving with milk: 110 cal., 34% (37 cal.) from fat; 4 g protein; 4.1 g fat (2.5 g sat.); 15 g carbo (0 g fiber); 67 mg sodium; 17 mg chol. ◆

JAMES CARRIER (3)

As smooth as … fudge?

For your valentine, use a chocolate maker's favorite recipe

BY LINDA LAU ANUSASANANAN

Premier chocolatier Alice Medrich, who knows fudge inside and out, likes it dense with dark chocolate, firm enough to cut neatly, and melt-in-your-mouth velvety smooth. Such fudge makes a perfect Valentine's Day gift.

Medrich's recipe for fudge is a keeper, but the tips at right ensure the best results for any recipe. Sweet science is the answer.

Dark Chocolate Fudge

PREP AND COOK TIME: About 1¾ hours

NOTES: Use a heavy pan to reduce the risks of sticking or burning. Fudge slices best and tastes creamiest if it's allowed to mellow overnight.

MAKES: 3 pounds (48 oz.)

> About 2 tablespoons **butter** or margarine
> 1½ cups **half-and-half** (light cream)
> 3½ cups **sugar**
> ¼ cup **light corn syrup**
> ½ teaspoon **salt**
> 8 ounces **bittersweet** or semisweet **chocolate,** chopped
> 4 ounces **unsweetened chocolate,** chopped
> 2 teaspoons **vanilla**
> 1½ cups **walnuts** or pecans

1. Smoothly line an 8- or 9-inch square pan with foil. Lightly butter foil.

2. In a 3- to 4-quart pan, mix half-and-half, sugar, corn syrup, and salt. Stir occasionally over high heat until simmering, about 3 minutes. With a brush dipped in water, frequently wipe off beads of syrup that form on the sides of the pan.

3. Reduce heat to medium. Add bittersweet and unsweetened chocolate; gently stir until chocolate melts and mixture begins to simmer, 3 to 6 minutes.

4. Insert a candy thermometer into mixture. Boil, occasionally stirring and washing sides of pan with wet brush, until mixture reaches 235° (or a drop of candy spooned into cold water forms a soft ball that flattens when removed from water), 30 to 40 minutes longer.

5. Immediately pour fudge mixture into a 10- by 15-inch rimmed pan. Dot with 2 tablespoons butter and vanilla.

6. Let stand undisturbed until a thermometer inserted in center of candy registers 115° (pan is warm to touch), 20 to 30 minutes. With a wide metal spatula, scrape mixture back and forth in pan until it becomes smooth and glossy and starts to thicken and mound but is still soft and malleable, 4 to 10 minutes. Add nuts and mix just enough to distribute.

7. Scrape fudge into foil-lined pan. Let stand until firm to touch, at least 2 hours. Invert pan to release candy. Peel off foil.

8. With a sharp knife, cut fudge into 1-inch squares and serve. Or wrap the uncut fudge airtight and store at room temperature up to 1 week.

Per ounce: 136 cal., 44% (60 cal.) from fat; 1.3 g protein; 6.7 g fat (2.7 g sat.); 20 g carbo (0.7 g fiber); 36 mg sodium; 4.3 mg chol. ◆

■ Food technologist George K. York explains the critical points of fudge making:

A. TO AVOID GRAININESS. The sugar (sucrose) in fudge is responsible for its texture. As sugar cooks, it physically changes, forming crystals, some tiny, some big. Graininess results when sugar crystals get large. To thwart the formation of large sugar crystals, York has three suggestions: Wash down the pan sides with water as the fudge cooks. Monitor the temperature carefully with an accurate thermometer to make sure the mixture does not overcook. And use corn syrup (glucose), which is not prone to crystallization.

B. FOR FUDGE THAT CUTS WELL. Agitating, or stirring, the fudge mixture after it is cooked affects the size of the sugar crystals, which controls the consistency of the finished fudge. If you stir when the mixture is too hot or too cold, it will either stay soft or get too firm to cut neatly. It is important to let the fudge mixture cool to 115° before the last stirring step (step 6 at left).

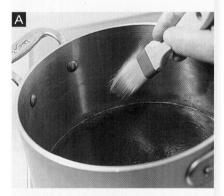

A

B

foodguide

BY JERRY ANNE DI VECCHIO

MILE-HIGH COOKING. *Sunset* is now testing leavened baked goods at high altitudes. Any needed adjustments will be included in recipes (following tests for doneness is essential).

A TASTE OF THE WEST

Rhubarb rhythm and blues

Tart, skinny stalks tingle with flavor

■ *Rhubarb* is such a funny collection of letters, I've never been able to take it seriously as a word or a food. Even though my grandmother made rhubarb into the pie that reigned supreme in Cowley County, Kansas, I never warmed up to it as a kid. But then I tasted rhubarb with strawberries—as a partner, it's a real asset. Paul Coumantaros, pastry chef at San Francisco's Savoy Brasserie, suggests another delectable union—rhubarb and almonds.

Rhubarb-Almond Tart

PREP AND COOK TIME: About 1½ hours (1¼ hours if using a convection oven)

NOTES: If making up to 1 day ahead, cool, cover, and chill; bring to room temperature to serve.

MAKES: 8 or 9 servings

  Butter pastry (directions follow)
1 pound **rhubarb**
1 cup **sugar**
1 cup **blanched almonds**
6 tablespoons (⅜ lb.) **butter** or margarine
2 **large eggs**
¼ teaspoon **almond extract**

1. Press butter pastry dough evenly over bottom and up sides of a 10-inch tart pan with removable rim.

2. Bake in a 300° oven until pale gold, about 20 minutes (about 15 minutes in a convection oven). Use hot or cool.

3. Rinse rhubarb, trim and discard dried ends, and cut stalks into 1-inch lengths. Put in a 10- to 12-inch frying pan and mix with 5 tablespoons sugar and ¼ cup water. Let stand 10 minutes, then stir and set over medium-low heat. When water boils, turn rhubarb pieces over once and cook about 2 more minutes. Remove from heat.

4. Meanwhile, in a food processor or blender, whirl nuts to a fine powder. To processor, add remaining sugar and the butter, eggs, and almond extract. Whirl until well blended. Or put the ground almonds in a bowl, add remaining sugar and the butter, eggs, and almond extract, and beat with a mixer until well blended.

5. Pour almond mixture into pastry. With a fork or slotted spoon, lift rhubarb pieces from cooking liquid (save liquid for other uses) and arrange in a pattern on filling.

6. Bake in a 350° oven until filling, which rises around rhubarb, is golden brown and center is firm when pan is gently shaken, 35 to 50 minutes (25 to 40 minutes in a convection oven).

7. Let cool at least 15 minutes; remove pan rim to cut. Serve warm or cool.

Per serving: 530 cal., 61% (324 cal.) from fat; 7.6 g protein; 36 g fat (17 g sat.); 47 g carbo (2.3 g fiber); 281 mg sodium; 140 mg chol.

Butter pastry. In a food processor or bowl, combine 1⅓ cups **all-purpose flour** and ¼ cup **sugar**. Add ½ cup (¼ lb.) **butter** or margarine, in chunks. Whirl, or rub with your fingers, until fine crumbs form. Add **1 large egg** yolk; whirl, or mix with a fork, until dough holds together. Firmly pat into a ball.

Mini rice

Teensy and tasty

■ Size does matter when it comes to rice. The grains of Kalijira, a fragrant basmati-like rice from Bangladesh, are only a third to half the size of basmati grains, and they cook in about half the time. Frankly, saving 10 minutes or so doesn't justify paying $4 to $6 a pound—the price of Kalijira. But its appealing size may seduce you. You'll find Kalijira rice where gourmet, specialty, and natural foods are sold.

Kalijira Pilaf with Pine Nuts

PREP AND COOK TIME: About 20 minutes

MAKES: 3¼ cups; 4 or 5 servings

1. Pour 1 cup **Kalijira rice** into a fine strainer. Rinse with cool water, draining often, until water is clear.

2. Meanwhile, in a 2- to 3-quart pan over medium-high heat, stir 1 tablespoon **butter** or margarine with ¼ cup **pine nuts** until butter begins to brown, about 3 minutes. Add rice and stir until a few grains are lightly toasted, about 2 minutes.

3. Add 1¼ cups fat-skimmed **chicken broth,** ½ teaspoon freshgrated **nutmeg,** and 1 teaspoon grated **orange** peel. Stir and bring to a boil, then reduce heat, cover, and simmer slowly until rice is tender to bite, 8 to 10 minutes. Add ¼ cup **orange juice,** stir, and season to taste with **salt.**

Per serving: 197 cal., 30% (60 cal.) from fat; 7.7 g protein; 6.7 g fat (2.1 g sat.); 31 g carbo (1.2 g fiber); 59 mg sodium; 6.2 mg chol.

PACKAGED GOODS

The envelope, please

■ "From-scratch" culinary purists have laid on enough guilt to push convenient old standbys from the cupboard into the closet. It's a bold cook who's willing to admit he or she likes to mix a packet of onion soup into a tub of sour cream for party dip. But even my friend Joan Nightingale (who loves to cook) pulls an envelope out of her closet regularly. "My family thinks the pot roast I make with oxtail soup mix and a can of beer is the best ever," she declares. "I think it's the easiest." She has some points. You be the judge.

Oxtail Soup Mix Pot Roast

PREP AND COOK TIME: About 3½ hours

NOTES: Beef rump is very lean. You can also use boned and tied beef chuck, which gets more succulent but doesn't slice as neatly. Serve the meat and gravy with mashed potatoes or hot fettuccine.

MAKES: 8 servings

    1 piece (about 3 lb.) **beef rump**

    1 teaspoon **salad oil** (optional)

    2 **onions** (1 lb. total), peeled and sliced

    1 bottle (12 oz.) **beer**

    1 package (1.8 oz.) **oxtail soup mix**

1. Wipe meat with a damp towel. Place a 5- to 6-quart pan over high heat and add oil (if desired). Add meat and brown lightly all over, turning as needed, about 5 minutes.

2. Transfer meat to a bowl. Add onions and 2 tablespoons water to pan. Stir frequently until onions are lightly browned, about 5 minutes.

3. Add beer, soup mix, and 1 cup water to pan; stir to release browned bits. Add beef and any juice. Bring to a boil, reduce heat, cover, and simmer gently until meat is very tender when pierced, about 3 hours.

4. Lift meat onto a platter and keep warm. Let stand at least 10 minutes to slice neatly. Meanwhile, if needed, boil sauce, uncovered, over high heat, stirringoccasionally, until reduced to 3 cups.

5. Slice roast and serve with gravy.

Per serving: 396 cal., 52% (207 cal.) from fat; 36 gprotein; 23 g fat (9 g sat.); 9.1 g carbo (0.8 g fiber); 506 mg sodium; 108 mg chol.

JAMES CARRIER (3)

Dowels square off

■ Ruth Garcia of San Jose uses matching plastic dowels to help her roll cookie dough, pie crust, and other foods that must be uniformly thick to bake evenly. Flanking the dough, they support the rolling pin, giving her full control. The transparent dowels, available at stores such as Tap Plastics, come in various diameters; Garcia's kit has ⅛- to ½-inch-thick pairs. They wash and store as easily as chopsticks—which triggered another idea: Why not use *square* plastic dowels to make uniform cuts in, but not all the way through, foods—coxcomb carrots and potatoes for roasting, radishes to fan in ice water? They cost about $1 per set. And you can use the square dowels with a rolling pin too.

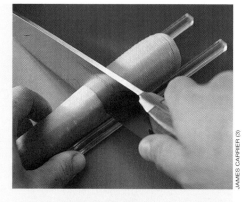

JAMES CARRIER (3)

Coxcomb Carrots

PREP AND COOK TIME: About 1½ hours (about 1¼ hours if using a convection oven)

MAKES: About 4 cups; 4 to 6 servings

1. Peel 3 pounds of **carrots** (about ¼ lb. each).

2. Set 1 carrot at a time, flattest side down, between and parallel to 2 matching square dowels (plastic or wood) about ⅜ inch thick and 10 to 12 inches long.

3. With a sharp knife, make crosswise cuts down to dowels, ¼ inch apart, along the length of the carrot. Then cut the carrot in half lengthwise through the center of the cross-cuts and cut or break each carrot half into 4 or 5 equal pieces.

4. Put carrots in a 10- by 15-inch rimmed pan. Mix with 2 tablespoons **olive oil** and 1½ tablespoons minced **fresh ginger.**

5. Bake in a 400° oven until carrots are well browned and taste slightly caramelized, 1 hour to 1 hour and 10 minutes (about 50 minutes in a convection oven). Turn often with a wide spatula and move pieces that are less cooked to perimeter of pan. Season with **salt** to taste.

Per serving: 128 cal., 34% (44 cal.) from fat; 2.1 g protein; 4.9 g fat (0.7 g sat.); 21 g carbo (6.5 g fiber); 71 mg sodium; 0 mg chol.

Salami takes a tasty stand

■ Food industry consultant François Vecchio stands by the slow, old-European ways of curing meats—salamis and other dried sausages in particular. His motive is simple: superior flavor. Such concentrated packets not only make good eating but also make a fine ingredient in savory dishes.

Potato, Fennel, and Salami Casserole

PREP AND COOK TIME: About 1 hour and 25 minutes (1 hour and 10 minutes if using a convection oven)

MAKES: 4 servings

1. Peel 1½ pounds **thin-skinned potatoes** and cut into ⅛- to ¼-inch-thick slices. Cover the bottom of a shallow 1½-quart casserole with half the potato slices.

2. Trim and discard stalks from 1 head fennel (about 3 in. wide), saving feathery green tops. Trim and discard any bruises and coarse fibers from fennel head, then rinse and thinly slice, using a hand slicer or food processor.

3. Discard casing from about 2 ounces **dried salami.** Cut meat into thin slices, then cut slices into slivers.

4. Mix half the salami with the sliced fennel and arrange evenly over potatoes in casserole. Cover with remaining potato slices. Add 1 cup fat-skimmed **chicken broth.** Cover casserole tightly with foil.

5. Bake in a 375° oven until potatoes are tender when pierced, 1 hour to 1 hour and 10 minutes (45 to 55 minutes in a convection oven). Uncover, sprinkle with ⅓ cup **finely shredded parmesan cheese,** and bake 5 minutes longer.

6. Finely chop fennel tops, mix 2 tablespoons (save rest for other uses) with remaining salami, and sprinkle over casserole. Add **salt** and **pepper** to taste.

Per serving: 241 cal., 29% (69 cal.) from fat; 12 g protein; 7.7 g fat (3.3 g sat.); 30 g carbo (3.3 g fiber); 521 mg sodium; 18 mg chol. ◆

The Wine Guide

BY KAREN MacNEIL-FIFE

RICK MARIANI

The West gets all the good vines

■ Quick: Name a famous place where wine is made. If you answered "Bordeaux" or even "Tuscany," you're in good company. But you could also have replied, "The American West."

It's ironic that most of us don't think of ourselves as living close to the land. We read books like *A Year in Provence* and imagine how magical it would feel to be immersed in the archetypal simplicity of vineyards and olive groves—to be nurtured by a daily routine of good meals and good local wine.

But think again: the American West *is* the New World's Provence and Tuscany. Drive an hour outside the city of Bordeaux and you're surrounded by vineyards. Drive an hour out of Los Angeles and it's the same thing.

Even more important, there's a similar sensibility. Part of what makes the West special is its celebrated lifestyle of pleasure. Some of that surely comes from being surrounded by so many places that produce great wine (just as in France, Italy, or Spain).

Place is inextricable from good wine. The oldest wine "labels" in the world—

GREAT WESTERN AVAs—A DELICIOUS SAMPLER

Note: By law, when a wine is labeled with an AVA, 85 percent of the grapes it was made from must have come from that place.

■ NAPA VALLEY. **Harrison Cabernet Sauvignon 1996,** $42. Top Napa Cabernets like Harrison are expensive but have incredible beauty and power. Less expensive but also outrageous: **Joseph Phelps Cabernet Sauvignon 1995,** $27.

■ SONOMA COUNTY. **Ferrari-Carano Fumé Blanc 1997,** $11.50. Sonoma County is big and geographically diverse enough to make legions of great wines. This feisty, peppery Fumé Blanc is a favorite.

■ MENDOCINO. **Hidden Cellars "Eaglepoint Ranch—Mendocino Heritage" Petite Syrah 1996,** $25. Top reds from Mendocino have saturated fruit and lots of power. The "yum" quotient in this one is high.

■ ALEXANDER VALLEY. **Silver Oak Cabernet Sauvignon 1994,** $45. Silver Oak makes the best wine from the Alexander Valley, in northern Sonoma County. This soft Cab is packed with ripe berry flavor.

■ DRY CREEK VALLEY. **Lambert Bridge Zinfandel 1997,** $22. Dry Creek, just west of Alexander Valley, is known for wonderful, mouth-filling Zins. This one is like falling into a pool of blackberry jam.

■ RUSSIAN RIVER VALLEY. **Rutz Cellars Pinot Noir 1996,** $20. Supple and nuanced, Rutz's Pinots (and several others from the Russian River Valley, which traverses central Sonoma County) have Burgundian sexiness.

■ CARNEROS. **Saintsbury Pinot Noir 1997,** $22. Classic Pinot Noir from Carneros, tucked below Napa and Sonoma, leans toward wonderful strawberry jam, black

cherry, and pomegranate flavors, and this elegant Saintsbury hits the mark.

■ SANTA BARBARA COUNTY. **Fess Parker Syrah 1996,** $18. Santa Barbara is known for Syrahs bursting with berry fruit. This one from Fess Parker (a.k.a. Daniel Boone) is terrific.

■ SIERRA FOOTHILLS. **Domaine de la Terre Rouge "Noir" 1995,** $18. The Sierra foothills (Gold Rush country) produce tasty, often rustic wines. This delicious blend of Grenache, Syrah, and Mourvèdre has loads of menthol and berry flavors.

■ WILLAMETTE VALLEY (OREGON). **Chehalem "Ian's Reserve" Chardonnay 1996,** $27. The best Chardonnays that have ever come out of Oregon are coming out now. Chehalem's is crème brûlée.

■ COLUMBIA VALLEY (WASHINGTON). **Hogue Chenin Blanc 1997,** $7. Chenin Blanc and Riesling are the Columbia Valley's best-kept secrets. This Chenin from Hogue, with lovely honeydew and apple, is a bargain. The valley's Merlot and Cabernet are also superlative; try **Covey Run Merlot 1995,** $10.

■ SONOITA (ARIZONA). **Callaghan Buena Suerte Cuvée 1997,** $28. Hard to believe, but the land of the Apaches is now burgeoning wine country. At the top of the pack: anything from winemaker Kent Callaghan, such as this Cabernet blend.

> ### SUNSET'S MONTHLY STEAL
> ■ **Paraiso Springs Gewürztraminer 1997 (Santa Lucia Highlands, Monterey County),** $9. Floral and full of exotic fruit flavors—terrific with Asian dishes. — *KAREN MacNEIL-FIFE*

the hieroglyphics on wine jars that belonged to the Egyptian king Tutankhamen (14th century B.C.)—indicate who made the wine *and* the vineyards where the grapes were grown. Because wines from some places are better than those from others, *place* is a clue to *quality.*

In the United States, the importance of place was codified into law by the Bureau of Alcohol, Tobacco and Firearms in 1980, when it designated the first American viticultural areas, or AVAs. An AVA is "a delimited grape-growing region, dis-

tinguishable by geographical features, the boundaries of which have been [recognized and defined]." On wine labels, names like Napa Valley, Carneros, and Columbia Valley are all AVAs.

Just as place is a clue to the quality of a wine, wine is a clue to the quality of life in a place. One day last year, standing on the desolate, windswept high desert of Arizona—land once ruled by Apache warriors—I looked out over new pastoral vineyards, and I knew: The West is wine country indeed. ◆

STIRRING IS ELIMINATED when Dungeness crab risotto cooks under pressure.

A PRESSURE COOKER, like this Fagor model (left), saves the day—or at least precious dinnertime minutes.

Perfect under pressure

For quick meals, turn to these versatile pans

BY SUZANNE CARREIRO • PHOTOGRAPHS BY LON CLARK

The pressure cooker has never been more timely. It gets foods to the table long before conventional cooking does; it is user-friendly, tenderizes tough cuts of meat, and requires little fat—which just about covers every modern cooking concern!

Extremely versatile (check out the manufacturer's instruction booklets), pressure cookers produce flavorful soups, stews, beans, grains, meats, fresh vegetables, and fruit dishes—even risotto.

Food cooks faster under pressure because it reaches higher temperatures. At sea level, food cooks at 212° (boiling); at a pressure cooker's maximum pressure (15 lb.), the temperature rises to 250°. The pressure is regulated by the amount of heat under the pan and by a valve or weight that controls the release of steam through a small vent. The type of valve varies among brands. Most models have a choice of settings that produce different temperatures. All pressure cookers are easy to operate, but for safety it is important to follow the manufacturer's instructions.

EXPLORING THE OPTIONS

Pressure cookers are available in 2- to 12-quart sizes, and range in price from $50 to more than $200. A 6-quart pan is adequate for recipes that serve six. If you frequently cook for large groups, however, choose an 8- to 12-quart pan.

Pressure cookers are sold in housewares sections of department stores and in cookware and hardware stores.

BEFORE YOU COOK

Learn how the lid and handle fit together, how the pressure valve works, and how to clean the steam release opening. Call the manufacturer or retailer if the owner's manual is unclear.

Most manufacturers advise filling the pan no more than two-thirds full. Foods that tend to foam and block the vent are not recommended for pressure cooking—for example, applesauce, cranberries, oatmeal and other cereals, pasta, barley, rhubarb, and split peas. In general, foods that you can braise or steam work well. To adapt your favorite recipes to the pressure cooker, consult the manufacturer's instructions for cooking times and liquid amounts.

If you have a vintage pressure cooker:
1. Make sure the pan bottom is flat and the handles and pressure vent are free of cracks and nicks.
2. Check the gasket. If it is dried out or won't seal, soak it in hot water for 20 minutes, then dry it and rub it with salad oil. If it's still stiff, discard it and buy a new gasket.

For information about Mirro and Wearever pressure cookers, call (800) 527-7727; to order new parts, call the Cook's Corner Factory Outlet at (800) 236-2433. For Presto pressure cooker information, call (800) 877-0441.

Dungeness Crab Risotto

PREP AND COOK TIME: About 25 minutes, including 6 minutes under pressure

MAKES: 4 main-dish servings

- 1 tablespoon **butter** or olive oil
- $\frac{3}{4}$ cup finely chopped **onions**
- 2 cloves **garlic,** minced
- 2 cups **arborio** or medium-grain white **rice**
- $1\frac{3}{4}$ cups fat-skimmed **chicken broth**
- $\frac{1}{2}$ cup **dry white wine**
- $\frac{3}{4}$ pound **shelled cooked Dungeness crab**
- $\frac{1}{2}$ cup finely shredded **parmesan cheese**
- 1 tablespoon minced **fresh sage** leaves
  Salt

1. In a 6-quart pressure cooker over high heat, frequently stir butter, onions, and garlic until onions are limp, about 3 minutes. Add rice and stir often until it is opaque, about 3 minutes longer. Add broth, wine, and 2 cups water. Stir occasionally until mixture boils, about 4 minutes.

2. Seal cooker. Following manufacturer's instructions, bring to maximum pressure (15 lb.); adjust heat to stabilize cooking rate. Cook 6 minutes. Release pressure quickly, running cold water over pan.

3. Open pan. Stir in crab, parmesan cheese, and sage. Add salt to taste.

Per serving: 489 cal., 16% (76 cal.) from fat; 31 g protein; 8.4 g fat (3.9 g sat.); 70 g carbo (6.3 g fiber); 491 mg sodium; 101 mg chol.

Lamb and Mushroom Stew

PREP AND COOK TIME: About 1 hour, including 20 minutes under pressure

MAKES: 6 servings

- 2 pounds **boned lamb shoulder** or beef chuck, fat-trimmed, cut into $1\frac{1}{2}$-inch chunks
- $\frac{1}{2}$ pound **common mushrooms**
- $\frac{1}{2}$ pound **fresh shiitake mushrooms** (or more common mushrooms)
- $\frac{3}{4}$ pound **onions,** peeled and coarsely chopped
- 1 cup thinly sliced **carrots**
- 4 cloves **garlic,** minced
- 2 ounces **thin-sliced pancetta** or bacon, chopped
- 1 cup **dry red wine**
- 3 tablespoons minced **fresh basil** leaves

- 1 tablespoon minced **fresh rosemary** leaves
- 5 whole **cloves**
- 1 package (10 oz.) **frozen peas**
- 1 tablespoon **cornstarch**
  Salt and **pepper**
  Mashed potatoes or hot cooked rice

1. In a 6-quart pressure cooker over high heat, frequently stir lamb until browned, about 15 minutes. With a slotted spoon, transfer lamb to a bowl.

2. Meanwhile, rinse common mushrooms, trim stem ends, and quarter mushrooms. Rinse shiitakes, discard stems, and slice caps.

3. In cooker, stir common mushrooms, shiitakes, onions, carrots, garlic, and pancetta until onions are lightly browned, about 10 minutes. Add lamb and juices, wine, basil, rosemary, and cloves.

4. Seal cooker. Following manufacturer's instructions, bring to maximum pressure (15 lb.); adjust heat to stabilize cooking rate. Cook 20 minutes. Release pressure quickly, running cold water over pan.

5. Open pan. If desired, discard cloves. Add peas to pan. Mix cornstarch with 2 tablespoons water and stir into mixture, then stir stew over high heat until boiling. Season to taste with salt and pepper.

6. Serve with mashed potatoes or cooked rice.

Per serving: 346 cal., 36% (126 cal.) from fat; 36 g protein; 14 g fat (4.8 g sat.); 19 g carbo (4.3 g fiber); 270 mg sodium; 105 mg chol.

Chicken, Linguisa, and Vegetable Soup

PREP AND COOK TIME: About 40 minutes, including 10 minutes under pressure

MAKES: 8 servings

- 6 **boned, skinned chicken thighs** (1 lb. total), fat-trimmed
- $\frac{3}{4}$ pound **linguisa sausage**
- 2 **onions** ($1\frac{1}{4}$ lb. total), peeled and thinly sliced
- $1\frac{1}{2}$ cups thinly sliced **carrots**
- 2 cups thinly sliced **celery**
- 2 quarts fat-skimmed **chicken broth**
- $\frac{1}{2}$ pound **Roma tomatoes,** rinsed, cored, and diced
- 2 cups thinly sliced **cabbage**
- 1 teaspoon grated **lemon** peel
- 1 package (10 oz.) **frozen peas**

- 3 tablespoons **lemon juice**
- $\frac{1}{3}$ cup finely chopped **fresh mint** leaves
  Salt and **pepper**

1. Rinse chicken and cut into 1-inch cubes. Cut linguisa into $\frac{1}{2}$-inch slices.

2. In a 6-quart pressure cooker over high heat, stir linguisa until lightly browned, about 5 minutes. With a slotted spoon, transfer to a bowl.

3. Discard all but 1 tablespoon fat from pan. Add onions, carrots, and celery. Stir occasionally until onions are limp, about 5 minutes. Add broth, chicken, linguisa with juices, tomatoes, cabbage, and lemon peel.

4. Seal cooker. Following manufacturer's instructions, bring to maximum pressure (15 lb.); adjust heat to stabilize cooking rate. Cook 10 minutes. Release pressure quickly, running cold water over pan.

5. Open pan, add peas, lemon juice, and mint. Stir occasionally over high heat until simmering. Add salt and pepper to taste.

Per serving: 343 cal., 52% (180 cal.) from fat; 24 g protein; 20 g fat (6.8 g sat.); 17 g carbo (4.6 g fiber); 453 mg sodium; 76 mg chol.

Pressure-Cooked Beans

PREP AND COOK TIME: About 1 hour and 40 minutes, including $1\frac{1}{2}$ hours under pressure

NOTES: Serve the cooked beans alone or incorporate them into other recipes. If making ahead, cool, cover, and chill up to 4 days.

MAKES: About 6 cups; 12 servings

1. In a 6-quart pressure cooker, combine 1 pound sorted, rinsed, and drained **dried Great Northern beans,** 2 chopped **onions** (1 lb. total), **1 dried bay leaf,** and 5 cups fat-skimmed **chicken broth.**

2. Seal cooker. Following manufacturer's instructions, bring to maximum pressure (15 lb.) over high heat, then adjust heat to stabilize cooking rate. Cook $1\frac{1}{2}$ hours. Release pressure quickly, running cold water over pan.

3. Open pan. Serve beans or, for less liquid, stir often over high heat until mixture has consistency desired, about 5 minutes. Add **salt** and **pepper** to taste.

Per serving: 157 cal., 2.9% (4.5 cal.) from fat; 12 g protein; 0.5 g fat (0.1 g sat.); 27 g carbo (16 g fiber); 38 mg sodium; 0 mg chol. ◆

Kitchen Cabinet

READERS' RECIPES TESTED IN SUNSET'S KITCHENS

BY LINDA LAU ANUSASANANAN

BROWNED PORK CHOPS sizzle with Southwestern flavors of cumin, chilies, and tequila.

Tequila Pork Chops

Al Zangri, Juneau

When Al Zangri visited Tucson, he fell in love with the food. Back home, he was inspired to create this dish with Southwestern flavors.

PREP AND COOK TIME: 20 minutes

MAKES: 4 servings

- 4 **center-cut loin pork chops** (each about ³⁄₄ in. thick)
- ¹⁄₂ teaspoon **cumin seed**
- ¹⁄₄ cup (¹⁄₈ lb.) **butter** or margarine
- 3 cloves **garlic,** pressed or minced
- ¹⁄₄ cup fat-skimmed **chicken broth**
- ¹⁄₂ cup **tequila**
- 2 tablespoons **lime juice**
- 2 to 4 teaspoons minced **fresh jalapeño chilies**

 Salt and **ground white pepper**

1. Trim and discard fat from chops. Wipe chops with a damp towel, then press cumin seed equally onto wide sides of each piece.

2. Place a 10- to 12-inch nonstick frying pan over high heat. When hot, add 1 teaspoon butter, tilting to coat pan. Add chops; brown well on each side, about 6 minutes total. Stir in garlic.

3. Remove pan from heat (away from a vent, fan, or inflammables). Stir broth, tequila, and lime juice into pan. Set over high heat. When liquids boil, reduce heat and simmer until meat is no longer pink in center (cut to test), about 4 minutes. Transfer chops to a platter; keep warm.

4. On high heat, boil pan juices until reduced to 3 to 4 tablespoons, about 2 minutes. Add remaining butter, in a lump, and stir until blended with sauce. Season to taste with chilies. Pour sauce over pork. Season to taste with salt and pepper.

Per serving: 450 cal., 66% (297 cal.) from fat; 35 g protein; 33 g fat (15 g sat.); 1.5 g carbo (0.1 g fiber); 230 mg sodium; 145 mg chol.

I Love You Fettuccine with Shrimp

Ana Maria Osorio, Dublin, California

When Ana Maria Osorio's special dinner guest asked for the name of the dish she had just served him, she responded, "I Love You Very Much." He was delighted.

PREP AND COOK TIME: About 20 minutes

MAKES: 4 servings

- 1 tablespoon **olive oil**
- 1 **onion** (5 to 6 oz.), peeled and chopped
- 3 cloves **garlic,** pressed or minced
- 1 cup **whipping cream**
- 1 can (14 oz.) **diced tomatoes**
- 1 pound **shrimp** (51 to 60 per lb.), peeled, deveined, and rinsed
- 1 tablespoon chopped **Italian** or curly **parsley**

 Salt and **pepper**
- 1 pound **fresh fettuccine**

1. In a covered 5- to 6-quart pan over high heat, bring about 3 quarts water to a boil.

2. Meanwhile, in a 10- to 12-inch frying pan over medium heat, frequently stir oil, onion, and garlic until onion is limp, about 5 minutes.

3. Add cream and tomatoes (with juice) to frying pan. Bring to a boil over high heat. Add shrimp and stir often until pink, 3 to 4 minutes. Add parsley and salt and pepper to taste. Remove from heat and keep warm.

4. When shrimp is in pan, add fettuccine to boiling water and cook just until pasta is tender to bite, 3 to 4 minutes. Drain well; return pasta to pan.

5. Stir shrimp mixture with pasta.

Per serving: 664 cal., 35% (234 cal.) from fat; 34 g protein; 26 g fat (13 g sat.); 73 g carbo (3.7 g fiber); 349 mg sodium; 289 mg chol.

Savory Squash and Leek Casserole

Beverly E. Allen, Coupeville, Washington

Some like golden winter squash sweetly seasoned like candied yams. But not Beverly Allen's husband. To suit his taste, she flavors this casserole with shallots and leeks from her garden.

PREP AND COOK TIME: 1¼ hours

MAKES: 4 servings

- 1½ pounds **banana** or hubbard **squash,** peeled and seeded
- 3 **leeks** (1¼ lb. total)
- 2 tablespoons **olive oil** or butter
- ½ cup chopped **shallots**
- ¼ teaspoon **ground nutmeg**
  About ¼ teaspoon **salt**
- ⅛ teaspoon **pepper**
- 1 **large egg,** beaten to blend

1. In a 2- to 3-quart pan over high heat, bring 4 to 6 cups water to a boil.

2. Cut squash into 1-inch chunks. Add to boiling water, cover, and simmer until tender when pierced, 12 to 14 minutes. Drain and mash squash with a potato masher or a mixer.

3. Meanwhile, cut off and discard tough green tops, root ends, and coarse outer layer of leeks. Split leeks in half lengthwise and rinse well. Thinly slice.

4. In a 10- to 12-inch frying pan over medium-high heat, combine oil, leeks, and shallots. Stir often, until vegetables are limp, 5 to 7 minutes. Remove from heat.

5. Add mashed squash, nutmeg, ¼ teaspoon salt, pepper, and egg; mix well. Spread in a shallow 1-quart casserole.

6. Bake, uncovered, in a 350° oven until lightly browned on top, about 45 minutes (35 minutes in a convection oven). Add salt to taste.

Per serving: 175 cal., 45% (79 cal.) from fat; 5.2 g protein; 8.8 g fat (1.4 g sat.); 22 g carbo (2.9 g fiber); 181 mg sodium; 53 mg chol.

Mediterranean Wheat Berry Salad

Gererdene Gibbons, Tigard, Oregon

"My husband is mad about wheat berries," says Gererdene Gibbons. So she cooks the chewy grain in big batches, then packs and freezes it in 2-cup portions, ready to use for this salad and in other dishes.

PREP AND COOK TIME: About 1 hour

MAKES: 9 servings

- ¾ cup **wheat berries**
- ¾ cup **long-grain brown rice**
- 1 jar (6 oz.) **marinated artichoke hearts**
- 6 tablespoons **balsamic** or red wine **vinegar**
- 2 tablespoons **olive oil**
- 2 teaspoons **Dijon mustard**
- 1 teaspoon **dried oregano**
- 2 **Roma tomatoes** (½ lb. total), rinsed, cored, and cut into ½-inch cubes
- 1 **cucumber** (¾ lb.), rinsed and cut into ½-inch cubes
- ¾ cup thinly sliced **green onions**
- ½ cup **crumbled feta cheese**
- ⅓ cup **calamata olives,** pitted and halved
- ⅓ cup chopped **fresh mint** leaves
- ¼ cup chopped **parsley**
  Salt and **pepper**

1. In a 3- to 4-quart pan, combine wheat berries, rice, and 6 cups water. Bring to a boil over high heat. Cover and simmer until grains are tender to bite, 30 to 35 minutes. Drain. Pour into a large bowl.

2. Drain artichoke marinade into bowl with grains. Coarsely chop artichokes and add to bowl along with vinegar, oil, mustard, and oregano. Mix well and let stand until cool, about 20 minutes.

3. Add tomatoes, cucumber, onions, cheese, olives, mint, and parsley; mix well. Add salt and pepper to taste.

Per serving: 207 cal., 36% (75 cal.) from fat; 5.4 g protein; 8.3 g fat (2 g sat.); 29 g carbo (4.8 g fiber); 304 mg sodium; 6.7 mg chol.

Three Cs Cookies

Patty Stearns, Fresno, California

Three flavors—coconut, cashew, and cardamom—are the foundation for these chewy-crisp cookies.

PREP AND COOK TIME: About 1¼ hours, including 30 minutes to chill

MAKES: About 5½ dozen

- About 1 cup (½ lb.) **unsalted butter** or margarine
- 1 cup **granulated sugar**
- ¾ cup firmly packed **brown sugar**
- 2 **large eggs**

CHEWY WHEAT BERRIES soak up salad seasonings.

- 2 teaspoons **vanilla**
- 1½ cups **all-purpose flour**
- 2 teaspoons **ground cardamom**
- 1 teaspoon **baking soda**
- 2 cups **sweetened flaked dried coconut**
- 1 cup **salted roasted cashews,** very coarsely chopped

1. In a bowl with a mixer, beat 1 cup butter, ¾ cup granulated sugar, and brown sugar until fluffy. Beat in eggs and vanilla until well blended.

2. In another bowl, mix flour, 1 teaspoon cardamom, and baking soda.

3. Add dry ingredients to butter mixture; stir to mix, then beat until blended.

4. Stir in coconut and cashews. Cover and chill dough until firm enough to shape, at least 30 minutes or up to 1 day.

5. In a small dish, mix ¼ cup granulated sugar and 1 teaspoon cardamom.

6. Shape dough into 1-inch balls, rolling each in cardamom sugar to coat. Set balls at least 3 inches apart on buttered baking sheets.

7. Bake in a 350° oven until golden brown, 9 to 12 minutes (7 to 10 minutes in a convection oven).

8. Cool on pans about 1 minute, then with a wide spatula, transfer to racks. Serve or store airtight up to 3 days; freeze to store longer.

Per cookie: 81 cal., 51% (41 cal.) from fat; 0.9 g protein; 4.6 g fat (2.6 g sat.); 9.4 g carbo (0.3 g fiber); 41 mg sodium; 14 mg chol. ◆

Mexican-inspired party (page 54) is easy on the cook. Make-ahead finger foods include fruit wands and pine nut cookies.

March

Sunday suppers

At home with family, friends, and mouthwatering meals

BY LINDA LAU ANUSASANANAN • PHOTOGRAPHS BY JAMES CARRIER

■ Some say the days when family and friends came together for a relaxed Sunday supper have disappeared. To all appearances, fast foods, fancy frozen meals, speedy microwaves, and take-out dishes have practically put home-cooked dinners on the endangered species list.

But simple, straightforward food designed to welcome rather than impress is timeless. A kitchen filled with mouthwatering aromas—from meat roasting in the oven, several pans gently simmering on the stove, a pie or cake cooling on the counter— is still inviting, maybe even more than ever in these hectic times. No rush, no pretension. Just cover the table with a fresh cloth and bring the good silver out of the sideboard. The family, your son's favorite playmate, and maybe the folks next door will still gather to wind down the weekend and plan for another week over a nurturing meal.

Here's how two families slow the pace, sit down, and break bread together, just for the pleasure of it.

Out on their farm—Pastures of Plenty, near Longmont, Colorado—Lyle Davis, his wife, Sylvia Tawse, and their four children dine together more often than city families perhaps. Davis, farmer and chief cook, has been influenced by the food-friendly cultures of France, Italy, and Greece. He cooks seasonally and simply, usually in a Mediterranean style, using many foods the farm produces. As a result, the Davis clan has been reared on a broad spectrum of flavors and international influences that have brought an adventurous spirit to the rituals of dining.

Asparagus with Watercress

PREP AND COOK TIME: About 30 minutes

NOTES: Up to 1 day ahead, cook asparagus; cool, cover, and chill. Mix dressing; cover and let stand. Radicchio di Trevisio leaves are long and narrow.

MAKES: 8 to 10 servings

2 pounds **asparagus**

1/3 cup **extra-virgin olive oil**

3 tablespoons **champagne** or white wine **vinegar**

1 tablespoon **Dijon mustard**

1 teaspoon **dried tarragon**

4 cups **tender watercress sprigs,** rinsed and crisped

About 1/2 pound **radicchio di Trevisio,** red Belgian endive, or regular radicchio, rinsed and crisped (optional)

Salt and **pepper**

1. Snap off and discard tough ends of asparagus. In a 5- to 6-quart pan over high heat, bring 2 quarts water to a boil. Add asparagus; cook, uncovered, until barely tender when pierced, about 5 minutes. Drain and immerse in cold water. When cool, in about 5 minutes, drain.

2. Meanwhile, in a small bowl, mix oil, vinegar, mustard, and tarragon.

3. Arrange watercress and radicchio (whole leaves or slivered) on a platter. Top with asparagus. Drizzle dressing over asparagus and greens. Add salt and pepper to taste.

Per serving: 83 cal., 82% (68 cal.) from fat; 2.6 g protein; 7.6 g fat (1.1 g sat.); 3.1 g carbo (1 g fiber); 43 mg sodium; 0 mg chol.

TENDER ASPARAGUS from the farm starts the meal.

pan over medium-high heat, stir nuts often until golden, 3 to 4 minutes. Add currants, stir, and pour mixture into a small bowl.

2. In a wide bowl, mix 2 tablespoons oil and the vinegar. Add arugula leaves and mix to coat. Mound equal portions on salad plates.

3. Pour 1 tablespoon oil into the frying pan and set over medium-high heat. Lay cheese in pan and heat just until warm, turning once with a wide spatula, ¾ to 1 minute total. Set a portion of cheese on each salad. Sprinkle with nuts and currants. Season to taste with salt and pepper.

Per serving: 164 cal., 71% (117 cal.) from fat; 7.8 g protein; 13 g fat (5.5 g sat.); 5.4 g carbo (1.2 g fiber); 122 mg sodium; 14 mg chol.

Roast Leg of Lamb with Balsamic Onions

PREP AND COOK TIME: About 1¾ hours
MAKES: 8 to 10 servings

- 4 **onions** (6 oz. each), peeled and quartered
- 3 tablespoons **olive oil**
- 3 tablespoons **balsamic vinegar**
  Salt and **pepper**
- 1 **leg of lamb** (5 to 6 lb.)
- 3 cloves **garlic,** slivered
- 3 tablespoons **lemon juice**
- 2 teaspoons **fresh rosemary** leaves or dried rosemary
- 1 teaspoon **dried oregano**
  Rosemary sprigs

1. In a bowl, mix onions with 2 tablespoons olive oil and the balsamic vine-

gar. Sprinkle lightly with salt and pepper. Let stand at least 5 minutes, stirring occasionally.

2. Meanwhile, rinse lamb; trim off and discard excess surface fat. Cut ½-inch slits all over the leg and insert garlic slivers. Rub lamb with 1 tablespoon olive oil and the lemon juice, then pat rosemary leaves and oregano onto meat. Sprinkle with salt and pepper. Set lamb in an 11- by 17-inch roasting pan. Spoon onions and marinade around lamb.

3. Roast in a 375° oven until a thermometer inserted in thickest part of leg to the bone registers 140° for medium-rare, 1 hour and 10 minutes to 1½ hours; or 150° for medium, 1 hour and 20 minutes to 1 hour and 40 minutes. If drippings begin to burn, add water ¼ cup at a time as needed.

4. Transfer lamb to a board or platter and, keeping warm, let stand 10 to 15 minutes. Keep onions warm in pan while lamb rests. Spoon onions and drippings around lamb; garnish with rosemary sprigs. Slice meat and serve with onions and juices. Add salt and pepper to taste.

Per serving: 475 cal., 66% (315 cal.) from fat; 33 g protein; 35 g fat (14 g sat.); 6.1 g carbo (1 g fiber); 104 mg sodium; 124 mg chol.

Cannellini Beans with Tomatoes

PREP AND COOK TIME: 30 to 35 minutes
MAKES: 8 to 10 servings

- 1 **onion** (¾ lb.), peeled and chopped
- 2 cloves **garlic,** thinly sliced
- 2 tablespoons **olive oil**

Arugula Salad with Goat Cheese Medallions

PREP AND COOK TIME: 20 to 25 minutes
MAKES: 8 to 10 servings

- ⅓ cup **pine nuts**
- ⅓ cup **currants**
- 3 tablespoons **extra-virgin olive oil**
- 1 tablespoon **white wine vinegar**
- 9 to 10 ounces (about 9 cups) small, tender **arugula** leaves or salad mix, rinsed and drained
- 1 to 3 logs (11 to 12 oz. total) **fresh chèvre** (goat) **cheese,** cut into 8 to 10 equal rounds
  Salt and **pepper**

1. In an 8- to 10-inch nonstick frying

FRESH GOAT CHEESE is the heart of the salad.

1 cup **dry white wine**

½ cup finely shredded **parmesan cheese**

Salt

1. Trim off feathery fennel greens and finely chop enough to make ¼ cup; reserve for garnish. Save remaining greens for other uses. Trim off and discard tough stems, root ends, and any bruised spots from fennel heads. Cut fennel lengthwise into ½-inch-thick slices.

2. In a 6- to 8-quart pan over medium-high heat, combine oil and onion. Stir often until onion is limp, 5 to 7 minutes.

3. Add sliced fennel and wine. Cover and simmer over medium heat, stirring occasionally, until fennel is just tender when pierced, about 25 minutes.

4. Arrange fennel slices neatly in a shallow 3- to 3½-quart casserole and add liquid. Cover tightly with foil.

5. Bake in a 375° oven until fennel is very tender when pierced, 1 hour and 10 minutes (1 hour in a convection oven).

6. Uncover fennel, sprinkle with cheese, and, if desired, broil about 4 inches from heat until slightly browned, 3 to 4 minutes. Sprinkle with reserved ¼ cup chopped green fennel tops. Season to taste with salt.

Per serving: 61 cal., 59% (36 cal.) from fat; 2.7 g protein; 4 g fat (1.1 g sat.); 3.9 g carbo (0.9 g fiber); 138 mg sodium; 3.2 mg chol.

Marinated Strawberries with Mint

PREP TIME: About 20 minutes

NOTES: For a nonalcoholic dessert, marinate the strawberries in white grape juice or a varietal grape juice such as Chardonnay or Gewürztraminer. Up to 3 hours ahead, complete step 1; let stand at room temperature until dessert time. Garnish with mint sprigs if desired.

MAKES: 8 to 10 servings

1 cup **dry white wine**

½ cup **sugar**

8 cups **strawberries**, rinsed and hulled

3 tablespoons chopped **fresh mint** leaves

1. In a large bowl, stir wine and sugar until sugar is mostly dissolved. Slice strawberries lengthwise and add to wine mixture. Mix gently to coat.

2. Sprinkle with mint; spoon into bowls.

Per serving: 92 cal., 4.9% (4.5 cal.) from fat; 0.8 g protein; 0.5 g fat (0 g sat.); 19 g carbo (3.3 g fiber); 3 mg sodium; 0 mg chol.

STRAWBERRY SLICES soak in white wine with sugar; fresh mint goes in at dessert time.

4 or 5 **Roma tomatoes** (¾ lb. total), rinsed, cored, and chopped

4 cans (15 oz. each) **cannellini** (white) **beans**, drained

1 teaspoon **fresh rosemary** leaves, chopped, or dried rosemary, crumbled

Salt and **pepper**

1. In a 4- to 5-quart pan over medium-high heat, stir onion, garlic, and oil often until onion is slightly browned, about 10 minutes.

2. Set aside ½ cup of the tomatoes and add the remainder to onion mixture. Stir often until tomatoes begin to soften, about 4 minutes.

3. Add beans and rosemary and stir occasionally over low heat to blend flavors, about 10 minutes. If bean mixture is

thicker than desired, thin with water and bring to a simmer. Pour into a bowl and sprinkle with reserved tomatoes. Season to taste with salt and pepper.

Per serving: 163 cal., 21% (34 cal.) from fat; 9.4 g protein; 3.8 g fat (0.4 g sat.); 23 g carbo (7.7 g fiber); 215 mg sodium; 0 mg chol.

Braised Fennel

PREP AND COOK TIME: About 1½ hours

NOTES: Up to 3 hours ahead, simmer fennel, arrange in casserole, cover, and let stand at room temperature; then bake in oven with the lamb.

MAKES: 8 to 10 servings

8 heads **fennel** (3 in. wide), rinsed

2 tablespoons **olive oil**

1 **onion** (½ lb.), peeled and finely chopped

SUBTLE TWEAKS make this meal anything but traditional. Chicken, salad, and macaroni are all offered in both adventurous and safe versions.

MENU TWO

Retro Roast Chicken Supper
for 8 to 10

• A Brace of Herb-Roasted Chickens

• Macaroni Casserole or Buttered Macaroni (for finicky eaters)

• Iceberg Lettuce–Wedge Salad with Old-Fashioned Cooked French Dressing or Extra-Virgin Olive Oil and Balsamic Vinegar

• Cream Puff Sundaes   • Chardonnay, Beer, and Lemonade

Renee Behnke, Seattle-based owner of the Sur La Table cookware stores, promotes family dining through flexibility. Routinely, her large table is surrounded by children, grandchildren, cousins, aunts, uncles, and friends, who enjoy the way she mixes the old with the new in meals that are "pleasing for all kids," as Behnke puts it.

Ironically, nostalgia appeals to the children; fresh touches please the grown-ups. For this meal, Behnke roasts two plump chickens, one with and one without goat cheese tucked under its crisp breast skin; reincarnates a macaroni casserole from her own childhood (plain noodles with butter for finicky eaters); and offers mild, crunchy iceberg lettuce wedges with style, to moisten with old-fashioned cooked French dressing or the finest of today's olive oils and balsamic vinegars. Big, crisp cream puffs stuffed with ice cream are dessert (plain ice cream for the very timid). Options, graciously offered, are Behnke's key to conviviality.

A Brace of Herb-Roasted Chickens

PREP AND COOK TIME: About 1½ hours

NOTES: To make your own poultry rub, mix 1½ teaspoons *each* dried thyme and dried oregano with 1 teaspoon *each* garlic powder, kosher or sea salt, and coarse-ground pepper. For adult tastes, spread a layer of goat cheese beneath the breast skin. If you have only one oven, roast the chickens, then keep them warm while the macaroni bakes.

MAKES: 8 to 10 servings

- 2 **chickens** (3½ to 4 lb. each)
- 2 tablespoons **packaged poultry rub** (or make your own; see notes)
- 1 **onion** (6 oz.), peeled and cut into 1-inch chunks
- 1 **lemon,** ends sliced off, cut into 1-inch chunks
- 4 **parsley sprigs**
- 10 ounces **fresh chèvre** (goat) **cheese** or 2 packages (5 oz. each) Boursin cheese (optional)
- 2 tablespoons **olive oil**

1. Reserve chicken giblets for other uses. Pull off and discard lumps of fat from chickens. Rinse birds inside and out and pat dry.

2. Sprinkle ½ teaspoon poultry rub in each bird's body cavity. Place ½ the onion, lemon, and parsley in each chicken. Pin body cavities shut with small metal skewers.

3. If using cheese, starting at the neck, gently push your fingers under skin of each breast to loosen skin. Spread 5 ounces cheese under skin of each chicken, pressing to form an even layer over breast.

4. Rub skin of each chicken all over with ½ the oil and ½ the remaining poultry rub. Set chickens, breasts up, at least 2 inches apart on a rack in an 11-by 17-inch roasting pan.

5. Roast in a 400° oven until a thermometer inserted through thickest part of thigh to joint registers 175°, about 65 minutes (about 55 minutes in a convection oven).

6. Using pot holders to protect your hands, tilt chickens to drain juices into pan. Set chickens on a platter and let rest in a warm place 10 to 15 minutes. Stir pan juices to release browned bits; skim and discard fat, and pour drippings into a small bowl. Carve chicken and serve with juices.

Per serving: 368 cal., 54% (198 cal.) from fat; 38 g protein; 22 g fat (5.7 g sat.); 2.2 g carbo (0.3 g fiber); 263 mg sodium; 123 mg chol.

Macaroni Casserole

PREP AND COOK TIME: 40 to 45 minutes

NOTES: Behnke duplicates her mom's casserole by baking it until it's very crusty, 10 minutes longer, but the pasta is less creamy-tasting.

MAKES: 8 to 10 servings

1 pound **dried small elbow macaroni**

About ⅓ cup (⅙ lb.) **butter** or margarine

2 cups (½ lb.) **shredded sharp** or medium **cheddar cheese**

½ cup **fine dried bread crumbs**

3 **large eggs**

2 cups **milk**

¼ to ½ teaspoon **hot sauce**

About ½ teaspoon **salt**

¼ teaspoon **pepper**

¼ teaspoon **paprika**

1. In a 5- to 6-quart pan over high heat, cook macaroni in about 2 quarts boiling water just until tender to bite, 4 to 6 minutes. Drain. Return macaroni to pan, off the heat, and add ⅓ cup butter; stir to melt.

2. Lightly butter a shallow 2½- to 3-quart casserole. Sprinkle ½ cup cheese and ¼ cup bread crumbs over casserole bottom.

3. Beat eggs, milk, hot sauce, ½ teaspoon salt, and pepper to blend. Add to macaroni, along with ¾ cup cheese, and mix well. Pour mixture into casserole. Sprinkle remaining cheese and bread crumbs evenly over top. Dust with paprika.

4. Bake in a 400° oven until top feels slightly crusty when touched, about 20 minutes (about 15 minutes in a convection oven). Add salt to taste.

Per serving: 391 cal., 41% (162 cal.) from fat; 16 g protein; 18 g fat (10 g sat.); 41 g carbo (1.3 g fiber); 418 mg sodium; 112 mg chol.

Iceberg Lettuce–Wedge Salad

PREP TIME: **About 5 minutes**

NOTES: **Make the dressing, buy a favorite, or offer oil and vinegar in attractive cruets. For small children, tear lettuce into bite-size pieces.**

MAKES: **8 to 10 servings**

2 heads (1¼ to 1½ lb. each) **iceberg lettuce**, rinsed and crisped

Old-fashioned cooked French dressing (recipe follows)

Salt and **pepper**

Trim and discard stem ends and bruised leaves from lettuce; cut lettuce, through core, into 8 to 10 equal wedges. Lay each wedge on a salad plate. Add salad dressing and salt and pepper to taste.

Per serving: 188 cal., 72% (135 cal.) from fat; 1.7 g protein; 15 g fat (1.9 g sat.); 14 g carbo (1.3 g fiber); 93 mg sodium; 0 mg chol.

CRISP CREAM PUFFS enclose ice cream; chocolate sauce cloaks the dessert.

Old-Fashioned Cooked French Dressing

PREP AND COOK TIME: **About 15 minutes**

NOTES: **If making up to 1 week ahead, cool, cover, and chill.**

MAKES: **About 1¾ cups**

In a 1- to 1½-quart pan, mix ⅓ cup **sugar** and 1 teaspoon **cornstarch**. Stir in ½ cup **cider vinegar**. Stir over high heat until mixture boils and thickens, about 2 minutes. Pour into a blender and add ⅓ cup chopped **onion**, 1 peeled clove **garlic**, ¼ cup **catsup**, 2 teaspoons **Worcestershire**, and ⅛ teaspoon **cayenne**; whirl until smooth. With blender running, gradually pour in ⅔ cup **salad oil**. Stir in ¼ teaspoon **celery seed**. Add **salt** to taste. Let cool.

Per tablespoon: 60 cal., 78% (47 cal.) from fat; 0.1 g protein; 5.2 g fat (0.7 g sat.); 3.5 g carbo (0.1 g fiber); 29 mg sodium; 0 mg chol.

Cream Puff Sundaes

PREP AND COOK TIME: **About 1½ hours**

NOTES: **If making up to 1 day ahead, cool cream puffs and store airtight at room temperature; freeze to store longer (thaw unwrapped).**

MAKES: **8 to 10 servings**

About 6 tablespoons **butter** or margarine, cut into ½-inch chunks

½ teaspoon **sugar**

¾ cup **all-purpose flour**

3 **large eggs**

1 quart **vanilla ice cream**

1 to 1¼ cups **chocolate sauce** or caramel topping, homemade or purchased

Sweetened **whipped cream** (optional)

About ½ cup chopped **pecans**

1. In a 2- to 3-quart pan, combine ¾ cup water, 6 tablespoons butter, and sugar. Bring to a boil over high heat.

2. When butter is melted, remove from heat and add flour all at once. Beat with a sturdy spoon until well blended. Return pan to heat and stir vigorously until mixture forms a ball and leaves sides of pan, 1 to 2 minutes. Let mixture cool for 5 minutes.

3. Transfer the mixture to a food processor, or leave in pan. Add eggs 1 at a time; whirl or beat until smooth after each addition. Let the batter cool 10 minutes.

4. With a spoon, drop batter in 8 (¼ cup) to 10 (slightly more than 3 tablespoons) portions at least 2 inches apart on a lightly buttered 14- by 17-inch baking sheet.

5. Bake in the center of a 375° oven until brown and firm when pressed, about 45 minutes (about 30 minutes in a convection oven). Remove pan from oven and quickly cut the top ⅓ off each puff, then set back in place. Return to oven and bake until puffs are crisper and slightly browner, about 10 more minutes. Cool on racks.

6. Scoop out and discard moist interiors of puffs and fill the hollows with ice cream. Set cream puff tops on the ice cream and set puffs on plates. Drizzle with chocolate sauce, add dollops of whipped cream, and sprinkle with nuts.

Per serving: 326 cal., 50% (162 cal.) from fat; 5.7 g protein; 18 g fat (8.8 g sat.); 39 g carbo (0.6 g fiber); 160 mg sodium; 106 mg chol. ◆

Mango-mint agua fresca

Romaine hearts with pipián

Sunchoke dip

The easiest party ever

"Little bites" mean little work

BY ANDREW BAKER • PHOTOGRAPHS BY LEIGH BEISCH

■ Imagine a party where all the foods are made ahead but stay fresh. Where guests serve themselves while you enjoy the conversation. And where napkins—no plates or utensils—do the job of dinnerware. This Mexican-influenced menu of *bocaditos* (little bites) is just that kind of gathering.

It's also a party designed for movement: Guests circulate to sample foods arranged at various stations. Begin with refreshing *agua fresca* and a selection of Mexican soft drinks and beers on a beverage tray positioned to greet arriving guests. Place a salad course of romaine hearts with *pipián* nearby, and a Jerusalem artichoke dip and morsels of mushroom *bocadillos* in separate locations. Grill the steak ahead, to serve cold—or just before guests arrive, to serve hot—and present it sliced to stuff into little rolls for two-or-three-bite sandwiches. Combine hand-held fruit wands and pine nut cookies for dessert.

MENU

• *Mango-Mint Agua Fresca*
• *Mexican Soft Drinks and Beers*
• *Romaine Hearts with Pipián*
• *Sunchoke Dip*
• *Mushroom Bocadillos*
• *Flank Steak Tortitas with Chipotle Crema and Sliced Tomatillos*
• *Fruit Wands with Vanilla-Rum Syrup*
• *Pine Nut Panecillos*

Flank steak tortitas with chipotle crema and sliced tomatillos

Romaine Hearts with Pipián

PREP AND COOK TIME: About **15** minutes

NOTES: If making dressing up to 1 day ahead, cover airtight and chill. Serve at room temperature. Buy romaine hearts or use tender inner leaves from heads of romaine lettuce.

MAKES: About 1½ cups pipián; 8 servings

- 3 **dried California** or New Mexico **chilies** (4 to 5 in.)
- ½ cup **shelled roasted pumpkin seeds** (*pepitas*)
- 2 cloves **garlic,** peeled
- 2 tablespoons **red wine vinegar**
- ¾ cup chopped **Roma tomatoes**
- ½ cup lightly packed **fresh cilantro** **Salt**
- 24 to 32 **romaine lettuce** leaves (6 to 7 in.), rinsed and crisped **Ice cubes**

1. Discard chili stems. Shake out and discard chili seeds. Put chilies in a bowl and pour 1½ cups boiling water over them. Let stand until soft, 6 to 7 minutes.

2. Meanwhile, in an 8- to 10-inch frying pan over high heat, stir or shake pumpkin seeds until they smell lightly toasted, 2 to 3 minutes.

3. Put pumpkin seeds in a blender or food processor. Lift chilies from soaking liquid and add to blender. Add garlic, vinegar, tomatoes, and cilantro. Whirl, adding enough chili-soaking liquid (about ½ cup) to make pipián mixture thin enough to scoop but not drippy. Add salt to taste. Scrape pipián into a small bowl.

4. Stand romaine lettuce leaves, stem ends down, in closely fitting bowl and drop ice cubes among the leaves to keep them crisp. To eat, scoop leaves into pipián dressing.

Per serving: 39 cal., 36% (14 cal.) from fat; 1.9 g protein; 1.5 g fat (0.3 g sat.); 6 g carbo (2 g fiber); 6.2 mg sodium; 0 mg chol.

Sunchoke Dip

PREP AND COOK TIME: About **40** minutes

NOTES: This hummus-like dip was created by Loretta Barrett Oden of Corn Dance Cafe in Santa Fe and Josiah Citrin of JiRaffe in Los Angeles for the Cuisines of the Sun program at the Mauna Lani Bay Hotel in Hawaii. Jerusalem artichoke (also known as sunchoke) is the root of a native American variety of sunflower. You'll need about 8 cups of chips.

MAKES: About 2 cups dip; 8 servings

Mango-Mint Agua Fresca

PREP TIME: About **20** minutes

NOTES: If making up to 4 hours ahead, cover and chill puréed mixture; add ice just before serving.

MAKES: About 12 cups; 8 servings

- 3 pounds **firm-ripe mangoes**
- 4 cups **orange juice**
- ½ cup lightly packed **fresh mint** leaves, rinsed and drained
  About ¼ cup **lemon juice**
  Ice cubes
  Mint sprigs

1. Cut and discard pits and peel from mangoes. Cut fruit into chunks.

2. In a blender or food processor, in batches, whirl the mangoes, orange juice, mint leaves, and 5 cups water until smoothly puréed; pour into a pitcher. Stir in ¼ cup lemon juice, or to taste.

3. Pour agua fresca into ice-filled glasses. Garnish with mint sprigs.

Per serving: 136 cal., 2.6% (3.6 cal.) from fat; 1.6 g protein; 0.4 g fat (0.1 g sat.); 34 g carbo (1.9 g fiber); 6.9 mg sodium; 0 mg chol.

1½ pounds **Jerusalem artichokes**

2 cloves **garlic,** peeled

3 tablespoons **lemon juice**

3 tablespoons **olive oil**

1 to 2 tablespoons minced **fresh jalapeño chilies**

Salt

Blue or red **corn chips** (or a combination)

1. Peel Jerusalem artichokes and rinse.

2. In a 5- to 6-quart pan over high heat, bring 2 quarts water to a boil. Add Jerusalem artichokes and cook until tender when pierced, about 12 minutes. Drain.

3. In a blender or food processor, whirl Jerusalem artichokes, garlic, lemon juice, and oil until smoothly puréed; scrape container sides as needed. Add chilies and salt to taste. Scrape into a bowl.

4. To eat, scoop up dip with corn chips.

Per serving: 92 cal., 50% (46 cal.) from fat; 1.3 g protein; 5.1 g fat (0.7 g sat.); 11 g carbo (1 g fiber); 3.8 mg sodium; 0 mg chol.

Mushroom Bocadillos

PREP AND COOK TIME: About 45 minutes (about 35 minutes in a convection oven)

NOTES: If making up to 1 day ahead, cool, cover, and chill. Serve at room temperature or reheat: bake, uncovered, in a 325° oven until warm, about 10 minutes.

MAKES: 8 servings

About 2 tablespoons **butter** or margarine

1 pound **sliced mushrooms**

¼ cup finely chopped **onion**

¼ teaspoon **ground nutmeg**

Salt and **pepper**

4 **large eggs**

¼ cup **fine dried bread crumbs**

½ cup minced **fresh cilantro**

½ pound **asadero** or jack **cheese,** shredded

1. In a 10- to 12-inch frying pan over high heat, melt 2 tablespoons butter. Add mushrooms, onion, and nutmeg. Stir often until mushrooms are lightly browned, about 10 minutes. Season to taste with salt and pepper. Let cool.

2. Meanwhile, in a bowl, beat eggs to blend with crumbs, cilantro, and all but ½ cup of the cheese.

3. Coarsely chop the mushroom mixture and stir into the egg mixture. Pour

Mushroom bocadillos

into a buttered 8-inch square pan.

4. Bake in a 325° oven until center feels firm when lightly pressed, about 30 minutes (about 20 minutes in a convection oven). Sprinkle evenly with remaining cheese and bake just until it begins to melt, 3 to 4 minutes more (1 to 2 minutes in a convection oven). Remove from oven and let stand in pan until warm, at least 15 minutes, or until cool. Cut into 1-inch pieces and arrange on a platter.

Per serving: 187 cal., 63% (117 cal.) from fat; 12 g protein; 13 g fat (7.4 g sat.); 5.9 g carbo (1 g fiber); 298 mg sodium; 140 mg chol.

Flank Steak Tortitas

PREP AND COOK TIME: About 35 minutes

NOTES: Spoon chipotle crema (recipe follows) into rolls stuffed with beef and onion, and add thinly sliced fresh tomatillos.

MAKES: 8 servings

¼ cup chopped **garlic**

½ cup chopped **green onions,** including tops

2 tablespoons minced **fresh jalapeño chilies**

1 teaspoon **ground cumin**

2 tablespoons **fresh oregano** leaves or 1 teaspoon dried oregano

2 tablespoons **balsamic vinegar**

1 **beef flank steak** (1½ to 1¾ lb.)

1 **red onion** (¾ lb.)

About 2 teaspoons **olive oil**

16 **round** or oval **rolls** (about 2 in. wide)

1. In a blender or food processor, whirl garlic, green onions, chilies, cumin, oregano, and vinegar until coarsely puréed.

2. Rinse flank steak and pat dry. Rub garlic mixture over meat.

3. Peel red onion; cut crosswise into ½-inch slices. Rub lightly with olive oil.

4. Cut rolls almost in half horizontally, leaving attached on one side. Pile into a basket.

5. Lay steak and onion slices on a barbecue grill over a solid bed of very hot coals or high heat on a gas grill (you can hold your hand at grill level only 1 to 2 seconds); close lid on gas grill. Cook meat, turning to brown evenly, until as done as desired in center of thickest part (cut to test), 12 to 15 minutes for rare, about 20 minutes for medium-rare. Grill onion slices, turning with a wide spatula, until lightly browned on each side, about 13 minutes. Transfer meat and onion to a carving board. Serve hot, warm, or cool.

6. Cut beef across the grain into thin, slanting slices. Tuck slices of meat and pieces of red onion into rolls.

Per serving: 349 cal., 34% (117 cal.) from fat; 22 g protein; 13 g fat (4.5 g sat.); 35 g carbo (1.9 g fiber); 353 mg sodium; 43 mg chol.

Chipotle Crema

PREP TIME: About 5 minutes

NOTES: If making up to 2 days ahead, cover airtight and chill. Freeze extra chilies and adobado sauce.

MAKES: About 1½ cups

2 **canned chipotle chilies in adobado sauce**

1½ cups **Mexican crema** or sour cream

1. Wearing kitchen gloves, pull out and discard seeds and veins from chilies. Mince chilies.

2. In a small bowl, mix chilies, 2 tablespoons of the adobado sauce, and the Mexican crema.

Per tablespoon: 36 cal., 89% (32 cal.) from fat; 0.5 g protein; 3.5 g fat (2.3 g sat.); 0.7 g carbo (0 g fiber); 18 mg sodium; 15 mg chol.

Fruit Wands with Vanilla-Rum Syrup

PREP AND COOK TIME: About 20 minutes, plus about 30 minutes to cool syrup

NOTES: You'll need about 50 thin wood skewers. If making up to 2 hours ahead, let fruit stand in syrup. Use leftover syrup to flavor glasses of iced sparkling water.

MAKES: 8 servings

1 cup **sugar**

1 **vanilla bean** (about 7 in.) or 2 teaspoons vanilla

¼ cup **rum**

2 tablespoons long, thin shreds of **orange** peel

2 **star fruit** (about 6 oz. total), rinsed

2 cups **pineapple chunks**

1 cup **strawberries,** hulled and rinsed

1. Put sugar in a 1½- to 2-quart pan. Using a small, sharp knife, slit vanilla bean lengthwise. Scrape seeds from pod into sugar; add pod to sugar. Stir in rum, orange peel, and 2 cups water.

2. Stir often over high heat until mixture boils and is reduced to 1¾ cups, about 12 minutes. Remove vanilla pod (let dry and store airtight for other uses). Let syrup cool to room temperature, about 30 minutes.

3. Meanwhile, trim and discard ends from star fruit; cut fruit crosswise into ½-inch slices. Using a small, sharp knife, remove any seeds.

4. Poke sharp end of 1 skewer through skin edge of each star fruit piece. Also poke 1 skewer through each pineapple chunk and strawberry.

5. Put skewers, fruit ends down, in a deep bowl. Pour syrup over fruit. Provide napkins to catch drips as guests pick up wands to eat.

Per serving: 149 cal., 1.8% (2.7 cal.) from fat; 0.4 g protein; 0.3 g fat (0 g sat.); 33 g carbo (1.2 g fiber); 1.4 mg sodium; 0 mg chol.

Fruit wands with vanilla-rum syrup

Pine Nut Panecillos

PREP AND COOK TIME: About 45 minutes (about 40 minutes in a convection oven)

NOTES: If making up to 1 day ahead, cool and store airtight. Freeze to store longer.

MAKES: 16 cookies

1¼ cups **pine nuts**

About ½ cup (¼ lb.) **butter** or margarine, at room temperature

½ cup firmly packed **brown sugar**

½ cup plus 4 teaspoons **granulated sugar**

1 **large egg**

1 teaspoon **vanilla**

1¾ cups **all-purpose flour**

½ teaspoon **baking soda**

1 teaspoon **ground cinnamon**

1. In a 10- to 12-inch frying pan over medium heat, stir or shake pine nuts until lightly toasted, 3 to 4 minutes. Pour into a bowl.

2. In a food processor or blender, whirl 1 cup pine nuts until smoothly puréed, scraping container sides frequently.

3. In food processor or a bowl with a mixer, whirl or beat pine nut purée, ½ cup butter, brown sugar, and ½ cup granulated sugar to blend. Add egg and vanilla; whirl or beat to blend.

4. In another bowl, stir together flour and baking soda. Add to butter mixture; stir, then whirl or beat to mix well. Divide dough into 2 equal portions. In a small bowl, mix 4 teaspoons granulated sugar and the cinnamon.

5. Press each portion of dough evenly into a buttered 9-inch-wide cake pan with removable rim (you'll need 2). Scatter remaining pine nuts over dough and, with your fingers, press them lightly but firmly into dough.

6. Bake in a 375° oven until cookies begin to pull from pan sides and centers spring back when lightly pressed, 16 to 17 minutes (350° in a convection oven for about 13 minutes). About 5 minutes before cookies are baked, sprinkle with sugar-cinnamon mixture. Let cool in pans about 10 minutes; remove rims. Cut each cookie into 8 wedges. Transfer to racks. Serve warm or cool.

Per cookie: 219 cal., 49% (108 cal.) from fat; 4.6 g protein; 12 g fat (4.9 g sat.); 25 g carbo (1.6 g fiber); 110 mg sodium; 30 mg chol. ◆

foodguide

BY JERRY ANNE DI VECCHIO

A TASTE OF THE WEST

A tribute to St. Patrick

Tender corned beef the smart, lazy way

■ Irish immigrants plunked corned beef and cabbage into our culinary melting pot because it was good, cheap food. In my youth, it was also good for a chuckle in the Sunday funnies with Maggie and Jiggs. The couple had won a bundle in the lottery, but Jiggs hankered for the simple life. Wife Maggie, on the other hand, had social aspirations; she planted a silk top hat on her husband's head and banned his beloved corned beef in their mansion. Invariably, though, her moments of triumph in society were blown by Jiggs's secret attempts to boil a hunk of corned beef. As its unmistakable low-brow aroma drifted among Maggie's grand guests, their noses tilted even higher, and they marched out. The last cartoon frame usually had Maggie pursuing Jiggs, flinging pans angrily and shouting something like "Where's the (corned) beef?"

If Jiggs had just used the oven, he could've joined Maggie and their guests and diverted their attention as his untended corned beef baked discreetly, with little bouquet but exceptionally tender results. It's a practical choice.

You can bake potatoes with the beef and make a handsome red cabbage salad (all of the recipes follow) for a St. Patrick's Day celebration fit for the classiest guest.

Oven-Braised Corned Beef Brisket

PREP AND COOK TIME: About 4½ hours
NOTES: The weight of the meat shrinks by about half as the brisket cooks.
MAKES: 6 to 8 servings

1 piece (about 4 lb.) **center-cut corned beef brisket**

1 **lemon,** ends trimmed

1 **onion** (about ½ lb.), peeled

1 teaspoon **black peppercorns**

½ teaspoon **whole allspice**

6 to 8 **whole cloves**

¼ cup **Dijon mustard**

¼ cup **brown sugar**

1. Trim and discard most of the surface fat from brisket. Rinse meat well under cool running water, rubbing gently to release its corning salt.

2. Lay meat, fattiest side up, in a 2-inch-deep, 11- by 15- or 16-inch roasting pan. Thinly slice lemon (discard seeds)

Putting cabbage in the red

Red Pear, Onion, and Cabbage Salad

PREP TIME: About 20 minutes

NOTES: You can substitute green cabbage, white onions, and yellow- or green-skin

■ Flaunting the hue of certain red vegetables is simple if you know what turns it on. The red in cabbage and onions is enhanced by acid, like that in vinegar, fruit juice, and wine. Without acid, red cabbage and onions turn purple-blue as they stand; when cooked, cabbage gets bluer, onions fade. The dressing in this recipe makes a salad brilliant.

pears. If making up to 1 day ahead, cover and chill.

MAKES: 6 to 8 servings

1 head **red cabbage** (about 1½ lb.)

About 6 tablespoons **rice vinegar**

1 tablespoon **sugar**

2 teaspoons **prepared horseradish**

½ cup finely chopped **red onion**

2 tablespoons coarsely chopped **crystallized ginger**

Salt

2 **firm-ripe red-skin pears** (5 to 6 oz. each)

½ cup chopped **chives** or green onions

1. Pull off and discard the bruised cabbage leaves. Rinse cabbage and thinly slice.

2. In a large bowl, mix 6 tablespoons rice vinegar, sugar, horseradish, red onion, and ginger. Add cabbage and then salt to taste; mix well. For mellower flavor, let salad stand at least 10 minutes, then mix again.

3. Rinse the pears, and core them. Coarsely chop 1 pear and mix with salad. Slice remaining pear, moisten with a little rice vinegar, and arrange on salad. Sprinkle with chives.

Per serving: 62 cal., 4.4% (2.7 cal.) from fat; 1.3 g protein; 0.3 g fat (0 g sat.); 15 g carbo (2.5 g fiber); 13 mg sodium; 0 mg chol.

---

and onion and lay slices over meat. Sprinkle with peppercorns, allspice, and cloves.

3. Set pan on middle rack in a 325° oven. Pour about 8 cups boiling water around brisket, seal the pan with foil, and bake until meat is very tender when pierced, about 4 hours. Uncover and drain off all but about 1 cup of the liquid. If desired, reserve the lemon and onion slices and rearrange them on top of the meat.

4. In a small bowl, mix the mustard and brown sugar; spread evenly over meat, on top of the onion-lemon mixture. Broil about 8 inches from heat until the mustard mixture begins to brown, 3 to 5 minutes. Transfer the brisket to a platter. Serve hot, warm, or cold; slice meat across the grain.

Per serving: 330 cal., 60% (198 cal.) from fat; 21 g protein; 22 g fat (7.2 g sat.); 9.8 g carbo (0.5 g fiber); 1,471 mg sodium; 111 mg chol.

St. Paddy's Potatoes with Green Sauce

PREP AND COOK TIME: About 1¼ hours

NOTES: Add potatoes to oven for the last hour the corned beef bakes. If the beef is done before the potatoes, let it continue cooking until potatoes are ready. If making green sauce up to 1 day ahead, cover and chill.

MAKES: 6 to 8 servings

12 to 16 **round red thin-skinned potatoes** (2½ in. wide; 2 to 2½ lb. total)

2 tablespoons **lemon juice**

¼ cup chopped **parsley**

¾ cup lightly packed rinsed and drained **watercress sprigs**

¼ teaspoon **dried tarragon**

¾ cup **sour cream** (or half sour cream and half plain yogurt)

Salt

1. Scrub potatoes and pierce each with a fork.

2. Set potatoes directly on the rack in a 325° oven and bake until soft when pressed, 1 to 1¼ hours (about 45 minutes in a convection oven).

3. Meanwhile, in a blender or food processor, combine lemon juice, parsley, watercress, tarragon, and sour cream. Whirl until mixture is smoothly puréed, scraping container sides as required.

4. Cut a slit across the top of each potato and pinch sides to pop open top. Set potatoes on a platter and spoon a little of the green sauce into each. Serve with remaining sauce and salt to add to taste.

Per serving: 140 cal., 30% (42 cal.) from fat; 3 g protein; 4.7 g fat (2.8 g sat.); 22 g carbo (2.1 g fiber); 24 mg sodium; 9.5 mg chol.

Metric help

■ Translating from American to metric standards is frustrating in the kitchen. When I'm up to my elbows in dough, I'm much more inclined to guess than dig up a chart. I found help at the hardware store: a washable-plastic Hempe conversion table. Slide a card back and forth in the sheath and a multitude of conversions are revealed: gallons to liters, degrees Fahrenheit to degrees Celsius. It lacks small measurements like quarts and cups, but it gives a quick basis for calculating them. The table costs about $5 at Restoration Hardware; (888) 243-9720.

BACK TO BASICS

In a jam

■ Quick breads, leavened with baking powder (and sometimes baking soda), are so named because all you do is mix and bake. No need to knead—except for biscuits and scones. For these breakfast favorites, you knead the dough just enough to create layers that separate slightly during baking (too much kneading makes them tough).

At the Grand Central Baking Company in Portland one day, I settled on the Jammer, a big, flaky biscuit with a well of jam in the center, recalling teaching my own daughter how to jam her thumb into the dough to make the sweet pockets.

Jammer Cream Scones

PREP AND COOK TIME: About 35 minutes
MAKES: 6 to 8 servings

About 2 cups **all-purpose flour**
1 tablespoon **baking powder**
About 3 tablespoons **sugar**
¼ teaspoon **salt**
About ¼ cup (⅛ lb.) **butter** or margarine
2 **large eggs**
⅓ cup **whipping cream**
¼ cup **raspberry jam**

1. In a bowl, mix 2 cups flour, baking powder, 2 tablespoons sugar, and salt.

2. Cut ¼ cup butter into chunks; add to bowl. With your fingers or a pastry blender, rub or cut in butter until dough forms pieces no larger than small peas.

3. In a small bowl, beat eggs with cream to blend; set aside 1 tablespoon. Add remaining liquid to flour mixture and stir with a fork just until dough is evenly moistened and sticks together.

4. Scrape dough onto a lightly floured board; turn over to coat with flour.

5. To knead, gently slide your fingers under side of dough opposite you, and lift and fold about half the dough over the portion on the board. Press down gently and push slightly forward.

6. Rotate the dough 90° so a pointed end is in front of you. Again slide your fingers under the farthest point and lift and fold about half the dough over the portion on the board. Press down gently and push slightly forward again. Keep turning and kneading just until dough forms a neat ball, 3 or 4 more times.

7. In a buttered, floured 10- by 15-inch pan, pat dough into a 1-inch-thick round. With a floured sharp knife, cut round into 6 to 8 equal wedges and leave in place.

8. Dust your thumb with flour and push it straight down and almost through the middle of the wide end of each wedge, wiggling to make a hole that is ½ to ¾ inch wide. Divide jam equally among the holes. Brush reserved egg mixture over dough and sprinkle evenly with 2 to 3 teaspoons sugar.

9. Bake in a 375° oven until richly browned, about 25 minutes (350° in a convection oven). Serve hot.

Per serving: 269 cal., 37% (99 cal.) from fat; 5.3 g protein; 11 g fat (6.3 g sat.); 37 g carbo (1 g fiber); 344 mg sodium; 82 mg chol. ◆

JAMES CARRIER (4)

Scone secrets

A. A little kneading creates tender layers.

B. Make a well with your thumb.

C. Fill with your favorite jam.

The Wine Guide

BY KAREN MacNEIL-FIFE

The urge to merge

■ Recently, a very bright friend of mine begged me to make her something to tape to her refrigerator. The "something" turned out to be a list of all the major wine regions of Europe, along with the grape variety (or varieties) in each wine. "Meursault, Pouilly-Fumé, Vouvray—it's so frustrating!" she sighed. "How am I supposed to know they're actually … ah …"

"Chardonnay, Sauvignon Blanc, and Chenin Blanc?" I finished her question.

I sympathize. Like lots of Westerners, my friend learned about different varieties by drinking the wines of California, Washington, and Oregon. Oh, the comforting simplicity of buying those wines! Mondavi Chardonnay—it's as easy to grasp as Häagen-Dazs vanilla: Name of producer. Name of flavor. End of issue.

In fact, a wine such as Mondavi Chardonnay exemplifies one of the noble philosophies of winemaking: namely, that given the right climate and site, a *single* grape variety can produce a delicious, complex wine. (Note: By U.S. law, a wine labeled with a single variety must be 75 percent that variety. In practice, however, many wines are 100 percent one variety.)

There is also, however, an opposite, equally noble view. And many American winemakers are now headed in this second direction. Rather than single-variety wines, they are making blends. Wine names such as "Rocks and Gravel," from the producer Edmunds St. John, or "Le Mistral," from Joseph Phelps, don't tell you what the grape variety is. And that's because there isn't *one*.

There are several—and for a good reason. When certain varieties are blended, an almost magical transformation takes place. The flavor of the resulting wine can be far greater than the sum of its parts. Some of the most exciting red wines now being made in the West, for example, are blends of Rhône grape varieties, including Syrah, Grenache, Mourvèdre, Carignan, and Cinsault.

RICK MARIANI

"When unblended, some varieties can be beautiful but ultimately not fully …" Steve Edmunds, proprietor and winemaker of Edmunds St. John, searches for the right word. "Well—*complete*," he says. Complete?

"Wholly satisfying," Edmunds tries to explain. "A complete wine has breadth, depth, balance, complexity, attractive fruit, and, beneath all that, mysterious layers of *other* flavors and aromas."

For him, many of the Rhône varieties verge on incomplete. But blend them together and bam! "Suddenly all kinds of flavors start happening that you couldn't possibly have imagined," he says.

The blending-toward-greatness idea is not new. In France's Rhône Valley itself, wines such as Châteauneuf-du-Pape have been blends as far back as they've been recorded. The philosophy is also deep-seated in Champagne and Bordeaux. For both areas, greatness hinges on blending.

In the United States, we're just getting used to this idea. Not knowing the grape varieties, after all, means you need to get

GREAT RHÔNE BLENDS

■ **Andrew Murray "Esperance" 1997 (Santa Barbara County)**, $18. Massive and muscular, with wonderful espresso, chocolate, and boysenberry flavors.

■ **Bonny Doon "Le Cigare Volant" 1996 (California)**, $23. One of the first Rhône blends, and still one of the best. Randall Grahm, proprietor and winemaker of Bonny Doon, is a man whose sense of the outrageous knows few bounds. This wine howls.

■ **Eberle "Côtes du Rôbles" 1997 (Paso Robles)**, $14. Modeled on the simple, rustic wines of the southern Rhône, this delicious red is begging for a homey stew or pasta dish.

■ **Edmunds St. John "Rocks and Gravel" 1997 (California)**, $16. Absolutely delicious—a dead ringer for a French Rhône. Rich, long, and very satisfying. Full of licorice, berry, and complex meaty flavors.

■ **Joseph Phelps "Le Mistral" 1996 (California)**, $25. Spicy pomegranate flavors. I could drink this lively wine anytime.

■ **Qupe "Los Olivos Cuvée" 1996 (Santa Barbara County)**, $18. Alive, intense, and dramatic. Massive black flavors—fabulous.

■ **T-Vine Rhône blend 1995 (Napa Valley)**, $18.50. Only a little was made, but it's worth keeping a lookout for. Saturated and delicious menthol, tar, and boysenberry flavors.

---

to know and trust the producer. Sometimes, of course, the producer spills the beans. The back label of "Le Cigare Volant" from Bonny Doon Vineyard, for example, lists the varieties.

But don't feel compelled to look, because in the best of senses, it doesn't matter that the wine is X percent Syrah plus Y percent Grenache and so on. The flavor of a great blend always goes beyond that of its components. It's the synergy that counts. And synergy has to be tasted to be believed. ◆

SUNSET'S STEAL OF THE MONTH
■**La Vieille Ferme 1995 (Côtes du Luberon)**, $7. La Vieille Ferme (*the old farm*) is consistently one of the best deals among southern French reds. Spicy and meaty, with good juicy flavors and notes of saddle leather. A real winner with all kinds of slow-cooked meats. Try it with lamb shanks! — *Karen MacNeil-Fife*

DELICATE FENNEL LEAVES accent the flavors of a creamy potato and fennel soup.

Soups from a Montana lodge

Thick enough to fill you up, smooth enough to sip, and right at home for dinner

BY ELAINE JOHNSON

As owners of Fly Fishers' Inn near Great Falls, Montana, Rick and Lynne Pasquale know how to warm up guests who come here for world-class fly-fishing. Their secret is soup. At the lodge, they pack a thermos of hot soup into the kits of anglers, to provide a warming lunch during a day wading the chilly waters of the Missouri River. Then back at the log cabin lodge, dinner begins with more hot soup.

Lynne takes pride in producing hearty soups that don't echo the meat-and-potatoes reputation of this part of Montana, such as faintly licorice-flavor fennel, double mushroom with wild rice, and sweet pea with tarragon, curried apple, and caramelized onion and shallot.

To serve one of these soups as an elegant starter, offer about $^3/_4$-cup por-tions. For a main-course serving, allow about $1^1/_2$ cups of soup with a light companion such as grilled shrimp or a toasted cheese sandwich.

Potato-Fennel Soup

PREP AND COOK TIME: About $1^1/_2$ hours
NOTES: Chop feathery green fennel leaves and sprinkle onto servings.
MAKES: 8 cups; 5 or 6 main-dish servings

- 2 heads **fennel** (each about $3^1/_2$ in. wide)
- $1^1/_4$ pounds **onions,** peeled and chopped
- 2 tablespoons **butter** or margarine
- $1^1/_4$ pounds **russet potatoes,** peeled and chopped
- 3 cups fat-skimmed **chicken broth**
- $1^1/_2$ cups **half-and-half** (light cream)
- 2 to 4 tablespoons **anise-flavor liqueur** such as sambuca or ouzo
  Salt and **pepper**

1. Rinse fennel. Trim and discard stems and bruised portions (save leaves; see notes). Chop fennel heads.

2. In a 4- to 5-quart pan over medium-high heat, frequently stir fennel, onions, and butter until vegetables are golden, about 25 minutes.

3. Add potatoes and broth. Cover and bring to a boil over high heat, then reduce heat and simmer, stirring occasionally, until potatoes mash easily when pressed, about 20 minutes.

4. In a blender, whirl soup mixture,

a portion at a time, until smoothly puréed. Return to pan. Add half-and-half, and liqueur to taste. Stir over medium-high heat until hot, about 3 minutes.

5. Ladle into bowls and season to taste with salt and pepper.

Per serving: 271 cal., 37% (99 cal.) from fat; 9.8 g protein; 11 g fat (6.7 g sat.); 32 g carbo (4 g fiber); 202 mg sodium; 33 mg chol.

Wild Rice and Mushroom Soup

PREP AND COOK TIME: About $1^1/_4$ hours
NOTES: Garnish soup with parsley.
MAKES: 7 cups; 4 or 5 main-dish servings

- $3^1/_4$ cups fat-skimmed **chicken** or beef **broth**
- $^1/_4$ cup **wild rice**
- 1 cup (1 oz.) **dried shiitake mushrooms**
- 2 tablespoons **butter** or margarine
- 1 **onion** ($^1/_2$ lb.), peeled and chopped
- $^1/_2$ pound **sliced common mushrooms**
- 1 tablespoon minced **garlic**
- $^1/_2$ teaspoon **dried rosemary**
- $^1/_2$ teaspoon **dried thyme**
- 1 **russet potato** ($^1/_2$ lb.), peeled and chopped
- $^1/_2$ cup **dry sherry**
- $^1/_2$ cup **half-and-half** (light cream) or whipping cream
  Salt and **pepper**

1. In a 1- to 2-quart pan, bring $1^1/_4$ cups broth and rice to a boil over high heat. Reduce heat, cover, and simmer until rice is just tender to bite, 45 to 50 minutes.

2. Meanwhile, in a bowl, soak shiitake mushrooms in $1^1/_2$ cups hot water until pliable, about 20 minutes. Squeeze mushrooms in water to loosen grit. Lift out mushrooms, reserving liquid. Cut off and discard stems, then thinly slice caps.

3. In a 5- to 6-quart pan over medium-high heat, stir shiitakes in 1 tablespoon butter until golden brown, about 5 minutes. With a slotted spoon, transfer shiitakes to a small bowl.

4. To a large pan, add remaining 1 tablespoon butter, onion, common mushrooms, garlic, rosemary, and thyme; stir often until vegetables are golden, about 10 minutes.

5. Carefully pour shiitake soaking

liquid into pan, discarding grit in bottom of bowl. To pan, add potato and remaining 2 cups broth. Cover, bring to a boil over high heat, then reduce heat and simmer until potato mashes easily when pressed, about 20 minutes.

6. In a blender, whirl soup, a portion at a time, until very smooth. Return to pan. Add shiitakes, wild rice with liquid, sherry, and half-and-half. Stir often over high heat until hot, about 2 minutes.

7. Ladle into bowls and season to taste with salt and pepper.

Per serving: 238 cal., 30% (71 cal.) from fat; 10 g protein; 7.9 g fat (4.6 g sat.); 27 g carbo (3.5 g fiber); 116 mg sodium; 21 mg chol.

TARRAGON and tender green peas blend suavely in a velvety soup.

Tarragon Pea Soup

PREP AND COOK TIME: About 45 minutes

NOTES: Garnish servings with fresh tarragon sprigs.

MAKES: 9 cups; 6 main-dish servings

1¼ pounds **onions,** peeled and chopped

1 tablespoon minced **garlic**

2 tablespoons **butter** or margarine

1 quart fat-skimmed **chicken broth**

¾ pound **russet potatoes,** peeled and chopped

1½ pounds **frozen petite peas**

3 tablespoons chopped **fresh tarragon** leaves or 1½ tablespoons dried tarragon

⅛ to ¼ teaspoon **cayenne**

Salt and **pepper**

1. In a 5- to 6-quart pan over medium-high heat, frequently stir onions, garlic, and butter until onions are limp, 10 to 12 minutes.

2. Add broth and potatoes. Cover, bring to a boil over high heat, then reduce heat and simmer until potatoes mash easily when pressed, about 20 minutes. Stir in peas and tarragon; add cayenne to taste.

3. In a blender, whirl soup, a portion at a time, until very smooth. Return to pan and stir over high heat until hot, 2 to 3 minutes.

4. Ladle into bowls and season to taste with salt and pepper.

Per serving: 218 cal., 19% (41 cal.) from fat; 13 g protein; 4.6 g fat (2.5 g sat.); 32 g carbo (8.7 g fiber); 239 mg sodium; 10 mg chol.

Senegalese Apple Soup

PREP AND COOK TIME: About 1 hour

NOTES: Top servings with thin apple slices and a drizzle of whipping cream.

MAKES: 10 cups; 6 or 7 main-dish servings

1¼ pounds **onions,** peeled and chopped

½ pound **Granny Smith apples,** peeled, cored, and chopped

1 cup chopped **carrots**

¼ cup **raisins**

1 clove **garlic,** minced

2 tablespoons **butter** or margarine

3 tablespoons **curry powder**

¼ cup **all-purpose flour**

2 quarts fat-skimmed **chicken broth**

½ cup **whipping cream** (optional)

Salt and **pepper**

Major Grey chutney

1. In a 5- to 6-quart pan over medium-high heat, frequently stir onions, apples, carrots, raisins, garlic, and butter until onions are limp, 10 to 12 minutes.

2. Add curry powder and flour and stir to mix well.

3. Stir in broth. Stir over high heat until boiling, then reduce heat and simmer, stirring occasionally, until carrots are very tender to bite, about 20 minutes.

4. In a blender, whirl soup, a portion at a time, until very smooth. Return to pan. Add cream and stir often over medium heat until hot, 4 to 5 minutes.

5. Ladle into bowls and add salt, pepper, and chutney to taste.

Per serving: 166 cal., 22% (36 cal.) from fat; 11 g protein; 4 g fat (2.1 g sat.); 23 g carbo (3.7 g fiber); 129 mg sodium; 8.9 mg chol.

Caramelized Onion and Shallot Cream Soup

PREP AND COOK TIME: About 2 hours

NOTES: To decorate servings, set aside a few caramelized onion pieces.

MAKES: 9 cups; 6 main-dish servings

1½ pounds **shallots** (about 1½ in. wide), peeled

2 teaspoons **olive oil**

3 pounds **onions,** peeled and thinly sliced

3 tablespoons **butter** or margarine

2 tablespoons firmly packed **brown sugar**

¾ cup **cream sherry**

5 cups fat-skimmed **beef broth**

1 tablespoon minced **fresh thyme** leaves or dried thyme

1½ teaspoons **dried rubbed sage**

3 cups **half-and-half** (light cream)

2 tablespoons chopped **parsley**

Hot sauce

Salt and **pepper**

Lemon wedges

1. In an 8- or 9-inch-wide pan, mix shallots with oil. Bake in a 375° oven until deep golden, shaking pan occasionally to turn pieces, about 1 hour.

2. Meanwhile, in a 5- to 6-quart pan over medium-high heat, frequently stir onions, butter, and sugar until onions are deep golden brown, about 45 minutes.

3. Add sherry to shallots, stirring to release browned bits in pan. Pour mixture into onions. In a blender, whirl vegetables, a portion at a time, until very smooth, adding enough broth to facilitate blending. Return puréed vegetables to pan. Add remaining broth, thyme, and sage.

4. Stirring often, bring to a boil over high heat, then reduce heat and simmer 20 minutes to blend flavors. Add half-and-half and stir over medium-high heat until hot, 2 to 3 minutes. Add parsley.

5. Ladle into bowls and season to taste with hot sauce, salt and pepper, and juice from lemon wedges.

Per serving: 428 cal., 46% (198 cal.) from fat; 13 g protein; 22 g fat (12 g sat.); 50 g carbo (4.5 g fiber); 190 mg sodium; 60 mg chol. ◆

Kitchen Cabinet

READERS' RECIPES TESTED IN SUNSET'S KITCHENS

BY LINDA LAU ANUSASANANAN

TOASTED HAZELNUTS and nutmeg perfume this quick bread with a rich, heady fragrance.

ONDINE VIERRA (2)

ter (it is very thick) into an oiled 5- by 9-inch loaf pan and spread level.

5. Bake in a 375° oven until bread is browned and just begins to pull from pan sides, and a toothpick inserted into center comes out clean, about 45 minutes (about 40 minutes in a convection oven).

6. Cool in pan on rack about 15 minutes. Invert loaf onto rack and let cool at least 1 hour. If making ahead, store airtight up to 2 days; freeze to store longer.

Per serving: 214 cal., 46% (99 cal.) from fat; 4.8 g protein; 11 g fat (1.3 g sat.); 24 g carbo (1.9 g fiber); 251 mg sodium; 16 mg chol.

Warm Mushroom Salad

Russell Ito, San Mateo, California

The pleasing contrast of warm sautéed mushrooms on a bed of cool, crisp greens brings sophistication to this salad created by Russell Ito.

PREP AND COOK TIME: About 25 minutes

MAKES: 4 servings

- ½ pound **fresh chanterelle, shiitake,** or common **mushrooms**
- 3 tablespoons **olive oil**
- 1½ teaspoons **butter** or margarine
- 2 tablespoons chopped **shallots**
- 2 tablespoons **dry white wine**
- 1 tablespoon chopped **parsley**
  Salt and **pepper**
- 1 tablespoon **red wine vinegar**
- 6 cups **salad mix,** rinsed and crisped
  About 1 ounce **parmesan cheese**

Toasted Hazelnut Bread

Heide G. Gohlert, Cheney, Washington

The recipe for this firm-textured quick bread densely laced with toasted hazelnuts came from Germany, reports Heide Gohlert.

PREP AND COOK TIME: About 1 hour

MAKES: 1¾-pound loaf; 14 servings

- 1¼ cups **hazelnuts**
- 2 cups **all-purpose flour**
- ½ cup **whole-wheat flour**
- ⅓ cup firmly packed **brown sugar**
- 1½ teaspoons **baking powder**
- 1 teaspoon **baking soda**
- ½ teaspoon fresh-grated or ground **nutmeg**
- ½ teaspoon **salt**
- ¼ teaspoon **pepper**

- 1 **large egg**
- 1 cup **buttermilk**
  About ¼ cup **salad oil**

1. Place nuts in an 8- or 9-inch-wide pan. Bake in a 375° oven until golden under skin, about 10 minutes. Pour nuts onto a towel and rub briskly to remove as much skin as possible. Let nuts cool about 5 minutes, then lift from towel; discard skins. In a food processor or blender, whirl nuts until finely ground.

2. In a bowl, mix nuts, all-purpose flour, whole-wheat flour, brown sugar, baking powder, baking soda, nutmeg, salt, and pepper.

3. In another bowl, beat egg to blend with buttermilk and ¼ cup oil.

4. Add egg mixture to flour mixture. Stir just to evenly moisten. Scrape bat-

1. Place mushrooms in a plastic bag and fill with water. Seal bag and shake to wash mushrooms. Drain well. Repeat if mushrooms are still gritty. Trim off and discard bruised stem ends (or tough shiitake stems). Cut mushrooms into ¼-inch-thick slices.

2. In a 10- to 12-inch frying pan over high heat, combine 1 tablespoon olive oil and the butter. When butter is melted, add shallots and mushrooms. Stir often until juices evaporate and mushrooms begin to brown, 6 to 7 minutes. Add wine and stir to release browned bits; boil until wine evaporates, about 1 minute. Add parsley, and salt and pepper to taste. Keep warm.

3. In a large bowl, mix remaining olive oil and vinegar. Add salad mix and stir to blend with dressing. Mound greens onto plates and top with equal portions of mushroom mixture.

4. With a vegetable peeler, shave thin curls of parmesan onto salads. Add salt and pepper to taste.

Per serving: 178 cal., 71% (126 cal.) from fat; 5.3 g protein; 14 g fat (3.6 g sat.); 8 g carbo (1.8 g fiber); 170 mg sodium; 9.5 mg chol.

Lemon-Oregano Chicken
Chuck Allen, Palm Springs

Chuck Allen whipped up this easy dinner entrée for guests in less than an hour.

PREP AND COOK TIME: About 45 minutes
MAKES: 4 servings

- ½ cup **lemon juice**
- 2 tablespoons **olive oil**
- 1 tablespoon **dried oregano**
- 2 cloves **garlic,** pressed or minced
- ¼ teaspoon **pepper**
- 4 **whole chicken legs** (thighs with drumsticks; 2⅓ lb. total)
  Salt

1. In a large plastic food bag (or bowl), combine lemon juice, oil, oregano, garlic, and pepper.

2. Trim and discard excess fat from chicken legs. Rinse chicken and place in bag (or bowl). Seal and turn bag to mix chicken with marinade (or mix in bowl and cover airtight). Let stand 10 to 20 minutes, turning occasionally. If making ahead, chill chicken in marinade up to 1 day.

3. Lift chicken from marinade and place pieces slightly apart on a rack in a 10- by 15-inch broiler pan; reserve marinade.

4. Broil about 6 inches from heat, turning as needed to brown evenly, until meat is no longer pink at bone (cut to test), 25 to 30 minutes total; up until the last 10 minutes, baste occasionally with the reserved marinade. Add salt to taste.

Per serving: 339 cal., 56% (189 cal.) from fat; 34 g protein; 21 g fat (5.3 g sat.); 1.6 g carbo (0 g fiber); 117 mg sodium; 120 mg chol.

CHICKEN LEGS stand up to fast-penetrating marinade of lemon, garlic, and oregano.

Mexican Clam Chowder
Jean Chaney, Sedona, Arizona

"I recently lost 18 pounds and was never hungry between meals," says Jean Chaney. The secret, she claims, is this low-fat but filling chowder.

PREP AND COOK TIME: About 30 minutes
MAKES: 16 cups; 8 servings

- 1 tablespoon **olive oil**
- 1 **onion** (½ lb.), peeled and chopped
- 2 cloves **garlic,** pressed or minced
- 1 tablespoon **chili powder**
- 6 cups fat-skimmed **chicken broth**
  About 1⅓ pounds **red thin-skinned potatoes,** scrubbed
- 1 can (14½ oz.) **diced tomatoes**
- 1 can (15 oz.) **low-fat vegetarian chili with beans**
- 1 package (10 oz.) **frozen corn kernels**
- 1 package (10 oz.) **frozen petite peas**
- 1 or 2 cans (10 to 12 oz. each) **baby clams**
- 2 to 3 tablespoons **lime juice**
- 1 to 2 teaspoons **hot sauce**
- 2 tablespoons chopped **fresh cilantro**
  Salt and **pepper**

1. In a 5- to 6-quart pan over high heat, stir oil, onion, and garlic until onion is limp, about 5 minutes. Add chili powder and stir just until fragrant, about 30 seconds. Add broth, cover, and bring to a boil.

2. Cut potatoes into ½-inch cubes.

3. Add potatoes to boiling broth. Cover and return to a boil, then reduce heat and simmer until potatoes are tender when pierced, about 10 minutes.

4. Add tomatoes with juice, chili, corn, peas, and clams with juice, stirring to mix. Turn heat to high, cover, and return to a boil.

5. Add lime juice, hot sauce, cilantro, and salt and pepper to taste. Ladle soup into bowls.

Per serving: 252 cal., 10% (26 cal.) from fat; 18 g protein; 2.9 g fat (0.3 g sat.); 39 g carbo (7 g fiber); 418 mg sodium; 12 mg chol.

Marmalade-glazed Carrots
Carol Hjelte, Greeley, Colorado

Lacking orange juice to flavor carrots the way she likes, Carol Hjelte made do, very well, with orange marmalade.

PREP AND COOK TIME: About 20 minutes
MAKES: 4 or 5 servings

- 1 pound **baby carrots,** peeled or scrubbed, or rinsed baby-cut carrots
- 1 tablespoon **butter** or margarine
- ¼ cup **orange marmalade**
- 1 teaspoon **ground ginger**
- ⅛ teaspoon **ground nutmeg**
- 1 tablespoon chopped **parsley**
  Salt and **pepper**

1. In a 10- to 12-inch frying pan over high heat, combine ¾ cup water and carrots. Cover, bring to a boil, then reduce heat to medium-high. Shake pan occasionally until carrots are tender when pierced, about 8 minutes. Drain.

2. Return carrots to pan over high heat. Add butter, orange marmalade, ginger, and nutmeg. Stir often until marmalade mixture clings to carrots, 5 to 6 minutes. Sprinkle with parsley, and add salt and pepper to taste.

Per serving: 96 cal., 24% (23 cal.) from fat; 0.9 g protein; 2.5 g fat (1.5 g sat.); 19 g carbo (2.6 g fiber); 61 mg sodium; 6.2 mg chol.

Blue Cheese Spread with Spiced Walnuts
Pam Miller, Somerset, California

When her winery, Single Leaf Vineyards & Winery, participates in big festivals, owner Pam Miller uses this appetizer, which can be made ahead and easily multiplied. It goes well with Single Leaf's Chardonnay.

PREP AND COOK TIME: About 15 minutes
MAKES: About 1½ cups; 6 to 8 servings

- 1 package (8 oz.) **cream cheese**
- ¼ cup crumbled **blue cheese**
- ¼ cup fresh **chèvre** (goat) **cheese**
- 2 tablespoons **butter** or margarine, at room temperature
- 2 tablespoons **brandy** or milk
- 3 tablespoons thinly sliced **chives** or green onions
- ¼ teaspoon **salt**
- ¼ teaspoon **pepper**
- ⅛ teaspoon **ground cumin**
- ⅛ teaspoon **ground cinnamon**
- ⅛ teaspoon **ground cardamom**
- 2 teaspoons **chili oil**
- 2 teaspoons **olive oil**
- ½ cup coarsely chopped **walnuts**
- 2 teaspoons **sugar**
- 3 dozen **unsalted water crackers** or thin apple slices

1. Beat cream cheese, blue cheese, chèvre, butter, and brandy until creamy. Stir in 2 tablespoons chives. Mound in a small, shallow dish. If making ahead, cover and chill up to 2 days.

2. In a small bowl, mix salt, pepper, cumin, cinnamon, and cardamom.

3. Pour chili oil and olive oil into an 8- to 10-inch nonstick frying pan over medium heat. Add walnuts. Stir often until toasted, 5 to 7 minutes. Add sugar and stir until it melts onto nuts, about 1 minute.

4. Pour hot nuts into bowl with spices and mix to coat. If making ahead, let cool and store airtight up to 2 days.

5. Sprinkle nuts and remaining 1 tablespoon chives over cheese. Spread mixture onto crackers.

Per serving: 299 cal., 69% (207 cal.) from fat; 6.9 g protein; 23 g fat (10 g sat.); 15 g carbo (0.8 g fiber); 356 mg sodium; 45 mg chol.

Parsley-Mint-Pistachio Pesto

Krista Painter and Amy French, Seattle

In culinary school Krista Painter and Amy French became cooking buddies. On weekly trips to Pike Place Market, they gathered fresh ingredients for their experiments. One outcome is this rich, green pesto. Try it on steak, fish, chicken, vegetables, and hot or cold pasta.

PREP TIME: About 5 minutes

MAKES: About 1⅔ cups

- 1 cup **shelled roasted, salted pistachios**
- 2 cups coarsely chopped **Italian parsley**
- 2 cups lightly packed **fresh mint** leaves
- 1 cup **olive oil**
  Salt

1. Rub nuts in a towel to remove any loose skins. Lift nuts from towel and place in a food processor or blender.

2. Add parsley, mint, and oil; whirl until finely ground. Add salt to taste. Use, or cover and chill up to 2 days. Freeze airtight in small portions to store longer.

Per tablespoon: 39 cal., 69% (27 cal.) from fat; 1.5 g protein; 3 g fat (0.4 g sat.); 2.4 g carbo (0.9 g fiber); 26 mg sodium; 0 mg chol.

Radish Slaw

Marilou Robinson, Portland

Marilou Robinson loves coleslaw. Her husband hates raw cabbage. The solution? Mild and crunchy radish slaw. Use a food processor or Japanese box shredder to cut the radishes.

PREP TIME: About 40 minutes

MAKES: 4 or 5 servings

- ¼ cup **rice vinegar**
- 2 tablespoons **olive oil**
- 2 teaspoons **whole-grain mustard**
- 1 teaspoon **soy sauce**
- ½ teaspoon **pepper**
- 2 cups peeled and shredded **daikon** (about ½ lb. total)
- 2 cups shredded **red radishes** (about ½ lb.)
- 1 cup thinly sliced **green onions,** including tops
  Salt
- 2 cups **salad mix**, rinsed and crisped (optional)

1. In a wide bowl, mix vinegar, oil, mustard, soy sauce, and pepper.

2. Add daikon, red radishes, and onions. Mix; add salt to taste.

3. Line plates with salad mix and spoon radish slaw on top.

Per serving: 73 cal., 70% (51 cal.) from fat; 1 g protein; 5.7 g fat (0.7 g sat.); 5.2 g carbo (1.5 g fiber); 116 mg sodium; 0 mg chol. ◆

High time for tea

BY ELAINE JOHNSON

Perfect Tea

PREP AND COOK TIME: About 10 minutes

NOTES: Taste the tea as it steeps, and remove leaves when the liquid tastes good to you, usually in 3 to 5 minutes— after 5 minutes tannins get bitter. For stronger tea use more leaves. To contain leaves for easy removal, place them in a tea ball or infuser (a metal basket or cloth bag) that allows plenty of room for leaf expansion. Or place loose leaves in a teapot; when the tea is ready, pour all of it through a fine strainer into cups or another heated pot.

MAKES: 1 or more cups

Pour **hot water** into teapot and let stand until pot is warm to touch.

For each 1 cup (8 oz.) of tea, place 1½ teaspoons **black tea leaves** in a tea ball or infuser, filling it no more than half full. Drain teapot and put tea leaves in it. For each 1½ teaspoons leaves, add 1 cup **boiling water.** Cover and let steep 3 to 5 minutes. Swirl tea ball through tea and lift out. Pour tea into cups and add **milk, lemon,** and/or **sugar** to taste.

Per cup (any tea, plain): 2.4 cal., 0% (0 cal.) from fat; 0 g protein; 0 g fat; 0.7 g carbo (0 g fiber); 7.1 mg sodium; 0 mg chol.

Falkland House Tea Blend

NOTES: Milk and sugar smooth the bold character of this intense blend.

MAKES: 1 cup leaves; 32 cups tea

Combine ½ cup (about 1 oz.) **lapsang souchong tea leaves** and ½ cup (about 1 oz.) **Earl Grey tea leaves.** Use, or store airtight up to 6 months. Prepare as directed for **Perfect Tea** (at left).

Wake-Up Tea Blend

MAKES: 1 cup leaves; 32 cups tea

Combine ½ cup (about 1 oz.) **Assam tea leaves** and ½ cup (about 1 oz.) **Ceylon tea leaves.** Use, or store airtight up to 6 months. Prepare as directed for **Perfect Tea** (at left). ◆

FRANCE RUFFENACH

"MY CANS FESTIVAL": That's what Gary Holloway of San Francisco calls his collection of nearly 1,200 tea tins. His favorite tea? His own Falkland House blend (left). One mail-order source for high-quality tea is Tea Time; (877) 328-2877 or www.tea-time.com.

The Low-Fat Cook

HEALTHY CHOICES FOR THE ACTIVE LIFESTYLE

BY ELAINE JOHNSON

LOW-FAT CHEESE stacks up for flavor on pizza topped with basil and capers.

Real cheese choices for cooking

■ A low-fat lifestyle and the pleasures of cheese don't have to be mutually exclusive. Some cheeses are naturally low in fat, and many of today's fat-trimmed cheeses have satisfying flavors, ranging from mild to sharp, although they tend to be less complex than their full-fat counterparts. And they do melt, if not quite as well.

Compared with its role model, a trimmed-down cheese may have only a few grams less fat per ounce (see chart at right). But if you cook with cheese by the cupful, this can make a difference. *Reduced-fat* cheese contains at least 25 percent less fat than regular. *Light* cheese contains one-third fewer calories or 50 percent less fat. *Low-fat* cheese must have no more than 3 grams of fat per ounce.

Part-skim mozzarella cheese has 26 percent less fat.

In a *Sunset* tasting, these lower-fat products all fared well for flavor, melting quality, and texture. However, cheeses processed to remove all fat tend to have an unusual, uncheeselike flavor, and they get gummy when heated.

Some cheeses don't need any adjusting to meet low-fat goals. Two regular cheeses you may not have considered for low-fat cooking are intensely flavored parmesan and sap sago—particularly the latter, which is made from whey and therefore naturally nonfat. Grated, a little of either hard cheese goes a long way toward enhancing the character of other cheeses. In combination with a fat-trimmed type, they can give traditionally high-fat pizza and toasted cheese sandwiches plenty of taste—and a trim profile.

Low-Fat Basil Pizza

PREP AND COOK TIME: About 25 minutes
MAKES: 4 servings

- 1 can (10 oz.) **refrigerated pizza crust dough**
- ⅓ cup **tomato paste**
- ½ teaspoon **dried oregano**
- 2 tablespoons drained **capers**
- 1 cup (4 oz.) shredded **low-fat, reduced-fat, light, or part-skim mozzarella,** jack, or Swiss **cheese**
- ¼ cup **grated parmesan** or sap sago **cheese**
- ½ to ¾ cup slivered **fresh basil** leaves
- ½ teaspoon **hot chili flakes**

1. Unfold dough. In a lightly oiled 12- to 14-inch pizza pan or on a 14- by 17-inch baking sheet, pat dough into a 12-inch-wide round with a slightly thicker ½-inch-wide rim.

2. Bake crust on lowest rack in a 425° oven until lightly browned on the bottom, 6 to 8 minutes (5 to 6 minutes in a convection oven).

3. In a bowl, combine tomato paste, 2 tablespoons water, and oregano.

4. Spread tomato mixture over crust, but not rim. Sprinkle with capers. Drop shredded mozzarella cheese in clusters onto tomato mixture, then sprinkle with parmesan.

5. Return pizza to lowest oven rack and bake until mozzarella softens, about 3 minutes (2 minutes in a convection oven). Scatter basil leaves and chili flakes over pizza.

Per serving: 370 cal., 29% (108 cal.) from fat; 15 g protein; 12 g fat (4 g sat.); 47 g carbo (4.8 g fiber); 900 mg sodium; 4 mg chol.

Cheese-Chutney Sandwich

For 1 serving, spread 1 slice **whole-grain bread** with 1 tablespoon **Major Grey chutney,** cover with ⅓ cup shredded **reduced-fat cheddar cheese,** and top with 1 more slice of whole-grain bread.

Place sandwich in an 8- to 10-inch nonstick frying pan over medium-high heat. Toast on each side, heating until cheese melts, 5 to 6 minutes total. Open sandwich and tuck in ¼ cup **watercress sprigs.**

Per sandwich: 297 cal., 26% (77 cal.) from fat; 17 g protein; 8.6 g fat (5 g sat.); 38 g carbo (3.9 g fiber); 717 mg sodium; 26 mg chol. ◆

Check the label of each cheese you buy for nutrition information. This chart gives ranges found in reduced-fat, light, low-fat, and part-skim cheeses.

FAT FACTS

CHEESE Per oz.	REGULAR Gm. fat	Cal.	FAT-TRIMMED Gm. fat	Cal.
Cheddar	9–10	110–120	1.5–6	50–90
Jack	8–9	100–110	6	80–90
Mozzarella	6	80	1.5–4.5	50–72
Parmesan	7–8	106–111	n/a	n/a
Sap sago	0	51	n/a	n/a
Swiss	7.8–8	107–110	4–6.5	80–90

Old World Easter: Paskha, a sweet molded cheese, and kulich, a rich yeast bread, break the symbolic Lenten fast (see page 76).

April

Spring
garden party

Celebrate the season
with a festive
alfresco buffet

BY ANDREW BAKER

PHOTOGRAPHS BY AMY NEUNSINGER

■ Although Helene Henderson caters parties for some of Hollywood's biggest names, her recipes are down-to-earth. Her own vegetable patch, in fact, inspired this casual but elegant meal, which she hosted in the garden for family and friends.

Kaleidoscopic tomatoes and potatoes, lanky beans, and fragrant herbs, including her trademark lavender (her company's name is Lavender Farms Catering), give the menu vivid color. Many do-ahead steps make it easy to set out the first tastes of spring.

SHRIMP ON ROSEMARY SKEWERS and potato salad—both from the grill—join orzo pasta and Caesar salad (left) at Helene Henderson's (right, seated in pink) afternoon feast in Los Angeles. Homegrown rhubarb bakes into the dessert crisp (above left). Just-picked radishes (above right) are for munching as guests arrive.

Per serving: 160 cal., 28% (44 cal.) from fat; 0.8 g protein; 4.9 g fat (4 g sat.); 12 g carbo (0.9 g fiber); 4.3 mg sodium; 0 mg chol.

Grilled Grapefruit-Rosemary Shrimp

PREP AND COOK TIME: About 45 minutes

NOTES: Use yellow or pink grapefruit juice, fresh-squeezed or bottled. To crush juniper berries, smash with the flat bottom of a glass or pan. Serve shrimp on basil butter orzo (recipe follows).

MAKES: 8 to 10 servings

- ¼ cup **grapefruit juice**
- ¼ cup **orange juice**
- 1 tablespoon minced or pressed **garlic**
- ¼ cup **olive oil**
- 1 tablespoon crushed **dried juniper berries** (see notes)
- 8 to 10 **rosemary sprigs** (about 10 in.) with straight stems
- 1 pound (26 to 30 per lb.) **shelled** (tails left on), **deveined shrimp,** rinsed

1. In a bowl, combine grapefruit juice, orange juice, garlic, oil, and juniper berries.

2. Pull most of the leaves from each rosemary stem, leaving about 2 inches

---

M E N U

Lavender Margaritas

PREP TIME: About 12 minutes

NOTES: For 10 servings, use the larger amounts of ingredients; whirl in batches, pouring each batch into a pitcher. Stir the coconut milk before measuring it. You can also use plain sugar or coarse salt to garnish glass rims.

MAKES: About 5½ to 7½ cups; 8 to 10 servings

- ¾ to 1 cup **tequila**
- ⅓ to ½ cup **blue curaçao** or other orange-flavor liqueur
- ¾ to 1 cup **canned coconut milk**
- ¼ to ⅓ cup **lime juice**

- 1½ to 2 cups **frozen unsweetened raspberries**
- 1½ to 2 cups **frozen unsweetened blueberries**
- 3 to 4 cups **ice cubes**
- 1 tablespoon **sugar**
- 1 teaspoon **fresh** or dried **lavender blossoms**

  Lime wedge

  Lavender sprigs, rinsed (optional)

1. In a blender, combine tequila, curaçao, coconut milk, and lime juice. Cover and turn to high speed, then gradually add raspberries, blueberries, and ice. Whirl until margarita mixture is smooth and slushy.

2. Put sugar and lavender blossoms in a small bowl. Rub with your fingers or mash with a spoon to release some of the lavender flavor. Rub glass rims with lime wedge to moisten. Dip rims in lavender sugar, coating evenly.

3. Pour margaritas into sugar-rimmed glasses. Garnish with lavender sprigs.

THE VIBRANT COLOR of lavender margaritas comes from blueberries and raspberries whirled to an icy slush.

at the tip of the sprig. Mince enough leaves to make 1 teaspoon; add to bowl. Reserve extra leaves for other uses.

3. Add shrimp to bowl and mix. Let stand at least 15 minutes, or cover and chill up to 2 hours.

4. Meanwhile, put rosemary stems in a bowl and cover with water.

5. Drain shrimp; discard marinade. Form 1 shrimp into a C and push thick end of a rosemary sprig through fat section, then through tail end of the shellfish. Continue skewering shrimp with remaining rosemary, distributing shrimp equally among sprigs.

6. Lay skewered shrimp on a barbecue grill over very hot coals or very high heat on a gas grill (you can hold your hand at grill level only 1 to 2 seconds); close lid on gas grill. Turn shrimp as needed to cook evenly until they are opaque but still moist-looking in center of thickest part (cut to test), about 4 minutes.

Per serving: 103 cal., 54% (56 cal.) from fat; 9.4 g protein; 6.2 g fat (0.9 g sat.); 2 g carbo (0 g fiber); 67 mg sodium; 69 mg chol.

Basil Butter Orzo

PREP AND COOK TIME: About 30 minutes

NOTES: If starting up to 4 hours ahead, cook and drain pasta (step 1), then immerse in cold water until cool; drain again, cover, and chill. Prepare peppers (step 2); cover and let stand at room temperature. Start at step 3 to complete dish.

MAKES: 8 cups; 8 to 10 servings

- 1 pound **dried orzo pasta**
- 1 **red bell pepper** (about ½ lb.)
- 1 **yellow bell pepper** (about ½ lb.)
- ½ cup (¼ lb.) **butter** or margarine
- 1½ cups lightly packed **fresh basil** leaves
- 2 cloves **garlic,** chopped
- ¾ pound **cherry tomatoes,** rinsed (cut in half if wider than ¾ in.)
- ¼ pound **crumbled feta cheese**
- 1 jar (4 oz.) **capers,** drained

1. In a 5- to 6-quart pan over high heat, bring 3 quarts water to a boil. Add orzo and cook just until tender to bite, about 10 minutes. Drain orzo and return to pan.

2. Meanwhile, rinse peppers; stem, seed, and finely chop.

3. In a food processor, purée butter, basil, and garlic.

4. Add butter mixture to orzo. Stir over medium heat until butter is melted and pasta is hot.

5. Stir in peppers, tomatoes, cheese, and capers. Pour onto a rimmed platter and serve hot, warm, or at room temperature.

Per serving: 307 cal., 38% (117 cal.) from fat; 8.6 g protein; 13 g fat (7.5 g sat.); 40 g carbo (2.9 g fiber); 536 mg sodium; 35 mg chol.

Grilled Baby-Potato Salad

PREP AND COOK TIME: About 1 hour and 25 minutes

NOTES: Use a combination of red, blue, and Yukon gold potatoes.

MAKES: 8 to 10 servings

- ½ pound **green beans**
- ¼ pound **red pearl onions** (about ¾ in. wide)
- 1¼ pounds **thin-skinned potatoes** (about 2 in. wide; see notes)
- 2 **yams** (about 1 lb. total)
- 2 cloves **garlic,** minced or pressed
- 2 tablespoons **Dijon mustard**
- ¼ cup **balsamic vinegar**
- ⅓ cup **olive oil**
- 2 cups (¾ lb.) **red cherry tomatoes**
- 2 cups (¾ lb.) **yellow cherry tomatoes**
- **Salt** and **pepper**
- ¼ pound **arugula,** tough stems removed, rinsed and drained
- 2 tablespoons chopped **fresh mint** leaves

1. Remove stem ends and any strings from beans. In a 6- to 8-quart pan over high heat, bring 2 quarts water to a boil. Add beans and cook until tender-crisp to bite, about 4 minutes. With a slotted spoon, transfer beans to a bowl of ice water to cover. When cool, lift beans out and put in a wide, shallow bowl.

2. Add onions to boiling water and cook just until tender when pierced, about 4 minutes. With slotted spoon, transfer to ice water.

3. Meanwhile, scrub potatoes and yams. Put in boiling water, adding more water if needed to cover. Cook until vegetables are tender when pierced, about 25 minutes. Drain.

4. While potatoes and yams cook, drain onions and peel.

5. In a bowl, whisk together garlic, mustard, vinegar, and oil.

6. Peel yams; cut potatoes and yams into ½-inch slices.

7. Place potato and yam slices on a barbecue grill over very hot coals or very high heat on a gas grill (you can hold your hand at grill level only 1 to 2 sec-

onds); close lid on gas grill. Cook, turning once, until grill marks develop on both sides, 2 to 4 minutes total.

8. Add potatoes, yams, onions, tomatoes, and garlic dressing to beans. Mix gently; season to taste with salt and pepper.

9. Arrange arugula on a platter, spoon salad onto leaves, and sprinkle with mint.

Per serving: 186 cal., 37% (68 cal.) from fat; 2.9 g protein; 7.6 g fat (1 g sat.); 27 g carbo (4 g fiber); 91 mg sodium; 0 mg chol.

FRIED GINGER SHREDS and ginger-infused oil brighten Caesar salad.

Caesar Salad with Fried Ginger

PREP AND COOK TIME: About 35 minutes

NOTES: Shred ginger with a shredder or finely julienne with a knife.

MAKES: 8 to 10 servings

- 6 tablespoons **olive oil**
- ½ cup finely shredded **fresh ginger**
- 6 ounces **parmesan cheese**
- 1 clove **garlic,** minced or pressed
- 3 tablespoons **lemon juice**
- 1 pound **romaine lettuce,** rinsed and crisped
- 1 cup **prepared toasted croutons**

1. In an 8- to 10-inch frying pan over high heat, stir oil and ginger until ginger is golden brown, 2 to 4 minutes. With a slotted spoon, transfer ginger to paper towels. Let oil cool.

2. With a vegetable peeler, shave about half the cheese into very thin slices. Grate remaining cheese.

TENDER CHUNKS of rhubarb and apple, under a buttery topping, cradle whipped cream.

Per tablespoon: 2.2 cal., 0% (0 cal.) from fat; 0.1 g protein; 0 g fat; 0.5 g carbo (0.1 g fiber); 0.9 mg sodium; 0 mg chol.

Apple-Rhubarb Crisp

PREP AND COOK TIME: About 1 hour and 15 minutes

MAKES: 8 to 10 servings

- 1½ pounds **Granny Smith apples**
- 1 pound **rhubarb**, rinsed
- 1 **orange** (about ½ lb.)
- 1 cup firmly packed **brown sugar**
- ½ teaspoon **ground cinnamon**
- ⅛ teaspoon **ground cloves**
- 2 teaspoons minced **fresh ginger**
  - About ¾ cup **all-purpose flour**
- ¼ cup **pecans**
- ½ cup **granulated sugar**
- 6 tablespoons (⅜ lb.) **butter** or margarine, in chunks
- 1 cup **whipping cream**
- 1 tablespoon **powdered sugar**
- 1 teaspoon **vanilla**

1. Peel and core apples. Cut into 1-inch chunks.

2. Trim and discard coarse ends and any bruised spots from rhubarb. Cut rhubarb into 1-inch pieces.

3. Grate 1 tablespoon peel from orange. Cut orange in half and ream ¼ cup juice.

4. In a shallow 3-quart (9- by 13-in.) casserole, combine apples, rhubarb, orange peel, orange juice, brown sugar, cinnamon, cloves, ginger, and 2 tablespoons flour. Mix well.

5. In a food processor, combine ¾ cup flour, pecans, and granulated sugar; whirl until nuts are finely ground. Or mince nuts with a knife and mix with flour and sugar in bowl. Add butter and whirl or rub mixture with your fingers until it forms fine crumbs. Squeeze crumbs into lumps and scatter over apple-rhubarb mixture.

6. Bake in a 375° oven until topping is well browned and juice bubbles at edges, about 40 minutes (35 minutes in a convection oven).

7. Meanwhile, in a chilled bowl with a mixer on high speed, whip cream until it holds soft peaks; add powdered sugar and vanilla. Serve, or cover and chill up to 4 hours; whisk before serving.

8. Let crisp cool 10 minutes. Serve warm or at room temperature. Spoon into bowls; top with whipped cream.

Per serving: 416 cal., 52% (216 cal.) from fat; 2.2 g protein; 24 g fat (14 g sat.); 52 g carbo (1.5 g fiber); 161 mg sodium; 64 mg chol. ◆

---

3. In a wide, shallow bowl, whisk oil, grated cheese, garlic, and lemon juice to blend.

4. Break romaine into bite-size pieces into bowl. Add croutons and mix gently.

5. Sprinkle fried ginger and shaved parmesan over salad.

Per serving: 173 cal., 73% (126 cal.) from fat; 8.2 g protein; 14 g fat (4.4 g sat.); 5 g carbo (1 g fiber); 343 mg sodium; 13 mg chol.

Barbecued Lavender Chicken

PREP AND COOK TIME: About 50 minutes

NOTES: Use one cut of chicken (breasts, wings, or leg-thigh combinations) or a mixture of pieces.

MAKES: 8 to 10 servings

- 4¾ to 5 pounds **chicken pieces**
- ¼ cup **olive oil**
  - About ¼ cup **dried** or rinsed fresh **lavender blossoms**
- 2 cloves **garlic**, minced or pressed
- ⅔ cup **prepared barbecue sauce**
  - **Salt**
  - **Cucumber salsa** (recipe follows)

1. Rinse chicken pieces, drain, and put in a large bowl with oil, ¼ cup lavender blossoms, garlic, and barbecue sauce. Mix well and let stand at least 15 minutes, or cover and chill up to 4 hours.

2. *On a charcoal barbecue:* Prepare a solid bed of coals and let burn until medium-hot (you can hold your hand at grill level only 4 to 5 seconds). Dot the surface of coals evenly with 10 charcoal briquets and set grill in place.

On a gas barbecue: Adjust heat to medium (you can hold your hand at grill level only 4 to 5 seconds).

Lay chicken on grill and cover with lid; open vents for charcoal. Cook chicken, turning to brown evenly, until no longer pink at bone in thickest part (cut to test), 25 to 35 minutes. If drippings flare up, move pieces to edge of grill. Transfer to a platter as cooked.

3. Sprinkle chicken lightly with more lavender blossoms. Add salt to taste. Serve with cucumber salsa.

Per serving: 303 cal., 56% (171 cal.) from fat; 27 g protein; 19 g fat (4.5 g sat.); 4.4 g carbo (0.4 g fiber); 220 mg sodium; 86 mg chol.

Cucumber Salsa

Rinse 1 **cucumber** (about ½ lb.) and 2 **Roma tomatoes** (about 6 oz. total). Peel cucumber and cut into ¼-inch chunks. Core tomatoes and cut into ¼-inch chunks. In a small bowl, mix cucumber and tomatoes with 2 tablespoons minced **fresh jalapeño chilies,** ¼ cup finely chopped **red onion,** and 2 tablespoons **lime juice.**

The Low-Fat Cook

HEALTHY CHOICES FOR THE ACTIVE LIFESTYLE

BY ANDREW BAKER

A classic wrap

■ Hardly any food escapes a wrapper these days—Thai chicken in a spinach tortilla, goat cheese and roasted peppers in won ton skins. But long before the current craze for encased edibles, cooks were wrapping the main course in cabbage leaves.

A Hungarian dish, cabbage rolls are traditionally filled with beef or pork and served with a light tomato sauce on a bed of sauerkraut. A no-fat cooking method—steaming—makes them comfort food with a clean (and lean) conscience.

Beef Cabbage Rolls

PREP AND COOK TIME: About 35 minutes

MAKES: 4 servings

- 1   head **savoy cabbage** (about 1¼ lb.)
- 1   jar (16 oz.) **sauerkraut,** rinsed, drained, and squeezed dry
- ½   teaspoon **paprika**
- 1   pound **ground lean beef** (7 to 10 percent fat)
- ¾   cup finely chopped **onion**
- 1   **large egg** white
- ¾   cup **dried precooked white rice**
- ¼   cup chopped **parsley**
- ¼   cup **fine dried bread crumbs**
-     About ½ teaspoon **salt**
-     About ¼ teaspoon **pepper**
- 1   cup **tomato juice**
- 1   cup fat-skimmed **beef broth**
-     **Nonfat** or low-fat **sour cream**

1. In a 2½- to 3-inch-deep 12-inch frying pan or 5- to 6-quart pan, bring about 1 inch of water to a boil over high heat.

2. Cut out and discard cabbage core. Carefully separate leaves from head, keeping them whole.

3. Add cabbage to pan, cover, and cook until leaves are wilted, 3 to 4 minutes. Drain water from pan and fill with cold water. Drain again.

4. Cut thickest parts of tough stems from the 8 largest leaves; set leaves

TRENDY TRADITION: Hearty low-fat cabbage rolls make a quick and easy dinner.

JULIE TOY

aside. Finely chop stems and remaining leaves.

5. In pan, mix chopped cabbage with sauerkraut and paprika; spread flat.

6. In a bowl, mix ground beef, onion, egg white, rice, parsley, bread crumbs, 3 tablespoons water, ½ teaspoon salt, and ¼ teaspoon pepper.

7. Mound ⅛ of the meat mixture at stem end of cupped side of each reserved cabbage leaf. Form the meat into a horizontal log 2½ to 3 inches long, fold leaf sides over meat, then roll from stem end to enclose. Set rolls, seams down, on sauerkraut mixture in pan.

8. Mix tomato juice and broth. Pour over cabbage rolls. Cover pan and bring to a boil over high heat. Reduce heat to medium-low and simmer until meat is no longer pink in center of thickest part (cut to test), about 15 minutes.

9. Spoon stuffed cabbage rolls and sauerkraut mixture into shallow rimmed bowls. Add sour cream, salt, and pepper to taste.

Per serving: 340 cal., 23% (79 cal.) from fat; 31 g protein; 8.8 g fat (3.1 g sat.); 35 g carbo (3 g fiber); 959 mg sodium; 65 mg chol.

More lean fillings

TURKEY CABBAGE ROLLS. Follow recipe for beef cabbage rolls, but omit ground beef and instead use 1 pound **ground lean turkey.** In step 8, simmer until meat is no longer pink in center of thickest part (cut to test), 10 to 12 minutes.

Per serving: 330 cal., 25% (83 cal.) from fat; 28 g protein; 9.2 g fat (2.4 g sat.); 35 g carbo (3 g fiber); 996 mg sodium; 83 mg chol.

SALMON CABBAGE ROLLS. Follow recipe for beef cabbage rolls, but omit ground beef, salt, and pepper. Instead, use 1 pound **seasoned ground-salmon patties** (thawed, if frozen). In step 8, simmer until salmon is opaque but still moist-looking in center of thickest part (cut to test), about 8 minutes.

Per serving: 279 cal., 5.4% (15 cal.) from fat; 29 g protein; 1.7 g fat (0.1 g sat.); 39 g carbo (2.9 g fiber); 981 mg sodium; 35 mg chol. ◆

An Old World Easter

For a traditional Russian celebration, there are markets to explore, a bread to bake, and a simple cheese to make

BY LINDA LAU ANUSASANANAN

RICHARD JUNG

MENU

Smoked Salmon

Fresh Salmon or Sturgeon Caviar

Pumpernickel Triangles

Butter • Sour Cream

Chopped Chives

Pickled and Marinated Herring

Baked Ham

Sour Cream Cucumber Salad*

Pickled Mushrooms*

Potato-Beet Salad*

Pickled Beets

Cabbage Slaw • Rye Bread

Vodka or Beer

Kulich (Russian Easter Bread)*

Paskha (Sweet Cheese)*

Colored Eggs • Coffee or Tea

recipe follows

■ On a balmy spring evening, Tanya Meyer waits with other Russian Orthodox parishioners along the pathway to Holy Virgin Mary Cathedral in Los Angeles. On a bench before her are dozens of loaves of tall, cylindrical *kulich*—a festive sweet yeast bread—including her own, which her mother taught her to make decades ago.

As the priest, Father Joseph, approaches to bless the loaves on this Russian Easter eve, Meyer hastily lights a candle atop her kulich. Later, her family will break their Lenten fast with a lavish buffet that includes the blessed bread.

The crowd swells to pack the cathedral, and minutes before midnight, a flame is passed to light candles members of the congregation are holding. At the stroke of 12, bells ring in joyful chorus, and the clergy leads worshipers

outside, through azalea-filled gardens and around the building. Then the procession reenters the brightly lit church for services that last until about 3 A.M.

On April 11 this year (1999), similar Russian Easter celebrations will take place across the land.

The earliest Russian settlements in Alaska date back to the 18th century, but it is 20th-century immigration that has swelled the number of Russian

LAVISH make-ahead buffets await Russian Orthodox families after Easter services.

Orthodox Americans—particularly in the Northwest, San Francisco, Los Angeles, and New York—who continue to observe the holiday traditions of the old country. Like Meyer's, most families include in their festivities a buffet of many dishes: fish (smoked, pickled, and marinated), warm or cold roasts (ham and turkey), and sausages; salads, pickled vegetables, and dark breads; colored eggs; and, most important, the rich kulich loaves and *paskha,* a sweet and simple homemade cream cheese spread to slather onto slices of the kulich.

A Russian Easter table is both a gracious and a relaxed way to entertain. In Russian Orthodox homes, the meal is served following midnight services, as a brunch, or as midday dinner. And it's an easy menu for Easter or any other party—composed of make-ahead dishes and presented like a smorgasbord, with little plates to refill at each diner's own pace.

Recipes follow for menu items with asterisks. Purchase remaining dishes from a deli (see Russian shopping information on page 79) or make them from favorite recipes. For each person, allow at least 2 tablespoons of caviar, ¼ pound total of cooked meat or fish, 1 to 1½ cups total of salads and/or pickled vegetables, and ¼ pound of dark bread.

Sour Cream Cucumber Salad

PREP TIME: About 20 minutes, plus at least 30 minutes to chill

NOTES: This recipe is adapted from Leda Voropaeff's *Russian-American Feasts*. The dressing can be made up to 1 day ahead.

MAKES: About 4 cups; 12 servings

- 2 **English cucumbers** (2 lb. total)
  About 1 teaspoon **salt**
- 3 hard-cooked **large eggs,** shelled
- ⅓ cup **sour cream**
- 2 tablespoons **white wine vinegar**
- 1 teaspoon **Dijon mustard**
- 1 teaspoon **sugar**
- ⅛ teaspoon **pepper**
- 1 tablespoon chopped **fresh dill** or 1 teaspoon dried dill weed
  Butter lettuce leaves, rinsed and crisped (optional)

1. Trim and discard cucumber ends. Cut cucumbers in half lengthwise and thinly slice. In a bowl, mix cucumbers with 1 teaspoon salt; cover and chill at least 30 minutes or up to 4 hours. Drain well and pat dry.

2. Separate egg yolks and whites. Cut whites into slivers. Add to cucumber.

3. In a blender or food processor, combine yolks, sour cream, vinegar, mustard, sugar, and pepper; whirl until smooth.

4. To serve, mix sour cream dressing and dill with cucumbers. Add salt to taste. Line a wide bowl with lettuce leaves and spoon cucumber salad onto leaves.

Per serving: 45 cal., 53% (24 cal.) from fat; 2.2 g protein; 2.7 g fat (1.2 g sat.); 3 g carbo (0.8 g fiber); 127 mg sodium; 56 mg chol.

Pickled Mushrooms

PREP AND COOK TIME: About 15 minutes, plus at least 20 minutes to cool

NOTES: If making ahead, cover and chill up to 1 week.

MAKES: About 4 cups; 12 servings

- 2 pounds **mushrooms** (2-in. caps)
- 1½ cups **white wine vinegar**
- 1 **dried bay leaf**
- 2 teaspoons **black peppercorns**
- 2 teaspoons **mustard seed**
- 2 teaspoons **dill seed**
- 2 teaspoons **salt**
- 2 cloves **garlic,** crushed

1. Rinse and drain mushrooms; trim off and discard discolored stem ends. Cut mushrooms into quarters through caps.

2. Meanwhile, in a 3- to 4-quart pan over high heat, bring ⅔ cup water, vinegar, bay leaf, peppercorns, mustard seed, dill seed, salt, and garlic to a boil.

3. Add mushrooms. Simmer, stirring occasionally, for 10 minutes. Let mixture cool, stirring occasionally. Serve cool or chilled.

Per serving: 28 cal., 16% (4.5 cal.) from fat; 1.8 g protein; 0.5 g fat (0 g sat.); 5.3 g carbo (1.1 g fiber); 392 mg sodium; 0 mg chol.

Potato-Beet Salad

PREP AND COOK TIME: About 40 minutes

NOTES: If making ahead, cover and chill up to 4 hours.

MAKES: About 6 cups; 12 servings

- 1½ pounds **thin-skinned potatoes** (about 3 in. wide)
- ⅓ cup **white wine vinegar**
- 2 tablespoons **salad oil**
- 2 tablespoons chopped **parsley**
- 1 tablespoon **Dijon mustard**
- 1 can (15 oz.) **baby beets,** rinsed and drained
- ½ cup chopped **red onion,** rinsed and drained
  Salt and **pepper**

1. Scrub potatoes.

2. In a 3- to 4-quart covered pan over high heat, bring 1½ quarts water to a boil. Add potatoes, cover, and simmer until they are just tender when pierced in thickest part, 20 to 30 minutes.

3. Drain potatoes and cover generously with cold water. Drain when cool, about 15 minutes.

4. Meanwhile, mix vinegar, oil, parsley, and mustard in a wide bowl.

5. Peel potatoes. Cut potatoes and beets into ½- to ¾-inch cubes and add to bowl. Add onion, mix gently, and season to taste with salt and pepper.

Per serving: 87 cal., 37% (32 cal.) from fat; 1.4 g protein; 3.5 g fat (0.4 g sat.); 12 g carbo (1.4 g fiber); 123 mg sodium; 0 mg chol.

Kulich

PREP AND COOK TIME: About 1¾ hours, plus 2 hours to rise

NOTES: Instead of vanilla bean and vodka, you can use 1 tablespoon vanilla; add with the milk. Tuck scraped vanilla

AT MIDNIGHT SERVICES for Russian Easter, candles glow in the hands of parishioners.

bean pod into an airtight jar of sugar to make vanilla sugar. If making bread ahead, don't ice; let cool, wrap airtight, and freeze. Thaw in wrapper, then unwrap and ice. For a Russian finale, sprinkle soft icing with colored candy sprinkles or set small rosebuds in it.

MAKES: A 1¾-pound loaf; 12 servings

- 1 envelope **active dry yeast**
- ½ cup **granulated sugar**
- 1 **vanilla bean** (6 to 8 in.)
- 1 tablespoon **vodka** or brandy
- ⅛ teaspoon **powdered saffron** (optional)
- 2 tablespoons **milk**
- ½ cup (¼ lb.) **butter** or margarine
- ¼ teaspoon **salt**
- 3 **large eggs**
- 2½ to 3 cups **all-purpose flour**
- 2 tablespoons finely chopped **candied orange peel**
- ½ cup **powdered sugar**
- 1½ teaspoons **lemon juice**

1. In a bowl, add yeast and ½ teaspoon granulated sugar to 2 tablespoons warm (110°) water. Let stand until yeast is soft, about 5 minutes.

2. Cut vanilla bean lengthwise; scrape out black seeds and add to vodka in a cup. Add saffron to milk in another cup.

3. In another bowl, beat to blend remaining granulated sugar, butter, and salt.

TERRENCE McCARTHY

PASKHA, A SWEET MOLDED CHEESE, and kulich, a rich yeast bread, break the symbolic Lenten fast.

4. Add yeast mixture, vodka-vanilla mixture, saffron mixture, eggs, 2¼ cups flour, and orange peel. Stir until thoroughly moistened.

5. With mixer on high speed, beat dough until stretchy and shiny, 4 to 5 minutes. Stir in ¼ cup flour until evenly moistened.

6. *With a dough hook,* beat on high speed until dough pulls fairly cleanly from sides of bowl, about 2 minutes. Dough will be soft and slightly sticky to touch. If necessary, add more flour, 1 tablespoon at a time, and beat longer.

Or with lightly oiled hands, knead dough in bowl until it feels smooth, pulls from your hands, and is just slightly sticky to touch, about 4 min-

utes. If necessary, add more flour, 1 tablespoon at a time.

7. Cover bowl with plastic wrap and let dough rise in a warm place until about doubled in volume, 1 to 2 hours.

8. Line the bottom of 1 juice or broth can (46-oz. size) with cooking parchment cut to fit. Then line sides of can with parchment, extending it about 2 inches above can rim; secure with paper clip. (Or use waxed paper, buttered heavily and dusted with flour.)

9. Punch dough down to expel air, then shape into a smooth-topped ball and drop into can. Cover can lightly with plastic wrap and let stand in a warm place until dough is about 1½ inches below can rim, 45 minutes to 1¼ hours.

10. Bake on lowest rack in a 325° oven until a long, thin wood skewer inserted into center of the loaf comes out clean, 1¼ to 1½ hours (45 minutes to 1¼ hours at 300° in a convection oven).

11. Let bread stand in can for 10 minutes, then remove from can and parchment. Lay the loaf on its side on a rack to cool.

12. Blend powdered sugar with lemon juice and ¾ teaspoon water until smooth. Stand kulich upright and drizzle top with icing.

13. To serve, cut bread into rounds.

Per serving: 245 cal., 34% (84 cal.) from fat; 4.6 g protein; 9.3 g fat (5.2 g sat.); 35 g carbo (0.9 g fiber); 144 mg sodium; 74 mg chol.

Paskha

PREP TIME: About 15 minutes, plus at least 1 hour to chill

NOTES: This dessert cheese is traditionally shaped in a flat-topped pyramid mold. A new 4- to 6-inch-wide clay flowerpot also works. Make cheese up to 4 days ahead. Instead of vanilla bean, you can use 1 tablespoon vanilla. To make the XB (*Christ is risen* in Russian) on sides, use decorator icing in a tube or toasted slivered almonds.

MAKES: 2¼ pounds; 12 to 16 servings

- 1 **vanilla bean** (6 to 8 in.)
- 1 cup (½ lb.) **unsalted butter,** at room temperature
- 1 package (8 oz.) **cream cheese,** at room temperature
- ½ cup **sugar**
- 1 carton (16 oz.) **ricotta cheese**
- 2 tablespoons finely chopped **candied orange peel**

1. Split the vanilla bean lengthwise with a sharp knife and scrape out black seeds.

2. In a bowl with a mixer, beat vanilla seeds, butter, cream cheese, and sugar until smooth. Add ricotta and orange peel; beat until blended.

3. Line a deep 5-cup mold with 2 layers of damp cheesecloth (if making more than 2 hours ahead, use a mold with a bottom drain—see notes—to get a firmer cheese). Spoon paskha mixture into cloth and pack down firmly. Set on a rack on a rimmed dish.

4. Cover airtight and chill until paskha is firm enough to hold its shape, at least 1 hour.

5. Lift cloth with paskha from mold. Peel back cloth, invert cheese onto a flat plate, and remove cloth.

Per serving: 231 cal., 78% (180 cal.) from fat; 4.4 g protein; 20 g fat (13 g sat.); 8.6 g carbo (0 g fiber); 67 mg sodium; 61 mg chol.

A taste of Russia

In communities with established Russian populations, you'll find specialized markets. Recent Jewish immigrants from the former Soviet Union have also opened food markets, and although Easter is not part of their culture, foods for the holiday are available: smoked fish, herring mixtures, sausages, cheeses, yogurts, salads, pickled vegetables, and breads.

PORTLAND
S & M Russian Food, 6433 S.E. Foster Rd.; (503) 771-8873. Kulich and paskha.

SAN FRANCISCO
Many Russian delicatessens line Geary Blvd. between 18th and 22nd avenues.

Gastronom Deli and Bakery, 5801 Geary; (415) 387-4211.

Katia's A Russian Tea Room, 600 Fifth Ave.; (415) 668-9292. Kulich and paskha; order ahead at this restaurant.

Moscow Bakery Store, 5540 Geary; (415) 668-6959. Kulich and paskha.

SEATTLE-BELLEVUE AREA
European Gourmet Cafe and Deli, 1882 136th Place N.E., Bellevue; (425) 641-0818.

WEST HOLLYWOOD
Santa Monica Blvd. has markets between N. Ogden Dr. and N. Crescent Heights Blvd.

Gastronom European Food, 7859 Santa Monica; (213) 654-9456. Kulich.

Royal Gourmet, 8151 Santa Monica; (213) 650-5001. Kulich and paskha.

Tatiana, 8205 Santa Monica; (213) 656-7500. Kulich.

Tblisi & Yerevan Bakery, 7862 Santa Monica; (213) 654-7427. Kulich. ◆

foodguide

BY JERRY ANNE DI VECCHIO

Egg cup encore

A high-ranking insider of a well-known cookware chain slipped me this tidbit: egg cups are hot. No, they aren't new. The passion for china models probably dates back to the 19th century, when, in their zeal to expand desire for their products, porcelain makers wooed the bourgeoisie with an astonishing array of special-function pieces. Now, varied materials and imaginative designs are giving this little container for an egg cooked in its shell a new round of popularity in cookware stores.

Perfect eggs in the shell: Place **large eggs** in a single layer in a straight-sided pan 6½ to 7 inches wide. Add **cold water** to cover eggs by 1 inch. Cook over high heat until water reaches 200°, 8 to 11 minutes; yolks will be liquid, whites firm. For entirely firm whites, cover pan, remove from heat, and let stand 2 to 4 minutes. For firm yolks, leave pan on burner but lower heat to keep water at 180° to 200° for 10 to 12 minutes longer.

Per egg: 78 cal., 62% (48 cal.) from fat; 6.3 g protein; 5.3 g fat (1.6 g sat.); 0.6 g carbo (0 g fiber); 62 mg sodium; 213 mg chol.

STEP BY STEP

Unsticking tamarind

■ Tart-sweet tamarind is the essential tang in many Mexican, Indian, and Southeast Asian dishes. It's sold in many forms, including bricks of paste and prepared concentrates, in specialty produce sections and ethnic markets. The "fresh" fruit looks like big, dried, and cracked bean pods. Extract the paste around the seeds to create a liquid base for marinades, sauces, and the cooler at right.

TAMARIND LIQUID
1. If using fresh tamarind, break off and discard pods (some bits will stick).

2. Put the sticky brown paste with seeds (or all or part of a brick of tamarind paste, which often has seeds too) in a bowl and add about 3 parts hot water to 1 part paste. Let stand 3 to 4 minutes to cool. Squeeze pulp from seeds.

3. Rub tamarind mixture through a fine strainer into a bowl; discard residue. Use liquid, or freeze to store.

Tamarind cooler. Mix together 1 part **tamarind liquid** (directions preceding) and 3 parts **sparkling water** or orange juice. Add **sugar** to taste and pour into a glass over **ice.**

Per cup with 2 teaspoons sugar: 41 cal., 0% (0 cal.) from fat; 0.1 g protein; 0 g fat; 11 g carbo (0 g fiber); 1.1 mg sodium; 0 mg chol.

1 to 2 tablespoons **shaved bonito** (optional)

½ pound **thin-sliced smoked salmon,** cut into strips

About ¼ cup **sliced pickled ginger**

About 1 ounce **radish** (or daikon) **sprouts,** rinsed and drained

2 to 3 tablespoons **tobiko caviar**

Chili mayonnaise (recipe follows)

1. Rinse a 1- to 2-cup bowl with cold water and lightly pack ¼ of the sushi rice salad into it. Invert onto a plate. Repeat to shape remaining portions.

2. Cut nori sheets into quarters. Moisten sliced avocado with rice vinegar.

3. Sprinkle sushi rice salads equally with shaved bonito. Alongside each, arrange ¼ of the nori, avocado, salmon, pickled ginger, and radish sprouts. Sprinkle servings with tobiko caviar.

4. To eat as sushi, put some of each ingredient on a piece of nori and add chili mayonnaise to taste; fold nori over filling. Or eat as a salad with a knife and fork, adding chili mayonnaise to taste.

Per serving without mayonnaise: 540 cal., 23% (126 cal.) from fat; 21 g protein; 14 g fat (2.1 g sat.); 82 g carbo (2.6 g fiber); 2,025 mg sodium; 60 mg chol.

Sushi rice salad. Rinse, drain, and discard stems from 4 **fresh shiitake mushrooms** (2-in. caps). Finely chop caps and put in a 6- to 8-inch frying pan with 2 tablespoons **water,** 1 tablespoon **salad oil,** and 1 tablespoon **soy sauce.** Stir over high heat until liquid evaporates, 3 to 4 minutes. Scrape into a large bowl. In a 2- to 3-quart pan, rinse 1½ cups **short-grain white rice** with cold water until water is clear. Drain. Add 1½ cups **water,** cover, and bring to a boil over high heat. Reduce heat to low and cook until water is absorbed, about 15 minutes. Dump rice into bowl with shiitake mixture. Sprinkle with 5 to 6 tablespoons **seasoned rice vinegar.** Mix with a spatula and let stand about 10 minutes. To rice add 4 teaspoons finely chopped **sliced pickled ginger,** ¼ cup diced **red bell pepper,** and ¾ cup diced **Japanese** or English **cucumber.** Mix.

Per serving: 344 cal., 9.9% (34 cal.) from fat; 6.8 g protein; 3.8 g fat (0.5 g sat.); 69 g carbo (1.8 g fiber); 651 mg sodium; 0 mg chol.

Chili mayonnaise. Mix 6 tablespoons **mayonnaise,** 1½ tablespoons **seasoned rice vinegar,** and **hot sauce** to taste.

Per tablespoon: 76 cal., 97% (74 cal.) from fat; 0.1 g protein; 8.2 g fat (1.2 g sat.); 0.8 g carbo (0 g fiber); 147 mg sodium; 6.1 mg chol.

Salmon stars in sushi role

■ Chef Katsuo "Naga" Nagasawa at Cafe Del Rey in Marina Del Rey, California, presents smoked salmon in a beautifully structured, time-honored sushi roll. But he goes beyond tradition by seasoning the rice like a salad. Inspired by his innovation but lacking his technical skill, I've borrowed the essentials of Naga's salmon roll for a simpler—but still traditional—*temaki* (hand-rolled sushi). I present the ingredients separately; diners put a little of each on a square of nori, then fold the seaweed over the filling—sort of a Japanese taco.

Smoked Salmon Sushi Salad

PREP AND COOK TIME: About 50 minutes

NOTES: Up to 1 day ahead, make sushi rice salad, cover, and chill; bring to room temperature to serve. Garnish with cucumber if desired. Specialty ingredients are available at Japanese markets.

MAKES: 4 servings

Sushi rice salad (recipe follows)

6 sheets **roasted** (or toasted) **nori** (about 7 by 9 in.)

1 **firm-ripe avocado** (about ½ lb.), peeled, pitted, and sliced

Seasoned rice vinegar

Crisp nonwheat popover treat

■ If you deal with wheat allergies in your family but crave a puffy morsel of bread, try these muffin popovers made with rice flour. Their steamy interiors and crisp crusts suit every taste.

Rice Muffin Popovers

PREP AND COOK TIME: About 40 minutes

NOTES: If batter stands, muffins won't be as crisp or puffy because the flour rapidly soaks up the liquid. And since there is no gluten in rice flour, the muffins won't pop as much as wheat-flour versions, and may sink as they cool.

MAKES: 8 pieces

In a bowl, beat together to blend 1½ teaspoons **butter** (if using cooked rice flour), 1 **large egg,** ½ cup **nonfat** or low-fat **milk,** ½ cup **sweet** or cooked **rice flour,** and ½ teaspoon **salt** (optional). At once, fill 8 well-buttered muffin cups (2½ in.) equally with batter. Bake in a 375° oven until popovers are well browned, about 35 minutes (about 30 minutes in a convection oven). Run a knife between pan and popovers and ease out of pan. Serve hot.

Per piece: 57 cal., 25% (14 cal.) from fat; 1.9 g protein; 1.5 g fat (0.7 g sat.); 8.7 g carbo (0.2 g fiber); 23 mg sodium; 29 mg chol.

CASSEROLE

The whole tomato story

■ A flavorful tomato casserole at the Indian Taj Restaurant in San Diego brought me an epiphany: you can use the carefully peeled ripe tomatoes from a can *whole.* (Obviously, I have been cutting up too much.) This fresh-tasting adaptation goes well with poultry, fish, lamb, and pork.

Taj Tomato Casserole

PREP AND COOK TIME: About 50 minutes

MAKES: 6 to 8 servings

- 2 cans (1 lb., 12 oz. each) **peeled whole plum tomatoes**
- 1 **onion** (½ lb.), peeled and chopped
- 1 tablespoon **salad oil**
- ⅛ teaspoon **cardamom seed,** crushed
- ½ teaspoon **cumin seed**
- 2 teaspoons minced **fresh ginger**
- 1 tablespoon **mustard seed**
- 2 tablespoons finely chopped **lemon,** including peel
- 1 teaspoon **curry powder**
- ¼ cup **lemon juice**
- 2 tablespoons **sugar**
- ¾ cup chopped **fresh cilantro**
- **Salt**

1. Drain tomatoes, reserving juice. Arrange tomatoes in a single layer in a shallow 9- or 10-inch square casserole. Measure 2 cups tomato juice; if less than 2 cups, add water. Reserve any extra juice for other uses.

2. In a 10- to 12-inch frying pan, combine onion, oil, cardamom seed, cumin seed, ginger, mustard seed, and chopped lemon. Stir over high heat until onion is limp, 3 to 5 minutes. Stir in curry powder and add tomato juice, lemon juice, sugar, and ¼ cup cilantro. Boil, stirring occasionally, until mixture is reduced to 3 cups, about 5 minutes. Pour over tomatoes in casserole.

3. Bake in a 375° oven until sauce is slightly reduced and flavors are well blended, about 45 minutes (35 minutes in a convection oven). Baste tomatoes with juices and gently mix in remaining cilantro. Add salt to taste. Serve hot or at room temperature.

Per serving: 88 cal., 27% (24 cal.) from fat; 2.6 g protein; 2.7 g fat (0.3 g sat.); 16 g carbo (2.3 g fiber); 327 mg sodium; 0 mg chol. ◆

JAMES CARRIER (2)

The Wine Guide

BY KAREN MacNEIL-FIFE

RICK MARIANI

What winemakers drink in private

■ Imagine that every night, of all the foods in the world, you ate only cornflakes, chicken, or, occasionally, walnuts. Wouldn't that be unthinkable? Virtually no one would eat so narrowly by choice.

As tragic as this food scenario is, however, it's precisely the way many of us drink wine. On any given night, we sip a Chardonnay, Merlot, or maybe Cabernet or Sauvignon Blanc. Four flavors. But do you know how many grape varieties there are? About 5,000. That's 5,000 taste experiences we could be having!

There is nothing wrong with Chardonnay, Merlot, Cabernet, and Sauvignon Blanc, of course. But in the same way that it's intriguing and enlightening to try, say, a guava or some couscous every now and then, it's also wonderful to taste wines that are not part of your usual repertoire.

Admittedly, 5,000 flavors can be daunting. How then could you experi-

ment tomorrow night without taking a total shot in the dark? I thought inspiration might lie with some of our best winemakers. What, after a day of tasting narrowly (mostly their own wines), do winemakers drink at home?

"The great German and Alsatian wines," said Bill Knuttel, winemaker at Chalk Hill Estate Vineyards and Winery in Sonoma County. "Rieslings, Pinot Gris, and Gewürztraminers are a real treat. They give me a new perspective on what I'm doing." (What Knuttel is "doing" is mostly Chardonnay and Cabernet Sauvignon.)

For Bob Lindquist, winemaker at Qupé Wine Cellars in Santa Barbara County, it's also German Rieslings. "They are the mirror opposites of California wines," he said. "They're about understatement, not power." (Lindquist's sensational Syrahs are most definitely not about understatement.)

I phoned Randall Grahm, iconoclastic winemaker at Bonny Doon Vineyard in the Santa Cruz Mountains. "Life is tough,"

he sighed. "I want wine to be comforting. So I spell relief R-I-E-S-L-I-N-G. A German Riesling—from the Mosel especially—is so lovely, so perfect."

Grahm has made some perfectly comforting wines himself, but I understand what he, Knuttel, Lindquist, and an amazing number of other German Riesling–drinking winemakers are getting at. Great German Riesling—light and exquisite—is about as different from California wines as conceivably possible. And therein lie its magic and its appeal.

What else do winemakers drink when left to their own devices? Paul Draper, winemaker at Ridge Vineyards in the Santa Cruz Mountains (famous for its Zinfandels and Cabernets), loves the wines of Piedmont, Italy, especially Barolos, Barbarescos, and Dolcettos.

At heart winemakers are insatiably curious. "Every time I read an article about a wine, I can't wait to see what it tastes like," said Daniel Baron from Napa Valley. He makes Silver Oak Cellars's luscious Cabernets but the night before had drunk a fabulous Spanish wine.

The more winemakers I spoke to, the more Germany, Italy, and Spain kept coming up. Even Robert Mondavi, 85-year-old patriarch and chairman of the Robert Mondavi winery in Napa Valley, named Italian and Spanish wines as his favorites. But not just any old Italian and Spanish wines. The simplest ones. "I like wines that are gentle, wines that are easy to drink and not too damned serious," said Mondavi, who, of course, has made more than a few serious wines of his own. ◆

SUNSET'S STEAL OF THE MONTH

Barwang Regional Selection Shiraz 1996, Coonawarra (Australia), $12. Talk about bang for your buck! This big, juicy Shiraz (the grape is also known as Syrah) is packed with velvety-soft boysenberry, chocolate, and licorice flavors. A great steal from Oz. — *Karen MacNeil-Fife*

Old World inspiration

Here are a few of the European wines Western winemakers admitted to loving. Although these specific wines might be a little hard to come by (look for them on good restaurant wine lists), you can get a sense of what the winemakers are talking about by buying wines from any top German, Alsatian, or Italian producers. Rely on a good wine shop for suggestions.

• **Domaine Zind Humbrecht Pinot Gris "Clos Saint Urbain" Vendange Tardive** (Alsace). From a top Alsatian producer, this wine may be one of the most concentrated Pinot Gris in the world.

• **Heyl Niersteiner Ölberg Riesling Spätlese, Rheinhessen** (Germany). A fresh, lively Riesling from a venerable estate.

• **Selbach-Oster Zeltinger Sonnenuhr Riesling Spätlese** (one star), **Mosel** (Germany). Selbach-Oster is a great

Mosel producer; the 1997 ($21) is a knockout.

• **Antinori Tenuta Belvedere "Guado al Tasso," Bolgheri** (Italy). Antinori blends Cabernet and Merlot in "Guado al Tasso."

• **Bodegas Julian Chivite "Gran Feudo" Reserva, Navarra** (Spain). Spain's rising star Julian Chivite makes this wine from the country's most revered red grape, Tempranillo, plus small amounts of Garnacha, Merlot, and Cabernet Sauvignon.

FILO NEST CAN REST in an elegant bowl or stand boldly on its own.

Ice cream "eggs"

BY ELAINE JOHNSON

T his dessert celebrates the natural look in the spirit of springtime. Buttery strands of sweetened filo dough stick together and bake crisp in a bowl-shaped form made of foil. The nests are amusing containers for egg-shaped scoops of ice cream. A cold apricot custard sauce enhances the ice cream and moistens the crunchy "nest." All components of this dessert can be made ahead.

Golden Filo Nests

PREP AND COOK TIME: About 1 hour
NOTES: Use vanilla, peach, green tea, or coconut ice cream or sorbet, or a combination. If making up to 2 days ahead, complete dessert through step 9; carefully wrap nests airtight and let stand at room temperature.
MAKES: 6 servings

About 2 pints **ice cream** or sorbet (see notes)

8 sheets **filo dough** (each 13 by 18 in., 7 oz. total)

5 tablespoons melted **butter** or margarine

½ cup **sugar**

Apricot custard sauce (recipe follows)

1. Put a rimmed 10- by 15-inch pan in the freezer until cold, at least 10 minutes. Shape ice cream into 18 egg-shaped ovals: to make each portion, dip an oval ice cream scoop in water, drain, and quickly scoop ice cream into a 3-tablespoon-size oval. As shaped, put each oval on cold pan. (Or use a round scoop, shape ice cream into balls, and set on pan. With a soup spoon, quickly press balls into ovals.) Immediately re-turn pan to freezer. If storing longer than 2 hours, wrap airtight when ice cream is hard and freeze up to 2 days.

2. Cut 6 sheets of foil, each 12 by 18 inches. From a narrow side, fold each sheet in half.

3. As a form, use a bowl about 2½ inches deep and 5 to 5½ inches wide. Center 1 foil rectangle over bowl, then press smoothly into bowl and fold foil ends over bowl rim. Lift out foil bowl and repeat to shape remaining foil rectangles. Set foil bowls on 2 baking sheets, each 12 by 15 inches.

4. Lay 1 filo sheet flat. Keep remaining filo dough covered with plastic wrap to prevent drying. With a pastry brush, quickly and lightly streak filo sheet with butter. Sprinkle evenly with 1 tablespoon sugar. Top with another filo sheet, brush with butter, sprinkle with sugar, and repeat to make 1 stack of 4 filo sheets.

5. From a long edge, fold filo stack in half. With a long, sharp knife, cut stack across the narrow width of filo to make ⅛-inch-wide strands. Divide strands into thirds.

6. Use a third of the cut filo to make 1 nest: Gently place a handful of cut filo into bottom of 1 foil bowl. Then gently drop remaining filo, bit by bit, against bowl sides, spiraling up to rim. Leave a few strands sticking up randomly around rim. Repeat to make 2 more nests.

7. Repeat steps 4 through 6 to shape 3 more nests.

8. Bake nests in a 350° oven until golden brown, about 15 minutes (10 minutes in a convection oven); switch pan positions halfway through baking.

9. Let nests cool in foil bowls on a rack. With a small metal spatula, gently ease nests from foil.

10. Set nests on dessert plates or in bowls. Place 3 ice cream ovals in each nest. Add apricot sauce to taste.

Per serving: 580 cal., 47% (270 cal.) from fat; 8.3 g protein; 30 g fat (16 g sat.); 71 g carbo (0.3 g fiber); 341 mg sodium; 258 mg chol.

Apricot custard sauce. In a 1½- to 2-quart pan over high heat, stir 1¼ cups **canned apricot nectar** and 6 tablespoons **whipping cream** until boiling, about 5 minutes. In a bowl, whisk 5 **large egg** yolks to blend. Whisk in about half of the hot apricot mixture. Put contents of bowl in pan. Stir over low heat until sauce thickly coats a metal spoon, 8 to 10 minutes. Set pan in a bowl of ice water and stir often until cool, about 8 minutes. If making ahead, chill airtight up to 2 days.

DIRECTIONS

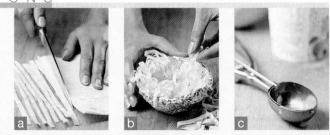

Cut buttered, sugared stack of filo dough sheets into thin strands (a). Gently and evenly fill foil bowls with filo strands, first covering bottoms, then building upward to cover bowl sides (b). Bake until golden. Use an oval scoop (c) to form ice cream or sorbet into egg shapes. ◆

A new dairy tale

How to choose and use nondairy alternatives

BY CHRISTINE WEBER HALE

Got milk? Even before the pervasive campaign by the California Milk Processor Board, most households would have answered "yes." But now, if the board pressed for details, it might be surprised at the *kind* of milk many of us are drinking.

Milk alternatives—nondairy milks made from soybeans, rice, oats, or almonds—are proliferating, particularly soybean and rice varieties. Many kinds are available for those who are allergic to milk, lactose intolerant, or on a strict vegetarian diet. Some brands even include many choices: enriched and unenriched, nonfat, and low-fat. In some well-stocked health food stores, entire aisles are devoted to nondairy milks. And at supermarkets, they are well represented in sections with canned and dried milk products or health foods.

How do they taste?

Nondairy milks have a wide range of flavors, so you may have to sample several to find a product you like. The milk's basic ingredient is often readily identifiable—more in some, less in others—depending on the manufacturer's process and what the milk is made from: Soy milks range from bland and mild to distinctly soylike and grassy. Rice and oat milks usually have a faint, natural sweetness with subtle overtones of the source grain. Almond milks have a delicate nutty character. Compare your own reactions with those of our panel on page 87.

How can I use them?

We tested the milks to learn if they curdle when boiled (they don't) or thicken when cooked with cornstarch (they do, but rice milks thicken a bit less than the others). We tried nondairy milks as beverages, in coffee, on cereal, in soups, in puddings, and for baking. Here's what we found.

For drinking. Although milk drinkers might spurn a tall, cold glass of a nondairy alternative—even with warm chocolate chip cookies—most of our tasters found one or more of the nondairy milks acceptable in fruit smoothies, especially those in the almond-, oat-, and rice-based group. We give recipes for two smoothies we particularly liked on page 87.

In coffee. Nondairy milks with a fat content equal to that of whole milk or reduced-fat milk are creamy enough to look appetizing in coffee. For flavor, mild soy, almond, and rice milks are the most acceptable, especially if the coffee is strong. Stronger-tasting soy milks emphasize coffee's inherent bitterness and add an unpleasant chalky, grassy flavor.

On cereal. Some nondairy milks are acceptable on cold and hot cereals—rice-, oat-, and almond-based milks in particular. Rice and oat milks pair especially well with cereals made from the same grain; likewise, almond milks set off cereals that contain almonds. Although a few of the mild-tasting soy milks are okay on cereal, most have a grassy flavor that is too strong for them to pair well.

In soups. Nondairy milks, including strong-tasting soy milks, make very acceptable soups. Try the cream of mushroom soup on page 87.

In puddings. Because chocolate masks any strong flavors in these milks, all make an excellent homemade chocolate pudding (see recipe on page 86).

Unfortunately, results are inconsistent with instant chocolate pudding mixes. Most do not thicken when made with a nondairy alternative. Quick-cooking tapioca pudding isn't a good option, either; if there are strong flavors in the milk, they predominate, and the

IT LOOKS LIKE MILK, and may taste like milk, but it's not from Bossy. These alternatives to cow's milk are made from soybeans, oats, rice, or almonds.

pudding doesn't always set.

For baking. In pancakes and in the hot milk cake on page 86, there were no significant differences in flavor or texture between those made with cow's milk and those that used a nondairy alternative.

How long do they last?

Most nondairy milks are sold in vacuum-sealed cartons and are shelf-stable for as long as a year. Once opened, they must be refrigerated, and stay fresh-tasting only as long as cow's milk does, about five days. Although most nondairy milks are sold in quarts, you'll find an occasional pint, as well as packs of three or more individual-size cartons, including chocolate-flavor milk.

A few brands of soy milk require refrigeration from the start. You'll find them in the dairy section. The shelf life of these products ranges from four to eight weeks, and once opened, they stay fresh for at least five days.

Are nondairy milks better for me than real milk?

No—unless you have a medical reason for avoiding milk. If you have philosophical objections to dairy products, nondairy milks can help fill the void. But if you drink milk alternatives simply because you think they're more nutritious, look at these hard facts.

Cup for cup, most nondairy milks

have less protein than cow's milk. Because they are vegetable-based, they are deficient in one or more of the amino acids that the body needs. Adults who eat a widely varied diet can get these amino acids from a combination of nondairy milks and other foods. But none of these milks should ever be used as a substitute for either a cow's-milk or a soy-based infant formula.

Some nutrition labels note whether a nondairy milk's calcium supplement is equal to the calcium in cow's milk. But most researchers agree that the supplements are not readily utilized by the body. Soy milks naturally contain phytates, which can inhibit the body's ability to use calcium. When you consume nondairy milks, eating foods high in vitamin C and phosphorus will improve calcium absorption.

Hot Milk Cake

PREP AND COOK TIME: About 35 minutes
NOTES: Serve wedges of plain cake with crushed, sweetened berries, or cover the layers with your favorite frosting.
MAKES: 12 to 14 servings

- 2 cups **all-purpose flour**
- 2 teaspoons **baking powder**
- 1 cup **plain soy** or other nondairy **milk**
  About ¼ cup (⅛ lb.) **margarine** or butter
- 4 **large eggs** or 1 cup egg substitute
- 2 cups **sugar**
- 2 teaspoons **vanilla**

1. In a bowl, mix flour and baking powder.
2. In a 1-quart glass measure in a microwave oven at full power (100%), or in a 1- to 1½-quart pan over medium heat, warm soy milk with ¼ cup margarine until margarine is melted, stirring occasionally.
3. In another bowl, with a mixer, beat eggs, sugar, and vanilla until foamy. Add flour and milk mixtures. Stir to mix, then beat until well blended.
4. Lightly coat 2 cake pans (each 9 in. wide) with margarine. Pour batter equally into pans.
5. Bake in a 350° oven until top of cake is browned and springs back when lightly pressed in the center, about 25

IT'S NOT MADE with the real thing, but you'd never know that this hot milk cake uses nondairy milk.

minutes (about 20 minutes in a convection oven). Invert cake from pans onto racks. Serve warm or cool.

Per serving: 242 cal., 21% (51 cal.) from fat; 4 g protein; 5.7 g fat (1.1 g sat.); 44 g carbo (0.5 g fiber); 141 mg sodium; 61 mg chol.

Chocolate Pudding

PREP AND COOK TIME: About 20 minutes
MAKES: About 4 cups; 8 servings

- 4 **large egg** yolks
- ¼ cup **all-purpose flour**
- 1 tablespoon **cornstarch**
- 1 cup **sugar**
- 3 cups **plain soy** or other nondairy **milk**
- 3 ounces chopped **unsweetened chocolate**
- 2 tablespoons **margarine** or butter

1½ teaspoons **vanilla**

1. In a bowl, beat egg yolks with a fork to blend.
2. In a 3- to 4-quart pan, mix flour, cornstarch, and sugar. Gradually whisk in soy milk until smooth.
3. Add chopped chocolate. Stir over high heat until mixture comes to a full boil, 6 to 10 minutes. Boil, stirring, for 1 minute.
4. Stir about ½ cup hot pudding into egg yolks, then pour yolk mixture into pan. Cook, stirring, for 1 minute more. Remove from heat. Add margarine and vanilla and stir until margarine is melted.
5. Pour pudding into a serving dish or individual dishes. Serve warm, or cover pudding surface with plastic wrap and chill up to 24 hours.

Per serving: 280 cal., 45% (126 cal.) from fat; 4.8 g protein; 14 g fat (5.1 g sat.); 39 g carbo (1.7 g fiber); 91 mg sodium; 106 mg chol.

Cream of Mushroom Soup

PREP AND COOK TIME: About $1/2$ hour

MAKES: About 3 cups; 2 servings

- $1/4$ cup ($1/8$ lb.) **margarine** or butter
- 1 **onion** ($1/2$ lb.), peeled and finely chopped
- $1/2$ pound **sliced mushrooms**
- 1 tablespoon **all-purpose flour**
- $1 1/2$ cups fat-skimmed **chicken broth**
- 1 cup **plain soy** or other nondairy **milk**
- **Salt** and **pepper**

1. In a 5- to 6-quart pan over high heat, combine margarine, onion, and mushrooms. Cover and cook, stirring occasionally, until liquid evaporates and vegetables are lightly browned, 6 to 10 minutes. Sprinkle vegetables with flour and stir 1 to 2 minutes more.

2. Stirring, add broth and bring to a simmer; cover and simmer 10 minutes, stirring occasionally. Stir in soy milk and add salt and pepper to taste. Ladle soup into bowls.

Per serving : 394 cal., 62% (243 cal.) from fat; 13 g protein; 27 g fat (4.5 g sat.); 27 g carbo (3.4 g fiber); 413 mg sodium; 0 mg chol.

Berry Rice Smoothie

PREP TIME: 3 to 5 minutes

MAKES: 2 servings

In a blender whirl 1 cup **rice milk,** 1 cup sliced **ripe banana,** $1/2$ cup **frozen unsweetened strawberries,** $1/2$ cup **ice cubes,** and $1/4$ teaspoon **vanilla** to a smooth slush. Add **honey** to taste.

Per serving: 144 cal., 9% (13 cal.) from fat; 1.4 g protein; 1.4 g fat (0.1 g sat.); 34 g carbo (1.2 g fiber); 47 mg sodium; 0 mg chol.

Oat Breakfast Smoothie

PREP TIME: 3 to 5 minutes

MAKES: 2 servings

In a blender whirl 1 cup **oat milk,** $1/2$ cup **ready-to-eat oat cereal,** 1 cup sliced **ripe banana,** $1/2$ cup **chopped dates,** $1/2$ cup **ice cubes,** and 1 tablespoon **lemon juice** to a smooth slush.

Per serving: 270 cal., 5.6% (15 cal.) from fat; 4.5 g protein; 1.7 g fat (0.2 g sat.); 65 g carbo (3.7 g fiber); 120 mg sodium; 0 mg chol.

Tasting notes

With so many nondairy choices, selecting a product that suits your taste can be as confusing as picking a long-distance phone service. That's why we conducted taste and cooking tests with 15 varieties of unflavored soy, rice, oat, and almond nondairy products. Here are the results.

Shelf-stable soy milks

Edensoy original. Light tan color and velvety texture. Sweet, almost malted flavor. Okay for drinking, good for cooking.

Pacific Original. Off-white color, somewhat watery texture. Fairly clean flavor with a faint chalky aftertaste. Most tasters found it unsuitable for drinking but good for cooking.

Vitasoy Creamy original. Tan color, whipping-cream texture. Slightly sweet, cooked-vegetable taste. Most found it unsuitable for drinking but fine for cooking.

Vitasoy Light original (1% fat). Pleasant, smooth texture. Slightly sweet flavor; tastes cleaner and less cooked than the creamy original version. Okay for drinking and good for cooking.

Westsoy Lite plain (1% fat). Odd tan color, watery texture. Bland flavor with faint bitter aftertaste. Okay on cereal, fine for cooking.

Westsoy nonfat plain. Not bad if you can get past the watery texture and slightly curdled appearance. Mild, sweet flavor with no noticeable aftertaste. Some found it okay for drinking; good for cooking.

Westsoy original (2% fat). Off-white color; thick, rich texture. Mild, sweet flavor, but strong soy aftertaste. A few thought it fine for drinking; very good for cooking.

Westsoy unsweetened (2% fat). Thick, creamy texture. Mildly grassy soy flavor and aroma, although not as strong as in ¡Yo Soy! (at right). Most tasters did not find it suitable for drinking; excellent for cooking.

Shelf-stable almond, oat, and rice milks

Amazake original (nonfat rice drink). Watery tan color, thin texture. Strong rice flavor with bitter aftertaste. Okay on cereal, fine for cooking.

Naturally Almond. Creamy white color; mild, nutty flavor. Good for drinking and cooking.

Naturally Oat. Creamy white color with a slight chalkiness. Pleasant, slightly sweet, mild oat flavor. Okay for drinking, good for cooking.

Rice Dream original. White color, somewhat watery texture. Sweet, pleasant, rice-like taste. Okay for drinking, fine for cooking.

Rice Dream original enriched. Similar to plain Rice Dream Original in color, flavor, and texture, but slightly chalky. Good on cereal and for cooking.

Refrigerated nondairy milks

White Wave Silk (1% fat). Soy-based. Similar to commercial eggnog in color and texture. Sweet flavor with faint aftertaste of soy and rice. Okay on cereal, good for cooking.

¡Yo Soy! plain. Definite soy aroma, somewhat watery texture. Flavor reminiscent of plain tofu's. Most tasters found it unsuitable for drinking but fine for cooking. ◆

COLUMBUS AVENUE'S Tavolino Ristorante.

North Beach's movable feast

Hot new restaurants add glamour
to San Francisco's favorite neighborhood

BY JONATHAN KING

I'm at a window table at Tavolino, making short work of some deep-fried olives—morsels so delicious they should be considered bar food of the gods. From my perch, I scan Columbus Avenue's passing parade: longtime Italian-American residents, newcomers from Asia, artists and musicians toting notebooks, canvases, guitars. In one direction I see St. Francis of Assisi, San Francisco's first Catholic parish church, founded in 1849. In another shines the sleek façades of the new high-energy restaurants that have revived this much-loved San Francisco neighborhood as a nightlife mecca.

This return to North Beach is a sentimental journey. I used to live in this neighborhood, and so have strong feelings about its character and future. In 1974, I moved into a tiny apartment

above the Basque Hotel on Romolo Alley, just a tassel throw from the bawdy corner of Broadway and Columbus. Carol Doda, her Condor club, and neighboring strip joints held little allure, but the markets, delis, and butcher shops of my new neighborhood surely did—for I was a serious young cook, and in those days the best ingredients in San Francisco could be found right here.

Now, after more than two decades away, I've returned to North Beach for several days of exploration. Throughout its history this 20-block urban enclave has been a haven for Italian fishermen, wayward Beats, and countless aspiring 20-somethings like myself. I wanted to see how the place had changed. And, I hoped, how it had not.

There are two distinct North Beaches.

The one garnering headlines is the nighttime neighborhood. Glamorous new restaurants have transformed streets that had started to seem frozen in time with their gaudy but tired strip clubs, bars, and pasta joints. Now the young, hip, and moneyed are thronging to places like Moose's, Rose Pistola (already a fixture on national magazines' best-restaurant lists), and Enrico's, a venerable hangout recently revitalized.

"It's a different crowd in North Beach now," says Rick Hackett, executive chef at Enrico's. "We've seen the change since we took over Enrico's in 1991. North Beach was popular on weekends then, but mostly with strip-club customers and serious drinkers. Now it's hopping every night with a different kind of clientele."

NORTH BEACH NIGHTS AND DAYS
These newcomers have pumped terrific energy into North Beach. And yet in some ways I prefer the other North Beach—the daytime North Beach—perhaps because the neighborhood it used to be shines through more clearly in the sunlight.

My advice: Enjoy your night on the

town. But try to take a morning stroll, too, fueled by strong coffee from one of the neighborhood's signature cafes. Amble through Washington Square, North Beach's green heart. Then walk down Columbus Avenue. Check your watch against R. Matteucci & Company jewelers' huge 1908 street clock. Soon it's lunchtime, and you'll find your own power table waiting for you at that restaurant whose waiting list you couldn't crack last Friday night.

Then stroll some more and hit some of the classics: Puccini, Trieste, Enrico's, and Roma among the cafes, Stella and Victoria for biscotti and pastries. Pay homage to the poetic and political clutter of City Lights Bookstore with its unwavering commitment to uncommercial literature, and to A. Cavalli & Company Italian Bookstore and its incomparable inventory of Italian CDs, not to mention its proud storefront banner proclaiming "Our 118th Year!" And somewhere along the way you begin to understand the North Beach that once was, in the words of one historian, "a magnet for radicals, anarchists, populists, Communists, Wobblies, bohemians, Abstract Expressionist painters, performance artists, poets, jazz musicians, playwrights in experimental theater, atheists, Buddhists, and street musicians." Wobblies are thin on the ground today, but you'll see that North Beach still harbors enough musicians, artists, and poets to guarantee a certain level of local color.

Now, dusk is falling, and the face of R. Matteucci's clock begins to glow. Here come the crowds: They're packed into Black Cat or Moose's; they're scoring sidewalk tables at Tavolino and Enrico's for an evening of conspicuous cappuccino consumption. Or they're just standing in clusters on the sidewalk, waiting to get in here or talking about the prospect of getting in over there instead. Even in the hubbub, they are aware of being in a place that is not like any other in San Francisco, or the world. Find a seat and savor the parade. You're in North Beach, after all.

North Beach travel planner

A roughly 20-block enclave near San Francisco's northeast corner, North Beach is bounded by Russian Hill on the west, Washington Street on the south, Bay Street to the north, and the steep slopes of Telegraph Hill to the east.

The North Beach Chamber of Commerce (556 Columbus Ave., 415/989-2220) publishes a good neighborhood map. For sample restaurant menus, information about special events, and other information, you can visit their Web site at www.sfnorthbeach.com.

Area code is 415 unless noted.

Restaurants: Superstars

Adolfo's Ristorante e Bar. This fairly new contemporary Italian restaurant offers a classic menu—antipasti, pasta, meat, and fish secondi—but gives most dishes a distinctive twist. The wine list is particularly strong. *570 Green St., 434-8080.*

Black Cat. Call in advance for reservations at chef Reed Hearon's newest addition to the San Francisco dining scene. The menu is a culinary salute to the varied threads that weave the fabric of North Beach life; that's why you'll find Italian-inspired shellfish dishes cheek by jowl with Singapore stir-fries. *501 Broadway, 981-2233.*

Enrico's Restaurant and Supper Club. A lovingly revived North Beach landmark, Enrico's functions simultaneously as a quality dining room, jazz club, neighborhood bar, and outdoor cafe. *504 Broadway, 982-6223.*

Moose's. There's nothing particularly Italian about crab cakes, grilled chicken, and ribeye steak, but Moose's can launch into a culinary aria when so moved: a recent plate of orecchiette with seared ahi tuna, aged balsamic, and ricotta salata cheese was a grand opera of assertive flavors. *1652 Stockton St., 989-7800.*

Rose Pistola. The cuisine of Italy's Liguria region is not well known hereabouts, though its emigrants helped populate North Beach. Rose Pistola fills that gap. It opened to great acclaim in 1996 and continues to hum with business lunchers and serious nighttime eaters. *532 Columbus, 399-0499.*

Tavolino Ristorante and Cicchetti Bar. Tavolino's flavorful *cicchetti* (roughly, *little plates*) are the Venetian version of tapas. The main dishes—also Venetian-inspired—include grilled fish in saor and baccala mantecato. *401 Columbus, 392-1472.*

Other attractions

Among Italian delis in North Beach, **Molinari Delicatessen** (373 Columbus, 421-2337) is the acknowledged standard-bearer.

For pastries, try **Stella Pastry** (446 Columbus, 986-2914) and **Victoria Pastry Company** (1362 Stockton, 781-2015); the latter is a time-honored provider of neighborhood wedding cakes.

North Beach runs on espresso and its variants. You'll want to visit legendary **Caffe Trieste** (601 Vallejo St., 392-6739). After that, assess the mood and the mocha at **Caffe Greco** (423 Columbus, 397-6261), **Caffe Puccini** (411 Columbus, 989-7033), or **Caffé Roma** (526 Columbus, 296-7662).

Other North Beach highlights include **City Lights Bookstore** (261 Columbus, 362-8193), **R. Matteucci & Company** (450 Columbus, 781-1063), and **A. Cavalli & Company Italian Bookstore** (1441 Stockton, 421-4219).

Lodging

You can find rooms—not always quiet, but always serviceable or better—at the **Washington Square Inn Hotel** (1660 Stockton, 800/388-0220; rooms 7 and 8 have park views) and the more recently opened **Hotel Bohème** (444 Columbus, 433-9111). The latter, with its elegant interior and walls adorned with historic North Beach photos, is a particularly attractive option in a location that couldn't be more central. ◆

The Quick Cook

MEALS IN 30 MINUTES OR LESS

BY ANDREW BAKER

JAMES CARRIER

MENU
Asian Hummus and Grilled-
Vegetable Sandwiches

Calamata Olives • Ginger Beer

Persian Melon Wedges and Baklava

Peanut sauce for timely dishes

■ In today's cyberspace-paced world, ingredients evolve from gourmet to everyday practically overnight. One marvelously convenient product that has recently proliferated in supermarkets is Asian peanut sauce, a blend of ground peanuts, chilies, ginger, garlic, and soy sauce. Traditionally, it's the seasoning sauce for satays—grilled skewered bits of pork or chicken—but it adapts to many quick dishes.

Try several brands of peanut sauce to find the one you like best (they vary considerably in flavor and texture depending on the manufacturer). Then make it a staple, ready for quick meals.

Asian Hummus and Grilled-Vegetable Sandwiches

PREP AND COOK TIME: About 30 minutes

NOTES: Garnish sandwiches with sprigs of fresh herbs if desired.

MAKES: 4 servings

- 1 can (15 oz.) **garbanzos**, rinsed and drained
- ½ cup **prepared Asian peanut sauce**
- 5 **zucchini** (about ¼ lb. each)
- 1 **red onion** (¾ lb.)
- 1 to 2 tablespoons **olive oil**
- 4 **pocket breads** (about 6 in.)
- 1 **firm-ripe tomato** (about ¾ lb.), rinsed, cored, and thinly sliced
- 1½ cups (about 2 oz.) **alfalfa sprouts**, rinsed and drained

1. In a blender or food processor, purée garbanzos and peanut sauce, scraping hummus mixture from container sides as needed.

2. Trim and discard zucchini ends. Cut zucchini lengthwise into ¼-inch slices. Cut onion crosswise into ½-inch slices. Brush vegetables lightly with olive oil.

3. Place zucchini and onion slices on a barbecue grill over a solid bed of hot coals or high heat on a gas grill (you can hold your hand at grill level only 2 to 3 seconds); close lid on gas grill. Cook vegetables, turning to brown evenly, 10 to 12 minutes, transferring to a plate as cooked.

4. Spread cupped side of each pocket bread with ¼ of the hummus and set on plates. Top each bread equally with zucchini, tomato, onion, and alfalfa sprouts. Eat with knife and fork.

Per serving: 442 cal., 26% (117 cal.) from fat; 16 g protein; 13 g fat (1.7 g sat.); 67 g carbo (8.2 g fiber); 1,170 mg sodium; 0 mg chol.

3 more quick recipes

Rice Bowl with Sauced Beef

MAKES: 4 or 5 servings

1. In a 2- to 3-quart pan over high heat, bring 4 cups **water** and ¼ cup **prepared Asian peanut sauce** to a boil. Stir in 4 cups **precooked dried white rice** and 1 cup shredded **carrots**. Cover, remove from heat, and let stand until liquid is absorbed, 5 to 7 minutes.

2. Meanwhile, in a bowl, mix ¾ pound thinly sliced **fat-trimmed cooked tender beef** (such as ribeye or tenderloin) and 6 tablespoons **prepared Asian peanut sauce**.

3. Spoon rice into bowls and top equally with sliced beef and ½ cup thinly sliced **green onions**. Add more prepared Asian peanut sauce to taste.

Per serving: 527 cal., 19% (99 cal.) from fat; 28 g protein; 11 g fat (3.8 g sat.); 74 g carbo (3.3 g fiber); 773 mg sodium; 54 mg chol.

Peanut-Coconut Soup with Shrimp

MAKES: 4 servings

1. In a 2- to 3-quart pan over high heat, frequently stir 1 can (14½ oz.; 1¾ cup) fat-skimmed **chicken broth**, 1 can (14 oz.) **reduced-fat coconut milk**, 5 tablespoons **prepared Asian peanut sauce**, and 1 cup **frozen peas** until mixture is simmering. Add ½ pound (26 to 30 per lb.) rinsed **peeled, deveined shrimp**.

2. Cover and remove from heat. Let stand until shrimp are opaque but still moist-looking in center of thickest part (cut to test), 3 to 4 minutes. Ladle soup into bowls and garnish with chopped **green onions**. Serve with **lime** wedges to squeeze into soup to taste.

Per serving: 208 cal., 36% (74 cal.) from fat; 19 g protein; 8.2 g fat (4 g sat.); 13 g carbo (2 g fiber); 626 mg sodium; 86 mg chol.

Oodles of Noodles Salad

MAKES: 6 servings

Mix 8 cups cold cooked **fresh linguine** (about 1 lb., 2 oz. uncooked) with 2½ cups shredded skinned **cooked chicken** and 1 cup *each* prepared **Asian peanut sauce**, thinly sliced **red bell pepper**, and **fresh cilantro** leaves. Mound onto plates and top servings equally with 1 cup chopped **papaya**. Serve with **lime** wedges to squeeze over salads to taste.

Per serving: 464 cal., 19% (90 cal.) from fat; 31 g protein; 10 g fat (2.1 g sat.); 60 g carbo (3.7 g fiber); 1,020 mg sodium; 114 mg chol. ◆

MAKES: About 2¾ cups; 4 servings

- 1 can (6 oz.) **frozen orange juice concentrate**
- 1 cup **frozen unsweetened peach slices**
- ¾ cup **gin**, vodka, or soda water
- 1 tablespoon **orange-flavor liqueur** (optional)
- 1 cup crushed **ice**

1. In a blender, combine orange juice concentrate, peaches, gin, orange liqueur, and ice. Whirl until smooth.

2. Pour into glasses and serve at once.

Per serving: 207 cal., 0.4% (0.9 cal.) from fat; 1.6 g protein; 0.1 g fat (0 g sat.); 25 g carbo (1.1 g fiber); 2 mg sodium; 0 mg chol.

Baked Spinach-Parmesan Dip

Alice Chazen, Perry Creek Vineyards, Somerset, California

This appetizer rates high with Alice Chazen, co-owner of Perry Creek Vineyards. Make the cheese mixture up to 2 days ahead, cover, and chill, then bake uncovered. To vary the results, replace the spinach with chopped artichoke hearts. Chazen serves a dry Chardonnay or fruity Riesling with either version.

PREP AND COOK TIME: About 40 minutes

MAKES: About 3 cups; 12 servings

- 1 package (10 oz.) **frozen chopped spinach,** thawed
- 1 cup **reduced-fat** or regular **mayonnaise**
- 1 package (3 oz.) **cream cheese**
- 1 **onion** (6 oz.), peeled and minced
- 1 clove **garlic,** pressed or minced
- 1 cup plus 2 tablespoons grated **parmesan cheese**
- ⅛ teaspoon **pepper**
- ½ teaspoon **paprika**
- 2 **baguettes** (8 oz. each), thinly sliced

1. Squeeze spinach to remove liquid. With a mixer, beat spinach, mayonnaise, cream cheese, onion, garlic, 1 cup parmesan cheese, and pepper until thoroughly combined.

2. Mound mixture in a 3- to 4-cup baking dish. Sprinkle evenly with 2 tablespoons parmesan cheese and the paprika.

3. Bake in a 350° oven until hot in center and lightly browned on top, 25 to 30 minutes.

4. Serve hot to spread on baguette slices.

Per serving: 227 cal., 39% (89 cal.) from fat; 7.8 g protein; 9.9 g fat (3.9 g sat.); 26 g carbo (1.7 g fiber); 569 mg sodium; 14 mg chol.

Irene's Cornish Hens with Tarragon and Calvados

Barbara Bennett, San Leandro, California

In France, Barbara Bennett was treated to a home-cooked meal by her Parisian friend Irene. The main course was Cornish hens in a creamy tarragon sauce. It's a dish Bennett has duplicated many times since—with fond memories.

PREP AND COOK TIME: About 1 hour

MAKES: 4 servings

- 2 **Cornish hens** (1¾ to 2 lb. each)
- 1 to 2 teaspoons melted **butter** or margarine
- ⅓ cup chopped **shallots**
- ½ cup **calvados** or dry white wine
- ⅓ cup fat-skimmed **chicken broth**
- ¼ cup chopped **fresh tarragon** or 1 tablespoon dried tarragon
- ¾ cup **crème fraîche** or whipping cream
  Tarragon or parsley **sprigs**
  Salt and **white pepper**

1. With poultry shears or a knife, cut each hen in half lengthwise through breastbone and backbone. Rinse and pat dry. Reserve giblets for other uses.

2. Set halves, skin side up, in a 9- by 13-inch pan. Brush skin with melted butter, then sprinkle with the shallots.

3. Bake in a 425° oven until meat at thigh bone is no longer pink (cut to test), about 40 minutes (35 minutes in a convection oven). Transfer hens to a platter; keep warm.

4. Spoon off and discard fat from pan drippings. Add calvados, broth, and tarragon to drippings. Set pan over medium-high heat and stir to scrape brown particles free.

5. Whisk in crème fraîche. Turn heat to high and boil until mixture is reduced to ¾ cup, 5 to 8 minutes. Pour sauce into a bowl. Garnish hens with tarragon sprigs and add salt and pepper to taste. Serve with sauce.

Per serving: 696 cal., 62% (432 cal.) from fat; 40 g protein; 48 g fat (20 g sat.); 4.3 g carbo (0.1 g fiber); 155 mg sodium; 259 mg chol.

Gooey Hazelnut-Chocolate Cake

Marie Yong, North Vancouver, B.C.

When Marie Yong travels, she always carries along a notebook to collect recipes. One she recorded gets a lot of mileage at home: an easy chocolate cake with a baked-in sauce made with cocoa-flavored hazelnut spread (such as Nutella). Look for the spread in well-stocked supermarkets alongside peanut butter or ice cream toppings.

PREP AND COOK TIME: About 1¼ hours

MAKES: 10 to 12 servings

- About 10 tablespoons (⅓ lb.) **butter** or margarine, at room temperature
- ½ cup **cocoa-flavored hazelnut spread**
- ½ cup **whipping cream**
- 1 cup **sugar**
- 2 **large eggs**
- 1½ cups **all-purpose flour**
- ⅓ cup **unsweetened cocoa**
- 2 teaspoons **baking powder**
- ½ teaspoon **baking soda**
- ½ teaspoon **salt**
- ¾ cup **milk**
  Strawberries
  Vanilla ice cream or sweetened softly whipped cream

1. Butter an 8-inch plain or fluted tube pan. In a bowl, mix hazelnut spread and whipping cream until smoothly blended. Pour evenly into bottom of pan.

2. In a large bowl with a mixer, beat 10 tablespoons butter and the sugar until well blended. Add eggs, 1 at a time, beating until fluffy after each addition.

3. Sift together flour, cocoa, baking powder, baking soda, and salt.

4. Add flour mixture and milk to butter mixture; stir to combine, then beat until well blended. Spoon evenly over hazelnut mixture in pan.

5. Bake in a 350° oven (325° in a convection oven) until cake begins to pull from pan sides and springs back when lightly pressed in the center, 50 to 60 minutes. Cool for 5 minutes in pan, then slip a thin-bladed knife between pan rim and cake. Invert a large plate over cake. Holding pan and plate together, invert again and shake gently to release cake onto plate. Let stand 2 to 3 minutes, then lift off pan. Scoop any hazelnut mixture left in pan onto top of cake. Garnish with strawberries.

6. Slice and serve warm with ice cream.

Per serving: 321 cal., 50% (162 cal.) from fat; 4.6 g protein; 18 g fat (9.3 g sat.); 37 g carbo (1.1 g fiber); 366 mg sodium; 76 mg chol. ◆

Discover the new artisan cheeses and ways to use them (see page 96); above, soft-ripened goat cheese and walnuts top a salad.

May

a renaissance of Western cheeses

A new wave of artisan cheeses, from gouda to dry jack, inspires 16 delicious recipes

BY ELAINE JOHNSON • PHOTOGRAPHS BY JAMES CARRIER
FOOD STYLING BY VALERIE AIKMAN-SMITH

■ The clock ticks at a different rate for a growing group of skilled Western cheesemakers. They are taking their time and using old-fashioned methods to handcraft Old World–style cheeses. They're starting with more kinds of milk—using sheep's milk as well as cow's and goat's milk—and some of it is coming from organically reared and fed animals. They're experimenting with fresh cheeses such as buttery crescenza. Sometimes they age them briefly, so a cheese like teleme can grow creamy and goat's-milk camellia can develop a delicate white bloom. Others they age longer, to get the best flavor from the likes of firm, full-cream cheddars and to develop the ideal density and texture in hard cheeses such as dry Monterey jack.

The results are piling up on our cheese counters—deep gold wedges, wheels as supple as suede, pyramids coated with molds, logs white as snow, and much more.

The cheese family tree

To help you find Western handcrafted cheeses to suit your taste, we've divided them into four families (shown opposite) based on how they're made and on their textures. In addition to selecting cheeses just for the pure pleasure of eating them, you can use this guide to choose cheeses for cooking. Tasting and shopping details are on page 103. Although many of the cheeses we list are made in limited quantities, if they're not available locally, you can probably order them from the dairy or a specialty shop. Fresh cheeses (opposite, top left). These young cheeses have the delicate flavor of fresh milk. Some, such as crème fraîche and mascarpone, are barely more than cooked, culture-thickened cream, drained just enough to spoon or spread. Others, like mild-tasting cow's-milk mozzarella and the more assertive fresh chèvres made from goat's milk, are drained more thoroughly of whey (the amber liquid that separates from the milk) and get firm enough to slice.

Store fresh cheeses, wrapped airtight,

LIAM CALLAHAN of Bellwether Farms cuts curds for carmody cheese.

in the refrigerator for no more than a few days. Discard any that are moldy or have a sour, wet-rag, or ammoniated odor. If airtight packaging around a cheese is swollen by gases (from deterioration), don't purchase or use.

FRESH CHEESES. 1. Fresh mozzarella, *California Mozzarella Fresca.* 2. Ricotta, *Bellwether.* 3. Crescenza, *Bellwether.* 4. Fromage blanc de Parma, *Rollingstone.* 5. Herb chevre, *Cypress Grove.* 6. Traditional quark, *Appel.* 7. Chèvre en marinade, *Haystack Mountain.* 8. Chevre in oil, *Sea Stars.*

SOFT-RIPENED CHEESES. 1. Bermuda Triangle, *Cypress Grove.* 2. Bûche, *Juniper.* 3. Schloss, *Rouge et Noir.* 4. Crottin, *Laura Chenel.* 5. Taupinière, *Laura Chenel.* 6. Camellia, *Redwood Hill.* 7. Breakfast cheese, *Rouge et Noir.* 8. Humboldt Fog, *Cypress Grove.* 9. Rice-flour teleme, *Peluso.*

SEMIFIRM TO FIRM CHEESES. 1. Carmody, *Bellwether.* 2. Toscano, *Bellwether.* 3. Tumalo tomme, *Juniper Grove.* 4. St. George, *Joe Matos.* 5. Feta, *Sea Stars.* 6. Cougar Gold, *WSU.* 7. San Andreas, *Bellwether.*

HARD CHEESES. 1. Aged goat curado, *Quillisascut.* 2. Dry Monterey jack, *Vella.* 3. Alpine Chevre shepherd's cheese, *Yerba Santa.*

fresh

semifirm to firm

hard

soft-ripened

Soft-ripened cheeses (page 97, bottom right). The surfaces of soft-ripened cheeses are treated in various ways to develop edible rinds, which create environments that determine what flavors and textures the cheeses develop as they ripen. Teleme that is aged unwrapped is coated with rice flour; the surface dries and becomes a little leathery, while the center gets creamier and the flavor richer. Uncoated teleme is vacuum-packed and ages differently. Bacteria or molds are applied to the surfaces of other soft-ripened cheeses to develop various textures, from moist to dry and velvety. Inside, the cheeses may soften or get firmer as they age, but all develop more intense flavor.

The cheeses that will soften—breakfast, camellia, chestnut leaf–aged goat, and some crottins—are often still firm when you buy them. To ripen, leave the whole cheese in its wrapper at room temperature until it gives to gentle pressure, up to three days.

Store soft-ripened cheeses in their original wrappers or wrap loosely in waxed paper (to prevent sweating), then enclose in plastic wrap or an airtight container. Chill cut pieces up to a week.

If a little mold or rust-colored patches form on a soft-ripened cheese, trim them off if you like. But discard cheeses that are thoroughly moldy or have an ammoniated odor.

Semifirm to firm cheeses (page 97, top right). The members of this diverse group—which includes easy-slicing cheddar and gouda, and the crumbly blues—have flavors ranging from mellow to robust. Semifirm to firm cheeses have less moisture than fresh or soft-ripened cheeses and can be aged for months to years. Some form hard, dry surfaces, which may be coated with a finish such as wax; others develop specific molds. The natural rinds are edible, although their taste doesn't please everyone; discard waxy coatings.

Store whole cheeses and large pieces in original packaging in the refrigerator. After you cut them, seal remainders in plastic wrap and chill. Whole cheeses keep many months; large cut pieces may keep up to a month if trimmed of

TO MAKE SPIEDINI DI MOZZARELLA, stack layers of sourdough bread and fresh mozzarella, spear stacks with fresh rosemary, and grill.

surface mold. Discard the cheese if it's penetrated with mold and smells or tastes unpleasant.

Hard cheeses (page 97, bottom left). These grating cheeses, including dry jack, are very hard and crumbly, with rich, nutlike flavors. Store as directed for semifirm to firm cheeses, trimming off any mold that develops. Whole and cut cheeses keep for months.

Spiedini di Mozzarella

PREP AND COOK TIME: About 25 minutes

NOTES: Cooks at the Culinary Institute of America at Greystone in St. Helena, California, use rosemary to skewer the bread for this appetizer. Or you can use wood skewers (at least 5 in. long).

MAKES: 16 appetizers

> About ³⁄₄ pound **sourdough** or other country-style **bread** (5-in.-wide loaf)
>
> ¹⁄₄ cup (¹⁄₈ lb.) **butter** or margarine, at room temperature
>
> ³⁄₄ to 1 pound **fresh mozzarella cheese** (about 3¹⁄₂ in. wide)

16 **fresh rosemary** sprigs (about 5 in. long)
Salt and **pepper**

1. Cut bread crosswise into 12 slices about ¹⁄₂ inch thick. Lightly spread both sides of each slice with butter. Cut cheese across the widest dimension into ¹⁄₄-inch-thick slices.

2. Layer 3 bread slices with enough cheese between slices to cover bread. Cut stack into quarters. Push cut end of a rosemary sprig through each quarter-stack of bread and cheese to hold layers together. Repeat to use remaining bread, cheese, and rosemary. If needed for stability, push toothpicks into stacks parallel to rosemary sprigs. Season to taste with salt and pepper.

3. Lightly oil a barbecue grill over a solid bed of hot coals or a gas grill on high heat (you can hold your hand at grill level only 2 to 3 seconds). Lay skewered bread and cheese on grill. Close lid on gas grill. Cook, turning often, until bread is lightly toasted, 2 to 5 minutes. Serve spiedini hot.

Per piece: 153 cal., 52% (80 cal.) from fat; 6.4 g protein; 8.9 g fat (5.4 g sat.); 11 g carbo (0.6 g fiber); 246 mg sodium; 27 mg chol.

Teleme Focaccia Sandwich

PREP AND COOK TIME: **About 25 minutes**

MAKES: **6 servings**

- 1 piece (1 lb.) **focaccia**
- About ½ pound **rice-flour teleme**, crescenza, or jack **cheese**
- About 3 ounces **thin-sliced prosciutto**
- 1½ cups lightly packed rinsed, drained **arugula**

1. Cut focaccia in half horizontally. Cut teleme or jack cheese into ½-inch-thick slices. Lay slices (or spread crescenza) on bottom half of focaccia and cover evenly with prosciutto. Place both focaccia pieces (the top, cut side up) on a 14- by 17-inch baking sheet.

2. Bake in a 450° oven until cheese begins to melt and bread is crusty, about 8 minutes (about 6 minutes in a convection oven).

3. Arrange arugula over prosciutto. Using a wide spatula, set focaccia top, cut side down, on arugula. Slide focaccia sandwich onto a board and cut into 6 pieces.

Per piece: 341 cal., 40% (135 cal.) from fat; 20 g protein; 15 g fat (5.8 g sat.); 34 g carbo (1.5 g fiber); 837 mg sodium; 29 mg chol.

Feta Sticks

PREP AND COOK TIME: **About 45 minutes**

NOTES: If making up to 1 day ahead, complete through step 4, then chill cylinders airtight. Uncover and continue.

MAKES: **24 pieces; 8 appetizer servings**

- ½ pound **feta cheese** (goat, cow, or sheep), crumbled
- 3 tablespoons minced **green onions**
- 1 tablespoon minced **fresh dill** or 1 teaspoon dried dill
- ½ teaspoon fresh-ground **pepper**
- 4 sheets (each 13 by 18 in.; 2 oz. total) **filo dough**
- About 2 tablespoons melted **butter** or margarine

1. In a bowl, mix cheese, onions, dill, and pepper.

2. Stack filo sheets. With a long, sharp knife, cut stack into 6 equal rectangles to make 24 pieces. Cover with plastic wrap to prevent drying.

3. Lay 1 filo piece flat and brush lightly with butter. Sprinkle 2 teaspoons cheese mixture along 1 edge, leaving about ½ inch bare at each end. Fold ends of filo over filling, then roll to enclose; if filo doesn't stick together at end of roll, brush edge with a little more butter.

4. Place cheese stick seam side down on a nonstick 12- by 15-inch baking sheet and brush lightly with butter. Repeat step 3 to shape remaining cheese sticks, and lay about ½ inch apart on pan.

5. Bake in a 400° oven until lightly browned, about 12 minutes (9 to 10 minutes in a convection oven). Serve hot or warm.

Per piece: 45 cal., 69% (31 cal.) from fat; 1.6 g protein; 3.4 g fat (2.2 g sat.); 2.1 g carbo (0 g fiber); 133 mg sodium; 12 mg chol.

Chèvre-Pepper Sticks

Follow directions for **feta sticks** (preceding), but instead of feta, use ½ pound crumbled **fresh chèvre** (goat) **cheese.** Omit dill and increase **green onions** to ¼ cup and fresh-ground **pepper** to 1½ teaspoons.

Per piece: 54 cal., 70% (38 cal.) from fat; 2.3 g protein; 4.2 g fat (2.7 g sat.); 2.1 g carbo (0.1 g fiber); 76 mg sodium; 11 mg chol.

Cheddar-Garlic Portabella Soufflés

PREP AND COOK TIME: **About 1 hour**

NOTES: Instead of cheddar you can use aged gouda or a robust, semifirm sheep's milk cheese such as Toscano or San Andreas. Garnish soufflés with additional chives.

MAKES: **4 servings**

- 4 **portabella mushrooms** (4- to 4½-in. caps; ¾ to 1 lb. total)
- About 2½ tablespoons **butter** or margarine
- 3 tablespoons **fine dried bread crumbs**
- 1½ tablespoons minced **garlic**
- ¼ cup **all-purpose flour**
- ¼ teaspoon **salt**
- ¼ teaspoon **pepper**
- ¾ cup **low-fat milk**
- 1¼ cups (5 oz.) shredded **sharp cheddar cheese**
- 2 tablespoons chopped **fresh chives**
- 4 **large eggs**, separated

1. Rinse and drain mushrooms. Trim stems off flush with caps. Trim discolored ends from stems, then finely chop

SHARP CHEDDAR–GARLIC SOUFFLÉ bakes to a rich brown inside a portabella cap.

stems. Set caps, cup sides up, on a 12- by 15-inch baking sheet.

2. Cut 4 sheets of foil, each 12 by 16 inches. Fold each sheet lengthwise in half, then in half again. Generously butter 1 side of each foil strip and dust with bread crumbs. Tightly wrap each foil strip, crumb side in, around a mushroom cap, overlapping ends; secure with metal paper clips.

3. In a 2- to 3-quart pan over medium heat, stir 2 tablespoons butter, garlic, and mushroom stems until stems are browned and limp, about 8 minutes. Add flour, salt, and pepper, and stir 1 minute more. Remove from heat and whisk in milk until mixture is smooth. Stir over high heat until boiling, about 1 minute.

4. Remove from heat, add 1 cup cheese, and stir until melted. Add chives and egg yolks, and stir to blend.

5. In a deep bowl with a mixer on high speed, whip egg whites until stiff, moist peaks form. Stir about ⅓ of the whites into cheese mixture, then gently fold cheese mixture into remaining whites just until blended.

6. Spoon mixture equally into mushroom caps. Sprinkle evenly with remaining cheese.

7. Bake in a 375° oven until soufflés are well browned, about 30 minutes (about 25 minutes in a convection oven). Quickly remove paper clips and pull foil free, easing away with a knife tip if necessary. With a wide spatula, transfer soufflés to plates.

Per serving: 376 cal., 60% (225 cal.) from fat; 20 g protein; 25 g fat (14 g sat.); 18 g carbo (1.7 g fiber); 570 mg sodium; 271 mg chol.

Orechiette with Chèvre, Peas, and Mint

PREP AND COOK TIME: About 20 minutes

NOTES: This pasta dish comes from Wildwood Restaurant & Bar in Portland. As a variation, use fromage blanc instead of chèvre (goat) cheese. For a creamier dish, stir in more hot broth.

MAKES: 4 servings

- 12 ounces **dried orechiette pasta**
- 1½ teaspoons minced **garlic**
- 2 teaspoons **olive oil**
- 1 cup (8 oz.) **fresh chèvre (goat) cheese**
- 1 cup fat-skimmed **chicken broth**
- 1 cup **frozen petite peas**
- ⅓ cup minced **fresh mint** leaves
  Salt and **pepper**
  Lemon wedges

1. Cook pasta in 3 quarts boiling water until just tender to bite, about 8 minutes.

2. Meanwhile, in a 10- to 12-inch frying pan over medium heat, stir garlic in oil until limp, about 2 minutes. Add cheese, broth, and peas and stir until simmering, 4 to 5 minutes.

3. Drain pasta; return to pan. Add cheese mixture to pasta and mix well. Add mint and mix again. Add to taste salt, pepper, and juice from lemon wedges.

Per serving: 534 cal., 27% (144 cal.) from fat; 26 g protein; 16 g fat (8.8 g sat.); 71 g carbo (5.3 g fiber); 299 mg sodium; 26 mg chol.

Orechiette with Ricotta and Basil

Follow directions for **orechiette with chèvre, peas, and mint** (preceding), but instead of chèvre, use 1 cup (8 oz.) **whole-milk ricotta cheese**. Omit mint and use ½ cup minced **fresh basil** leaves instead.

Per serving: 492 cal., 22% (108 cal.) from fat; 23 g protein; 12 g fat (5.8 g sat.); 72 g carbo (5.2 g fiber); 141 mg sodium; 33 mg chol.

Soft-Ripened Goat Cheese and Walnut Salad

PREP AND COOK TIME: About 20 minutes

MAKES: 4 servings

- ½ cup **walnut halves** or pieces
- 2 tablespoons **walnut oil**
- 1 tablespoon **lemon juice**
- 2 quarts (about 8 oz.) **salad mix**, rinsed and crisped
  Salt and **pepper**
- 4 to 6 ounces **soft-ripened goat cheese** such as Bermuda Triangle or Humboldt Fog

1. Bake walnuts in an 8- or 9-inch pan in a 400° oven until golden, 5 to 8 minutes (about 4 minutes in a convection oven).

2. In a large bowl, combine oil and lemon juice. Add salad mix and stir, adding salt and pepper to taste. With 2 large spoons, divide salad equally among plates.

3. Cut cheese into thin slices and divide evenly among salads. Sprinkle evenly with walnuts.

Per serving: 226 cal., 84% (189 cal.) from fat; 7.4 g protein; 21 g fat (5.4 g sat.); 4 g carbo (0.9 g fiber); 113 mg sodium; 13 mg chol.

EXPLORE THE BERMUDA TRIANGLE: It's a striking soft-ripened cheese to top a salad.

The return of the cheese and wine course

To brie or not to brie—that is the question facing diners at many of the West's trendiest restaurants. The cheese course is booming on menus. And giving a few glorious cheeses a setting they deserve can also enhance a special meal at home. For a strong visual presentation, use whole or large cheese pieces that represent an interesting spectrum of tastes and textures.

Fresh goat and cow cheeses are good with fresh and dried sweet-tart fruits such as nectarines and apricots. Semifirm cheeses with mellow, nutlike flavors pair well with these, other stone fruits, and fresh or dried apples. Sweet dates and dried figs complement soft-ripened cheeses with pungent flavors. Wine suggestions follow.

Cheese Course

1. To serve 6, set **cheeses** (1 to 4 kinds; ¾ pound total) such as camellia, Tumalo tomme, extra-aged gouda, and Oregon blue on a platter or board, allowing enough space to cut easily. If cheeses are chilled, let stand at room temperature 2 to 3 hours.

2. Rinse and slice about 1 pound **fresh fruit** such as apples and/or pears and arrange around cheeses. Add ½ pound **dried fruit** such as nectarines. Accompany with at least ¾ pound **bread**, such as sweet French and/or walnut, sliced.

Per serving for 1 oz. *each* Oregon blue and gouda, 2½ oz. apples, 1 oz. dried nectarines, and 2 oz. French bread: 465 cal., 35% (162 cal.) from fat; 19 g protein; 18 g fat (11 g sat.); 58 g carbo (5.4 g fiber); 829 mg sodium; 62 mg chol.

Wines for cheese

Select one wine that's compatible with a wide range of cheeses, or several, each suited to specific cheeses.

The wines that go best with the greatest number of cheeses are fruity and on the sweet side, but with plenty of acid to stand up to the richness of cheese. At the sweetest end of this profile is Elysium, a dessert wine compatible with nearly all of these Western handcrafted cheeses. Chardonnays and other dry white wines with a lot of oak didn't rate well in our tastings. Nor did robust Cabernet Sauvignons, Zinfandels, or the classic standby, port.

Try some of the cheese-friendly wines that follow. If you can't find one of these, ask your wine merchant to suggest another of similar character.

■ **Bonny Doon Vineyard Fraise**, $10. Intense, sweet-tart strawberry flavor. Delightful with chèvres and mellow, nutlike cheeses like carmody, aged gouda and cheddar, and St. George.

■ **Cambria Julia's Vineyard Pinot Noir 1996**, $24. Delicate red with soft berry flavors. Good with mellow, nutty cheeses, Oregon blue, and schloss.

■ **Quady Winery Elysium 1997**, $12. Moderately sweet, fruity red dessert wine made from Black Muscat grapes. Goes well with most cheeses, especially mild, buttery crescenza, teleme, and breakfast cheese.

■ **Quady Essensia 1997**, $12. Sweet apricot flavors in a golden wine made from Or-

TRY EARTHY, WHITE camellia and tangy Tumalo tomme with an elegant Pinot Noir.

ange Muscat grapes; particularly suited to sharp chèvres, blue cheeses, and dry jack.

■ **Thomas Fogarty Winery Monterey Gewürztraminer 1997**, $12.50. Floral, soft, and refreshing with good acid balance. Excellent with mellow, nutty cheeses like tome, aged gouda, and sheep's milk cheese.

■ **Wente Vineyards Sauvignon Blanc 1997**, $9. Crisp, fresh-tasting white wine with plenty of acid and no oak. Particularly good with mild, buttery cheeses like crescenza, teleme, breakfast cheese, and dry jack, and mellow, nutty cheeses.

■ **Domaine Drouhin Oregon Pinot Noir 1996**, $35. Well-balanced, elegant red with berry and black pepper overtones. Suits mellow, nutty cheeses and most goat cheeses.

Cheese and Almond Salad

Follow directions for **soft-ripened goat cheese and walnut salad** (preceding), but instead of walnuts, use ⅓ cup **blanched almonds**; instead of walnut oil, use **olive oil**; and instead of soft-ripened goat cheese, use 4 ounces **soft-ripened cow cheese** such as breakfast cheese or schloss.

Per serving: 233 cal., 81% (189 cal.) from fat; 8.6 g protein; 21 g fat (1.5 g sat.); 3.8 g carbo (1.7 g fiber); 187 mg sodium; 28 mg chol.

Blue Cheese–Date Salad

PREP AND COOK TIME: About 20 minutes

MAKES: **4 servings**

12 **medjool dates** (about ⅔ lb. total)

¾ cup crumbled **Oregon blue** or other blue **cheese**

6 slices (4½ oz. total) **bacon**, cut in half crosswise

1½ tablespoons **extra-virgin olive oil**

1½ tablespoons **balsamic vinegar**

2 quarts (about 8 oz.) **baby spinach leaves**, rinsed and crisped

Salt and **pepper**

1. Slit dates lengthwise down 1 side and remove pits. Squeeze dates from ends to open slits, and fill equally with blue cheese. Press dates to close around cheese. Wrap a piece of bacon around each date, securing with a toothpick. Place dates in a 10- by 15-inch pan.

2. Bake in a 450° oven until bacon is well browned, about 10 minutes (about 6 minutes in a convection oven); after about 4 minutes, use a wide spatula to ease dates loose from pan and turn over.

3. Meanwhile, in a bowl, combine oil and vinegar. Add spinach and mix gently, seasoning to taste with salt and pepper.

4. Spoon spinach mixture onto plates. Remove toothpicks from dates and set an equal number on each salad.

Per serving: 405 cal., 38% (153 cal.) from fat; 11 g protein; 17 g fat (7 g sat.); 58 g carbo (5 g fiber); 532 mg sodium; 27 mg chol.

CREAMY DESSERT FONDUE of mascarpone cheese and wine crowns pound cake.

In a bowl, stir ¾ cup **crème fraîche** (cow or goat), mascarpone, fromage blanc, or quark with 2 tablespoons **orange marmalade** and 1 to 2 tablespoons **honey,** to taste.

Per tablespoon with crème fraîche: 51 cal., 73% (37 cal.) from fat; 0.4 g protein; 4.1 g fat (2.6 g sat.); 3.1 g carbo (0 g fiber); 9 mg sodium; 9.4 mg chol.

Per tablespoon with fromage blanc: 16 cal., 0% (0 cal.) from fat; 0.9 g protein; 0 g fat; 3.1 g carbo (0 g fiber); 20 mg sodium; 0.6 mg chol.

Mascarpone Dessert Fondue

PREP AND COOK TIME: **About 20 minutes**

MAKES: **6 servings**

- 1½ quarts (about 10 oz.) 1-inch cubes **pound cake**
- ¾ cup **Orange Muscat wine** such as Essensia
- 1 cup **mascarpone**
- 2 **Fuji apples** (½ lb. each), rinsed, cored, and sliced

1. Spread cake in a single layer in a 9- by 13-inch pan. Bake in a 450° oven until lightly toasted, 5 to 7 minutes. Place in a small bowl.

2. Meanwhile, in a 1- to 2-quart pan or fondue pan over high heat, boil wine until reduced to ¼ cup, 6 to 8 minutes.

3. Reduce heat to medium-high, add mascarpone, and stir until boiling, about 4 minutes. Set pan over a candle or on an electric warming tray.

4. Use forks or thin wood skewers to spear cake and apple slices and dunk them into fondue.

Per serving: 443 cal., 55% (243 cal.) from fat; 5.4 g protein; 27 g fat (17 g sat.); 39 g carbo (2 g fiber); 211 mg sodium; 138 mg chol.

Chèvre Appetizer Fondue

PREP AND COOK TIME: **About 20 minutes**

NOTES: **This recipe comes from Seattle's Palace Kitchen.**

MAKES: **6 servings**

Follow directions for **mascarpone dessert fondue** (preceding), but instead of pound cake, use 6 ounces **sourdough bread** cut into 1- to 1½-inch chunks (1½ qt.); instead of Orange Muscat wine, use a **dry Johannisberg Riesling** and, if desired, add ½ teaspoon **dried lavender blossoms** as wine boils; and instead of mascarpone, use 1 cup (8 oz.) **herb-flavor fresh chèvre** (goat) **cheese.** Add **pepper** to taste.

Per serving: 238 cal., 49% (117 cal.) from fat; 5.3 g protein; 13 g fat (8.6 g sat.); 16 g carbo (0.8 g fiber); 426 mg sodium; 35 mg chol.

Chèvre-Prune Salad

Follow directions for **blue cheese–date salad** (page 101), but instead of dates, use 20 **prunes** (8 oz. total); instead of blue cheese, use ½ cup **fresh chèvre** (goat) **cheese;** and instead of bacon, use 3 ounces **thin-sliced prosciutto** cut into 1- by 6-inch strips.

Per serving: 285 cal., 38% (108 cal.) from fat; 12 g protein; 12 g fat (4 g sat.); 37 g carbo (5.2 g fiber); 491 mg sodium; 25 mg chol.

Cheese and Dried-Fruit Appetizers

Follow steps 1 and 2 for **blue cheese–date or chèvre-prune salad** (preceding), and omit spinach and vinaigrette.

Per serving with dates: 350 cal., 31% (108 cal.) from fat; 9.6 g protein; 12 g fat (6.3 g sat.); 57 g carbo (3.9 g fiber); 498 mg sodium; 27 mg chol.

Pastis-marinated Chèvre

PREP TIME: **About 5 minutes,** plus at least 24 hours to marinate

NOTES: **Campagne restaurant in Seattle serves this French-style appetizer. Pastis, such as Pernod or Ricard, is an unsweetened anise-flavor liqueur.**

MAKES: **About 1½ cups; 12 appetizer servings**

1. Cut 1 log (10 oz.) **fresh chèvre** (goat) **cheese** crosswise into ½-inch-thick slices. Fit slices into a 2-cup jar with an airtight lid. Add 5 teaspoons **herbes de provence** (or 1 teaspoon *each* fennel seed and dried basil, rosemary, sage, and thyme), 2 tablespoons **pastis,** and ¾ cup **extra-virgin olive oil.** Close jar tightly and tilt to mix herbs and oil. Chill at least 24 hours or up to 1 month (oil thickens when chilled but liquefies at room temperature).

2. Bring to room temperature to serve. Spread cheese and a little oil onto toasted **bread** or crackers. Save leftover oil for salad dressings.

Per 1 teaspoon cheese with ½ teaspoon oil: 22 cal., 82% (18 cal.) from fat; 0.7 g protein; 2 g fat (0.7 g sat.); 0.2 g carbo (0 g fiber); 15 mg sodium; 1.8 mg chol.

Fresh Cheese with Orange Honey

PREP TIME: **About 5 minutes**

NOTES: **Spread onto warm croissants, brioche, or toasted raisin bread.**

MAKES: **About 1 cup**

Our favorite artisan cheeses

Western cheesemakers produce a myriad of fine cheeses; the following examples got high ratings at a *Sunset* tasting. Some styles of cheese are made by many producers; others are one of a kind. Many small manufacturers sell by phone.

Two stores that stock and ship a wide variety of Western cheeses are Tomales Bay Foods (80 Fourth St., Point Reyes Station, CA; 415/663-9335 or www.cowgirlcreamery.com) and Brie & Bordeaux (2227 N. 56th St., Seattle; 206/633-3538).

The designation of cow, goat, or sheep indicates the type of milk used. Cheeses marked with asterisks are pictured on page 97. **D** indicates cheeses are sold at the dairy. If no phone number is listed, the cheesemaker doesn't sell by mail.

fresh cheeses

Chèvre in oil. Goat cheese pieces in olive oil with seasonings. **Chèvre en marinade, Haystack Mountain Goat Dairy*;** garlicky; **D:** Niwot, CO; (303) 581-9948. **Chèvre in oil, Sea Stars Goat Cheese*;** fruity oil with herbs and sun-dried tomatoes. **Cabecou, Laura Chenel's Chèvre;** high-quality olive oil with herbs.

Crème fraîche. Thick cream; buttery, tangy. **Cowgirl Creamery;** cow; **D:** Point Reyes Station, CA; (415) 663-9335. **Kendall Farms;** cow.

Crescenza. **Bellwether Farms*;** cow; soft and buttery, melts in your mouth; slightly tangy; **D:** near Valley Ford, CA; (888) 527-8606.

Fresh chèvre. Goat; soft, spreadable, and creamy; mildly tangy. **Chabis, Laura Chenel's Chèvre. Plain chèvre, Skyhill Napa Valley Farms;** (707) 255-4800.

Fresh mozzarella. **California Mozzarella Fresca*;** cow; mild, sweet, nice chewy bite.

Fromage blanc de Parma. **Rollingstone Chèvre*;** goat; soft, smooth, and spreadable; tangy and salty. **D:** Parma, ID; (208) 722-6460.

Herb-flavor chèvre. Goat cheese with herb coating. **Herb chevre, Cypress Grove Chèvre*;** dense, coated with lavender and fennel; (707) 839-3168. **Herb chabis, Laura Chenel's Chèvre;** lots of thyme.

Mascarpone. **Cowgirl Creamery;** cow; sinfully rich and tangy; **D:** Point Reyes Station, CA; (415) 663-9335.

Queso crema. **Bodega Goat Cheese;** goat; rich, smooth; (707) 876-3483; sold at the Gourmet Goat, Bodega, CA; (707) 876-9686.

Ricotta. Cow; sweet. **Bellwether Farms*;** chewy; **D:** near Valley Ford, CA; (888) 527-8606. Whole milk **California Mozzarella Fresca.**

Traditional quark. **Appel Farm, Langerfeld Imports*;** cow; thick, creamy, tangy; we also liked Appel's low-fat quark; (360) 354-1125.

soft-ripened cheeses

Bermuda Triangle. **Cypress Grove Chèvre*;** goat; triangular, coated with ash and white mold, dense, rich flavor; (707) 839-3168.

Breakfast cheese. **Rouge et Noir, Marin French Cheese Company*;** cow; mild, buttery, and nutty; **D:** Petaluma, CA; (800) 292-6001.

Bûche. **Juniper Grove Farm*;** goat; thin-crusted log flecked with blue, tangy, buttery, smooth; **D:** Redmond, OR; (541) 923-8353.

Camellia. **Redwood Hill Farm*;** goat; similar to camembert, disk with delicate rind of white mold and flowing interior; very complex and nutty; **D:** Sebastopol, CA (by reservation only; no mail order; 707/823-8250).

Chestnut leaf–aged goat. **Quillisascut Cheese Co.;** dense and creamy, pungent, complex flavors; available July-November; (509) 738-2011.

Cow's milk tome. **Quillisascut Cheese Co.;** moldy rind, runny center, rich, complex, earthy flavors; (509) 738-2011.

Crottin. **Laura Chenel's Chèvre*;** goat; classic puck shape with delicate rind and slightly runny interior, creamy, bold flavor.

Humboldt Fog. **Cypress Grove Chèvre*;** goat; center layer of ash, outside coated with ash and white mold; complex and earthy, with a nice tang; (707) 839-3168.

Rice-flour teleme. **Peluso Cheese*;** cow; edible rind coated with rice flour, smooth, buttery, tangy; **D:** Los Baños, CA; (209) 826-3744.

Schloss. **Rouge et Noir, Marin French Cheese Company*;** cow; beautifully pungent and nutty; **D:** Petaluma, CA; (800) 292-6001.

Taupinière. **Laura Chenel's Chèvre*;** goat; mound-shaped cheese coated with ash and white mold; nutty, tangy, and rich.

semifirm to firm cheeses

Aged sheep's milk cheese in chestnut leaves. **Sally Jackson Cheeses;** moist bite, mellow chestnut flavor; available March-November.

Carmody. **Bellwether Farms*;** cow; golden, aged wheel; mellow, rich, and smooth; **D:** near Valley Ford, CA; (888) 527-8606.

Cheddar. Cow. **Cougar Gold, WSU Creamery*;** aged at least one year; sharp, nutty, and sweet; **D:** Pullman, WA; (800) 457-5442. **Full-cream medium cheddar, Bandon Cheese;** creamy, mellow, rich; we also liked Bandon's full-cream sharp, regular sharp, and extra-sharp cheddars; **D:** Bandon, OR; (800) 548-8961. **Vintage white extra-sharp cheddar,**

Tillamook County Creamery Association; 90th-anniversary cheese, aged three years; nutty, sharp; **D:** Tillamook, OR; (800) 542-7290.

Extra-aged gouda. **Winchester Cheese Co.;** cow; pleasant grainy texture; rich, complex, lively; we also gave high marks to Winchester's gouda with cumin and medium-aged gouda; **D:** Winchester, CA; (909) 926-4239.

Feta (or feta-type). Goat; tangy and salty. **Feta, Sea Stars Goat Cheese*;** smooth, salty. **Feta, Hamakua Goat Cheese Co.;** nice bounce, pungent; (808) 775-9207. **Feta with calamata olives and rosemary, Rollingstone Chèvre;** in olive oil; very salty; **D:** Parma, ID; (208) 722-6460. **Feta, Redwood Hill Farm;** creamy and nutty; **D:** Sebastopol, CA (by appointment only; no mail order; 707/823-8250). **Alpine chevre chevito, Yerba Santa Goat Dairy;** dry and rich; (707) 263-8131.

Oregon blue. **Rogue River Valley Creamery;** cow; very creamy and rich; salty and pungent; **D:** Central Point, OR; (541) 664-2233.

Pepato. **Bellwether Farms;** sheep; firm, mildly tangy, with whole peppercorns; **D:** near Valley Ford, CA; (888) 527-8606.

San Andreas. **Bellwether Farms*;** sheep; semifirm and dense, very buttery and nutty; **D:** near Valley Ford, CA; (888) 527-8606.

St. George. **Joe Matos Cheese Factory*;** cow; aged two months; firm, rich, medium-sharp; **D:** Santa Rosa, CA; (707) 584-5283.

Tome. Goat; smooth, dense, and mellow. **Tumalo tomme, Juniper Grove Farm*;** lightly tangy; **D:** Redmond, OR; (541) 923-8353. **Tome, Laura Chenel's Chèvre;** nutty.

Toscano. **Bellwether Farms*;** sheep; dry and slightly crumbly; nutty, sharp; **D:** near Valley Ford, CA (888) 527-8606.

hard cheeses

Aged goat curado. **Quillisascut Cheese Co.*;** goat; hard, dry; complex; (509) 738-2011.

Alpine Chevre shepherd's cheese. **Yerba Santa Goat Dairy*;** goat; aged three to six months; firm, flaky, mellow; (707) 263-8131.

Dry Monterey jack. **Vella Cheese Co.*;** cow; sweet, nutty flavor; **D:** Sonoma, CA; (800) 848-0505. ◆

Solo

Meridol

Green Papaya

INTERIOR SECRETS: Solo papayas are golden (Kapoho, Rainbow) or rosy (Kamia, Sunrise, Sunset, SunUp) inside; Meridol is reddish orange. Ripe papayas can be scooped with a spoon. Green-skinned, immature papayas are white and crisp inside; use raw or cooked.

A passion for papayas

Eight ways to love this tropical fruit, from salad to dessert

BY LINDA LAU ANUSASANANAN

PHOTOGRAPHS BY JAMES CARRIER

■ Remember your first bite of papaya? Its smooth, melting flesh, subtle floral taste, and musky aroma might have seemed seductive—or strange. (Regardless, a squeeze of lime made it more enjoyable.)

Papayas' growing presence in the market is evidence that they've seduced a good share of their audience. Small (1 to 1½ lb.) pear-shaped Solo papayas, primarily from Hawaii, and large (1½ to 7 lb.) football-shaped Meridol (also spelled Maradol) fruit from Mexico dominate the supply in Western markets. Other Meridol sources are Belize, Costa Rica, Brazil, and the Caribbean. As a result, papayas of one variety or another are available here year-round.

Although sweetness and color vary slightly with variety and ripeness (some think Solo has a more intense flavor and

Meridol a muskier taste), papayas can be used interchangeably. After harvest, fruit will soften and get juicier, but sugar content will not change.

Buy papayas with some golden color and smooth, unblemished skin. To ripen, store at room temperature until most of the skin turns gold and the flesh gives slightly when gently pressed. Eat, or refrigerate up to several days. Chilling before fruit is ready to eat can stop the ripening process.

Green, or immature, papayas are firm and unripe. Southeast Asians use green papaya as a vegetable, raw or cooked, for its crunchy texture and cool flavor, reminiscent of cucumbers and chayotes. Look for green papayas in Asian food markets. To keep fruit firm, store at cool room temperature (about 55°) or refrigerate.

Papaya–Kiwi Fruit Sundaes with lemon-ginger sauce (page 107)

Papaya Gazpacho

PREP TIME: About 35 minutes

NOTES: Up to 8 hours ahead, complete recipe through step 2; cover and chill.

MAKES: 6 servings

2 pounds chilled **ripe papayas**

½ to 1 teaspoon minced seeded **fresh habanero chili** or 1 to 2 teaspoons minced seeded fresh red Fresno chili

⅔ cup **orange juice**

¾ cup **vegetable broth**

½ cup **lime juice**

¼ cup minced **shallots**, rinsed and drained

½ pound **shelled cooked tiny shrimp** (optional)

½ cup diced (¼ in.) peeled, seeded **green papaya** or cucumber (about ¾ lb.)

½ cup diced (½ in.) peeled, pitted **firm-ripe avocado**

Salt

2 tablespoons **fresh cilantro** leaves

1. Peel, seed, and cut enough ripe papaya into ½-inch cubes to make ½ cup; reserve for garnish. Cut remaining papayas into 1-inch chunks. In a blender or food processor, combine 1-inch papaya chunks, ½ teaspoon chili, and orange juice; purée until smooth.

2. Pour purée into a bowl; add broth, lime juice, shallots, and additional chili to taste; mix well.

3. Ladle into wide bowls. To each bowl, add equal portions shrimp, reserved ripe papaya cubes, diced green papaya, and avocado. Add salt to taste and sprinkle with cilantro.

Per serving: 90 cal., 22% (20 cal.) from fat; 1.4 g protein; 2.2 g fat (0.3 g sat.); 18 g carbo (1.4 g fiber); 18 mg sodium; 0 mg chol.

Green Papaya–Turkey Tumble

Green Papaya–Turkey Tumble

PREP AND COOK TIME: About 30 minutes

NOTES: Serve as a first course or accompany with rice for a main dish. Garnish with green onion slivers.

MAKES: 6 first-course or 3 main-dish servings

- 1 tablespoon **salad oil**
- 1 **onion** (6 oz.), peeled and chopped
- 1 pound **ground turkey** or ground lean pork
- 1 tablespoon **curry powder**
- 1½ cups diced (¼ in.) peeled, seeded **green papaya**
- ¾ cup fat-skimmed **chicken broth**
- 3 tablespoons **chutney**, chopped
- 1 teaspoon **cornstarch**
  Salt
- 12 **iceberg** or butter **lettuce** leaves (about 3 by 4 in.), rinsed and crisped

1. In a 10- to 12-inch frying pan over high heat, stir oil, onion, and turkey until meat is browned and crumbly, about 7 minutes.

2. Add curry powder; stir until fragrant, about 30 seconds. Add papaya, broth, and chutney. Cover and cook over medium heat, stirring occasionally, until papaya is tender when pierced, 5 to 7 minutes.

3. Mix cornstarch and 2 tablespoons water; stir into pan. Keep stirring until sauce boils, about 1 minute. Add salt to taste. Scrape into a bowl.

4. To eat, spoon turkey mixture into lettuce leaves and roll up.

Per first-course serving: 187 cal., 40% (74 cal.) from fat; 15 g protein; 8.2 g fat (1.8 g sat.); 13 g carbo (1.3 g fiber); 102 mg sodium; 55 mg chol.

Spice-dusted Papaya

PREP AND COOK TIME: About 10 minutes

NOTES: Serve as a salad, or as a relish with grilled chicken, fish, or pork.

MAKES: 3 or 4 salad servings

- 1 to 1½ pounds **firm-ripe papayas**, peeled and seeded
- ½ teaspoon **ground cumin**
- ⅛ teaspoon **cayenne**
- ⅛ teaspoon **ground nutmeg**
- ⅛ teaspoon **pepper**
  Salt
- 1 **lime**, cut in half

1. Cut papayas into ¼-inch-thick slices and arrange on a platter.

2. In a 6- to 8-inch frying pan over low heat, stir ground cumin, cayenne, ground nutmeg, and pepper until the spices are fragrant, about 3 minutes. Remove the pan from heat.

3. Sprinkle papaya slices evenly with spice mixture and lightly with salt. Squeeze lime over papayas.

Per serving: 33 cal., 5.5% (1.8 cal.) from fat; 0.5 g protein; 0.2 g fat (0 g sat.); 8.2 g carbo (0.7 g fiber); 2.8 mg sodium; 0 mg chol.

Papaya-Watercress Salad

PREP TIME: About 10 minutes

NOTES: Ellie Stepo of Kailua, Hawaii, uses local fruit to make this colorful salad. If desired, reserve some of the peppery seeds from the papayas to use in the dressing.

MAKES: 6 servings

- 3 cups diced (about ¾ in.) peeled, seeded **firm-ripe papayas** (about 1 lb. total)
- 5 cups (about ½ lb.) **watercress sprigs,** rinsed and crisped
- ½ cup thinly sliced **sweet onion** such as Maui, Walla Walla, or Vidalia
- ¼ cup **white** or red **balsamic vinegar**
- 1 tablespoon **honey**
- 1 tablespoon **poppy seed** or papaya seeds
- 2 tablespoons minced **fresh mint** leaves
- ½ teaspoon **ground coriander**
  Salt

1. In the center of a wide, shallow bowl, mound papayas, surround with watercress, and arrange onion slices on top.

2. In a small bowl, mix vinegar, honey, poppy seed, mint, and coriander; pour over papaya salad. To serve, mix gently and add salt to taste.

Per serving: 60 cal., 12% (7.2 cal.) from fat; 1.9 g protein; 0.8 g fat (0.1 g sat.); 13 g carbo (2 g fiber); 21 mg sodium; 0 mg chol.

Green Papaya and Carrot Slaw

PREP TIME: About 20 minutes

NOTES: Use the shredding blade of a food processor or a hand-shredder to cut papayas for this traditional Southeast Asian salad.

MAKES: 4 servings

- ¼ cup **rice vinegar**
- 1 tablespoon thin slivers **fresh ginger**
- 1 teaspoon **sugar**
- 2 cups shredded peeled, seeded **green papayas** (about ¾ lb. total)
- 1 cup shredded **carrots**
- ¼ cup thinly sliced **green onions,** including tops
  Asian fish sauce (*nuoc mam* or *nam pla*) or salt

1. In a large bowl, mix vinegar, ginger, and sugar.

2. Add papayas, carrots, and onions; mix to blend. Add fish sauce to taste.

Per serving: 52 cal., 3.5% (1.8 cal.) from fat; 0.9 g protein; 0.2 g fat (0 g sat.); 13 g carbo (1.8 g fiber); 13 mg sodium; 0 mg chol.

Papaya Pie

Papaya Pie

PREP AND COOK TIME: About 1½ hours, plus 1 hour to cool

NOTES: Serve pie plain or with vanilla ice cream.

MAKES: 8 servings

> About 3 pounds **firm-ripe papayas**
> ¾ cup **sugar**
> ¼ cup **cornstarch**
> 1 teaspoon **ground coriander**
> ½ teaspoon **ground cardamom**
> ¼ teaspoon **ground nutmeg**
> 2 teaspoons grated **lemon** peel
> 3 tablespoons **lemon juice**
> 1 package (15 oz.) **refrigerated pastry for double-crust 9-inch pie,** at room temperature
> **All-purpose flour**

1. Peel papayas, cut in half lengthwise, and discard seeds. Cut papayas lengthwise into 2- to 3-inch-wide slices, then cut crosswise into ¼-inch-thick strips.

Measure 8 cups of fruit; reserve extra for other uses.

2. In a large bowl, mix sugar, cornstarch, coriander, cardamom, nutmeg, and lemon peel. Add papayas and lemon juice, and mix.

3. Unfold 1 pastry round and ease into a 9-inch pie pan. Fill pastry with fruit mixture.

4. Unfold remaining pastry on a lightly floured board and roll into a 13-inch-wide round.

5. Center round over fruit. Pinch pastry at rim to seal, then fold edge under itself, flush with pan rim, and pinch to flute. Slash pastry top decoratively. Set pie on a foil-lined baking sheet.

6. Bake on the bottom rack of a 375° oven until juices bubble near center, 1 hour and 10 minutes to 1 hour and 20 minutes (55 to 65 minutes in a convection oven). If pastry edges get too dark, cover loosely with foil. Cool at least 1 hour. Cut into wedges.

Per serving: 375 cal., 36% (135 cal.) from fat; 2.7 g protein; 15 g fat (6 g sat.); 58 g carbo (1.1 g fiber); 272 mg sodium; 14 mg chol.

Papaya–Kiwi Fruit Sundaes

PREP TIME: About 30 minutes
MAKES: 6 servings

> 2 pounds **firm-ripe papayas**
> 3 **firm-ripe kiwi fruit** (10 oz. total)
> 2 teaspoons grated **lemon** peel
> ⅓ cup **lemon juice**
> 3 tablespoons **honey**
> 2 tablespoons minced **crystallized ginger**
> 2 to 3 cups **vanilla ice cream**
> **Mint sprigs**

1. Peel papayas, cut in half lengthwise, and discard seeds. Thinly slice papayas lengthwise and arrange on plates.

2. Peel kiwi fruit and thinly slice crosswise; arrange kiwi slices on papayas.

3. In a small bowl, mix lemon peel, lemon juice, honey, and ginger. Scoop ice cream into balls and place equally on fruit. Drizzle honey mixture over desserts. Garnish with mint sprigs.

Per serving: 206 cal., 23% (47 cal.) from fat; 2.6 g protein; 5.2 g fat (3 g sat.); 40 g carbo (2.5 g fiber); 48 mg sodium; 19 mg chol.

Papaya Sorbet

PREP TIME: About 45 minutes

NOTES: For best flavor, use fully ripe, slightly soft fruit. If making sorbet up to 5 days ahead, let soften in the refrigerator about 15 minutes before serving.

MAKES: 3¾ cups; 6 servings

> About ½ cup **sugar**
> About ½ cup **lime juice**
> 4½ cups diced (½ in.) peeled, seeded **ripe papayas** (about 1¾ lb. total)

1. In a blender or food processor, combine ½ cup sugar and ½ cup lime juice. Add papayas, in batches if necessary, and whirl until smooth. Pour mixture as puréed into a bowl. Stir, taste, and if desired, add more sugar and lime juice.

2. Nest bowl in ice and stir often until mixture is cold, 10 to 12 minutes.

3. Pour purée into an ice cream maker (minimum capacity 1 qt.). Freeze according to manufacturer's directions until sorbet is firm, dasher is hard to turn, or machine stops, 15 to 20 minutes. Serve, or freeze airtight up to 5 days.

Per serving: 120 cal., 1.5% (1.8 cal.) from fat; 0.9 g protein; 0.2 g fat (0.1 g sat.); 31 g carbo (1.2 g fiber); 7.4 mg sodium; 0 mg chol. ◆

foodguide

BY JERRY ANNE DI VECCHIO

Asparagus tips for spring

■ In the produce department, the change of seasons is growing less and less evident. Thanks to farms in the tropics and south of the equator, where fall is our spring, many "seasonal" fruits and vegetables are available year-round. However, the price of asparagus clarifies the calendar. Rarely is it a better bargain—or the source more local—than in May. To take advantage of the consummate spring vegetable, I couldn't resist giving it two settings this month.

Asparagus first won me over when I was a young thing, just into high heels. I was terribly impressed by a dish in vogue at the time called veal Oscar. Reputedly named for a Scandinavian king, the veal, topped with crab, asparagus, and a velvety butter sauce, had royal cachet.

Chef Bradley Ogden recently revived this forgotten pleasure at one of his annual crab festival dinners at Lark Creek Inn in Larkspur, California. But he presented a different Oscar, this one with chicken. Here's an adaptation that works well for a cook without a staff.

Chicken Oscar

PREP AND COOK TIME: About **25 minutes**
NOTES: Up to 6 hours ahead, pound chicken; cover and chill. Cook asparagus, drain, chill at once in ice water, then drain again. Immerse in simmering water for 1 to 2 minutes to reheat.
MAKES: 4 servings

- 12 **asparagus spears** (equal size; about 1 lb. total)
- 4 **boned, skinned chicken breast halves** (about ¼ lb. each)
- 3 to 4 tablespoons **fine dried bread crumbs**
- 2 tablespoons **butter** or margarine
- ¼ pound **shelled cooked crab**
- ½ to ⅔ cup **hollandaise sauce** (recipe follows), hot, warm, or at room temperature
- **Chive spears** or minced chives

1. Snap tough ends from asparagus and discard. Rinse asparagus and, if desired, peel stems with a vegetable peeler.

2. Rinse chicken, pat dry, and lay pieces 4 to 5 inches apart on a sheet of plastic wrap. Cover with more plastic wrap. Pound chicken with a flat mallet until it is ⅜ to ½ inch thick.

3. Put bread crumbs in a shallow pan. Turn chicken in crumbs to coat evenly, patting to make them stick.

4. Set an 11- to 12-inch ovenproof nonstick frying pan over high heat. When hot, add butter and swirl until melted. Add chicken and cook until browned on bottom, shaking pan to avoid scorching butter, about 2 minutes. Turn pieces over and cook 1 minute more.

5. Set pan in a 350° oven and bake until chicken is no longer pink in center (cut to test), 7 to 9 minutes.

6. Meanwhile, in a 10- to 12-inch frying pan over high heat, bring about 1 inch water to a boil. About 3 minutes before chicken is done, add asparagus to boiling water and cook just until tender when pierced; drain.

7. Quickly transfer each chicken breast half to a warm plate. Top with equal amounts of the crab and asparagus, and pour hollandaise sauce over each portion. Garnish with chives.

Per serving: 334 cal., 49% (162 cal.) from fat; 36 g protein; 18 g fat (9.8 g sat.); 7.2 g carbo (1.1 g fiber); 370 mg sodium; 173 mg chol.

Give hollandaise a quick whirl

■ The secret of exquisitely smooth hollandaise sauce is forming a perfect emulsion. Egg yolks are naturally emulsified, and when melted butter is whipped or whirled into them, the fat and liquid won't separate if the eggs aren't overcooked. The trick is to get the mixture to a bacteria-safe temperature without cooking the yolks enough to solidify them and make the sauce separate. If this happens, you can save it by putting 2 tablespoons of water in a blender or another bowl and whirling or whisking in the broken sauce.

Hollandaise Sauce

PREP AND COOK TIME: About 10 minutes

NOTES: To keep hollandaise sauce warm up to 2 hours, seal in a thermos. If making up to 4 days ahead, pour into a jar and chill airtight. To serve, let stand about 2 hours at room temperature, then whisk to soften.

MAKES: 2 cups

- 3 **large egg** yolks
- 3/4 cup (3/8 lb.) **butter** or margarine
- 2 tablespoons **lemon juice**
- 1 tablespoon **Dijon mustard**

1. Put yolks in a blender or food processor **(a)**. Cut butter into chunks and put in a 1- to 2-quart pan over medium-high heat. Heat until melted and a little of the foam is beginning to brown (about 230°), 3 to 4 minutes.
2. Turn on blender or food processor and pour 1/4 cup boiling water into yolks, then add lemon juice and mustard. At once, pour hot butter into yolks in a steady stream **(b)**, taking about 10 seconds (sauce will be thin). Sauce should be 160°. If it's not, pour into a metal bowl (about 3 qt.) or round-bottomed pan and nest over slightly simmering water in another pan. Whisk **(c)** for 3 minutes.
3. Serve sauce hot or warm.

Per tablespoon: 45 cal., 98% (44 cal.) from fat; 0.3 g protein; 4.9 g fat (2.9 g sat.); 0.1 g carbo (0 g fiber); 57 mg sodium; 32 mg chol.

■ Layer asparagus and roasted vegetables on a crisp pastry for a colorful main-dish salad. Alain Giraud describes it as a tart on his spring menu at Lavande in Santa Monica.

Lavande Spring Vegetable Tart

PREP AND COOK TIME: About 2 hours

MAKES: 4 servings

- 6 **Roma tomatoes** (about 1/4 lb. each)
- 2 heads **fennel** (each 3 1/2 in. wide)
- 2 **garlic** cloves
- 3 tablespoons **olive oil**
- 2 **artichokes** (3 in. wide)
- 12 **asparagus spears** (equal size; about 1 lb. total)
- 4 **frozen puff pastry shells** (2/3 of a 10-oz. package), thawed
- 1 tablespoon **balsamic vinegar**

  About 1/4 cup **prepared tapenade** (olive paste)

  Salad (recipe follows)

  Salt and fresh-ground **pepper**

1. Rinse tomatoes, core, and cut in half lengthwise. Trim off and discard fennel tops, root ends, and any bruised spots. Rinse heads and cut lengthwise into 1/4-inch slices. Peel and chop garlic.

2. Rub 1 tablespoon olive oil over bottom of 10- by 15-inch pan. Sprinkle garlic over half the pan and set tomatoes, cut side down and close together, on garlic. Lay fennel slices in other side of pan and drizzle with 1 tablespoon oil; mix gently with your hands to coat, then spread fennel evenly in half of pan.

3. Bake in a 350° oven until tomatoes are shriveled and fennel is translucent, about 1 hour (about 50 minutes in a convection oven). Let cool.

4. Meanwhile, rinse artichokes, drain, and trim discolored ends from stems. Put artichokes in a 4- or 5-quart pan. Add about 3 inches water, cover pan, and bring to a boil over high heat. Reduce heat and simmer until artichoke bottoms are tender when pierced, about 40 minutes.

5. Snap off and discard tough ends of asparagus. Rinse spears. Lift artichokes from pan and let cool. Add asparagus to water and turn heat to high. Cook, uncovered, until spears are tender-crisp when pierced, about 3 minutes. Drain and immerse at once in ice water until cold, about 2 minutes; drain again.

6. On a lightly floured board, roll each puff pastry shell into a 6- to 7-inch-wide round. Set rounds side by side on a 12-by 15-inch baking sheet; set another pan of the same size on top of the pastries.

7. Bake pastries in a 350° oven until well browned (lift top pan to check), 25 to 30 minutes (about 25 minutes in a convection oven).

8. As pastries bake, break leaves from artichokes and reserve for other uses. Scoop out and discard fuzzy centers from artichoke bottoms; also trim any coarse fibers from artichoke stems. Cut bot-toms vertically into ⅛- to ¼-inch-thick slices. In a bowl, mix with 1 tablespoon olive oil and vinegar.

9. Spread each warm pastry lightly with tapenade and set on a plate. Top each with 3 tomato halves and equal portions of fennel (don't wash pan; set aside), artichoke bottoms, and asparagus.

10. Top vegetables with equal portions of green salad (including dressing). Add salt and pepper to taste.

Per serving: 595 cal., 62% (369 cal.) from fat; 13 g protein; 41 g fat (5.1 g sat.); 49 g carbo (9.3 g fiber); 792 mg sodium; 0 mg chol.

Salad. Rinse and crisp 4 cups (2 to 3 oz.) **baby salad mix.** In pan used to bake tomatoes and fennel, preceding, stir 2 tablespoons **extra-virgin olive oil,** 1½ tablespoons **balsamic vinegar,** 1 teaspoon chopped **fresh thyme** leaves, and ½ teaspoon chopped **fresh rosemary** leaves, incorporating drippings in pan. Add salad mix and stir, seasoning to taste with **salt** and **pepper.**

JAMES CARRIER

It's about thyme— and parsley and sage...

Although McCormick & Company has been in the spice and herb business for more than 100 years, its newest product couldn't be fresher: cut herbs sold in water-filled vessels to preserve their quality and extend their life. The herbs can be kept at room temperature (the water should be replaced when it gets murky). However, *Sunset's* tests over the years have demonstrated that cut herbs in water—with the exception of basil—stay fresh even longer in the refrigerator, loosely covered with a plastic bag. McCormick's selection of fresh herbs—basil, dill, Italian parsley, marjoram, mint, oregano, rosemary, and sage—is available at major supermarket chains and natural-food stores. A bunch costs about $2; for more information, call (800) 632-5847. ◆

Gourmet's guide to Mountain View

Eat around the globe at this unsung South Bay destination

Just as Silicon Valley created itself by compressing vast amounts of information onto tiny computer chips, the city of Mountain View, at its heart, squeezes a world of cuisines and sophisticated entertainment into its five-block downtown strip.

Anchored by the architecturally stunning City Hall and the Mountain View Center for the Performing Arts, where TheatreWorks stages performances , Castro Street yields fine meals and other small-town delights. Among your best dining options:

In a renovated Victorian home one block off the strip, *Chez T.J.* (938 Villa St.; 650/964-7466) is the classiest restaurant in town, with a seasonal, French-inspired, fixed-price menu. *Chef Wang's* (212 Castro; 969-4574) bustles with locals who don't need to look at the menu to order. Try the hand-pulled noodles (la mien) or the seaweed salad. The chicken tikka masala at *Sue's Indian Cuisine* (216 Castro; 969-1112) is a longtime favorite. And the heady mushroom risotto and other Italian classics are packing the tables at chic *Don Giovanni* (235 Castro; 961-9749).

At the recently opened *Rio Grande* (228 Castro; 988-6700), buffalo heads, calfskin rugs, and Western murals get you in the mood for all-American dining (ribs and steaks) and line dancing to country music. For mellower toe-tapping, check out one of Mountain View's many coffeehouses. **Cuppa Joe** (194 Castro; 967-2294) has spirited bluegrass jams Monday and Wednesday nights, and live music most weekends.

Mountain View Chamber of Commerce; 968-8378. TheatreWorks; 903-6000.

— *Sara Schneider and Lisa Taggart* ◆

STEVE CASTILLO

Chef Chang Chiang makes hand-pulled noodles at Chef Wang's .

The Wine Guide

BY KAREN MacNEIL-FIFE

A word about wine

■ "There's just one thing I don't get," said one of my wine students recently. "Wine tastes like cherries, apples, pears, even pomegranates. How come it almost never tastes like grapes?"

It was a great question. It's ironic that wine—which by nature ought to taste like grapes—usually doesn't. Instead, it can taste like all sorts of unexpected things, from leather boots to pineapple.

In part, the reason lies in the mind-bendingly complex process of fermentation, when all kinds of chemical transformations take place. Many compounds we know in other contexts are created. Diacetyl, for example, the compound that makes butter taste buttery, can be created. And if it is, the wine literally tastes buttery.

Wine, in fact, seems to have no vocabulary of its own; we use the language of food, nature, even fabrics. A wine can be raspberrylike, earthy, or silky—or (as in the case of many Pinot Noirs) all three.

That said, there are terms used by just about everybody to describe wine.

BODY. Wines are described as *light-bodied* or *full-bodied,* depending on how heavy they are on your tongue. Imagine, for example, the relative weights of skim milk, whole milk, and half-and-half. Light-bodied, medium-bodied, and full-bodied wines correspond. But don't confuse body with flavor intensity. A wine can be light-bodied yet extremely intense in flavor the way a sorbet is.

COMPLEXITY. A *complex* wine has multiple layers of flavors and aromas. Each sip reveals something you didn't notice before. Complex wines are more fascinating than their opposites—*simple* wines.

EARTHINESS. *Earthy* describes a range of flavors and aromas, from soil to mushrooms and truffles. Professional wine tasters also use the word when comparing the aroma of a wine to the sweet, slightly sweaty smell of the human body. Pinot Noirs tend to be earthy.

FRESHNESS. A wine that tastes clean and lively is often described as *fresh,* a sense that often stems from its natural acidity. A wine with too little acidity frequently tastes bland and dull, or *flabby.*

FRUIT. *Fruity* means simply that the wine has pronounced flavors or aromas of fruit. Some wines—usually unexpressive ones like Pinot Grigio—aren't particularly fruity. On the other hand, Gewürztraminer, Gamay (the grape in beaujolais), Zinfandel, and California Riesling all can be very fruity.

LENGTH. *Long* wines have flavors that linger in your mouth even after you've swallowed (these end-run flavors are called the wine's finish). A long finish is one of the hallmarks of a great wine.

TANNIN. A compound found in grape skins, *tannin* gives wine a firm structure—its skeleton. It also acts as a preservative, helping wine age gracefully. Red wine, which is fermented with skins, has more tannin than white wine, which is fermented without skins. Unfortunately, if red grapes are picked before they're fully ripe, their tannin can make the wine bitter and astringent. But if the grapes are picked ripe, the tannin creates a good structure; the wine does not taste dry and astringent.

TOAST. Many wines that have been fermented and/or aged in new oak barrels take on a *toasty* character not unlike that of buttered toast. The reason: during the barrelmaking process, the oak staves are toasted over fire to make them more malleable. While many wine drinkers like some toastiness (especially in Chardonnay), wines that taste exclusively of toast are poorly made.

Karen MacNeil-Fife teaches wine classes at the Culinary Institute of America at Greystone in the Napa Valley.

RICK MARIANI

WINES FOR THE WORDS

Here are some wines that define the terms discussed here particularly well.

Light-bodied: Waterbrook Sauvignon Blanc 1997 (Columbia Valley, WA), $12. Beautifully light, almost evanescent.

Full-bodied: Beringer Chardonnay 1997 (Napa Valley), $16. Round and creamy—positively buxom.

Complex: Qupé "Los Olivos Cuvee" 1996 (Santa Barbara County), $18. A fascinating, multilayered blend of Mourvèdre, Syrah, and Grenache.

Earthy: Robert Mondavi Pinot Noir 1996 (Napa Valley), $20. Primordially dark—the forest floor.

Fresh: Covey Run Fumé Blanc 1996 (Columbia Valley), $7. Bright, fresh, and lemony. Very easy to pair with food.

Fruity: Beaulieu Zinfandel 1996 (Napa Valley), $12. Like boysenberry jam.

Long: Long Vineyards Chardonnay 1997 (Napa Valley), $35. Elegant crème brûlée and vanilla flavors that just don't end.

Tannic: Markham Merlot 1996 (Napa Valley), $20. Ripe tannins give this wine impressive structure.

Toasty: Chateau St. Jean Chardonnay 1997 (Sonoma County), $12. Full and yeasty, with opulent toasty overtones. ◆

SUNSET'S STEAL OF THE MONTH

Bookwalter Chenin Blanc 1998 (Columbia Valley, WA), $7. Possibly the best Chenin Blanc in America, at an unbelievable price! Lovely peach and mineral flavors; perfect balance and elegance.
— KAREN MacNEIL-FIFE

POBLANO CHILI halves make mellow cups for pungent cheese and mashed potatoes.

The right stuff for chiles rellenos

Tradition includes a free hand with flavor and form

BY ELAINE JOHNSON

A fresh large chili filled with melting cheese, dipped in frothy egg batter, and sizzled golden brown in bubbling oil is an authentic chile relleno. But so is a deep-fried jalapeño stuffed with mozzarella cheese—the "poppers" savored by brew pub and ball-park crowds. A casserole of chilies baked in a cheese custard also qualifies for the name. *Relleno* is the Spanish word for *stuffed*. And the term *chiles rellenos*, here and in Mexico, covers a spectrum of imaginative dishes in which the "stuff" may be in, over, or around the chili.

Sunset readers regularly expand the chile relleno tradition, often by lowering the fat. In these four dishes, a baked filled chili is the common denominator.

Low-Fat Jalapeño Bites

PREP AND COOK TIME: About 1 hour and 10 minutes

NOTES: Midge Stapleton of Anacortes, Washington, often starts these appetizers 1 day ahead. Complete the recipe through step 3; cover and chill poppers. To serve, uncover and continue.

MAKES: 28 pieces

$\frac{1}{2}$ cup (4 oz.) **fat-free cream cheese** or neufchâtel (light) cream cheese

2 teaspoons minced **garlic**

$\frac{1}{3}$ cup minced **green onions**

3 tablespoons **shredded cheddar cheese**

1 tablespoon **lime juice**

About $\frac{3}{4}$ pound **fresh jalapeño chilies** (14 or 15, equal-size), rinsed

2 **large egg** whites

1 cup **cornflake crumbs**

1. In a bowl, use a fork to blend cream cheese, garlic, onions, cheddar cheese, and lime juice.

2. Wearing rubber gloves, cut chilies in half lengthwise. With a knife, cut seed lump from beneath the stem inside each chili, leaving stem end in place (to form a cup). Pull out and discard veins. Fill chili halves equally with cheese mixture, spreading surface smooth.

3. In a small bowl, whisk egg whites until slightly frothy. Put cornflake crumbs in another small bowl. Dip filled chili halves, 1 at a time, in egg whites, then roll in crumbs. Set chilies slightly apart on a 12- by 15-inch baking sheet, filling the sheet.

4. Bake in a 350° oven until crumbs are slightly darker brown and crisp, about 20 minutes. Serve hot or warm.

Per piece: 28 cal., 9.6% (2.7 cal.) from fat; 1.5 g protein; 0.3 g fat (0.2 g sat.); 4.8 g carbo (0.2 g fiber); 79 mg sodium; 1.2 mg chol.

Potato Cheese Chilies

PREP AND COOK TIME: About 1$\frac{3}{4}$ hours

NOTES: Barbara Schack of Medford, Oregon, stuffs chilies with seasoned mashed potatoes. You can mash fresh potatoes or use frozen or instant. To get maximum space for stuffing, select straight poblano chilies.

MAKES: 4 servings

2 cups **mashed potatoes,** hot or cold (see notes)

$\frac{1}{2}$ cup **fresh chèvre** (goat) **cheese**

$\frac{1}{2}$ cup crumbled **cotija** or feta **cheese**

1 can (4 oz.) **diced green chilies**

1 tablespoon chopped **green onion**

Salt

About 1 pound **fresh poblano chilies** (also called pasillas; 6 to 8, equal-size), rinsed

Bell pepper salsa (recipe follows) or 1 cup purchased red salsa

1. In a bowl, use a fork or mixer to blend potatoes, chèvre, $\frac{1}{4}$ cup cotija, canned chilies, onion, and salt to taste.

2. Wearing rubber gloves, cut poblanos in half lengthwise. With a knife, cut seed lump from beneath the stem inside each chili, leaving stem end in place (to form a cup). Pull out and discard veins. Fill chilies equally with potato mixture. Set chilies in an oiled 9- by 13-inch casserole, filling it. Cover tightly with foil.

3. Bake in a 350° oven for 30 minutes. Uncover, sprinkle with remaining ¼ cup cotija, and return to oven. Bake until stuffing is dotted with brown, 20 to 25 minutes longer.

4. Serve chilies with a wide spatula. Add salsa and salt to taste.

Per serving: 358 cal., 48% (171 cal.) from fat; 17 g protein; 19 g fat (10 g sat.); 33 g carbo (4.5 g fiber); 1,094 mg sodium; 38 mg chol.

Bell pepper salsa. In an 8- or 9-inch square pan, combine 1 cup coarsely chopped **firm-ripe tomatoes,** 1 cup coarsely chopped **red bell peppers,** 2 cloves chopped **garlic,** and 1 teaspoon **olive oil.** Cover tightly with foil.

Bake in a 350° oven until tomatoes mash easily, 50 to 60 minutes. Pour vegetable mixture into a blender or food processor. Add ½ cup **fresh cilantro,** ⅓ cup chopped **green onions,** 1½ teaspoons **balsamic vinegar,** and ¼ teaspoon **sugar.** Whirl until coarsely puréed. Add **salt** to taste. Makes 1 cup.

Per ¼ cup: 33 cal., 36% (12 cal.) from fat; 0.9 g protein; 1.3 g fat (0.2 g sat.); 5.1 g carbo (1.3 g fiber); 6.8 mg sodium; 0 mg chol.

Chicken and Cheese Chilies

PREP AND COOK TIME: About 1½ hours

NOTES: Steve Tomasek of Castle Rock, Colorado, fills poblanos with shredded chicken, cheese, and vegetables.

MAKES: 5 or 6 servings

2　**boned, skinned chicken breast halves** (¾ lb. total), each cut into quarters

½　cup chopped **onion**

¼　cup chopped **tomato**

1　tablespoon **olive oil**

2　teaspoons minced **garlic**

½　teaspoon **ground cumin**

¼　cup chopped **red bell pepper**

1　can (4 oz.) **diced green chilies**

1¼　cups (5 oz.) shredded **jack cheese with chilies**

　　About 1 pound **fresh poblano chilies** (also called pasillas; 6 to 8, equal-size), rinsed

　　Crème fraîche or sour cream

　　Salt

1. Rinse chicken and pat dry. In a 10- to 12-inch nonstick frying pan over medium heat, combine chicken, onion, tomato, oil, garlic, and cumin. Stir often until chicken is slightly pink in center of thickest part (cut to test), 6 to 10 minutes.

2. Let stand until chicken is cool enough to touch, then tear meat into shreds. Return to pan. Add bell pepper, canned chilies, and cheese; mix.

3. Wearing rubber gloves, cut poblanos in half lengthwise. With a knife, cut seed lump from beneath the stem inside each chili, leaving stem end in place (to form a cup). Pull out and discard veins.

4. Mound chicken mixture equally in

chili halves. Set chilies in an oiled 9- by 13-inch casserole, filling it. Cover tightly with foil.

5. Bake in a 375° oven until the poblanos are tender when pierced, about 35 minutes.

6. Serve chilies with a spatula. Add crème fraîche and salt to taste.

Per serving: 211 cal., 47% (99 cal.) from fat; 21 g protein; 11 g fat (4.7 g sat.); 9.4 g carbo (1.4 g fiber); 316 mg sodium; 58 mg chol.

Beef and Jack Chiles Rellenos

PREP AND COOK TIME: About 50 minutes

NOTES: James Hayes of Ridgecrest, California, suggests any tender cut of grilled or roasted beef for this casserole. Garnish with chopped tomatoes and cilantro.

MAKES: 5 or 6 servings

2　cans (7 oz. each) **whole green chilies**

½　pound **thin-sliced jack cheese**

¼　pound fat-trimmed **cooked roast beef,** cut into 1/16- to ⅛-inch-thick slices

6　**large eggs**

1　cup **low-fat milk**

¼　cup **all-purpose flour**

2　cloves **garlic,** peeled

　　About ½ teaspoon **salt**

⅓　cup **shredded jack cheese**

　　Purchased avocado and chili salsa

1. Count chilies and divide sliced cheese and beef into as many portions. Roll each portion of cheese around a portion of beef and stuff into a chili. Lay chilies side by side in an oiled shallow 9- by 13-inch casserole.

2. In a blender, whirl eggs, milk, flour, garlic, and ½ teaspoon salt to blend. Pour over chilies.

3. Bake in a 350° oven for 25 minutes. Sprinkle with shredded jack cheese and continue to bake until egg mixture no longer jiggles around chilies when casserole is gently shaken, about 2 minutes more.

4. Scoop onto plates and add salsa and salt to taste.

Per serving: 328 cal., 55% (180 cal.) from fat; 25 g protein; 20 g fat (10 g sat.); 11 g carbo (0.9 g fiber); 929 mg sodium; 276 mg chol. ◆

CRUSTY JALAPEÑO BITES are baked, not fried.

SEASON EACH BOWL of Indonesian chicken soup to taste with crisp raw vegetables, shrimp chips, a squeeze of lime, fried shallots, and chili paste.

JAMES CARRIER

Chicken soup for a party

Crunch and Asian flavors come from imaginative additions

BY LINDA LAU ANUSASANANAN

Indonesia's chicken soup is tailor-made to taste, with a freewheeling style that's uniquely hospitable—and distinctive. Guests select the fillings for their own bowls, from an expansive array of readily available and quickly assembled ingredients: shredded chicken, transparent noodles, tender rice, crisp bean sprouts, fiery chilies, crunchy cabbage, even potato chips. Then hot broth (*soto*) is ladled over all, warming the room-temperature fillings, which in turn fill the aromatic liquid with contrasting flavors and textures.

Here we offer two delicious versions of the chicken soup—the classic soto ayam is light and refreshing, and soto resah is spicier and creamier.

Each soup is truly a meal in a bowl.

And the array of condiments gathered on a tray are party decorations in themselves. To complete an easily organized menu, start with vegetables to dip in a purchased peanut sauce and serve tropical fruit for dessert. Iced tea, fruit juice, or beer go down well with either soup.

Soto Ayam

PREP AND COOK TIME: About 1¾ hours
NOTES: This version of the classic Indonesian chicken soup comes from the Hyatt Regency in Yogyakarta, Indonesia. Up to 2 days ahead, cook, cover, and chill chicken in seasoned broth.
MAKES: 6 to 8 servings

⅓ cup peeled **garlic** cloves

1 cup sliced **shallots**

¼ cup **salted, roasted macadamia nuts** or blanched almonds

6 thin slices (the size of a quarter) **fresh galangal** or fresh ginger

1 teaspoon **ground turmeric**

1 tablespoon **salad oil**

2½ quarts fat-skimmed **chicken broth**

1 stalk (12 to 15 in.) **fresh lemon grass** or 3 strips (½ by 4 in.) lemon peel, yellow part only

1½ pounds **boned, skinned chicken breasts,** rinsed

4 to 6 ounces **dried bean thread noodles** (*saifun*)

Salt and **pepper**

3 cups finely shredded **cabbage**

3 cups **bean sprouts,** rinsed and drained

1 cup thinly sliced **green onions,** including tops

1 cup diced **Roma tomatoes**

1 cup chopped **fresh cilantro**

4 hard-cooked **large eggs,** shelled and cut into wedges

2 cups **potato chips** or shrimp chips (optional)

½ cup **fried shallots** (recipe follows)

Lime wedges

Chili sambal, Asian red chili paste, or minced fresh hot chilies

1. In a food processor, combine garlic, sliced shallots, macadamia nuts, galangal, and turmeric. Whirl mixture to a paste, scraping container sides as needed. (Or chop ingredients with a knife, then whirl in a blender to a paste.)

2. In a 5- to 6-quart pan over high heat, stir the paste and the oil until mixture barely begins to brown, about 3 minutes. Stir in broth, cover, and bring to a boil.

3. Meanwhile, trim stem end and any tough leaves off lemon grass and pull off coarse outer layer. Crush stalk with the back of a knife, then cut into 3-inch pieces. Add to broth.

4. Add chicken breasts to broth. Cover, bring to a boil, then reduce heat to low and simmer until the breasts are no longer pink in center of thickest part (cut to test), 15 to 20 minutes. Lift out chicken and let cool at least 10 minutes. Skim fat from broth. (Or if making ahead, cover and chill the broth and the chicken separately. Lift off and discard fat from the chilled broth.)

5. In a bowl, pour 5 cups hot water over bean thread noodles. Let stand until the noodles are tender to bite, about 5 minutes; drain. If desired, snip through noodles with scissors to make shorter strands.

6. Season broth with salt and pepper to taste. Return to a boil over high heat.

7. Tear the chicken into shreds. In individual small bowls, mound shredded chicken, bean thread noodles, cabbage, bean sprouts, green onions, tomatoes, cilantro, egg wedges, potato chips, fried shallots (recipe far right), lime wedges, and chili sambal. Pour hot broth into a tureen or pitcher.

8. Let guests place desired portions of the chicken, noodles, cabbage, bean sprouts, green onions, tomatoes, cilantro, and eggs in wide bowls. Ladle or pour hot broth into bowls. Sprinkle with potato chips and fried shallots. Add juice from lime wedges, chili sambal, and more salt and pepper to taste.

Per serving: 385 cal., 33% (126 cal.) from fat; 37 g protein; 14 g fat (2.4 g sat.); 28 g carbo (2.5 g fiber); 218 mg sodium; 156 mg chol.

Soto Resah

PREP AND COOK TIME: About 1¾ hours

NOTES: Kasih, owner and chef of Lotus River Rafting and Guest House in Borobudur, Jawa Tengah, Indonesia, is famous for her spicy coconut milk soup. She offers fried chicken and potato patties; we've simplified with poached chicken and potato chips.

MAKES: 6 to 8 servings

Follow recipe for Soto Ayam (preceding), but in step 1, add 1 teaspoon *each* **ground cumin** and **ground coriander** and ¼ teaspoon *each* **white pepper** and **ground nutmeg**. Also, reduce chicken broth to 1½ quarts and add 2 cans (14 oz. each) **coconut milk.** Instead of bean thread noodles, use 4 to 6 cups **hot cooked rice.**

Per serving: 598 cal., 53% (315 cal.) from fat; 35 g protein; 35 g fat (21 g sat.); 38 g carbo (1.5 g fiber); 186 mg sodium; 156 mg chol.

Fried Shallots

PREP AND COOK TIME: About 12 minutes

NOTES: If making up to 1 day ahead, cover and chill.

MAKES: ½ cup

In an 8- to 10-inch frying pan over medium-high heat, stir 1 cup thinly sliced **shallots** in 3 tablespoons **salad oil** until golden and crisp, 7 to 9 minutes. Drain on paper towels. Use warm or at room temperature.

Per tablespoon: 60 cal., 77% (46 cal.) from fat; 0.5 g protein; 5.1 g fat (0.6 g sat.); 3.4 g carbo (0.2 g fiber); 2.4 mg sodium; 0 mg chol. ◆

Bake and take treat

Easy-to-make energy bars for hikers

BY LINDA LAU ANUSASANANAN

Packed with nuts, dried fruit, and rolled oats, these nutritious bars provide a high-energy snack for hikers. Wrap individual bars airtight, and pack a supply in knapsacks for on-the-trail snacks.

Honey Toasted Oat and Fruit Bars

PREP AND COOK TIME: About 1 hour

NOTES: Store airtight for up to a week. Wrap bars individually.

MAKES: 15 bars

- 3½ cups **rolled oats**
- ½ cup **sesame seed**
- ½ cup chopped **almonds**
- About ¾ cup (⅜ lb.) **butter** or margarine
- ½ cup *each* **honey** and firmly packed **brown sugar**
- ½ teaspoon **ground nutmeg**
- ½ cup chopped **dried apricots**
- ½ cup **golden raisins**
- ½ cup **sweetened flaked dried coconut**

1. Combine oats, sesame seed, and almonds in a 10- by 15-inch rimmed pan. Bake in a 350° oven, stirring occasionally, until nuts begin to brown, about 20 minutes (about 15 minutes in a 325° convection oven).

2. In a 4- to 5-quart pan over low heat, melt ¾ cup butter. Remove from heat and add honey, brown sugar, and nut-

meg; stir until blended. Stir in oat mixture, apricots, raisins, and coconut.

3. Butter and flour the 10- by 15-inch pan. Scrape oat mixture into pan; press firmly into an even layer.

4. Bake in a 350° oven until evenly browned and bubbly in center, 20 to 25 minutes (10 to 15 minutes in a 325° convection oven).

5. Cool on a rack 20 minutes. Cut into 2- by 5-inch bars. When cool, lift from pan with wide spatula.

Per bar: 307 cal., 47% (144 cal.) from fat; 5.2 g protein; 16 g fat (7.3 g sat.); 39 g carbo (3.7 g fiber); 146 mg sodium; 25 mg chol. ◆

The Low-Fat Cook

HEALTHY CHOICES FOR THE ACTIVE LIFESTYLE

BY CHRISTINE WEBER HALE

RICHARD JUNG

LINGUINE TANGLES tastefully with shrimp and dried tomatoes in a one-pan main dish.

Pour and cook

■ Sweet, tender shrimp are naturally lean, which makes them ideal for low-fat cooking. They also can be exceptionally convenient if you buy them by the bag—shelled, deveined, and individually frozen so each shrimp is separate. Just pour the shrimp from the container right into flavorful sauces to make quick, elegant main dishes. Seal remaining shrimp in the bag and return to the freezer. Shrimp come in many sizes; those that are 38 to 50 per pound work best in these one-pan entrées. More shrimp per pound means they are smaller and will cook a little faster.

Shrimp with Dried Tomatoes and Linguine

PREP AND COOK TIME: About 25 minutes
MAKES: 4 servings

- 2 teaspoons **olive oil**
- 1 clove **garlic**, minced
- 2 tablespoons **lemon juice**
- ⅓ cup **dry white wine**
- 2 cups fat-skimmed **chicken broth**
- ½ cup (¾ oz.) **dried tomato slices**
- 9 ounces **fresh linguine**
- 1 pound (38 to 50 per lb.) **frozen uncooked shelled, deveined shrimp**
- 3 **green onions,** ends trimmed, thinly sliced

1. In a 5- to 6-quart pan over medium-high heat, stir olive oil and garlic until garlic is limp but not browned, 2 to 3 minutes. Add lemon juice, wine, broth, and tomatoes.

2. Turn heat to high and stir often until sauce boils, about 2 minutes. Add pasta, return to a boil, then add shrimp. Stir often until pasta is tender to bite and shrimp are opaque but moist-looking in center of thickest part (cut to test), 5 to 8 minutes. Ladle into wide bowls and sprinkle with onions.

Per serving: 377 cal., 14% (51 cal.) from fat; 36 g protein; 5.7 g fat (0.9 g sat.); 41 g carbo (2.7 g fiber); 232 mg sodium; 219 mg chol.

Shrimp Provençal

PREP AND COOK TIME: About 25 minutes
NOTES: Serve toasted slices of crusty bread to dunk into sauce.
MAKES: 4 servings

- ½ teaspoon shredded **lemon** peel
- 1 teaspoon shredded **orange** peel
- ½ cup **orange juice**
- ½ teaspoon **hot chili flakes**
- 1 jar (25 oz.) **marinara sauce**
- 1 pound (38 to 50 per lb.) **frozen uncooked shelled, deveined shrimp**
- 2 tablespoons chopped **fresh basil leaves**

1. In a 12-inch frying pan or 5- to 6-quart pan over high heat, combine lemon peel, orange peel, orange juice, chili flakes, and marinara sauce. Stir often until boiling.

2. Add shrimp and stir often until shrimp are opaque but moist-looking in the center of the thickest part (cut to test), 5 to 8 minutes. Add basil and ladle into wide bowls.

Per serving: 257 cal., 28% (72 cal.) from fat; 26 g protein; 8 g fat (1.2 g sat.); 23 g carbo (3 g fiber); 1,283 mg sodium; 173 mg chol.

Lemon-Basil Shrimp with Rice

PREP AND COOK TIME: About 25 minutes
NOTES: Start rice, then cook shrimp.
MAKES: 4 servings

- ½ teaspoon **hot chili flakes**
- 1½ teaspoons shredded **lemon** peel
- 2 tablespoons **lemon juice**
- 3 cups fat-skimmed **chicken broth**
- 1 pound (38 to 50 per lb.) **frozen uncooked shelled, deveined shrimp**
- 3 tablespoons **cornstarch** mixed with 3 tablespoons water
- 2 tablespoons chopped **fresh basil leaves**
- 3 cups hot, **cooked white rice**

1. In a 12-inch frying pan or 5- to 6-quart pan over high heat, combine chili flakes, lemon peel, lemon juice, and broth.

2. When broth mixture boils, add shrimp and stir often until shrimp are opaque but moist-looking in the center of the thickest part (cut to test), 5 to 8 minutes. Stir cornstarch mixture into pan; stir until boiling again. Add basil.

3. Mound rice equally into wide bowls. Ladle shrimp mixture around rice.

Per serving: 326 cal., 6.4% (21 cal.) from fat; 32 g protein; 2.3 g fat (0.5 g sat.); 41 g carbo (0.6 g fiber); 228 mg sodium; 173 mg chol.

Shrimp with Black Bean Sauce

PREP AND COOK TIME: About 25 minutes

MAKES: 4 servings

2 teaspoons **olive oil**

1 clove **garlic,** minced

2 tablespoons **prepared Asian black bean sauce**

2 tablespoons **lemon juice**

⅓ cup **dry white wine**

2 cups fat-skimmed **chicken broth**

9 ounces **fresh linguine**

1 pound (38 to 50 per lb.) **frozen uncooked shelled, deveined shrimp**

⅓ cup **fresh cilantro** leaves

1. In a 5- to 6-quart pan over medium-high heat, stir olive oil and garlic until garlic is limp but not browned, 2 to 3 minutes. Add black bean sauce, lemon juice, wine, and broth.

2. Turn heat to high and stir often until sauce boils, about 2 minutes. Add pasta, return to a boil, then add shrimp. Stir often until pasta is tender to bite and shrimp are opaque but moist-looking in center of thickest part (cut to test), 5 to 8 minutes. Ladle into wide bowls and sprinkle with cilantro.

Per serving: 370 cal., 15% (56 cal.) from fat; 35 g protein; 6.2 g fat (0.9 g sat.); 38 g carbo (1.8 g fiber); 860 mg sodium; 219 mg chol. ◆

BUCKET BRIGADE: Young visitors to Bright Ranch enjoy a 30-year-old ritual.

Ripe for the picking

Enjoy the season's sweet and sour cherries at Leona Valley's U-pick orchards

BY NORMAN KOLPAS

For a few weeks in late spring and early summer, families gather at more than two dozen small U-pick cherry orchards that dot Leona Valley, a tiny enclave secluded in the western foothills of vast Antelope Valley. Harvest usually extends from early June through mid-July, with sweet varieties followed by sour cherries (best for pies and preserves). For cherry growers' recorded updates, call (805) 266-7116.

"There's nothing like the experience of picking fruit fresh off the tree," offers Ron Bright, whose 20-acre ranch makes him one of the area's largest growers.

To get to Leona Valley, take Interstate 5 north from Los Angeles to State 14 east. Exit at Palmdale Blvd., turn left, and drive west approximately 10 miles (Palmdale Blvd. becomes Elizabeth Lake Rd.). Pick up a free orchards map at Rancher's Market, 9001 Elizabeth Lake Rd.; (805) 270-0615.

Orchards provide buckets or cans. Some growers also provide picnic areas, so consider taking lunch with you. ◆

Bright Ranch Cherry Pie

PREP AND COOK TIME: 1½ hours, plus 2 hours to cool

NOTES: You can use your favorite pastry recipe instead.

MAKES: 8 or 9 servings

About ¾ cup **sugar**

5 tablespoons **cornstarch**

7 cups **dark sweet cherries** (about 2¼ lb.), rinsed and pitted

½ teaspoon **almond extract**

¼ teaspoon **ground cinnamon**

1 package (15 oz.) **refrigerated pastry for double-crust 9-inch pie**

1. In a large bowl, mix ¾ cup sugar and cornstarch; add cherries, almond extract, and cinnamon; mix gently.

2. Ease 1 pastry round into a 9-inch pie pan. Scrape cherry mixture into pastry, mounding in the center.

3. With the tip of a sharp knife, cut the shape of a cherry (at least 1½ in. wide; plus a stem) in the center of remaining pastry. Center pastry over fruit. Press pastry edges together, then fold under at rim and pinch edge decoratively. Lightly brush pastry with water, then sprinkle with about 1 teaspoon sugar. Set pie pan in a larger, shallow rimmed pan lined with foil (to catch any drips).

4. Bake pie on pan in a 375° oven on the lowest rack until pastry is richly browned and filling bubbles in the center, 1 to 1¼ hours. Let cool at least 2 hours for filling to firm. Serve warm or at room temperature.

Per serving: 367 cal., 34% (126 cal.) from fat; 2.9 g protein; 14 g fat (5.5 g sat.); 59 g carbo (1.6 g fiber); 238 mg sodium; 12 mg chol.

— Jerry Anne Di Vecchio

Kitchen Cabinet

READERS' RECIPES TESTED IN SUNSET'S KITCHENS

BY LINDA LAU ANUSASANANAN

THIN WON TON NESTS hold a combination of cheese and crab.

Chili Crab in Won Ton Cups

Louise Ross, Elk Grove, California

Liking the look of desserts baked in crisp cups made from won ton skins, Louise Ross adapted the idea to a savory crab appetizer. If making up to 1 day ahead, let the crab cups cool out of pan on a rack, then cover and chill. To reheat, set slightly apart on a baking sheet and bake in a 375° oven until hot, 6 to 8 minutes.

PREP AND COOK TIME: About 45 minutes

MAKES: 16 appetizers

16 **won ton skins** (3¼ in. square)

About 2 tablespoons **olive oil**

⅓ cup minced **green onions,** including tops

1 can (4 oz.) **diced green chilies**

6 ounces **shelled cooked crab**

2 tablespoons **mustard-mayonnaise blend** (or 1 tablespoon *each* mayonnaise and Dijon mustard)

½ cup shredded **jack cheese with chilies**

1. Lightly brush 1 side of each won ton skin with oil. Center each square, oiled side down, on a muffin cup (1¼-in. across bottom). Gently press skin down to line cup smoothly; skin will extend above pan rim.

2. In a 6- to 8-inch frying pan over medium-high heat, stir ½ teaspoon oil and onions until onions are limp, about 1 minute. Remove from heat. Stir in chilies, crab, and mustard-mayonnaise.

3. Fill each won ton cup equally with crab mixture. Sprinkle filling evenly with cheese.

4. Bake in a 350° oven until rims of won ton skins are golden and crisp, 8 to 10 minutes (7 to 9 minutes in a convection oven). Lift from pan and serve hot.

Per serving: 70 cal., 46% (32 cal.) from fat; 3.9 g protein; 3.5 g fat (0.9 g sat.); 5.7 g carbo (0.3 g fiber); 169 mg sodium; 15 mg chol.

Lemon Wild Rice Salad

Camilla V. Saulsbury, Albany, California

For graduate student Camilla Saulsbury, potlucks are a way of life. When the creations of the cooks are compared, this fresh-tasting but easy grain salad keeps Saulsbury's ratings high.

PREP AND COOK TIME: About 45 minutes

MAKES: 6 to 8 servings

2 packages (about 6 oz. each) **long grain and wild rice pilaf mix**

1 jar (6 oz.) **marinated artichokes**

1 pound **firm-ripe tomatoes,** rinsed, cored, and coarsely chopped

1 **red bell pepper** (½ lb.), rinsed, stemmed, seeded, and coarsely chopped

½ cup chopped **parsley**

3 tablespoons drained **capers** (optional)

1½ teaspoons grated **lemon** peel

3 tablespoons **lemon juice**

2 teaspoons **sugar**

Salt and **pepper**

1. Cook rice until tender to bite, according to package directions, then pour into a large bowl.

2. Drain marinade from artichokes into bowl with rice. Chop artichokes and add to rice. Mix, then stir occasionally until rice is cool, 30 to 45 minutes.

3. Mix tomatoes, bell pepper, parsley, capers, lemon peel, lemon juice, and sugar with cool rice mixture. Season to taste with salt and pepper.

Per serving: 212 cal., 22% (46 cal.) from fat; 5.8 g protein; 5.1 g fat (2 g sat.); 39 g carbo (3.5 g fiber); 723 mg sodium; 7.8 mg chol.

Cinnamon Streusel Buttermilk Coffee Cake

Janet Hausmann, Beaverton, Oregon

This recipe was handed down to Janet Hausmann from her grandmother, Helen Whipple. It's now beloved by all generations. At mile-high altitude, increase flour to 2¼ cups and reduce baking powder to 1½ teaspoons; bake as directed, allowing about 55 minutes.

PREP AND COOK TIME: About 50 minutes, plus at least 20 minutes to cool

MAKES: 8 to 10 servings

1 cup firmly packed **brown sugar**

½ cup **granulated sugar**

2 cups **all-purpose flour**

LEIGH BEISCH (2)

½ teaspoon **ground nutmeg**

About ⅔ cup (⅓ lb.) melted **butter** or margarine

½ cup chopped **pecans** or almonds

1 teaspoon **ground cinnamon**

1 **large egg**, beaten to blend

1 cup **buttermilk**

2 teaspoons **baking powder**

1 teaspoon **baking soda**

1. In a large bowl, mix brown sugar, granulated sugar, flour, nutmeg, and ⅔ cup butter.

2. Transfer 1 packed cup of the sugar mixture to a small bowl. Add nuts and cinnamon, mixing well.

3. To the mixture in the large bowl, add egg, buttermilk, baking powder, and baking soda; mix well. Pour batter into a buttered 9-inch cheesecake pan with removable rim. Sprinkle cinnamon-nut mixture evenly over batter.

4. Bake in a 350° oven until toothpick inserted in center comes out clean and cake begins to pull from pan sides, about 40 minutes (about 35 minutes in convection oven).

5. Cool on a rack at least 20 minutes. Remove pan rim. Serve warm or cool.

Per serving: 378 cal., 41% (153 cal.) from fat; 4,5 g protein; 17 g fat (8.4 g sat.); 53 g carbo (1 g fiber); 393 mg sodium; 56 mg chol.

Pork Tenderloin with Rosemary Cream Sauce

Theresa M. Cross, Corrales, New Mexico

"This is the ultimate 'to die for' pork dish that will make your company think you went to cooking school in France!" writes Theresa Cross. It's fast, easy, and low-fat compared with her original version, which used whipping cream.

PREP AND COOK TIME: About 50 minutes

MAKES: 6 servings

1½ pounds **pork tenderloin,** fat-trimmed

1 tablespoon **olive oil** or butter

1 cup **dry vermouth** or dry white wine

1 teaspoon chopped **fresh rosemary** leaves or crumbled dried rosemary

½ teaspoon **fresh thyme** leaves or dried thyme

¼ teaspoon **pepper**

About ⅓ cup fat-skimmed **chicken broth** (optional)

½ cup **milk**

2 teaspoons **cornstarch**

Salt

1. Rinse meat and pat dry. If needed, cut tenderloin in half crosswise to fit a 10- to 12-inch frying pan.

2. Place empty frying pan over high heat. Add oil; when hot, add tenderloin and turn as needed to brown well on all sides, 5 to 8 minutes total.

3. Reduce heat to medium-low. Add vermouth, rosemary, thyme, and pepper. Cover and simmer, turning pork after 5 minutes, until a thermometer inserted in thickest part reaches 155°, 10 to 12 minutes total. Transfer pork to a platter and keep warm.

4. Measure pan juices. If less than ½ cup, add broth to make ½ cup. If more than ½ cup, boil on high heat, uncovered, until reduced to ½ cup.

5. Blend milk and cornstarch. Mix into pan and stir over high heat until boiling. Add salt to taste. Pour into a bowl.

6. Cut pork into diagonal slices and pour sauce around or over meat.

Per serving: 209 cal., 27% (57 cal.) from fat; 24 g protein; 6.3 g fat (1.8 g sat.); 2.2 g carbo (0 g fiber); 69 mg sodium; 75 mg chol.

Lemon Pudding Cake

Jeanette Hennings,
Lake Havasu City, Arizona

"This light and tangy lemon dessert satisfies my longing for lemon pie," says Jeanette Hennings. And it certainly weighs in with fewer calories and fat than a traditional lemon pie.

PREP AND COOK TIME: About 1 hour

MAKES: 4 servings

½ cup **sugar**

3 tablespoons **all-purpose flour** or baking mix

1 teaspoon grated **lemon** peel

3 tablespoons **lemon juice**

About 2 tablespoons melted **butter** or margarine

2 **large eggs,** separated

1 cup **milk**

⅛ teaspoon **cream of tartar**

Raspberries, rinsed and drained (optional)

1. In a bowl, mix sugar and flour. Add lemon peel, juice, and 2 tablespoons butter; mix well. In a small bowl, beat yolks to blend with milk and stir into lemon mixture.

2. In a deep bowl with a mixer on high speed, beat egg whites and cream of tartar until they hold stiff, moist peaks. Gently fold egg whites into lemon mixture.

3. Butter a 4- to 5-cup straight-sided shallow baking dish or soufflé dish and set dish in a slightly larger baking pan. Pour lemon mixture into dish and set pan with dish on oven rack. Fill outer pan with boiling water to the depth of 1 inch.

4. Bake in a 350° oven until pudding top springs back when lightly touched, 35 to 40 minutes. Lift dish from water.

5. Serve dessert warm, scooping down to bottom of the dish to include pudding that forms beneath cake. Serve with berries.

Per serving: 243 cal., 37% (89 cal.) from fat; 5.8 g protein; 9.9 g fat (5.3 g sat.); 34 g carbo (0.2 g fiber); 133 mg sodium; 127 mg chol. ◆

TENDER CAKE is topped with nut and spice streusel.

Create the romance of tropical Bali with an island barbecue (see page 122); dessert is black rice pudding (recipe on page 129).

June

Island
sizzle

Bring the romance of Bali home.
Spicy aromas from the barbecue
and luscious fruits and flowers
evoke the spirit of the
Island of the Gods

BY LINDA LAU ANUSASANANAN

PHOTOGRAPHS BY JUST LOOMIS

FOOD STYLING BY DAN BECKER

■ NATIVES AND VISITORS ALIKE CALL BALI the Island of
the Gods. The reason: it's obviously blessed. Scenes
of celestial beauty surround you there—riotous tropical foliage punctuated by vivid blossoms; wide, sandy
beaches; velvety green hillsides stair-stepped with rice
fields. The warm, wet climate and fertile volcanic soil
yield an abundance of life-sustaining rice, bewitching
fruits, vibrant vegetables, and fragrant spices. • Some
of Bali's charms transport beautifully. And they are the
inspiration for this lush, tropical setting, which you
can create in your own garden, and this menu for 10
to 12. The heart of the party is the street food of
Southeast Asia: *satay* (*saté* in Bali)—marinated meats,
poultry, and seafood skewered on thin sticks and
grilled—as common in that part of the world as Big
Macs are here. A spicy peanut dipping sauce makes the
grilled morsels addictive. The recipes are from chef
Lother Arsana at the Grand Hyatt Bali. Our shopping
guide to ingredients (page 126) will take you on a culinary adventure.

party

DELECTABLE SATAY SKEWERS from the grill and coconut-scented rice anchor a South Seas meal for a warm summer evening. Simple, colorful decorations create an island paradise in your own backyard.

Chili in Soy Sauce
(TABIA LALAH MANI)

Tomato Sambal
(SAMBEL TOMAT)

Spicy Peanut Sauce
(BUMBU KACANG)

tastes

Fruit Salad with Palm Sugar Syrup
(RUJAK)

Beef Satay
(SATÉ SAMPI)

Yellow Rice
(NASI KUNING)

Vegetables for Satay
(LALAB)

Minced Chicken Satay
(SATÉ LILIT)

Shrimp Satay
(SATÉ UDANG)

balinese satay party for 10 to 12

For a simpler meal, make only one kind of satay (triple the recipe) and the peanut sauce. Serve with vegetables, white rice, and plain fruit salad for dessert.

Shrimp Chips

PREP AND COOK TIME: About 25 minutes

NOTES: Fried in oil, *krupuk* puff into crisp, featherweight, bubble-filled chips. The chips can be fried up to 1 day ahead; store airtight.

MAKES: 10 to 12 servings

1. Measure 3 to 4 ounces **uncooked shrimp-flavor crackers** (krupuk; about 1½ cups 2-in.-wide rounds, or 12 rectangular pieces 4½ by 1½ in.).

2. In a wok (at least 14 in.) or 5- to 6-quart pan, pour **salad oil** to a depth of about 1½ inches. Set pan over high heat and bring oil to 350° on a thermometer. Adjust heat to maintain oil temperature.

3. Drop 3 to 5 rounds or 1 rectangular cracker into oil and, with a slotted spoon, turn to cook other sides; they puff almost immediately. At once, lift from oil and drain in paper towel–lined pans. Repeat step to cook remaining krupuk.

Per serving: 56 cal., 57% (32 cal.) from fat; 0.3 g protein; 3.5 g fat (0.5 g sat.); 5.8 g carbo (0.1 g fiber); 48 mg sodium; 1.4 mg chol.

Fruit Salad with Palm Sugar Syrup

PREP AND COOK TIME: About 50 minutes

NOTES: Make the spicy syrup for salad up to 3 days ahead; cover and chill. Wear kitchen gloves when handling fresh hot chilies.

MAKES: 10 to 12 servings

- ½ teaspoon **anchovy paste**
- 1½ cups (10 oz.) chopped **palm sugar** or firmly packed brown sugar
- ¼ cup **liquid tamarind concentrate** or lemon juice
- 1 to 2 tablespoons thinly sliced **fresh Thai** or serrano **chilies**
- ¼ teaspoon **salt**
- 6 to 8 cups bite-size pieces mixed **fresh fruit** (pineapple, mango, honeydew, seedless watermelon, star fruit, grapefruit or orange segments, unripe or ripe papaya, green apple)

1. In a 1½- to 2-quart pan over medium heat, stir anchovy paste until warm, about 30 seconds.

2. Add 1 cup water, palm sugar, tamarind concentrate, chilies, and salt. Bring to a boil over high heat. Reduce heat to medium and cook, stirring occasionally, until mixture is reduced to 1 cup, about 20 minutes.

3. Pour through a strainer into a bowl; discard residue. Cover and chill syrup until cool, about 30 minutes.

4. Up to 30 minutes before serving, mix syrup with fruit.

Per serving: 121 cal., 1.5% (1.8 cal.) from fat; 0.4 g protein; 0.2 g fat (0 g sat.); 31 g carbo (0.8 g fiber); 71 mg sodium; 0.1 mg chol.

Beef Satay

PREP AND COOK TIME: About 40 minutes

NOTES: Instead of making spice paste, you can use ¼ cup purchased Thai red curry paste mixed with 2 tablespoons salad oil; stir in a 6- to 8-inch frying pan over medium heat until fragrant, about 5 minutes, then add sugar. You will need about 12 thin wood or metal skewers. If using wood, soak in water at least 30 minutes just before using. Up to 1 day ahead, coat meat with spice mixture and thread onto skewers; wrap airtight and chill.

MAKES: 10 to 12 servings

- 1½ pounds **boned beef top sirloin**, fat-trimmed
- ¼ cup **spice paste** (recipe follows)
- 2 tablespoons chopped **palm sugar** or firmly packed brown sugar

1. Cut meat into ¾-inch chunks.

2. Mix spice paste and sugar. Coat meat with mixture.

3. Thread meat equally onto skewers.

4. Lay skewers on a lightly oiled grill over hot coals or high heat on a gas grill (you can hold your hand at grill level only 2 to 3 seconds) and cook, turning to brown on all sides, 6 to 8 minutes. Serve hot or at room temperature.

Per serving: 106 cal., 33% (35 cal.) from fat; 13 g protein; 3.9 g fat (1.3 g sat.); 3.9 g carbo (0.1 g fiber); 32 mg sodium; 38 mg chol.

Spice paste. Trim and discard tough top and root end of 1 stalk (12 in.)

PARTY DECOR

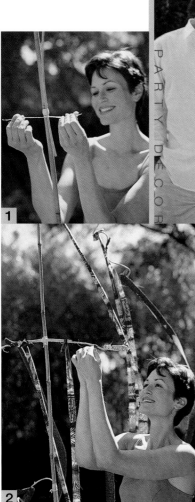

BALINESE STREAMERS: Use raffia to attach two or three bamboo whirligigs—parallel or at right angles—to upper half of 10- to 12-foot bamboo poles (1). Tie several 1-inch by 3-foot strips of fabric to each whirligig (2). Hang amid foliage (3). Design by Françoise Kirkman.

Per tablespoon: 42 cal., 52% (22 cal.) from fat; 0.8 g protein; 2.4 g fat (0.3 g sat.); 5 g carbo (0.3 g fiber); 7.3 mg sodium; 0 mg chol.

Minced Chicken Satay

PREP AND COOK TIME: About 30 minutes
NOTES: Instead of spice paste, you can use ¼ cup purchased Thai red curry paste mixed with 2 tablespoons water. And instead of fresh lemon grass stalks, you can mold chicken around 20 to 24 thin wood or metal skewers; if using wood, soak in water at least 30 minutes just before using. Up to 1 day ahead, shape satay, wrap airtight, and chill.
MAKES: 10 to 12 servings

- ¾ cup **dried sweetened flaked coconut**
- 1 to 1½ teaspoons sliced **fresh Thai** or serrano **chilies**
- ½ cup **spice paste** (recipe precedes)
- 1 teaspoon **salt**
- ½ teaspoon **pepper**
- 1¼ pounds **ground chicken** or turkey
- 10 to 12 stalks (about 12 in.) **fresh lemon grass**

fresh lemon grass. Remove and discard tough outer layers. Thinly slice tender inner part, then whirl in a food processor until finely chopped. Add 2 cups sliced **shallots**, 3 tablespoons sliced **garlic**, ½ cup sliced **fresh red** or green **jalapeños**, 3 tablespoons sliced peeled **fresh galangal** (optional), 2 tablespoons thinly sliced peeled **fresh ginger**, 1½ teaspoons **coriander seed**, 1 teaspoon **ground dried turmeric**, and 6 **salted roasted macadamia nuts**; whirl until finely ground. Put spice paste and 2 tablespoons **salad oil** in an 8- to 10-inch frying pan over high heat. Stir until paste is slightly darker and drier, 6 to 8 minutes. Use hot or cool. If making up to 3 days ahead, cover and chill; freeze to store longer.

MAKES: About 1 cup

shopping guide

You can buy most of these ingredients—and their readily available substitutes—in a good supermarket. But for a culinary adventure, explore Asian, Indian, and Mexican food markets.

Galangal *(isen):* Fresh root, also known as *laos* or *galingale*. Resembles fresh ginger but has a thinner, translucent skin and more astringent flavor.

Lemon grass *(sereh):* Thick, rough, pale green stalks with a citrus scent and flavor.

Liquid tamarind concentrate: Tart brown fruit purée sold ready to use in Indian supermarkets (do not substitute the almost black, pastelike concentrate). You can make your own from tamarind pulp. Soak about ¼ cup pulp in ½ cup hot water until pulp is soft, 3 to 4 minutes. With your hand, squeeze pulp off seeds, then rub mixture through a fine strainer into a bowl. Makes about ¼ cup. Measure amount needed and chill or freeze remainder for other uses.

Palm sugar *(gula bali):* Ivory- to light-caramel-colored cakes of sugar with flavor extracted from coconut flower or palm; similar to brown sugar.

Shrimp-flavor crackers *(krupuk):* Dried crackers typically made from shrimp and various flours, such as tapioca. Ready-to-eat chips are sometimes sold alongside snack foods like potato chips. But for freshest flavor, fry uncooked crackers or chips. The Indonesian versions are large cream-colored rectangles or small wafers with a strong shrimp flavor. Milder-flavored Chinese chips are thin, translucent, white or pastel wafers.

Sweet rice *(nasi ketan):* Glutinous rice that cooks up sticky and sweet. The unhulled rice is black and turns purplish black when cooked. The hulled rice is white.

Sweet soy sauce *(kecap manis):* Sweetened, slightly thick soy sauce.

Thai chilies *(hang prik):* Fresh, explosive chilies 3 to 4 inches long, ½ to ¾ inch wide.

Thai red curry paste: Ready-to-use paste made from chilies, lemon grass, garlic, and spices. Tends to be very hot.

1. In a food processor, whirl coconut, chilies, and 2 tablespoons hot water until finely ground.

2. Add spice paste, salt, pepper, and chicken; whirl until well mixed.

3. Trim root ends from lemon grass. Trim tops to make stalks 6 to 8 inches long. Remove coarse outer leaves.

4. Dipping hands in cool water often to reduce sticking, mound about ¼ cup chicken mixture around thick end of each lemon grass stalk (or 2 tablespoons on one end of each soaked wood skewer). Gently squeeze chicken mixture around each stalk (or skewer) into a 4-inch log. Place chicken sticks in a single layer in a flat pan.

5. Lay chicken satay on a lightly oiled grill over hot coals or high heat on a gas grill (you can hold your hand at grill level only 2 to 3 seconds). Cook, turning as needed to brown evenly, 5 to 6 minutes. Serve hot or at room temperature.

Per serving: 123 cal., 54% (66 cal.) from fat; 9 g protein; 7.3 g fat (2.6 g sat.); 5.5 g carbo (0.5 g fiber); 249 mg sodium; 39 mg chol.

Shrimp Satay

PREP AND COOK TIME: About 20 minutes

NOTES: Instead of spice paste, you can use ¼ cup prepared Thai red curry paste. You will need about 24 thin wood or metal skewers; if using wood skewers, soak them in water at least 30 minutes just before using. Up to 1 day ahead, coat shrimp with spice mixture and thread onto skewers; wrap airtight and chill.

MAKES: 10 to 12 servings

¼ cup **spice paste** (recipe, page 125)

2 tablespoons **tomato paste**

2 tablespoons **lemon juice**

1½ pounds (21 to 25 per lb.) **frozen shelled, deveined shrimp,** thawed, rinsed, and drained

1. Mix spice paste, tomato paste, and lemon juice. Coat shrimp with mixture.

2. Lay 2 or 3 shrimp flat, parallel to each other, and run 2 skewers about 1 inch apart through center of shrimp (see photo, page 124). Repeat to skewer remaining shrimp.

3. Lay shrimp on a lightly oiled grill over hot coals or high heat on a gas grill (you can hold your hand at grill level only 2 to 3 seconds). Cook, turning occasionally, until shrimp are opaque but moist-looking in center of thickest part (cut to

test), 5 to 6 minutes. Serve hot or at room temperature.

Per serving: 77 cal., 21% (16 cal.) from fat; 12 g protein; 1.8 g fat (0.3 g sat.); 2.8 g carbo (0.2 g fiber); 109 mg sodium; 86 mg chol.

Yellow Rice

PREP AND COOK TIME: About 30 minutes

MAKES: About 4 quarts; 10 to 12 servings

3 stalks (about 12 in.) **fresh lemon grass** or 3 strips lemon peel (yellow part only; ½ by 4 in.)

12 thin slices (the size of a quarter) peeled **fresh galangal** or ginger

4 **dried bay leaves**

2 teaspoons **ground dried turmeric**

3 cans (14 oz. each) **reduced-fat** or regular **coconut milk**

4 cups fat-skimmed **chicken broth**

5½ cups **jasmine** or long-grain white **rice**

1 teaspoon **salt**

1. Trim and discard tough tops and root ends of lemon grass stalks. Remove and discard tough outer leaves. With the flat side of a knife, gently crush lemon grass

and galangal. Wrap lemon grass, galangal, and bay leaves in a piece of cheesecloth.

2. In a 5- to 6-quart pan, mix turmeric with ¼ cup water. Stir in coconut milk, broth, rice, salt, and lemon grass bundle. Bring to a boil, uncovered, over high heat; lower heat to medium and simmer, stirring occasionally, until most of the liquid is absorbed, 10 to 15 minutes. Cover pan and cook over low heat, stirring occasionally, until rice is tender to bite, 10 to 15 minutes more. Remove and discard lemon grass bundle.

3. Pour rice in a mound on a platter. Or, if desired, shape rice by spooning into a large cone-shaped basket or mold and inverting onto platter.

Per serving: 350 cal., 14% (48 cal.) from fat; 9.5 g protein; 5.3 g fat (3.3 g sat.); 67 g carbo (0 g fiber); 246 mg sodium; 0 mg chol.

Vegetables for Satay

PREP AND COOK TIME: About 45 minutes

NOTES: Up to 1 day ahead, arrange vegetables (except tomato) on platter, cover airtight, and chill. Season to taste with peanut sauce (recipe follows, or

LEMON GRASS VASES: Start with straight-sided narrow vases. Trim stalks of fresh lemon grass so they are slightly taller than vases. Separate stalk layers (1). Position one lemon grass stalk against vase and secure with a rubber band. Slip more stalks under band to cover vase (2). Wrap raffia around rubber band to camouflage (3). Design by Ann Bertelsen.

island**sizzle**

the game plan

C O U N T D O W N

☐ **Up to 3 days ahead:**
Make syrup for fruit salad, spice paste for satay, and tomato sambal.

☐ **Up to 2 days ahead:**
Make peanut sauce.

☐ **Up to 1 day ahead:**
Fry shrimp chips. Season and skewer beef, chicken, and shrimp satay. *Prepare* vegetables for satay (except tomato). *Make* chili in soy sauce.

☐ **1½ hours ahead:**
Prepare fruit for fruit salad.

☐ **1 hour ahead:**
Cook rice pudding.

☐ **40 minutes ahead:**
Ignite briquets if using a charcoal barbecue. *Reheat* peanut sauce if desired.

☐ **30 minutes ahead:**
Cook yellow rice. *Mix* fruit salad with syrup and chill. *Add* tomato to vegetable platter.

☐ **20 minutes ahead:**
Heat barbecue if using a gas grill. *Pour* sauces and sambal into bowls.

☐ **10 minutes ahead:**
Grill satay.

☐ **Just before serving:**
Arrange yellow rice and satay on platters. *Set out* the shrimp chips and fruit salad.

☐ **Before dessert:**
Warm rice pudding; top with coconut milk, fruit, and ice cream.

use a purchased peanut sauce) and serve with grilled foods.

MAKES: 10 to 12 servings

- ¾ pound **Chinese long beans** or regular beans, rinsed
- 2½ cups matchstick-size strips **carrots**
- 2½ cups matchstick-size strips **cucumbers**
- ½ pound **bean sprouts,** rinsed and drained
- 3 to 4 cups finely shredded **cabbage**
- 1 **firm-ripe tomato** (10 oz.), rinsed, cored, and cut into thin wedges

1. In a 5- to 6-quart pan over high heat, bring about 2½ quarts water to a boil. Trim ends off beans; cut beans into 3-inch lengths. Add beans to boiling water and cook until they are bright green and just tender to bite, 2 to 3 minutes. Drain and immerse in ice water until cool, about 2 minutes. Drain again.

2. Mound beans, carrots, cucumbers, sprouts, cabbage, and tomato on a platter.

Per serving: 36 cal., 5% (1.8 cal.) from fat; 1.8 g protein; 0.2 g fat (0 g sat.); 8 g carbo (2.3 g fiber); 16 mg sodium; 0 mg chol.

Spicy Peanut Sauce

PREP AND COOK TIME: About 35 minutes

NOTES: Serve as a dipping sauce for beef, chicken, and shrimp satay and to spoon onto vegetables for satay. If making sauce up to 2 days ahead,

cover and chill; reheat in a microwave oven or stir over low heat. If sauce has thickened or looks slightly curdled, stir in a little water. Prepared Asian-style peanut sauce is a quick alternative.

MAKES: About 4½ cups

- ½ pound **salted roasted peanuts**
- 3 cloves **garlic,** peeled
- 1 to 1½ teaspoons chopped **fresh Thai chili** or 1 to 2 tablespoons chopped fresh serrano chilies
- 2 tablespoons sliced peeled **fresh galangal** or fresh ginger
- ¼ cup chopped **palm sugar** or firmly packed brown sugar
- 2 cans (14 oz. each) **coconut milk**
- ¼ cup **sweet soy sauce** (*kecap manis*) or 2 tablespoons *each* soy sauce and sugar
- About 3 tablespoons **lime juice**
- About ½ teaspoon **salt**

1. In a food processor, whirl peanuts, garlic, chili, galangal, and sugar until finely ground.

2. In a 2- to 3-quart pan over high heat, combine peanut mixture, coconut milk, and sweet soy sauce. Bring to a boil, stirring constantly. Reduce heat and simmer, uncovered, stirring occasionally, until sauce is slightly darker and thicker, about 15 minutes. Add lime juice and salt to taste. Serve warm or at room temperature.

Per tablespoon: 45 cal., 78% (35 cal.) from fat; 1.1 g protein; 3.9 g fat (2.3 g sat.); 2.1 g carbo (0.3 g fiber); 60 mg sodium; 0 mg chol.

Tomato Sambal

PREP AND COOK TIME: About 40 minutes

NOTES: If making up to 3 days ahead, cover and chill. Seed chilies if you want less heat. If fresh red chilies are not available, use 1 cup chopped red bell pepper and ⅓ to ½ cup chopped fresh green jalapeño or serrano chilies. If time is short, purchase a prepared sambal or Asian red chili paste.

MAKES: 1⅓ cups

- 2 tablespoons **salad oil**
- ½ cup sliced **shallots**
- ⅓ cup sliced **garlic**

BANANA LEAF–WRAPPED BOWL: Wrap a banana leaf (thawed, if frozen) around a straight-sided bowl; secure with a rubber band. Trim leaf so it is flush with bottom of bowl and extends 1 to 2 inches above top (1). Cover rubber band with raffia; knot to secure (2). Use to serve spicy peanut sauce, tomato sambal, and chili in soy sauce (see page 124). Design by Françoise Kirkman.

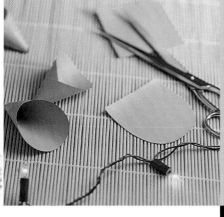

PARTY DECOR

PARTY LIGHTS: Shape colored self-stick removable notes (about 3 in. square) into cones by wrapping adhesive edges over nonadhesive edges, leaving a small opening just large enough to fit over white twinkle lights; press to seal. For rounded shades, trim off the pointed corners. Slip cones over lights. Design by Dennis Leong.

1⅓ cups (about 6 oz.) sliced **fresh red Fresno** or jalapeño **chilies**

2 teaspoons **anchovy paste**

1½ cups chopped **Roma tomatoes**

About 1 tablespoon **lime juice**

Salt

1. In a 10- to 12-inch frying pan over medium-high heat, combine oil, shallots, garlic, and chilies. Stir often until vegetables are limp, 5 to 7 minutes. Add anchovy paste and stir until fragrant, about 1 minute. Add tomatoes and stir occasionally until soft, 8 to 10 minutes.

2. Coarsely purée mixture in a food processor. Add lime juice and salt to taste. Serve warm or cold.

Per tablespoon: 25 cal., 52% (13 cal.) from fat; 0.6 g protein; 1.4 g fat (0.2 g sat.); 2.9 g carbo (0.4 g fiber); 29 mg sodium; 0.2 mg chol.

Chili in Soy Sauce

PREP TIME: About 7 minutes

NOTES: Make this hot-sweet-salty sauce up to 1 day ahead; cover and chill. Offer it as a condiment for any of the dishes in this menu. If sweet soy sauce is not available, substitute ¼ cup regular soy sauce mixed with ¼ cup sugar.

MAKES: About 1 cup

Mix ½ cup *each* soy sauce and **sweet soy sauce**. Add 2 tablespoons thinly sliced **fresh Thai chilies** or 3 to 4 tablespoons minced fresh serrano chilies, or to taste.

Per tablespoon: 20 cal., 0% (0 cal.) from fat; 0.7 g protein; 0 g fat; 4.4 g carbo (0 g fiber); 772 mg sodium; 0 mg chol.

Black Rice Pudding

PREP AND COOK TIME: About 30 minutes

NOTES: If black rice is unavailable, use all sweet white rice and cook only 10 to 15 minutes. Make pudding up to 1 hour ahead. It thickens as it stands; if desired, stir in a little hot water to thin. Reheat, covered, in a microwave oven. Garnish with mint sprigs if desired.

MAKES: 10 to 12 servings

1 cup **sweet** (glutinous) **black rice**

¾ cup **sweet** (glutinous) **white rice**

½ cup chopped **palm sugar** or firmly packed brown sugar

Salt

1 can (14 oz.) **coconut milk**

1½ to 2 cups bite-size chunks **mango** or fresh or drained canned litchis

Coconut ice cream (optional)

1. Place black and white rice in a fine strainer and rinse well under cool running water until water runs clear. Place rice in a 2- to 3-quart pan and add 5 cups water. Bring to a boil over high heat; reduce heat and simmer, uncovered, until rice is tender to bite, stirring occasionally, 18 to 20 minutes. If rice begins to stick, stir in a little more water.

2. Mix sugar and ¼ cup hot water. Stir into rice. Add salt to taste.

3. Serve the rice pudding warm or at room temperature. Spoon the pudding into stemmed glasses or small bowls. Stir the coconut milk and pour it equally over portions. Top each serving with fruit and a small scoop of coconut ice cream.

Per serving: 213 cal., 31% (65 cal.) from fat; 2.6 g protein; 7.2 g fat (6.3 g sat.); 35 g carbo (1 g fiber); 10 mg sodium; 0 mg chol. ◆

foodguide

BY JERRY ANNE DI VECCHIO

Salzburg's sweet soufflé

The city knows the sound of music and the shape of dessert

■ Long ago in Mozart's birthplace, I tasted the city's most famous dessert, Salzburger nockerln. The puffy baked eggs, simply served with whipped cream, sounded so easy to make that I tucked away an approximate formula in my head: separate the eggs and use 1 tablespoon of sugar for each white and 1 teaspoon of flour for each yolk. Whip them separately, fold together, and bake. At home I embellish the idea but not the process. The result is golden and velvety, like a sun-drenched cloud—a stellar main dish for brunch.

Raspberry-Macaroon Soufflé

PREP AND COOK TIME: 30 to 35 minutes

NOTES: If you serve with whipped cream, another delicious addition is grated semisweet chocolate; sprinkle over servings.

MAKES: 6 servings

- 6 **large eggs**
- 6 tablespoons **sugar**
- 2 tablespoons **all-purpose flour**
- 2 tablespoons **butter** or margarine
- ⅓ cup **apricot jam**
- ¾ cup (2 to 3 oz.) coarsely crushed **amaretti** or almond macaroons
- 3 cups **raspberries,** rinsed and drained

  Sweetened whipped cream (optional)

1. Separate egg whites and yolks. Put whites in a large, deep bowl, and yolks in a medium bowl. With a mixer on high speed, whip whites until they hold soft peaks; gradually adding sugar, beat on high speed until whites hold stiff peaks,

WHIPPING UP A SOUFFLÉ

Stir a portion of the whipped egg whites into the yolks, then fold the mixture into the rest of the whites **(a).** Scoop the whipped eggs over fruit and butter in a hot pan **(b),** then bake the soufflé.

JAMES CARRIER (4)

3 to 5 minutes total. Scrape whites off beaters but don't wash.

2. With mixer on high speed, whip yolks for 1 minute. Add flour and beat on high speed until mixture is very thick, 2 to 3 minutes more.

3. Put an 8½- to 9-inch-wide (or 7- by 10-in. oval) ovenproof frying pan or shallow metal pan over medium heat; add butter and jam. Heat until butter is melted, stirring occasionally, about 3 minutes. Turn heat to low and sprinkle about half the cookie crumbs and 1 cup of the berries into pan.

4. Stir about ¼ of the egg whites into the yolks, then fold yolk mixture into whites (top left); some streaking is fine.

5. Turn heat to medium-high and quickly mound egg mixture in pan (bottom left). Sprinkle with remaining cookie crumbs. Cook about 1 minute.

6. Set pan in a 350° oven and bake until

Liver, bacon, and onions

■ Once viewed as a wholesome necessity to be consumed under duress, liver, bacon, and onions have nonetheless always had a loyal following. In our house, only my father and I had a taste for this combination, so I mastered the dish early on—and felt healthier for the effort. Today's fans, however, must deal with the guilt of cholesterol overload, and pace the indulgence. Here's a top-notch version that will make it a rare treat.

Lemon Bacon and Red Onions with Calf's Liver

PREP AND COOK TIME: 45 minutes

NOTES: Up to 4 hours ahead, bake the bacon; cool, wrap airtight (don't stack), and let stand at room temperature. Serve with watercress salad.

MAKES: 4 servings

- 8 slices (about ⅔ lb.) **thick-cut bacon**
- ¼ cup firmly packed **brown sugar**
- 1½ teaspoons grated **lemon** peel
- ½ to ¾ pound **calf's liver**, cut into ½-inch-thick slices
- 2 **red onions** (1 lb. total), peeled and thinly sliced
- 3 tablespoons **lemon juice**
- 2 tablespoons **butter** or olive oil
- 1 cup minced **parsley**
  About ¼ cup **all-purpose flour**
  Salt and **pepper**

1. In a 10- by 15-inch rimmed pan, lay bacon slices side by side.

2. Bake in a 350° oven for 15 minutes. Drain and save fat.

3. Mix sugar and lemon peel. With your fingers, evenly pat mixture onto bacon slices, covering completely.

4. Return pan to oven and bake until bacon is well browned, 12 to 15 minutes. With a wide spatula, transfer bacon to a rack; scrape sugar drippings from pan and put on bacon.

5. Meanwhile, rinse liver, pat dry, and trim off and discard any tough membrane. Cut liver into 4 equal portions.

6. In a 10- to 12-inch nonstick frying pan, combine onions, lemon juice, and butter. Stir over high heat until onions are limp and slightly browned, about 15 minutes. Add parsley and stir until wilted. Mound onions on an ovenproof platter; arrange bacon in a single layer alongside. Put in a 150° oven. Wipe frying pan clean.

7. Set frying pan over high heat and add reserved bacon fat. Coat liver with flour, shaking off excess. When fat is hot, add liver. Brown on each side, turning as needed until just barely pink in center (cut to test), about 5 minutes total. Drain liver briefly on towels, then add to platter. Add salt and pepper to taste.

Per serving: 394 cal., 48% (189 cal.) from fat; 20 g protein; 21 g fat (8.7 g sat.); 33 g carbo (2.5 g fiber); 469 mg sodium; 210 mg chol.

eggs are tinged with brown and set, but still slightly creamy, in the center (jiggle to test), 15 to 18 minutes (10 to 12 minutes in a convection oven).

7. Meanwhile, divide remaining berries equally among wide bowls. Serve soufflé immediately, dipping to bottom of pan to spoon sauce and soufflé into bowls. Add whipped cream to taste.

Per serving: 280 cal., 32% (90 cal.) from fat; 7.8 g protein; 10 g fat (3.9 g sat.); 41 g carbo (3.2 g fiber); 114 mg sodium; 223 mg chol.

Cheese whiz

■ If you enjoy the delicate, short-lived flavors of really fresh mozzarella and ricotta as much as I do, the cheese kit from the New England Cheesemaking Supply Company is for you. Included are vegetable rennet tablets, citric acid, and other supplies for about 20 batches, each of which uses 1 gallon of milk to produce about ¾ pound of cheese.

Order the kit ($19.95, plus $4.75 shipping) from the New England Cheesemaking Supply Company, Box 85, Ashfield, MA 01330; (413) 628-3808 or www.cheesemaking.com.

The perfect partner for fresh homemade mozzarella is homegrown tomatoes. Since those in my garden aren't ready yet, I've been using the vine-ripened tomatoes from Mexico in my supermarket. On a recent trip to Sinaloa, I saw them being fastidiously grown, harvested, and packed to meet FDA and USDA standards. The Mexican-grown tomatoes bring garden-fresh flavor to a classic summer combo: **Tomatoes and fresh mozzarella salad.** Alternate layers of sliced **tomatoes** and **fresh whole-milk mozzarella** on a platter, drizzle with **extra-virgin olive oil** and **balsamic vinegar,** and season to taste with **salt** and **pepper.**

JAMES CARRIER (3)

Hot off the grill

■ For barbecue enthusiasts, *Weber's Art of the Grill: Recipes for Outdoor Living,* by Jamie Purviance (Chronicle Books, San Francisco, 1999; $35; 800/722-6657), is a rich resource. Practical—as expected from master barbecue manufacturer Weber-Stephen Products Co.—and handsome, this book is full of imaginative recipes and beautiful photographs. Its chapters are devoted to courses, with bonus wine suggestions and entertaining ideas.

Venerable vegetable

■ Creamed spinach endures. It's holding its own on menus in restaurants weathered by time and tradition. One such institution is the charmingly rustic, century-old Saddle Peak Lodge tucked into the hills of Calabasas, California. Chef Alex Scrimgeour gives creamed spinach an unexpected dash of panache by adding a touch of anise flavor.

Creamed Spinach with Pernod

PREP AND COOK TIME: About 15 minutes

NOTES: Buy trimmed, cleaned spinach. If you don't have anise-flavor liqueur, add ½ teaspoon anise seed to the boiling cream mixture instead.

MAKES: 2 cups; 4 to 6 servings

1 pound (4 to 4½ qt.) **spinach leaves,** rinsed and drained

1 cup **whipping cream**

About ¾ teaspoon fresh-grated or ground **nutmeg**

About 2 tablespoons **Pernod** or other dry anise-flavor liqueur

Salt and **pepper**

1. In a 5- to 6-quart pan over high heat, stir spinach until wilted, about 5 minutes. Drain, saving liquid. Purée about half the spinach in a food processor or blender.

2. Return reserved spinach liquid to pan and add cream, ½ teaspoon nutmeg, and 1 tablespoon Pernod. Boil over high heat until mixture is reduced to about ½ cup, about 10 minutes. Stir in puréed and whole spinach and additional nutmeg and Pernod to taste; stir until bubbling. Season to taste with salt and pepper.

Per serving: 141 cal., 83% (117 cal.) from fat; 3 g protein; 13 g fat (7.8 g sat.); 5.5 g carbo (2 g fiber); 73 mg sodium; 44 mg chol. ◆

The Wine Guide

BY KAREN MacNEIL-FIFE

RICK MARIANI

Summer's best red

■ I have just spent what otherwise would have been an unremarkable Saturday with 5,500 possessed people, all of whom had unnervingly purple teeth. This was the consequence of their having consumed something in the neighborhood of 54,300 glasses of Zinfandel with what can only be described as abandon. Zinfandel—more than any other wine—does this sort of thing to people. It makes them giddy with obsession. Drinking Zin is kind of like falling in love for the first time.

The Zinfandel fanatics and I were in San Francisco at a ZAP event, possibly the most hedonistic wine tasting in the country. ZAP stands for Zinfandel Advocates & Producers. As a descriptor, *advocates* only scratches the surface; these were enthusiasts who could comparatively taste two Zinfandels, eat little cubes of orange cheese, and talk on a cell phone at the same time.

What was amazing to me—and the reason I bring up this tasting (which is open to the public*)—is this: out of more than 360 Zinfandels from 181 producers, a huge number were absolutely stellar. You just don't taste this kind of

across-the-board success in a mass of Chardonnays or Merlots. But quietly, steadily, and without attracting much notice, Zinfandel has become astonishingly good. The top Zins are now wines of depth and complexity. Not to mention irresistible crushed-velvet textures and ripe, spicy boysenberry flavors.

Why this upswing in quality? The short answer is money. Because Zinfandel now commands higher prices than it once did, growers can afford to plant the grapes in the best vineyard sites and winemakers can use top-quality barrels and equipment.

Zinfandel is often called "America's grape." As early as 1830, for example, it was showing up in nursery catalogs around New England, where it was eaten as a table grape.

Then, serendipitously, something happened in the West: the Gold Rush. Thousands of European immigrants, heady with dreams of wealth, poured into Northern California. When their hopes of getting rich quick died, they turned to what, in many cases, were the only occupations they knew: farming and winemaking. Zinfandel was a sturdy grapevine, requiring very little special equipment to turn its fruit into satisfying wine. By the late 1860s, Zin was growing in the Sierra foothills, Sacramento, the Napa Valley, Sonoma, and the Santa Clara Valley. By the 1870s and 1880s, the time of the vast post–Gold Rush grape plantings, Zinfandel was the leading red grape in California.

It still is. As of 1997, Zinfandel, with 50,498 acres, is the most widely planted red variety in the state. Cabernet Sauvignon, its more aristocratic cousin, comes in second with 45,307 acres.

Given Zinfandel's significance in

SUNSET'S STEAL OF THE MONTH
Beaulieu Zinfandel 1996 (Napa Valley), $12. A juicy, rustic Zin with mouth-filling berry-spice flavors. Zinfandels in this price range seldom have this much personality.
— KAREN MacNEIL-FIFE

BACKYARD BLISS IN A BOTTLE

Here, after extensive ZAP research, are some of my current favorite Zinfandels.

- **Eberle "Steinbeck Vineyard" 1997 (Paso Robles),** $16
- **Folie à Deux Old Vine 1996 (Amador),** $18
- **Green & Red "Chiles Mill Vineyard" 1997 (Napa Valley),** $20
- **Hidden Cellars "Mendocino Heritage—Eaglepoint Ranch" 1996 (Mendocino),** $28
- **Lolonis Estate 1996 (Redwood Valley),** $17
- **Ridge "Geyserville" 1997 (Alexander Valley),** $27.50
- **Saucelito Canyon 1997 (Arroyo Grande),** $19.50
- **Tria 1997 (Napa Valley),** $18

American history, it's startling to realize what scientists themselves discovered only months ago—that Zinfandel is probably of Croatian origin. Using the new technique of DNA fingerprinting, they've found that it's a close relative of a grape grown on the Dalmatian coast.

In the end, though, the single most important fact about Zin may be this: it's the absolute best all-around summertime red. When it comes to grilled steaks, grilled leg of lamb, or, say, barbecued chicken, most white wines just don't cut it. Zin, on the other hand, is massively fruity—a delicious contrast to the char of grilled meats. Plus it's less tannic than Cabernet or Merlot, making it refreshing and easy to drink.

There's one more thing: backyard pleasures imply "backyard prices." Somehow, drinking a $40 Cabernet while sitting out on the deck seems a tad indulgent. And while the price of Zin is higher than it once was, dollar for dollar the wine is still one of the West's most affordable pleasures.

ZAP tastings are held annually throughout the country. For more information, call (530) 432-8964. ◆

Flower power

From the garden or market,
edible blossoms add a riot
of color to summer salads

BY ELAINE JOHNSON

PHOTOGRAPHS BY
JAMES CARRIER

■ A rose is a rose is a rose, until it's in your salad bowl. Then it becomes an ingredient with alluring color, delicate flavor, and Monet impact. Other edible blossoms, including herb flowers, can be equally effective.

Many palatable flower varieties, grown without pesticides and chemicals to preserve their edibility, are sold in the produce section. They may seem a bit pricey, but a few go a long way to enhance other foods. If you raise these tasty posies with identical care, you can pluck them from your own garden for dining. However, the same flowers from a florist can be harmful if consumed because of what's added.

Edible flowers you are apt to encounter at the market are listed on page 136. Don't experiment with other varieties without expert guidance. Some flowers are poisonous; others just taste bad. If you need a local source for edible flowers, contact HerbThyme Farms

ROSE PETALS and Johnny-jump-ups garnish blueberry and nectarine salad (below). An assortment of flowers turns leafy greens into an edible bouquet (right).

in South San Francisco at (650) 952-4372 or www.herbthyme.com. They distribute throughout the West.

Rose Petal Fruit Salad

PREP TIME: About 10 minutes

NOTES: Rose flower water is available in liquor stores, Middle Eastern food markets, and fancy supermarkets.

MAKES: 6 servings

1½ cups **blueberries,** rinsed

3½ cups sliced **nectarines**

¼ cup **rose petals,** rinsed and drained

¼ cup **Johnny-jump-ups** (stems pinched off), rinsed and drained

2 tablespoons **raspberry vinegar**

About 1½ teaspoons **rose flower water**

Salt (optional)

1. Arrange berries and nectarines on a platter; sprinkle flowers over fruit.

2. In a small bowl, mix vinegar with rose flower water to taste. Spoon evenly over salad. Season to taste with salt.

Per serving: 61 cal., 7.4% (4.5 cal.) from fat; 1 g protein; 0.5 g fat (0 g sat.); 15 g carbo (2.1 g fiber); 2.3 mg sodium; 0 mg chol.

¾ cup **English cucumber** sticks (see notes)

Salt

½ cup **calendula** or marigold **petals** (see notes)

3½ cups **nasturtium blossoms,** rinsed and drained

3½ cups tender **nasturtium leaves** or butter lettuce leaves, rinsed and drained

1. Cook pasta in about 3 quarts boiling water over high heat until tender to bite, about 10 minutes. Drain, immerse in cold water, and drain when cool, about 3 minutes.

2. In large bowl, mix lemon juice, oil, and pepper. Add pasta, feta, and cucumber. Mix and season to taste with salt. Add calendula petals and nasturtium blossoms; mix gently.

3. Line a platter or plates with nasturtium leaves. Spoon salad onto leaves.

Per serving: 571 cal., 41% (234 cal.) from fat; 16 g protein; 26 g fat (7.1 g sat.); 70 g carbo (3 g fiber); 333 mg sodium; 25 mg chol.

Purple Flash Spinach Salad

PREP AND COOK TIME: About 15 minutes

NOTES: Other purple-blue flowers you can use include borage, chive, and sage. Rinse and drain flowers. Pull petals from dianthus, and blossoms from rosemary and lavender.

MAKES: 6 servings

⅓ cup **slivered almonds**

2 tablespoons **extra-virgin olive oil**

1 tablespoon **red wine vinegar**

1 teaspoon **Dijon mustard**

2 quarts (6 to 8 oz.) **baby spinach leaves,** rinsed and drained

2 tablespoons **rosemary blossoms** (see notes)

1 cup **purple** or pink **dianthus** petals (see notes)

1½ tablespoons chopped **fresh lavender blossoms** (see notes) or 2¼ teaspoons dried lavender

Salt and **pepper**

1. In an 8- to 10-inch frying pan over medium heat, shake or stir almonds until golden, about 3 minutes. Pour from pan into a wide shallow bowl.

2. To bowl, add oil, vinegar, 1 tablespoon water, and mustard; mix.

3. Add spinach, rosemary blossoms,

Bouquet Mix Salad

PREP TIME: About 10 minutes

NOTES: Use a combination of flowers including Johnny-jump-ups and pansies (stems pinched off), nasturtiums (with stems), and rose petals.

MAKES: 6 servings

¼ cup **orange juice**

1 tablespoon **lemon juice**

1 tablespoon **extra-virgin olive oil**

½ teaspoon grated **orange** peel

2 quarts (6 to 8 oz.) **salad mix,** rinsed and drained

3 cups **edible blossoms** or petals (see notes), rinsed and drained

Salt and **pepper**

In a wide bowl, combine orange juice, lemon juice, oil, and orange peel. Add salad mix and blossoms. Mix and season to taste with salt and pepper.

Per serving: 36 cal., 58% (21 cal.) from fat; 0.6 g protein; 2.3 g fat (0.3 g sat.); 3.1 g carbo (0.3 g fiber); 7.7 mg sodium; 0 mg chol.

Nasturtium Pasta Salad

PREP AND COOK TIME: About 20 minutes

NOTES: To cut cucumber sticks, slice cucumber into ⅛-inch-thick rounds, stack rounds, and cut into ¼-inch-wide pieces. Rinse and drain calendula or marigold flowers, then pull off petals.

MAKES: 4 entrée servings

¾ pound **dried farfalle** (bow-tie) **pasta**

⅓ cup **lemon juice**

⅓ cup **extra-virgin olive oil**

1½ teaspoons fresh-ground **pepper**

1 cup (4 oz.) **crumbled feta cheese**

Flowers grown for eating

Flower	Color	Flavor
Begonia, tuberous	orange, pink, red, yellow, white	lemon
Borage	blue-lavender	cucumber
Calendula	orange, yellow	spicy, pepper
Carnation	lavender, pink, red	pepper, cloves
Chive	lavender	onion
Chrysanthemum	many colors	faint to distinct bitterness
Daisy, English	pastels, white	tangy lettuce
Dianthus	many colors	cloves
Fuchsia	many colors	tart
Geranium	pink, peach, red, white	differs with variety
Hollyhock	lavender, pink, red, white	mild lettuce
Johnny-jump-up	purple, white, yellow	mild lettuce
Lavender	purple	floral, pungent
Marigold	orange, yellow	spicy, mildly bitter
Nasturtium	orange, red, yellow	horseradish
Pansy	many colors	sweet, mild
Rose	many colors	floral, delicate
Rosemary	light blue	pine resin
Sage	many colors	sage, differs with variety
Squash blossom	yellow	faintly sweet, mild lettuce
Stock	pink, purple, white, yellow	spicy, sweet
Thyme	purple, white	thyme
Viola	many colors	mild lettuce

dianthus petals, and lavender. Mix and season with salt and pepper to taste.

Per serving: 94 cal., 83% (78 cal.) from fat; 2.6 g protein; 8.7 g fat (1 g sat.); 3.1 g carbo (1.3 g fiber); 51 mg sodium; 0 mg chol.

Strawberry-Begonia Salad

PREP TIME: About 10 minutes

MAKES: 6 servings

- ¼ cup **balsamic vinegar**
- 1 tablespoon **honey**
- 1 teaspoon grated **lemon** peel
- 2 quarts **butter lettuce leaves,** rinsed and drained
- 2 cups **strawberries,** rinsed and hulled
- 1¼ cups **begonia blossoms,** rinsed and drained
- 2 tablespoons **fresh tarragon** leaves, rinsed and drained
- **Salt** and **pepper**

1. In a wide shallow bowl, mix vinegar, honey, and lemon peel.

2. Place lettuce in bowl. Cut strawberries in ⅓-inch-thick slices and scatter over lettuce. Top with begonias and tarragon.

3. Mix salad and season to taste with salt and pepper.

Per serving: 40 cal., 9% (3.6 cal.) from fat; 1.5 g protein; 0.4 g fat (0 g sat.); 9.1 g carbo (2 g fiber); 5.7 mg sodium; 0 mg chol.

Rice and Rosemary Blossom Salad

PREP AND COOK TIME: About 25 minutes, plus about 30 minutes for rice to cool

NOTES: Other suitable blue flowers are chive and sage blossoms. Garnish salad with herb sprigs of the flower you choose.

MAKES: 6 servings

- 1 cup **long-grain white rice**

  About ½ teaspoon **salt**
- ½ cup **walnut pieces**
- 2 tablespoons **extra-virgin olive oil**
- 3 tablespoons **lemon juice**
- ¼ cup chopped **chives**
- ¼ cup **Italian parsley** leaves, rinsed and drained

  Salt
- 3 tablespoons **rosemary blossoms,** rinsed and drained

1. In a 3- to 4-quart pan over high heat, bring rice, ½ teaspoon salt, and 2 cups water to a boil. Cover, reduce heat, and simmer until rice is tender to bite, about 20 minutes. Scrape rice into a wide shallow bowl, fluff with a fork, and let stand until cool, about 30 minutes.

2. Meanwhile, in an 8- to 10-inch frying pan over medium heat, frequently stir walnuts with 1 tablespoon oil until nuts are golden beneath skins, about 5 minutes.

3. Pour nut mixture over rice. Add remaining olive oil, and lemon juice, chives, and parsley; add salt to taste. Mix with a fork. Sprinkle salad with rosemary blossoms.

Per serving: 220 cal., 45% (99 cal.) from fat; 3.7 g protein; 11 g fat (1.3 g sat.); 27 g carbo (1 g fiber); 198 mg sodium; 0 mg chol. ◆

The Low-Fat Cook

HEALTHY CHOICES FOR THE ACTIVE LIFESTYLE

BY ELAINE JOHNSON

APRICOTS and freshly candied lemon slices bake with the beauty of a fruit tart but without a crust.

RICHARD JUNG

Rustic fruit gratins

■ Technically, a gratin has a topping that gets brown when broiled or baked. These fruit desserts brown with the same appetizing appeal, are speedy to assemble, and have the look of a carefully arranged fruit tart—minus the calorie-laden crust. Their flavors are surprisingly complex, the result of a combination of high-heat baking that concentrates the taste of the fruit and the addition of syrup-saturated fresh citrus slices. Serve hot gratins plain or with justifiable scoops of nonfat frozen yogurt.

Apricot Gratin

PREP AND COOK TIME: About 45 minutes

NOTES: Serve with scoops of vanilla nonfat frozen yogurt.

MAKES: 4 to 6 servings

- 1 **lemon** (about ¼ lb.)
- ½ cup **sugar**
- 1¼ to 1½ pounds **ripe apricots**
- 2 tablespoons **apricot-flavor brandy**, brandy, or orange juice
- ¼ cup **apricot jam**

1. Rinse lemon, slice off and discard ends, then cut fruit crosswise into paper-thin slices, and discard seeds.

2. In a 10- to 12-inch nonstick frying pan over high heat, bring 1 cup water to a boil. Add lemon and cook for 1 minute. Drain. Repeat step.

3. In pan, combine lemon and ¼ cup sugar. Stir often over medium-high heat until liquid evaporates, 4 to 5 minutes; take care not to scorch fruit.

4. Rinse apricots, pit, and cut fruit lengthwise into ¾-inch slices. In a 10-inch-wide (about 8-cup) round quiche dish or shallow casserole, snugly arrange apricots in a single layer. Tuck lemon pieces among apricot slices. Spoon brandy over fruit, then sprinkle evenly with remaining ¼ cup sugar.

5. Bake in a 450° oven until fruit edges are tinged with dark brown, 25 to 30 minutes.

6. Stir apricot jam to soften; dot evenly over fruit.

7. Return dish to oven and bake until jam is bubbling, about 5 minutes. Spoon portions onto plates.

Per serving: 156 cal., 2.3% (3.6 cal.) from fat; 1.5 g protein; 0.4 g fat (0 g sat.); 38 g carbo (1.3 g fiber); 6.9 mg sodium; 0 mg chol.

Apple Gratin

PREP AND COOK TIME: About 45 minutes

MAKES: 4 to 6 servings

Follow directions for **apricot gratin** (preceding), but instead of apricots, use peeled, cored **Golden Delicious apples**. In step 4, decrease sugar to 2 tablespoons, and mix with ½ teaspoon fresh-grated or ground **nutmeg.**

Per serving: 112 cal., 3.2% (3.6 cal.) from fat; 0.4 g protein; 0.4 g fat (0.1 g sat.); 28 g carbo (1.7 g fiber); 5.9 mg sodium; 0 mg chol.

Pear-Orange Gratin

PREP AND COOK TIME: About 50 minutes

NOTES: If desired, splash a little cassis over servings of the dessert.

MAKES: 4 to 6 servings

Follow directions for **apricot gratin** (at left), but instead of lemon, use 1 **orange** (6 oz.), rinsed and cut in half lengthwise, then sliced crosswise. Omit step 2. In step 3, add 2 tablespoons **water.**

Instead of apricots, use peeled, cored **firm-ripe pears** such as d'Anjou or Bartlett. Mix fruit with 1½ tablespoons **lemon juice.** In step 4, decrease sugar to 2 tablespoons.

Per serving: 126 cal., 3.6% (4.5 cal.) from fat; 0.8 g protein; 0.5 g fat (0 g sat.); 32 g carbo (2.8 g fiber); 6.7 mg sodium; 0 mg chol. ◆

Kitchen Cabinet

READERS' RECIPES TESTED IN SUNSET'S KITCHENS
BY LINDA LAU ANUSASANANAN

GRILLED APRICOTS bring the sweet tang of summer to barbecued steaks.

Lift steaks from bag and discard the marinade.

3. Lay steaks on a grill over a solid bed of hot coals or high heat on a gas barbecue (you can hold your hand at grill level only 2 to 3 seconds). Lay apricot halves on grill and brush with some of reserved apricot sauce. Cook steak, turning once, until done to your liking, 8 to 10 minutes total for medium-rare (pink in center, cut to test). Cook apricots until hot and lightly browned, about 5 minutes total; as cooked, transfer to a platter and keep warm.

4. Heat the rest of the reserved apricot sauce until boiling in a microwave-safe bowl in a microwave oven at full power (100%) or in a pan on direct heat. Serve sauce with steaks and apricots, adding salt and pepper to taste.

Per serving: 406 cal., 51% (207 cal.) from fat; 30 g protein; 23 g fat (9.1 g sat.); 17 g carbo (0.9 g fiber); 173 mg sodium; 98 mg chol.

The Other Slaw

Jane Roush, Shelton, Washington

Jane Roush took a fresh look at an old-fashioned vegetable from her garden, kohlrabi, and came up with this crunchy slaw. You can also use broccoli stems, which taste much like kohlrabi.

PREP TIME: About 30 minutes

MAKES: 5 or 6 servings

- 1/4 cup **lime juice**
- 2 tablespoons **salad oil**
- 3 tablespoons chopped **red onion**
- 3 tablespoons chopped **fresh cilantro**
- 1/2 teaspoon **sugar**
- 1 clove **garlic,** pressed or minced
- 1 to 2 teaspoons minced **fresh jalapeño chili**
- 1 1/2 cups shredded peeled **kohlrabi** or broccoli stems
- 1 1/2 cups shredded peeled **carrots**
- 1 1/2 cups shredded **zucchini**
  Salt and **pepper**

1. In a bowl, mix lime juice, oil, onion, cilantro, sugar, garlic, and chili to taste.

2. Add kohlrabi, carrots, and zucchini. Mix and season with salt and pepper to taste.

Steak with Apricots

Margaret Pache, Mesa, Arizona

The joy of cooking, says Margaret Pache, is trying new things for her family. Here she pairs the season's fresh apricots with grilled steaks.

PREP AND COOK TIME: About 25 minutes

MAKES: 4 servings

- 3/4 cup **canned apricot nectar**
- 1/4 cup **orange juice**
- 1 1/2 tablespoons **honey**
- 1 1/2 tablespoons **Dijon mustard**
- 2 teaspoons **prepared horseradish**
- 4 **beef tenderloin steaks** (1 in. thick; 6 oz. each), fat-trimmed
- 4 **firm-ripe apricots** (1/2 to 3/4 lb. total), rinsed
  Salt and **pepper**

1. In a bowl, mix apricot nectar, orange juice, honey, mustard, and horseradish. Rinse meat and put in a plastic food bag; add 1/3 cup of the apricot sauce. Seal bag and let stand 15 to 20 minutes, turning occasionally. Reserve remaining apricot sauce.

2. Cut apricots in half and discard pits.

Per serving: 73 cal., 58% (42 cal.) from fat; 1.4 g protein; 4.7 g fat (0.6 g sat.); 7.6 g carbo (1.5 g fiber); 20 mg sodium; 0 mg chol.

Orange Russian Cream

Stephen Nagy, Klamath Falls, Oregon

"Here's a high-fat and utterly wonderful dessert recipe that is quick, easy to make, and decadent. Your guests will moan with delight after the first taste, and die from pleasure shortly after—but not before they've finished eating!" says Stephen Nagy.

PREP AND COOK TIME: About 12 minutes, plus 3 hours to chill

MAKES: 6 servings

- ¾ cup **sugar**
- 1 envelope **unflavored gelatin**
- 1 teaspoon grated **orange** peel
- 1 cup **whipping cream**
- 1½ cups **vanilla** or plain **nonfat yogurt**
- 1 teaspoon **vanilla**
- 1 tablespoon finely chopped **semisweet chocolate**

1. In a 1½- to 2-quart pan, mix sugar and gelatin. Add ½ cup water and orange peel; stir over high heat until boiling, about 2 minutes.

2. Remove from heat, add cream, yogurt, and vanilla. Whisk to blend smoothly. Pour into ramekins or custard cups (6-oz. size). Chill until firm, at least 3 hours; cover airtight if storing up to 1 day.

3. Uncover desserts and sprinkle equally with chocolate.

Per serving: 278 cal., 42% (117 cal.) from fat; 4.9 g protein; 13 g fat (8 g sat.); 37 g carbo (0.1 g fiber); 56 mg sodium; 46 mg chol. ◆

CURLS OR BITS of chocolate garnish bowls of rich, orange-scented cream.

Steaming and just cooked corn is ready to be sprinkled or brushed with flavorings.

Give a glorious corn feast

Butter and salt for the purists, imaginative seasonings for the adventurous, a potluck spread for all

BY LINDA LAU ANUSASANANAN

For the last 31 years, Neil and Susan Hall and Allan and Barbara Fredrickson have taken corn to the ultimate level in eating, sharing the experience annually with about 150 friends. The process begins in late spring at the Halls' nursery in Mount Vernon, Washington, when they plant four 200-foot-long rows of corn. The variety they currently favor is Platinum Lady, a sweet white hybrid well suited to their climate.

Then, on party day, they serve up a feast of succulent corn cooked within minutes of harvest—right in the field where it grew.

As 500 or so ears of corn are stripped from their stalks, guests lend a hand to husk them. In a 32-quart pan of water boiling over a powerful portable propane burner, Neil cooks a batch of 20 ears about every four minutes. And how quickly these sweet, tender ears disappear, as one and all chomp into tight rows of plump kernels, squirting sweet, milky nectar.

The rest of the meal, for those who can manage, is roast chickens and a potluck spread of entrées, salads, and desserts, which the guests help supply.

Sounds like fun, but you didn't plant any corn? Not to worry. Farm stands and urban farmers' markets are a ready resource for contemporary varieties of corn bred to stay sweet for days, not just minutes. You can follow the simple Mount Vernon menu plan. But to focus due attention on the corn, we suggest

CRAIG HARROLD

FROM FIELD TO FEAST IN MINUTES— Neil Hall harvests more than 500 ears to feed 150 guests.

adding a collection of spreads and sprinkles to enhance it.

Corn for a Crowd

PREP AND COOK TIME: About 10 minutes

NOTES: If cooking more than 1 batch of corn, use tongs to lift out hot ears, then add more to boiling water. Replenish water as needed, and return to boiling before adding more corn.

MAKES: 12 ears; allow at least 2 or 3 for a serving

  12 **ears corn** (7 to 8 in.)

      Flavor bar (recipes at right)

      Butter or margarine

      Salt and **pepper**

1. In a covered 10- to 12-quart pan over high heat, bring 5 to 6 quarts water to a boil.

2. Meanwhile, pull off and discard corn-husks and silks. Immerse ears in boiling water. Cover and cook until corn is hot, 3 to 5 minutes.

3. Drain, or lift ears from water with tongs. Season hot corn with choices from the flavor bar, or butter ears and add salt and pepper to taste.

Per unseasoned ear of corn: 77 cal., 13% (9.9 cal.) from fat; 2.9 g protein; 1.1 g fat (0.2 g sat.); 17 g carbo (2.9 g fiber); 14 mg sodium; 0 mg chol.

10 seasonings to spread or sprinkle

Select 1 or more of the following combinations. Each covers at least a dozen ears of corn.

Chili salt and lime. Mix 1 tablespoon **salt** and 1½ teaspoons **chili powder.** Cut 3 **limes** into wedges. Rub corn with lime wedge, then sprinkle with chili salt to taste.

Per serving: 1.7 cal., 53% (0.9 cal.) from fat; 0 g protein; 0.1 g fat (0 g sat.); 0.4 g carbo (0.1 g fiber); 585 mg sodium; 0 mg chol.

Sesame teriyaki. Mix ¾ cup **purchased thick teriyaki sauce** or glaze and 1 tablespoon **Asian** (toasted) **sesame oil.** In an 8- to 10-inch frying pan over medium heat, stir about ⅓ cup **sesame seed** until golden, about 3 minutes. Brush corn with sauce and sprinkle with sesame seed.

Per serving: 45 cal., 56% (25 cal.) from fat; 1.7 g protein; 2.8 g fat (0.4 g sat.); 3.8 g carbo (0.6 g fiber); 691 mg sodium; 0 mg chol.

Pesto. In a blender or food processor, combine 1⅓ cups **fresh basil** leaves, ⅔ cup **olive oil,** ⅓ cup **grated parmesan cheese,** and 2 cloves **garlic;** whirl until mixture is smooth. Add **salt** and **pepper** to taste. Spread on corn.

Per serving: 120 cal., 98% (117 cal.) from fat; 1.2 g protein; 13 g fat (2 g sat.); 0.6 g carbo (0.4 g fiber); 41 mg sodium; 1.7 mg chol.

Mexican cheese and chili. Mix ½ cup **mayonnaise** with 2 tablespoons **milk.** Put ¾ cup finely crumbled **cotija** or grated parmesan **cheese** and 1 tablespoon **ground dried California** or New Mexico **chilies** or chili powder in individual bowls. Brush corn with mayonnaise mixture and sprinkle with cheese and chilies.

Per serving: 86 cal., 91% (78 cal.) from fat; 1.5 g protein; 8.7 g fat (2 g sat.); 0.7 g carbo (0.1 g fiber); 141 mg sodium; 9.7 mg chol.

Cilantro-chili-garlic butter. Mix ¾ cup (⅜ lb.) melted **butter** or margarine with ⅓ cup finely chopped **fresh cilantro,** 1½ to 2 tablespoons minced **fresh jalapeño chili,** and 2 or 3 pressed or minced cloves **garlic.** Brush on corn.

Per serving: 103 cal., 96% (99 cal.) from fat; 0.2 g protein; 11 g fat (7.2 g sat.); 0.3 g carbo (0 g fiber); 117 mg sodium; 31 mg chol.

Lemon-thyme butter. Mix ½ cup (¼ lb.) melted **butter** or margarine with ¼ cup minced **chives** or green onions, 1 tablespoon minced **fresh** or 1 teaspoon dried **thyme,** 1 teaspoon grated **lemon** peel, and 2 tablespoons **lemon juice.** Brush butter on corn.

Per serving: 69 cal., 100% (69 cal.) from fat; 0.1 g protein; 7.7 g fat (4.8 g sat.); 0.3 g carbo (0.1 g fiber); 79 mg sodium; 21 mg chol.

Mustard-tarragon sauce. Mix 6 tablespoons **olive oil,** 3 tablespoons **white wine vinegar,** 1½ tablespoons **Dijon mustard,** 1½ tablespoons minced **shallot,** 2 teaspoons chopped **fresh** or ¾ teaspoon dried **tarragon,** and 1 pressed or minced clove **garlic.** Add **salt** and **pepper** to taste. Brush on corn.

Per serving: 64 cal., 95% (61 cal.) from fat; 0.1 g protein; 6.8 g fat (0.9 g sat.); 0.5 g carbo (0 g fiber); 45 mg sodium; 0 mg chol.

Spiced salt. In a 6- to 8-inch frying pan over medium heat, stir ½ teaspoon *each* **cumin seed, coriander seed, mustard seed,** and **black peppercorns** until mustard seed begins to pop, about 3 minutes. Pour into a blender with 1 tablespoon **coarse salt** and grind to a powder. Sprinkle on buttered ears of corn.

Per 1/4 teaspoon: 0.7 cal., 0% (0 cal.) from fat; 0 g protein; 0 g fat; 0.1 g carbo (0 g fiber); 184 mg sodium; 0 mg chol.

Curry butter. In a 6- to 8-inch frying pan over low heat, stir 1½ tablespoons **curry powder,** ¾ teaspoon **ground coriander,** and ¼ teaspoon **cayenne** until spices are fragrant, about 1 minute. Add ¾ cup (⅜ lb.) **butter** or margarine and stir until melted. Brush on corn.

Per serving: 104 cal., 95% (99 cal.) from fat; 0.2 g protein; 11 g fat (7.2 g sat.); 0.5 g carbo (0.3 g fiber); 118 mg sodium; 31 mg chol.

Dried tomato–basil butter. In a food processor, whirl ¼ cup drained **dried tomatoes packed in oil** until finely chopped. Add ½ cup (¼ lb.) **butter** or margarine (at room temperature) and 1 teaspoon **dried basil;** whirl to blend. Or finely chop tomatoes with a knife and mix with butter and basil in a bowl. Add **salt** and **pepper** to taste. Spread on corn.

Per serving: 80 cal., 94% (75 cal.) from fat; 0.4 g protein; 8.3 g fat (4.8 g sat.); 1.4 g carbo (0.3 g fiber); 98 mg sodium; 21 mg chol. ◆

The Quick Cook

Go with the grain

■ Grains in minutes? The smallest ones just naturally cook fast. Others are specially treated in processing to make them speedy.

Bulgur (cracked) wheat is steamed. It gets soft enough to eat when soaked but stays chewy when cooked.

Quinoa (pronounced *keen*-wah), a fine, round, high-protein grain, is native to the Andes and was prized by ancient farmers because it grows at high altitudes. It has a slightly bitter natural coating that needs to be rinsed off.

Barley labeled quick-cooking has had its outer hull removed so that moisture can penetrate faster.

Quick-cooking brown rice has been cooked and dried, and needs to be rehydrated. It's ready to eat in three-quarters the time it takes to cook regular brown rice.

Pilaf with Baked Eggs

PREP AND COOK TIME: About 30 minutes

NOTES: For an interesting grain mix, combine equal parts quick-cooking barley, quick-cooking brown rice, bulgur, and rinsed quinoa.

MAKES: 4 servings

- 1 tablespoon **butter** or margarine
- ²/₃ cup finely chopped **shallots**
- 1¹/₃ cups **grain mix** or any individual quick-cooking grain (see notes)
- 2 cups fat-skimmed **chicken broth**
- ³/₄ teaspoon **dried marjoram**
- 1 cup (¹/₄ lb.) **shredded Swiss cheese**
- 4 **large eggs**
- **Roma tomato** slices
- **Salt** and **pepper**

1. In a 10- to 12-inch ovenproof frying pan over high heat, stir butter and shallots often until shallots are lightly browned, about 3 minutes.

2. Add grain mix and stir until grains are lightly toasted, about 2 minutes.

GREAT GRAINS: An egg baked in a mixed-grain pilaf nest makes a quick supper main dish.

Add broth and marjoram, stir, and bring to a boil. Cover, reduce heat, and simmer until grains are tender to bite, about 12 minutes, stirring occasionally.

3. Mix ¹/₂ cup cheese with pilaf. Using the back of a spoon, make 4 deep wells in mixture. Slide 1 egg into each well. Lay tomato slices around eggs.

4. Bake in a 400° oven until egg whites are opaque and yolks have desired texture, about 8 minutes for liquid yolks. About 3 minutes before eggs are cooked, sprinkle mixture with remaining cheese.

5. Use a wide spatula to scoop out pilaf and eggs, 1 at a time, and put on plates. Add salt and pepper to taste.

Per serving: 413 cal., 37% (153 cal.) from fat; 24 g protein; 17 g fat (8.5 g sat.); 42 g carbo (6.1 g fiber); 223 mg sodium; 246 mg chol.

3 more quick grain recipes

Lamb Soup. In a 4- to 5-quart pan over high heat, stir 1 pound **ground lean lamb,** 1 cup chopped **onion,** and 1 cup chopped **carrots** until lamb is well browned, 8 to 10 minutes. Spoon off and discard any fat. Add 1¹/₃ cups **grain mix** (see notes at left), 5¹/₂ cups fat-skimmed **beef broth,** and 1 cup **dry sherry.** Bring to a boil, cover, reduce heat, and simmer until grains are tender to bite, about 12 minutes. Stir in ¹/₄ cup chopped **parsley.** Makes about 9 cups; 4 servings.

Per serving: 521 cal., 29% (153 cal.) from fat; 32 g protein; 17 g fat (6.5 g sat.); 44 g carbo (7.5 g fiber); 194 mg sodium; 76 mg chol.

Shrimp Tumble with Lettuce. In a 10- to 12-inch frying pan over high heat, combine 1¹/₃ cups **grain mix** (see notes at left) and 2 cups fat-skimmed **chicken broth.** Bring to a boil. Cover, reduce heat, and simmer until grains are tender to bite, about 12 minutes, stirring occasionally. Meanwhile, rinse and finely chop ¹/₂ pound **shelled cooked tiny shrimp.** Stir shrimp, ¹/₂ cup minced **green onions,** 2 tablespoons **oyster sauce,** and 1 tablespoon minced **fresh ginger** into grains. Spoon into 8 rinsed and crisped large **iceberg lettuce** leaves (about ¹/₂ lb. total). Roll to eat. Makes 4 servings.

Per serving: 263 cal., 7.6% (20 cal.) from fat; 23 g protein; 2.2 g fat (0.3 g sat.); 39 g carbo (6.5 g fiber); 543 mg sodium; 111 mg chol.

Sausage Pilaf. In a 10- to 12-inch frying pan over high heat, frequently turn 3 or 4 **cooked sausages** (about 14 oz. total) until lightly browned. Set aside. Add to pan 1¹/₃ cups **grain mix** (see notes at left), 2 cups fat-skimmed **chicken broth,** and ¹/₂ cup minced **parsley.** Bring to a boil. Cover, reduce heat, and simmer about 8 minutes, stirring occasionally. Push sausages down into grains, cover, and continue simmering until grains are tender to bite, about 5 minutes more; stir occasionally. Sprinkle with about 2 tablespoons **shredded parmesan cheese** and fresh-ground **pepper** to taste. Makes 3 or 4 servings.

Per serving: 562 cal., 53% (297 cal.) from fat; 30 g protein; 33 g fat (11 g sat.); 36 g carbo (5.9 g fiber); 1,385 mg sodium; 84 mg chol. ◆

Reminiscent of an early-California fiesta, this rancho-style barbecue grows as your party grows. Article begins on page 144.

July

Fiesta barbecue

rancho-style

A San Diego buffet that grows as your party does

BY LINDA LAU ANUSASANANAN

FOOD PHOTOGRAPHS BY JAMES CARRIER

■ When Elena Cota, a 78-year-old San Diego native, welcomes you to her table, it's a bountiful experience reminiscent of legendary early-California hacienda hospitality. She describes her entertaining style as California rancho. The description fits. It's an imaginative blend of Mexican heritage, from her mentor-mother, with the multiethnic influences and rich ingredient resources that are a vital aspect of her community. Cota, an energetic cooking instructor and home economist, shifts from small to large parties easily. The barbecue gives her flexibility. She may grill one or several entrées—beef, pork, poultry, seafood—on one or more barbecues. She rounds out the buffet with appetizers, salsas, salads, and vegetable dishes, some of which also cook on the grill. Guests often tuck custom combinations into warm tortillas. • If Cota expects a mere 8 to 10 guests, the lead menu on page 146 comes into play. As the party grows, she adds more main dishes and flavorful companions. The second and third tiers of the menu show how she combines the 22 recipes that follow to create a lively balance for gatherings of as many as 30. Thinking bigger? Make dishes in multiple proportions. • Cota shops in San Diego's Barrio Logan, a long-established neighborhood, for Mexican foods. However, most of the ingredients are readily found in well-stocked supermarkets. For authentic buy-and-serve desserts and beverages, shop at Latino markets.

ELENA COTA entertains with (far left, clockwise from front) skirt steaks, chipotle pork, watermelon, chilies, corn, salsa, Josefinas, and beans. She buys frozen paletas (above) for dessert.

STEPHEN SIMPSON

MENU

San Diego barbecue buffet

for 8 to 10:

Guacamole* and Tortilla Chips

Jalapeños en Escabeche*

Tomato Cucumber Salad with Panela Cheese*

Fiesta Barbecue Tacos*

Orange-Soy Skirt Steaks* and/or Garlic Butterflied Shrimp*

Salsa Cruda*

Salsa Chilpequín*

Grilled Vegetables with Tomato Oil*

Mexican Rancho Pinto Beans*

Warm Flour and Corn Tortillas

Watermelon Wedges

Mexican Sodas   Red Wine

Sangría   Beer

for up to 20, add:

Josefinas*

California Fruit Salad* with Poppy Seed Dressing*

Chipotle Pork Roast* and/or Herbed Beef Tri-Tip Roast*

Salsa de Tomatillo*

Grilled Corn with Onion and Cheese*

Refried Beans with Spinach*

Fruit Platter with Guava Paste and Panela Cheese

Pineapple Juice

Aguas Frescas (Fruit Drinks)

for up to 30, add:

Tomato Salad* with Guacamole Dressing*

Apple Honey-glazed Chicken Legs*

Salsa Verde*

Paletas (Frozen Juice Bars)

*recipe follows

appetizers

Guacamole

PREP TIME: About 5 minutes

NOTES: If making up to 4 hours ahead, cover and chill.

MAKES: About 2½ cups

- 1½ pounds **firm-ripe** to ripe **avocados**
- ⅓ to ½ cup **salsa verde**, salsa cruda, or salsa de tomatillo (recipes on pages 149 and 150) or prepared tomatillo salsa
- 3 to 4 tablespoons **lemon juice**

  Salt and **pepper**

Peel and pit avocados. Coarsely mash with a fork or beat with a mixer. Add salsa, lemon juice, and salt and pepper to taste.

Per tablespoon: 21 cal., 81% (17 cal.) from fat; 0.3 g protein; 1.9 g fat (0.3 g sat.); 1.1 g carbo (0.3 g fiber); 1.5 mg sodium; 0 mg chol.

Josefinas
(Toast with Chili Cheese)

PREP AND COOK TIME: About 15 minutes

NOTES: Serve this chili- and cheese-topped toast as an appetizer or a bread.

MAKES: 8 to 10 appetizer servings

- 1 **slender baguette** (½ lb.)
- 1 cup (¼ lb.) **shredded jack cheese**
- 2 cans (4 oz. each) **diced green chilies**
- ½ cup minced **sweet onion** (such as Maui or Walla Walla)
- ½ cup **sour cream**
- 3 cloves **garlic,** peeled and minced

  About ¼ teaspoon **paprika**

1. Cut baguette in half horizontally.

2. In a bowl, mix shredded cheese, chilies, onion, sour cream, garlic, and ¼ teaspoon paprika.

3. Spread mixture evenly over cut sides of baguette; dust lightly with more paprika. Set, cheese mixture up, on a 14- by 17-inch baking sheet.

4. Broil 4 inches from heat until topping is puffy and lightly browned, about 6 minutes. For appetizers, cut into 1¼- to 1½-inch-long pieces; to serve as a bread, cut into 3- to 4-inch sections. Serve warm.

Per serving: 140 cal., 42% (59 cal.) from fat; 5.5 g protein; 6.6 g fat (3.6 g sat.); 15 g carbo (1 g fiber); 345 mg sodium; 17 mg chol.

Jalapeños en Escabeche (Pickled Chilies)

PREP AND COOK TIME: About 30 minute

NOTES: If making these pickled chilie up to 2 months ahead, cover and chill Or buy canned jalapeños en escabeche

MAKES: 8 to 10 servings

- 1 pound **fresh jalapeño chilies**
- 2 **carrots** (6 oz. total)
- 1 **onion** (6 oz.)
- 2 cups **distilled vinegar**
- ½ cup **salad oil** (or ¼ cup *each* salad oil and olive oil)
- 3 or 4 **garlic** cloves, peeled
- 1 teaspoon **dried oregano,** crumble
- 1 **dried bay leaf**

  Salt and **pepper**

1. Rinse jalapeños and pierce each with a fork. Peel carrots and cut crosswise into ¼-inch slices. Peel onion and cu vertically into ¼-inch slivers.

2. In a 3- to 4-quart pan over high heat combine jalapeños, carrots, onion, 2 cups water, vinegar, oil, garlic, oregano and bay leaf. Bring to a boil.

3. Reduce heat and simmer just until carrots are tender-crisp when pierced, 5 to 8 minutes. Add salt and pepper to taste.

4. Pour into jars, cover, and refrigerate at least 1 day. Use a slotted spoon to serve

Per serving: 130 cal., 76% (99 cal.) from fat; 1 g protein; 11 g fat (1.4 g sat.); 8.8 g carbo (1.2 g fiber); 8.7 mg sodium; 0 mg chol.

salads

Tomato Cucumber Salad with Panela Cheese

PREP TIME: About 10 minutes

NOTES: Panela, a mild Mexican-style cheese that tastes much like fresh mozzarella, is available in well-stocked su permarkets and Latino food markets Use fresh mozzarella as an alternative.

MAKES: 8 to 10 servings

- 3 **firm-ripe tomatoes** (6 oz. each), rinsed, cored, and sliced
- 1 **cucumber** (½ lb.), peeled and thinly sliced
- ¾ pound **panela cheese,** thinly slice
- ¼ cup **lime juice**
- 2 tablespoons **olive oil**

  Salt and **pepper**

1. Arrange tomatoes, cucumber, and cheese on a platter.

2. Mix lime juice and oil; pour evenly over salad. Add salt and pepper to taste.

Per serving: 133 cal., 81% (108 cal.) from fat; 6.5 g protein; 12 g fat (6.4 g sat.); 3.1 g carbo (0.8 g fiber); 222 mg sodium; 12 mg chol.

Tomato Salad with Guacamole Dressing

Follow recipe for **tomato cucumber salad with panela cheese** (preceding), omitting cheese, lime juice, and olive oil. Spoon **guacamole dressing** (following) onto individual portions.

Per serving: 53 cal., 57% (30 cal.) from fat; 1.6 g protein; 3.3 g fat (0.5 g sat.); 5.6 g carbo (1.1 g fiber); 17 mg sodium; 0.2 mg chol.

Guacamole Dressing

PREP TIME: About 5 minutes

NOTES: If making up to 1 day ahead, cover and chill.

MAKES: About 1¾ cups

1 cup **guacamole** (recipe on page 146)

½ cup **plain nonfat yogurt**

2 tablespoons **lemon juice**

1 tablespoon minced **fresh cilantro**

1 to 2 tablespoons minced **fresh jalapeño chilies** (optional)

Salt and **pepper**

In a blender or food processor, combine 3 tablespoons water, guacamole, yogurt, lemon juice, cilantro, and chilies to taste. Whirl until smooth. If dressing is thicker than desired, thin with 1 or 2 tablespoons water. Add salt and pepper to taste.

Per tablespoon: 15 cal., 66% (9.9 cal.) from fat; 0.4 g protein; 1.1 g fat (0.2 g sat.); 1 g carbo (0.1 g fiber); 4.2 mg sodium; 0.1 mg chol.

California Fruit Salad

PREP AND COOK TIME: About 30 minutes

NOTES: Up to 6 hours ahead, cut all the fruit except avocados; cover and chill. Up to 15 minutes before serving, slice avocados and coat with fruit juices.

MAKES: 8 to 10 servings

3 tablespoons **pine nuts** or slivered almonds

4 **oranges** (½ lb. each)

2 **ruby** or pink **grapefruit** (¾ lb. each)

2 **firm-ripe avocados** (1 lb. total)

Large butter, green-, or red-leaf **lettuce leaves**, rinsed and crisped

1 **firm-ripe papaya** (1 lb.), peeled, seeded, and sliced

2 cups **red** or black **grapes**, rinsed

Poppy seed dressing (recipe follows)

Salt and **pepper**

1. In a 6- to 8-inch frying pan over medium heat, stir or shake nuts until golden, 3 to 5 minutes. Pour from pan and let cool.

2. Cut peel and white membrane from oranges and grapefruit. Over a bowl, cut between membranes to release fruit segments; put in bowl.

3. Peel, pit, and slice the avocados; coat slices with some of the citrus juice from the bowl.

4. Line a large platter with lettuce leaves. Arrange oranges, grapefruit, avocados, papaya, and grapes on leaves. Sprinkle with nuts. Moisten with a little of the poppy seed dressing, then spoon portions of salad onto plates and add more dressing and salt and pepper to taste.

Per serving: 245 cal., 66% (162 cal.) from fat; 2.4 g protein; 18 g fat (2.5 g sat.); 22 g carbo (3.4 g fiber); 117 mg sodium; 0 mg chol.

Poppy Seed Dressing

PREP TIME: About 5 minutes

NOTES: If making up to 1 week ahead, cover and chill. For a clinging consistency, whirl dressing in a blender just before using.

MAKES: About 1 cup

½ cup **salad oil** (or ¼ cup *each* salad oil and olive oil)

¼ cup **rice vinegar**

1½ tablespoons **Dijon mustard**

1½ tablespoons **lemon juice**

1½ tablespoons **honey**

2 teaspoons **poppy seed**

¼ teaspoon *each* **salt** and **pepper**

In a bowl or a blender, whisk or whirl oil, vinegar, mustard, lemon juice, honey, poppy seed, salt, and pepper.

Per tablespoon: 70 cal., 90% (63 cal.) from fat; 0.1 g protein; 7 g fat (0.9 g sat.); 1.8 g carbo (0 g fiber); 70 mg sodium; 0 mg chol.

SALADS INCLUDE a fresh fruit combination and tomatoes with panela cheese.

HONEY GLAZES a grilled chicken leg that was marinated in apple juice.

entrées

Fiesta Barbecue Tacos

Offer warm **flour** or corn **tortillas** with any of the following, cut into thin strips: **orange-soy skirt steaks** (as shown on the cover), apple honey-glazed chicken legs, chipotle pork roast, herbed beef tri-tip roast, and garlic butterflied shrimp (leave whole). Have guests build their own tacos, adding **Mexican rancho pinto beans** or refried beans with spinach, **grilled vegetables with tomato oil, guacamole, salsa,** and other **condiments** of choice. See recipes on pages 146 through 151.

Orange-Soy Skirt Steaks

PREP AND COOK TIME: 25 minutes, plus at least 4 hours to marinate

NOTES: Up to 1 day ahead, marinate the steaks.

MAKES: 8 to 10 servings

- 2 **beef skirt steaks** (2½ lb. total), fat-trimmed
- 2 cups **orange juice**
- ¼ cup **soy sauce**
- 4 to 5 cloves **garlic,** peeled, pressed or minced
- 1 teaspoon **coarse-ground pepper**
- 1 teaspoon **dried oregano**
- ½ teaspoon **ground cumin**
  Salt and **pepper**

1. Rinse steaks and pat dry. In a 1-gallon heavy plastic food bag, combine steaks, orange juice, soy sauce, garlic, pepper, oregano, and cumin. Seal bag, set in a bowl, and chill at least 4 hours or up to 1 day; turn occasionally.

2. Weave 2 long metal skewers (18 to 24 in.) parallel through center of each steak. Lay steaks on a barbecue grill over a solid bed of hot coals or high heat on a gas grill (you can hold your hand at grill level only 2 to 3 seconds). Close lid on gas grill. Cook, turning once, until done to your liking, 6 to 8 minutes for medium-rare (cut to test).

3. Transfer steak to a platter, remove skewers, and cut meat into portions. Add salt and pepper to taste.

Per serving: 134 cal., 42% (56 cal.) from fat; 17 g protein; 6.2 g fat (2.7 g sat.); 1.6 g carbo (0 g fiber); 150 mg sodium; 41 mg chol.

Apple Honey-glazed Chicken Legs

PREP AND COOK TIME: About 1 hour, plus at least 4 hours to marinate

NOTES: Up to 1 day ahead, marinate chicken. There may not be enough indirect-heat space for 10 legs on one barbecue. If so, cook in 2 batches, or simultaneously on 2 barbecues.

MAKES: 8 to 10 servings

- 8 to 10 **whole chicken legs** (thighs and drumsticks attached, about 4½ lb. total)
- 2 cups **apple juice**
- 3 cloves **garlic,** peeled, pressed or minced
- ½ teaspoon **pepper**
- ¼ cup **honey**
  Salt

1. Rinse chicken and pat dry. In a 1-gallon heavy plastic food bag, combine chicken, apple juice, garlic, and pepper. Seal bag, set in a bowl, and chill at least 4 hours or up to 1 day; turn over occasionally.

2. Lift chicken from marinade. Barbecue as directed for chipotle pork roast (following, steps 3 and 4), basting with marinade occasionally during the first 20 minutes. Cook chicken until no longer pink at bone of thickest part (cut to test), 40 to 45 minutes. Discard marinade.

3. Brush all sides of chicken with honey. Cook until browned, turning as needed, 3 to 4 minutes longer. Transfer to a platter. Add salt to taste.

Per serving: 278 cal., 45% (126 cal.) from fat; 26 g protein; 14 g fat (3.7 g sat.); 11 g carbo (0.1 g fiber); 90 mg sodium; 93 mg chol.

Chipotle Pork Roast

PREP AND COOK TIME: About 2 hours, plus at least 4 hours to marinate

NOTES: Up to 1 day ahead, marinate pork.

MAKES: 8 to 10 servings

- 1 **boned center-cut pork loin** (3 lb.), fat-trimmed
- 10 cloves **garlic,** peeled
- 2 cups **orange juice**
- ⅓ cup **canned chipotle chilies,** including sauce
- 1 tablespoon chopped **fresh oregano** leaves or dried oregano
- 1 tablespoon **salad oil**
  Oregano sprigs (optional)
  Orange wedges
  Salt and **pepper**

1. Rinse pork; pat dry. Cut garlic into ½-inch slices. Cut ½-inch slits all over meat; insert garlic in them. Place meat in a 1-gallon heavy plastic food bag.

2. In a blender, whirl orange juice, chilies with sauce, chopped oregano, and oil until smooth. Pour over pork, seal bag, and turn to coat. Set bag in a bowl. Chill at least 4 hours or up to 1 day, turning occasionally.

3. *Prepare barbecue.* If using charcoal briquets, mound and ignite 60 briquets on the firegrate of a barbecue with a lid. When briquets are dotted with gray ash, in 15 to 20 minutes, push equal amounts to opposite sides of firegrate. Add 5 more briquets now, and every 30 minutes of cooking, to each mound of coals. If using a gas barbecue, turn heat to high and close lid for 10 minutes. Adjust burners for indirect cooking (no heat down center) and keep on high. Set a drip pan on firegrate between coals or burners. Set barbecue grill in place.

4. Lift pork from marinade and lay on grill, not over heat. Cover barbecue open vents for charcoal. During the first hour, baste meat with marinade occasionally. Cook pork until a thermometer reaches 155° in center of thickest part 1¼ to 1¾ hours. Discard remaining marinade.

5. Transfer pork to a platter, keep warm and let rest about 10 minutes. Garnish with oregano sprigs and orange wedges. Cut meat into thin slices, squeeze juice from orange wedges over slices, and add salt and pepper to taste.

Per serving: 232 cal., 35% (82 cal.) from fat; 31 g protein; 9.1 g fat (3.1 g sat.); 4.4 g carbo (0.2 g fiber); 97 mg sodium; 84 mg chol.

FLOUR TORTILLA is wrapped around grilled garlic shrimp and salsa cruda.

3 to 4 tablespoons minced **garlic**

Salt and **pepper**

Lime wedges

1. Peel shrimp, then cut each down the back, from neck to tail, almost all the way through. Pull out and discard veins. Rinse shrimp and lay open, cut sides down, pressing gently to flatten. For easier handling and to hold shrimp flat, run thin metal skewers, in parallel pairs, crosswise through shellfish, filling skewers.

2. In a 6- to 8-inch frying pan over low heat, stir butter and garlic occasionally until butter melts, about 4 minutes. Remove from heat. Mix or brush shrimp with ²⁄₃ cup of the butter mixture.

3. Lay shrimp, spread open, on a barbecue grill over a solid bed of hot coals or over high heat on a gas grill (you can hold your hand at grill level only 2 to 3 seconds). Close lid on gas grill. Cook, turning once, until shrimp are opaque but still moist-looking in thickest part (cut to test), 5 to 7 minutes. Transfer to a platter as cooked.

4. Warm remaining garlic butter and spoon over shrimp. Add salt and pepper to taste. Squeeze lime onto shrimp to taste.

Per serving: 265 cal., 68% (180 cal.) from fat; 19 g protein; 20 g fat (12 g sat.); 1.8 g carbo (0.1 g fiber); 324 mg sodium; 190 mg chol.

salsas

Salsa Cruda

PREP TIME: About 25 minutes

NOTES: If making up to 1 day ahead, cover and chill.

MAKES: About 4 cups

3 **fresh Anaheim chilies** (9 oz. total)

3 **firm-ripe tomatoes** (1½ lb. total)

2 **green onions,** ends trimmed, thinly sliced

2 cloves **garlic,** peeled, pressed or minced

2 tablespoons chopped **fresh cilantro**

1 to 3 tablespoons minced **fresh serrano chilies** (optional)

Salt and **pepper**

1. Rinse, stem, seed, and chop Anaheim chilies. Rinse, core, and chop tomatoes.

2. In a bowl, mix Anaheim chilies, tomatoes, onions, garlic, cilantro, and

Herbed Beef Tri-Tip Roast

PREP AND COOK TIME: About 1 hour, plus at least 1 hour to marinate

NOTES: Up to 5 hours ahead, start meat preparation.

MAKES: 8 to 10 servings

1 **beef tri-tip** (about 2½ lb.), fat-trimmed

3 or 4 cloves **garlic,** peeled

1 tablespoon **dried Italian herb blend** or herbes de Provence blend

1 cup **beer** or apple juice

Salt and **pepper**

1. Rinse meat and pat dry. Cut ½-inch-wide slits all over roast. Cut garlic into ½-inch slices and tuck into meat slits. Rub meat with herbs. Place in 1-gallon heavy plastic food bag, add beer, and seal bag. Set in a bowl and chill at least 1 hour, or up to 4 hours; turn over occasionally.

2. Lift meat from marinade. Barbecue as directed for chipotle pork roast (facing page, steps 3 and 4), basting with marinade occasionally during the first 30 minutes. Cook beef until a thermometer inserted in the center of thickest part reaches 135° for medium-rare, 35 to 40 minutes. Discard remaining marinade.

3. Transfer beef to platter or board, keep warm, and let rest about 10 minutes. Cut meat into thin slices; add salt and pepper to taste.

Per serving: 157 cal., 24% (38 cal.) from fat; 27 g protein; 4.2 g fat (1.4 g sat.); 0.8 g carbo (0 g fiber); 55 mg sodium; 72 mg chol.

Garlic Butterflied Shrimp

PREP AND COOK TIME: About 1 hour

NOTES: Up to 1 day ahead, butterfly shrimp, cover, and chill.

MAKES: 8 to 10 servings

2½ to 3 pounds **shrimp** (12 to 15 per lb.)

1 cup (½ lb.) **butter** or margarine

ZEST BY THE BOWL: Fresh salsas, green and red, and pickled jalapeños.

2 **green onions,** ends trimmed, thinly sliced

2 tablespoons chopped **fresh cilantro**

2 cloves **garlic,** peeled, minced or pressed

Salt and **pepper**

1. Discard husks and rinse tomatillos In a 1- to 1½-quart pan, combine tomatillos and 2 cups water. Bring to a boil over high heat. Cover and simmer until tomatillos are soft when pressed, 7 to 10 minutes. With a slotted spoon transfer tomatillos to a blender or food processor; reserve cooking water.

2. Rinse, stem, and, if desired for less heat, seed chili. Coarsely chop chili and add to tomatillos along with 2 tablespoons cooking water; whirl until smooth. Pour into a bowl.

3. When cool, add onions, cilantro, garlic, and salt and pepper to taste. For thinner salsa, add more of the cooking water.

Per tablespoon: 4.3 cal., 21% (0.9 cal.) from fat; 0.2 g protein; 0.1 g fat (0 g sat.); 0.8 g carbo (0 g fiber); 0.3 mg sodium; 0 mg chol.

Salsa Verde

PREP AND COOK TIME: About 20 minutes

NOTES: If making up to 1 day ahead, cover and chill.

MAKES: About 1½ cups

4 **fresh Anaheim chilies** (¾ lb. total), rinsed

3 **firm-ripe tomatoes** (1½ lb. total), rinsed

3 **green onions,** ends trimmed, thinly sliced

2 cloves **garlic,** peeled, pressed or minced

¼ cup chopped **fresh cilantro**

Salt and **pepper**

1. Place chilies and tomatoes in a 10- by 15-inch pan. Broil about 4 inches from heat, turning as needed, until vegetables are charred on all sides, about 5 minutes. Cool. Peel and stem chilies; for less heat, discard seeds. Peel tomatoes, cut in half crosswise, and squeeze out and discard seeds. Finely chop tomatoes and chilies and place in a bowl.

2. Add onions, garlic, cilantro, and salt and pepper to taste. If thicker than desired, add a little water to thin.

Per tablespoon: 11 cal., 8.2% (0.9 cal.) from fat; 0.5 g protein; 0.1 g fat (0 g sat.); 2.4 g carbo (0.5 g fiber); 3.4 mg sodium; 0 mg chol.

serrano chilies with salt and pepper to taste.

Per tablespoon: 3.5 cal., 0% (0 cal.) from fat; 0.1 g protein; 0 g fat; 0.8 g carbo (0.2 g fiber); 1.2 mg sodium; 0 mg chol.

Salsa Chilpequín

PREP AND COOK TIME: About 10 minutes

NOTES: If making up to 3 days head, cover and chill. If the tiny fiery chilpequín and chiltepín are unavailable, use ½ cup of another dried hot chili such as *chiles de árbol;* discard stems and seeds before toasting.

MAKES: About ½ cup

½ cup (about 1 oz.) **dried chilpequín** or dried chiltepín

2 teaspoons **salad oil**

2 cloves **garlic,** peeled, pressed or minced

Salt

1. In an 8- to 10-inch frying pan over medium heat, stir chilies in oil until chilies smell toasted, about 3 minutes; take care not to scorch. Pour from pan into a blender.

2. Add garlic and ½ cup water. Whirl until a smooth purée. If desired, thin with 1 or more tablespoons water. Add salt to taste.

Per tablespoon: 22 cal., 68% (15 cal.) from fat; 0.5 g protein; 1.7 g fat (0.3 g sat.); 2.2 g carbo (1 g fiber); 1.2 mg sodium; 0 mg chol.

Salsa de Tomatillo

PREP AND COOK TIME: About 10 minutes

NOTES: If making up to 1 day ahead, cover and chill.

MAKES: About 1½ cups

¾ pound **tomatillos**

1 **fresh jalapeño,** güero, or Santa Fe Grande **chili** (½ oz.)

vegetables

Grilled Corn with Onion and Cheese

PREP AND COOK TIME: About 50 minutes, plus at least 30 minutes to soak

NOTES: Up to 1 day ahead, prepare corn to cook, wrap airtight, and chill. For faster and steamier corn, instead of tying husk to hold in place, seal each ear with its husk in foil. Depending on barbecue grill space, the corn can cook over direct or indirect heat.

MAKES: 8 to 10 servings

- 8 to 10 **ears corn** (about ¾ lb. each)

  About ½ cup (¼ lb.) melted **butter** or margarine

  About ½ cup **grated parmesan cheese**

- ¾ cup very thinly sliced **onion**

  Salt and **pepper**

1. Soak corn in water to cover at least 30 minutes or up to 4 hours.

2. Remove 3 or 4 pieces of husk from 1 or 2 corn ears; tear these pieces lengthwise into ¼-inch-wide strips (you'll need at least 16 to 20 strips).

3. Pull back but don't remove the husk on each ear. Discard corn silk. Brush each ear lightly with butter and sprinkle with 1 tablespoon cheese. Pull husk up on 1 side of each ear and set husk-covered side on a flat surface. Arrange equal portions of onion slices on corn; pull remaining husk up to enclose onion and corn. Tie tip end of each ear with a husk strip (knot strips if pieces are too short). Tie another husk strip around center of each ear.

4. Lay corn on a barbecue grill over a solid bed of hot coals or high heat on a gas grill (you can hold your hand at grill level only 2 to 3 seconds). Close lid on gas grill. Cook, turning often, until corn is hot, about 20 minutes.

5. Pull open husks and season corn with salt and pepper to taste.

Per serving: 210 cal., 51% (108 cal.) from fat; 5.8 g protein; 12 g fat (6.7 g sat.); 24 g carbo (4.1 g fiber); 187 mg sodium; 28 mg chol.

Grilled Vegetables with Tomato Oil

PREP AND COOK TIME: About 30 minutes

NOTES: If there's not enough barbecue grill space for vegetables alongside cooking meats, cook vegetables first and serve at room temperature.

MAKES: 8 to 10 servings

- 2 **sweet onions** (6 oz. each), such as Maui or Walla Walla, peeled
- ¾ to 1 pound **Asian** or regular **eggplant**
- 2 or 3 **zucchini** (¼ lb. each)
- 2 or 3 **bell peppers** (½ lb. each), red, yellow, or green
- 2 **portabella mushrooms** (4-in.-wide caps)

  About ⅓ cup **olive oil**

- 3 tablespoons drained minced **dried tomatoes packed in oil**

  Salt and **pepper**

1. Cut onions crosswise in ¾-inch-thick slices. Run a slender skewer across and through center of each slice to hold rounds flat and secure; put as many slices on skewer as will fit.

2. Rinse eggplant, discard stem, and cut crosswise into ¾-inch-thick rounds. Thread skewers across and through rounds as directed for onions.

3. Rinse zucchini, trim ends, and cut crosswise into ¾-inch-thick rounds. Thread on skewers as directed for onions.

4. Rinse peppers, cut into quarters lengthwise, stem, and seed. Thread thin skewers through center of slices, leaving about ¼ inch between pieces.

5. Rinse mushrooms, trim stems flush with caps, and save stems for other uses.

6. Mix olive oil and tomatoes. Brush mixture onto vegetables.

7. Set vegetables on a barbecue grill over a solid bed of hot coals or high heat on a gas grill (you can hold your hand at grill level only 2 to 3 seconds). Close lid on gas grill. Cook, turning as needed, until vegetables are browned and tender when pierced, 8 to 10 minutes. Transfer to a platter as cooked.

8. Slice mushrooms. Remove vegetables from skewers. Add mushrooms to platter and season vegetables to taste with salt and pepper. Serve hot or at room temperature.

Per serving: 117 cal., 62% (72 cal.) from fat; 2.3 g protein; 8 g fat (1 g sat.); 11 g carbo (2.4 g fiber); 25 mg sodium; 0 mg chol.

Mexican Rancho Pinto Beans

PREP AND COOK TIME: About 30 minutes

NOTES: For speed, start with canned beans. To cook your own dried beans, start with 2 pounds. If making up to 2 days ahead, cover and chill. Reheat in a microwave oven or stir occasionally over medium heat.

MAKES: 8 to 10 servings

- 2 **firm-ripe** to ripe **tomatoes** (1 lb. total), rinsed, cored, and chopped
- 1 **onion** (¾ lb.), peeled and chopped
- 3 **fresh Anaheim chilies** (½ lb. total), rinsed, stemmed, seeded, and chopped
- 5 cloves **garlic**, peeled and chopped
- 6 cans (about 15 oz. each; 10 to 11 cups total) **pinto beans**, drained

  Salt and **pepper**

1. In a 5- to 6-quart pan over medium-high heat, combine tomatoes, onion, chilies, and garlic. Stir often until onion is slightly browned, about 10 minutes.

2. Add beans. Cover and simmer, stirring occasionally, until hot, about 10 minutes. Season to taste with salt and pepper. Pour into a bowl.

Per serving: 211 cal., 5.2% (11 cal.) from fat; 12 g protein; 1.2 g fat (0.2 g sat.); 39 g carbo (11 g fiber); 793 mg sodium; 0 mg chol.

Refried Beans with Spinach

PREP AND COOK TIME: About 40 minutes

NOTES: If making up to 2 days ahead, cover and chill bean mixture and bacon separately. Reheat in a microwave oven or stir often over medium heat.

MAKES: 8 to 10 servings

- ½ pound **bacon**, coarsely chopped

  Mexican rancho pinto beans (preceding)

- 2 quarts (6 oz.) **spinach leaves** or mustard greens, rinsed and drained
- 1 cup (¼ lb.) **shredded cheddar cheese**

  Salt and **pepper**

  Chicken broth or water (optional)

1. In a 5- to 6-quart pan over medium-high heat, stir bacon until crisp, about 10 minutes. Lift out with a slotted spoon and drain on towels.

2. Add beans to drippings in pan; mash with a potato masher or beat with a mixer until creamy. Stir often over medium heat until hot, about 6 minutes.

3. Meanwhile, coarsely chop spinach. When beans are hot, add spinach; cover and stir occasionally, until wilted, about 3 minutes. Stir in half the cheese. Add salt and pepper to taste. If beans are not as creamy as you like, stir in a little broth. Pour into a bowl and sprinkle with remaining cheese and bacon.

Per serving: 224 cal., 68% (153 cal.) from fat; 8.1 g protein; 17 g fat (7.3 g sat.); 9.6 g carbo (2.9 g fiber); 419 mg sodium; 27 mg chol. ◆

In a Vancouver Island garden

Barbecued lamb, fragrant herbs, and blueberries make a party menu

BY LINDA LAU ANUSASANANAN • PHOTOGRAPHS BY TERRENCE McCARTHY

■ Fresh herbs perfume every course of this leisurely meal, and it's not by happenstance. The menu's creator, cookbook author Noël Richardson, lives on a 10-acre herb farm on sunny Vancouver Island in British Columbia. Inspiration grows all around her. "We eat out of our garden year-round," she explains.

Richardson's husband, Andrew Yeoman, a writer and the head gardener at their Ravenhill Herb Farm, supplies the just-picked herbs and a delectable assortment of vegetables. Daughter Jenny Cameron, chef and food stylist, lends a hand with the cooking. Collectively they presented this garden party for eight to celebrate the glories of their island in summer.

The party is easy to duplicate in spirit and detail elsewhere in the West. You can purchase fresh ingredients at a well-stocked supermarket, but a farmers' or specialty produce market will offer more variety. Richardson bakes her own bread, decorating the surface of the dough with fresh herbs. You can do the same or purchase plain or herb-flavor crusty French bread. To emphasize the regional richness of the area, the family serves locally produced wine, but the same varietals from other areas are suitable.

Richardson's most recent book, *In a Country Garden: Life at Ravenhill Farm* (Graphic Arts Center Publishing, Portland, 1996; $12.95; 800/452-3032), offers more inspiration from the land.

Noël Richardson (on left in photo below) and daughter Jenny Cameron (on right) prepare a meal from the bounty of British Columbia, including farm-fresh tomatoes and lemon cucumbers with a nasturtium vinaigrette (left) and grilled lamb with cilantro (right).

Ravenhill Herb Farm Supper

Tapenade with Basil

Roasted Garlic with Rosemary

Summerhill Estate Winery 'Cipes' Brut nonvintage
Okanagan Valley, British Columbia

Tomato Cucumber Salad with Nasturtium Vinaigrette

Barbecued Lamb with Cilantro

Grilled Zucchini with Basil Balsamic Vinaigrette

Roasted Baby Potatoes with Tarragon Aioli

French Bread with Herbs • Butter

Nichol Vineyard 1994 Pinot Noir,
Okanagan Valley, British Columbia

Sugar-glazed Blueberries • Lemon Verbena Sabayon

Quails Gate Estate Winery 1997 Gewürztraminer,
Okanagan Valley, British Columbia

Tapenade with Basil

PREP TIME: About 20 minutes

NOTES: If making up to 1 week ahead, chill airtight. Spread tapenade onto crusty bread to serve as an appetizer.

MAKES: About 1¼ cups

- 1 cup **calamata olives**
- 3 cloves **garlic,** peeled
- 1 can (2 oz.) **anchovy fillets,** drained and rinsed
- ¾ cup chopped **fresh basil** leaves
- ½ cup **extra-virgin olive oil**

Pit olives. In a food processor, whirl olives, garlic, anchovies, and basil until finely chopped. Add olive oil and whirl until smooth. (Or with a knife, mince olives, garlic, anchovies, and basil; mix with oil.)

Per tablespoon: 74 cal., 91% (67 cal.) from fat; 0.8 g protein; 7.4 g fat (1 g sat.); 1.2 g carbo (0.1 g fiber); 204 mg sodium; 1.2 mg chol.

FRESH HERBS PERMEATE every dish: Tarragon seasons the aioli for potatoes, and rosemary scents the garlic (above). Guests sip local sparkling wine (left).

Tender **nasturtium** or romaine lettuce **leaves,** rinsed and drained

Nasturtium vinaigrette (recipe follows)

Dill sprigs (optional), rinsed

8 **nasturtium sprigs** and **flowers,** or watercress sprigs, rinsed and drained

Salt and **pepper**

1. Slice cucumber and tomatoes into ¼-inch-thick rounds.

2. Line a platter with nasturtium leaves. Arrange sliced tomatoes and cucumbers on leaves.

3. Drizzle salad with vinaigrette. Garnish with dill and nasturtium sprigs or flowers. Add salt and pepper to taste.

Per serving: 151 cal., 83% (126 cal.) from fat; 1.7 g protein; 14 g fat (1.3 g sat.); 6.1 g carbo (2.1 g fiber); 54 mg sodium; 0 mg chol.

Nasturtium Vinaigrette

PREP TIME: About 10 minutes

NOTES: Up to 30 minutes ahead, make dressing.

MAKES: About 1 cup

¼ cup **lemon juice**

¼ cup thinly sliced **chives** or chopped green onions

2 tablespoons finely chopped **nasturtium flowers** or watercress

1 tablespoon **Dijon mustard**

½ cup **salad** or extra-virgin olive **oil**

In a bowl, mix lemon juice, chives, nasturtiums, and mustard. Add oil, whisking to blend.

Per tablespoon: 62 cal., 98% (61 cal.) from fat; 0 g protein; 6.8 g fat (0.6 g sat.); 0.3 g carbo (0 g fiber); 23 mg sodium; 0 mg chol.

Barbecued Lamb with Cilantro

PREP AND COOK TIME: About 1 hour

NOTES: Up to 1 day ahead, marinate lamb.

MAKES: 8 servings

2 cups **dry red wine**

¾ cup **soy sauce**

½ cup **extra-virgin olive oil**

3 cloves **garlic,** peeled and minced

1½ cups chopped **fresh cilantro**

2 **fresh** or dried **bay leaves**

1 **leg of lamb** (6 lb.), boned, butterflied, and fat-trimmed

Cilantro sprigs

Salt and **pepper**

Roasted Garlic with Rosemary

PREP AND COOK TIME: About 1 hour

NOTES: Up to 4 hours ahead, bake garlic. For an appetizer, spoon garlic onto thin baguette slices. For a condiment, present with the main part of the meal.

MAKES: 8 servings

3 heads **garlic** (about 9 oz. total)

¼ cup **extra-virgin olive oil**

2 tablespoons **balsamic vinegar**

2 tablespoons **dry wine** (red or white)

1 tablespoon minced **fresh rosemary** leaves or crumbled dried rosemary

Salt and **pepper**

1. Peel garlic and put cloves in a 6- to 8-inch-wide pan.

2. Add oil, balsamic vinegar, wine, and rosemary; mix.

3. Cover and bake in a 400° oven 25 minutes. Uncover and continue to bake until garlic is light gold and soft to touch, 10 to 15 minutes longer.

4. Add salt and pepper to taste. Serve hot, warm, or at room temperature.

Per serving: 105 cal., 61% (64 cal.) from fat; 1.8 g protein; 7.1 g fat (1 g sat.); 9.4 g carbo (0.6 g fiber); 5.1 mg sodium; 0 mg chol.

Tomato Cucumber Salad

PREP TIME: About 30 minutes

NOTES: Up to 1 hour ahead, assemble salad. Add dressing when serving. Buy nasturtium flowers and leaves, grown for eating, in the produce section. Or, if you grow nasturtiums without chemicals or pesticides in your own garden, you can pick and use them.

MAKES: 8 servings

½ pound **English** or lemon **cucumber,** rinsed

6 **firm-ripe tomatoes** (½ lb. total), rinsed and cored

1. In a 9- by 13-inch baking dish, mix wine, soy sauce, oil, garlic, chopped cilantro, and bay leaves. Spread lamb open in the marinade and turn to coat. Cover and chill, turning meat occasionally, at least 4 hours or up to 1 day.

2. Lift lamb from marinade (reserve marinade) and lay flat (open) on a barbecue grill over a solid bed of medium coals or medium heat on a gas grill (you can hold your hand at grill level only 4 to 5 seconds). Close lid on gas grill. Cook, turning as needed to brown meat evenly, until a thermometer inserted in thickest part is 135° to 140° for rare, 30 to 45 minutes; thin portions will be well-done. Brush meat occasionally with marinade up until the last 10 minutes of cooking.

3. Transfer meat to a platter, keep warm, and let rest 5 to 15 minutes. Garnish with cilantro sprigs. Thinly slice meat. Add salt and pepper to taste.

Per serving: 383 cal., 47% (180 cal.) from fat; 47 g protein; 20 g fat (5.5 g sat.); 2 g carbo (0.1 g fiber); 895 mg sodium; 145 mg chol.

Grilled Zucchini with Basil Balsamic Vinaigrette

PREP AND COOK TIME: About 20 minutes

NOTES: Cook zucchini on grill beside the lamb.

MAKES: 8 servings

- ¼ cup chopped **fresh basil** leaves
- 3 tablespoons **balsamic vinegar**
- 1 tablespoon **Dijon mustard**
- 1 teaspoon **honey** or maple syrup
- 2 cloves **garlic,** minced or pressed
- ⅓ cup **extra-virgin olive oil**
- 8 **yellow** or green **zucchini** (3 lb. total), rinsed, ends trimmed, and cut into ½-inch-thick rounds

  Basil sprigs

  Salt and **pepper**

1. In a small bowl, mix chopped basil, vinegar, mustard, honey, and garlic. Whisking, blend in oil.

2. Thread zucchini on thin skewers so rounds lie flat and pieces touch. Brush generously with basil vinaigrette.

3. Place zucchini on a barbecue grill over a solid bed of medium coals or medium heat on a gas grill (you can hold your hand at grill level only 4 to 5 seconds). Close lid on gas grill. Cook until brown on each side, 5 to 7 minutes total; turn once.

4. Push zucchini from skewers onto a platter. Drizzle with remaining vinaigrette. Garnish with basil sprigs. Add salt and pepper to taste.

Per serving: 110 cal., 78% (86 cal.) from fat; 2.1 g protein; 9.5 g fat (1.4 g sat.); 6.2 g carbo (1 g fiber); 51 mg sodium; 0 mg chol.

Roasted Baby Potatoes

PREP AND COOK TIME: About 50 minutes

NOTES: Richardson uses a mixture of red and white thin-skinned small potatoes from her garden. Roast potatoes in the oven as lamb is cooking.

MAKES: 8 servings

- 3 pounds **thin-skinned potatoes** (1½ in. wide), scrubbed
- 3 tablespoons **olive oil**

  Salt and **pepper**

  Tarragon aioli (recipe follows)

1. In a 10- by 15-inch pan, mix potatoes and oil. Lightly sprinkle with salt and pepper.

2. Roast potatoes in a 400° oven, shaking pan occasionally, until tender when pierced, 45 to 50 minutes (35 to 40 minutes in convection oven).

3. Serve potatoes hot or warm with tarragon aioli.

Per serving without aioli: 182 cal., 27% (49 cal.) from fat; 3.3 g protein; 5.4 g fat (0.7 g sat.); 31 g carbo (2.8 g fiber); 13 mg sodium; 0 mg chol.

Tarragon Aioli

PREP TIME: About 15 minutes

NOTES: Up to 1 day ahead, mix, cover, and chill the aioli. Serve with potatoes and, if desired, the lamb.

MAKES: 1⅓ cups

- 1¼ cups **mayonnaise**
- 1 to 2 tablespoons minced **garlic**
- 2 tablespoons minced **fresh tarragon** leaves
- 1 teaspoon grated **lemon** peel
- 3 tablespoons **lemon juice**
- 1 teaspoon **Dijon mustard**

  Salt

In a bowl, mix mayonnaise, garlic, tarragon, lemon peel, lemon juice, and mustard. Add salt to taste.

Per tablespoon: 96 cal., 94% (90 cal.) from fat; 0.2 g protein; 10 g fat (1.5 g sat.); 0.7 g carbo (0 g fiber); 81 mg sodium; 7.7 mg chol.

Sugar-glazed Blueberries

PREP AND COOK TIME: About 12 minutes

NOTES: Measure ingredients before dinner. Heat just before serving.

MAKES: 8 servings

- 1 **lemon** (5 oz.)
- ⅔ cup **sugar**
- ¼ teaspoon **ground cinnamon**
- 8 cups **blueberries** (3 lb.), rinsed and drained

  Lemon verbena sabayon (recipe follows)

1. With a vegetable peeler, pare off yellow peel from lemon and mince. Ream juice from lemon.

2. In a 5- to 6-quart pan, mix 3 tablespoons lemon juice (save extra for other uses), sugar, and cinnamon. Stir over high heat until mixture is boiling vigorously, 2 to 3 minutes. Remove from heat and stir in lemon peel and blueberries.

3. Serve warm or cool. Spoon into bowls and top with lemon verbena sabayon.

Per serving: 233 cal., 12% (29 cal.) from fat; 2.6 g protein; 3.2 g fat (0.8 g sat.); 50 g carbo (4 g fiber); 16 mg sodium; 106 mg chol.

Lemon Verbena Sabayon

PREP AND COOK TIME: About 15 minutes to assemble; about 5 minutes to cook

NOTES: Measure ingredients before dinner, then cook just before serving. Jenny Cameron whips up the sabayon while her mother prepares the berries.

MAKES: About 4 cups; 8 servings

- 4 **large egg** yolks
- ⅓ cup **sugar**
- 2 tablespoons **lemon** juice
- 6 tablespoons **late-harvest Riesling** or white grape juice
- 1½ tablespoons finely chopped **fresh lemon verbena,** lemon balm, or mint leaves

1. In the top of a double boiler or metal bowl (4 to 6 qt.), whisk to blend egg yolks, sugar, lemon juice, and Riesling.

2. Set double boiler over boiling water, or nest bowl in a pan over boiling water. Whisk egg mixture (or beat with a mixer on medium speed) until it is thick enough to hold a mound for a few seconds, 5 to 7 minutes total. Add lemon verbena, whisk, and serve at once.

Per ½ cup: 70 cal., 33% (23 cal.) from fat; 1.4 g protein; 2.6 g fat (0.8 g sat.); 8.8 g carbo (0.1 g fiber); 5.3 mg sodium; 106 mg chol. ◆

foodguide

BY JERRY ANNE DI VECCHIO

PHOTOGRAPHS BY JAMES CARRIER

No cows in this corn

The kernel gets no respect in France but turns to gold on an American table

■ In France, corn is mostly grown to feed cattle—not a bad cause, of course; that cow's milk makes great cheese. But what few ears I see in French markets for human consumption look very old and tired. However, Ronald Zappardino, proprietor of French-influenced Top o' the Cove restaurant in La Jolla, California, more than meets American standards when it comes to corn. Sweet ears take a direct route from the field to his door. • One night, from a romantic corner of the restaurant, I was watching the sun slip over the Pacific Rim (a justifiably praised view) when, lo and behold, another golden orb appeared before me—a bowl of rich corn chowder to shift my attention to dinner. As I savored the soup, it struck me that French influence on an American classic is not a bad thing. It manages to make coziness elegant.

Top o' the Cove Corn Chowder

PREP AND COOK TIME: About 1 hour

NOTES: Executive chef Guy Sockrider makes the chowder with about three times as much whipping cream as broth. This somewhat less indulgent version is still very smooth and creamy; in fact, it's quite velvety even if you reduce the cream to only 1 cup and add 1 more cup chicken broth. Garnish bowls with chive spears, if desired, and edible flowers such as blue rosemary blossoms or golden calendula petals.

MAKES: About 7½ cups; 6 to 8 servings

    4 **ears corn** (7 to 8 in.)

    2 tablespoons **butter** or olive oil

    ⅔ cup chopped **celery**

    ⅔ cup chopped **onion**

    1 teaspoon **fresh thyme** leaves or dried thyme

    1 clove **garlic,** peeled

    1 **potato** (½ lb.), peeled and diced

    3 cups fat-skimmed **chicken broth**

    2 cups **whipping cream**

       Salt and **pepper**

1. Husk the corn and discard the silk. Rinse corn. In a 5- to 6-quart pan over high heat, brown 2 ears, turning as needed to toast all sides, until kernels are speckled dark brown, about 10 minutes. Let corn cool. Rinse out pan.

2. With a sharp knife or corn cutter, cut the toasted corn from the cobs; set aside ¹⁄₂ cup of the kernels. Also cut corn from remaining cobs.

3. Return pan to high heat; add butter, celery, onion, thyme, and garlic. Stir often until vegetables are slightly browned, 3 to 5 minutes.

4. Add all of the corn except for the reserved ¹⁄₂ cup toasted kernels. Also add potato, broth, and cream. Stir to mix, then bring to a boil, cover, and reduce heat. Simmer gently, stirring occasionally, until potatoes are easy to mash, about 20 minutes.

5. In a blender, whirl the cooked mixture, a portion at a time, until smoothly puréed. Rub the purée through a fine strainer back into the pan. Add salt and pepper to taste. Bring to a boil over high heat, stirring often.

6. Ladle the soup into bowls and top equally with the reserved browned corn kernels.

Per serving: 291 cal., 68% (198 cal.) from fat; 7 g protein; 22 g fat (13 g sat.); 19 g carbo (2.7 g fiber); 98 mg sodium; 74 mg chol.

Short cuts

■ Beef short ribs are tasty, but they're also full of long strips of connective tissue. This tough stuff melts away if you give ribs the long, slow cooking treatment. You can get to the ribs' rich flavor faster, however, if you cut them Korean-style, with strategic slashes parallel to the bone. Pulled out to a thin layer—butterflied—and browned quickly on the barbecue, the meat is juicy and tender, and the gristly strips can be trimmed off easily with a sharp steak knife. The diagram below is an end view of the rib showing how to make the cuts.

Korean Barbecued Short Ribs

PREP AND COOK TIME: About 30 minutes, plus 30 minutes to marinate ribs

NOTES: Buy ribs with bones whole, not cracked. Serve with dressed bitter greens or braised bok choy and rice.

MAKES: 4 servings

- 4 **beef short ribs** (about 1 lb. each)
- ¹⁄₄ cup **soy sauce**
- ¹⁄₄ cup **dry sherry**
- 1 tablespoon **sugar**
- 1 tablespoon minced **fresh ginger**

1. Trim thick outer layer of fat from ribs; discard. Rinse meat and pat dry.

2. On the meaty side of each rib, ¹⁄₄ inch in from the edge opposite the bone, make a cut the length of the rib, down into meat but not quite through it **(a)**. Turn the rib over. About halfway between bone and first cut, make another lengthwise cut almost through meat **(b)**. Flip the rib over again and make a third lengthwise cut parallel to and around the bone almost through meat, leaving bone attached **(c)**. Pull out to unfold meat.

3. In a 1-gallon heavy plastic food bag, combine soy, sherry, sugar, and ginger; shake to mix. Add short ribs to bag, seal, and turn over to coat meat with marinade.

4. Set bag in a bowl; chill at least 30 minutes or up to 1 day, turning several times. Remove ribs and discard marinade.

5. Lay ribs, pulled open so meat is flat, on a barbecue grill over a solid bed of hot coals or high heat on a gas grill (you can hold your hand at grill level only 2 to 3 seconds). Close lid; open vents for charcoal. Brown meat, turning once, 7 to 10 minutes. Transfer to a platter.

Per serving: 728 cal., 73% (531 cal.) from fat; 44 g protein; 59 g fat (25 g sat.); 2.8 g carbo (0 g fiber); 628 mg sodium; 164 mg chol.

CUT ON THE DOTTED LINES

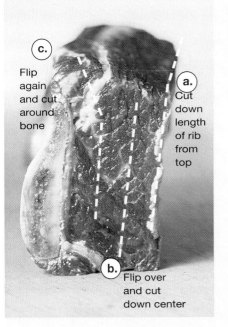

c. Flip again and cut around bone

a. Cut down length of rib from top

b. Flip over and cut down center

Worldly fish

■ The obstacle to preparing *moqueca,* Brazil's great fish stew, has been one of its most characteristic ingredients: *dendê,* a red palm oil. Prone to rancidity, it's rarely at its best by the time it travels here. However, Joao Victor Barbosa of Joao's Restaurant in Santa Clara, California, captures remarkably authentic moqueca flavor, sans dendê, in this simple version made with a fillet of salmon.

Salmon Moqueca

PREP AND COOK TIME: About 25 minutes

NOTES: Leaving the skin on makes salmon easier to cook; lift from skin to eat.

MAKES: 3 servings

- 1 pound **salmon fillet with skin**
- 2 teaspoons **butter** or olive oil
- 1 clove **garlic,** chopped
- ¼ cup chopped **green onions**
- ¼ cup chopped **tomato**
- 1 teaspoon **paprika**
- ½ cup **canned coconut milk**
- ½ cup **sour cream**
- 3 tablespoons chopped **fresh cilantro**
- 3 cups hot cooked **rice**
  Salt and **pepper**

1. Rinse salmon; pat dry. In a 10- to 11-inch frying pan over high heat, melt butter. Lay salmon, flesh down, in pan and brown lightly, about 2 minutes. Turn over with a wide spatula and brown skin lightly, about 2 minutes. Lift fish out and set on a plate.

2. To pan add garlic, onions, and tomato. Stir until juices evaporate, about 2 minutes. Add paprika; stir. Add coconut milk; mix well. Set fish, skin down, in sauce. Cover pan and simmer over medium heat until salmon is opaque but still moist-looking in center of thickest part (cut to test), 5 to 7 minutes, stirring sauce around fish occasionally.

3. With spatula, transfer fish to a platter; keep warm. Add sour cream to pan and stir over high heat until sauce is boiling. Stir in 2 tablespoons cilantro and pour sauce over fish. Sprinkle with remaining cilantro. Serve fish and sauce over rice. Season to taste with salt and pepper.

Per serving: 671 cal., 48% (324 cal.) from fat; 37 g protein; 36 g fat (17 g sat.); 49 g carbo (1.1 g fiber); 145 mg sodium; 113 mg chol.

Ever green

■ The most famous vegetarian dining establishment in the West—possibly the country—is celebrating its 20th birthday this month. San Francisco's Greens Restaurant is still going strong without meat, thanks to chef Annie Somerville's fresh dishes, such as this salad.

Greens Salad with Roasted Peppers

PREP AND COOK TIME: About 30 minutes

NOTES: Greens roasts the red peppers on-site, but canned ones work well.

MAKES: 6 to 8 servings

- 1 cup **canned roasted red peppers**
  About ¼ cup **extra-virgin olive oil**
  About 3 tablespoons **balsamic vinegar**
- 1 clove **garlic,** minced
- 10 to 12 **niçoise** or calamata **olives**
- 8 to 12 **baguette** slices (about ¼ in. thick)
- ½ cup thinly sliced **mild red onion**
- 10 cups (about 10 oz.) **spinach leaves,** rinsed and drained
- 2 cups (about 2 oz.) **frisée** or curly endive, rinsed and drained
  Salt
- ⅓ cup fresh-grated **parmesan cheese**

1. Cut peppers into ¼-inch-wide strips and put in a wide salad bowl. Add 1 teaspoon olive oil, 3 tablespoons vinegar, garlic, and olives; mix.

2. Brush baguette slices lightly on 1 side with olive oil (about 1 tablespoon total). Lay oiled side up in a 10- by 15-inch pan. Bake in a 375° oven until lightly toasted, about 8 minutes; cool on a rack.

3. To bowl, add onion, spinach, and frisée; mix, and season to taste with more vinegar and salt.

4. Heat 2 tablespoons oil in a 6- to 8-inch frying pan over high heat, about 1 minute. Pour over salad and mix. Add cheese and baguette slices; mix again.

Per serving: 137 cal., 61% (83 cal.) from fat; 4.1 g protein; 9.2 g fat (1.9 g sat.); 11 g carbo (1.8 g fiber); 231 mg sodium; 3.2 mg chol. ◆

The Wine Guide

BY KAREN MacNEIL-FIFE

RICK MARIANI

Season of rosés

■ This time of year in southern France, people are drinking something special we Americans rarely do. The same is true in southern Italy. And certainly in Spain. It's something so glorious and so perfect for warm weather that it is totally baffling why we remain largely oblivious to its pleasures.

This something is pink wine—or, as it is traditionally known, rosé.

Okay, I know we are only in the third paragraph, but I suspect some of you are already on the verge of flipping the page. "Rosé?" you're thinking. "Not for me."

Well, hold on. This could be the summer you convert.

Our collective American hang-up with rosé is not a matter of the wine's quality—it's a matter of its image. And rosé's image is anything but rosy. To begin with, in every one of the last several decades, there was at least one popular rosé that wine connoisseurs loved to hate. In the '60s it was Lancers and Mateus (about which I have fond memories). In the '70s it was Riunite. And by the '80s, "white" Zinfandel (a pink wine showing the depth of

its identity crisis) was known coast to coast. With one brush stroke, pink became the lowbrow drink.

It's now, of course, the end of the '90s, and in this last summer of the century, the tide has begun to turn. Refreshing top-notch rosés abound here, and convincing Americans of their merits may just be a matter of getting them to take that first chilled sip. "If we can get people to try rosé, 80 percent of them will love it," says Bill Hart, assistant winemaker at Hart Winery in Temecula, California, "and the rest of them will be lying."

Like all of the other top domestic rosé producers, tiny Hart has had an uphill battle turning people on to its scrumptious rosé. In the end it's the makers' passion for the wine that keeps them going—and their wacky humor. "Our newest promotional campaign is a T-shirt," Hart explains. "It says, 'Rosé has gotten a bad rap because people always drink it with their clothes on.'"

Ahem.

Though many wine drinkers assume that rosé is fairly simple to make, that's not exactly the case. *Mediocre* rosé may be a cinch, but the great rosés possess an uncanny balance of crispness and fruitiness that is not easy to achieve. Moreover, rosé is not like chocolate milk; to make it, you can't just mix half a vat of red wine with half a vat of white.

The winemaker has two main options. In scenario one, he or she crushes red grapes and puts the soupy mass into a tank. The skins begin to tint the juice red (red or white, grapes always have white juice). When the juice is pink—but before it's red—the winemaker drains it off the skins so it won't get any darker.

Scenario two is a French method called *saignée* (French for *bleeding*). Here, the winemaker's primary goal is

> ### SUNSET'S STEAL OF THE MONTH
>
> **McDowell Grenache Rosé 1997 (Mendocino), $8** (Grenache, Cinsault, Syrah). While most top rosés are a steal, for just $8 it's hard to beat this one—snappy and refreshing, with a rush of berry fruit.
>
> — KAREN MacNEIL-FIFE

ROSÉ SENSATIONS

Rosés (which can be still or sparkling) are consummate warm-weather dinner wines. Nothing could be better with salads and simple grilled chicken or shrimp. Here are some of my favorites.

■ **Chateau Potelle "Riviera" 1997 (Amador County),** $12 (Zinfandel, Cabernet Sauvignon). Bold, simple, and tasty—much like a southern French rosé.

■ **Hart Grenache Rosé 1998 (Cucamonga Valley),** $10 (Grenache). A spicy, strawberry-like stunner. (Available mostly through the winery; 909/676-6300.)

■ **Joseph Phelps "Vin du Mistral" Grenache Rosé 1997 (California),** $12.50 (Grenache, Mourvèdre). Lively and fresh; strawberry and watermelon flavors.

■ **Simi Rosé of Cabernet 1997 (Sonoma County),** $10 (Cabernet Sauvignon). Fresh and delicious—like a Shirley Temple for grown-ups.

■ **Zaca Mesa "Z Gris" 1997 (Santa Barbara County),** $10 (Grenache, Counoise, Viognier, Cinsault, Mourvèdre, Syrah). Totally scrumptious, with elegant flavors reminiscent of rose petals, peaches, and apricots.

to make a rich *red* wine. To do this, he or she "bleeds off" some pink juice early in the process so that the rest of the liquid has more contact with the skins. The result is two wines: a concentrated red and, as a bonus, a wonderful rosé.

Rosés can be made from any single red grape variety or a combination. Simi's tasty Rosé of Cabernet, for example, is made from only Cabernet Sauvignon, while Zaca Mesa's sensational Z Gris is made from a veritable rainbow of grapes—Grenache, Counoise, Viognier, Cinsault, Mourvèdre, and Syrah.

So experiment to find the wines you like. Here's the plan: Some night this week, imagine you are on the Riviera, where everything is beautiful, everyone is in love, and just about everyone is drinking pink. ◆

The Low-Fat Cook

HEALTHY CHOICES FOR THE ACTIVE LIFESTYLE

BY ELAINE JOHNSON

FROSTY DRINK FLAVORS include, from left, coffee, four-fruit, chocolate, and blueberry.

Dessert in a glass

■ The days are hot. The clothes are skimpy. You crave something decadent. What fills you up and cools you off, but won't fill you out? Four choices follow.

Frozen Cappuccino

PREP TIME: About 5 minutes, plus 20 minutes to chill

NOTES: Theresa Loverro of Carlsbad, California, shared this recipe with us.

MAKES: 1 serving

1. Put ⅓ cup finely ground **espresso-roast coffee** or other dark-roast coffee in a paper-lined coffee filter set over a mug. Pour 1 cup hot (190°) **water** into filter and let drip through. Chill until cool, about 20 minutes.

2. In a blender, whirl coffee, ¾ cup **vanilla nonfat frozen yogurt**, ½ cup **ice cubes**, and 1½ tablespoons **sugar** until smoothly puréed. Pour into a glass.

Per serving: 227 cal., 0% (0 cal.) from fat; 3.2 g protein; 0 g fat; 53 g carbo (0 g fiber); 72 mg sodium; 0 mg chol.

Four-Fruit Smoothie

PREP TIME: About 5 minutes, plus at least 1 hour to freeze fruit

NOTES: This recipe came from Cerrith-wen Genetti of Cazadero, California. To freeze fruit pieces, set them slightly apart on a baking sheet. Put in the freezer until firm, 1 to 2 hours. To store longer, transfer frozen fruit to a freezer container. Or buy individually quick-frozen fruit pieces or berries by the bag, pour out the amount of fruit you need, then seal bag and store in the freezer.

MAKES: 3½ cups

In a blender, whirl 1½ cups **apple juice**, 1¾ cups **frozen banana** chunks (cut into 1-in. pieces), 1 cup **frozen strawberries**, and 1 cup **frozen peach** slices until smoothly puréed. Add ⅛ to ¼ teaspoon **almond extract** (optional) to taste. Pour into glasses to serve.

Per cup: 155 cal., 3.5% (5.4 cal.) from fat; 1.3 g protein; 0.6 g fat (0.2 g sat.); 39 g carbo (2.1 g fiber); 4.8 mg sodium; 0 mg chol.

Iced Mexican Chocolate

PREP TIME: About 5 minutes

NOTES: Elizabeth Monroe of Seattle contributed this recipe.

MAKES: 4½ cups

In a blender, whirl 1 cup **nonfat milk,** 1½ ounces **unsweetened chocolate** (coarsely chopped), 2 tablespoons **honey,** ½ teaspoon grated **orange** peel, and ½ teaspoon **ground cinnamon** until chocolate is finely ground. Add 1 pint **vanilla nonfat frozen yogurt** and 2 cups **ice cubes;** whirl until smoothly puréed (chocolate forms streaks). Pour into glasses.

Per cup: 187 cal., 26% (48 cal.) from fat; 4.6 g protein; 5.3 g fat (3.1 g sat.); 33 g carbo (1.4 g fiber); 70 mg sodium; 1.1 mg chol.

Blueberry-Lemon Shake

PREP TIME: About 5 minutes, plus at least 1 hour to freeze berries

NOTES: Freeze blueberries as directed in notes for Four-Fruit Smoothie (preceding). Or buy unsweetened frozen blueberries.

MAKES: 3½ cups

In a blender, whirl 3 cups **frozen blueberries,** 1½ cups **buttermilk,** ½ cup **sugar,** ½ teaspoon grated **lemon** peel, and 2 tablespoons **lemon juice** until smoothly puréed. Pour into glasses to serve.

Per cup: 224 cal., 5.8% (13 cal.) from fat; 4.3 g protein; 1.4 g fat (0.6 g sat.); 52 g carbo (2.9 g fiber); 120 mg sodium; 4.2 mg chol. ◆

A food lover's treasure trove

Shopping along Artesia's Pioneer Boulevard

BY ANDREW BAKER

Some of the best food shopping in the West is served up along Pioneer Boulevard in the L.A. suburb of Artesia. Foodstuffs of every sort—all the essentials for an Indian meal, plus everyday produce and spices—are sold here at bargain prices. Interspersed among the grocers are sari shops and jewelers as well as snack stops and restaurants offering immediate gratification to shoppers.

Area code is 562; addresses are on Pioneer unless noted.

SHOPPING

Forget expensive tiny tins of spices: This neighborhood sells in quantity. For example, cloves come in 14-ounce packages (about $1.70).

Beyond spices, the choices vary from store to store: basmati rice in 10-pound sacks (about $9), fenugreek-flavor flatbreads, fresh turmeric, and rose syrup. Among the best: **Farm Fresh** (18612; 865-8171) carries produce like fresh fenugreek and baby eggplant, plus British food products for hungry expatriates. **House of Spices** (18550; 860-9919) is an emporium of flavorful edibles, including tea, beans, and rice. **Novelty's** (18607; 865-5664) gleams with stainless steel cooking and serving pieces; it also sells bracelets and fashion accessories.

SNACKING

Indian snacks and sweets come in a rainbow array, from green pistachio candy topped with edible silver to neon-orange *jalebi,* a crispy fritter soaked in a saffron syrup. Many start with familiar flavors and textures: Think of *sev* and *chevra* as Chex mix flavored with turmeric or cayenne. **Surati Farsan Mart** (11814 E. 186th St.; 860-2310 or www.suratifarsan.com) has a full line of treats (also available by mail order), as well as light meals.

South of Los Angeles, Artesia offers rich culinary resources.

DAVID ZAITZ (3)

SHOPPERS' REWARDS: Cashew-pistachio rolls for a nibble (top); lunch at Udupi Palace (top right); a pot for every purpose at Novelty's.

EATING

The following restaurants serve lunch and dinner.

Ambala Dhaba (18413; 402-7990) offers *ludhiana* chicken—marinated in a spicy yogurt sauce and cooked in a tandoori oven. It's a steal at $6. Soothe scorched taste buds with housemade pistachio *kulfi* (ice cream).

Jay Bharat (18701; 924-3310) specializes in *dosas* and *uttapas* (thin rice-flour pancakes) with savory fillings. Add chutney and sambar soup for a hearty snack.

Udupi Palace (18635; 860-1950). Sari-clad waitresses serve vegetarian cuisine here. The tamarind rice is a mountain of spiced basmati with cashews. Honey-infused desserts, made with almonds or carrots, are a rich, sweet ending. Generous servings at reasonable prices. ◆

Artesia is about 20 miles south of downtown Los Angeles. From State 91, exit at Pioneer Blvd. and drive south about ½ mile. Most shops and restaurants are open 11–8 Tue-Sun. Ample parking.

The Quick Cook

MEALS IN 30 MINUTES OR LESS

BY BARBARA GOLDMAN

JAMES CARRIER

MENU

Pan-Grilled Tuna Steaks*

Chinese Noodles with Shiitakes*

Cucumber Kimchi   Green Salad

Litchi or Vanilla Ice Cream

Ginger Cookies

*Recipe follows

New take on tuna and noodles

■ Fresh tuna with noodles is as far removed from the clichéd canned-tuna casserole as oysters on the half-shell are from fish and chips. And the fresh fish dish can be just as quick and easy. Varying the noodle foundation makes it a perennial adventure. Fresh, thick Asian-style noodles, kimchi, and litchi ice cream are available at Asian food markets and in many well-stocked supermarkets.

Pan-Grilled Tuna Steaks

PREP AND COOK TIME: 5 to 10 minutes

NOTES: Start the noodles (recipes follow), and as they cook, prepare the

fish. For moist texture, serve the tuna with a red interior. If you don't want it red, cover browned fish in pan (step 2), remove from heat, and let stand until gray-white in the center (cut to test).

MAKES: 4 servings

1¼ pounds **tuna** (ahi), cut 1 inch thick, rinsed and patted dry

Noodle mixture (see notes)

2 tablespoons **reduced-sodium soy sauce**

2 teaspoons **Asian** (toasted) **sesame oil**

1. Cut tuna into 4 equal pieces.

2. Place a 10- to 12-inch nonstick frying pan over high heat. When pan is hot, add tuna and cook on each side, turning once, until browned on the surface, gray to about ¼ inch in, and still red in the center (cut to test), 4 to 5 minutes total.

3. Spoon noodle mixture equally onto plates and top with tuna. Mix soy sauce and sesame oil, then drizzle over tuna to taste.

Per serving tuna: 178 cal., 18% (32 cal.) from fat; 34 g protein; 3.6 g fat (0.7 g sat.); 0.8 g carbo (0 g fiber); 352 mg sodium; 64 mg chol.

The noodles

Chinese noodles with shiitakes. In a 10- to 12-inch nonstick frying pan over high heat, stir ½ pound stemmed, rinsed,

drained, and sliced **fresh shiitake mushrooms,** ½ cup chopped **onion,** and 1 tablespoon minced **fresh ginger** until onion is limp, about 5 minutes. Add 2 cups fat-skimmed **chicken broth,** 2 cups **water,** and 1 pound rinsed and drained **fresh Chinese,** Shanghai-style, or udon **noodles** (about ¼ in. thick). Bring to a boil and stir occasionally until noodles are barely tender to bite, 6 to 7 minutes. Meanwhile, rinse, stem, and string ½ pound **Chinese pea pods.** Add to pan, stir, and cook 1 minute more. Stir in ⅓ cup **prepared oyster sauce** and 2 teaspoons **Asian** (toasted) **sesame oil.** PREP AND COOK TIME: About 25 minutes.

Per serving: 436 cal., 11% (46 cal.) from fat; 22 g protein; 5.1 g fat (0.7 g sat.); 75 g carbo (4.8 g fiber); 1,013 mg sodium; 83 mg chol.

Buckwheat noodles with macadamias. In a 10- to 12-inch nonstick frying pan over high heat, frequently stir ⅓ cup coarsely chopped **roasted, salted macadamia nuts** until golden brown, 3 to 4 minutes. Pour from pan; set aside. In same pan over high heat, bring 1½ cups fat-skimmed **chicken broth** and 2 cups **water** to a boil. Add ½ pound **dried buckwheat noodles** (soba) and cook until just tender to bite, 6 to 7 minutes. Stir in 3 tablespoons **lime juice,** ⅓ cup thinly sliced **green onions,** and ¼ cup chopped **fresh cilantro.** Sprinkle each serving with macadamias and garnish with **cilantro sprigs** and **lime wedges.** PREP AND COOK TIME: About 20 minutes.

Per serving: 287 cal., 27% (77 cal.) from fat; 12 g protein; 8.6 g fat (1.3 g sat.); 45 g carbo (2.7 g fiber); 529 mg sodium; 0 mg chol.

Spinach noodles provençal. In a 10- to 12-inch nonstick frying pan over high heat, stir 1 tablespoon **olive oil,** 6 minced drained **anchovy fillets,** 3 minced cloves **garlic,** and 1 cup sliced **onion** until onion is limp, about 5 minutes. Stir in 1 can (28 oz.) **diced tomatoes** with juice, 2 cups **water,** ½ pound **dried spinach noodles,** ½ cup chopped pitted **calamata olives,** and 1 tablespoon chopped **fresh thyme** leaves. Stir occasionally until noodles are just tender to bite, 10 to 12 minutes. Stir in ¼ cup chopped **parsley.** PREP AND COOK TIME: About 25 minutes.

Per serving: 364 cal., 24% (89 cal.) from fat; 12 g protein; 9.9 g fat (1.4 g sat.); 58 g carbo (8.5 g fiber); 871 mg sodium; 3.3 mg chol. ◆

Vancouver dining

New chefs transform the B.C. food scene

BY LINDA LAU ANUSASANANAN

SPIT-ROASTED DELICACIES rotate on display in Chinatown.

Over the last decade, Vancouver's restaurant scene has transformed itself. A cadre of talented chefs inspired by superb regional ingredients (including British Columbia's increasingly good wines) and an influx of new residents from the four corners of the globe have lifted the city into the ranks of world culinary capitals. • Area code is 604.

Best of B.C.

The following restaurants reflect the best of Vancouver dining. They're not inexpensive—menu prices are comparable to the most expensive restaurants in Los Angeles or San Francisco. Convert the prices to American dollars, though, and you'll be pleasantly surprised.

Bishop's. This beloved local favorite is run by John Bishop, who makes every diner feel like a personal friend. Meals start with fine homemade breads, then move on to dishes such as grilled salmon with sesame ginger glaze and wild rice risotto. *2183 W. Fourth Ave.; 738-2025.*

C Restaurant. This newcomer on the shores of False Creek boasts a gorgeous view and a winning way with fresh seafood. Dishes include the playfully named grilled halibut T-bone and halibut baby back ribs; if you want beef you have to order "the catch of the day." *1600 Howe St.; 681-1164.*

Lumière. One of the hottest chefs in town, Robert Feenie, mixes fine Northwestern ingredients with meticulous French technique in this sleek, austere bistro. Choose from three tasting menus—chef's, seafood, or vegetarian—whose prices range from $50 to $70 for six to eight courses. Any item on the tasting menu is also available à la carte. *2551 W. Broadway; 739-8185.*

Raincity Grill. This casual beachside restaurant is less expensive than others in this list, and it takes a nice approach to Northwest ingredients. But the wine list is the real attraction. Raincity offers 100 wines by the glass and 400 vintages for tasting, with a tilt toward the wines produced in British Columbia's Okanagan Valley. *1193 Denman St.; 685-7337.*

Sun Sui Wah. On weekends, both branches—one in Vancouver, one in suburban Richmond—of a long-established Hong Kong restaurant bustle with activity as Chinese families flag down carts to order dim sum. If they're available, be sure to try the fresh spot prawns panfried with soya sauce. *3888 Main St., Vancouver; 872-8822. 4940 Alexander Rd. (Alderbridge Plaza), Richmond; 273-8208.*

Tojo's. This Japanese restaurant is spacious; some tables have lovely views. But insiders advise you to head to the 10-seat sushi bar, domain of sushi master Hidekazu Tojo. "Sit there and forget the menu," we were told. "Tojo will take care of you." Highlights of our eight-course dinner included braised halibut cheeks with chili, lobster sushi, and Tojo's trademark egg crêpe–wrapped golden rolls. Even at $75 (about $51 U.S.), the food seemed a bargain; but if you're nervous about cost, set the price before you order. *777 W. Broadway; 872-8050.*

Vij's. Flavors explode in your mouth, bright colors dance on whimsically plated food—dinner at Vikram Vij's restaurant is not just a meal but a near-psychedelic experience. In dishes like chicken curry decorated with fresh currants and blueberries, Vij injects fusion fun into East Indian food; the results are light, bright, and unlike anything you've eaten before. Prices are moderate for such delicious originality. Come early—Vij doesn't take reservations. *1480 W. 11th Ave.; 736-6664.*

Chopstick choices

The arrival of new immigrants from Hong Kong has given Vancouver some fine Chinese restaurants. Among them:

Hon's Wun Tun House. Come here for fresh, fast Chinese food at bargain prices—noodles, vegetarian dim sum, Chinese barbecued meats. *1339 Robson St.; 685-0871. 268 Keefer St.; 688-0871.*

Shanghai Chinese Bistro. This modern bistro hosts a nightly noodle-pulling show and serves great food. Try Shanghai-style hand-pulled noodles, chili won tons, dim sum. *1124 Alberni St.; 683-8222.*

Victoria Chinese Restaurant. Inventive dim sum is made to order from an extensive menu. *1088 Melville St., at Royal Centre; 669-8383.*

Hotel excellence

Hotel dining in Vancouver is unusually sophisticated. These restaurants uses seasonal ingredients in intriguing ways.

Bacchus Lounge & Restaurant. The richly appointed dining room serves Northern Italian food. Afternoon tea is also worth attending. *Wedgewood Hotel, 845 Hornby St.; 608-5319.*

Chartwell. The dining room has a private-club elegance; the menu includes creative meat-free choices. *Four Seasons Hotel, 791 W. Georgia St.; 844-6715.*

Diva at the Met. With an open kitchen, the atmosphere is airy and inviting, the menu combinations inventive. *Metropolitan Hotel, 645 Howe St.; 602-7788.*

900 West. Handsome dining room; the wine list has 75 wines by the glass. *Hotel Vancouver, 900 W. Georgia; 669-9378.* ◆

Ravioli runaways

Southwestern flavors in Asian wraps

BY ELAINE JOHNSON

WON TON SKINS, sealed around chorizo filling, make quick ravioli.

Italy may claim ravioli, but reader Ann Beck of Tucson gives the dish a more worldly twist. Her fillings and sauces come right out of the American Southwest, from chilies to chorizo. And we've given them an Asian spin with ready-made won ton wrappers.

Won Ton Ravioli

PREP AND COOK TIME: About 55 minutes

NOTES: Serve chili-cheese-filled ravioli with chipotle-cream sauce. Serve chorizo-tomatillo-filled ravioli with lime sauce. If making ravioli ahead, complete through step 2, cover, and chill up to 1 day. Or freeze in a single layer until firm, transfer to an airtight container, and freeze up to 1 month; cook frozen, allowing 6 to 8 minutes.

MAKES: About 20 pieces; 4 servings

All-purpose flour

About 40 (8 oz. total) **won ton skins**

Chili-cheese filling or chorizo-tomatillo filling (recipes follow)

Chipotle-cream sauce or lime sauce (recipes follow)

1. In a small bowl, blend 1½ teaspoons flour with 1½ tablespoons water.

2. On a lightly floured board, lay 4 to 6 won ton skins flat. Spoon 1 tablespoon filling onto center of each. Brush edges of skins with flour-water mixture. Align another won ton skin over each one on the board; firmly press edges together to seal. If desired, trim edges slightly with a zigzag ravioli cutter.

3. Lay filled ravioli, side by side but not touching, on a flour-dusted baking sheet. Cover with plastic wrap to prevent drying. Repeat to fill remaining ravioli, using additional pans as required.

4. In a 5- to 6-quart pan, bring 3 quarts water to a boil over high heat. Add half the ravioli at a time; cook until wrappers are just tender to bite, 2 to 3 minutes.

5. As ravioli cook, spoon hot chipotle sauce equally onto heated plates (or spoon half the lime sauce onto plates).

6. With a slotted spoon, lift 1 ravioli at a time from water, drain and lay on plates. If using lime sauce, spoon remainder equally over ravioli.

Per serving with chili-cheese filling and chipotle-cream sauce: 583 cal., 52% (306 cal.) from fat; 21 g protein; 34 g fat (21 g sat.); 48 g carbo (2.3 g fiber); 1,373 mg sodium; 163 mg chol.

Per serving with chorizo-tomatillo filling and lime sauce: 628 cal., 57% (360 cal.) from fat; 22 g protein; 40 g fat (13 g sat.); 44 g carbo (2 g fiber); 953 mg sodium; 53 mg chol.

Chili-Cheese Filling

In a food processor, whirl 1 can (4 oz.) **diced green chilies,** 2 tablespoons chopped **onion,** 1½ teaspoons chopped **garlic,** 1½ cups (6 oz.) grated **cotija** or parmesan **cheese,** and 1 **large egg** until smooth. Or mince vegetables, place in a bowl, and mix with cheese and egg.

Chipotle-Cream Sauce

NOTES: If making sauce ahead, chill airtight up to 1 day. Or freeze up to 1 month. Thaw sauce, whirl smooth in a blender, then reheat.

⅓ cup chopped **onion**

2 tablespoons chopped **canned roasted red bell pepper**

1½ teaspoons chopped **garlic**

2 teaspoons **butter** or margarine

¼ teaspoon **ground cumin**

¼ cup fat-skimmed **chicken broth**

2 tablespoons **canned chipotle chilies in adobado sauce,** seeds and veins removed

1 cup **whipping cream**

1. In a 10- to 12-inch frying pan over medium heat, frequently stir onion, roasted pepper, garlic, butter, and cumin until onion is limp, 6 to 8 minutes.

2. Whirl mixture in a blender or food processor with broth and chipotles.

3. Scrape purée back into frying pan. Add cream and stir often over high heat until simmering, about 3 minutes.

Chorizo-Tomatillo Filling

⅓ pound **hot chorizo sausage,** casings removed

⅓ cup chopped **onion**

1½ teaspoons chopped **garlic**

½ teaspoon **ground cumin**

⅓ cup drained **canned tomatillos**

½ cup **fresh chèvre** (goat) **cheese**

1½ teaspoons **lime juice**

1. In a 10- to 12-inch frying pan over medium heat, crumble chorizo; stir with onion, garlic, and cumin until browned, about 8 minutes. Discard fat.

2. In a food processor, whirl sausage mixture, tomatillos, cheese, and lime juice until smooth. Or mince meat mixture and tomatillos, put in a bowl, and stir in cheese and lime juice.

Lime Sauce

In a bowl, mix ⅓ cup **extra-virgin olive oil,** 3 tablespoons **lime juice,** and 1½ tablespoons grated **parmesan cheese.** Add **salt** and **cracked pepper** to taste. ◆

Plum dandy

Turn up the heat for a burst of flavor

BY ANDREW BAKER

SWEET-TART PLUM SLICES bake into rich almond cake.

LEIGH BEISCH

As summer rolls along, the plum scene shifts constantly. No sooner does a variety hit its harvest peak than it begins to slide away, replaced by newcomers. But regardless of the many kinds of plums available, those with skin in the red to purple spectrum share a common virtue—their flavor brightens and intensifies when they're heated, even briefly. In catsup, their tang is pronounced; in salad, their flavor is livelier; and in cake, they are juicier.

Plum Catsup

PREP AND COOK TIME: About 35 minutes

NOTES: Serve as you would tomato catsup, with meats, poultry, and fish. If making ahead, cover and chill sauce up to 1 week.

MAKES: 1½ cups

- ½ pound **firm-ripe red-skin plums**
- ½ pound **Roma tomatoes**
- 2 tablespoons chopped **fresh ginger**
- ½ cup finely chopped **onion**
- ¼ cup firmly packed **brown sugar**
- 2 teaspoons **soy sauce**
- 1 cup fat-skimmed **chicken broth**

1. Rinse plums and tomatoes. Pit plums and cut into chunks. Core tomatoes and cut into chunks. In a blender or food processor, purée plums, tomatoes, and ginger.

2. In a 10- to 12-inch frying pan over high heat, combine purée, onion, brown sugar, soy sauce, and broth. Stir often until reduced to 1½ cups, 15 to 18 minutes.

Per tablespoon: 19 cal., 4.7% (0.9 cal.) from fat; 0.5 g protein; 0.1 g fat (0 g sat.); 4.2 g carbo (0.4 g fiber); 34 mg sodium; 0 mg chol.

Sweet plum sauce. Follow directions for **plum catsup** (preceding), but omit onion, soy sauce, and broth. Increase **brown sugar** to ½ cup; add ⅛ teaspoon **ground cloves**, ¼ teaspoon **ground cinnamon**, and 1 cup **orange juice.**

Per tablespoon: 29 cal., 3.1% (0.9 cal.) from fat; 0.2 g protein; 0.1 g fat (0 g sat.); 7.2 g carbo (0.3 g fiber); 2.7 mg sodium; 0 mg chol.

Plum-Almond Cake

PREP AND COOK TIME: About 1 hour

MAKES: 8 or 9 servings

- 3 **firm-ripe red-skin plums** (about 2 in. wide; ¾ lb. total)
- About ½ cup (¼ lb.) **butter** or margarine
- About 1 cup **all-purpose flour**
- ⅓ cup **granulated sugar**
- 8 ounces (¾ cup) **almond paste**
- 2 **large eggs**
- **Powdered sugar**

1. Rinse plums, pit, and cut into ½-inch-thick slices.

2. Butter and flour a 10-inch cake pan that has a removable rim.

3. In a bowl, combine ½ cup butter, granulated sugar, and almond paste. With a mixer at high speed, beat until mixture is blended, about 2 minutes. Add eggs and beat until fluffy, 2 or 3 minutes. Add 1 cup flour, stir to mix, then beat until well blended.

4. Scrape batter into cake pan. Arrange plum slices evenly on batter.

5. Bake in a 350° oven until cake just begins to pull from pan sides and is golden brown, about 45 minutes.

6. Cool in pan at least 10 minutes. Run a thin-bladed knife between cake and pan rim; remove rim. Dust cake with powdered sugar. Cut into wedges.

Per serving: 321 cal., 53% (171 cal.) from fat; 6.2 g protein; 19 g fat (7.4 g sat.); 34 g carbo (1.1 g fiber); 121 mg sodium; 75 mg chol.

Hot Plum and Spinach Salad

PREP AND COOK TIME: About 25 minutes

MAKES: 4 servings

- 4 slices (¼ lb.) **thick-cut bacon**
- 8 cups (about ½ lb.) **baby spinach leaves,** rinsed and drained
- 2 **firm-ripe red-skin plums** (about ½ lb. total)
- 4 teaspoons **coarse-grain Dijon mustard**
- 2 tablespoons **red wine vinegar**
- 1 teaspoon **sugar**
- **Salt**

1. Cut bacon crosswise into ¼-inch pieces. In a 10- to 12-inch frying pan, stir bacon frequently until browned, 4 to 5 minutes. With a slotted spoon, transfer bacon to drain on towels. Reserve 2 tablespoons drippings in pan.

2. Put spinach in a large bowl. Rinse and pit plums and cut into ½-inch-thick slices.

3. Set pan with drippings over high heat. Add mustard, vinegar, and sugar; stir, then add plums. Heat until boiling, about 1 minute; turn plums over once.

4. Pour hot plum mixture over spinach. Mix and lift with salad fork and spoon. Sprinkle with bacon and add salt to taste.

Per serving: 144 cal., 60% (86 cal.) from fat; 4.5 g protein; 9.5 g fat (3 g sat.); 10 g carbo (2.6 g fiber); 324 mg sodium; 11 mg chol. ◆

Kitchen Cabinet

READERS' RECIPES TESTED IN SUNSET'S KITCHENS

BY LINDA LAU ANUSASANANAN

LEIGH BEISCH

1. With a serrated knife, horizontally slice 1 inch off the top of the loaf. Pull soft center from bottom half of loaf, making a shell with ½-inch-thick walls. Reserve soft bread for other uses.

2. In a bowl, mix vinaigrette dressing, cucumber, tomato, and chives. Brush or spoon about half the dressing evenly over interior of the hollowed shell. Also spoon enough dressing on cut side of loaf top to moisten.

3. Layer cheese, bell pepper, turkey, salami, and onion in shell. Drizzle remaining dressing over filling. Set bread top over filling. Wrap sandwich in foil or plastic wrap and refrigerate at least 3 hours or up to 1 day.

4. Unwrap; cut into equal portions.

Per serving: 394 cal., 30% (117 cal.) from fat; 23 g protein; 13 g fat (5.1 g sat.); 44 g carbo (2.6 g fiber); 970 mg sodium; 48 mg chol.

Raspberry and Candied Walnut Salad

Rebecca Casper, Avondale, Arizona

This salad is loaded with surprises—raspberries, candied walnuts, and feta cheese. Rebecca Casper finds that it never fails to make an impression.

PREP AND COOK TIME: About 30 minutes
MAKES: 6 to 8 servings

Salad oil

⅓ cup **sugar**

½ cup **walnut halves** or large pieces

¼ cup **raspberry vinegar**

2 tablespoons **olive oil**

2 teaspoons **honey**

1 tablespoon **mayonnaise**

¼ teaspoon fresh-ground **pepper**

3 quarts (¾ lb.) **butter lettuce,** leaf lettuce, or salad mix (1 kind or a combination), rinsed, crisped, and torn into bite-size pieces

⅓ cup thinly sliced **red onion,** rinsed and drained

1 cup **raspberries,** rinsed and drained

1 cup (8 oz.) **crumbled feta cheese**

Salt

1. Lay a 10- to 12-inch-long sheet of foil

Picnic Deli Sandwich

Audrey Thibodeau, Mesa, Arizona

This meal-scale sandwich not only is easy to transport but also gets better if made up to 1 day ahead. Audrey Thibodeau often takes it to summer picnics and Super Bowl parties.

PREP AND COOK TIME: About 20 minutes
MAKES: 6 servings

1 loaf (1 lb.; about 4½ in. wide, 14 to 16 in. long) **sourdough bread**

½ cup **vinaigrette-style salad dressing,** homemade or purchased

½ cup finely chopped **cucumber**

½ cup finely chopped **tomato**

2 tablespoons thinly sliced **chives** or green onion

3 to 4 ounces **thin-sliced Swiss cheese**

12 thin **green bell pepper** rings, seeds removed

6 to 9 ounces **thin-sliced cooked turkey breast**

12 pieces **thin-sliced salami** (about 3 oz. total)

3 thin **red onion** slices, separated into rings

on a heatproof surface and rub lightly with oil.

2. In an 8- to 10-inch frying pan over medium-high heat, combine sugar and walnuts. Shake and tilt pan often until sugar is melted and amber-colored and until nuts are coated, 4 to 5 minutes total. At once pour walnut candy onto foil. Let candy cool until hard, 12 to 15 minutes. Discard foil; break candy into chunks, put in a heavy plastic food bag, and hit gently with a flat mallet to break into small pieces. If making ahead, store airtight up to 2 days.

3. In a wide shallow bowl, whisk vinegar with oil, honey, mayonnaise, and pepper.

4. Add lettuce, onion, raspberries, cheese, and walnut candy. Mix and season to taste with salt.

Per serving: 211 cal., 64% (135 cal.) from fat; 5.7 g protein; 15 g fat (5.2 g sat.); 16 g carbo (1.6 g fiber); 330 mg sodium; 26 mg chol.

Grilled Eggplant Parmesan

Ann Beck, Tucson

Summer in Arizona is hot enough, says Ann Beck. She escapes a hot kitchen by cooking a family favorite, eggplant parmesan, on the barbecue. She tops her preparation with a homemade olive-tomato sauce. Make your own sauce, or use a purchased one.

PREP AND COOK TIME: About 30 minutes

MAKES: 4 servings

- 2 **eggplant** (1 lb. each)
- 1/3 cup **olive oil**
- 1 tablespoon **dried Italian herb mix** or dried oregano
- 10 to 12 ounces **mozzarella cheese**
- 1 jar (about 26 oz.) **marinara** or pasta **sauce**
- 1/3 cup **grated parmesan cheese**
- 3 tablespoons chopped **parsley**
  Salt and **pepper**

1. Rinse eggplant, cut each crosswise into 3/4-inch rounds, and discard stems and smooth ends. Lay slices side by side on a large tray or 2 or 3 baking sheets, about 12 by 15 inches.

2. In a small bowl, mix oil and Italian herb mix. Brush cut sides of eggplant with oil mixture.

3. Cut mozzarella cheese into thin slices, making 1 piece for each eggplant round.

4. In a 1 1/2- to 2-quart pan over medium heat, stir marinara sauce occasionally

PEACHES, blueberries, and cream fill shortcake.

RICHARD JUNG

until warm.

5. Set eggplant rounds on a grill over a solid bed of medium-hot coals or medium-high heat on a gas barbecue (you can hold your hand at grill level for only 3 to 4 seconds). Close lid of gas barbecue. Cook until eggplant is very soft when pressed, creamy inside (cut to test), and browned, 6 to 8 minutes; turn once. Set marinara sauce on cool area of grill to keep warm.

6. Top each eggplant round with a slice of mozzarella cheese. Cover barbecue until cheese softens, about 1 minute. Transfer to a platter. Spoon marinara sauce onto slices, then sprinkle with parmesan cheese and parsley. Season to taste with salt and pepper.

Per serving: 577 cal., 66% (378 cal.) from fat; 22 g protein; 42 g fat (14 g sat.); 36 g carbo (6.5 g fiber); 1,569 mg sodium; 60 mg chol.

English Shortcake

Carolyn T. Black, Bountiful, Utah

Years ago, at a little tearoom in the English countryside, Carolyn Black fell in love with true English shortcake. Her replica is more like a scone than a sweet biscuit shortcake.

PREP AND COOK TIME: About 45 minutes

MAKES: 6 to 8 servings

- 2 1/2 cups **all-purpose flour**
  About 3/4 cup **sugar**
- 2 teaspoons **baking powder**
- 1/2 teaspoon **baking soda**
- 1/2 teaspoon **salt**
- 1/2 cup (1/4 lb.) **butter** or margarine
- 2/3 cup **low-fat buttermilk**
- 2 **large egg** yolks

- 4 cups sliced peeled **peaches,** plums, or nectarines; or rinsed and drained raspberries, blueberries, or hulled strawberries (1 or more kinds of fruit)

  About 1 cup **whipping cream**

1. In a bowl, mix flour, 1/2 cup sugar, baking powder, baking soda, and salt.

2. With a pastry blender or your fingers, cut or rub butter until no pieces are larger than 1/4 inch.

3. In a small bowl, mix buttermilk and egg yolks; add to flour mixture. Stir with a fork until evenly moistened, then press into a ball.

4. On a lightly floured board, knead until dough forms a smooth ball, 5 to 10 turns. Pat dough into a 1-inch-thick oval. With a floured round cutter (2 1/4 to 2 3/4 in. wide), cut dough; place pieces about 2 inches apart on a baking sheet, about 12 by 17 inches. Press scraps together, knead briefly, and repeat to cut more rounds. Sprinkle cut dough evenly with sugar, using about 1 tablespoon total.

5. Bake in a 400° oven (or a 375° convection oven) until golden, 12 to 15 minutes. Transfer to racks.

6. In a bowl, mix fruit with sugar to taste. In another bowl, whip cream with a mixer on high speed until it holds soft peaks. Sweeten to taste with sugar.

7. Split warm or cool shortcakes in half. Set bottom halves on plates and spoon about half the fruit and juices onto cakes. Top each with a spoonful of cream. Set a cake top on each base and spoon remaining fruit and cream equally over each.

Per serving: 468 cal., 44% (207 cal.) from fat; 6.8 g protein; 23 g fat (13 g sat.); 61 g carbo (2.4 g fiber); 497 mg sodium; 118 mg chol. ◆

Golden caramel, juicy sweet peaches, and crunchy pecans fill nut shortbread crusts in these dessert tarts (recipe on page 201).

August

the new Wine Countries

From the canyons of Colorado to the shores of Puget Sound, pioneer winemakers are planting where few grapes have gone before. And they're triumphing

GRANDE RIVER
Vineyards flourishes
amid Colorado
mesas.

THE GRAND VALLEY OF WESTERN COLORADO DOESN'T LOOK MUCH LIKE NAPA OR SONOMA OR THE West's other classic wine regions. There are no palatial tasting rooms. In place of rolling, oak-studded hills, red rock cliffs jut into a cobalt Colorado sky. Grand Valley still feels like a frontier more suited to saddles than Chardonnays. And yet a posse of pioneering wine-makers is producing wine here. • These winemakers are not alone. The desert near Sonoita, Arizona, now nurtures Pinot Noir grapes. Around Walla Walla, Washington, Mer-lot plantings rival the region's fabled sweet onions for horticultural fame. • What's more, many of these wines are earning accolades from wine critics and consumers alike. We won't say that every bottle from the West's new wine countries ranks with Napa's finest—not yet. Still, the best of their vintages will delight you. • For the traveler, touring these regions has the low-key appeal of visiting Napa Valley 30 years ago. Tasting rooms are uncrowded. The person pouring your Pinot is likely to be the person who has spent the last 10 years making a dream come true. Lift your glasses, then, to the West's new crop of winemakers and to the new wine countries they call home.

JACK DYKINGA

Here comes T. Red

CHECK YOUR WINE SNOBBERY AT the door when you visit Colorado's Grand Valley wineries. The region's anything-but-stuffy attitude shows up right away on the names of some of the wines. Plum Creek Cellars's winemaker, Erik Bruner, is a former geologic engineer, co-owner Sue Phillips a rockhound: They named Plum Creek's Bordeaux-style red Redstone, after the iron-stained basalt near the winery.

The sense of fun prevails even on some wine labels, like those for Carlson Vineyards: A dinosaur raises a wineglass on a bottle of Tyrannosaurus Red (a bow to dig sites nearby); a cheerful rodent wears a grape-leaf crown on a bottle of Prairie Dog White. "Wine is something to have fun with," claims Mary Carlson, the vineyard's co-owner. Standing beside a stuffed jackalope (the mythical antlered jackrabbit of postcard fame), she says, "We're not pretentious. But we are serious about quality in this region."

For a winery to survive in the Grand Valley, it has to be serious at least part of the time—notably when it comes to grape growing. This sere land of mesas and buttes hard by the Colorado-Utah border is among the highest and most challenging wine-grape growing regions in the world. Altitude ranges from 4,600 to more than 5,000 feet, so bud-killing spring frosts are an annual threat. Rainfall varies from pitiful to ridiculous (6 to 9 inches annually). In winter, the dormant grapevines must sometimes endure temperatures down to -8°.

There hadn't been wine grapes grown here since Prohibition, but in 1974, Colorado State University began researching the area's vineyard potential. "For wine-grape growers, this is no place for wimps," says former CSU viticulturist Rick Hamman. But Hamman is quick to point out the area's pluses. Its low humidity reduces grape-mold problems. During August and September, when grapes mature, temperatures can

"**Wine is** something to have fun with. But we are serious **about quality.**"

swing 30°. That means the day's high heat helps grapes build sugar, while the extremely cool nights help them retain good acidity. The result, when everything is ideal: a fruity, crisp wine.

A few years after its research began, CSU's work bore fruit, and the winery now known as Colorado Cellars swung open its doors. Now the Grand Valley is home to seven wineries (six open to the public). Vineyards spread over 263 acres.

Growers largely stick to the basics: Chardonnay and Merlot are the dominant varietals. But winemakers aren't afraid of stretching the region's potential. Among their efforts: honey wine (Rocky Mountain Meadery), Rhône varietals (Grande River), sparkling wine

JAMES CARRIER

JAY DICKMAN

■LEFT: Sharon Smith of Grande River Vineyards holds a bounteous bunch of Colorado grapes.

■ABOVE RIGHT: Beef (or buffalo) meets red wine with savory results in Plum Creek Cellars tenderloin.

(Colorado Cellars), and Gewürztraminer and fruit wines (Carlson Vineyards).

Visitors find a wine country where traffic is nil. Inns and restaurants are good but relatively new and few in number. Think of the Grand Valley as a kind of Leonardo DiCaprio of wine regions—young and brash, but bursting with potential. — *Lora J. Finnegan*

Plum Creek Cellars Grilled Tenderloin

PREP AND COOK TIME: About 1¾ hours

NOTES: Buffalo tenderloin, which can be pricey, is the preference of Doug Phillips, co-owner of Plum Creek Cellars; order it at least 1 week ahead from a meat market. But beef also works quite well. If making the sauce up to 3 weeks ahead, cover and chill.

MAKES: 8 servings

¾	cup **apple cider vinegar**
⅓	cup firmly packed **brown sugar**
⅓	cup **dry red wine** such as Merlot or Cabernet Sauvignon
⅓	cup **catsup**
¼	cup **Worcestershire**
¼	cup minced **onion**
1½	tablespoons **cornstarch**
2	teaspoons minced **fresh rosemary** leaves or 1 teaspoon dried rosemary
1½	tablespoons **hot sauce**
	About ½ teaspoon **salt**
½	teaspoon **pepper**
8	**beef tenderloin steaks** (2 in. thick; about 4 lb. total), fat-trimmed

1. In a 2- to 3-quart pan, combine vinegar, sugar, wine, catsup, Worcestershire, onion, cornstarch, rosemary, hot sauce, ½ teaspoon salt, and pepper. Stir over high heat until boiling, about 2 minutes. Let marinade cool, or to chill quickly, nest pan in a bowl of ice water and stir until cold, about 5 minutes.

2. Rinse steaks, pat dry, and put in a 1-gallon heavy plastic food bag. Pour marinade into bag, seal, and rotate to mix well. Chill at least 1 hour or up to 1 day.

3. Lightly oil a barbecue grill over a solid bed of hot coals or gas grill on high heat (you can hold your hand at grill level only 2 to 3 seconds). Lift steaks from marinade and lay on grill. Close lid on gas grill. Pour marinade into a 1- to 1½-quart pan.

4. Turn steaks every 2 to 3 minutes to brown evenly, basting with marinade up until 2 minutes before meat is cooked to desired doneness, 10 to 12 minutes for rare (cut to test). Stir marinade in pan (on grill or over high heat) until boiling. Spoon sauce onto steaks; season to taste with salt.

Per serving: 334 cal., 35% (117 cal.) from fat; 37 g protein; 13 g fat (4.8 g sat.); 16 g carbo (0.3 g fiber); 503 mg sodium; 107 mg chol.

— *Recipes by Elaine Johnson*

PUGET SOUND, WASHINGTON

The wine islands

THERE IS SOMETHING STIRRING about taking a ferry to go wine touring. Sea breezes and blue skies whet the appetite for the vintages that wait across the water. A more enjoyable transition from city to wine country is hard to imagine.

While some of Washington state's largest and best-known wineries are located just east of Seattle, other vintners have settled near the water, in what has been designated the Puget Sound appellation. Even within the appellation, many winemakers produce wines made exclusively from grapes grown elsewhere, notably eastern Washington's Columbia Valley. But an increasing number are planting vineyards here on the shores of Puget Sound. Their cool-weather varieties sometimes puzzle the palates of Chardonnay lovers, but the popularity of Puget Sound's locally grown wine rises each year.

Gerard and Jo Ann Bentryn's Bainbridge Island Vineyards & Winery is a half-hour ferry ride from downtown Seattle. Subscribing to an unbending philosophy of local wine production, Bainbridge Island Winery produces Madeleine Angevine, Müller-Thurgau, Pinot Gris, Pinot Noir, and Siegerrebe, all from grapes grown at the winery. Intensely flavored strawberry and raspberry wines are made seasonally from fruit grown elsewhere on Bainbridge Island. The fruit wines vary each year, say the Bentryns, taking on the sweetness and flavor of that season's crop.

The Bentryns are happy to have visitors. They offer wine tasting and a self-guided vineyard tour Wednesdays through Sundays. And Gerard leads a winegrower's vineyard tour each Sunday, rain or shine.

To reach another of Puget Sound's wineries, take the ferry from Mukilteo

■ RIGHT: Bainbridge Island winemakers Gerard and Jo Ann Bentryn pose with pal Pinot.
■ FAR RIGHT: Jo Ann's prize dish is an emphatic garlic chicken.

(southwest of Everett) to Whidbey Island Vineyards & Winery, near the artists community of Langley. Greg and Elizabeth Osenbach raise Siegerrebe and Madeleine Angevine grapes to produce local wine, but they also bring red grapes from eastern Washington's warmer Yakima Valley to make their Lemberger and Cabernet Sauvignon. A flavorful rhubarb wine provides another dimension for tasters. Just north, Whidbey Island Greenbank Farm

offers wine tasting and picnicking.

The north end of Whidbey stops at Deception Pass, where swift-running tidal waters make for exciting viewing from the bridge above. Just north, another ferry leaves from Anacortes to serve the San Juan Islands. The ferry's first stop is Lopez Island, home to Brent Charnley's Lopez Island Vineyards. Charnley founded the winery in 1987, and he grows Madeleine Angevine and Siegerrebe grapes on the site. Like Greg

Bainbridge Island Vineyards Greek Garlic Chicken

PREP AND COOK TIME: About 2 hours

NOTES: Vineyard co-owner Jo Ann Bentryn uses considerably more salt to give the sauce the quality she likes. But our taste panel preferred less; you can always add more when serving. For speed, buy peeled or minced garlic; or with the flat side of a knife, lightly smash cloves and pull off skin.

MAKES: 8 servings

- 8 **chicken legs** (thighs and drumsticks attached; about 5 lb. total)
- $\frac{2}{3}$ cup minced **garlic** (about 3 heads)
- $\frac{1}{2}$ cup **lemon juice**
- $\frac{1}{4}$ cup **olive oil**
- $2\frac{1}{2}$ tablespoons **dried oregano**
- 2 tablespoons **coarse-ground pepper**
- 1 to 2 teaspoons **salt** (see notes)
- $\frac{1}{4}$ cup chopped **parsley**

  Parsley sprigs

1. Rinse chicken, pat dry, and pull off and discard lumps of fat. Put legs in a rimmed 12- by 17-inch pan.

2. In a bowl, mix minced garlic, lemon juice, olive oil, oregano, pepper, and salt. Smear garlic mixture evenly over chicken, then arrange legs, cut side down, in a single layer.

3. Bake in a 375° oven until skin is well browned, about $1\frac{1}{2}$ hours ($1\frac{1}{4}$ hours in a convection oven). After 45 minutes, baste chicken with pan juices every 10 to 15 minutes.

4. Transfer chicken to a warm platter. Skim and discard fat from drippings. Add $\frac{1}{2}$ cup boiling water to pan, stir to loosen browned bits, and pour sauce into a bowl.

5. Scatter chopped parsley over chicken; garnish with parsley sprigs. Add sauce to taste.

Per serving: 419 cal., 56% (234 cal.) from fat; 38 g protein; 26 g fat (6.1 g sat.); 7.5 g carbo (0.8 g fiber); 420 mg sodium; 129 mg chol.

PHIL SCHOFIELD

JAMES CARRIER

Osenbach, Charnley chooses to make his reds (Merlot and a Cabernet and Merlot blend) from Columbia Valley fruit, and offers local fruit wines—apple-pear and blackberry—as well.

A few stops farther on the island ferry milk run is San Juan Island, the largest in the archipelago. At Friday Harbor you'll find a pleasing mix of nautical shops and art galleries, along with the excellent Whale Museum. Just up the hill is San Juan Vineyards. It began wine-making operations last year. The owners planted an 8-acre vineyard with hopes for a first commercial harvest in 2000.

Bellingham, on the mainland, is the jumping-off point for Mount Baker Vineyards. Owner Randy Finley is joined by his winemaker son, Maitland, in producing a wide selection of local wines. Chasselas, Madeleine Angevine, Müller-Thurgau, Pinot Gris, Pinot Noir, and Siegerrebe are made from grapes grown on the estate's 7-acre vineyard, while other red varieties derive from grapes imported from the Yakima Valley. Apple, blackberry, blueberry, plum, raspberry, and rhubarb wines, all from local fruits, round out Finley's offerings.

More fine fruit wines can be had west of Seattle, off U.S. 101 near Hood Canal. Here Hoodsport Winery's offerings include a delicious raspberry wine, along with the historic Island Belle grape wine from some of Washington's oldest vines, on nearby Stretch Island. — *Chuck Hill*

The taste of greatness

SAY "OREGON WINE" AND SAGE heads nod: the Willamette Valley, lots of rain, Pinot Noir. But in the baking summer heat of the Rogue Valley, 43 miles north of the California border, Clay Shannon and Lee Traynham are turning heads with a different vision of wine in the Beaver State.

At Del Rio Vineyards, there's not a Pinot Noir vine in sight. The wispy young vines are sun-worshipping, muscle-flexing reds: Cabernet Franc, Cabernet Sauvignon, Grenache, Merlot, Sangiovese, Syrah. There are whites, too: Chardonnay, Pinot Blanc, Pinot Gris, and Viognier. These are grapes you would find in Bordeaux or the Rhône Valley in France, or in Sonoma, California, Shannon explains.

Shannon and Traynham came to the Rogue from California, bringing big bucks and business brawn. Traynham, a rancher and farmer, and Shannon, who runs a vineyard development and management company, know their stuff.

Typical vineyards in the Rogue weigh in at 30 to 40 acres and run on a shoe-string. So you can't help but take seriously a site planned for 350 acres. The advent of Del Rio brings the Rogue Valley what it may need most: attention.

That's music to the ears of the Rogue's seven wineries. Says Sarah Powell, winemaker at Foris Vineyards Winery, "We're still no-man's-land in terms of recognition. We've had to pay our dues through quality, consistency, and value."

The Rogue was established as a wine region in the 1860s; after Prohibition's interruption, it resurged in the 1970s. Wineries like Foris, Valley View, and Troon make wine to rival the best of any region in the country. But the Rogue struggles with its distance from a major metropolitan area, and with differentiating itself from the Willamette Valley.

The banks of the Rogue River make up three subappellations. The southwesternmost, Illinois Valley, near Cave Junction, is cooled by the Pacific Ocean. This is Pinot Noir country—proof that the Rogue can grow Pinot Noir very nicely, though in a riper style than in the Willamette Valley. Head northeast into the Applegate Valley outside Jacksonville, and rain gets scarcer. The Siskiyou Mountains embrace the narrow valley, trapping plenty of heat. Here, and in the third subappellation—the Rogue Valley that parallels Interstate 5 from Ashland to Grants Pass—reign grapes such as the ones Del Rio grows. These hotter subappellations are experiencing the region's fastest growth.

Despite that growth, wine touring in

MARK GAMBA

the Rogue Valley remains a pleasantly low-key experience. The scenery is gorgeous and the small-town charms of Ashland and Jacksonville beguiling. The wineries are modest, hospitable, family run.

The ambitious giant Del Rio isn't selling wine as yet. Its first order of the day is to sell grapes. Wineries in the Willamette Valley are hungry for the fruit this region can produce. But the partners have bigger plans.

Shannon looks out over Del Rio's 200,000 vines and the historic, picture-postcard stagecoach house that sits at their base. "This is too beautiful, too perfect a site not to have a winery," he says. — *E. J.*

■ **ABOVE LEFT:** Clay Shannon (left) and Lee Traynham survey new Del Rio Vineyards.
■ **RIGHT:** Meri Gerber of Foris Vineyards created this fruitful berry-port cake.

Foris Vineyards Winery Berry-Port Cake

PREP AND COOK TIME: About 1¼ hours

NOTES: For the cake, mile-high bakers need to increase flour to 1¼ cups, reduce sugar to ¾ cup, and reduce baking powder to ¾ teaspoon.

MAKES: 6 to 8 servings

- ½ cup **blackberries,** rinsed and drained
- ¾ cup **raspberries,** rinsed and drained
- ¼ cup **port wine**

  About 1 cup plus 1 tablespoon **sugar**

  About ½ cup (¼ lb.) **butter** or margarine, at room temperature

  About 1 cup **all-purpose flour**

- 2 **large eggs**
- 1 teaspoon **baking powder**

  Vanilla ice cream or sweetened whipped cream

1. In a bowl, gently mix blackberries, ½ cup raspberries, port, and 1 tablespoon sugar.

2. Butter and flour a 9-inch cake pan with removable rim.

3. In a bowl with a mixer on high speed, beat 1 cup sugar and ½ cup butter until well blended, 2 to 3 minutes. Add eggs and beat until fluffy, 2 to 3 minutes.

4. Add 1 cup flour and baking powder. Stir to combine, then beat on high speed until the stiff batter is well blended, about 2 minutes.

5. Scrape batter into cake pan and spread top smooth. Drain wine marinade from berries and save. Evenly spoon berries and 2 tablespoons of the marinade over batter.

6. Bake in a 350° oven until cake begins to pull from pan rim, 50 to 55 minutes (40 to 45 minutes in a convection oven). Run a thin-bladed knife between cake and pan rim. Let cool at least 10 minutes.

7. Remove pan rim and sprinkle cake with a little more sugar. Top with remaining raspberries, cut into wedges, and moisten portions with reserved wine marinade. Accompany with scoops of ice cream.

Per serving: 310 cal., 38% (117 cal.) from fat; 3.6 g protein; 13 g fat (7.9 g sat.); 43 g carbo (1.4 g fiber); 200 mg sodium; 85 mg chol.

JAMES CARRIER

SOUTHEAST ARIZONA
Pinots and burros

WHEN THE APACHE WARRIOR chief Cochise envisioned the destiny of his homeland, he probably wasn't imagining it as wine country. But the parched, blindingly bright high desert of southeast Arizona has indeed been so transformed. About 20 miles from the Mexican border, the villages of Sonoita, Patagonia, and Elgin are sprouting the improbable: small green vines that clutch the earth with true-grit tenacity. (Yes, John Wayne westerns were filmed here.)

Desert beauty aside, the first thing a visitor notices about this corner of the West is that it doesn't seem even remotely suitable for grape growing. Daytime temperatures can hover above 100°, plunging the vines into drought shock. The elevation— around 5,000 feet above sea level—virtually guarantees a high risk of killing springtime frosts. In early summer, torrential monsoon rains can pelt the grapes with ferocious power. Then, of course, there are the coyotes that not only adore grapes but also possess a special fondness for the flavor of irrigation hoses, without which no Arizona winery could survive.

It's enough to dissuade any but the most resolute—and clever— winemakers. Which Arizona seems to have its share of. By finding the best patches of ground and by farming the grapes with extraordinary care, these winemakers intend to make wine an Arizona reality.

That said, *finding* Arizona's wineries can be an odyssey all its own. Although there are now 12 of them in the state, all are tiny and only a scant few are open to the public. Luckily, most of the

wines are easily found in local (and very loyal) restaurants and wine shops. And if you don't find yourself in southeast Arizona, don't worry. Many hip Tucson and Phoenix restaurants also now carry the state's best wines.

Given the small size of the Arizona wine industry (with just 300 acres, the state has less than 0.1 percent the vine-

yard acreage of California), it's perhaps surprising to discover that grape growing here may well have predated vineyards in California. The first Arizona vines were planted by Franciscan missionaries in the late 17th century. Thanks to severe climate conditions however, a viable wine industry didn't emerge until the 1980s, when Gordon

---

Callaghan Vineyards Chili-Cheese Chicken

PREP AND COOK TIME: About 40 minutes

NOTES: Cut any extra canned chilies into thin strips to drape over cooked chicken. Karen Callaghan, Kent's mother, shares this recipe.

MAKES: 4 servings

- 6 tablespoons **green jalapeño jelly**
- 3 tablespoons **white wine vinegar**
- 2 tablespoons **Dijon mustard**
- 2 tablespoons **honey**
- 4 **boned, skinned chicken breast halves** (1½ lb. total), rinsed and patted dry
- 1 can (7 oz.) **whole green chilies**
- 5 ounces **sliced jack cheese**
- **Salt** and **pepper**

1. In a 9- by 13-inch pan, combine jelly, vinegar, mustard, and honey. Put in a 375° oven and occasionally whisk until jelly is melted and sauce blended, 5 to 10 minutes.

2. Turn chicken over in jelly sauce in pan, arranging pieces side by side.

3. Bake in a 375° oven for 15 minutes.

4. Pull 4 chilies open on 1 side and lay flat. Put 1 chili over each chicken piece. Reserve extra chilies for other uses (see notes). Lay cheese on chili and chicken, covering evenly; baste with jelly sauce.

5. Continue to bake chicken until it is no longer pink in thickest part (cut to test), 5 to 10 minutes more.

6. Put chicken on plates and spoon sauce around portions. Season to taste with salt and pepper.

Per serving: 448 cal., 26% (117 cal.) from fat; 48 g protein; 13 g fat (6.8 g sat.); 30 g carbo (0.5 g fiber); 791 mg sodium; 136 mg chol.

■ LEFT: Wine pioneer Kent Callaghan tends his southeast Arizona vineyard.

JACK DYKINGA

Dutt, a Ph.D. in soil science at the University of Arizona, planted grapes near Sonoita. Today, Sonoita Vineyards sits atop a knoll, giving wine tasters a breathtaking 360° view of the majestic landscape while they sip.

If Dutt is the founding father of Arizona winemaking, Kent Callaghan is its heir apparent. A 33-year-old native who looks like a young Robert Redford, Callaghan makes rich, expressive wines that could easily compete with the best wines made anywhere in California or Europe. He was the winemaker behind Dos Cabezas; now he concentrates on his own Callaghan Vineyards. These are two labels not to be missed!

As Southwest lovers know, the power of the desert dawns on one slowly. So plan to stay a few days. The aptly named Vineyard Bed & Breakfast, a restored hacienda in Sonoita, is invitingly homespun with wonderful breakfasts, warmly gracious proprietors, and Pepperoni, a burro who possesses remarkable charm. Just don't let him sip your Arizona Pinot Gris.

— *Karen MacNeil-Fife*

Other rising stars

■ WALLA WALLA VALLEY, WASHINGTON

COMPARED WITH THE RELAXED PACE OF growth in the Puget Sound region, the Walla Walla Valley has red-hot wine fever. The success of L'Ecole No 41, Waterbrook Winery, and Woodward Canyon Winery generated the first wave of growth about 15 years ago, but today a veritable tsunami of investing, building, and planting is transforming the industry as could never have been imagined.

Walla Walla has become best known for rich red wines: Merlot, Cabernet Sauvignon, Sangiovese, and Syrah. To meet demand for them, a number of new wineries have recently started up. Success stories include Canoe Ridge Vineyard, Glen Fiona (blended wines based on Syrah), and Walla Walla Vintners (Merlot and Cabernet Sauvignon blends). This year will see releases of wines from new ventures like Cayuse Vineyards, Dunham Cellars, and Bunchgrass Winery.

But perhaps the best is yet to come. Over the next few years, new plantings of red wine grapes will let local vintners use increased quantities of Walla Walla Valley fruit. (Today, many of them must depend in part on grapes grown elsewhere.) Says Norm McKibben, whose Pepper Bridge Winery had its first crush last year, "I believe that Walla Walla could someday be another Napa Valley." — *C.H.*

■ SNAKE RIVER VALLEY, IDAHO

FRAMED ON THE WALL in THE NEW TASTING room at Indian Creek Winery is a *New Yorker* cartoon showing a hostess presenting a bottle for dinner guests to inspect.

"It's a little white wine Stuart brought back from Idaho," she's saying. "Are you game?"

Winemaker Bill Stowe hears me chuckle as he opens a bottle of his award-winning 1994 Pinot Noir. "Are you game?" he asks, pouring a taste for each of us.

Stowe and his wife, Mui, are pioneer Idaho grape growers now making some of the best wines in the Snake River country southwest of Boise. Containing more than half the state's wineries, it's a region that hasn't had to apologize for its wines in some time.

Although grapes were being grown in Idaho more than a century ago, federal Prohibition laws in 1919 killed winemaking until 1976, when Ste. Chapelle Winery—the 500-pound gorilla among 17 boutique wineries scattered throughout the state—opened its doors on the sloping high-desert benches north of the Snake River.

Young as it is, the Snake River wine region is rapidly coming of age. Over the last few years, four of Ste. Chapelle's neighbors have expanded production and built new tasting rooms. Winemakers quickly admit that in most cases they are still refining their red wines, although some, like Bill Stowe, are already making impressive reds as well as whites.

How impressive? During a Sunday afternoon of wine tasting I found six bottles I liked well enough to lug them home on the plane. Anyone game?

— *Jeff Phillips*

■ AMADOR COUNTY, CALIFORNIA

SAVVY AMERICAN WINE DRINKERS INSTANTLY recognize this region in California's Sierra foothills as one of the state's best-kept wine secrets. For this is one of the oldest "homes" of Zinfandel. And not just any Zinfandel—the kind of rustic, gutsy, teeth-staining, King Kong–size Zin that for decades has had a cult following.

Amador's wine story begins in the middle of the last century, well before the rise of Napa and Sonoma. At the time, California's wine industry was centered around Los Angeles. Only a scant few wineries existed in the northern counties, most of them tiny, noncommercial ventures.

But in 1848, with the discovery of gold near the town of Coloma in the foothills of the Sierra Nevada, the wine industry took off in a new direction. Mining camps sprang up everywhere and, in their wake, so did vineyards and small wineries begun mostly by Italian immigrants seeking their fortunes. By the 1860s there were nearly 200,000 vines growing in the "gold counties" of Northern California, including Amador. Notably, these were the first wineries in the state to forgo the humble mission grape (planted earlier by Spanish missionaries) in favor of better varieties such as Zinfandel.

In time, of course, the gold supply diminished and eventually dried up. The population shrank. Winemaking and grape growing slowed considerably, then virtually disappeared following the double blows of phylloxera and Prohibition. By the end of World War II, Amador County was home mostly to ghost wineries and abandoned vineyards. Only one winery managed to remain continuously in operation—the D'Agostini Winery, now Sobon Estate.

A renaissance began in the early 1970s and has continued unabated since. There are now more than 2,200 acres of wine grapes in Amador. Best of all, this includes many of the state's old prized Zinfandel vineyards, which, for decades, were kept in production thanks to home winemakers.

One of the first wineries to realize the true value of these old Amador Zinfandel vineyards was Sutter Home Winery in the Napa Valley. In 1971, Sutter Home released its first Amador County Zinfandel—a stunning wine made from the now-famous Deaver Ranch in the Shenandoah Valley. Today, Amador's leading wineries include Amador Foothill Winery, Deaver Vineyards, Domaine de la Terre Rouge, Karly Wines, Montevina Winery, Renwood Winery, Shenandoah Vineyards, and Sobon Estate. What these wineries are discovering would probably make the old European pioneers proud: Amador, as it turns out, is not just a good place for Zinfandel. Some of the most exciting up-and-coming Rhône and Italian grapes thrive too. Amador's real "gold" is wine. — *K.M.-F.*

■ GRUET, NEW MEXICO

WHEN THE GRUET FAMILY INTRODUCED THEIR New Mexico sparkling wine in 1989, it was greeted with the skepticism usually reserved for upstart wineries. "Is it made from cactus juice?" vice president Farid Himeur remembers being asked. Three years later at the San Francisco Fair, Gruet's Blanc de Noir took the double gold medal over heavyweights such as Domaine Chandon and Carneros. Nobody is laughing now.

Actually, it should come as no surprise that good wine is being made in New Mexico. It is the oldest wine-producing state in the nation. European wine grapes brought to New Mexico by Spanish missionary priests nearly four centuries ago thrived in the sunny days and cool nights of the Rio Grande Valley.

In 1981 the Gruet family, newly arrived from France, decided to take advantage of these favorable winemaking conditions.

Gruet grows its Chardonnay and Pinot Noir grapes on 90 acres of high-altitude alkaline sandy loam just east of Elephant Butte Reservoir in south-central New Mexico. The grapes are harvested in August and immediately placed in refrigerated trucks for the trip to Gruet's new 36,000-square-foot state-of-the-art winery in Albuquerque. Using the traditional eight-step *méthode champenoise*, the grapes are pressed and the juice is put in stainless steel tanks for the first fermentation.

The results? Well, hear what wine writer Robert Parker has to say. In reviewing Gruet's Brut and Blanc de Noirs, he notes, "These wines are among the best domestic sparkling wines." Quite an accolade for a wine from a region better known for tamales. "People still look at you when you say it's from New Mexico," says winemaker Laurent Gruet, "so most of the time we don't say New Mexico. We just say, 'Taste it.'" — *Joe Wise*

Western
The top 34 wines

As the saying goes, it was a tough job, but someone had to do it. We asked vintners from the eight emerging Western wine regions in this story to send us their finest efforts. In a blind tasting, a panel of eight judges sampled 86 wines and chose the best each region has to offer.

Judges were wine writers Karen MacNeil-Fife of St. Helena, California, and Chuck Hill of Seattle; beverage manager/sommelier Traci Dutton and assistant beverage manager Michael Pryor of the Culinary Institute of America at Greystone in St. Helena; Michele Valence, Greystone bartender; Jerry Anne Di Vecchio, *Sunset* senior food editor; Sara Schneider, *Sunset* senior editor; and Elaine Johnson, *Sunset* senior writer. Rebecca Murphy, a Portland-based consultant, ran the tasting.

Our recommended wines show particular promise. But many are still works in progress. Winemakers are constantly improving their efforts. Stay tuned for the next vintage. Many of our favorites are available only in small quantities and are sold primarily at the wineries—a great reason to visit.

■ GRAND VALLEY, COLORADO

Canyon Wind Cabernet Sauvignon 1996, Palisades, $20. Pleasing pine, eucalyptus, cassis, and smoke; a bit rough around the edges.
Canyon Wind Merlot 1996, Palisades, $18. Spicy ripeness, lots of new oak.
Grande River Meritage 1995, Grand Valley, $13. Bordeaux-style blend. Lean, tight, sleek, and smoky.
Plum Creek Redstone Reserve Chardonnay 1997, $13. Apple, banana, and butterscotch with lemony brightness, hot finish.

wine winners...
from *Sunset's* taste-off

■ PUGET SOUND, WASHINGTON

Bainbridge Island Late Harvest Botrytised Siegerrebe 1996, Puget Sound, $22. Apricots, honey, and tea.

Hoodsport Raspberry Wine, $9. Also sold under Whidbey Island Greenbank Farms label. Essence of raspberries; light and fresh.

Lopez Island Siegerrebe 1997, San Juan County, $12. Spicy, gingery; great for Asian food.

Mount Baker Madeleine Angevine, Washington State, $14. Off-dry, spicy baked pears.

■ ROGUE VALLEY, OREGON

Bridgeview Pinot Gris Cuvée Speciale 1997, Oregon, $10. Lean and fresh with lively acidity.

Foris Pinot Noir 1996, Siskiyou Terrace, Rogue Valley, $19. Earthy cherries and blackberries, tart finish.

Troon Vintage Select, Proprietor's Reserve Cabernet Sauvignon 1996, $18. Light cassis, earthy.

Valley View Anna Maria Merlot 1995, Rogue Valley, $28. Soft, dead-ripe cherries, toasty oak, bright acidity.

■ SOUTHEAST ARIZONA

Callaghan Cabernet Sauvignon 1997, Buena Suerte Vineyard, $18. Light-bodied cherry and herb flavors, forthright tannins.

Dos Cabezas Reserve Chardonnay 1997, $18. Buttery apples and pears, but a short finish.

■ WALLA WALLA VALLEY, WASHINGTON

Canoe Ridge Vineyard Merlot 1996, Columbia Valley, $19. Warm, earthy tones, light finish.

Dunham Cabernet Sauvignon III 1997, Columbia Valley, $45. Smoky eucalyptus and cassis; young tannins.

Leonetti Cabernet Sauvignon Reserve 1996, Seven Hills Vineyard, Walla Walla Valley, $75. Big and meaty, cassis and berries, well balanced.

Patrick M. Paul Merlot 1997, Conner Lee Vineyards, Columbia Valley, $15. Sweet and spicy raspberries, plenty of acidity.

Seven Hills Syrah 1997, Walla Walla Valley, $25. Young tannins with meaty cherries and plums.

Walla Walla Cabernet Franc 1997, Spring Valley Vineyard, Walla Walla Valley, $25. Complex blend of licorice, oak, dill, violets, and berries.

Walla Walla Merlot 1997 Spring Valley Vineyard, Walla Walla Valley, $25. Lots of oak with cassis and baked cherries.

Waterbrook Chardonnay 1997, Columbia Valley, $9. Sweet apples, crème brûlée; good value.

Woodward Canyon Chardonnay 1997, Columbia Valley, $28. Plenty of vanilla and toasty oak.

■ SNAKE RIVER VALLEY, IDAHO

Carmela Barrel-fermented Chardonnay 1997, Idaho, $12. Woody nose, nice buttery and lemony personality.

Carmela Proprietor Grown Cabernet Franc 1995, Idaho, $12. Bright cherries, lots of old wood and earth.

Hells Canyon Artists Conservation Series Reserve Merlot 1997, Idaho, $42. Scratchy but hefty, full of ripe cherries; begs for a steak.

Ste. Chapelle Johannisberg Riesling 1998, Idaho, $6. Light, refreshing apricots and peaches; a steal.

■ AMADOR COUNTY, CALIFORNIA

Easton Zinfandel 1996, Shenan- doah Valley, California, $18. Ripe brambleberries, robust tannins.

Karly El Alacrán 1997, Amador County, $30. Mourvèdre grapes. Young, earthy, toasty berries.

Karly Sadie Upton Zinfandel, 1997, Amador County, $22. Intense color, subtle raspberries and cherries.

Noceto Sangiovese 1997, Shenandoah Valley, California, $13. Fragrant, spicy plums, good structure, easy drinking.

Terre Rouge Noir 1995, Sierra Foothills, $18. Rhône-style blend of Grenache, Mourvèdre, and Syrah. Fruity plums and berries; earthy.

■ GRUET, NEW MEXICO

Gruet Blanc de Blanc 1995, $22. Toasty yeast with notes of pear and citrus; tiny bubbles.

Gruet Brut, $13. Flint, smoke, and citrus; tiny bubbles. *— E.J.*

JAY DICKMAN

New wine countries travel planner

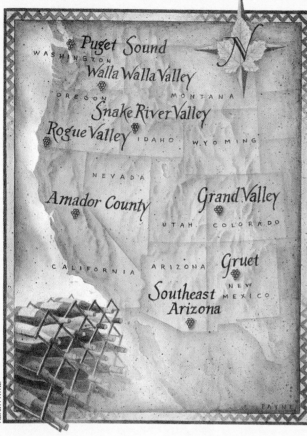

Puget Sound
Walla Walla Valley
Snake River Valley
Rogue Valley
Amador County
Grand Valley
Southeast Arizona
Gruet

ADAIR PAYNE

■ GRAND VALLEY, COLORADO

WHERE. Wineries are in Palisade, just east of Grand Junction and about 250 miles west of Denver via I-70. Area code is 970 unless noted.

WINERIES. All are open daily except for Canyon Wind Cellars (call for appointment). **Canyon Wind Cellars,** 3907 N. River Rd.; 464-0888. **Carlson Vineyards,** 461 35 Rd.; 464-5554. **Colorado Cellars Winery,** 3553 E Rd.; (800) 848-2812. **Confre Cellars/Rocky Mountain Meadery,** 3701 G Rd.; 464-7899. **Grande River Vineyards,** 787 Elberta Ave.; 464-5867. **Plum Creek Cellars,** 3708 G Rd.; 464-7586. One more should be open this month: **St. Kathryn Cellars,** 888 Elberta; 464-9288.

MAIN EVENT. Colorado Mountain Winefest, Palisade. September 17–19; $15. (800) 704-3667.

LODGING. Orchard House Bed and Breakfast (from $65; 3573 E½ Rd.; 464-0529) puts you right in the wine country. The elegant **Los Altos Bed & Breakfast** (from $80; 375 Hillview Dr.; 256-0964 or 888/774-0982) offers 360° views.

DINING. Dolce Vita (336 Main St.; 242-8482) for Italian food. Pick up picnic fixings at the **Westside Delicatessen** (2454 U.S. 6 and U.S. 50; 241-3100).

CONTACT. For a map, call 523-1232. Also helpful is the **Grand Junction Visitor & Convention Bureau;** (800) 962-2547 or www.grand-junction.net.

■ PUGET SOUND, WASHINGTON

WHERE. Wineries are scattered over Bainbridge, Lopez, Whidbey, and San Juan islands, with two on the mainland. Area code is 360 unless noted.

WINERIES. All are open Saturdays, most Sundays, some daily. **Bainbridge Island Vineyards & Winery,** 682 State 305, Bainbridge Island; (206) 842-9463. **Hoodsport Winery,** 23501 N. U.S. 101, Hoodsport; 877-9894. **Lopez Island Vineyards,** 724 Fisherman Bay Rd., Lopez Island; 468-3644. **Mount Baker Vineyards,** 4298 Mt. Baker Hwy., Everson; 592-2300. **San Juan Vineyards,** 2000 Roche Harbor Rd., Friday Harbor; 378-9463. **Whidbey Island Greenbank Farm,** 765 Wonn Rd., Greenbank; 678-7700. **Whidbey Island Vineyards & Winery,** 5237 S. Langley Rd., Langley; 221-2040.

LODGING. Good choices abound. On Whidbey Island, the **Inn at Langley** (from $199; 400 First St., Langley; 221-3033) has luxurious rooms and a good restaurant.

DINING. On Lopez Island, **Bay Cafe** (Lopez Village; 468-3700) adroitly pairs local wines with regional cuisine.

FERRIES. For information on service to Bainbridge, Whidbey, Lopez, and San Juan islands, call (206) 464-6400.

CONTACT. Washington Wine Commission; (206) 667-9463 or www.washingtonwine.org.

■ ROGUE VALLEY, OREGON

WHERE. The Rogue Valley is about 170 miles south of Eugene. Ashland and Jacksonville make excellent bases of operation. A good road map is helpful. Area code is 541 unless noted.

WINERIES. Through Labor Day,

most wineries are open daily, except for the Academy of Wine and Troon Vineyards, which are open by appointment only. Other times of year, call for hours. **Academy of Wine of Oregon,** 18200 State 238, Grants Pass; 846-6817. **Ashland Vineyards,** 2775 E. Main St., Ashland; 488-0088. **Bridgeview Vineyards,** 4210 Holland Loop Rd., Cave Junction; (877) 273-4348. **Foris Vineyards Winery,** 654 Kendall Rd., Cave Junction; (800) 843-6747. **Troon Vineyards,** 1475 Kubli Rd., Grants Pass; 846-6562. **Valley View Winery,** 1000 Upper Applegate Rd., Ruch; (800) 781-9463; there's also a tasting room at **Anna Maria's,** 130 W. California St., Jacksonville; 899-1001. **Weisinger's of Ashland,** 3150 Siskiyou Blvd., Ashland; 488-5989.

LODGING. In Ashland, **Winchester Country Inn** (from $140; 35 S. Second St.; 488-1115) is an elegant downtown Victorian. The grande dame of Jacksonville lodgings is the 138-year-old **Jacksonville Inn** (from $115; 175 E. California St.; 800/321-9344). Both also have good restaurants.

DINING. In Ashland, **Monet Restaurant and Garden** (36 S. Second; 482-1339) shines with spinach-wrapped salmon fillet and a choice of a dozen local wines. The **Apple Cellar** (2255 State 66; 488-8131) offers picnic fare like polenta–goat cheese salad, panini, and almond shortbread tart.

WINE SHOPS. Jacksonville Inn Wine Shop (see lodging above) and **Chateaulin Wine & Gourmet Foods** in Ashland (52 E. Main; 488-9463) carry Rogue Valley wines and will ship them.

CONTACT. For a guide to most Oregon wineries, call (800) 242-2363 or visit www.oregonwine.org. Also helpful are the **Ashland Chamber of Commerce** (482-3486) and the **Jacksonville Chamber of Commerce** (899-8118).

■ SOUTHEAST ARIZONA

WHERE. Wineries are clustered near Sonoita and Elgin, about 50 miles southeast of Tucson, with one in Willcox, about 80 miles east of Tucson. Area code is 520.

WINERIES. Most are open weekends; still, with the distances involved, it's wise to call ahead. **Callaghan Vineyards,** 3 miles south of Elgin on Canelo Rd.; 455-5322. **Dos Cabezas WineWorks,** Kansas Settlement; by appointment only, 455-5285. **Village of Elgin Winery,** the Elgin Complex, Elgin; 455-9309. **Kokopelli Winery,** 2060 N. Haskell Ave., Willcox; 384-3800. **Santa Cruz Winery,** 315 McKeown Ave., Patagonia; 394-2888. **Sonoita Vineyards,** 3 miles south of Elgin on Canelo; 455-5893.

LODGING. In Sonoita, the **Vineyard Bed & Breakfast** (from $85; 92 S. Los Encinos Rd.; 455-4749) has three rooms and one casita ($95). You'll also find numerous motels in Sierra Vista, 30 miles southeast of Sonoita.

DINING. Good for Italian is **Cose Buono** in Patagonia (436 Naugle Ave.; 394-2366; reopens for the season Sept. 4).

CONTACT. Sonoita Chamber of Commerce; 455-5498.

■ WALLA WALLA VALLEY, WASHINGTON

WHERE. The wineries are near Walla Walla (with one across the border in Oregon), about 275 miles southeast of Seattle, 235 miles east of Portland. Area code is 509 unless noted.

BAINBRIDGE Island Vineyards & Winery typifies the new breed of small, pioneering vineyards.

PHIL SCHOFIELD

WINERIES. All are open to the public on weekends, many on weekdays as well. **Canoe Ridge Vineyard,** 1102 W. Cherry St., Walla Walla; 527-0885. **Cayuse Vineyards,** 17 E. Main St., Walla Walla; 526-0686. **L'Ecole No 41,** 41 Lowden School Rd., Lowden; 525-0940. **Patrick M. Paul Vineyards,** 1554 School Ave., Walla Walla; 526-0676. **Waterbrook Winery,** 31 E. Main, Walla Walla; 522-1262. **Woodward Canyon Winery,** 1920 W. State 12, Touchet; 525-4129. The following wineries are open by appointment only. **Dunham Cellars,** Walla Walla; 520-8463. **Glen Fiona,** Walla Walla; 522-2566. **Seven Hills Winery,** Milton-Freewater, OR; (541) 938-7710. **Walla Walla Vintners,** Walla Walla; 525-4724.

LODGING AND DINING. Mill Creek Inn (from $85; Box 251, Mill Creek Rd., Walla Walla; 522-1234) is a great place for wine-minded guests; Glen Fiona winery occupies the carriage house. For lunch, try

Merchants Delicatessen & French Bakery (21 E. Main; 525-0900).

CONTACT. Walla Walla Chamber of Commerce; 525-0850.

■ SNAKE RIVER VALLEY, IDAHO

WHERE. The valley follows the Snake River west of Boise to Twin Falls. Area code is 208.

WINERIES. All are open weekends; call for weekday hours. **Carmela Vineyards,** 795 W. Madison Ave., Glenns Ferry; 366-2313. **Hells Canyon Winery,** 18835 Symms Rd., Caldwell; 454-3300. **Indian Creek (Stowe) Winery,** 1000 N. McDermott Rd., Kuna; 922-4791. **Koenig Distillery & Winery,** 20928 Grape Lane, Caldwell; 455-8386. **Sawtooth Winery,** 13750 Surrey Lane, Nampa; 467-1200. **Ste. Chapelle Winery,** 19348 Lowell Rd., Caldwell; 459-7222.

LODGING. In Boise, try the Idaho Heritage Inn (from $60; 109 W. Idaho; 342-8066).

DINING. Before leaving Boise, get your picnic supplies at **Villano's Specialty Market & Deli** (712 W. Idaho St.; 331-3066).

CONTACT. For a guide to all Idaho wineries, call (888) 223-9463 or check www.winesnw.com/idhome.html.

■ AMADOR COUNTY, CALIFORNIA

WHERE. Amador County is about 50 miles southeast of Sacramento. Area code is 209 unless noted.

WINERIES. All are in Plymouth. **Amador Foothill Winery,** 12500 Steiner; 245-6307. **Deaver Vineyards,** 12455 Steiner Rd.; 245-4099. **Domaine de la Terre Rouge,** 10801 Dickson Rd.; 245-4277. **Karly Wines,** 11076 Bell Rd.; 245-3922. **Montevina Winery,** 20680 Shenandoah School Rd.; 245-6942. **Renwood Winery,** 12225 Steiner; 245-6979. **Shenandoah Vineyards,** 12300 Steiner; 245-4455. **Sobon Estate,** 14430 Shenandoah Rd.; 245-4455. **Vino Noceto;** open by appointment only, 245-6556.

LODGING. In Plymouth, **Amador Harvest Inn** (from $95; 12455 Steiner; 245-5512) shares its grounds with Deaver Vineyards (above).

DINING. In Sutter Creek, **Zinfandels at Sutter Creek** (51 Hanford St./State 49; 267-5008) is a good bet. In Amador City, the **Imperial Hotel** (14202 State 49; 800/242-5594) offers fine dining in a restored 1879-vintage hotel.

CONTACT. Amador Vintners' Association; (209) 245-4309 or www.amadorwine.com.

— K.M.-F.

■ GRUET, NEW MEXICO

WHERE. Gruet Winery, 8400 Pan-American Hwy., Albuquerque; (505) 821-0055. ◆

hooked on the grill

A fearless guide for barbecuing your favorite seafood— even the hardest to tackle

BY ANDREW BAKER • PHOTOGRAPHS BY JAMES CARRIER

*"I like the fishes, swimmin'
round in the sea,
I like to plop 'um on the grill
And I cook 'um up for me
with a big pat of butter
Man it can't get better than this."*

— *"Moloka'i Slide," by Tad Suckling*

■ THOSE WORDS FROM A CATCHY HAWAIIAN tune echo the sentiments I felt on my first trip to Hawaii. Everywhere I ate, seafood was in abundance, prepared as easily as the song says: grilled and served with a simple sauce. • But while the serendipity of throwing together a beachside meal makes for good lyrics, in practice, grilling seafood successfully takes a little know-how. • The challenge lies in the physical makeup of fish, which is more fragile than a hunk of meat. Success is based on how you "plop 'um on the grill." • Dense, firm fish in pieces that are at least 1 inch thick and small enough to slide onto a wide spatula (or thread onto skewers) can be placed directly on the grill. Turn them once, carefully. • But even for firm fish, as well as others that are more delicate, a little support works wonders. Set the fish (or piece) on foil trimmed to fit the outline of the fish, then lift the two together on and off the grill. No sticking. No falling apart. You don't need to turn the pieces over. Cover the grill so thick pieces will cook through. • Most fish cooks well over direct heat (see "How to Grill Fish," page 186). For large, thicker pieces, such as whole trout or salmon, indirect heat provides temperature controls more like baking. • Shellfish presents few problems on the barbecue: Clams, oysters, and mussels pop open to eat. Barbecue shrimp and lobster in or out of the shell. Crab is best if cooked first, then warmed on the grill. • Try these 11 special fish recipes, and for that simple sauce, 14 choices almost as easy as "a big pat of butter" follow.

BOUNTY FROM THE SEA, by way of the grill: Lobster (right) is paired with potato salad and salmon caviar. Tuna (left) rests on cashew pilaf.

Grilled Lobster with Potato Salad

PREP AND COOK TIME: About 45 minutes
NOTES: Use direct heat.
MAKES: 4 servings

- 1½ pounds **Yukon Gold potatoes,** peeled
- ⅓ cup thawed **frozen orange juice concentrate**
- ¼ cup **lemon juice**
- 4 teaspoons **Dijon mustard**
- ⅔ cup finely chopped **green onions,** including tops
  Salt
- 4 **spiny** or rock **lobster tails** (½ lb. each), thawed if frozen
- ¼ cup **fresh salmon caviar** (*ikura,* optional)

1. In a 5- to 6-quart pan over high heat, bring potatoes and 3 quarts water to a boil. Cover and simmer until potatoes are tender when pierced, 30 to 35 minutes. Drain. When potatoes are cool enough to touch, cut into ¼- to ½-inch chunks.

2. Meanwhile, in a large bowl, stir together orange juice concentrate, lemon juice, Dijon mustard, and green onions. Add potato chunks and mix gently. Add salt to taste.

3. With scissors, cut lengthwise down the center of the top of each lobster shell. Set each tail, underside down, on a cutting board. Force a heavy knife through the cut in each shell to slice each lobster tail in half. Rinse lobster in shell.

4. Have barbecue ready with *direct heat* at *hot* (see page 186). Lightly oil grill and lay lobster on it. Turn once to cook evenly until lobster is opaque but moist-looking in center of thickest part (cut to test), about 7 minutes.

5. Mound potato salad equally onto plates; top with caviar. Place 2 lobster halves around each salad portion.

Per serving: 297 cal., 3.3% (9.9 cal.) from fat; 29 g protein; 1.1 g fat (0.1 g sat.); 40 g carbo (3.1 g fiber); 613 mg sodium; 90 mg chol.

Tuna with Coconut-Curry Sauce

PREP AND COOK TIME: About 25 minutes
NOTES: Use direct heat. Purchase tamarind concentrate in Latino or Middle Eastern food markets. The concentrate and curry paste are also sold in Southeast Asian groceries and well-stocked supermarkets.

MAKES: 4 servings

  1 cup **canned coconut milk**

  4 teaspoons **tamarind concentrate** or lime juice

1½ teaspoons **Thai red curry paste** or curry powder

  2 tablespoons minced **fresh cilantro**

1 ½ pounds **boned tuna** (ahi, 1¼ to 1½ in. thick)

  ½ cup chopped **salted roasted cashews**

  4 cups **hot cooked rice**

  ¼ cup slivered **fresh basil** leaves **Salt**

1. In a bowl, mix coconut milk, tamarind concentrate, and curry paste; stir in cilantro.

2. Rinse tuna, pat dry, and turn over in coconut milk sauce. Lift out fish; save the sauce.

3. Pour sauce into a 1- to 1½-quart pan; bring to a boil over high heat, stirring. Or bring to a boil in a microwave-safe container in a microwave oven at full power (100%). Keep warm.

4. Have barbecue ready with *direct heat* at *very hot* (see right). Lightly oil grill and set fish on it. Cook tuna until bottom is pale color about ¼ inch into fish (cut to test; center is red), about 2 minutes. Turn tuna with a wide spatula and cook until side on grill is the same color as it is on the top, and center is still pink to red, about 1 minute longer.

5. Stir cashews into rice, spoon onto plates, and top with equal portions tuna. Sprinkle with basil. Serve with warm coconut-curry sauce and add salt to taste.

Per serving: 610 cal., 34% (207 cal.) from fat; 48 g protein; 23 g fat (13 g sat.); 52 g carbo (2.3 g fiber); 251 mg sodium; 77 mg chol.

Salmon with Ginger-Banana Sauce

PREP AND COOK TIME: About 20 minutes
NOTES: Use direct heat.
MAKES: 4 servings

1 can (8 oz.) **crushed pineapple**

1 **ripe banana** (½ lb.), peeled and cut into chunks

SWEET, SPICY ginger-banana sauce sets off salmon from the grill.

How to grill fish

Heat grill while you prepare the fish to cook.

DIRECT HEAT—beneath the food
1. If using charcoal briquets, cover firegrate with a single, solid layer of ignited coals. Let briquets burn down to desired heat.

If using a gas barbecue, turn burners to high and close lid for 10 minutes. Adjust the burners to desired heat.

Set the barbecue grill in place and measure heat:

VERY HOT (you can hold your hand at grill level only 1 to 2 seconds)

HOT (you can hold your hand at grill level only 2 to 3 seconds)

MEDIUM-HOT (you can hold your hand at grill level only 3 to 4 seconds)

MEDIUM (you can hold your hand at grill level only 4 to 5 seconds)

MEDIUM-LOW (you can hold your hand at grill level only 5 to 6 seconds)

LOW (you can hold your hand at grill level only 6 to 7 seconds)

2. To oil grill, brush with salad oil. Lay food on grill, cook as recipe directs.

3. Cover gas barbecue. Do not cover charcoal barbecue unless recipe specifies.

INDIRECT HEAT—on opposite sides of the food

1. If using charcoal briquets, mound and ignite 60 briquets on the firegrate of a barbecue with a lid. When briquets are dotted with gray ash, in 15 to 20 minutes, push equal amounts to opposite sides of firegrate. Add 5 more briquets to *each* mound of coals now and every 30 minutes while cooking. Set a drip pan on firegrate between coals.

If using a gas barbecue, turn all burners to high and close lid for 10 minutes. Adjust burners for indirect cooking (no heat down center) and keep on high unless recipe specifies otherwise.

Set barbecue grill in place.

2. To oil grill, brush with salad oil. Lay food on grill, but not over heat source.

3. Cover grill (open vents for charcoal). Cook as recipe directs.

Firm, dense fish that can go directly onto the grill: mackerel, mahi mahi, opah (moonfish), orange roughy, salmon (with skin), shark, sturgeon, swordfish, and tuna.

Fish that need support: barracuda, bass, butterfish, catfish, Chilean seabass, cod, flounder, halibut, lingcod, rockfish, sablefish, salmon (without skin), sand dab, snapper, sole, tilapia, and trout.

4 teaspoons minced **fresh ginger**

1 tablespoon minced **fresh jalapeño chili**

2 tablespoons **lime juice**

½ cup finely chopped **onion**

½ cup finely chopped **red bell pepper**

½ teaspoon **salad oil**

2 cans (15 oz. each) **black beans,** rinsed and drained

1½ pounds **boned, skinned salmon fillet** (1½-in. maximum thickness)

Lime wedges

Salt

1. Drain pineapple and save ¼ cup of the juice.

2. In a blender or food processor, whirl the ¼ cup pineapple juice, banana, ginger, chili, and lime juice until puréed. Scoop into a small bowl.

3. In a 10- to 12-inch nonstick frying pan over high heat, stir onion, bell pepper, and oil until vegetables are limp, 3 to 5 minutes. Add crushed pineapple and beans; stir just until hot, about 2 minutes. Cover and keep warm.

4. Rinse salmon and pat dry. Lay fish, skin down, on a sheet of foil. Trim foil to fit salmon.

5. Have barbecue ready with *direct heat* at *hot* (see above). Lay foil with salmon on grill. Cook fish until opaque but moist-looking in center of thickest part (cut to test), 6 to 8 minutes.

6. Cut salmon into equal portions. Spoon bean mixture equally onto plates; top with salmon and ginger-banana sauce. Add lime juice from wedges and salt to taste.

Per serving: 518 cal., 35% (180 cal.) from fat; 43 g protein; 20 g fat (3.9 g sat.); 41 g carbo (7.4 g fiber); 447 mg sodium; 100 mg chol.

Butterflied Salmon with Mustard Sauce

PREP AND COOK TIME: About 1 hour
NOTES: Use indirect heat. Order a whole salmon that is boned and butterflied (attached at back), with skin left on. If your gas grill does not have enough space to cook the salmon using indirect heat, cut fish lengthwise into 2 fillets and cook 1 fillet at a time.
MAKES: 18 to 20 servings

- ½ cup finely chopped **onion**
- 1 cup **dry vermouth**
- 6 tablespoons **coarse-grain mustard**
- 2 teaspoons **dried tarragon**
- 2 tablespoons **sugar**
- 1 **salmon,** head removed (6 to 7 lb. total), filleted but still attached down the back

    Salt

1. In a 10- to 12-inch frying pan, combine onion, vermouth, mustard, tarragon, and sugar. Stirring often, boil over high heat until reduced to ¾ cup, 5 to 8 minutes.

2. Rinse salmon and pat dry. Lay fish open, skin down, on a sheet of foil (about 12 by 17 in.). Trim foil to fit salmon. Spread onion mixture over top of salmon.

3. Have barbecue ready with ***indirect heat*** (see page 186). Set foil with salmon on grill but not over heat. Cover barbecue as directed. Cook until fish is opaque but moist-looking in thickest part (cut to test), 30 to 40 minutes.

4. Slide a rimless baking sheet under salmon and foil, then slide fish onto a large flat platter or board. Cut salmon and lift portions from skin with a wide spatula. Season to taste with salt.

Per serving: 175 cal., 49% (86 cal.) from fat; 18 g protein; 9.6 g fat (1.9 g sat.); 2.2 g carbo (0.1 g fiber); 162 mg sodium; 52 mg chol.

Smelt and Fennel in Prosciutto

PREP AND COOK TIME: About 1 hour
NOTES: Use direct heat. If desired, use 1 pound (12 to 15 per lb.) shelled, deveined, and rinsed shrimp instead of smelt.
MAKES: 6 appetizer servings

- 1 pound **smelt** (4 to 5 in.)
- 1 head **fennel** (3 to 3½ in. wide)
- 12 pieces **thin-sliced prosciutto** (about 4 by 7 in.; 6 oz. total)

    Lemon wedges

TENDER SMELT, wrapped in thinly sliced fennel and prosciutto, then grilled, make an adventurous appetizer. Bones are soft enough to eat, or pull out easily.

1. Using a small, sharp knife, slit open smelt bellies, discard innards, rinse fish, and pat dry.

2. Rinse fennel. Trim and discard stalks and bruised spots. Rinse, drain, and chop feathery leaves. Using a slicer, cut fennel into ¹⁄₁₆-inch-thick pieces.

3. Lay prosciutto slices flat. Lay equal portions of smelt across narrow width of prosciutto slices, then mound sliced fennel equally onto fish. Roll prosciutto to enclose fish and fennel, and secure with 2 parallel thin metal skewers crosswise through fish. Or cut prosciutto into strips. Wrap 1 smelt at a time with equal portions of fennel on a prosciutto strip. Thread crosswise onto skewers.

4. Have barbecue ready with ***direct heat*** at ***hot*** (see page 186). Lightly oil grill and lay skewers on it. Cook until smelt are opaque but moist-looking in thickest part (cut 1 to test), about 6 minutes; after 3 minutes, turn skewers.

5. Place skewers on a platter or plates and sprinkle with chopped fennel greens. Pull out skewers and add juice from lemon wedges to taste. Smelt bones are edible, if you like, but the skeletons can be lifted out whole and discarded.

Per serving: 114 cal., 40% (46 cal.) from fat; 16 g protein; 5.1 g fat (1.2 g sat.); 1.5 g carbo (0.5 g fiber); 600 mg sodium; 52 mg chol.

Swordfish Mole Tacos

PREP AND COOK TIME: About 30 minutes
NOTES: Use direct heat. Shop for canned mole sauce (in cans or jars) in well-stocked supermarkets or Latino food markets. Purchase mole that requires additional liquid (see label), but use amount specified in step 1.
MAKES: 4 servings

sauces for fish

SAUCES and salsas (from bottom): Baby tomato, kiwi fruit, mango-masala, and grilled two-chili.

Each sauce requires 5 to 15 minutes to prepare, and makes 4 to 6 servings. Serve sauces with any fish suggested for grill cooking on page 186. With the exception of the grapefruit beurre blanc, all the sauces can be made at least 1 day ahead, covered, and chilled.

■ **Artichoke Tapenade.** In a blender or food processor, combine 1 jar (6.5 oz.) **marinated artichokes** with marinade, ¼ cup **sliced black ripe olives**, ¼ cup drained **oil-packed dried tomatoes**, ½ cup chopped **parsley**, and 1 teaspoon grated **lemon** peel. Whirl until smooth, scraping

container sides as needed. Makes about 1 cup.

Per tablespoon: 23 cal., 61% (14 cal.) from fat; 0.6 g protein; 1.6 g fat (0.1 g sat.); 2.2 g carbo (0.8 g fiber); 93 mg sodium; 0 mg chol.

■ **Baby Tomato Vinaigrette.** Rinse 1 cup **tiny cherry tomatoes** (about ¾ in. wide; red, yellow, orange, or a mixture). Cut tomatoes into halves and put in a bowl. Add 1 tablespoon minced **mild onion**, 1 tablespoon minced **fresh tarragon** leaves, 2 teaspoons **olive oil**, and 1 teaspoon **white wine vinegar**. Stir to mix; add **salt** to taste. Makes about 1 cup.

Per tablespoon: 6.8 cal., 79% (5.4 cal.) from fat; 0.1 g protein; 0.6 g fat (0.1 g sat.); 0.4 g carbo (0.1 g fiber); 0.7 mg sodium; 0 mg chol.

■ **Caesar Tartar Sauce.** In a bowl, mix ½ cup **mayonnaise**, 2 tablespoons **sweet pickle relish**, 2 tablespoons minced **onion**, 2 tablespoons grated **parmesan cheese**, and ¾ teaspoon **anchovy paste**. Makes about ¾ cup.

Per tablespoon: 74 cal., 92% (68 cal.) from fat; 0.5 g protein; 7.6 g fat (1.2 g sat.); 1.3 g carbo (0 g fiber); 103 mg sodium; 6.2 mg chol.

■ **Cracked Pepper Aioli.** Coarsely grind or crush ½ teaspoon **dried peppercorns** (black, green, or pink). In a bowl, mix pepper, ½ cup **mayonnaise**, ½ teaspoon minced **garlic**, ¾ teaspoon grated **lemon** peel, and 1 ta-

blespoon **lemon juice**. Makes about ½ cup.

Per tablespoon: 100 cal., 99% (99 cal.) from fat; 0.2 g protein; 11 g fat (1.6 g sat.); 0.7 g carbo (0 g fiber); 79 mg sodium; 8.1 mg chol.

■ **Crisp Jicama Guacamole.** Peel and pit 1 **firm-ripe avocado** (½ lb.). In a bowl, mash avocado, then stir in ½ cup finely chopped peeled **jicama**, 2 tablespoons **lime juice**, 2 tablespoons minced **fresh cilantro**, 1 tablespoon minced **fresh jalapeño chili**, and 2 teaspoons grated **orange** peel. Add **salt** to taste. Makes about 1¼ cups.

Per tablespoon: 15 cal., 80% (12 cal.) from fat; 0.2 g protein; 1.3 g fat (0.2 g sat.); 1.1 g carbo (0.3 g fiber); 1.2 mg sodium; 0 mg chol.

San Francisco Bay Area restaurateur Faz Pourshoi serves this sauce with sturgeon, but it goes well with any grilled fish.

■ **Faz's Herb Sauce.** In a blender or food processor, combine 2 cups lightly packed, rinsed and drained **fresh basil** leaves; ½ cup lightly packed, rinsed and drained **Italian parsley**; ½ cup chopped **chives**; ¼ cup **olive oil**; 2 tablespoons **lemon juice**; 4 teaspoons drained **capers**; 1 teaspoon **anchovy paste**; and ½ teaspoon chopped **garlic**. Whirl until puréed smooth, scraping container sides as needed. Makes about ¾ cup.

⅓ cup **canned mole sauce**

1½ pounds **boned, skinned swordfish**

½ cup **mayonnaise**

8 **corn tortillas** (6 in.)

1½ cups thinly shredded **red** or green **cabbage**

¾ cup chopped **tomatoes**

Lime wedges

Salt

1. In a bowl, mix mole and ⅓ cup water.

2. Rinse fish and pat dry; cut into 1-inch chunks and mix with mole sauce. Thread swordfish, pieces touching, onto thin metal skewers.

3. In a small bowl, mix mayonnaise with 2 tablespoons water.

4. Have barbecue ready with ***direct heat*** at ***hot*** (see page 186). Lay tortillas on grill and turn to heat both sides, 1 to 2 minutes total. When tortillas are hot, stack in a towel-lined basket to keep warm.

5. Lightly oil grill and lay skewers on it. Barbecue fish until opaque but moist-looking in center of thickest part (cut to test), about 8 minutes; turn once to cook evenly.

6. Put skewers on plates. To assemble each taco, top a tortilla with fish chunks, cabbage, tomatoes, mayonnaise mixture, and lime juice and salt to taste. Fold tortilla around filling to eat.

Per serving: 680 cal., 53% (360 cal.) from fat; 39 g protein; 40 g fat (6.6 g sat.); 35 g carbo (4.9 g fiber); 700 mg sodium; 83 mg chol.

Halibut with Zahtar and Mint Couscous

PREP AND COOK TIME: About 30 minutes

NOTES: Use direct heat. Zahtar is a Middle Eastern seasoning made with sumac, a dried sour berry. Dried tart cherries have a similar tang.

MAKES: 4 servings

¾ cup **dried sour cherries**

1 tablespoon **dried oregano**

1 tablespoon **ground cumin**

1½ teaspoons **paprika**

3 tablespoons **olive oil**

6 tablespoons **lemon juice**

Salt

Per tablespoon: 44 cal., 93% (41 cal.) from fat; 0.2 g protein; 4.6 g fat (0.6 g sat.); 0.6 g carbo (0.3 g fiber); 67 mg sodium; 0.1 mg chol.

■ Grapefruit Beurre Blanc.

In a 10- to 12-inch frying pan over high heat, boil 2 cups **ruby grapefruit** juice until reduced to ⅓ cup, about 10 minutes. Turn heat to low and whisk in ¾ cup (⅜ lb.) **butter** or margarine, in chunks. Serve at once; sauce separates as it stands. Makes about 1 cup.

Per tablespoon: 89 cal., 89% (79 cal.) from fat; 0.2 g protein; 8.8 g fat (5.4 g sat.); 2.8 g carbo (0 g fiber); 89 mg sodium; 24 mg chol.

■ Grilled Two-Chili Salsa.

Rinse 2 **fresh Anaheim chilies** (about 6 oz. total) and 2 **fresh habanero chilies** (½ oz. total). Wearing kitchen gloves, cut chilies in half lengthwise; remove and discard seeds, veins, and stems. Rinse ½ pound **green onions** and trim ends. Rinse 4 **Roma tomatoes** (about 14 oz. total), and cut in half. Prepare barbecue for **direct heat** at **hot** (see page 186). Lay vegetables on grill and turn as needed until lightly browned, about 3 minutes for green onions and habaneros, about 8 minutes for tomatoes, and 12 to 15 minutes for Anaheims. Remove from grill as cooked. When vegetables are cool, coarsely chop them. In blender or food processor, combine chopped vegetables, any juices, and 1 tablespoon **red wine vinegar**; whirl until smooth. Add **salt** to taste. Makes about 1½ cups.

Per tablespoon: 8.8 cal., 10% (0.9 cal.) from fat; 0.4 g protein; 0.1 g fat (0 g sat.); 2 g carbo (0.5 g fiber); 3.4 mg sodium; 0 mg chol.

■ Kiwi Fruit Salsa Verde.

Peel 2 **kiwi fruit** (about 7 oz. total). Cut 1 kiwi fruit into ¼-inch chunks and place in a bowl. In a blender or food processor, combine remaining kiwi fruit, cut into chunks, ¼ cup lightly packed **fresh cilantro**, and 1 tablespoon **lime juice**. Whirl until puréed; mix with fruit in bowl. Stir in 1 tablespoon minced **fresh red jalapeño** or Fresno **chili** and **salt** to taste. Makes about 1 cup.

Per serving: 7 cal., 0% (0 cal.) from fat; 0.1 g protein; 0 g fat; 1.7 g carbo (0.4 g fiber); 0.8 mg sodium; 0 mg chol.

■ Macadamia Pesto.

In a blender or food processor, whirl 1 tablespoon **lemon juice**, 3 tablespoons **olive oil**, and ¼ cup **salted, roasted macadamia nuts** until coarsely ground. Add 3 tablespoons **grated parmesan cheese** and 1½ cups lightly packed rinsed and drained **fresh basil** leaves. Whirl until smooth, scraping container sides as needed. Add **salt** to taste. Makes about ½ cup.

Per tablespoon: 90 cal., 88% (79 cal.) from fat; 1.7 g protein; 8.8 g fat (1.5 g sat.); 1.8 g carbo (0.9 g fiber); 54 mg sodium; 1.5 mg chol.

■ Mango-Masala Sauce.

Peel and pit 1 firm-ripe mango (about ¾ lb.). Cut mango into chunks. In a blender combine mango, 1 tablespoon chopped **fresh jalapeño chili**, 1½ teaspoons **garam masala** or curry powder, and 2 tablespoons **lime juice**; whirl until puréed. Add **salt** to taste. Makes about 1 cup.

Per tablespoon: 10 cal., 0% (0 cal.) from fat; 0.1 g protein; 0 g fat; 2.7 g carbo (0.2 g fiber); 3.1 mg sodium; 0 mg chol.

■ Pickled Cabbage Relish.

In a 2-cup glass measure, mix 1 cup **seasoned rice vinegar** and 2 teaspoons broken **star anise**. Heat in a microwave oven at full power (100%) until vinegar boils, about 3 minutes. Pour through a fine strainer into a bowl with 2 cups shredded **red cabbage**, 1 cup diced (¼ in.) **English cucumber**, 1 tablespoon minced **garlic**, and 1 teaspoon **salt**; discard star anise. Mix and let stand at least 10 minutes. Serve warm or cool, or cover and chill up to 2 days. Makes about 2 cups.

Per tablespoon: 8.6 cal., 0% (0 cal.) from fat; 0.1 g protein; 0 g fat; 2 g carbo (0.1 g fiber); 222 mg sodium; 0 mg chol.

■ Roasted Tomato–Caper Sauce.

Thread 1 pound rinsed **cherry tomatoes** (about 1 in. wide), touching, onto thin metal skewers. Thread ½ pound unpeeled **pearl onions** (about 1 in. wide), touching, onto thin metal skewers. Have barbecue ready with **direct heat** at **hot** (see page 186). Lay skewers on grill. Turn often until vegetables are charred, 5 to 8 minutes for tomatoes, 8 to 10 minutes for onions. Pull off and discard onion skins. In a blender or food processor, coarsely purée tomatoes, onions, ¼ cup lightly packed **parsley**, and 4 teaspoons drained **capers**. Add **salt** to taste. Makes about 1⅓ cups.

Per tablespoon: 8.6 cal., 10% (0.9 cal.) from fat; 0.3 g protein; 0.1 g fat (0 g sat.); 2 g carbo (0.3 g fiber); 27 mg sodium; 0 mg chol.

■ Sherry-Almond Sauce.

In an 8- to 10-inch frying pan over medium-high heat, stir or shake 1 tablespoon **slivered almonds** until golden, about 3 minutes. Pour from pan. Add ½ cup minced **shallots** or onion and 1 tablespoon **butter** or margarine. Stir over high heat until shallots are limp, about 2 minutes. Add 1 tablespoon **all-purpose flour** to pan and stir until mixture is lightly browned, 2 to 3 minutes. Add 1 cup **dry sherry**, 1 cup fat-skimmed **chicken broth**, and ¼ teaspoon **dried thyme**. Boil, stirring often, until sauce is reduced to 1 cup, about 7 minutes. Finely chop almonds and stir into sauce. Makes about 1 cup.

Per tablespoon: 20 cal., 45% (9 cal.) from fat; 0.8 g protein; 1 g fat (0.5 g sat.); 1.9 g carbo (0.1 g fiber); 14 mg sodium; 1.9 mg chol.

- 1 cup **couscous**
- 1½ cups fat-skimmed **chicken broth**
- 1½ pounds **boned, skinned halibut** (1 in. thick)
- 1 cup finely chopped **English cucumber**
- ¼ cup chopped **fresh mint** leaves

1. In a blender or food processor, combine dried cherries, oregano, cumin, paprika, oil, and lemon juice. Whirl until puréed, scraping container sides as necessary. Add salt to taste.

2. In a 1½- to 2-quart pan, combine couscous and broth. Bring to a boil over high heat, cover, remove pan from heat, and let stand until liquid is absorbed, about **5 minutes**. Keep warm.

3. Meanwhile, rinse halibut, pat dry, and coat with cherry mixture. Set each piece of halibut on a slightly larger piece of foil. Cut foil to fit fish.

4. Have barbecue ready with **direct heat** at **hot** (see page 186). Set foil with fish on grill. Cover barbecue with lid (open vents for charcoal), and cook until fish is opaque but moist-looking in thickest part (cut to test), 8 to 10 minutes.

5. Stir chopped cucumber and chopped mint into couscous; spoon onto plates. Cut grilled halibut into equal portions and set onto couscous. Season to taste with salt.

Per serving: 549 cal., 25% (135 cal.) from fat; 45 g protein; 15 g fat (2 g sat.); 58 g carbo (2.4 g fiber); 135 mg sodium; 54 mg chol.

Sole with Creamed Mushrooms

PREP AND COOK TIME: About 35 minutes
NOTES: Use direct heat.
MAKES: 4 servings

- ½ pound minced **mushrooms**
- ¼ cup finely chopped **shallots**
- 2 tablespoons **butter** or margarine
- ½ teaspoon **dried thyme**
- ½ cup **marsala** or dry white wine
- ¾ cup **whipping cream**
  About 1 pound **boned, skinned sole fillets** (8 of equal size)
- ½ cup shredded **gruyère** or Swiss **cheese**
  Thyme sprigs (optional)
  Salt

1. In a 10- to 12-inch frying pan over high heat, stir mushrooms and shallots in butter until mushrooms are browned, about 10 minutes. Add thyme, marsala, and cream. Stirring often, boil until mixture is pale gold color and there is no free-flowing liquid, 6 to 7 minutes. Let cool to room temperature.

2. Rinse sole, pat dry, and lay fillets flat. Spoon mushroom mixture equally onto fillets and spread to coat evenly. Roll fillets from narrow end and set seam down on a sheet of foil (about 9 by 13 in.).

3. Have barbecue ready with *direct heat* at *hot* (see page 186). Set foil with fish on grill and cover with lid (open vents for charcoal). Cook until sole is opaque but moist-looking in thickest part (cut to test), about 8 minutes. The last 2 minutes, sprinkle cheese evenly on fish.

4. Slide a rimless baking sheet under foil and lift from grill. With a wide spatula, transfer sole to plates; scrape any drippings from foil and spoon onto fish. Garnish with thyme sprigs. Add salt to taste.

Per serving: 380 cal., 62% (234 cal.) from fat; 28 g protein; 26 g fat (15 g sat.); 9.3 g carbo (0.8 g fiber); 220 mg sodium; 135 mg chol.

Barbecued Oysters

PREP AND COOK TIME: About 25 minutes
NOTES: Use direct heat.
MAKES: 8 appetizer servings

- ¼ cup **tomato-based chili sauce**
- 1 tablespoon **oyster** or soy **sauce**
- 1 tablespoon **lemon juice**
- 2 teaspoons minced **fresh cilantro**
- 16 **oysters in shells** (about 4 in. long), scrubbed

1. In a small bowl, mix chili sauce, oyster sauce, lemon juice, and cilantro.

2. To shuck each oyster, place shell, cupped side down, on a heavy towel. Grip curved end of shell with a towel and hold oyster level. Firmly insert an oyster knife into hinge at narrow end of oyster between top and bottom shell; twist to open. Slide oyster knife along underside of top shell to cut adductor muscle and free oyster. Remove top shell. Slide knife under oyster to cut free. Leave in shell and set shell side down on a tray.

3. Spoon an equal portion of the chili sauce mixture onto each oyster.

4. Have barbecue ready with *direct heat* at *hot* (see page 186). Set oysters in shells on grill and cook until juices bubble, about 4 minutes.

5. Serve hot oysters in shells.

SHELL GAME: Chili-sauced oysters capture the smoky essence of the grill.

Per serving: 93 cal., 23% (21 cal.) from fat; 9.9 g protein; 2.3 g fat (0.5 g sat.); 7.6 g carbo (0 g fiber); 310 mg sodium; 55 mg chol.

Grilled Scallop and Shrimp Salad

PREP AND COOK TIME: 15 to 20 minutes
NOTES: Use direct heat. This salad is adapted from one presented by Chef Staffan Terje at Scala's Bistro in San Francisco.
MAKES: 4 servings

- 8 **scallops** (about 2 in. wide; ¾ to 1 lb. total), rinsed and drained
- ½ pound **peeled, deveined shrimp** (26 to 30 per lb.), rinsed and drained
- 1 head **radicchio** (about 5 oz.)
- 1 head **Belgian endive** (4 to 5 oz.)
- 4 cups **arugula** (about ¼ lb.)
- 6 tablespoons **lemon-flavor olive oil**
- 3 tablespoons **white wine vinegar**
- 1 tablespoon chopped **chives**
- **Salt** and **pepper**

1. Thread scallops, through width of the rounds and touching, onto a thin metal skewer. Push a second metal skewer through scallops, parallel to and about ½ inch from the first. Thread shrimp, touching, onto thin metal skewers.

2. Rinse and drain radicchio, Belgian endive, and arugula. Separate leaves from radicchio and endive heads. Discard tough arugula stems.

3. In a large bowl, mix oil, vinegar, and chives.

4. Have barbecue ready with *direct*

heat at *hot* (see page 186). Lay scallops and shrimp on grill. Turn as needed until scallops are lightly browned and shrimp are pink, and both are opaque but moist-looking in center of thickest part (cut to test), 5 to 7 minutes for scallops, about 5 minutes for shrimp.

5. Add radicchio, arugula, and endive to dressing; mix. Lift salad, draining briefly, onto plates, dividing equally. Push scallops and shrimp from skewers into bowl. Mix, then spoon onto salads. Add salt and pepper to taste.

Per serving: 335 cal., 59% (198 cal.) from fat; 27 g protein; 22 g fat (3 g sat.); 6.4 g carbo (1.4 g fiber); 239 mg sodium; 114 mg chol.

Clams with Garlic Sauce

PREP AND COOK TIME: About 40 minutes
NOTES: Use direct heat. You can cook the clams in a pan directly on the barbecue, on a gas barbecue's side burner, or in the kitchen. Tap any open clams; discard if they don't close.
MAKES: 4 servings

- 2 heads **garlic** (about 6 oz. total)
- ¼ cup (⅛ lb.) **butter** or margarine
- ¼ cup **dry white wine**
- ¼ cup fat-skimmed **chicken broth**
- 1 tablespoon **balsamic vinegar**
- 6 dozen **clams in shells** (about 2 in. wide), suitable for steaming, scrubbed
- 1 loaf (1 lb.) **sourdough bread**

1. Place garlic on a flat surface. Press each head firmly to separate cloves. Discard root end and loose peels; do not peel cloves. Thread cloves, touching, onto thin metal skewers.

2. Have barbecue ready with *direct heat* at *very hot* (see page 186). Lay skewers on grill and turn as needed until garlic is soft when pressed and peels are charred, about 10 minutes.

3. When cool enough to touch, in 3 to 4 minutes, push garlic off skewers and squeeze cloves from peels; discard peels.

4. In a blender or food processor, whirl garlic, butter, wine, broth, and vinegar until puréed. Scrape into a 5- to 6-quart pan. Add clams; cover pan.

5. Bring to a boil over high heat (see notes) and cook until clams open, about 10 minutes. Ladle clams and broth into wide bowls. Serve with chunks of bread to dip into sauce.

Per serving: 684 cal., 24% (162 cal.) from fat; 47 g protein; 18 g fat (8.4 g sat.); 78 g carbo (3.8 g fiber); 976 mg sodium; 124 mg chol. ◆

The Low-Fat Cook

HEALTHY CHOICES FOR THE ACTIVE LIFESTYLE

BY ELAINE JOHNSON

PORK TENDERLOIN with Asian flavors teams up with baby bok choy and rice.

Steam for lean, the Chinese way

■ Steaming, a basic cookery method in Chinese cuisine, makes it extremely easy to cook low-fat with lots of flavor. Just start with a lean cut of meat, such as pork tenderloin, and no-fat seasonings, such as ginger and black beans, for results that are both virtuous and delicious. Kate Blood of Oakland, California, shares the recipe.

Cantonese Steamed Pork

PREP AND COOK TIME: About 30 minutes

NOTES: You can also use regular bok choy cut into 2- to 3-inch pieces.

MAKES: 4 servings

- 1½ cups **long-grain white rice**
- ½ cup fat-skimmed **beef broth**

  About 2 tablespoons **reduced-sodium soy sauce**
- 1 tablespoon **dry sherry**
- 1 tablespoon **salted fermented black beans,** rinsed and chopped
- 1 tablespoon minced **fresh ginger**
- 1 large clove **garlic,** minced
- 2 teaspoons firmly packed **brown sugar**
- ¼ teaspoon **hot chili flakes**

- 1 pound **fat-trimmed pork tenderloin,** cut into ½-inch crosswise slices

  About 1⅓ pounds **baby bok choy** (each 2 to 3 in. long), rinsed

1. In a 3- to 4-quart pan over high heat, bring rice and 3 cups water to a boil. Reduce heat and simmer, covered, until rice is tender to bite, about 20 minutes.

2. Meanwhile, in an 8- to 10-quart pan or a 14-inch wok, set a rack over at least 1 inch boiling water. Choose a shallow, rimmed pan about 8 inches wide that fits on the rack and can be lifted out (fashion a string harness, if needed).

3. In the shallow pan, combine beef broth, 2 tablespoons soy sauce, sherry, black beans, ginger, garlic, brown sugar, chili flakes, and pork. Turn the meat over in the seasonings.

4. Cover pan with foil and set pork pan on rack; cover larger pan. Steam on high heat until pork is no longer pink in center (cut to test), about 12 minutes. Protecting hands, lift out pork pan and rack. Keep pork warm.

5. Add enough water to pan to make 1 inch deep and bring to a boil. Add bok choy, cover, and boil until just tender when pierced, 2 to 4 minutes. Drain.

6. Serve rice in bowls with pork and juice, and bok choy. Add soy to taste.

Per serving: 436 cal., 9.9% (43 cal.) from fat; 33 g protein; 4.8 g fat (1.5 g sat.); 63 g carbo (2.2 g fiber); 578 mg sodium; 74 mg chol.

Cantonese Steamed Tofu

1. Follow the directions for **Cantonese steamed pork,** preceding, but use 14 to 16 ounces **firm low-fat** or regular **tofu** instead of pork, **vegetable broth** instead of beef broth, and 5 cups rinsed **broccoli florets** instead of bok choy.

2. Drain tofu on towels and cut into ½- by 1½-inch pieces. Turn tofu over in seasonings in pan. Proceed as directed in step 4, steaming tofu until hot, about 10 minutes. Then cook broccoli as directed for bok choy, step 5.

Per serving: 373 cal., 6.7% (25 cal.) from fat; 17 g protein; 2.8 g fat (0.5 g sat.); 70 g carbo (5.5 g fiber); 575 mg sodium; 0 mg chol. ◆

foodguide

BY JERRY ANNE DI VECCHIO

PHOTOGRAPHS BY JAMES CARRIER

A TASTE OF THE WEST

Of Persian persuasion

One of the spice boys plays chicken

■ There's an old boys' network in the spice world—behind the scenes and faceless, yet powerful. Turmeric is a major player. This rhizome, a ginger look-alike, gives a dark orange color to many everyday mixtures, like curry powders and some pickle relishes. In cautious Western cuisines, turmeric's individuality is usually masked; it rarely ventures on its own. But in Middle Eastern foods, the spice becomes a bold and visible presence. Faz Poursohi, who serves foods with Persian flair in his San Francisco Bay Area restaurants, uses turmeric to give an earthy intensity and golden sheen to normally passive chicken.

CHICKEN STICKS: Ground meat is flavored with turmeric and smoke from the grill.

Persian Chicken on Skewers

PREP AND COOK TIME: About 45 minutes

NOTES: Serve with basmati rice, grilled tomatoes, and a spray of herbs: parsley, basil, tarragon, cilantro, and dill.

MAKES: 4 servings

- 1 pound **ground chicken**
- 6 tablespoons **fine dried bread crumbs**
- 1 **large egg** yolk
- 2 tablespoons minced **onion**
- ½ teaspoon **ground dried turmeric**

    About ¼ teaspoon **salt**

1. In a bowl, mix chicken, crumbs, egg yolk, onion, turmeric, and ¼ teaspoon salt. Cover and chill at least 30 minutes or up to 1 day.

2. Divide chicken mixture into 4 equal portions. Dip-ping your hands frequently in water to keep mixture from sticking, pat each portion around a skewer (flat metal ones are easiest to handle) to form a log 1 inch thick and about 7 inches long.

3. One skewer at a time, lay chicken on a lightly oiled barbecue grill over a solid bed of hot coals or high heat on a gas grill (you can hold your hand at grill level only 2 to 3 seconds) and rotate quickly to firm up the surface of the meat. When all skewers are on the grill, close lid of gas grill. Rotate skewers every 2 to 3 minutes until meat is lightly browned and firm, not squishy, at skewer (cut to test), about 10 minutes total.

4. Cut or push meat off skewers. Add salt to taste.

Per serving: 240 cal., 49% (117 cal.) from fat; 21 g protein; 13 g fat (4.1 g sat.); 8 g carbo (0.5 g fiber); 278 mg sodium; 190 mg chol.

A different cornbread

■ *Piki* is the Hopi name for an unusual, tissue-thin bread. It's traditionally made on a hot stone griddle, but you can also swirl the corn-meal batter in a nonstick frying pan. The process, I've found, holds the attention of summer-bored youngsters; they're fascinated by the bubbling brew that dries, turns into a crackly, pop-corn-flavor bread, and melts away in your mouth. No kids? Piki makes an entertaining appetizer with a cool beverage.

Hopi Paper Bread

PREP AND COOK TIME: 10 to 14 minutes per piece

NOTES: To speed up the process, use 2 frying pans at once.

MAKES: 13 or 14 pieces

- ¼ cup **blue cornmeal**
- ¼ teaspoon **baking soda**
- ¼ teaspoon **salt**
- ¼ cup **cornstarch**

    Lard, shortening, or salad oil

1. In a 3- to 4-quart pan, whisk 7 cups water with the cornmeal, baking soda, and salt until well blended. Bring the mixture to a boil over high heat,

Thanks for the memory

■ In "The Gastronomical Me" from *The Art of Eating*, Mary Frances Kennedy Fisher made compelling prose out of a simple cauliflower dish she dreamily prepared in a most inadequate kitchen in Dijon, France, in the early '30s. When I read it, my taste buds were so entranced by the description, I attempted to duplicate the gratin, even though I had no access to the thick French cream she'd used; I had to boil down fresh cream to make the proper sauce. Years later, when Mary Frances became my friend, she confirmed that my efforts to turn her graceful phrases into real food had worked. Here's the recipe.

M.F.K. Fisher Memorial Cauliflower Casserole

PREP AND COOK TIME: About 25 minutes

MAKES: 6 servings

- 1 **cauliflower** (about 2½ lb.) or 2 quarts cauliflower florets
- 1 cup **whipping cream**
- ½ teaspoon fresh-ground **pepper**
- 1½ cups (6 oz.) shredded **gruyère cheese**
  Salt

1. Break cauliflower into florets, discarding core and leaves. Rinse florets.

2. In a 4- to 5-quart pan over high heat, bring about 3 quarts water to a boil. Add cauliflower and cook until just tender when pierced, 5 to 8 minutes.

3. Drain cauliflower and arrange in a shallow 1½-quart casserole.

4. Add cream to the empty pan and boil over high heat until it's reduced to ½ cup, stirring often, about 5 minutes.

5. Drizzle cream over cauliflower, sprinkle with pepper, and cover evenly with cheese.

6. Bake in a 425° oven just until cheese is lightly browned, 4 to 6 minutes. Add salt to taste.

Per serving: 252 cal., 79% (198 cal.) from fat; 11 g protein; 22 g fat (13 g sat.); 5 g carbo (1.8 g fiber); 120 mg sodium; 75 mg chol.

---

stirring. Reduce heat and simmer, uncovered, about 10 minutes, stirring occasionally.

2. Mix 1 cup water with cornstarch until smooth. Whisk into cornmeal mixture. Turn heat to high and stir until boiling again; stir 1 minute longer. Remove from heat.

3. Place a nonstick frying pan, 9½ to 10 inches across the bottom, over medium heat.

4. When pan is hot, rub lightly with lard, then pour in ¼ cup of the cornmeal mixture. Tilt pan, swirling batter to coat bottom (see photo). Cook until batter stops bub-

bling, begins to curl away from pan sides and is dry, 5 to 7 minutes. Slide a wide spatula under sheet of paper bread (the first sheet may be hard to handle), lift out, and lay flat (if bread breaks, lift out and save pieces).

5. Repeat step 4 with more

batter, but when edges of bread begin to curl from pan sides and bread is still bubbling a little in the center, lay the first piece, along with any broken pieces, on top of the piece in the pan. Cook until bread feels dry in the center when touched, pressing flat if it puffs up, 5

to 7 minutes. Lift bread out with spatula and fold up opposite sides, overlapping to make a loose roll (at left). (If bread is not cooked dry, it loses its crispness when it cools; if this happens, unroll, return to pan, and toast again until dry.) Set roll on a rack.

6. Repeat steps 4 and 5 with remaining batter to make each double sheet of paper bread. Serve immediately, or store airtight at room temperature up to 1 week.

Per piece: 29 cal., 41% (12 cal.) from fat; 0.2 g protein; 1.3 g fat (0.5 g sat.); 4 g carbo (0.1 g fiber); 63 mg sodium; 1.2 mg chol.

STEP-BY-STEP

SEASONAL NOTE

Tomatoes to relish

■ Bart, my son-in-law, is gifted with a green thumb. But until the family moved to Colorado last summer and acquired a big backyard, his nurturing went toward house plants. Now he has a vegetable garden, where sons Henry, 2½, and Jack, 1 plus a tad, like to watch things grow. Most promising at the moment are tomatoes. They're taking

shape, and some are bound to end up in this simple relish, which my daughter, Angela, likes in toasted brie cheese sandwiches. Bart prefers it with pork chops. The vote's still out with the wee laddies.

Denver Summer Relish

PREP AND COOK TIME: About 30 minutes, plus at least 20 minutes to cool

NOTES: If making up to 3 weeks ahead, cover and chill.

MAKES: 3 cups

- 1 pound **Roma tomatoes,** rinsed, cored, and cut into ¼-inch dice
- 2 cups diced (¼ in.) **onions**
- 1 cup **golden raisins**
- 1 cup **white vinegar** (distilled, rice, or wine)
- 1 cup **sugar**
- 2 tablespoons minced **fresh ginger**
- 2 **fresh jalapeño chilies** (1½ to 2 oz. total), rinsed, stemmed, seeded, and chopped

  Salt

1. In a 5- to 6-quart pan, combine tomatoes, onions, raisins, vinegar, sugar, ginger, and chilies. Boil over high heat, stirring often, until mixture is reduced to 3 cups, about 20 minutes.

2. Let cool at least 20 minutes. Season to taste with salt; stir and serve.

Per tablespoon: 31 cal., 0% (0 cal.) from fat; 0.3 g protein; 0 g fat; 7.9 g carbo (0.4 g fiber); 1.5 mg sodium; 0 mg chol.

Cool tool puts dessert under pressure

■ There's a tool that whips up more than cream. Even nonfat and reduced-fat dairy products, combined with whipping cream, will puff delectably. It's the Isi whipped cream and dessert maker ($45 to $65 for pint size, about $75 quart size), available in fancy cookware stores like Sur La Table and Williams-Sonoma.

Just fill the container with liquid ingredients (don't add anything lumpy—the nozzle will

jam), load with a gas capsule (about 75 cents each), then shake and squirt. If you start with fresh ingredients, you can keep the mixture in the refrigerator up to a week.
Whipped dessert cream. *All ingredients except sugar must be cold.* In a bowl, whisk until smooth ½ cup **plain nonfat yogurt,** ½ cup **reduced-fat** or regular **sour cream,** ½ cup **whipping cream,** ½ cup **powdered sugar,** and 2 tablespoons **liquid flavoring** such as a

liqueur (coffee, hazelnut), a fruit syrup (raspberry, strawberry), or thawed frozen juice concentrate (orange, apple). Pour into a chilled whipped dessert maker, seal, and load with a gas capsule. If making up to 1 week ahead, chill. Shake vigorously before each use. Serve as a dessert or topping. Makes about 4 cups.

Per tablespoon with coffee liqueur: 14 cal., 51% (7.2 cal.) from fat; 0.3 g protein; 0.8 g fat (0.5 g sat.); 1.4 g carbo (0 g fiber); 3 mg sodium; 2.7 mg chol. ◆

The Wine Guide

BY KAREN MacNEIL-FIFE

RICK MARIANI

Vines to watch

■ Drive through wine country and you're struck by how timeless it seems, how pastoral and immutable. Given the technodrama of modern life, it's a comforting feeling.

It's also a grand illusion. The American wine industry today is a hotbed of innovation. Not only are new wine regions emerging across the West (see "The New Wine Countries," page 170), but a brave new world of grape varieties has begun to emerge as well.

Not so long ago, the varieties that caused the most excitement were Chardonnay, Cabernet Sauvignon, and Merlot. Today, once-obscure grapes such as Viognier and Syrah are being crushed. And on their heels, still-obscure varieties like Arneis and Albariño are beginning to be planted.

What's causing this minirevolution?

First, a new global perspective. In the pivotal 1960s and '70s, when the American fine-wine industry was establishing itself, winemakers looked for inspiration to France's two premier wine regions: Burgundy (known for Chardonnay and Pinot Noir) and Bordeaux (known for

UP-AND-COMERS

Great wines based on emerging varieties.

■ Arneis: **Il Podere dell'Olivos 1997 (Central Coast)**, $16

■ Marsanne: **McDowell Valley 1997 (Mendocino)**, $16

■ Pinot Gris: **WillaKenzie 1997 (Willamette Valley, OR)**, $15

■ Roussanne: **Zaca Mesa 1997 (Santa Barbara County)**, $16.50

■ Tocai Friulano: **Monte Volpe 1997 (Mendocino)**, $12

■ Viognier: **Alban "Estate" 1997 (Edna Valley, CA)**, $28

■ Mourvèdre: **Jade Mountain 1997 (California)**, $20

■ Petite Syrah: **Stag's Leap Wine Cellars 1996 (Napa Valley)**, $30

■ Sangiovese: **Turnbull 1996 (Napa Valley)**, $20

■ Syrah: **Edmunds St. John "Durell Vineyard" 1996 (Sonoma Valley)**, $25

Cabernet Sauvignon and Merlot). Today, however, there is increasing enthusiasm about dozens of grapes grown in other parts of France, and in Spain and Italy.

Second, many winemakers in California—where about 90 percent of American wine is made—have realized that much of the state shares more commonalities of climate and soil with the Mediterranean than it does with Bordeaux and Burgundy.

"The world," explains Randall Grahm, president of Bonny Doon Vineyard in Santa Cruz, California, "can be divided into two: that which is Continental and that which is Mediterranean. Continental is butter, Cary Grant, Protestant work ethic, Cabernet. Mediterranean is olive oil, Anthony Quinn, mañana, Grenache."

Here's a list of great varieties beginning to be produced in the West.

Emerging whites

Albariño. Snappy, fresh, and lemony, this is the most exciting white wine in all of Spain. The grape is just beginning to be planted in California.

Arneis. This sassy, fresh, and light-bodied *little rascal* (*arneis* in Italian) from Piedmont, Italy, makes a delicious summertime wine. A few makers now produce it in Oregon and California.

Marsanne. This is the main white grape of the Rhône region of France, where it's blended with Roussanne into blockbuster, honeyed-almond whites. California Marsannes are usually softer.

Pinot Gris. This creamy, lemony French grape is better known in Italy as Pinot Grigio. Dozens of producers in Oregon and California now make it.

Roussanne. This is the more elegant "sister" of Marsanne. A few gorgeous Roussannes with delicious melon, peach, and rosewater flavors are now being made in California.

Tocai. Only a few vintners in California are producing Tocai Friulano (its full name), but with terrific results. Native to northern Italy, Tocai is refreshing, with hints of mint and more body than Pinot Grigio.

Viognier. Rich and oozing with passion fruit and honeysuckle, Viognier can be enormously sensual; alas, it's also expensive. A common Rhône variety, Viognier is being planted in Washington and all over California.

Emerging reds

Grenache. Several of the best rosés in California are made from this variety (see July Wine Guide, page 159).

Mourvèdre. Popular in southern France, this grape makes black, smoky, juicy wine. In California, Mourvèdre is often included in top Rhône blends.

Petite Syrah. Massive and masculine, Petite Syrah is undergoing a renaissance in California.

Sangiovese. The grape in Tuscany's Chianti, it has been a challenge in California, but many good Sangioveses—sleek and medium-bodied—are emerging.

Syrah. No longer exactly up-and-coming, Syrah has arrived, with dozens of producers in California and a few in Washington: deeply berried, meaty, and earthy—powerfully delicious. ◆

Fresh bean bounty

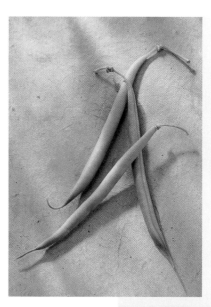

Relish these popular vegetables in all their colors, sizes, and shapes

BY LINDA LAU ANUSASANANAN

PHOTOGRAPHS BY JAMES CARRIER

■ PO-PO, MY GRANDMOTHER, TAUGHT ME TO LOVE FRESH BEANS. Well, technically, bean pods—beans that are bred and grown to be eaten before the seeds inside are fully developed, while the pod that cradles them is still tender, plump, and fleshy.

A passionate gardener, Po-Po planted the kinds of beans she liked to eat, none of which we found at the local grocer's. She also was an exacting cook who prepared beans tender-crisp and brightly colored—hardly the olive drab, mushy norm of the mid-'50s.

Her fresh beans grew fast, sometimes rambling, sometimes in bushes. The ones I remember most fondly were dark green, round, skinny, and almost the yard long their name promised. She also grew a bean that was short, plump, and a translucent gold. She would slice the pods into bite-size lengths, briefly boil or steam them, then stir-fry them—with ingredients like pork and a pungent sauce—until they were full of flavor, yet still so crunchy they squeaked when chewed.

Times have changed. The beans that Po-Po grew, as well as many others that are equally colorful and tasty, are readily available in farmers' markets and well-stocked supermarkets: long or short, thin or wide, rounded or flat. Some are distinguished by a variety name, others by their physical characteristics like color and shape. And some beans have pronounced flavor, while others are more delicate in taste. Some are chewier than others (though all fresh beans are tender); past their prime, beans get tough and fibrous.

Regardless, the simplest, freshest way to deal with beans is to cook them to crunchy tenderness. Then enjoy them, lightly seasoned or vividly sauced, as a vegetable or salad, with pasta, or in soup. These recipes take advantage of the color, texture, size, and shape of the beans in today's market—while duly honoring Po-Po's stringent cooking standards.

■ ROUND-POD GREEN BEAN (includes Blue Lake and other market varieties), top: Pods are round and plump, flesh is tender, and flavor is mild. Blue Lakes have no strings.

■ YELLOW WAX OR YELLOW BEAN, above: Color class, not a variety; many flat or round-pod beans are yellow. The color tints the whole bean and does not fade (as green does) when beans are cooked or put in acidic dressings.

TARRAGON, Dijon mustard, and shallots dress a two-tone bean salad.

■ **YARD-LONG BEAN** (also called Chinese long bean or asparagus bean), above left: Tender, skinny pods, 1½ to 2 feet long; intense bean flavor. Technically a cowpea (*Vigna unguiculata*) and related to black-eyed peas, but sold and prepared as a fresh bean. No strings.

■ **SMALL ROUND-POD GREEN BEAN** (also called French haricot vert or fillet-type), center: Pods are round; beans are short, very slender, very tender, and slightly sweet. Few if any strings.

■ **KENTUCKY WONDER GREEN BEAN**, right: Slightly flat, fleshy green pods with distinctive bean flavor and moderately firm, dense texture. This old-fashioned variety may have some strings.

SESAME-SEASONED yard-long beans and plump noodles tangle in this playful dish.

Cooked Fresh Beans

PREP AND COOK TIME: 12 to 18 minutes

NOTES: Serve cooked beans plain or use as directed in the following recipes. If making up to 1 day ahead, wrap the cool beans airtight and chill. To reheat, immerse the cooked beans in boiling water until hot, 1 to 2 minutes; drain.

MAKES: 4 cups; 4 servings

1. In a 5- to 6-quart pan over high heat, bring 2½ to 3 quarts **water** to a boil.

2. Trim stem ends and pull any strings from 1 pound **fresh beans** (for choices, see photographs and descriptions on pages 196 to 199). Rinse beans and drain; leave whole or cut into 2- to 3-inch lengths.

3. Add beans to boiling water and cook until just tender to bite, 3 to 7 minutes. Drain.

4. Serve hot. Or immerse the beans at once in ice water until cool, to preserve texture (and, if green, their bright color). Drain and serve, or cover and chill up to 1 day.

Per serving: 35 cal., 2.6% (0.9 cal.) from fat; 2.1 g protein; 0.1 g fat (0 g sat.); 8.1 g carbo (2 g fiber); 6.8 mg sodium; 0 mg chol.

Long Beans and Noodles

PREP AND COOK TIME: About 25 minutes

MAKES: 2 servings

1. In a 5- to 6-quart pan over high heat, bring about 3 quarts **water** to a boil.

2. Meanwhile, trim stem ends from ½ pound **yard-long beans;** rinse beans.

3. To boiling water, add beans and 8 ounces **fresh udon** or fresh Shanghai (about ¼ in. thick) **noodles.** Cook just until beans and noodles are tender to bite, 4 to 5 minutes. Drain.

4. Mix **sesame dressing** (recipe follows; prepare through step 2) with hot beans and noodles.

Per serving: 703 cal., 28% (198 cal.) from fat; 26 g protein; 22 g fat (2.4 g sat.); 104 g carbo (11 g fiber); 1,200 mg sodium; 0 mg chol.

Beans with Sesame Dressing

PREP AND COOK TIME: About 20 minutes

NOTES: This spicy dressing is very attractive on yellow beans, and goes well with Kentucky Wonder green beans.

MAKES: 4 servings

1. In a 6- to 8-inch frying pan over medium heat, combine 2 tablespoons *each* **salad oil** and **sesame seed.** Shake pan often until seed is golden, 3 to 5 minutes. Add 1 tablespoon *each* minced **fresh ginger,** minced **garlic,** and minced **fresh red jalapeño** or serrano **chili** (or ¼ to ½ teaspoon hot chili flakes). Stir, remove from heat, and let cool about 2 minutes.

2. Add 3 tablespoons **rice vinegar,** 2 tablespoons **soy sauce,** and ½ teaspoon **sugar** and stir to blend.

3. Pour dressing over 1 pound hot or cool **cooked fresh beans** (recipe at left; see notes) and mix.

Per serving: 134 cal., 62% (83 cal.) from fat; 3.5 g protein; 9.2 g fat (1.2 g sat.); 12 g carbo (2.7 g fiber); 522 mg sodium; 0 mg chol.

Beans with Tarragon Vinaigrette

PREP AND COOK TIME: About 20 minutes

NOTES: This fresh-tasting herb dressing, tangy with mustard, suits tender, small whole beans such as haricots verts, and round-pod yellow and green beans.

MAKES: 4 servings

1. Mix ¼ cup **rice vinegar,** 2 tablespoons **olive oil,** 2 tablespoons finely

THIN, PEELED LEMON slices make a piquant garnish for cold, cooked Italian green beans with basil gremolata.

■ ITALIAN GREEN BEAN (Romano), far left: Flat, broad, fleshy pods have full herbaceous flavor and no strings.

■ PURPLE BEAN, left: Another color class, not a variety. Many beans are purple. The water-soluble color disappears when beans are cooked; the underlying color is green.

flavor **olive oil** or extra-virgin olive oil, and 2 teaspoons minced **garlic**.

2. Combine mixture with 1 pound cool **cooked fresh beans** (page 198; see notes). Add **salt** and **pepper** to taste.

Per serving: 70 cal., 46% (32 cal.) from fat; 2.4 g protein; 3.5 g fat (0.5 g sat.); 9.2 g carbo (2.3 g fiber); 7.5 mg sodium; 0 mg chol.

Cumin-Orange Beans with Linguine

PREP AND COOK TIME: About 35 minutes

NOTES: Nicole Perzik blends North African flavors in this bean and pasta dish. She prefers to use whole tiny haricots verts, but the seasonings also blend well with larger fresh beans cut into 3-inch lengths.

MAKES: 3 or 4 servings

- 1 pound **fresh beans** (see notes)
- 1 **orange** (6 oz.), rinsed
- ½ pound **dried linguine**
- 1 tablespoon **olive oil**
- 1 tablespoon **cumin seed**
- 1 clove **garlic**, peeled and pressed or minced
- 1 cup thinly sliced **green onions**
- 1 cup **cherry tomatoes**, rinsed and cut in half
- 1 cup **vegetable** or fat-skimmed chicken **broth**

  Salt and **pepper**

1. In a 5- to 6-quart pan over high heat, bring about 3 quarts water to a boil.

2. Trim ends and pull any strings from beans; rinse beans.

3. With a vegetable peeler, cut thin peel (colored part only) from orange. Cut enough of the peel into fine shreds to make 1 tablespoon. Cut orange into wedges.

4. When water boils, add linguine and cook 6 minutes. Add beans and cook until pasta and beans are tender to bite, 5 to 7 minutes longer. Drain and pour into a wide, shallow bowl.

5. Meanwhile, in a 10- to 12-inch frying pan over high heat, stir olive oil and cumin until seed is fragrant, about 1 minute. Add garlic, onions, and cherry tomatoes; stir until tomatoes are hot, about 2 minutes.

6. Add broth and orange peel; bring to a boil. Pour over noodles and beans, mix, and season to taste with salt and

chopped **shallot**, 1 tablespoon **Dijon mustard**, and 1 tablespoon minced **fresh tarragon** leaves or 1 teaspoon dried tarragon.

2. Combine the tarragon vinaigrette with 1 pound cold **cooked fresh beans** (page 198, see notes). Mix beans and dressing; add **salt** and **pepper** to taste.

Per serving: 103 cal., 60% (62 cal.) from fat; 2.3 g protein; 6.9 g fat (0.9 g sat.); 9.1 g carbo (2.1 g fiber); 98 mg sodium; 0 mg chol.

Beans with Basil Gremolata

PREP AND COOK TIME: About 20 minutes

NOTES: Small round-pod yellow wax, Romano, and Blue Lake beans are complemented by this lemon-scented dressing.

MAKES: 4 servings

1. Mix ⅓ cup chopped **fresh basil** leaves, 1 tablespoon finely shredded **lemon** peel, 1 tablespoon **lemon-**

pepper. Serve with orange wedges to squeeze juice onto each portion.

Per serving: 320 cal., 14% (45 cal.) from fat; 11 g protein; 5 g fat (0.6 g sat.); 60 g carbo (5.2 g fiber); 38 mg sodium; 0 mg chol.

Curry Spice Beans

PREP AND COOK TIME: About 20 minutes

NOTES: Use Kentucky Wonder green, yard-long, round-pod green, yellow wax, or Italian green beans.

MAKES: 4 servings

1. Set a 10- to 12-inch frying pan over medium heat. When pan is hot, add 2 tablespoons **salad oil** and 1 tablespoon *each* **cumin seed** and **mustard seed**. Shake pan often until seeds sizzle and begin to pop, 30 to 60 seconds. Add ⅓ cup chopped **shallots** and stir until limp, about 2 minutes. Stir in 1 teaspoon **curry powder** and ½ teaspoon **hot chili flakes**.

2. Add 1 pound hot or cool **cooked fresh beans** (page 198; see notes) to pan. Stir beans until coated with seasonings and hot, 2 to 3 minutes. Add **salt** and **pepper** to taste.

Per serving: 126 cal., 59% (74 cal.) from fat; 3.4 g protein; 8.2 g fat (0.9 g sat.); 12 g carbo (2.9 g fiber); 11 mg sodium; 0 mg chol.

Long Beans with Black Bean Sauce

PREP AND COOK TIME: About 30 minutes

NOTES: Pungent Chinese black bean sauce, flavored with garlic, is found in the international section of well-stocked supermarkets or in Asian grocery stores. Yard-long beans are traditionally used in this dish, but round-pod and Kentucky Wonder green beans are equally satisfactory.

MAKES: 4 servings

1 pound **fresh beans** (see notes)

¼ cup **black bean sauce**

2 teaspoons **cornstarch**

1 tablespoon **salad oil**

½ pound **ground lean pork**

1 **onion** (6 oz.), peeled and chopped

1. Trim stem ends from beans, remove any strings, and cut beans into 3-inch lengths; rinse.

2. Set a wok or 5- to 6-quart pan over high heat. When pan is hot, add 1 cup water and beans. Cover and stir occasionally until beans are tender to bite, 4 to 5 minutes. Drain beans and pour into a bowl.

3. Meanwhile, in a small bowl, mix black bean sauce, ¾ cup water, and cornstarch.

4. Return pan to high heat and add oil. When hot, add pork and stir-fry until meat is crumbled and lightly browned, about 3 minutes.

5. Add onion and stir-fry 1 minute. Add black bean sauce mixture and beans. Stir until sauce boils, about 1 minute.

Per serving: 269 cal., 31% (84 cal.) from fat; 20 g protein; 9.3 g fat (2.1 g sat.); 28 g carbo (5.5 g fiber); 1,323 mg sodium; 38 mg chol.

Bean Bundles

PREP AND COOK TIME: About 15 minutes

NOTES: Assemble up to 1 day ahead; add dressing when ready to serve.

MAKES: 4 servings

1. Prepare 1 pound **yard-long beans,** following directions for **cooked fresh beans** (page 198). Drain and immerse in ice water.

2. When beans are cool, drain and lay full length on a platter with stem ends together. With a hand at each end of the beans, pull them close together to form a log. Remove 4 beans and slide each under the log, equally spaced. Loosely tie each of the 4 beans over the log to hold it together.

3. In a small bowl, mix ¼ cup **soy sauce** with 2 tablespoons **Asian** (toasted) **sesame oil** and pour over beans. Or omit this mixture and moisten beans with sesame dressing or tarragon vinaigrette (page 198).

4. To serve, cut across bean log between tied beans to make 4 bundles. With a wide spatula, transfer beans to plates.

Per serving: 177 cal., 37% (65 cal.) from fat; 8.1 g protein; 7.2 g fat (1.1 g sat.); 22 g carbo (4.1 g fiber); 1,038 mg sodium; 0 mg chol.

Bean Knots

PREP AND COOK TIME: About 15 minutes

NOTES: Assemble up to 1 day ahead; add dressing when ready to serve.

MAKES: 6 to 8 servings

1. Prepare 1 pound **yard-long beans** following directions for **cooked fresh beans** (page 198). Drain and immerse in ice water. When cold, drain.

2. For each portion, gather 6 to 8 beans by the stem end and loosely coil or tie into a loose knot.

3. Season as suggested for **bean bundles** (preceding).

Per serving: 88 cal., 36% (32 cal.) from fat; 4 g protein; 3.6 g fat (0.5 g sat.); 11 g carbo (2.1 g fiber); 519 mg sodium; 0 mg chol.

Zuppa di Pasta e Fagioli Freschi
(Pasta and Fresh Bean Soup)

PREP AND COOK TIME: About 40 minutes

NOTES: Thick, fleshy Romano beans pair well with pasta in this fresh bean version of an Italian classic. You can also use thinner beans.

MAKES: 4 or 5 servings

1 tablespoon **olive oil**

1 **onion** (6 oz.), peeled and chopped

¾ cup chopped **carrot**

½ cup chopped **celery**

1 clove **garlic,** peeled and minced

8 cups fat-skimmed **chicken** or vegetable **broth**

2 cups (6 oz.) **dried penne pasta**

1 pound **fresh beans** (see notes)

2 teaspoons chopped **fresh basil** leaves or ½ teaspoon dried basil

1 ounce **thin-sliced prosciutto,** cut into thin strips

Grated **parmesan cheese**

Salt and **pepper**

1. In a 4- to 5-quart pan over medium-high heat, combine oil, onion, carrot, celery, and garlic; stir often until onion is limp, about 5 minutes.

2. Add broth, cover, and bring to a boil over high heat.

3. Stir penne pasta into broth and cook 7 minutes.

4. Meanwhile, trim stem ends and pull any strings from beans. Rinse beans and cut into 2-inch lengths. Add beans to pasta; cook until both are tender to bite, 5 to 6 minutes longer. Add basil and mix.

5. Ladle into bowls and scatter prosciutto evenly over portions. Add parmesan cheese and salt and pepper to taste.

Per serving: 269 cal., 14% (38 cal.) from fat; 21 g protein; 4.2 g fat (0.7 g sat.); 37 g carbo (3.7 g fiber); 250 mg sodium; 4.6 mg chol. ◆

GOLDEN CARAMEL, juicy peaches, and pecans fill nut shortbread crusts.

Sweet summer fruit tarts

Use succulent, ripe peaches or figs for flavorful desserts

BY ELAINE JOHNSON

Some desserts are too good to forget. Miles apart and years ago, I sampled two fruit tarts that bore delicious similarities. Each had a buttery shortbread crust filled with summer fruit and a sticky nut sauce. One used peaches, the other figs. You can have both of these desserts by making a few changes in a basic recipe, to create individual pastries or a large tart.

Peach-Caramel Tarts

PREP AND COOK TIME: About 1¼ hours, plus 30 minutes to cool

NOTES: To peel peaches, immerse fruit in boiling water for about 15 seconds, then pull off skins.

MAKES: 6 individual tarts or 1 large tart; 6 or 8 to 9 servings

Nut shortbread crusts or crust (recipe follows)

½ cup **sugar**

½ cup **whipping cream**

⅔ cup **pecan halves**

1½ teaspoons grated **lemon** peel

1¾ pounds **ripe peaches**

Vanilla ice cream or sweetened whipped cream (optional)

1. Bake nut shortbread crusts (set individual crusts in a 12- by 15-inch pan) in a 350° oven (or a 325° convection oven) until golden at edges, 20 to 25 minutes.

2. While crusts bake, make nut sauce in a 10- to 12-inch frying pan. Over medium-high heat, shake sugar in pan until melted and amber-colored, 4 to 6 minutes. Add whipping cream and stir until caramelized sugar melts, 1 to 2 minutes. Stir in pecans and lemon peel; remove from heat.

3. Peel peaches, if desired (see notes). Cut into halves, pit, then cut into ½- to ¾-inch-wide slices. Arrange peach slices, slightly overlapping, in hot crusts or crust. Save extra fruit for other uses.

4. Spoon nut sauce equally over fruit; if sauce has thickened too much to spoon, stir and heat until fluid.

5. Bake in a 350° oven (or a 325° convection oven) until sauce is bubbling and crust is deep golden, 20 to 24 minutes for individual tarts, 50 to 55 minutes for a large tart.

6. Cool in pan or pans on a rack at least 30 minutes. If making ahead, chill airtight up to 1 day. Remove pan rims. Serve with ice cream.

Per individual tart: 279 cal., 55% (153 cal.) from fat; 2.9 g protein; 17 g fat (7.3 g sat.); 30 g carbo (1.7 g fiber); 83 mg sodium; 49 mg chol.

Nut shortbread crusts. In a food processor, mince ⅓ cup **pecans** with 1¼ cups **all-purpose flour** and ¼ cup **sugar**. Add ½ cup (¼ lb.) **butter** or margarine, in chunks, and whirl until fine crumbs form. Add 1 **large egg** yolk and whirl until dough holds together. (Or mince nuts with a knife, then put in a bowl. Rub in flour, butter, and sugar until fine crumbs form; then, with a fork, mix in yolk. Pat into a ball.) In 6 tart pans (4½ in. wide) with removable rims, or an 11-inch tart pan, press dough evenly over bottom and up sides, flush with rims.

Fig-Honey Tarts

PREP AND COOK TIME: About 1¼ hours

MAKES: 6 individual tarts or 1 large tart; 6 or 8 to 9 servings

Follow directions for **peach-caramel tarts,** but in nut shortbread crusts, use ⅓ cup **hazelnuts** instead of pecans.

For nut sauce (step 2), use 6 tablespoons **honey** instead of sugar, decrease **whipping cream** to 6 tablespoons, and use ⅔ cup coarsely chopped **hazelnuts** instead of pecans. Do not cook; just mix.

Instead of peaches (step 3), use about 1¾ pounds **ripe black-skinned figs.** Rinse figs, trim stems, and cut into pieces that are about 1 inch wide. Arrange figs, tips and cut side up, in crusts. Continue from step 4.

Per individual tart: 300 cal., 51% (153 cal.) from fat; 3.6 g protein; 17 g fat (6.8 g sat.); 37 g carbo (3.3 g fiber); 83 mg sodium; 47 mg chol. ◆

A French affair with fresh tomatoes

Pick them ripe and full of color, then dress them with flavor

BY LINDA LAU ANUSASANANAN

NICOLE PERZIK (above) selects choice tomatoes to bake with cheese and anchovies in a tart reminiscent of her native France.

I n the hands of Nicole Perzik, tomatoes speak with a French accent. Perzik, born in France, works the magic of her heritage on vine-ripened summer beauties from neighborhood Santa Monica and Westwood farmers' markets. Big, meaty, juicy beefsteak tomato types make a handsome, savory first-course or main-dish tart. Hollowed out, they load up with turkey filling to bake. Even petite tomatoes perform well. Some sizzle with a basil-crumb topping, others go into a casserole or get wrapped into an omelet. These dishes may not improve your French, but they'll add a style to hot-weather menus.

French Tomato Tart

PREP AND COOK TIME: About 1 hour

NOTES: Up to 1 day ahead, bake crust, cool, wrap airtight, and keep at room temperature.

MAKES: 6 or 7 servings

1½ cups **all-purpose flour**

½ cup (¼ lb.) **butter** or margarine

1 **large egg**

4 **firm-ripe tomatoes** (each 3 in. wide; about 1½ lb. total), rinsed and cored

2 tablespoons **Dijon mustard**

2 cups (½ lb.) **shredded Swiss cheese**

3 tablespoons **olive oil**

3 tablespoons **tomato paste**

3 tablespoons chopped **shallots**

1 clove **garlic,** peeled and minced

2 teaspoons **fresh thyme** leaves or dried thyme

2 teaspoons chopped **fresh marjoram** leaves or 1 teaspoon dried marjoram

1 teaspoon chopped **fresh oregano** leaves or ½ teaspoon dried oregano

6 to 8 **canned anchovy fillets,** drained

6 to 8 **niçoise** or calamata **olives,** pitted

Salt and **pepper**

1. In a food processor or bowl, combine flour and butter. Whirl or rub with your fingers until fine crumbs form. Add egg and whirl or stir with a fork until dough holds together. Pat dough into a ball, then press evenly over bottom and sides of a 10-inch tart pan with removable rim.

2. Bake in a 325° oven until crust is pale gold, about 30 minutes (about 25 minutes in a convection oven).

3. Meanwhile, cut tomatoes in half and gently squeeze out seeds. Cut tomatoes crosswise into 1-inch-thick slices, and lay on towels to drain. Save ends.

4. Remove baked crust from oven and turn oven to 400°. Spread mustard over bottom of crust, then sprinkle evenly with 1½ cups cheese. Fit largest tomato slices snugly in a single layer on cheese. Cut remaining tomato slices into pieces to fill the gaps; reserve extra tomato pieces for other uses.

5. In a small bowl, mix oil to blend with tomato paste, shallots, garlic, thyme, marjoram, and oregano. Spread over tomatoes. Sprinkle with remaining cheese. Arrange anchovies and olives on tomatoes.

6. Bake in a 400° oven until cheese is lightly browned, about 25 minutes (about 18 minutes in a convection oven). Remove pan rim. Cut the tart into wedges and serve hot or warm. Add salt and pepper to taste.

Per serving: 441 cal., 61% (270 cal.) from fat; 15 g protein; 30 g fat (15 g sat.); 28 g carbo (2.3 g fiber); 531 mg sodium; 98 mg chol.

Layered Tomato-Vegetable Casserole

PREP AND COOK TIME: About 1 hour
NOTES: If assembling casserole up to 4 hours ahead, cover and let stand at room temperature until ready to bake.
MAKES: 8 servings

2 **red onions** (1 lb. total), peeled and thinly sliced

¼ cup **olive oil**

Salt and **pepper**

2 pounds **firm-ripe red** or yellow **tomatoes**

¼ cup chopped **fresh basil** leaves

2 teaspoons **fresh thyme** leaves or dried thyme

2 cloves **garlic,** peeled and chopped

1 pound **zucchini,** rinsed, ends trimmed, and thinly sliced

1. In a 10- to 12-inch frying pan over medium-high heat, frequently stir onions and 1 tablespoon olive oil until onions begin to brown, 12 to 15 minutes. Season to taste with salt and pepper.

2. Meanwhile, rinse tomatoes, core, cut in half, and squeeze out seeds. Thinly slice tomatoes crosswise.

3. Combine basil, thyme, and garlic. Mix ½ of the herbs with zucchini.

4. Spread cooked onions in a shallow 2-

to 3-quart casserole. Distribute zucchini evenly over onions.

5. Layer tomato slices over sliced zucchini. Sprinkle evenly with remaining herb mixture and lightly with salt and pepper. Drizzle vegetables with remaining olive oil.

6. Bake in a 400° oven until tomatoes are browned and zucchini slices are tender when pierced, 35 to 40 minutes (30 to 35 minutes in a convection oven). Add salt and pepper to taste.

Per serving: 114 cal., 57% (65 cal.) from fat; 2.6 g protein; 7.2 g fat (1 g sat.); 12 g carbo (2.7 g fiber); 17 mg sodium; 0 mg chol.

Tomatoes Provençal

PREP AND COOK TIME: About 30 minutes
NOTES: Serve with grilled fish, chicken, or beef.
MAKES: 5 servings

5 **firm-ripe tomatoes** (each 2½ in. wide; about 1¾ lb. total)

2 tablespoons **olive oil**

¾ cup coarse fresh **French bread** crumbs

1 clove **garlic,** peeled and minced

1 tablespoon chopped **parsley**

2 tablespoons chopped **fresh basil** leaves

1 tablespoon chopped **fresh chervil** or more parsley

Salt and **pepper**

1. Rinse tomatoes, core, cut in half crosswise, and gently squeeze out seeds. Drain cut side down on towels.

2. Pour 1 tablespoon oil into a 10- to 12-inch frying pan over medium-high heat. When oil is hot, set as many tomatoes as will fit in a single layer, cut side down, in pan. Cook, turning once, until lightly browned on both ends, 6 to 8 minutes total. Set tomatoes, cut side up, in a shallow 2½- to 3-quart casserole. Brown any remaining tomato halves.

3. In a bowl, mix crumbs with remaining 1 tablespoon olive oil, garlic, parsley, basil, and chervil. Pat mixture evenly over tomatoes.

4. Broil tomatoes 4 inches from heat until crumbs are golden, 4 to 6 minutes. Add salt and pepper to taste. Serve hot or warm.

Per serving: 95 cal., 57% (54 cal.) from fat; 1.8 g protein; 6 g fat (0.8 g sat.); 9.9 g carbo (2 g fiber); 53 mg sodium; 0 mg chol.

Turkey-filled Tomatoes

PREP AND COOK TIME: About 1 hour
NOTES: Use leftover tomato pulp and juices to make tomato sauce or salsa.
MAKES: 4 servings

4 **firm-ripe tomatoes** (each about 3½ in. wide; about 3 lb. total)

1 pound **ground lean turkey** or beef

½ cup finely chopped **shallots**

1 clove **garlic,** peeled and minced

1 **large egg**

3 tablespoons chopped **fresh basil** leaves

2 tablespoons chopped **parsley**

1 tablespoon chopped **fresh marjoram** leaves or 1 teaspoon dried marjoram

1 teaspoon chopped **fresh oregano** leaves or ½ teaspoon dried oregano

⅓ cup **fine dried bread crumbs**

About ½ teaspoon **salt**

About ¼ teaspoon **pepper**

Basil, marjoram, or oregano sprigs

1. Rinse tomatoes; cut ½ inch horizontally off the top of each and save. With a spoon, scoop soft pulp and seeds from tomatoes, leaving a ¼- to ⅓-inch-thick wall; save pulp mixture. Drain tomatoes, cut side down, on towels.

2. Chop enough pulp mixture to make ⅔ cup; reserve remainder for other uses. In a bowl, mix pulp, turkey, shallots, garlic, egg, basil, parsley, marjoram, oregano, bread crumbs, ½ teaspoon salt, and ¼ teaspoon pepper.

3. Fill tomatoes equally with the seasoned turkey mixture; set cut side up in a 2- to 3-quart shallow casserole. Set tomato tops, cut side down, between tomatoes.

4. Bake in a 375° oven until filling is firm when gently pressed in center, 35 to 40 minutes (30 to 35 minutes in a

SAUTÉED TOMATOES, shallots, chives, basil, and tangy chèvre cheese make an elegant omelet.

convection oven). Set tomato tops on filling. Add salt and pepper to taste. Garnish with herb sprigs.

Per serving: 281 cal., 35% (99 cal.) from fat; 25 g protein; 11 g fat (2.9 g sat.); 21 g carbo (3.8 g fiber); 513 mg sodium; 136 mg chol.

Tomato Omelets

PREP AND COOK TIME: About 20 minutes

NOTES: Garnish with cherry tomatoes.

MAKES: 2 servings

   1   **ripe tomato** ($^1\!/_2$ lb.)

   2   teaspoons **olive oil**

   2   tablespoons thinly sliced **shallots**

   3   tablespoons thinly sliced **chives**

   1   tablespoon chopped **fresh basil** leaves

Salt and **pepper**

   4   **large eggs**

$^1\!/_4$ cup **fresh chèvre** (goat) **cheese**

   2   teaspoons **butter** or margarine

1. Rinse tomato, core, cut in half crosswise, and squeeze out seeds. Chop tomato.

2. In an 8- to 10-inch frying pan over medium-high heat, combine oil and shallots. Stir often until shallots are limp, 3 to 4 minutes. Add tomato, 2 tablespoons chives, and basil; stir until tomato juices evaporate, 3 to 5 minutes. Add salt and pepper to taste. Keep warm.

3. In a bowl, beat eggs to blend with 1 tablespoon water and $^1\!/_8$ teaspoon salt. Also, break goat cheese into small pieces.

4. In a 6- to 7-inch nonstick frying pan over medium-high heat, melt 1 tea-

spoon butter. When sizzling, add $^1\!/_2$ the egg mixture. As eggs firm on the bottom, lift with a spatula to let uncooked portion flow beneath. Shake pan often to keep eggs freely moving. When eggs are softly set, in 1 to 2 minutes, spoon half the tomato mixture and chèvre down center of omelet, in line with pan handle.

5. To fold, tilt pan at about a 45° angle parallel to filling. With spatula, fold about $^1\!/_3$ of upper side of omelet down over the filling. Hold pan over plate and shake so unfolded edge slips out onto it, then quickly flip pan over to fold omelet out onto dish. Keep warm and repeat to cook remaining omelet. Sprinkle omelets with remaining chives. Add salt and pepper to taste.

Per serving: 299 cal., 66% (198 cal.) from fat; 17 g protein; 22 g fat (8.6 g sat.); 8.2 g carbo (1.7 g fiber); 238 mg sodium; 443 mg chol. ◆

The Quick Cook

MEALS IN 30 MINUTES OR LESS

BY LINDA LAU ANUSASANANAN

WHAT'S FOR DINNER?
Mexican Hero Sandwiches*
Cucumber Sticks   Radishes
Beer or Lemonade   Watermelon Wedges
*Recipe follows

A Mexican hero makes dinner

■ In Mexico, one answer to a quick meal is an amply stuffed hero-style sandwich called a *torta*. Vendors pack hollowed crusty rolls with refried beans, avocado, pickled chilies, tomato, shredded cabbage, and a choice of fillings—from meat to eggs or cheese. They flip the packed sandwiches on hot griddles to toast, then serve them with salsa. For the home cook, it's easier to toast the rolls first, then fill. All the ingredients you need are at the supermarket. Explore Mexican markets for the traditional rolls, cheeses, and canned chilies.

Mexican Hero Sandwiches

PREP AND COOK TIME: About 30 minutes

NOTES: *Bolillos* and *taleras* are crusty oval Mexican sandwich rolls. Instead of pickled jalapeño chilies, you can use 3 or 4 canned chipotle chiles in sauce, cut into thin slices.

MAKES: 4 sandwiches

- 4   **crusty sandwich rolls,** bolillos, or taleras (about 3 by 6½ in.)

- 1   can (15 oz.) **refried beans**

    Filling (recipes follow)

- 4   to 6 thin **red onion** slices, separated into rings

- 1   **firm-ripe tomato** (½ lb.), rinsed, cored, and thinly sliced

- 16 to 20 pieces drained **sliced pickled jalapeño chilies** (*jalapeños en escabeche*)

- 2   cups **finely shredded cabbage** or iceberg lettuce

    Salt and **pepper**

- 1   **firm-ripe avocado** (½ lb.)

    Salsa

1. Cut rolls in half horizontally. Pull out

JAMES CARRIER

MEXICAN TORTA is a meal on a bun. To eat the towering combination of refried beans, ham, cheese, onion, tomato, chilies, and cabbage, squish it down.

soft centers, making bread shells about ½ inch thick. Reserve soft bread for another use. Set rolls in a single layer on a 14- by 17-inch baking sheet.

2. Broil rolls about 4 inches from heat, turning once, until lightly toasted on both sides, about 3 minutes total.

3. Meanwhile, scoop beans into a microwave-safe bowl; cover. Heat in a microwave oven at full power (100%) until hot, about 2 minutes; stir at least once.

4. Spread refried beans equally on cut sides of each roll section. In bottom section of each roll, tuck equal portions of the filling, onion, tomato, chilies, and cabbage. Sprinkle lightly with salt and pepper.

5. Cut avocado in half lengthwise; discard pit. With a large spoon, scoop avocado from shell (or pull off peel), chopping slightly. Place equal portions of avocado on cut sides of the roll tops and spread to cover; sprinkle lightly with salt and pepper. Set tops, avocado down, on sandwich bases. Press down to secure filling. Serve with salsa to add to taste.

Egg-chorizo filling. Chop ⅓ pound **cooked** or smoked **chorizo** or linguisa **sausage.** In a bowl, beat 8 **large eggs** to blend with 2 tablespoons **water** and

¼ teaspoon **salt.** In a 10- to 12-inch nonstick frying pan over medium-high heat, stir chorizo until lightly browned, 3 to 4 minutes. Add egg mixture. As mixture sets, use a wide spatula to push cooked eggs aside and let uncooked liquid flow to pan bottom. Cook until eggs are softly set, about 2 minutes. Add **salt** and **pepper** to taste.

Per sandwich: 737 cal., 43% (315 cal.) from fat; 37 g protein; 35 g fat (10 g sat.); 68 g carbo (3.9 g fiber); 1,804 mg sodium; 458 mg chol.

Ham and cheese filling. Use ¾ pound **thinly sliced cooked ham** and ¼ pound sliced **asadero** or jack **cheese.**

Per sandwich: 659 cal., 36% (234 cal.) from fat; 42 g protein; 26 g fat (9.1 g sat.); 66 g carbo (3.9 g fiber); 2,549 mg sodium; 75 mg chol.

Chicken filling. Use ¾ pound purchased **cooked, seasoned chicken breast strips** or sliced, cooked chicken breasts.

Per sandwich: 522 cal., 22% (117 cal.) from fat; 36 g protein; 13 g fat (2.7 g sat.); 67 g carbo (3.9 g fiber); 1,537 mg sodium; 56 mg chol.

Cheese filling. Use ¾ pound **panela** or fresh mozzarella **cheese,** cut into ¼-inch-thick slices.

Per sandwich: 658 cal., 48% (315 cal.) from fat; 31 g protein; 35 g fat (17 g sat.); 66 g carbo (3.9 g fiber); 1,613 mg sodium; 30 mg chol. ◆

MAKING A STAND: Sanford Farms in Modesto, California, has been a popular roadside stop for visitors—and the friendly neighborhood market for locals—for 27 years.

Big valley farm stands

Now's the best time to enjoy the produce of California's fertile soil, fresh from the fields

BY MATTHEW JAFFE

So often we think of California as the ocean. The mountains and the desert. Hollywood or the Golden Gate. They are unforgettable places. But so, too, is the Central Valley, the great plain consisting of the Sacramento and San Joaquin valleys that extends from the edge of the Tehachapis to the waters of Shasta Lake, from the foothills of the Sierra to the Coast Range. It is perhaps the most productive agricultural region in the history of mankind.

That's a fact that people don't fully appreciate, says Shawn S. Stevenson, a Clovis citrus grower and former president of the Fresno County Farm Bureau; his family first arrived here back in the 1840s. "Most Americans are two to four generations removed from the farm," he says. "The general public has very little idea of what agriculture is about. Food is cheap and plentiful. Everyone takes it for granted."

I'm two generations removed from a chicken farm, and may take food production for granted, but not food. In fact, with a few days to meander between Los Angeles and San Francisco, I'm hunting the southern half of the Central Valley, the San Joaquin, for quality tomatoes, always a summer treat.

It's just the kind of trip my father would have taken. He often drove across the city for a loaf of bread from a favorite bakery and loved any excuse for getting off the interstate. He also never passed up an opportunity to add a "slice tomata" to whatever he was eating and would rhapsodize about a batch of tomatoes he had picked up from some farm stand on a vacation years before.

And be it nature or nurture or some combination thereof, I am my father's son. My plan of attack for killer tomatoes is simple. Drive around. Ask around. See the small towns, take the backroads, and hit those farm stands hard.

SUMMER IN THE VALLEY

As I drop down from the Tehachapis, it's hot in the Central Valley. Muggy hot, under hazy skies that wash out the hills of the Coast Range on the west and the Sierra to the east. It's the dead of summer, the doldrums.

There's no breeze, and the farmland never changes. Generically named roads—Avenue 104, Avenue 112, Avenue 120—count their way up from the Kern-Tulare county line. The farmland pays no heed to such jurisdictions. It spreads toward some distant unseen point. It can't go on forever, can it?

There is a majesty to the valley, and farther along, considerable diversity, too. You won't see it from Interstate 5 or State 99—you have to get out onto the two-lane roads.

Soon I'm in raisin country, and on both sides of the road, vines grow thick and green, fully leafed out. The farmland feels lush and fertile, with an almost Mediterranean-style romance to it.

Northeast of Fresno is another kind of landscape, one that would feel unmistakably familiar to Southern Californians of earlier generations. When development and progress came to Southern California, many citrus growers sold their farms and retreated to the foothill country along the valley's eastern boundary. The dark green of the orange groves set against the summer golden hills brings to mind the citrus heartland of Andalusia.

Unlike oranges, tomatoes don't redefine landscapes. You don't hear references to "Tomato Country" or to the "Tomato Empire." And so my quest meets with mixed success: wonderful cantaloupes and amazing white nectarines, but only a few memorable tomatoes.

As I drive through the valley—stopping to see the murals and shop for antiques in the picture-perfect farming town of Exeter, walking around Reedley, and catching the farmers' market in the historic town square in Hanford—the backseat begins to resemble some upholstered horn of plenty.

I spend nights at minor-league ballparks, grab a shake in Visalia at Mearle's College Drive In, and remind myself that it is the journey, not the destination, that counts. Process, not produce, in this instance.

Then, in Modesto, my quest suddenly seems as if it might bear fruit, and quite literally. Someone downtown mentions "the tomato place." Another person at a breakfast spot refers to "the tomato guys." They're out on Roselle Avenue.

It's getting late and I'm due in San Francisco tonight. As I head out, Modesto rides shotgun. This is an area of new subdivisions, exactly the kind of spreading urbanization that many people worry could pose a threat to agriculture.

I pull up to Sanford Farms and there are tomatoes. Lots of tomatoes. And not just the bright red ones of my imaginings. There are yellow and green tomatoes. There are red tomatoes with black markings and amber tomatoes with green stripes. There are hybrids, heirlooms, and big old beefsteaks. And they bear names that hint at some exotic, perhaps even secret, past: Cherokee Purple,

Black Prince, and the Arkansas Traveler.

The tomato guys are two brothers, Jim and Richard Sanford. Their ancestors came to the valley as dust-bowl migrants in the 1930s and, like many others, got their first jobs picking fruit. Their mother, Bessie, opened the farm stand in 1972; today, the 9-acre farm is still very much a family operation.

The subdivisions have crept within $\frac{1}{4}$ mile, but Jim isn't worried. People commuting home stop by the stand, he says. Jim even knows of a produce manager at a local supermarket who buys most of his fruits and vegetables here.

"I like to think of our stand as these people's fresh neighborhood market,"

Central Valley travel planner

Instead of blasting through the San Joaquin Valley on the way to the Sierra or Southern California, consider stopping along the way for a literal taste of what the valley has to offer. Accommodations, other than the ones we've noted, tend to be motel chains; local chambers of commerce can provide a list of options.

Fresno County

While summer is not blossom season, by following the 62-mile-long **Eastside Blossom Trail** you'll see county ag lands and several farm stands, such as **Simonian Farms** (2629 S. Clovis Ave.; 559/237-2294), which displays antique farm equipment. Also en route, **Reedley's** old-fashioned downtown boasts an opera house built in the early 1800s. Call (559) 638-3548 for information.

Blossom trail maps and other ag information are available through the Fresno County Farm Bureau at (559) 237-0263.

Kings County

Hanford features some grand public buildings (notably the courthouse and the old sheriff's office and jail), beautiful neighborhoods, and **China Alley,** remnant of the original Chinese railroad settlement here. China Alley is also home to the landmark **Imperial Dynasty Restaurant** (2 China Al-

ley; 559/582-0196). **Irwin Street Inn** (from $70; 522 N. Irwin; 559/583-8000) is a handsome restored Victorian. For more Hanford information, call (559) 582-5024 or the event line at (800) 722-1114.

For more information, contact the Kings County Farm Bureau at (559) 584-3557.

Merced County

For another side of local agriculture, the **Hilmar Cheese Visitor Center** will let you see an old-fashioned cheese operation (9001 Lander Ave.; 209/667-6076). If you're looking for a steak to balance out all that produce, have dinner at the **Branding Iron Restaurant** (640 W. 16th St.; 209/722-1822), a longtime Merced favorite.

Stanislaus County

The county farm bureau publishes a guide that highlights farmers who sell directly to consumers in Stanislaus, Merced, and San Joaquin counties. Contact the bureau at (209) 522-7278.

Tomato aficionados will definitely want to make a stop at Modesto's **Sanford Farms** (3248 Roselle Ave.; 209/551-4332).

For a beer and some pub grub in Modesto, drop in at **St. Stan's Micro Brewery Restaurant & Pub** (821 L St.; 209/524-4782).

Tulare County

The county's nicest agricultural drive is

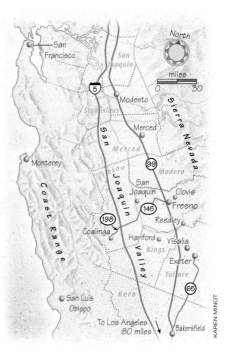

along State 65. It passes citrus groves and small farm towns. **Exeter** has several antiques stores and has undertaken a mural-painting program that celebrates the local farming tradition. For information, contact the Exeter Chamber of Commerce at (559) 592-2919.

In Visalia, the **Ben Maddox House** (from $85; 601 N. Encina St.; 800/401-9800) is a lovely 1870s home redone as a bed-and-breakfast. Don't miss one of the West's great drive-ins: **Mearle's College Drive In** (604 S. Mooney Blvd.; 559/734-4447).

says Jim. "It just amazes me how much everyone wants the fresh stuff. Anything you pick ripe and sell ripe is different from what they find in the store."

The Sanfords load me down with tomatoes, melons, and peppers. I also get a bag of dehydrated tomatoes for good measure. I eat them like candy on the way to San Francisco, finishing the last one on the Bay Bridge.

Double-parked on Russian Hill, I have to make several trips to carry the produce into my friends' apartment. Vegetables and fruit spread across the kitchen counter. The smell of ripe tomatoes fills the air. Dad would be proud.

SEAN ARBABI

Farmers' markets

Here's a pick of the crop of markets that are held all over the valley. If you're headed to a town not listed, be sure to contact the local chamber of commerce to see if the community hosts one.

•**Fresno.** At Blackstone and Shaw avenues; 2–6 P.M. Wed, 6–noon Sat year-round. (559) 222-0182.

•**Hanford.** Civic Center Park; 4–7 P.M. Thu through Sept. (559) 582-9457.

•**Merced.** W. Main St., between Martin Luther King Way and M St.; 6–9 P.M. Thu through Sept. (209) 383-6908.

•**Reedley.** G Street, between 10th and 11th streets. 4:30–7:30 P.M. Wed through Aug. (559) 638-5484.

•**Visalia.** At Church and Main streets; 5–8 P.M. Thu through Sept. At Caldwell Ave. and Mooney Blvd.; 8–11:30 A.M. Sat year-round. (559) 747-0095. ◆

Fizzy floats

Start with a bubbly new generation of sodas

BY ELAINE JOHNSON

With the inventiveness of the microbrewers, today's soft-drink makers are adding fizz to traditional favorites and diving into new tastes. Flavor renovations have hit root beer, sarsaparilla, ginger beer (nonalcoholic), and more.

These beverages not only make for fine sipping but also bring a cool dimension to another old-fashioned delight: an ice cream float. Serve floats with straws and long spoons.

Coffee-Hazelnut Floats

PREP TIME: About 15 minutes
NOTES: If coffee soda is unavailable, mix ¼ cup instant espresso powder with ½ cup cream soda. Pour equally into glasses; fill with cream soda.
MAKES: 4 servings

Scoop 2½ cups *each* **vanilla ice cream** and **coffee ice cream** equally into 4 glasses (each 16 oz.). Add 2 tablespoons **hazelnut liqueur** (½ cup total) or 1 tablespoon hazelnut syrup (¼ cup total) to each glass, then slowly fill with cold **coffee soda**, about 2 bottles (12 oz. each) total. Sprinkle 4 teaspoons **chocolate-covered coffee beans** equally onto ice cream.

Per serving: 527 cal., 32% (171 cal.) from fat; 6.1 g protein; 19 g fat (12 g sat.); 75 g carbo (0.3 g fiber); 155 mg sodium; 73 mg chol.

Deluxe Root Beer Floats

PREP TIME: About 10 minutes
NOTES: This drink is also good made with cherry soda instead of root beer. Garnish glasses with maraschino cherries and thin strips of orange peel.
MAKES: 4 servings

Scoop 5 cups **vanilla ice cream** equally into 4 glasses (16 oz. each). Sprinkle evenly with ⅓ cup chopped **bittersweet chocolate** and 1 teaspoon grated **orange** peel. Slowly fill glasses with cold **root beer** or sarsaparilla, about 2 bottles (12 oz. each) total.

Per serving: 477 cal., 43% (207 cal.) from fat; 6.8 g protein; 23 g fat (14 g sat.); 67 g carbo (0.3 g fiber); 156 mg sodium; 73 mg chol.

Double Ginger Floats

PREP TIME: About 10 minutes, plus 1½ hours to refreeze ice cream
MAKES: 4 servings

1. To slightly soften 5 cups **vanilla ice cream,** heat in a microwave oven at 30 percent power for 5 seconds, or let stand at room temperature about 15 minutes. Scoop ice cream into a large bowl.
2. Add ¼ cup chopped **crystallized ginger,** ¾ teaspoon **ground cardamom,** and ½ teaspoon **ground cinnamon;** stir quickly to swirl ingredients together. Place bowl in freezer until ice cream is firm enough to scoop, at least 1½ hours; if storing up to 1 week, cover airtight.
3. Scoop up the ice cream equally into 4 glasses (each 16 oz.). Slowly fill glasses with cold **ginger beer** or ginger ale, about 2 bottles (12 oz. each) total.

Per serving: 449 cal., 36% (162 cal.) from fat; 5.8 g protein; 18 g fat (11 g sat.); 69 g carbo (0.5 g fiber); 157 mg sodium; 73 mg chol.

Rum-Almond Floats

PREP TIME: 10 to 15 minutes
MAKES: 4 servings

1. Form ¼ cup (2¼ oz.) **almond paste** into ¼-inch balls.
2. Scoop 5 cups **vanilla frozen yogurt** equally into 4 glasses (each 16 oz.) and top equally with almond paste balls. Add 2 tablespoons **rum** (½ cup total) to each glass, then slowly fill with cold **cream soda,** about 2 bottles (12 oz. each) total.

Per serving: 423 cal., 17% (73 cal.) from fat; 9.4 g protein; 8.1 g fat (2.9 g sat.); 65 g carbo (0 g fiber); 165 mg sodium; 12 mg chol. ◆

PURE JAVA JOY: Coffee and vanilla ice creams percolate in coffee soda.

In Phoenix, oldies but goldies

Escape summer heat and modern conceits
at these four retro metro restaurants

LIGHTING UP the patio at El Chorro
Lodge (left); sampling Durant's pleasures
(top); the Pink Pony's still in style (above).

■ All things swing are back again. At these classic Phoenix-area restaurants the food is good, the wait staff well-seasoned, and the Sinatra-era ambience is genuine.

Since 1950 the city's movers and shakers have cut many a deal against **Durant's** backdrop of red flocked wallpaper, tufted booths, and dim lighting. If you want to make like a regular, park in the back and enter through the boisterous kitchen. Order prime rib or lobster and something shaken, not stirred. *2611 N. Central Ave., Phoenix; (602) 264-5967.*

El Chorro Lodge started out in 1934 as a girls' school in what was then the middle of the desert. Dine outside on the patio, flanked by citrus and palms, with views of Camelback Mountain. Sticky buns and a relish tray will tide you over while you wait for your shrimp Louie, shad roe, or chateaubriand. *5550 E. Lincoln Dr., Scottsdale; (480) 948-5170.*

Half the population of Arizona, it seems, has celebrated a birthday, graduation, or anniversary at **Monti's La Casa Vieja.** The rustic steakhouse's adobe building dates back to 1871, and it's housed various restaurant operations since 1890. Before you sit down to your sirloin, wander through the rambling rooms and check out the historic photographs. *1 W. Rio Salado Parkway, Tempe; (480) 967-7594.*

The **Pink Pony** has been a baseball hangout since 1950. World Series bats line the wall behind the bar, and players' uniforms are framed over the tables. During spring training the place is packed with fans, managers, sportswriters, and, yes, players. The menu doesn't strike out when it comes to the classics: liver and onions, prime rib, lamb chops, lobster. *3831 N. Scottsdale Rd., Scottsdale; (480) 945-6697.* ◆   — *Nora Burba Trulsson*

Kitchen Cabinet

READERS' RECIPES TESTED IN SUNSET'S KITCHENS

BY LINDA LAU ANUSASANANAN

FLUFFY, GOLDEN pancakes stack up for fresh blueberries and blueberry syrup.

LEIGH BEISCH (2)

Lemon Soufflé Pancakes with Blueberry Maple Syrup

Carolyn Kane, Daly City, California

As a professional chef, Carolyn Kane works most weekends. But on one rare free Sunday morning, she offered her fiancé a choice of dishes for brunch: Austrian crêpes, corn clafouti with smoked salmon, or frittata with goat cheese and artichokes. His answer: "All I really want is good old-fashioned blueberry pancakes with maple syrup." This is what she served, and he's now her husband.

PREP AND COOK TIME: About 35 minutes

MAKES: 8 pancakes; 3 or 4 servings

- 2 cups **all-purpose flour**
- 2 tablespoons **sugar**
- 1 teaspoon **baking soda**
- ½ teaspoon **salt**
- 2 **large eggs,** separated
- 1½ cups **buttermilk**
- 2 teaspoons grated **lemon** peel
- 3 tablespoons **lemon juice**
  About ¼ cup (⅛ lb.) melted **butter** or margarine
- 1 cup **maple syrup**
- 1 cup **blueberries,** rinsed

1. In a large bowl, mix flour, sugar, soda, and salt.

2. In a small bowl, whisk together egg yolks, buttermilk, lemon peel, lemon juice, and 2 tablespoons butter.

3. In a deep bowl with a mixer on high speed, whip egg whites until they hold stiff, moist peaks.

4. Pour buttermilk mixture into flour mixture; stir to blend. Add egg whites and fold gently to blend.

5. On a buttered griddle or 10- to 12-inch frying pan over medium heat, pour batter in ½-cup portions, without portions touching. Cook until golden brown on each side, turning once, 4 to 5 minutes total. Keep warm. Repeat to cook remaining pancakes.

6. Meanwhile, in a 1- to 2-quart pan over medium heat, combine 2 tablespoons butter, syrup, and blueberries. Heat, stirring occasionally, until butter melts, about 3 minutes.

7. Serve pancakes with blueberry syrup.

Per serving: 687 cal., 25% (171 cal.) from fat; 13 g protein; 19 g fat (11 g sat.); 118 g carbo (2.5 g fiber); 897 mg sodium; 150 mg chol.

Garlic Flank Steak

Cathy Herholdt, Bothell, Washington

In the opinion of Cathy Herholdt, "you can never use too much garlic in this marinade." But we suggest starting with the amount that follows. For convenience, Herholdt freezes steaks individually in the marinade, thawing the package overnight in the refrigerator.

PREP AND COOK TIME: About 1¼ hours

MAKES: 6 to 8 servings

- ⅓ cup **soy sauce**
- 2 tablespoons **balsamic vinegar**
- 2 tablespoons **olive oil**
- 3 to 5 cloves **garlic,** peeled, pressed or minced
- ¼ teaspoon **cayenne** (optional)
- 1 **beef flank steak** (about 2 lb.)

1. In a 1-quart or larger heavy plastic food bag, combine soy sauce, vinegar, oil, garlic, and cayenne.

2. Trim excess fat from steak. Rinse meat and pat dry. Add steak to marinade. Seal bag and set in a bowl. Chill at least 1 hour or up to 1 day, turning occasionally.

3. Lift steak from bag; save marinade. Lay steak on a grill above a solid bed of hot coals or over high heat on a gas grill (you can hold your hand at grill level only 2 to 3 seconds). Close lid on gas grill. Cook, turning once, until steak is browned and rare to medium-rare in the center of thickest part (cut to test), 8 to 10 minutes total. Transfer to a carving board. Let rest about 5 minutes.

4. Pour marinade into a 1- to 1½-quart pan. Bring to a boil over high heat. Cut meat diagonally across grain into thin slices and serve with marinade.

Per serving: 214 cal., 50% (108 cal.) from fat; 24 g protein; 12 g fat (4.2 g sat.); 1.5 g carbo (0 g fiber); 750 mg sodium; 57 mg chol.

Southwest Orzo and Bean Salad

Polly Parkinson, Salt Lake City

Polly Parkinson models this recipe after a rice salad she enjoyed at a cafe, but she prefers using rice-shaped pasta. Her brother recommends the salad as an appetizer, scooped onto corn tortilla chips.

PREP AND COOK TIME: About 20 minutes

MAKES: 4 main-dish servings

- ⅔ cup **dried orzo pasta**
- 1 can (15 oz.) **black beans**, rinsed and drained
- 1½ cups **corn kernels**, fresh-cut, thawed frozen, or drained canned
- 1 **firm-ripe tomato** (½ lb.), rinsed, cored, and chopped
- ⅓ cup chopped **fresh cilantro**
- ¼ cup thinly sliced **green onions** or chives
- 1 teaspoon grated **lime** peel
- ⅓ cup plus 1 tablespoon **lime juice**
  About ½ teaspoon **pepper**
  Salt
- 1 **ripe avocado** (10 oz.), peeled and pitted
- ¼ cup **nonfat sour cream**
  Corn tortilla chips (optional)

1. In a 3- to 4-quart pan over high heat, bring 1½ to 2 quarts water to a boil. Add pasta and cook until barely tender to bite, 9 to 11 minutes. Drain and rinse with cold water.

2. In a large bowl, mix pasta, beans, corn, tomato, cilantro, onions, lime peel, ⅓ cup lime juice, ½ teaspoon pepper, and salt to taste.

3. In a small bowl, mash avocado with 1 tablespoon lime juice and sour cream. Add salt and pepper to taste.

4. Equally mound pasta salad on dinner plates. Top with dollops of the avocado mixture. Surround or accompany with tortilla chips.

Per serving: 335 cal., 27% (89 cal.) from fat; 12 g protein; 9.9 g fat (1.5 g sat.); 54 g carbo (7.4 g fiber); 210 mg sodium; 1.5 mg chol.

Cardamom-Pistachio Ice Cream

Farah Ahmed, Sunnyvale, California

In India, *kulfi* is a dense, smooth ice cream that's sold in many flavors from street stalls. Farah Ahmed shares a quick version of her favorite kulfi, cardamom-pistachio. If your ice cream maker holds only 1 quart, prepare a half-recipe or freeze in batches; you can cover and chill the liquid mixture up to 2 days.

PREP TIME: About 25 minutes

MAKES: About 7¼ cups

- 1 can (12 oz.) **evaporated milk**, chilled
- 1 can (14 oz.) **sweetened condensed milk**, chilled
- 1 cup **unsalted roasted pistachios**
- ½ teaspoon **ground cardamom**
- 2 cups **whipping cream**
  Strawberry syrup (optional)
  Strawberries, rinsed and hulled, whole or sliced (optional)

1. In a blender, combine evaporated milk, condensed milk, pistachios, and cardamom; whirl until nuts are finely ground.

2. In a large bowl with a mixer at high speed, whip cream until it holds distinct peaks.

3. Add nut mixture to cream; fold to blend well.

4. Pour into a 2-quart (or larger) ice cream maker. Freeze according to manufacturer's directions until mixture is firm enough to scoop, dasher is hard to turn, or machine stops.

5. Serve softly frozen ice cream. Or package airtight and freeze up to 1 week. Scoop ice cream into bowls. Add strawberry syrup and whole strawberries to taste.

Per ½ cup: 273 cal., 63% (171 cal.) from fat; 5.9 g protein; 19 g fat (9.6 g sat.); 21 g carbo (1 g fiber); 74 mg sodium; 53 mg chol.

PALE GREEN pistachios flavor smooth ice cream.

Tisane

Rofina Wilenchik, San Anselmo, California

"I was first introduced to tisane at Chez Panisse in Berkeley. I loved the bright flavors that fresh herbs gave to tea," says Rofina Wilenchik, who makes this herbal tea contribution.

PREP AND COOK TIME: About 15 minutes, plus at least 5 minutes to steep

MAKES: About 4 cups; 4 servings

- 2 stalks **fresh lemon grass** (about 12 in.), rinsed
- 2 **lemon thyme** or regular thyme sprigs (3 to 4 in.), rinsed
- 24 **spearmint**, peppermint, or mint sprigs (6 to 8 in.; use 1 kind or a combination), rinsed
- 4 slices (size of a quarter) **fresh ginger**, crushed
- 5 thin **lemon** or lime slices
- 1 bag (about 1½ teaspoons) **peppermint tea**

1. In 2- to 3-quart pan over high heat, bring 4 cups water to a boil.

2. Meanwhile, trim off and discard tough ends of lemon grass and pull off coarse outer leaves. Thinly slice stalks.

3. Add lemon grass, thyme, mint, ginger, lemon slices, and tea to boiling water. Cover and remove from heat. Let stand (steep) 5 to 10 minutes.

4. Pour tisane liquid through a fine strainer into a teapot or pitcher. Serve hot, or cool with ice.

Per serving: 9.9 cal., 9.1% (0.9 cal.) from fat; 0.3 g protein; 0.1 g fat (0 g sat.); 3.3 g carbo (0 g fiber); 8.3 mg sodium; 0 mg chol. ◆

Inspired by Spanish tradition, our tapas party includes lamb chops dipped into a Spanish romesco sauce (recipe on page 217).

September

A tableful of small plates,
in the Spanish tradition,
sets the perfect tempo

■ SPANIARDS KNOW HOW TO SAVOR LIFE—
every delicious morsel of it. Especially in
the neighborhood bar, a beloved institution that nourishes the soul as well as the
stomach of the community. During the
day, regulars stop by for a quick bite and
local gossip. At night, families and friends
stroll from bar to bar to meet and share
appetizers and a drink before going
home to a late dinner. It's a progressive
happy hour. • Centuries ago the bar-
tenders began placing covers (*tapas*)
over the glasses of wine to keep flies out.
Sometimes the cover was a slice of bread,
cheese, or chorizo. Customers came to
expect a little bite with their drink, and
the tradition of tapas was born. • Now
Westerners have embraced the tradition.
Tapas bars and cafes have sprung up
throughout the region. They embody the
conviviality of the custom: Eat a little, eat
a lot. Choose from a wide range of foods,
from olives to marinated clams. And always do it with friends. • This freewheeling nibbling and noshing pattern is a
wonderful concept for entertaining at
home. Small plates of many foods accommodate all tastes and create the perfect
party pace. Most of these dishes can be
made ahead. Or, in the spirit of sharing,
you can ask each guest to bring one tapa,
homemade or purchased.

BY LINDA LAU ANUSASANANAN
PHOTOGRAPHS BY JAMES CARRIER
FOOD STYLING BY VALERIE AIKMAN-SMITH

party
bites

tapas spread invites grazing and expands easily for a casual, Spanish-style party. Combine simple homemade dishes with a few purchased items, and offer Spanish wines and sherries. From left on the raised pedestal: marinated clams, garlic mushrooms, fried green pimientos, salted roasted almonds, and roasted red peppers with garlic, olive oil, and sherry vinegar. Continuing clockwise on the table: grilled lamb chops, olives, pimiento sauce, tomatoes and capers with olive oil, roasted grapes with serrano ham, country bread, Spanish herbed fries, and honeyed figs and serrano ham on nut toast.

tapas
for 12

To serve between 12 and 24 guests, add any or all of the following buy-and-serve options. Or for a really quick, impromptu party, use this menu on its own, adding sliced baguettes.

- Spanish-style Olives
- Black and Green Ripe Olives
- Salted Roasted Almonds
- Sliced Tomatoes and Capers Drizzled with Olive Oil
- Grilled Shrimp or Swordfish on Skewers
- Grilled Sausages such as Chorizo, Linguisa, or Italian
- Smoked Salmon with Capers and Lemon Wedges
- Roasted Red Peppers and Minced Garlic Drizzled with Olive Oil and Sherry Vinegar
- Sliced Quince Paste with Sliced Queso Fresco (or Fresh Mozzarella)
- Cheese Wedges: Ibérico, Cabrales, Manchego, Mahón, Tetilla, Idiazábal

DIP GRILLED LAMB chops into a Spanish romesco sauce based on red peppers and almonds.

Honeyed Figs and Serrano Ham on Nut Toast

PREP AND COOK TIME: About 30 minutes, plus at least 2 hours to marinate

NOTES: This savory concept comes from Heidi Krahling, chef-owner of Insalata's restaurant in San Anselmo, California. Up to 1 day ahead, marinate figs. Up to 1 hour before serving, assemble toasts.

MAKES: 12 appetizers

6   **fresh** or dried **mission figs**, rinsed

½   cup **honey**

1   **rosemary sprig** (about 4 in.) or 1 teaspoon dried rosemary

3   tablespoons **balsamic vinegar**

¼   pound **cabrales** (Spanish blue) **cheese** or other blue cheese, at room temperature

¼   cup **cream cheese**, at room temperature

12   slices **firm walnut bread** (2 by 3 in., ½ in. thick), toasted

12   pieces **thin-sliced serrano ham** or prosciutto (each about 2 by 3 in.; about 2 oz. total)

1. Cut off and discard fig stems. Slice figs in half lengthwise and place in a small bowl.

2. In a 1- to 1½-quart pan, combine honey and ⅓ cup water. Bring to a boil over high heat. Add rosemary, reduce heat to medium-high, and boil until reduced to ½ cup, 6 to 12 minutes. Discard rosemary. Add vinegar and stir until boiling. Pour over figs. Let stand at least 2 hours, or cover and chill up to 1 day; stir occasionally.

3. In a bowl with a mixer, beat blue cheese and cream cheese until smoothly blended.

4. Spread cheese mixture thickly on toast. Lay 1 slice of ham on each toast.

Drain figs (reserve syrup for another use) and set 1 fig half on each toast.

Per serving: 148 cal., 34% (51 cal.) from fat; 6.6 g protein; 5.7 g fat (3 g sat.); 20 g carbo (1.8 g fiber); 334 mg sodium; 16 mg chol.

Garlic Mushrooms

PREP AND COOK TIME: About 20 minutes

NOTES: If making up to 6 hours ahead, keep at room temperature.

MAKES: 12 appetizer servings

- 1 tablespoon **olive oil**
- 1 tablespoon chopped **garlic**
- 1 pound **mushrooms** (1½- to 2-in.-wide caps), rinsed and drained
- 3 tablespoons **dry sherry**
- ¼ teaspoon **hot chili flakes**
- 1 tablespoon chopped **parsley**

  Salt and **pepper**

1. In a 10- to 12-inch frying pan over high heat, stir oil, garlic, and mushrooms until garlic is limp, about 2 minutes. Add sherry and chili flakes; cover and simmer over medium-high heat, stirring occasionally, until most of the liquid is evaporated and mushrooms are browned, 7 to 10 minutes.

2. Stir in parsley. Add salt and pepper to taste. Serve hot or at room temperature.

Per serving: 26 cal., 46% (12 cal.) from fat; 0.8 g protein; 1.3 g fat (0.2 g sat.); 2.2 g carbo (0.5 g fiber); 2.1 mg sodium; 0 mg chol.

Grilled Lamb Chops with Romesco Sauce

PREP AND COOK TIME: About 40 minutes

NOTES: This recipe was inspired by *A Taste of Spain,* by Anne Aguilar Santucci (Club Español, Rocklin, CA, 1998; $18; 916/488-3044). If making sauce up to 1 day ahead, cover and chill. Sauce also complements grilled beef, pork, poultry, and seafood.

MAKES: 12 appetizer servings

- 2 tablespoons **slivered almonds**
- 2 tablespoons **olive oil**
- 1 **onion** (½ lb.), peeled and chopped
- 2 cloves **garlic,** peeled and minced or pressed
- 1 **ripe tomato** (6 oz.), rinsed, cored, and chopped
- ¾ cup chopped **canned red peppers**
- ¼ to ½ teaspoon **hot chili flakes**
- 3 tablespoons **red wine vinegar**

  Salt and **pepper**
- 12 **lamb rib chops** (each about ¾ in. thick and 3 to 4 oz.)

1. In a 10- to 12-inch frying pan over medium heat, stir almonds until golden, about 5 minutes. Whirl nuts in a food processor or blender until finely ground.

2. Add oil, onion, and garlic to pan; stir over high heat until onion is limp, about 3 minutes. Add tomato, red peppers, chili flakes, and vinegar. Simmer over medium heat, stirring occasionally, until most of the liquid is evaporated, 6 to 8 minutes.

3. Stir ground almonds into tomato mixture; add salt and pepper to taste. Pour romesco sauce into a bowl.

4. Rinse lamb and pat dry. Trim and discard excess surface fat. Lay chops on a barbecue grill over a solid bed of hot coals or high heat on a gas grill (you can hold your hand at grill level only 2 to 3 seconds); close lid on gas grill. Cook, turning once until browned on both sides but still pink in center of thickest part (cut to test), 8 to 10 minutes total. Add salt and pepper to taste.

5. Serve with hot or cool romesco sauce.

Per serving: 106 cal., 56% (59 cal.) from fat; 8.1 g protein; 6.6 g fat (1.6 g sat.); 3.5 g carbo (0.6 g fiber); 42 mg sodium; 25 mg chol.

Spanish Herbed Fries

PREP AND COOK TIME: About 40 minutes

NOTES: Eat potatoes plain, or dip into pimiento sauce (recipe follows).

MAKES: 12 appetizer servings

- 4 **russet potatoes** (½ lb. each), peeled or scrubbed
- ¼ cup **olive oil**
- 2 tablespoons coarsely chopped **Italian parsley**
- 1 tablespoon chopped **fresh rosemary** leaves

  About ¼ teaspoon **salt**

  About ⅛ teaspoon **pepper**

1. Cut potatoes lengthwise into ½-inch-thick sticks.

2. In a 10- by 15-inch pan, mix potato sticks, oil, parsley, rosemary, ¼ teaspoon salt, and ⅛ teaspoon pepper. Pour ½ the mixture into another 10- by 15-inch pan. In each pan, spread potatoes slightly apart in a single layer.

3. Bake in a 425° oven for 15 minutes. With a wide spatula, turn potatoes; switch pan positions in oven. Continue to bake until potatoes are well browned and give readily when pressed, about 15 minutes more. With spatula, transfer to a platter. Add salt and pepper to taste. Serve hot or warm.

Per serving: 95 cal., 43% (41 cal.) from fat; 1.3 g protein; 4.6 g fat (0.6 g sat.); 12 g carbo (1.2 g fiber); 53 mg sodium; 0 mg chol.

Pimiento Sauce

PREP AND COOK TIME: About 30 minutes

NOTES: For a shortcut, skip steps 1 and 2, and instead of fresh bell peppers, use 1½ cups drained, chopped canned red peppers; season with raw garlic. If making up to 1 day ahead, cover and chill.

MAKES: About 1 cup; 12 servings

- 2 **red bell peppers** (1 lb. total), rinsed
- 1 clove **garlic**
- 2 tablespoons **whipping cream**
- 2 tablespoons **olive oil**
- ¼ teaspoon **cayenne**

  Salt

1. Place peppers and garlic in an 8- or 9-inch square pan. Broil 3 to 4 inches from heat, turning as needed to char all sides, 20 to 25 minutes for peppers, 14 to 16 minutes for garlic. Remove from pan as charred.

2. When peppers are cool, discard stems, seeds, and skin; coarsely chop peppers. Peel garlic.

3. In a food processor or blender, whirl peppers, garlic, cream, oil, and cayenne until smooth. Add salt to taste.

Per serving: 36 cal., 78% (28 cal.) from fat; 0.3 g protein; 3.1 g fat (0.8 g sat.); 2.2 g carbo (0.5 g fiber); 1.5 mg sodium; 2.8 mg chol.

Roasted Grapes with Serrano Ham

PREP AND COOK TIME: About 30 minutes

NOTES: If desired, put ham and grapes on baguette slices to eat.

MAKES: 12 appetizer servings

- 1 or 2 bunches **Red Flame grapes** (1½ lb. total), rinsed
- 6 ounces **thin-sliced serrano ham** or prosciutto

1. Lay grape bunch (or bunches, slightly apart) in a 10- by 15-inch pan. Bake in a 425° oven until grapes begin to shrink and brown, about 30 minutes.

2. Set warm or cool grapes on a platter.

tapas. wines

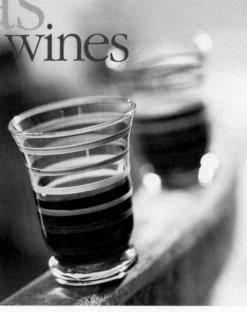

Spain has more vineyard land than any other country in the world. From the mountains in the north to the sun-drenched coasts of the south, vines flourish virtually everywhere. As a result, wine drinking is an inescapable part of Spanish culture—a part Spaniards are passionate about.

With tapas, almost any Spanish wine will do, though the Spaniards themselves tend to drink the great classics: soft, sensual red wines from Rioja and Ribera del Duero; the snappy white wine known as Albariño from Galicia; cava, Spain's sparkling wine; plus a wonderful assortment of spicy rosés (called rosados in Spain), especially from the province of Navarra.

But no wine epitomizes tapas more than sherry. I know—you're thinking: Sherry? Unfortunately, most of us have never tasted the great sherries of Spain (which bear no resemblance to the cheap stuff). But now's the time to change that. Try a rich, nutty oloroso sherry with the honeyed figs and serrano ham on nut bread. Just one sip and one bite, and you'll think you're in Spain itself.

Here are some of my favorite wines with tapas.

CAVA (Spanish sparkling wine)

■**Cavas Jaume Serra "Cristalino" Brut NV (Cava),** $9. Simply delicious. Lively crisp apple fruit.

■**Segura Viudas "Reserva Heredad" Brut NV (Penedes),** $12 to $15. Soft and creamy. A terrific sparkler for a party.

WHITE AND ROSÉ

■**Martin Codax Albariño 1998 (Rias Baixas),** $14. Albariño is Spain's most exciting white grape. Fresh and racy, it's terrific with tapas.

■**Julian Chivite "Gran Feudo" Rosé 1998 (Navarra),** $7. One of the best rosés made in Europe. Fresh and bursting with berries.

REDS

■**Bodegas Muga Reserva 1995 (Rioja),** $16. A classically beautiful Rioja with soft cherry and dried-leaf flavors.

■**Finca Retuerta "Abadia Retuerta" 1996 (Sardon de Duero),** $24. Spicy black fruits. Mouth-filling and wonderfully earthy.

■**Torres Gran Sangre de Toro Reserva 1995 (Vilafranca del Penedes),** $11. Rustic and bold, with good juicy red fruit flavors.

■**Viña Mayor Crianza 1996 (Ribera del Duero),** $11. Soft, spicy cherries; very easy to drink.

SHERRIES

■**Hidalgo "La Gitana" Manzanilla (Sanlucar de Barrameda),** $11. Bracingly fresh and bone-dry. A classic way to begin an evening of tapas.

■**Hidalgo Oloroso Especial (Sanlucar de Barrameda),** $18. Mesmerizingly rich, with a profound nuttiness.

■**Osborne "Coquinero" Fino/Amontillado (Jerez),** $15. Rich, deeply flavorful, and nutty; absolutely delicious.

— *Karen MacNeil-Fife*

If desired, snip into smaller bunches. Ripple ham slices alongside grapes. To eat, pick up a small portion of ham and wrap around a few grapes.

Per serving: 68 cal., 29% (20 cal.) from fat; 4.4 g protein; 2.2 g fat (0.6 g sat.); 9.7 g carbo (0.9 g fiber); 263 mg sodium; 12 mg chol.

Fried Green Pimientos

PREP AND COOK TIME: **About 15 minutes**

NOTES: In Spain, chilies and sweet peppers are both called *pimientos,* or peppers. If chilies are small, pick up stems to hold and eat. Or serve with knife and fork, pulling chili skin off if tough.

MAKES: **12 appetizer servings**

12 **slender mild chilies** or peppers (each 3 to 5 in. and ¾ to 1½ oz.) with stems, such as Anaheim, pepperoncini, or sweet Hungarian

2 tablespoons **olive oil**

Salt and **pepper**

1. Rinse chilies and pat dry.

2. Pour oil into a 10- to 12-inch frying pan over medium-high heat. Add chilies in a single layer and brown on all sides, turning as needed, 6 to 8 minutes total. Remove from pan; repeat to cook any remaining chilies. If desired, pull off loose skin.

3. Serve hot or cool. Add salt and pepper to taste.

Per serving: 26 cal., 81% (21 cal.) from fat; 0.3 g protein; 2.3 g fat (0.3 g sat.); 1.5 g carbo (0.2 g fiber); 1.1 mg sodium; 0 mg chol.

Marinated Clams

PREP AND COOK TIME: **About 20 minutes, plus at least 1 hour to chill**

NOTES: If making up to 4 hours ahead, chill cooked clams in seasonings.

MAKES: **12 appetizer servings**

1 cup **dry white wine**

3 cloves **garlic,** peeled and pressed or minced

3 dozen **clams in shells, suitable for steaming** (1½ to 2 in. wide), scrubbed

½ cup **white wine vinegar**

1 tablespoon **olive oil**

½ cup chopped **red bell pepper**

3 tablespoons chopped **fresh cilantro**

1. In a 5- to 6-quart pan over high heat, combine 1 cup water, wine, and garlic. Bring to a boil. Add clams. Cover and

dessert

Fine shreds of orange peel, slices of toasted almonds, and honey transform ricotta into a sweet last bite. Scoop the soft fresh cheese onto fruit or cookies.

cook until clams pop open, **5 to 10 minutes.** Discard any that don't open. With a slotted spoon, transfer clams to a bowl. Reserve clam juices.

2. Mix 2 cups reserved clam juice with vinegar and oil (reserve extra juice for other uses). Pour clam juice mixture over clams. Cover and chill, stirring occasionally, at least 1 and up to 4 hours.

3. Mix in red bell pepper and cilantro.

Per serving: 60 cal., 23% (14 cal.) from fat; 5.8 g protein; 1.6 g fat (0.2 g sat.); 2.1 g carbo (0.1 g fiber); 26 mg sodium; 15 mg chol.

Catalan Tomato Bread

PREP AND COOK TIME: **About 10 minutes**

NOTES: If making up to 30 minutes ahead, rub toast with garlic and oil. Rub toast with tomato just before serving.

MAKES: **20 to 24 pieces; 10 to 12 appetizer servings**

- 1 loaf (1 lb.) **French** or Italian **bread**
- 1 or 2 large cloves **garlic,** peeled
- 2 to 3 tablespoons **olive oil**

1 large (about ½ lb.) **ripe tomato,** rinsed

1. Slice loaf in half horizontally. Set halves, cut side up, on a 12- by 15-inch baking sheet. Broil about 4 inches from heat until toasted, about 2 minutes. If crust side is soft, turn over and toast 1 to 2 minutes longer.

2. Cut garlic clove in half. Rub clove over cut surface of bread. Brush or drizzle bread with oil.

3. Cut tomato in half horizontally; rub cut sides over toast, squeezing slightly to release juices.

4. Cut bread into 1½-inch-wide wedges.

Per serving: 128 cal., 24% (31 cal.) from fat; 3.5 g protein; 3.4 g fat (0.5 g sat.); 21 g carbo (1.3 g fiber); 232 mg sodium; 0 mg chol.

Fresh Cheese with Honey and Almonds

PREP AND COOK TIME: **About 10 minutes**

NOTES: Scoop cheese mixture onto dried apricots, fresh nectarine wedges, water crackers, or plain, dense cookies such as *petits beurres.*

MAKES: **12 servings**

- ¼ cup chopped **almonds**

    About 1 pound **ricotta** or large-curd cottage cheese

- 2 to 3 tablespoons **honey**
- 1 teaspoon finely shredded **orange** peel

1. In a 6- to 8-inch frying pan over medium heat, stir or shake almonds until toasted, about 5 minutes. Pour from pan.

2. Drain any liquid from ricotta or cottage cheese. Run a spatula around ricotta carton and unmold cheese onto a plate; or mound cottage cheese in a shallow bowl.

3. Drizzle honey onto cheese, then sprinkle with nuts and orange peel.

Per serving: 93 cal., 61% (57 cal.) from fat; 4.8 g protein; 6.3 g fat (3.3 g sat.); 4.7 g carbo (0.3 g fiber); 32 mg sodium; 19 mg chol. ◆

CHRISTINA RICCI (above, left) totes tender spinach leaves and a garlicky dressing separately, then tosses them together at the park (above).

A food lovers' picnic

Neighbors rise above the hectic times to meet—every week—over strategically simple potluck fare

BY ANDREW BAKER
AND ELAINE JOHNSON

PHOTOGRAPHS BY
FRANCE RUFFENACH

Every Thursday through the summer, Christina Ricci and about 25 of her neighbors in Albany, California, head to the local park for dinner. The kids play, the grown-ups talk, and everyone eats great home-made food—just like in the good ol' days. What's remarkable in *these* days is that this group of friends, who are just as busy as you and I are, have been gathering weekly from May into October for four years.

The weekly picnic tradition was Ricci's response to the realization that summers just didn't feel as special as they did when she was growing up. The park offered space for a large number of people (and diversion for the younger set), and sharing dishes kept the com-

mitment light. "Everybody came, and kept coming," Ricci remembers.

Over the years, plans and preparations have been streamlined to accommodate tight schedules. The group chooses recipes that can be either made ahead or pulled together quickly after work or soccer practice. (See the box on page 221 for some helpful potluck picnic strategies.)

"The picnics really fit our lifestyle," says Ricci. "Some Thursdays there are only three or four families. Other evenings there's a real crowd—even visiting relatives. If it's been a hectic week, some come empty-handed. They know it's all right to just show up—there will be ample food, and *they* might carry the ball next time."

In fact, now the potlucks just fall together. "We know more or less what everyone's going to bring," Ricci says. "I

make spinach salad almost every week. A couple of people always bring kids' food. It's a very low-maintenance thing."

At the same time, the weekly gatherings have become highly important to these neighbors otherwise isolated by urban work patterns. "It makes you feel like you have a big community," says Ricci, "a big group of people who are part of your life." Satisfying results from such a simple plan.

Chutney Mustard for Sausages

PREP TIME: About 10 minutes

NOTES: If making up to 1 day ahead (and to transport), cover and chill. Serve with 1 pound cooked chicken-apple sausages (minisausages, or large sausages cut into 1-in. pieces), warm or at room temperature.

MAKES: About ⅔ cup; 8 servings

In a bowl, mix ¼ cup **Major Grey chutney** (chop pieces if they are large),

2 tablespoons **Dijon mustard,** 2 tablespoons **coarse-grain mustard,** 2 tablespoons minced **green onion,** and 2 teaspoons **honey,** or to taste.

Per tablespoon: 35 cal., 0% (0 cal.) from fat; 0 g protein; 0 g fat; 6.8 g carbo (0 g fiber); 176 mg sodium; 0 mg chol.

Sweet-Spiced Yogurt Dip for Fruit

PREP TIME: About 10 minutes

NOTES: Kathy Sprague brings this appetizer because "kids love dipping." If making sauce up to 1 day ahead (and to transport), cover and chill. Serve with a total of 4 cups cut-up fruit—banana, cantaloupe, honeydew melon, pineapple, and/or rinsed strawberries.

MAKES: About 1 cup; 8 servings

In a bowl, mix ½ cup **vanilla-flavor nonfat yogurt,** ½ cup **reduced-fat sour cream,** 1 to 2 tablespoons firmly packed **brown sugar,** and ¼ teaspoon **ground cinnamon.**

Per tablespoon: 22 cal., 41% (9 cal.) from fat; 0.9 g protein; 1 g fat (0.5 g sat.); 2.5 g carbo (0 g fiber); 9.3 mg sodium; 2.7 mg chol.

Cocktail Sauce for Shrimp

PREP TIME: About 5 minutes

NOTES: If making dip up to 1 week ahead (and to transport), cover and chill. Christina Ricci serves it with 1 pound (30 to 35 per lb.) cooked shrimp.

MAKES: ½ to ⅔ cup; 8 servings

In a bowl, mix ⅓ cup **catsup** and 2 to 4 tablespoons **prepared cream-style horseradish,** to taste.

Per tablespoon: 12 cal., 0% (0 cal.) from fat; 0.2 g protein; 0 g fat; 3.1 g carbo (0.2 g fiber); 121 mg sodium; 0 mg chol.

Spinach Salad

PREP TIME: About 25 minutes

NOTES: This salad is Christina Ricci's weekly offering. For the picnic, mix dressing in a jar, close lid tightly, and carry along. Put remaining ingredients in the salad bowl, cover, and chill en route. Add dressing and mix to serve.

MAKES: 8 servings

6 tablespoons **basil-flavor** or regular **olive oil**

3 tablespoons **balsamic vinegar**

1 teaspoon minced or pressed **garlic**

3 quarts (10 to 12 oz.) **washed spinach leaves,** stems removed

3 hard-cooked **large eggs**

1½ cups **garlic-flavor croutons**

¾ cup **finely shredded parmesan cheese**

Salt and **pepper**

1. In a large bowl, mix olive oil, vinegar, and garlic. Add spinach.

2. Shred or finely chop eggs. Scatter eggs, croutons, and cheese onto spinach.

3. Mix salad, adding salt and pepper to taste.

Per serving: 185 cal., 73% (135 cal.) from fat; 7.2 g protein; 15 g fat (3.5 g sat.); 6.2 g carbo (1.2 g fiber); 231 mg sodium; 86 mg chol.

Potluck picnic savvy

■ Choose dishes that can be either made ahead or assembled at the last minute, and that taste good at room temperature.

■ Supplement with buy-and-serve items like breads, cheeses, olives, pickled vegetables, fruit, deli salads, or selections from a market's salad bar.

■ Keep a picnic bag, basket, or box packed with basic supplies: plates, cutlery, cups, napkins, tablecloth, bottled water or other beverages, salt, pepper, sugar, paper towels, moist wipes, and trash bags. Include a thermos and insulated bags for hot and cold items. Store a supply of frozen gel packs in the freezer to keep foods cold for transport; return the packs to the freezer when you get home.

■ Foods that are transported cold or hot can stand on the table up to two hours.

■ To serve eight, you'll need one appetizer, one salad, one entrée, and one dessert. For 16: two of each item. For 24: three of each.

■ Allow one bottle of wine for three or four adults. (Barry Snyder sets a $10-per-bottle limit to encourage lighthearted experimentation in the spirit of the picnic.) Have a couple of bottled soft drinks each for kids and adults not drinking wine.

Green Beans with Balsamic Sauce

PREP AND COOK TIME: About 30 minutes

NOTES: Kris Cardall carries the nuts in an airtight container, and the chilled beans with dressing in an insulated bag. If cooking beans up to 1 day ahead, cover and chill.

MAKES: 8 servings

1½ pounds **green beans**

⅓ cup **sliced almonds**

1 tablespoon **olive oil**

⅓ cup finely chopped **shallots** or onion

¼ cup **balsamic vinegar**

4 teaspoons **sugar**

1½ teaspoons **fresh tarragon** leaves or dried tarragon

Salt

1. Remove and discard ends and strings from beans. Rinse and drain beans. In a 5- to 6-quart pan over high heat, bring 3 quarts water to a boil. Add beans and cook until tender-crisp when pierced, about 6 minutes. Drain and immerse in ice water until cold, about 12 minutes. Drain again.

2. In the same pan over medium-high heat, stir or shake almonds until lightly browned, 1 to 2 minutes. Pour nuts from pan.

3. Add oil and shallots to pan. Stir often over medium-high heat until shallots are limp, about 2 minutes. Add vinegar, sugar, and tarragon. Boil over high heat until reduced to ¼ cup, 3 to 4 minutes.

4. Add beans to sauce, stir until hot, and pour into a bowl. Serve hot or at room temperature, sprinkling with nuts and adding salt to taste.

Per serving: 75 cal., 45% (34 cal.) from fat; 2.3 g protein; 3.8 g fat (0.4 g sat.); 9.6 g carbo (1.6 g fiber); 6.2 mg sodium; 0 mg chol.

Jicama-Cucumber Tabbouleh

PREP AND COOK TIME: About 35 minutes

NOTES: Susan Smith likes to bring this durable, easy-to-make salad. If making up to 1 day ahead, cover and chill. For best crunch, cut the jicama, cucumber, and tomato into ¼- to ½-inch pieces.

MAKES: About 6 cups; 8 servings

3 cups fat-skimmed **chicken broth**

1½ cups **bulgur wheat**

½ cup minced **Italian parsley**

1 cup diced peeled **jicama**

1 cup diced peeled **cucumber**

1 cup diced **firm-ripe tomato**

½ cup **lemon juice**

¼ cup **olive oil**

Salt and **pepper**

1. In a 2- to 3-quart pan over high heat, bring broth to a boil. Add bulgur, cover, and remove from heat. Let stand until bulgur is tender to bite, about 10 minutes. Drain and reserve liquid.

2. Pour bulgur into a wide bowl and let cool to room temperature, 10 to 15 minutes. Add parsley, jicama, cucumber, tomato, lemon juice, and oil; mix and add reserved liquid to moisten to taste. Serve at room temperature or chilled. Add salt and pepper to taste.

Per serving: 180 cal., 36% (65 cal.) from fat; 6.7 g protein; 7.2 g fat (1 g sat.); 24 g carbo (6.1 g fiber); 41 mg sodium; 0 mg chol.

Lentil–Goat Cheese Salad

PREP AND COOK TIME: About 1¾ hours

NOTES: The original model for Robert Uomini's salad came from Alice Waters's *Chez Panisse Menu Cookbook*. He uses green lentils (also called French or Le Puy), but regular (brown) lentils work, too. If cooking lentils up to 2 days ahead, pour into bowl and season; cover and chill. When cool, add toppings, cover, and transport chilled.

MAKES: 8 servings

2 cups (1 lb.) **dried lentils** (see notes)

1 cup finely chopped **onion**

1 cup diced (¼ in.) peeled **carrot**

½ cup diced (¼ in.) **celery**

4 teaspoons minced **garlic**

About ½ teaspoon **salt**

¼ cup **extra-virgin olive oil**

¼ cup **red wine vinegar**

⅔ cup **fresh chèvre** (goat) **cheese,** crumbled

⅓ cup thinly sliced **green onions** (including tops)

⅓ cup chopped **Italian parsley**

⅓ cup chopped **fresh basil** leaves

Pepper

1. Sort lentils and discard debris. Rinse, drain, and put in a 4- to 5-quart pan. Add onion, carrot, celery, garlic, ½ teaspoon salt, and 1 quart water. Bring to a boil over high heat; reduce heat, cover, and simmer until lentils are tender to bite, about 30 minutes.

2. Drain liquid from lentil mixture and save. Pour lentil mixture into a bowl and

stir in oil and vinegar. Let stand until cool, 45 to 50 minutes; stir occasionally. Add reserved cooking liquid, and mix.

3. Arrange the cheese, onions, parsley, and basil in decorative bands on lentils.

4. To serve, mix and season to taste with salt and pepper.

Per serving: 348 cal., 36% (126 cal.) from fat; 21 g protein; 14 g fat (5.5 g sat.); 38 g carbo (7.7 g fiber); 274 mg sodium; 17 mg chol.

Teriyaki Steak Sandwich Platter

PREP AND COOK TIME: About 2 hours

NOTES: When Kris Cardall has time, she marinates the steak up to 1 day ahead in the refrigerator. She grills the steak and mushrooms the day of the picnic and, if her schedule permits, chills them before transporting. She puts the crisped lettuce and other salad ingredients in individual heavy plastic food bags and the dressing in a jar, transports them in an insulated bag, then assembles everything on a platter at the party.

MAKES: 8 servings

⅓ cup **soy sauce**

2 tablespoons **salad oil**

2 tablespoons firmly packed **brown sugar**

1 tablespoon **dry sherry**

1 tablespoon minced **fresh ginger**

1 tablespoon minced **garlic**

1 **beef flank steak** (1½ lb.), fat-trimmed

4 **portabella mushroom caps** (about 4 in. wide; ¾ lb. total), rinsed and drained

1 head **romaine lettuce** (1 lb.), rinsed and crisped

1½ pounds **firm-ripe tomatoes** (1 or more colors), rinsed, cored, and sliced ¼ inch thick

1 **English cucumber** (⅔ lb.), rinsed and sliced ¼ inch thick

¾ cup **crumbled blue cheese**

3 tablespoons **olive oil**

3 tablespoons **balsamic vinegar**

8 **pocket breads** (6 in. wide)

Salt and **pepper**

1. In a 1-gallon heavy plastic food bag, combine soy sauce, salad oil, sugar, sherry, ginger, and garlic. Rinse flank steak, add to bag, seal, and set in a bowl. Chill at least 1 hour and up to 1 day, occasionally turning bag over.

2. Lightly oil a barbecue grill over a solid bed of medium-hot coals or a gas grill on medium-high heat (you can hold your hand at grill level only 3 to 4 seconds).

BALSAMIC-DRESSED GREEN BEANS and mushroom lasagna are posh picnic fare.

Lift steak from marinade and lay on grill. Coat each mushroom with marinade and lay, gills down, on grill; discard remaining marinade. Close lid on gas grill. After 5 minutes, turn meat and mushrooms over, and continue to cook until meat is done to your taste—5 to 7 minutes more for medium-rare (cut to center of thickest part to test)—and mushrooms are flexible, 5 to 7 minutes more.

3. Transfer steak and mushrooms to a cutting board. Let cool at least 10 minutes; or cover and chill meat and mushrooms up to 8 hours. Cut steak in half lengthwise, then cut crosswise into slanting ⅛- to ¼-inch-thick slices. Cut mushrooms into ¼-inch-thick slices. Save juices from meat and mushrooms.

4. Line a large platter with romaine leaves. Arrange steak in the center and surround with mushrooms, tomatoes, and cucumber. Scatter cheese over vegetables.

5. In a jar with a lid, or in a bowl, mix olive oil, vinegar, and any meat and mushroom juices.

6. Pour oil and vinegar dressing over vegetables. Cut pocket breads in half. To eat, fill pockets with meat and vegetables, adding salt and pepper to taste.

Per serving: 468 cal., 37% (171 cal.) from fat; 29 g protein; 19 g fat (6.3 g sat.); 45 g carbo (3.9 g fiber); 1,077 mg sodium; 52 mg chol.

Asian Chicken Salad

PREP AND COOK TIME: About 25 minutes
NOTES: This quick main-dish salad is Edith Muroga Morrow's specialty. A purchased cooked chicken (1½ to 2 lb.) yields enough meat to make it. If making up to 1 day ahead (and to transport), seal chicken and water chestnuts with seasonings in a heavy plastic food bag; in separate bags, seal salad mix, salad mix noodles, and nuts. Chill, and carry chilled. Mix at the picnic.

If you can't locate Asian salad mix, use a combination of shredded iceberg lettuce, shredded cabbage, and shredded carrots (8 cups total); add 1 cup canned chow mein noodles.

MAKES: 8 servings

   3   to 4 cups boned, skinned **cooked chicken** (see notes)

   1   can (8 oz.) **sliced water chestnuts,** drained

   ⅓   cup **seasoned rice vinegar**

   3   tablespoons **soy sauce**

READY FOR DESSERT: This berry-stuffed angel food cake can be made a day ahead.

   1½   tablespoons **Asian** (toasted) **sesame oil**

   2   teaspoons **sugar**

   1½   teaspoons **hot chili oil**

   2   packages (10 oz. each) **Asian salad mix with chow mein noodles**

   ½   cup **salted, roasted cashews**

1. Tear chicken into ½-inch chunks. Place in a large bowl and add water chestnuts, vinegar, soy sauce, sesame oil, sugar, and hot chili oil. Mix.

2. Set aside noodles; rinse and drain salad mix. Add salad mix, noodles, and cashews to bowl, and mix.

Per serving: 323 cal., 53% (171 cal.) from fat; 19 g protein; 19 g fat (3.6 g sat.); 19 g carbo (2.8 g fiber); 986 mg sodium; 47 mg chol.

Three-Mushroom Lasagna

PREP AND COOK TIME: About 1¾ hours
NOTES: Edith Muroga Morrow often brings lasagna. If making up to 1 day ahead, assemble through step 7; cover and chill. To heat, cover tightly with foil and bake for 30 minutes; uncover and bake until hot in the center, about 30 minutes longer. Seal casserole in foil again and transport in an insulated bag or container.

MAKES: 8 servings

   ½   cup (½ oz.) **dried porcini mushrooms**

   1   pound **common mushrooms**

   ½   pound **fresh chanterelle mushrooms** (or additional common mushrooms)

   2½   cups chopped **onions**

   1   tablespoon minced **garlic**

   3   tablespoons **butter** or margarine

   ¾   cup **dry white wine**

   1   jar (7 to 8 oz.) **roasted red peppers,** drained and coarsely chopped

   1   package (8 oz.) **dried lasagna**

   ⅓   cup **all-purpose flour**

   ¼   teaspoon **ground nutmeg**

   1½   cups fat-skimmed **chicken broth**

   1   cup **low-fat milk**

   3½   cups (about ¾ lb.) **shredded parmesan cheese**

1. In a small bowl, combine porcini and ¾ cup hot water; let stand until mushrooms are soft, 15 to 20 minutes. Squeeze porcini gently in water to release grit, then lift out and squeeze dry; reserve liquid. Chop porcini.

2. Meanwhile, rinse and drain common and chanterelle mushrooms; trim and discard discolored stem ends, spots, and debris. Chop ½ the common mushrooms. Slice remaining common and the chanterelle mushrooms ⅓ inch thick.

3. In a 5- to 6-quart pan over high heat, frequently stir porcini, common, and chanterelle mushrooms with 1½ cups onions, garlic, and 1 tablespoon butter until liquid evaporates and mushrooms are well browned, about 15 minutes.

4. Carefully pour most of the porcini soaking liquid into pan, discarding remainder with sediment. Stir in wine and red peppers. Boil mushroom mixture over high heat, stirring occasionally, until reduced to 4 cups, 2 to 5 minutes.

5. Meanwhile, in a 6- to 8-quart pan over high heat, bring 3 quarts water to a boil. Add lasagna and stir occasionally until tender to bite, 10 to 15 minutes. Drain and immerse in cold water until cool, about 2 minutes; drain again.

6. In the same pan over medium-high heat, combine remaining butter and onions; stir often until onions are limp, 5 to 8 minutes. Add flour and nutmeg and stir for 1 minute. Whisk in broth and milk. Stir until boiling. Remove from heat and stir in 2 cups cheese.

7. In a 9- by 13-inch pan, layer ⅓ of the cheese sauce, ⅓ of the noodles, and ½ the mushroom mixture. Repeat layers, then top with remaining noodles and cheese sauce. Sprinkle with remaining parmesan.

8. Bake in a 375° oven until hot in the center (cut to test), 30 to 35 minutes.

9. Let cool about 10 minutes. Cut portions and lift out with a wide spatula.

Per serving: 402 cal., 40% (162 cal.) from fat; 23 g protein; 18 g fat (12 g sat.); 38 g carbo (3.3 g fiber); 384 mg sodium; 50 mg chol.

Overnight Blackberry Cream Cake

PREP AND COOK TIME: About 20 minutes, plus at least 2 hours to chill

NOTES: If making up to 1 day ahead, cover and chill. Dust with powdered sugar, wrap, and transport chilled. Carry berry sauce in a jar. At the picnic, garnish cake with mint sprigs and more berries.

MAKES: 8 servings

    1 angel food cake (about 8 in. wide; 1⅔ lb.)
    6 cups blackberries, rinsed and drained
    ⅔ cup granulated sugar
    1½ teaspoons grated lemon peel
    1½ cups blueberries, rinsed and drained
    ¾ cup whipping cream
       Powdered sugar

1. With a long serrated knife, cut off top ¾ inch of cake horizontally. Lift top off and set aside. Cutting down into, but not through, cake, make a ¾-inch-thick rim around center and outer edges of cake. Pull cake from center in chunks. Tear cake chunks into 1-inch pieces and place in a bowl.

2. In a 3- to 4-quart pan over medium heat, frequently stir blackberries and granulated sugar until mixture is boiling, 5 to 10 minutes. Rub through a fine strainer into another bowl; discard

seeds. Cover and chill 1 cup of the strained berry sauce.

3. Pour remaining sauce over cake chunks. Stir in lemon peel and blueberries.

4. In bowl used for berry sauce (no need to wash), with a mixer on high speed, whip cream until it holds soft peaks. Fold cream into berry-cake mixture.

5. Set cake, hollowed-out side up, on a rimmed platter. Spoon all the cream mixture into cake cavity, spreading evenly. Set cake top in place. Gently pat cake to make sides and top straight and even. Wrap airtight and chill at least 2 hours and up to 1 day.

6. Unwrap cake and dust liberally with powdered sugar. Cut into thick slices and serve with reserved berry sauce.

Per serving: 454 cal., 16% (74 cal.) from fat; 7 g protein; 8.2 g fat (4.4 g sat.); 92 g carbo (6.9 g fiber); 719 mg sodium; 24 mg chol.

Brown Butter Chocolate Brownies

PREP AND COOK TIME: About 1 hour

NOTES: Use extra-large or regular chocolate chips. If making up to 1 day ahead, let brownies cool in pan, wrap airtight, and let stand at room temperature.

MAKES: 8 pieces

       About ¼ cup (⅛ lb.) butter or margarine
    1 cup firmly packed brown sugar
    1 large egg
    1 teaspoon vanilla
    1 teaspoon baking powder
    ¼ teaspoon salt
       About 1 cup all-purpose flour
    1 cup (6 oz.) semisweet chocolate chips (see notes)
    ¾ cup coarsely chopped walnuts

1. In a 2- to 3-quart pan over medium-high heat, melt ¼ cup butter until it begins to brown, 3 to 5 minutes (if using margarine, melt but do not brown). Let cool, 20 to 25 minutes.

2. Add sugar, egg, vanilla, baking powder, and salt; stir to mix well. Add 1 cup flour and stir until incorporated; mixture will be stiff. Stir in ½ the chocolate and ½ the nuts.

3. Butter and flour an 8-inch square pan. Spread batter level in pan; sprinkle with remaining chocolate and nuts.

4. Bake in a 350° oven until edges begin to pull from pan sides and brownies are firm to touch in the center, about 30

minutes (25 minutes in a convection oven).

5. Cool in pan on a rack at least 30 minutes. Cut into 8 equal pieces. Serve warm or cool.

Per piece: 404 cal., 45% (180 cal.) from fat; 5 g protein; 20 g fat (8.2 g sat.); 56 g carbo (1 g fiber); 219 mg sodium; 44 mg chol.

Apple-Pecan Noodle Kugel

PREP AND COOK TIME: About 1½ hours

NOTES: Helene Class uses her mother's recipe for this dish. Transport hot or chilled.

MAKES: 8 servings

    ½   pound dried wide egg noodles
    2   Granny Smith apples (1 lb. total), rinsed
    1   package (3 oz.) cream cheese
    ¼   cup granulated sugar
    1   carton (½ lb.; 2 cups) nonfat cottage cheese
    3   large eggs
    ¾   cup milk
    1½ teaspoons ground cinnamon
    ½   cup raisins
    ¼   cup (⅛ lb.) melted butter or margarine
    ¼   cup pecan halves
    ¼   cup firmly packed brown sugar

1. In a 5- to 6-quart pan over high heat, bring 3 quarts water to a boil. Add noodles, stir, and cook until tender to bite, about 8 minutes. Drain and immerse in cold water until cool, about 2 minutes. Drain again.

2. Meanwhile, core and shred apples.

3. In a large bowl with a mixer, beat cream cheese with sugar. Add cottage cheese, eggs, milk, and 1 teaspoon cinnamon. Beat to blend. Add noodles, shredded apples, raisins, and 3 tablespoons butter; stir to mix.

4. Rub sides and bottom of a 9-inch square pan with remaining butter. Add noodle mixture and spread level.

5. Mix remaining ½ teaspoon cinnamon with pecans and brown sugar. Sprinkle evenly over noodle mixture.

6. Bake in a 350° oven until top is golden brown, about 45 minutes (about 35 minutes in a convection oven). Cool at least 10 minutes. Serve warm or at room temperature, cut into rectangles.

Per serving: 390 cal., 37% (144 cal.) from fat; 12 g protein; 16 g fat (7.6 g sat.); 52 g carbo (2.6 g fiber); 238 mg sodium; 140 mg chol. ◆

The Low-Fat Cook

HEALTHY CHOICES FOR THE ACTIVE LIFESTYLE

BY ANDREW BAKER

POTATOES and sausage stack up surprisingly lean in this frittata.

TUCKER & HOSSLER

The myth about eggs

■ The name *frittata* hardly evokes low-fat images. For one thing, its basic ingredients are eggs and cheese—no lean reputations there. Then the whole thing is cooked up in a frying pan; visions of oil and butter follow.

Yet shattering stereotypes and shedding fat is actually easy for this versatile omelet. First, let a nonstick frying pan—not oil or butter—release the eggs effortlessly.

Reduce the fat in the mixture by combining whole eggs and egg whites. Include nonfat milk to keep the dish moist. And cook any added vegetables in broth or water.

These flavorful low-fat frittatas even include sausage, crab, and chicken—indulgences calculated to keep the illusion of richness alive.

Turkey Sausage Frittata

PREP AND COOK TIME: About 55 minutes
MAKES: 4 servings

- 1 cup thinly sliced **red onion**
- 2 tablespoons **distilled white vinegar**
- ½ pound **red thin-skinned potatoes**
- 1 cup fat-skimmed **chicken broth**
- 5 **large eggs**
- 5 **large egg** whites
- ½ cup **nonfat milk**
- 2 tablespoons minced **parsley**
- ¼ pound diced **cooked fat-free sausage** such as turkey kielbasa (Polish) sausage
- 2 tablespoons **shredded** or grated **parmesan cheese**

1. In a 10- to 12-inch ovenproof nonstick frying pan, combine onion, vinegar, and 2 cups water. Stir often over high heat until liquid is evaporated and onion is limp, 20 to 25 minutes. Remove onion from pan.

2. Meanwhile, scrub potatoes and cut into ½-inch chunks. Add potatoes and broth to pan. Stir often over high heat until potatoes are tender when pierced, 12 to 15 minutes.

3. In a bowl, beat eggs, egg whites, and milk to blend; stir in parsley.

4. Turn heat to medium and pour egg mixture into pan; add onion and sausage. As egg mixture sets on pan bottom, push aside with a wide spatula to let liquid flow down. Cook until frittata is set to the middle but still slightly liquid on top, 3 to 5 minutes. Sprinkle with cheese.

5. Set pan in a 350° oven and bake until top of frittata is firm when pressed and bottom is set (lift with a small spatula to check), 8 to 12 minutes.

6. Cut into wedges and serve.

Per serving: 241 cal., 28% (67 cal.) from fat; 23 g protein; 7.4 g fat (2.5 g sat.); 20 g carbo (1.7 g fiber); 588 mg sodium; 281 mg chol.

Crab and potato frittata. Follow directions for **turkey sausage frittata,** preceding, but omit sausage. Instead, use ⅓ pound **shelled cooked crab.** Remove any bits of shell from crab.

Per serving: 249 cal., 29% (72 cal.) from fat; 26 g protein; 8 g fat (2.6 g sat.); 17 g carbo (1.7 g fiber); 353 mg sodium; 306 mg chol.

Chicken chilaquiles frittata. Stack 4 **fat-free corn tortillas** (6 in.) and cut into ¼- by 2-inch strips. In a 10- to 12-inch ovenproof nonstick frying pan over high heat, stir tortillas until crisp, about 5 minutes. In a bowl, beat 5 **large eggs,** 5 **large egg** whites, and ½ cup **nonfat milk** to blend; stir in 2 tablespoons minced **parsley.** Turn heat to medium and pour egg mixture into pan; add 1 cup shredded skinned **cooked chicken breast,** 1 can (7 oz.) **diced green chilies,** and ½ cup chopped **green onions.** Cook as directed for turkey sausage frittata, step 4 (above). Sprinkle with 2 tablespoons **shredded reduced-fat jack cheese** and bake as directed in step 5. Cut into wedges and serve with ½ to 1 cup **tomatillo salsa.**

Per serving: 270 cal., 30% (80 cal.) from fat; 27 g protein; 8.9 g fat (2.8 g sat.); 20 g carbo (2.2 g fiber); 762 mg sodium; 298 mg chol. ◆

foodguide

BY JERRY ANNE DI VECCHIO

PHOTOGRAPHS BY JAMES CARRIER

Barbecue a cross-rib roast

A braising cut
breaks out of the pan

■ The beef shoulder, or chuck, gets lots of use, so the muscles in it—albeit flavorful—are well developed; they usually do best when braised until tender. But there's one chuck cut I consider a choice contender for the barbecue: a boned beef cross-rib roast. Cooked just to rare or medium-rare, it delivers the chuck's rich taste with succulence (roasted longer, the lean roast gets dry and chewy). According to meat authorities, the cross rib comes from the arm half of a square-cut chuck. This bare-bones fact can be helpful when you shop, because the cross rib has other poetic but unapproved (by the meat industry) names: boneless Boston cut, boneless English roast, or English roll. Regardless, it's a fairly inexpensive roast, easy to carve, and marvelous with curried potatoes.

Cross-Rib Roast with Curried Potatoes

PREP AND COOK TIME: About 2 hours

NOTES: Cook the potatoes while the roast is on the barbecue.

MAKES: 8 servings, plus left-over meat

1   **boned, tied beef cross-rib roast** (about 4 lb.)

3   tablespoons **soy sauce**

2   tablespoons **Worcestershire**

2   tablespoons **brown sugar**

1   tablespoon **dry mustard**

2   teaspoons **fresh thyme** leaves or dried thyme

Curried potatoes (recipe follows)

Salt

1. Rinse meat and pat dry. In a deep bowl, mix soy sauce, Worcestershire, brown sugar, mustard, and thyme. Add beef and turn to coat. Cover and chill at least 1 hour and up to 24 hours, turning meat occasionally.

2. Ignite 70 charcoal briquets on the firegrate of a barbecue with a lid. When coals are spotted with gray ash, in about 20 minutes, push equal amounts to opposite sides of firegrate. Add 10 more briquets to each mound of coals now and every 30 minutes of cooking. Or turn gas barbecue to high, cover, and heat 10 minutes, then adjust for indirect cooking.

3. Lift meat from marinade; discard liquid. Set meat on center of grill, not directly over heat. Cover barbecue (open vents for charcoal). Cook until a thermometer inserted in the center of the thickest part registers 130° for rare, 50 minutes to 1 hour, or 135° for medium-rare, 1 to 1¼ hours.

4. Set meat on a carving board and let rest at least 20 minutes. Slice, and serve with curried potatoes. Season to taste with salt.

Per serving of beef: 418 cal., 62% (261 cal.) from fat; 34 g protein; 29 g fat (11 g sat.); 2.9 g carbo (0 g fiber); 330 mg sodium; 120 mg chol.

Curried potatoes. Scrub 3 pounds **thin-skinned potatoes** (about 1½ in. wide), and bring 3 quarts **water** to a boil in a 4- to 5-quart pan over high heat. Add potatoes, cover, and simmer until tender when pierced, 20 to 30 minutes. Drain and let cool at least 15 minutes or until roast is cooked.

While the roast rests, cut potatoes into quarters. Melt ¼ cup (⅛ lb.) **butter** or margarine with 2 tablespoons **olive oil** in a 12- to 14-inch frying pan over high heat.

Add potatoes and turn often with a wide spatula until they are just beginning to brown, 6 to 8 minutes. Reduce heat to medium and push potatoes to sides of pan. In the center of the pan, stir 2 tablespoons **curry powder** and 1 tablespoon **mustard seed** about 30 seconds, then mix with potatoes. Add 2 cups chopped **green onions** (including tops) and mix until hot, about 2 minutes.

Per serving: 240 cal., 38% (90 cal.) from fat; 4.3 g protein; 10 g fat (4.2 g sat.); 34 g carbo (4.2 g fiber); 79 mg sodium; 16 mg chol.

Seeds of change

■ Nothing is new under the sun, but sometimes the word is slow to circulate. For years, to avoid stains and spatters when peeling a pomegranate, I've scored the thick skin, then held the fruit underwater in a bowl to break it apart and rub the edible seeds free. But a Persian friend showed me an old trick that speeds up the process. It's surprisingly neat, but working in a deep bowl is still a wise precaution.

Cut the pomegranate in half with a sharp knife **(a)**. Along the cut edge of each half, make 4 equally spaced vertical cuts ¾ to 1 inch long and deep **(b)**. Hold a pomegranate half, seeds down, over a deep bowl and pull the fruit open but not apart, using equal pressure from both hands **(c)**. Holding the pomegranate half, seeds down, in the palm of one hand, whack the top of the fruit with the back of a large spoon **(d)**. The seeds will just fall out **(e)**.

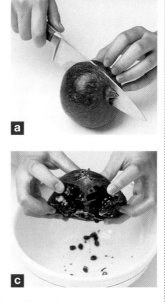

A zippy Asian herb

■ Rau ram (pronounced rau-*room*) is also known as Vietnamese coriander or mint. But the herb (*Polygonum odoratum*) is actually a member of the buckwheat family. To my palate, rau ram resembles a blend of coriander and purple basil, with a unique electric zing and curiously pleasant aftereffect. It's a taste adventure to seek out in Southeast Asian markets, many farmers' markets, and, sometimes, supermarkets.

Rau Ram Chicken Salad

PREP AND COOK TIME: About 20 minutes
NOTES: Garnish this Vietnamese-style salad with rau ram leaves or sprigs. If you can't find this herb, season the salad with 2 tablespoons *each* chopped fresh basil (green or purple) leaves and fresh cilantro.
MAKES: 4 servings

- 6 ounces **dried capellini pasta**
- 2 cups **boned, skinned cooked chicken**
- ⅓ cup **seasoned rice vinegar**
   About 2 tablespoons **Asian fish sauce** (*nuoc mam* or *nam pla*)
- 1½ tablespoons minced **fresh ginger**
- 2 to 3 tablespoons chopped **fresh rau ram**
- ½ cup chopped **salted roasted peanuts**

1. In a 4- to 5-quart pan over high heat, bring 2 quarts water to a boil. Add the pasta, stir, and cook until tender to bite, 5 to 6 minutes. Drain, immerse in cold water until cool, about 3 minutes, and then drain again.

2. Meanwhile, tear chicken into shreds and place in a bowl. Add vinegar, fish sauce, ginger, cool noodles, and 2 tablespoons rau ram. Mix, and add more rau ram to taste. Mound salad onto plates and sprinkle equally with peanuts.

Per serving: 433 cal., 33% (144 cal.) from fat; 32 g protein; 16 g fat (2.9 g sat.); 41 g carbo (2.8 g fiber); 831 mg sodium; 62 mg chol.

Cheese in the news

■ Chef Gayle Tanner baked the unique cheesecake that took first place at a recent Quady Winery dessert pairing competition. As judges, we were captivated by its refreshing tang, which came from fresh goat cheese. Tanner's recipe specifies a mild one. A kinder, gentler goat cheese the Norwegians have recently sent us is perfect. Soft, white, delicately tart Snofrisk (*snow fresh* in Norwegian) is made with 80 percent goat's milk and 20 percent cow's cream. It's available at supermarkets in 4.4-ounce triangular plastic tubs, priced comparably to fresh chèvre cheeses. This cheesecake—lighter and more cakelike than most versions—made with Snofrisk, will convert all those who think *mild goat cheese* is an oxymoron.

Tanner Cheesecake

PREP AND COOK TIME: 1¼ hours, plus 2 hours to chill
MAKES: 8 or 9 servings

- 2 cups **orange muscat wine,** such as Essencia, or 2 tablespoons *each* thawed frozen orange juice concentrate and water
- 3 packages (4.4 oz. each) **fresh cheese made with goat's milk and cow's cream,** or 11 ounces fresh chèvre (goat) cheese or cream cheese
- About ¾ cup **sugar**
- 3 tablespoons **all-purpose flour**
- 1 teaspoon grated **orange** peel
- 1 teaspoon **vanilla**
- 6 **large eggs,** separated

1. In a 3- to 4-quart pan over high heat, boil wine until reduced to ¼ cup (add water if reduced too much; if using orange juice concentrate, mix with water but do not reduce). In a bowl, with a mixer, beat reduced wine, cheese, ¼ cup sugar, flour, orange peel, and vanilla until well blended.

2. Butter a 9-inch cheesecake pan with removable rim; dust pan with sugar.

3. Put egg whites in a large, deep bowl and yolks in the cheese mixture. Beat cheese mixture. Wash beaters.

4. Whip egg whites on high speed until thick and foamy. Gradually add ½ cup sugar and continue to beat until whites hold soft, round peaks, 1 to 2 minutes longer.

5. Fold into cheese mixture. Scrape batter into pan.

6. Bake in a 325° oven until cake just begins to pull from pan sides and jiggles but isn't soupy in center when pan is gently shaken, 35 to 45 minutes (30 to 35 minutes in a convection oven). Cool on a rack (cake settles) about 1 hour; cover and chill until cold, at least 1 hour and up to 2 days. Remove pan rim.

Per serving: 265 cal., 54% (144 cal.) from fat; 7.5 g protein; 16 g fat (6.6 g sat.); 30 g carbo (0.1 g fiber); 303 mg sodium; 165 mg chol.

Measured steps

■ They say anyone can follow a recipe. But even experienced cooks know things don't always work out. Often the problem lies in how the ingredients are measured—and what they're measured in.

•**Clear cups,** with pour spouts, are primarily for liquids. They come in multiple-quart and 1-, 2-, and 4-cup sizes, with measurements marked on the sides. Set on a level surface and pour in ingredients; read markings at eye level. The larger sizes also work well for chunky foods like vegetables (cherry tomatoes, broccoli florets, hunks of squash), cut-up fruit, and berries.

•**Metal or plastic cups,** for measuring dry ingredients, come in sets of ¼, ⅓, ½, and 1 cup; some sets also include a ⅛-cup or 2-cup or larger unit. Fill to the brim and scrape the ingredient level with a spatula or straight-sided knife. How you fill the cup depends on the ingredient. Pour or spoon in granulated sugar, salt, grains, cornmeal, and other substances that don't pack down. Pack in brown sugar, soft cheeses, and solid fats. Spoon or drop in shredded cheeses and leafy vegetables (unless recipe says to pack). To measure fluffy items like flour, powdered sugar, or cornstarch, stir them first, then gently spoon into cup; if you scoop them with the cup or tap it to settle the contents, you can get as much as 25 percent more in the cup.

•**Standard measuring spoons** come in sets of 1 tablespoon, 1, ½, and ¼ teaspoon, and sometimes ⅛ teaspoon. Use these for both liquid and dry ingredients, pouring liquids to the rim and scraping dry ingredients level with rim. ◆

The Wine Guide

BY KAREN MACNEIL-FIFE

RICK MARIANI

A matter of taste

■ The idea that any of us needs to learn how to taste seems almost ludicrous. By adulthood, after all, we've had considerable practice.

But does simply having mastered eating and drinking really mean we know how to taste? I would submit that it doesn't. When it comes to wine, if you don't taste and smell correctly, you miss a lot of delicious pleasure in the glass.

Now I admit that wine tasting seems to invite affectation. But wine-snob exhibitions aside, there is a way of tasting that professionals use to maximize a wine's flavors. Look at the wine. When I first started studying wine 20 years ago, I'd watch the experts examining glasses

so intently you'd think there was buried treasure in them. I'd wonder what they could possibly be looking for.

Primarily color, as it turns out. Color is a clue to the wine's age. White wines get darker as they get older. Red wines do just the opposite; they get lighter.

A MINI WINE COURSE

Compare the pairs. In the "finish" category, which do you think has the longer?

BODY
■ **Bonny Doon Pacific Rim Riesling 1997 (America)**, $9. A super-crisp Riesling, so light-bodied it's almost sheer.

■ **St. Francis "Old Vine" Zinfandel 1997 (Sonoma County)**, $24. Big, exuberant, jamlike fruit gives this wine a round, full body.

MOUTH-FEEL
■ **Covey Run Fumé Blanc 1997 (Washington)**, $7. Zingy, snappy, and tart, this wine has a thirst-quenching texture.

■ **Turnbull Cabernet Sauvignon 1996 (Napa Valley)**, $22. As soft as a blanket, this Cabernet is also packed with juicy red fruits.

FINISH
■ **Domaine Grand Archer Chardonnay 1997 (Sonoma County)**, $15. Beautiful balance, with creamy apple-tart flavors and a (you decide) finish.

■ **Grgich Hills Chardonnay 1996 (Napa Valley)**, $30. The wine equivalent of French vanilla ice cream, with a (you decide) finish.

Color is also a clue to the grape variety. Because the pigments of grape skins differ from variety to variety, so do the ultimate colors of the wines. Pinot Noir grapes make brick-colored wine. Gamay is Jell-O red. Zinfandel can be electric purple, Nebbiolo almost black. Observing the color prepares your mind for the sensory experience to come.

Swirl it. Prove to yourself how critical swirling is: Pour the same wine into two glasses. Swirl one glass; don't swirl the other. See which one you can taste better. I guarantee it's the swirled one.

Swirling "opens up" a wine by mixing it with molecules of oxygen, which makes the flavors and aromas more pronounced. Hence, more pleasure. Almost all wines—whites, reds, rosés—should be swirled before you taste them. The only exceptions are sparkling wines and Champagnes. Swirling these might cause the bubbles to go flat, and the bubbles themselves, rising in the

tall, thin flute, help open up the wine. **Smell it.** Some chemists have suggested that wine is a virtually tasteless liquid that happens to be deeply fragrant. Whether that's true or not, smelling a wine is critical to tasting it. The highly exposed receptor nerve cells in your nose, which absorb every aroma molecule you breathe in, flash information to the olfactory bulb of the brain. If you do not smell a wine, very little information about it goes to your brain.

How do you smell correctly? Get your nose into the glass near the liquid, then take a series of short, quick sniffs. Nothing is achieved by holding your nose 2 inches above the glass and taking one polite whiff. Since the nose fatigues quickly, try to assess the aromas immediately. **Taste it.** A wine's "taste" is made up of body, mouth-feel, and flavor.

The body of a wine is its weight in the mouth. Wines can be light-, medium-, or full-bodied, depending on alcohol content (the more alcohol, the fuller the body). A light-bodied wine, like skim milk, slides easily down your throat. A medium-bodied wine has more viscosity, like whole milk. A full-bodied wine seems to coat your palate, like half-and-half.

A wine's mouth-feel is its texture, or the tactile impression it leaves. Fabrics are often used as metaphors. Wines can be as smooth as silk, as scratchy as wool, or as soft as flannel.

And finally, there's flavor, perceived by taste buds—groups of receptor cells clustered together on your tongue. They can pick up a seemingly infinite number of wine flavors: apples, butterscotch, olives, blackberries, mushrooms—you name it.

The single most important aspect of tasting, however, is simply this: You must hold the wine in your mouth long enough to register an impression—a few seconds, at least. And with great wines, the flavors have an almost magical ability to last and last, even after you've swallowed. This is called a "long finish," and it's one of the most seductive attributes a wine can possess. ◆

Amazing grapes

How sweet the rounds—
and perfect for tucking into
harvest-rich recipes

BY LINDA LAU ANUSASANANAN

PHOTOGRAPHS BY JAMES CARRIER

SALAD ON THE GREEN: Lettuce leaf cradles basil-flecked grapes, pear, and shrimp.

■ Green, red, or bluish black; firm and crisp or soft and sensuous; seeded or seedless—there's a grape to suit every taste. And Western vines are swinging into full production right now.

California supplies 97 percent of the nation's commercially grown table grapes. In 1839 at a pueblo now known as Los Angeles, a trapper from Kentucky, William Wolfskill, planted the first vineyard of grapes designated for eating, not winemaking. Today the state produces as many as 18 major table grape varieties (the photo on page 232 shows just a few), each distinctive and interesting. Starting in late spring, early varieties begin to ripen in the Coachella Valley; then the harvest slowly moves north, ending in the San Joaquin Valley in late fall. High-tech storage keeps some fresh California grapes in the market until February. (Fruit from Chile overlaps in winter and fills in the gaps to make grapes a year-round presence.)

For sweetest flavor, grapes should be picked fully ripe. Their color is a good indication of whether they have been or not. Red grapes should be—well, predominantly red. Blue-black fruit should have a very deep color. Green varieties should be tinged with yellow. Store them unwashed in the refrigerator for several days; rinse shortly before serving.

The diversity that makes grapes perennially interesting to eat plain also makes them widely versatile for cooking. Our recipes show off individual characteristics in unexpected ways, but feel free to substitute similar varieties.

Grape and Pear Salad Cups

PREP TIME: About 25 minutes
NOTES: Use green, red, or dark seedless grapes for this appetizer. To make a dinner salad for 10, combine the fruit mixture with 10 cups rinsed and crisped salad mix. Spoon onto plates.
MAKES: 10 to 12 appetizer servings

1. Rinse 3 cups **seedless grapes** (see notes) and cut in half. Peel 1 **Asian pear** ($\frac{1}{2}$ lb.); cut into matchstick-size pieces.
2. In a bowl, gently mix grapes, pear, $\frac{1}{2}$ cup **seasoned rice vinegar**, $\frac{1}{4}$ cup chopped **fresh basil** leaves, and $\frac{1}{2}$ pound rinsed, drained **shelled cooked tiny shrimp**. Add **salt** to taste.
3. Spoon equally into 30 to 36 rinsed and crisped tender **butter lettuce** leaves and arrange on a platter.

Per serving: 66 cal., 6.8% (4.5 cal.) from fat; 4.6 g protein; 0.5 g fat (0.1 g sat.); 12 g carbo (1.6 g fiber); 242 mg sodium; 37 mg chol.

Grape–Blue Cheese Bites

PREP TIME: About 15 minutes
NOTES: Use large grapes such as Red Globe or Ribier. If making up to 4 hours ahead, cover and chill.
MAKES: 18 pieces; 6 appetizer servings

1. In a bowl, mix 2 tablespoons *each* **whipped cream cheese** and **crumbled blue cheese**.
2. Rinse 18 large **grapes** (about 1 in. long; see notes), drain, and pat dry. From stem end, cut a slit $\frac{3}{4}$ of the way through each grape, leaving opposite end attached. Fill each slit with about $\frac{1}{2}$ teaspoon cheese mixture. Squeeze grape gently so it clings to cheese. Dip cheese edge in minced **salted roasted almonds** or pecans (about 2 tablespoons total).

Per serving: 71 cal., 58% (41 cal.) from fat; 1.9 g protein; 4.5 g fat (1.8 g sat.); 7.4 g carbo (1 g fiber); 79 mg sodium; 7.3 mg chol.

Grape Salsa

PREP TIME: About 15 minutes
NOTES: Green grapes are particularly attractive and fresh-looking in this mixture. If making up to 4 hours ahead, cover and chill. Serve with grilled fish, chicken, pork, ham, or lamb.
MAKES: 2 cups

1. Rinse 2 cups **seedless grapes** (see notes) and cut in half or quarters ($\frac{1}{2}$- to $\frac{3}{4}$-in. pieces).

2. In a bowl, mix the grapes with 3 tablespoons **lime juice**, 2 tablespoons thinly sliced **green onions**, 2 tablespoons chopped **fresh cilantro**, 1 tablespoon minced **fresh ginger**, and 1 to 2 tablespoons minced **fresh jalapeño chili**, to taste.

Per $\frac{1}{4}$ cup: 31 cal., 5.8% (1.8 cal.) from fat; 0.3 g protein; 0.2 g fat (0.1 g sat.); 7.8 g carbo (0.7 g fiber); 2.2 mg sodium; 0 mg chol.

Grilled Grapes in Salami Bonnets

PREP AND COOK TIME: About 10 minutes

NOTES: Use large grapes of any color, rinsed; varieties that work well include Red Globe, Christmas Rose, and Ribier. Soak wood skewers in water at least 30 minutes before using.

MAKES: 12 pieces; 3 or 4 appetizer servings

1. Lay 12 **thin slices dry salami** ($2\frac{1}{2}$ in. wide) flat. Set 1 **grape** ($\frac{3}{4}$ to 1 in. long; see notes) on each slice. Fold salami edges around each grape and run a thin wood skewer through salami on one side, into grape, and out through salami on the other side.

2. Set skewers on a barbecue grill over hot coals or high heat on a gas grill (you can hold your hand at grill level only 2 to 3 seconds); close lid on gas grill. Cook, turning once, until salami is lightly browned, about 3 minutes total.

Per serving: 78 cal., 58% (45 cal.) from fat; 3.4 g protein; 5 g fat (1.8 g sat.); 5.5 g carbo (0.5 g fiber); 264 mg sodium; 11 mg chol.

CONFETTI of fresh ginger, chili, and cilantro jazzes up juicy grape salsa.

Grape–Bulgur Wheat Salad

PREP AND COOK TIME: About 35 minutes

NOTES: Any grape suits this salad.

MAKES: 5 or 6 servings

- 1 cup **bulgur wheat**
- 3 cups **grapes** (see notes), rinsed, cut in half, and seeded if desired
- $\frac{2}{3}$ cup chopped **red onion**
- 2 teaspoons finely shredded **orange peel**
- 1 cup **orange juice**
- $\frac{1}{3}$ cup chopped **fresh mint** leaves
- 3 tablespoons **lemon juice**
- 1 teaspoon **ground coriander**
  Salt and **pepper**
  Romaine lettuce leaves, rinsed and crisped

1. In a large bowl, combine bulgur and 2 cups boiling water. Let stand until bulgur is tender to bite, about 30 minutes. Pour into a fine strainer to drain.

2. Return bulgur to bowl. Add grapes, onion, orange peel, orange juice, mint, lemon juice, and coriander. Mix, and season to taste with salt and pepper.

3. Line a platter or wide bowl with romaine leaves. Mound salad on leaves.

Per serving: 139 cal., 3.9% (5.4 cal.) from fat; 3.9 g protein; 0.6 g fat (0.1 g sat.); 33 g carbo (5.7 g fiber); 10 mg sodium; 0 mg chol.

Grape Pizza

PREP AND COOK TIME: About 45 minutes

NOTES: For colorful results, combine green, red, and dark-skinned grapes.

MAKES: 8 appetizer servings

- 1 tablespoon **olive oil**
  All-purpose flour
- 1 pound **frozen bread dough**, thawed
- $1\frac{1}{2}$ cups **seedless grapes** (see notes), rinsed
- 2 tablespoons **grated parmesan cheese**
- 1 teaspoon **fresh rosemary** leaves or dried rosemary
- 1 teaspoon **sugar**
- 2 tablespoons **thin-sliced prosciutto**, slivered (optional)

1. Rub a 12-inch pizza pan with $\frac{1}{2}$ the olive oil.

2. On a lightly floured board, knead dough into a ball; roll into a 10- to 12-inch round. Put dough in pan, and press or stretch to edges; if dough springs

back, let rest a few minutes, then press again. Rub dough with remaining oil. Let stand in a warm place, uncovered, until slightly puffy, 10 to 15 minutes.

3. Scatter grapes, cheese, rosemary, and sugar evenly over dough.

4. Bake on the bottom rack of a 450° oven for 10 minutes (8 minutes in a convection oven). Sprinkle prosciutto evenly over pizza. Continue baking until crust is well browned on top and bottom, 12 to 15 minutes longer (7 to 10 minutes in a convection oven). Cut into wedges and serve warm or cool.

Per serving: 172 cal., 18% (31 cal.) from fat; 5 g protein; 3.4 g fat (0.5 g sat.); 31 g carbo (1.4 g fiber); 353 mg sodium; 1 mg chol.

Chicken with Grapes

PREP AND COOK TIME: About 25 minutes

NOTES: Large Red Globe and Christmas Rose grapes are handsome in this dish, but green grapes also work well.

MAKES: 4 servings

- 4 **boned, skinned chicken breast halves** (5 to 6 oz. each)
  About $\frac{1}{4}$ cup **all-purpose flour**
- 2 tablespoons **butter** or margarine
- $\frac{1}{3}$ cup chopped **shallots**
- $\frac{1}{2}$ cup **dry white** or rosé **wine**
- $\frac{1}{3}$ cup **whipping cream**
- $\frac{1}{4}$ cup fat-skimmed **chicken broth**
- 1 tablespoon chopped **fresh tarragon** leaves or 1 teaspoon dried tarragon
- 2 cups **red** or green **grapes** (see notes), rinsed
  Salt and **pepper**
  Tarragon sprigs (optional)

1. Place breast halves between sheets of plastic wrap. With a flat mallet, gently but firmly pound breasts to $\frac{1}{4}$ inch thick. Coat chicken with flour, shake off excess, and lay in a single layer on plastic wrap.

2. In a nonstick 10- to 12-inch frying pan over medium-high heat, melt $\frac{1}{2}$ the butter. Fill pan with chicken; without overlapping, add more as pieces shrink, using about $\frac{1}{2}$ the chicken. Cook, turning as needed, until chicken is lightly browned on each side and no longer pink in center (cut to test), 3 to 4 minutes total. Transfer to a platter and keep warm. Add remaining butter and chicken and repeat step to brown all the pieces.

3. Add shallots to pan; stir until limp, 1 to 2 minutes. Add wine, cream, broth, and chopped tarragon. Boil over high

3. Add eggs, 1 at a time, beating thoroughly after each addition. Beat in lemon peel and vanilla.

4. Add 1 cup flour and mix well. Spread batter evenly in tart pan.

5. Rinse grapes, cut in half, and seed if desired. Arrange grapes, cut side up, evenly over batter. Sprinkle with about 1 tablespoon granulated sugar.

6. Bake in a 375° oven until cake feels firm in the center when lightly pressed, 30 to 35 minutes (about 20 minutes in a convection oven). Cool on a rack at least 30 minutes. Remove pan rim. Sift powdered sugar generously over warm or cool cake just before cutting.

Per serving: 262 cal., 48% (126 cal.) from fat; 4.3 g protein; 14 g fat (8.1 g sat.); 30 g carbo (0.7 g fiber); 147 mg sodium; 112 mg chol.

Frosty Grape Cooler

PREP TIME: About 7 minutes, plus 1 hour to freeze

NOTES: Frozen grapes keep this punch cold, but they thaw enough in minutes to nibble as you sip. Use one or several colors of grapes. If freezing grapes up to 1 week ahead, when solid, transfer to a freezer container and freeze.

MAKES: 6 to 8 servings

1. Rinse 3 cups **seedless grapes** (see notes), drain, and pat dry. Place in a single layer in a 10- by 15-inch pan. Freeze until hard, at least 1 hour.

2. In a 2- to 3-quart pitcher or bowl, combine 1 can (12 oz.) thawed **frozen white grape juice concentrate** and 1 bottle (33.8 oz.) chilled **soda water.** Add grapes and stir to blend. Pour into glasses.

Per serving: 155 cal., 1.7% (2.7 cal.) from fat; 0.4 g protein; 0.3 g fat (0.1 g sat.); 38 g carbo (1 g fiber); 31 mg sodium; 0 mg chol.

Grape Sparkler

PREP TIME: About 1 minute

NOTES: Use a fruity sparkling wine such as Asti Spumante, Blanc de Noir, or domestic brut.

MAKES: 1 serving

Rinse and drain 1 or 2 small clusters (about 2 in. long) **Black Corinth** (Champagne) **grapes** and hang over the rim of a champagne flute or wine glass. Add about ⅓ cup chilled **sparkling wine** (see notes) to glass, then 1 to 2 tablespoons chilled **Moscato di Canelli,** to taste. Nibble grapes as you sip wine.

Per serving: 91 cal., 1% (0.9 cal.) from fat; 0.2 g protein; 0.1 g fat (0 g sat.); 6.1 g carbo (0.3 g fiber); 5.7 mg sodium; 0 mg chol. ◆

Grape choices
(by row, top to bottom)

- **Crimson Seedless:** Bright red; oblong; sweet-tart and spicy; firm-crisp.
- **Autumn Royal:** Purple-black to jet black; oval; sweet; firm flesh; seedless.
- **Christmas Rose:** Dark red; large tear-drop shape; sweet; has seeds.

- **Thompson Seedless:** Light green to yellow-green; oblong; sweet-tart; crisp.
- **Flame Seedless:** Deep red; round; sweet-tart; crunchy with tender skin.
- **Black Corinth** (also called Champagne): Dark red to reddish black; tiny; sweet; fragile, with tender skin; seedless.
- **Ribier:** Blue-black to jet black; large, round; mild; tough skin; has seeds.

- **Red Globe:** Bright to dark red; cherry size; sweet, juicy; meaty; has seeds.
- **Niabell:** Purple to black with frosty blush; round, Concord type; earthy and rich; thick skin; has seeds.
- **Italia:** Light green; round; floral, sweet-tart; firm skin; has seeds.
- **Ruby Seedless:** Deep red; round to oval; sweet; crunchy with tender skin.

heat, stirring often, until reduced to ⅔ cup, 2 to 3 minutes.

4. Add grapes and shake pan often until fruit is hot, about 1 minute. Pour sauce over chicken. Add salt and pepper to taste. Garnish with tarragon sprigs.

Per serving: 355 cal., 35% (126 cal.) from fat; 35 g protein; 14 g fat (7.9 g sat.); 17 g carbo (1.1 g fiber); 166 mg sodium; 120 mg chol.

Butter Kuchen with Grapes

PREP AND COOK TIME: About 50 minutes, plus 30 minutes to cool.

NOTES: Dark Niabell grapes stand out boldly in this buttery cake. If making up to 1 day ahead, cool, cover, and chill.

MAKES: 8 servings

About ½ cup (¼ lb.) **butter** or margarine, at room temperature

About 1 cup **all-purpose flour**

About ½ cup **granulated sugar**

3 large **eggs**

¾ teaspoon grated **lemon** peel

½ teaspoon **vanilla**

1½ to 2 cups **blue-black grapes** (see notes)

Powdered sugar

1. Butter and flour an 11-inch tart pan with removable rim.

2. In a bowl with a mixer, beat ½ cup butter with ½ cup granulated sugar until smooth.

The Quick Cook

MEALS IN 30 MINUTES OR LESS

BY ANDREW BAKER

JAMES CARRIER

MENU

Penne with Mustard Greens and
Italian Oven-fried Meatballs

Tomato Wedges with Lemon-flavor Oil
and Fresh-Ground Black Pepper

Grissini Breadsticks

Purchased Tiramisu

Beef gets a round

■ If you love meatballs but hate the mess of pan-browning them, turn to the oven for a quick fix. Shaped and baked, oven-fried meatballs are ready in minutes. Spice up basic ground beef with Italian sausage, or give it an aromatic Middle Eastern spin with pine nuts and cinnamon. Ground turkey with sage and cranberries makes an all-American blend.

Mix and match any of the meatball flavor variations with the serving suggestions that follow: tossed with penne and pungent mustard greens, sandwiched with cheese and arugula in a French roll, or wrapped with lettuce and dolloped with yogurt in pocket bread.

Italian Oven-fried Meatballs

PREP AND COOK TIME: About 20 minutes

NOTES: Serve meatballs plain or use them in the main dishes that follow.

MAKES: 4 servings

1 **large egg**

½ pound **hot Italian sausages**

½ pound **ground lean beef**

3 tablespoons **fine dried bread crumbs**

3 tablespoons fat-skimmed **chicken broth** or water

⅓ cup finely chopped **green onions**

Salt

1. In a large bowl, beat egg with a fork to blend. Squeeze sausages from casings into bowl; discard casings. Add beef, bread crumbs, broth, and green onions. Mix well with your hands.

2. Shape mixture into 1½-inch balls. Set balls slightly apart in a rimmed 10- by 15-inch pan.

3. Bake in a 450° oven until no longer pink in the center (cut to test), about 12 minutes (about 9 minutes in a convection oven). Add salt to taste.

Per serving: 289 cal., 62% (180 cal.) from fat; 21 g protein; 20 g fat (7.2 g sat.); 5 g carbo (0.4 g fiber); 470 mg sodium; 118 mg chol.

Turkey-Sage Meatballs. Follow directions for **Italian Oven-fried Meatballs** (preceding), but instead of sausages and beef use 1 pound **ground turkey.** Add 3 tablespoons chopped **fresh sage** leaves or 1 teaspoon dried sage and ¼ cup chopped **dried cranberries.**

Per serving: 255 cal., 46% (117 cal.) from fat; 23 g protein; 13 g fat (3.6 g sat.); 10 g carbo (0.8 g fiber); 133 mg sodium; 110 mg chol.

Kofte Meatballs. Follow directions for **Italian Oven-fried Meatballs** (preceding), but omit sausages and increase **ground lean beef** to 1 pound. Add 3 tablespoons **pine nuts,** 1 teaspoon **ground cumin,** ½ teaspoon **ground cinnamon,** and ½ teaspoon **pepper.**

Per serving: 306 cal., 59% (180 cal.) from fat; 25 g protein; 20 g fat (7 g sat.); 6 g carbo (1.3 g fiber); 113 mg sodium; 119 mg chol.

3 quick meatball entrées

Penne with Mustard Greens and Meatballs. While **meatballs** (preceding) bake, in a 5- to 6-quart pan, combine ¾ pound **dried penne pasta,** 2½ cups fat-skimmed **chicken broth,** and 2½ cups **water** and stir frequently over high heat until pasta is tender to bite, about 15 minutes. Add 11 cups (about ¾ pound) chopped **mustard greens** (leaves only), 1 more cup fat-skimmed chicken broth, and cooked meatballs. Stir until greens are wilted and meatballs are hot, about 3 minutes. Transfer to a wide bowl; scatter 1½ cups (about 6 oz.) shredded **fontina cheese** over pasta. MAKES: 4 servings.

Per serving with Italian meatballs: 823 cal., 38% (315 cal.) from fat; 52 g protein; 35 g fat (16 g sat.); 73 g carbo (3 g fiber); 903 mg sodium; 168 mg chol.

Meatball Sandwich. Slice open 4 **French rolls** (about 6 in. long) and toast cut sides. Place ½ cup (2 cups total) rinsed and crisped **arugula** on 1 cut side of each roll. Set hot **meatballs** (preceding) on arugula and top with thinly sliced **gouda cheese** (about 4 oz. total). Add **Dijon mustard** to taste. MAKES: 4 servings.

Per serving with turkey-sage meatballs: 529 cal., 39% (207 cal.) from fat; 36 g protein; 23 g fat (8.9 g sat.); 43 g carbo (2.7 g fiber); 745 mg sodium; 143 mg chol.

Meatball-stuffed Pocket Breads. Cut 4 **pocket breads** (6 in.) in half crosswise, fill halves with cooked **meatballs** (preceding), and add **plain nonfat yogurt** (½ to 1 cup total) and shredded **lettuce** (about 2 cups total) to taste. MAKES: 4 servings.

Per serving with kofte meatballs: 492 cal., 38% (189 cal.) from fat; 32 g protein; 21 g fat (7.2 g sat.); 43 g carbo (2.5 g fiber); 458 mg sodium; 119 mg chol. ◆

Coconut Chutney

PREP TIME: About 10 minutes

NOTES: Chill airtight up to 1 week.

MAKES: About 1 cup

- 1 cup **sweetened shredded** or flaked **dried coconut**
- 2/3 cup chopped **green bell pepper**
- 1/4 cup chopped **fresh jalapeño chilies**
- 1 tablespoon **lime juice**
- 2 tablespoons chopped **fresh cilantro**
  Salt and **pepper**

In a blender, whirl coconut, bell pepper, chilies, lime juice, cilantro, and 1/4 cup water until smoothly puréed, about 4 minutes. Scrape container often. Season to taste with salt and pepper.

Per tablespoon: 24 cal., 58% (14 cal.) from fat; 0.2 g protein; 1.5 g fat (1.3 g sat.); 2.7 g carbo (0.4 g fiber); 12 mg sodium; 0 mg chol.

Peanut Chutney

PREP TIME: 5 minutes

NOTES: Chill airtight up to 1 week.

MAKES: About 1 cup

- 1 cup **salted roasted peanuts**
- 1 tablespoon **chili powder**
- 1 teaspoon **sugar**

In a blender or food processor, whirl peanuts, chili powder, and sugar until nuts are very finely ground, but not a paste; scrape container as needed.

Per tablespoon: 55 cal., 75% (41 cal.) from fat; 2.4 g protein; 4.5 g fat (0.6 g sat.); 2.2 g carbo (1 g fiber); 44 mg sodium; 0 mg chol.

Saffron-Mango Chutney

PREP AND COOK TIME: About 10 minutes

NOTES: Chill airtight up to 1 week.

MAKES: 2 cups

- 1/16 teaspoon crumbled **saffron threads**
- 1/4 teaspoon **ground cardamom**
- 2 cups **powdered sugar**
- 2 cups diced **mango**

In a 2- to 2 1/2-quart pan over high heat, mix saffron, 1/4 cup water, cardamom, and sugar until sugar dissolves, 1 to 2 minutes. Add mango and stir until boiling rapidly. Serve warm or cool.

Per tablespoon: 36 cal., 0% (0 cal.) from fat; 0.1 g protein; 0 g fat; 9.2 g carbo (0.1 g fiber); 0.3 mg sodium; 0 mg chol.

Cranberry Chutney

PREP AND COOK TIME: About 10 minutes

NOTES: Chill airtight up to 1 week.

MAKES: 2 cups

- 2 tablespoons **salted roasted peanuts**
- 2 teaspoons **coriander seed**
- 2 cups (1/2 lb.) **dried cranberries**
- 1 cup firmly packed **brown sugar**
- 1 tablespoon **chili powder**
- 1 teaspoon **ground coriander**
- 1/2 teaspoon **ground cumin**
- 1/4 teaspoon **ground pepper**
- 1/8 teaspoon **ground cinnamon**
- 1/8 teaspoon **ground cloves**
  Salt

1. Place peanuts and coriander seed in a blender or spice grinder; whirl or grind until mixture is minced.

2. In a 2- to 2 1/2-quart pan, combine peanut mixture, dried cranberries, brown sugar, chili powder, coriander, cumin, pepper, cinnamon, cloves, and 2 cups water. Stir over high heat until mixture boils for 1 minute. Add salt to taste. Serve warm or cool.

Per tablespoon: 51 cal., 7.1% (3.6 cal.) from fat; 0.2 g protein; 0.4 g fat (0 g sat.); 12 g carbo (0.5 g fiber); 5.2 mg sodium; 0 mg chol.

Garbanzo Chutney

PREP AND COOK TIME: About 10 minutes

NOTES: Chill airtight up to 1 day.

MAKES: About 2 cups

- 1 **Granny Smith apple** (1/2 lb.)
  About 1 tablespoon **lime juice**
- 1 can (about 15 oz.) **garbanzos,** rinsed and drained
- 1 tablespoon **cumin seed**
- 1 teaspoon **salad oil**
- 1 **small dried hot chili**
- 1/4 teaspoon **ground dried turmeric**
- 1 tablespoon **sweetened shredded** or flaked **dried coconut**
- 2 tablespoons chopped **fresh cilantro**
  Salt

1. Rinse, core, peel, and shred apple into a bowl; mix with 1 tablespoon lime juice.

2. In a blender or food processor, whirl garbanzos until coarsely puréed, scraping container as necessary. Add to apple.

3. In an 8- to 10-inch frying pan over medium-high heat, stir cumin seed in oil until it sizzles. Add chili and turmeric and stir until chili smells toasted, about 1 minute. Add to bowl.

4. Add coconut and cilantro to bowl; mix, adding lime juice and salt to taste. Remove and discard chili.

Per tablespoon: 15 cal., 24% (3.6 cal.) from fat; 0.5 g protein; 0.4 g fat (0.1 g sat.); 2.4 g carbo (0.5 g fiber); 15 mg sodium; 0 mg chol. ◆

SPRINKLE, SPREAD, or spoon a chutney (clockwise from top): peanut, coconut, garbanzo, and saffron-mango.

LEIGH BEISCH

Chutneys to relish

India's essential condiment comes in many guises

BY ANDREW BAKER

Like *salsa,* the term *chutney* is used to describe many kinds of sauces. But chutneys range, perhaps, a bit wider—from sweet jamlike mixtures to uncooked savory toppings. India-born Hema Kundargi of Cupertino, California, prepares particularly simple chutneys, some fresh, some cooked. She spreads coconut or garbanzo chutney on sandwiches, sprinkles peanut chutney on tomato-and-cucumber salads, spoons saffron chutney over ice cream or onto grilled chicken, and serves cranberry chutney with curries or any dish that will benefit from a flavor boost.

Seeking the holey grail

Three standout Bay Area mom-and-pop shops still make perfect doughnuts.
Treat yourself at these bakeries in San Jose, Castro Valley, and San Francisco

A good doughnut is hard to find. For one thing, there's not much demand anymore, what with the proliferation of bagels and bran muffins, those oh-so-'90s breakfast foods. For another, there's not much supply; most independent bakeries have faded in the shadow of Dunkin' Donuts and other chains. But if you know where to look, you can still find that perfect jelly roll or maple-glazed treat. And you might also discover a new hangout.

Lou's Living Donut Museum, a San Jose institution since 1955, is an unusual place. As the name indicates, it *is* a museum (albeit a tiny one) commemorating original owner Lucius Ades, a World War II B-24 pilot and decorated war hero. But perhaps even more entertaining than Lou's WWII paraphernalia is the sight of owners Ralph and Connie Chavira and son Richard up to their elbows in a vat of doughnut dough, surrounded by milled organic flour, fresh eggs, and potatoes. That's right, potatoes. According to the Chaviras, the unexpected ingredient is what makes Lou's doughnuts so moist—and a scant amount of oil is what makes them so light. Choose from peanut crumb, coconut, maple, chocolate-glazed, pumpkin, honey wheat, or blueberry. Chocolate-chocolate-glazed are made only on Thursdays and Saturdays. *387 Delmas Ave., San Jose; 6 A.M. until doughnuts sell out, typically around 12, Mon-Sat; (408) 295-5887.*

Rudy's Donut House has been helping Castro Valley residents jump-start their mornings since 1960. About 40 varieties of doughnuts are made here, including glazed, chocolate, and sugar among the raised types, and blueberry, peanut, coconut, and maple among the cake choices. Apple fritters and cinnamon rolls are also baked on the premises, as are muffins and croissants. The bustling coffee room is a favorite meeting place. *3692 Castro Valley Blvd., Castro Valley; 5–4 daily; (510) 889-1109.*

Bob's Donuts & Pastries is hard to pass up at any time of day or night—especially when you see its big window, showcasing trays of doughnuts, cinnamon rolls, apple fritters, and apple pandowdy. Once you've smelled the just-baked apple fritters, there's no going back. Open since the 1950s, this Polk Street shop is the kind of friendly place where locals have been sipping coffee for generations. Everything is homemade, hence the doughnuts' irregular shapes. *1621 Polk St., San Francisco; 24 hrs. daily; (415) 776-3141.* ◆

— *Lolly Winston*

EVERY DAY OF THE WEEK except Sunday, Connie Chavira, part-owner of Lou's Living Donut Museum, bakes and serves warm, light-as-air doughnuts: everything from peanut crumb to chocolate-glazed to pumpkin to plain.

TERRENCE McCARTHY

ROSY STRAWBERRY slices float in a cool, tall glass of Ruth's best lemonade.

Stir occasionally, or screw lid on jar and shake occasionally, until sugar is dissolved, 1 to 2 minutes.

2. Meanwhile, grate 1 tablespoon lemon peel (yellow part only) from 2 or 3 lemons. Add peel to warm sugar mixture; let cool about 10 minutes.

3. Cut all lemons in half and ream enough juice to make 1¾ cups. Add to sugar mixture. Use, or cover and chill up to 3 days.

4. To make each serving, slice a strawberry into a glass (about 12 oz.). Add ice cubes, ⅓ cup lemon syrup, and ⅔ cup water; stir. Garnish glass rim with lemon slices, or stir slices into lemonade.

Per serving: 106 cal., 0% (0 cal.) from fat; 0.1 g protein; 0 g fat; 28 g carbo (0.1 g fiber); 0.6 mg sodium; 0 mg chol.

Berry-Oat Muffins

Kristen L. Dillon, Grand Junction, Colorado

"My parents had a giant raspberry patch, so we were always looking for ways to use the fresh berries," says Kristen Dillon. These hearty muffins show them off deliciously.

PREP AND COOK TIME: About 40 minutes

MAKES: 12 muffins

About ½ cup (¼ lb.) **butter** or margarine, at room temperature

½ cup firmly packed **brown sugar**

1 **large egg**

½ cup **plain nonfat yogurt**

1 cup **all-purpose flour**

1 teaspoon **baking powder**

¼ teaspoon **baking soda**

¼ teaspoon **ground cinnamon**

2 cups **rolled oats**

1 cup **raspberries**, blueberries, or blackberries, rinsed and drained

1. In a bowl with a mixer on high speed, beat ½ cup butter and the sugar until well blended. Beat in egg and yogurt.

2. Add flour, baking powder, baking soda, and cinnamon. Mix on low speed until incorporated. Stir in oats. Add raspberries and stir gently to distribute evenly through very stiff batter.

3. Fill buttered muffin cups (2½ in. wide) equally with batter.

Ruth's Best Lemonade

Ruth Garcia, San Jose, California

"If life gives you too many lemons, make lemonade" is Ruth Garcia's old saw. She turns the fruit that comes from her parents' and their neighbors' trees into a simple concentrate. Then, when she needs a quick drink to serve, she dilutes the concentrate with water to make lemonade. Garcia often slices strawberries into a glass before mixing the lemonade in it. More lemonade, frozen in cubes, cools pitcher-size batches without diluting the taste.

PREP TIME: 10 minutes

MAKES: About 1 quart concentrate; 12 servings

1½ cups **sugar**

8 or 9 **lemons** (2¾ to 3¼ lb. total), rinsed

Strawberries, rinsed and hulled (optional)

Ice cubes

Thin **lemon** slices (optional)

1. In a bowl or a 1-quart or larger jar, combine sugar and 1¼ cups hot water.

4. Bake in a 350° oven until muffins are browned, 25 to 30 minutes (20 to 25 minutes in a convection oven). Let cool about 5 minutes in pan, remove, and serve warm or cool.

Per muffin: 217 cal., 41% (90 cal.) from fat; 4.5 g protein; 10 g fat (5.6 g sat.); 28 g carbo (2.2 g fiber); 171 mg sodium; 41 mg chol.

Honey-Dijon Barbecued Chicken

Karin Armstrong, Salem, Oregon

Karin Armstrong blends honey and mustard to make a quick, intriguing alternative to the typical red barbecue sauce. With her family, it's a hit every time on chicken.

PREP AND COOK TIME: About 40 minutes

MAKES: 6 servings

- 12 **chicken drumsticks** (2½ to 3 lb. total)
- ⅓ cup **honey**
- 2 tablespoons **Dijon mustard**
- 1 teaspoon grated **fresh ginger**
- 1 clove **garlic,** peeled and pressed or minced
- 1 teaspoon **Worcestershire**
- **Salt** and **pepper**

1. *If using charcoal,* ignite 60 briquets on the firegrate of a barbecue with a lid. When briquets are dotted with gray ash, in 15 to 20 minutes, push equal amounts to opposite sides of firegrate. Set a drip pan on firegrate between mounds.

If using a gas barbecue, turn all burners to high and close lid for 10 minutes. Adjust burners for indirect cooking (heat on opposite sides of grill, not down center); keep heat on high.

2. Rinse chicken and pat dry. Set chicken on grill, not directly over heat. Cover (open vents for charcoal) and cook 20 minutes.

3. Meanwhile, in a small bowl, mix honey, mustard, ginger, garlic, and Worcestershire. Brush drumsticks generously with honey mixture. Cover and cook another 5 minutes.

4. Turn drumsticks; baste with honey mixture. Cover and cook until meat is no longer pink at bone in thickest part (cut to test), about 5 minutes longer. Transfer to a platter. Add salt and pepper to taste.

Per serving: 296 cal., 36% (108 cal.) from fat; 29 g protein; 12 g fat (3.3 g sat.); 16 g carbo (0 g fiber); 227 mg sodium; 98 mg chol.

HOT OFF THE GRILL: Drumsticks glazed with honey-and-mustard sauce.

Angel Hair Pasta with Tomatoes and Feta

Alycia Oh, Moorpark, California

Alycia Oh developed this simple, light pasta for her sister's wedding reception. It's good warm or at room temperature.

PREP AND COOK TIME: About 30 minutes

MAKES: 8 servings

- 3 tablespoons **olive oil**
- 1 **onion** (½ lb.), peeled and chopped
- 3 tablespoons thinly sliced **garlic**
- 1 pound **dried angel hair pasta**
- 2 pounds **firm-ripe Roma tomatoes,** rinsed, cored, and chopped
- ¾ cup chopped **fresh basil** leaves
- ½ cup chopped **parsley**
- ½ pound **feta cheese,** crumbled
- **Salt** and **pepper**

1. In a covered 6- to 8-quart pan over high heat, bring 3 to 4 quarts water to a boil.

2. Meanwhile, in a 10- to 12-inch frying pan over medium-high heat, frequently stir oil, onion, and garlic until onion is limp, 5 to 7 minutes.

3. Add pasta to boiling water. Stir often and cook, uncovered, until pasta is barely tender to bite, 3 to 5 minutes. Drain and put in a wide, shallow bowl.

4. Meanwhile, add tomatoes to frying pan and stir just until warm, about 2 minutes. Stir in basil and parsley, and heat just until basil wilts, about 1 minute.

5. Pour tomato mixture over pasta. Add cheese and mix. Add salt and pepper to taste. Serve hot or cool.

Per serving: 371 cal., 29% (108 cal.) from fat; 13 g protein; 12 g fat (5.1 g sat.); 52 g carbo (3.6 g fiber); 333 mg sodium; 25 mg chol.

Di's Dipping Oil

Diane Hudson, Dublin, California

When friends stop by to chat over a glass of wine, Diane Hudson presents this dipping oil with good crusty bread.

PREP TIME: About 10 minutes

MAKES: 1¾ cups

- 1 cup **olive oil**
- ½ cup **balsamic vinegar**
- ½ cup **grated parmesan cheese**
- 1½ tablespoons **dried basil**
- ½ teaspoon **salt**
- ½ teaspoon **pepper**
- 4 to 5 cloves **garlic,** peeled and pressed or minced
- **Crusty bread**

1. In a jar with a lid, combine oil, vinegar, cheese, basil, salt, pepper, and garlic. Stir, or cover and shake. Use, or cover and chill up to 1 month (bring to room temperature to serve).

2. Mix oil to blend seasonings, and pour into small, shallow bowls or rimmed plates. Slice or tear bread into pieces and dip into oil to eat.

Per tablespoon without bread: 77 cal., 95% (73 cal.) from fat; 0.6 g protein; 8.1 g fat (1.3 g sat.); 0.5 g carbo (0 g fiber); 68 mg sodium; 1.1 mg chol. ◆

Oven-sautéed onions give this make-ahead French onion soup its deep color and flavor (recipe on page 242).

October

Dinner's ready!

Devote a weekend to simmering and sautéing, and fill the freezer with a month's worth of easy meals

BY ELAINE JOHNSON AND SARA SCHNEIDER

PHOTOGRAPHS BY JAMES CARRIER

■ If only we had a month of Sundays, cooking would be easy. It's all those Wednesdays and Thursdays that are a bear. Come 6 o'clock, there are no aromatic sauces simmering on the stove, no meats braising their way to tenderness—just the temptation to order takeout for your family to spoon out of cardboard at will.

Are daily home-cooked meals, thoughtfully planned and calmly executed, still possible? Dinners that rejuvenate tired bones and cement family relationships? Cooking instructor and cookbook author Stephanie Stephens of San Leandro, California, has developed a method to achieve them in the face of hectic schedules.

Once a month this mother of four devotes a block of time to cooking enough dinner fare for at least 20 weeknights, then loading it all in an average-size refrigerator freezer. Each day she pulls out one entrée to reheat and serve with a salad or fresh vegetable—the effect is as if she'd been cooking all afternoon.

Inspired by Stephens's concept, we've organized 11 entrées—from old family favorites to innovative international combinations—into three categories. One set shares a pan of lively tomato sauce. Another starts with a huge batch of sautéed onions and garlic. The third is a group of meats packed in simple seasonings. Each recipe makes enough for two main dishes (except a leg of lamb, which is geared for a crowd or tasty leftovers) to be thawed, one at a time, for family meals. All also make fine company fare; just serve both portions.

To save time, the basic preparation tasks for all the dishes in each category are consolidated, and you can do most of a month's food shopping at once (plus quick stops, as needed, for dairy products and fresh produce).

Comprehensive shopping also saves money. You can buy in warehouse-store volume and take advantage of bulk bargains. The tab for all the dishes in this story came to about $250—much less than a month's worth of weeknight takeout.

The cooking schedule itself is flexible. Prepare all the foods in two consecutive days (see "Game Plan" strategy one, page 242), or tackle one section a day as time permits (strategy two). Either way, use the tips to organize and assemble supplies and time. Refer to the advice on page 246 for freezing and thawing foods.

Why cook all day and have nothing to eat? Spare one dish from the freezer and enjoy it for dinner. One batch of the long-baked lamb shanks is a most satisfying reward—and proof that even your Wednesday night meals are going to be special this month.

One great homemade tomato sauce is the base for these entrées.
• Chicken Cacciatore
• Spinach and Sausage Manicotti
• Eggplant Parmesan
You need 3 quarts of sauce to make the dishes; freeze the remainder in 1-cup portions to mix with pasta for emergency meals.

Grandma's Tomato Sauce

PREP AND COOK TIME: About 1¾ hours

NOTES: If making sauce up to 3 days ahead, cool, cover, and chill.

MAKES: About 4 quarts

- 2 cans (28 oz. each) **crushed tomatoes with basil and oregano**
- 5 cans (6 oz. each) **tomato paste**
- 3 cups chopped **Roma tomatoes** (about 1¼ lb.)
- 1½ cups **dry red wine**
- 1 cup chopped **onion**
- 2 tablespoons chopped **fresh basil** leaves or 2 teaspoons dried basil
- 1 tablespoon minced **garlic**
- 5 **dried bay leaves**
- 1 teaspoon **dried oregano**
- 1 teaspoon **pepper**
- **Salt**

1. In an 8- to 10-quart pan, combine 3 cups water, canned tomatoes with their liquid, tomato paste, Roma tomatoes, wine, onion, basil, garlic, bay leaves, oregano, and pepper.

2. Bring to a boil over high heat, stirring often; reduce heat, cover, and simmer,

CHUNKY CHICKEN CACCIATORE, browned and sauced on cooking day, can be ready anytime. Boil pasta and pour a glass of wine.

stirring occasionally, until reduced to 4 quarts, 45 minutes to 1 hour.

3. Remove bay leaves and add salt to taste. Use hot or cool.

Per cup: 81 cal., 6.7% (5.4 cal.) from fat; 3.4 g protein; 0.6 g fat (0.1 g sat.); 17 g carbo (3.8 g fiber); 605 mg sodium; 0 mg chol.

Chicken Cacciatore

ASSEMBLY TIME: About 1¼ hours

REHEAT TIME: 1 to 1¼ hours

NOTES: Thaw overnight (see page 246) or bake directly from the freezer, allowing about 1½ hours. Serve with hot cooked wide noodles and shredded parmesan cheese.

MAKES: 2 main dishes, 4 servings each

16 **chicken thighs** (4½ to 5 lb. total), skinned and fat-trimmed

Salt and **pepper**

3 tablespoons **olive oil**

2½ cups chopped **onions**

1 pound **mushrooms,** rinsed, drained, and quartered

1 tablespoon minced **garlic**

2 teaspoons **dried oregano**

¼ cup chopped **parsley**

1 quart **Grandma's tomato sauce** (page 240)

1 cup **dry white wine**

1 cup **salt-cured olives,** pitted

1. Rinse chicken and pat dry. Sprinkle lightly with salt and pepper.

2. Pour 1 tablespoon oil into a 10- to 12-inch nonstick frying pan over medium-high heat. When hot, add ½ the chicken and brown well, 6 to 8 minutes total. As thighs are browned, transfer to a foil pan (8 to 9 in. square). Add 1 more tablespoon oil to frying pan and repeat to brown remaining chicken. Transfer to another foil pan (8 to 9 in. square).

3. To frying pan, add remaining 1 tablespoon oil and the onions, mushrooms, garlic, oregano, and parsley. Stir often over medium-high heat until vegetables are limp, 12 to 15 minutes.

4. Stir in tomato sauce and wine. Bring to a boil over high heat, stirring often; reduce heat, cover, and simmer about 20 minutes to blend flavors.

Before the cooking weekend

- Read all recipes and the game plan (below).
- Make a shopping list.
- Buy groceries and supplies: You'll need a permanent marker; foil; 24 plastic freezer bags that are 1-gallon size, 4 that are 1-quart size, and 12 that are 1-pint size; and 8 foil pans that are 8 to 9 inches square, and 2 that are 9 by 13 inches.

Cooking weekend

- Assemble all ingredients before beginning to cook.
- Use the food processor to chop and slice as many ingredients as possible.

Game plan

Strategy one: Two cooking days. On the first day, make tomato sauce, prepare all the dishes that use the sautéed onions and garlic, and marinate the meats. Allow 8 hours total.

1. First, start oven-sautéing the onions and garlic.

2. While they bake, prepare and freeze the marinated meats.

3. When the onion and garlic mixture is done, season the lamb shanks with sherry and onions and put them in the oven.

4. As the shanks bake, make the tomato sauce.

5. While the sauce simmers, complete the dishes that use the onions and garlic, and freeze (including half the lamb shanks). Cool tomato sauce, cover, and chill.

On the second day, assemble and freeze all of the dishes using the tomato sauce, and the companion dishes: gruyère croutons and garlic mashed potatoes. Allow about 5½ hours total.

Strategy two: Three cooking days. Tackle one segment of recipes each day. Allow about 6 hours for the sautéed onion and garlic dishes, 2 hours for the marinated meat dishes, and 5½ hours for the tomato sauce dishes.

Note: Assembly time for each recipe does not include any steps in master recipes, or cooling the dish to room temperature. Heating time does not include thawing.

---

5. Add olives to sauce. Let cool to room temperature, 45 minutes to 1 hour. Pour evenly over chicken in pans.

6. Seal pans with foil, and freeze (see page 246).

7. Thaw 1 pan (see notes). Bake, covered, in a 375° oven until chicken is no longer pink at bone (cut to test), 1 to 1¼ hours.

Per serving: 376 cal., 43% (162 cal.) from fat; 33 g protein; 18 g fat (2.9 g sat.); 18 g carbo (3.5 g fiber); 1,026 mg sodium; 121 mg chol.

Spinach and Sausage Manicotti

ASSEMBLY TIME: About 1 hour

REHEATING TIME: About 55 minutes

NOTES: Thaw overnight (see page 246) or bake directly from the freezer, allowing about 1¼ hours. If desired, sprinkle hot manicotti with shredded parmesan cheese and bake 5 minutes more. Serve with sautéed carrots and zucchini.

MAKES: 2 main dishes, 4 servings each

- 10 ounces **mild** or hot **turkey** or pork **Italian sausages**
- 16 **dried manicotti pasta shells** (3½ to 4 in. long; 8 to 10 oz. total)
- 1 package (9 to 10 oz.) thawed **frozen chopped spinach,** squeezed dry
- 1¾ cups (15 oz.) **ricotta cheese**
- ½ cup **grated parmesan cheese**
- ½ teaspoon **ground nutmeg**

Salt

- 4 **large eggs**
- 1 quart **Grandma's tomato sauce** (page 240)

Pepper

1. Discard sausage casings. In a 10- to 12-inch frying pan over medium-high heat, stir and crumble sausage until lightly browned, 5 to 10 minutes. Discard any fat. Let cool 10 minutes.

2. Meanwhile, in a 5- to 6-quart pan over high heat, bring 3 quarts water to a boil. Add manicotti and cook until barely tender to bite (test 1 at edge), 5 to 8 minutes. Drain and immerse in cold water until cool, about 2 minutes, then drain.

3. To sausage, add spinach, ricotta, parmesan, and nutmeg; mix, and add salt to taste. In a small bowl, beat eggs to blend. Stir into sausage mixture.

4. Spoon 1 cup tomato sauce evenly into each of 2 foil pans (9 by 13 in.).

5. With a spoon, fill manicotti shells equally with spinach mixture (about ¼ cup in each). Arrange in a single layer in sauce, and spoon remaining sauce evenly over manicotti.

6. Drizzle ½ cup water over pasta in each pan. Seal pans with foil, and freeze (see page 246).

7. Thaw 1 pan (see notes). Bake, covered, in a 375° oven until steaming in center (cut to test), 50 to 55 minutes. Season to taste with salt and pepper.

Per serving: 366 cal., 39% (144 cal.) from fat; 23 g protein; 16 g fat (7.3 g sat.); 34 g carbo (3.2 g fiber); 729 mg sodium; 156 mg chol.

Eggplant Parmesan

ASSEMBLY TIME: About 45 minutes

REHEATING TIME: About 1 hour

NOTES: Thaw overnight (see page 246) or bake directly from the freezer, allowing about 1½ hours. Serve with a salad of Belgian endive and marinated red peppers.

MAKES: 2 main dishes, 4 servings each

- 2¾ pounds **eggplant**
- ¼ cup **olive oil**
- 1½ pounds **mozzarella cheese**
- 1 quart **Grandma's tomato sauce** (page 240)
- ½ cup **Italian-style fine dried bread crumbs**
- 1 cup (4 to 5 oz.) **shredded parmesan cheese**

1. Rinse eggplant; trim and discard ends. Cut eggplant crosswise into ⅓-inch-thick slices. Arrange ½ the slices in a single layer on each of 2 baking sheets (14 by 17 in.). Lightly brush eggplant slices on both sides with oil.

2. Bake in a 500° oven until eggplant is soft when pressed and lightly browned, about 18 minutes (10 to 15 minutes in a convection oven); switch pan positions halfway through baking.

3. Meanwhile, cut mozzarella into ¼-inch-thick slices.

4. Arrange ¼ of the eggplant in a single layer in each of 2 foil pans (8 to 9 in. square). Cover eggplant in each pan with ¼ of the mozzarella and top with 1 cup tomato sauce. Repeat layers, using all the ingredients.

5. Seal pans with foil (see page 246). Combine crumbs and parmesan cheese; put ½ the mixture in each of 2 plastic freezer bags (1-pt. size). Seal bags, tape 1 to each pan, and freeze.

6. Thaw 1 pan (see notes). Remove bag with crumb mixture.

7. Bake eggplant, covered, in a 375° oven until steaming in center (cut to test), 50 minutes to 1 hour and 10 minutes. Uncover pan and sprinkle crumb mixture over eggplant. Bake until well browned, 5 to 10 minutes more.

Per serving: 459 cal., 57% (261 cal.) from fat; 26 g protein; 29 g fat (15 g sat.); 25 g carbo (4.3 g fiber); 1,052 mg sodium; 76 mg chol.

M A S T E R   R E C I P E

Sautéing such a large amount of onions and garlic in frying pans atop the range is unwieldy, and the mixture gets mushy. In large, shallow pans in the oven, the onions are easier to handle and retain their texture. They go into the following recipes.

• French Onion Soup
• Chicken Pot-au-Feu
• Lamb Shanks with Sherry and Onions
• Chard, Bean, and Pancetta Soup
• Lentil-Barley Stew

OVEN-SAUTÉED ONIONS give French onion soup deep color and flavor.

Oven-Sautéed Onions and Garlic

PREP AND COOK TIME: About 1¾ hours

NOTES: If you buy garlic heads, you'll need about ¾ pound total. Cooked, 1⅓ pounds onions and 2½ tablespoons minced garlic make about 1 cup. A food processor significantly speeds up prep time.

MAKES: About 8 cups

  9½ pounds **onions,** peeled and sliced (9 qt.)

  1⅓ cups (8 oz.) **peeled garlic cloves,** minced

  ½ cup **olive oil**

1. In a large bowl, mix ½ the onions, ½ the garlic, and ½ the oil. Pour into a shallow, rimmed pan (12 by 15 in. to 15 by 17 in., and 1 to 1½ in. deep). Repeat with remaining onions, garlic, and oil, and pour into another same-size pan.

2. Bake in a 400° oven until onions are limp and well browned, 1 to 1½ hours, switching pan positions and stirring mixture from pan sides into center with a wide spatula every 15 minutes to avoid scorching or burning.

3. Use as directed in recipes that follow. Or let cool to room temperature and freeze in 1-cup portions in plastic freezer bags (1-pt. size; see page 246).

Per cup: 346 cal., 36% (126 cal.) from fat; 7.4 g protein; 14 g fat (2 g sat.); 51 g carbo (8.4 g fiber); 19 mg sodium; 0 mg chol.

French Onion Soup

ASSEMBLY TIME: About 1 hour

REHEATING TIME: About 10 minutes

NOTES: Thaw overnight or quick-thaw (see page 246). Use 1½ quarts of broth to complete each batch of soup. Serve with a butter lettuce salad.

MAKES: 2 main dishes, 4 servings each

  2 teaspoons **sugar**

  1 tablespoon **balsamic vinegar**

  3 cups **oven-sautéed onions and garlic** (recipe precedes)

  1 tablespoon minced **fresh thyme** leaves or dried thyme

  ½ cup **dry red wine**

  3 quarts fat-skimmed **chicken broth** (see notes)

  Gruyère croutons (recipe follows)

  Salt and **pepper**

1. In a 3- to 4-quart pan over medium-high heat, shake and tilt sugar until melted and amber, 2 to 3 minutes. Immediately add vinegar, sautéed onions and garlic, and thyme. Stir until onions are deep amber, about 5 minutes.

2. Stir in wine. Let mixture cool to room temperature, about 20 minutes.

3. Put ½ the onion mixture in each of 2 plastic freezer bags (1-qt. size). Seal bags and freeze (see page 246).

4. Thaw 1 bag (see notes). Pour onion mixture into a 3- to 4-quart pan and add 1½ quarts chicken broth. Bring to a boil over high heat, stirring often; reduce heat and simmer to blend flavors, about 10 minutes.

5. Ladle soup into bowls and add 1 gruyère crouton to each. Season to taste with salt and pepper. Serve with remaining croutons.

Per serving: 197 cal., 25% (49 cal.) from fat; 15 g protein; 5.4 g fat (0.7 g sat.); 21 g carbo (3.2 g fiber); 121 mg sodium; 0 mg chol.

Gruyère croutons. Trim ends from 1 loaf (1 lb.; about 4½ in. wide) **French bread.** Cut crosswise into 16 equal slices. Arrange slices in a single layer on a 14- by 17-inch baking sheet.

Bake in a 350° oven until lightly browned, about 25 minutes. Let cool to room temperature, about 10 minutes. Put ½ the slices in each of 2 plastic freezer bags (1-gal. size). Seal bags and freeze (see page 246).

To serve 4, remove frozen toasts from 1

bag and lay in a 10- by 15-inch pan. Cut ½ pound **gruyère cheese** into ¼-inch-thick slices. Cover toasts evenly with cheese. Bake in a 400° oven until cheese melts, 8 to 10 minutes.

Per crouton: 191 cal., 47% (90 cal.) from fat; 11 g protein; 10 g fat (5.5 g sat.); 14 g carbo (0.7 g fiber); 260 mg sodium; 31 mg chol.

Chicken Pot-au-Feu

ASSEMBLY TIME: About 1 hour

REHEATING TIME: About 1½ hours

NOTES: Thaw overnight (see page 246). Serve with garlic mashed potatoes (recipe follows) and hot cooked broccoli or sugar snap peas.

MAKES: 2 main dishes, 4 servings each

- 8 **chicken legs** (drumsticks and thighs attached; 4 lb. total), skinned and fat-trimmed

  Salt and **pepper**

- 2 tablespoons **olive oil**

- 3 cups diced (¼ to ½ in.) **carrots** (about 1¼ lb.)

- 1½ tablespoons minced **fresh thyme** leaves or 1½ teaspoons dried thyme

- ⅓ cup **all-purpose flour**

- 1 cup **oven-sautéed onions and garlic** (page 243)

- 1½ cups **dry white wine**

- 2 cups fat-skimmed **chicken broth**

- ½ cup **port**

1. Rinse chicken and pat dry. Sprinkle lightly with salt and pepper.

2. Put 1 tablespoon oil in a 5- to 6-quart pan over medium-high heat. When hot, add ½ the chicken and brown on all sides, about 10 minutes total. As chicken is browned, transfer to a platter and add remaining chicken. Let cool to room temperature, about 10 minutes.

3. Add carrots, thyme, and remaining oil to frying pan. Stir often until carrots are slightly browned, about 10 minutes. Add flour and stir 1 minute longer. Add sautéed onions and garlic, white wine, broth, and port, and stir until boiling, about 5 minutes. Let cool to room temperature, about 40 minutes.

4. Put ½ the chicken in each of 2 foil pans (8 to 9 in. square). Spoon sauce evenly over chicken. Seal pans with foil, and freeze (see page 246).

5. Thaw 1 pan (see notes). Bake, covered, in a 375° oven until chicken is no longer pink at bone in thickest part (cut to test), about 1½ hours (about 1 hour in a convection oven).

Per serving: 288 cal., 34% (99 cal.) from fat; 29 g protein; 11 g fat (2.2 g sat.); 19 g carbo (3 g fiber); 164 mg sodium; 104 mg chol.

Garlic Mashed Potatoes

ASSEMBLY TIME: About 45 minutes

REHEATING TIME: About 40 minutes

NOTES: Thaw overnight (see page 246) or bake directly from freezer, allowing about 1½ hours.

MAKES: 2 side dishes, 4 servings each

- 4 pounds **Yukon Gold potatoes**

- 2 packages (about 5 oz. each) **garlic-flavor Boursin**, Rondelé, or Alouette **cheese**

- 1¼ cups **low-fat milk**

  Salt and **pepper**

1. Peel potatoes, rinse, and cut into 2-inch chunks. Combine potatoes and about 2 quarts water in a 5- to 6-quart pan. Cover and bring to a boil over high heat; reduce heat. Simmer until potatoes mash very easily, 20 to 25 minutes. Drain potatoes and return to pan.

2. Add cheese and milk to potatoes. Mash with a potato masher or a mixer until smooth. Season to taste with salt and pepper. Let cool to room temperature, about 40 minutes.

3. Put ½ the mashed potatoes in each of 2 foil pans (8 to 9 inch square). Seal pans with foil, and freeze (see page 246).

4. Thaw 1 pan (see notes). Bake, covered, in a 375° oven until potatoes are steaming, about 40 minutes (about 30 minutes in a convection oven).

Per serving: 295 cal., 40% (117 cal.) from fat; 7.1 g protein; 13 g fat (8.8 g sat.); 39 g carbo (3.4 g fiber); 205 mg sodium; 35 mg chol.

Lamb Shanks with Sherry and Onions

ASSEMBLY TIME: About 2 hours

REHEATING TIME: About 1½ hours

NOTES: Thaw overnight (see page 246). Cook instant polenta and frozen petite peas to serve with shanks.

MAKES: 2 main dishes, 4 servings each

- 8 **lamb shanks** (8 lb. total), fat-trimmed

- 3 cups fat-skimmed **beef broth**

- 2 cups **oven-sautéed onions and garlic** (page 243)

- 1 cup **dry sherry**

- 1 jar (12 oz.) **roasted red peppers**, drained and coarsely chopped

- 2 tablespoons **sherry vinegar** or red wine vinegar

  Salt and **pepper**

1. Rinse lamb shanks and pat dry.

2. In an 11- by 17-inch roasting pan, combine broth, sautéed onions and garlic, and sherry. Arrange lamb in a single layer in mixture. Cover pan tightly with foil.

3. Bake in a 400° oven until meat is very tender when pierced, 2 to 2½ hours.

4. With tongs, transfer shanks to a platter. Skim and discard fat from pan juices. Stir in red peppers and vinegar. Let lamb and red pepper sauce cool to room temperature, about 40 minutes.

5. Put ½ the shanks in each of 2 foil pans (9 by 13 in.). Spoon sauce evenly over lamb. Seal pans with foil, and freeze (see page 246).

6. Thaw 1 pan (see notes). Bake, covered, in a 400° oven until lamb is steaming, about 1 hour. Uncover and bake until meat is well browned, about 10 minutes longer. Season to taste with salt and pepper.

Per serving: 501 cal., 31% (153 cal.) from fat; 68 g protein; 17 g fat (5.2 g sat.); 17 g carbo (2.3 g fiber); 280 mg sodium; 200 mg chol.

Chard, Bean, and Pancetta Soup

ASSEMBLY TIME: About 30 minutes

REHEATING TIME: About 15 minutes

NOTES: Thaw overnight or quick-thaw (see page 246). Serve with shredded parmesan cheese, breadsticks, and a crisp salad.

MAKES: 2 main dishes, 4 servings each

- ¾ pound **Swiss chard**

- 6 ounces **pancetta** or bacon, diced (¾ cup)

- 1 cup **oven-sautéed onions and garlic** (page 243)

- 2 quarts fat-skimmed **chicken broth**

- ⅓ cup **lemon juice**

- 3 tablespoons **tomato paste**

- 1½ teaspoons **fresh thyme** leaves or dried thyme

- 5 cans (15 oz. each) **cannellini** (white) **beans**, rinsed and drained

  Salt and **pepper**

1. Rinse and drain chard. Trim discolored ends from stems. Thinly slice stems and coarsely chop leaves.

2. In a 5- to 6-quart pan over medium-high heat, stir pancetta often until lightly browned, about 5 minutes.

3. Stir in chard, sautéed onions and garlic, broth, lemon juice, tomato paste, and thyme. Bring to a boil over high heat, stirring frequently. Reduce heat, cover, and simmer until chard stems are tender-crisp to bite, 2 to 4 minutes; stir occasionally.

4. Stir in beans. Let cool to room temperature, about 1½ hours.

5. Ladle ½ the soup into each of 2 plastic freezer bags (1-gal. size). Seal bags and freeze (see page 246).

6. Thaw 1 bag (see notes). Empty soup into a 3- to 4-quart pan and bring to a boil over high heat, stirring frequently, about 15 minutes. Season to taste with salt and pepper.

Per serving: 399 cal., 36% (144 cal.) from fat; 26 g protein; 16 g fat (4.9 g sat.); 40 g carbo (13 g fiber); 695 mg sodium; 14 mg chol.

Lentil-Barley Stew

ASSEMBLY TIME: About 50 minutes

REHEATING TIME: About 10 minutes

NOTES: Thaw overnight or quick-thaw (see page 246). Serve with cabbage slaw and crusty sourdough bread.

MAKES: 2 main dishes, 4 servings each

1 cup **lentils**

2½ quarts **vegetable** or fat-skimmed chicken **broth**

2 cups sliced **celery** (about 10 oz.)

1¾ cups sliced **carrots** (about ½ lb.)

1 cup **barley**

About 1 cup **oven-sautéed onions and garlic** (page 243)

2 teaspoons **dried rosemary**

5 cups coarsely chopped **tomatoes** (about 2¼ lb.)

Salt and **pepper**

1. Sort lentils, discard debris, and rinse.
2. In a 6- to 8-quart pan, combine lentils, broth, celery, carrots, barley, sautéed onions and garlic, and rosemary. Bring to a boil over high heat, stirring frequently. Reduce heat, cover, and simmer, stirring occasionally, 15 minutes.

3. Add tomatoes, cover, and stir occasionally until lentils are tender to bite, about 15 minutes longer. Let cool to room temperature, about 1½ hours.

4. Ladle ½ the stew into each of 2 plastic freezer bags (1-gal. size). Seal bags and freeze (see page 246).

5. Thaw 1 bag (see notes). Empty stew into a 3- to 4-quart pan and bring to a boil over high heat, stirring frequently, about 10 minutes. Season to taste with salt and pepper.

Per serving: 290 cal., 11% (32 cal.) from fat; 13 g protein; 3.5 g fat (0.5 g sat.); 55 g carbo (11 g fiber); 148 mg sodium; 0 mg chol.

MASTER MARINADES

These meats freeze in flavorful seasonings that often double as sauces.
• Moroccan Pork Loin with Dried Fruit and Lemons
• Grilled Rosemary-Mustard Lamb
• Soy and Ginger Flank Steak

Moroccan Pork Loin with Dried Fruit and Lemons

ASSEMBLY TIME: About 45 minutes

COOKING TIME: About 50 minutes

NOTES: Thaw overnight (see page 246). Serve with couscous and hot cooked green beans.

MAKES: 2 main dishes, 4 servings each

2 **lemons** (¾ lb. total)

1 tablespoon **ground coriander**

1 tablespoon **ground dried turmeric**

1½ teaspoons **ground ginger**

1½ teaspoons **ground cumin**

1 teaspoon **salt**

⅔ cup **honey**

PETITE PORK ROAST and dried fruit freeze and bake in a sweet-tart sauce.

1½ cups chopped **red onion** (about ½ lb.)

1 cup **dried apricots**

1 cup **dried pitted prunes**

2 **boned center-cut pork loin roasts** (1¼ lb. each)

2 cups fat-skimmed **beef broth**

1. Rinse lemons and trim ends. Cut lemons into ⅛-inch-thick slices and discard seeds.

2. Put ½ the coriander, turmeric, ginger, cumin, salt, honey, onion, apricots, prunes, and lemon slices in each of 2 plastic freezer bags (1-gal. size). Squeeze bags to mix ingredients.

3. Rinse pork. Trim and discard most of the fat. Add 1 pork roast and ½ the broth to each bag. Seal bags, turn to mix, and freeze (see page 246).

4. Thaw 1 bag (see notes). Pour pork and sauce into a 9- by 13-inch pan. Turn pork fat side up.

5. Bake in a 400° oven until a thermometer inserted in center of thickest part of roast reaches 155°, about 40 minutes; frequently stir sauce and baste meat.

6. Transfer pork to a platter and let rest about 5 minutes. Slice meat and serve with sauce.

Per serving: 445 cal., 26% (117 cal.) from fat; 33 g protein; 13 g fat (4.4 g sat.); 54 g carbo (3.2 g fiber); 407 mg sodium; 92 mg chol.

Grilled Rosemary-Mustard Lamb

ASSEMBLY TIME: About 20 minutes

COOKING TIME: About 30 minutes

NOTES: Keep this dish on hand for guests. Thaw overnight (see below). When you purchase ingredients for the cooking day, also buy shelf-stable or refrigerated cooked polenta. As the lamb grills, cut polenta into 3/4- to 1-inch-thick slices and brush with olive oil. Lay slices over direct heat beside the lamb. Brown well on each side, 10 to 15 minutes total. Serve lamb and polenta with a green salad. Any leftover lamb is excellent another day, thinly sliced, in sandwiches.

MAKES: 1 main dish, 8 servings with leftovers

- 1 **boned leg of lamb** (4 lb.), fat-trimmed
- 2/3 cup **Dijon mustard**
- 2/3 cup **dry vermouth**
- 1/4 cup **olive oil**
- 1/4 cup **Worcestershire**
- 2 tablespoons **lemon juice**
- 1 tablespoon minced **fresh rosemary** leaves or 1 teaspoon dried rosemary
- 2 tablespoons minced **garlic**
- 1 cup **whipping cream**

1. Rinse lamb and pat dry. Lay flat, cut side up. Make long cuts lengthwise into, but not quite through, leg. Press out and pat meat so it's as evenly thick as possible, making additional cuts as required.

2. Put lamb in a plastic freezer bag (1-gal. size). Add mustard, vermouth, oil, Worcestershire, lemon juice, rosemary, and garlic. Seal bag, turn to coat meat, and freeze (see below).

3. Thaw (see notes).

4. Lightly oil a barbecue grill over a solid bed of medium-hot coals or medium-high heat on a gas grill (you can hold your hand at grill level only 3 to 4 seconds). Lift lamb from bag; save marinade. Lay meat on grill. Close lid on gas grill. Cook until lamb is well browned on bottom, about 8 minutes. Turn meat and cook until as done as you like, about 20 minutes longer for medium-rare (pink in center; cut in thickest part to check). Transfer lamb to a platter and let rest at least 10 minutes.

5. Meanwhile, in a 2- to 3-quart pan, combine reserved marinade and cream; bring to a boil over high heat and stir often until mixture is reduced to 2 1/4 cups, about 10 minutes. Add any meat juices from platter.

6. Slice lamb and accompany with sauce.

Per serving: 508 cal., 51% (261 cal.) from fat; 49 g protein; 29 g fat (11 g sat.); 4.3 g carbo (0.1 g fiber); 694 mg sodium; 185 mg chol.

Soy and Ginger Flank Steak

ASSEMBLY TIME: About 20 minutes

COOKING TIME: About 15 minutes

NOTES: Thaw overnight (see below). Use the marinade to season corn and red and green bell peppers: Remove steak from 1 bag and add 4 husked corn ears (8 to 9 in. each) and 2 halved and seeded bell peppers (1 lb. total) to marinade. Mix, lift out vegetables, and cook on grill beside steak, turning occasionally, until slightly browned, about 10 minutes.

MAKES: 2 main dishes, 4 servings each

- 2 **flank steaks** (about 1 1/4 lb. each), fat-trimmed
- 2 tablespoons minced **fresh ginger**
- 4 teaspoons minced **garlic**
- 1/2 cup **reduced-sodium soy sauce**
- 6 tablespoons **dry red wine**
- 3 tablespoons **honey**

1. Rinse meat and pat dry.

2. Put 1 steak in each of 2 plastic freezer bags (1-gal. size). Add 1/2 the ginger, garlic, soy, wine, and honey to each bag. Seal bags, turn to coat meat, and freeze (see below).

3. Thaw 1 bag (see notes).

4. Lightly oil a barbecue grill over a solid bed of hot coals or high heat on a gas grill (you can hold your hand at grill level only 2 to 3 seconds). Lift steak from bag; save marinade (see notes). Lay meat on grill. Close lid on gas grill. Cook, turning once, until as done as you like, about 15 minutes for medium-rare (slightly pink in center; cut in thickest part to check).

5. Transfer steak to a board and cut crosswise into thin slices.

Per serving: 347 cal., 36% (126 cal.) from fat; 31 g protein; 14 g fat (5.7 g sat.); 26 g carbo (3.1 g fiber); 697 mg sodium; 71 mg chol.

COLD FACTS

Packaging: Freezer bags and foil pans

- If ingredients include liquid, set each plastic freezer bag upright in a bowl, then fill.
- Squeeze out all air and seal bag.
- For better protection of frozen foods during storage, seal each bag inside a second one.
- Lay bags flat in freezer until solid so they will stack.
- Seal foil pans with a double layer of foil to protect foods for storage.
- Label each dish with a permanent marker.
- Make a master list of the dishes. As you remove each from the freezer, cross it off the list.
- For best quality, freeze meat mixtures no longer than six weeks, others three months.

Thawing

Cooking times are for thawed, chilled foods.

- *Overnight:* The night before serving, place container of frozen food in the refrigerator.
- *Quick-thaw:* Heat frozen foods in plastic bags in a microwave oven at 50% power just until pliable, then cook as recipe directs or empty food into a microwave-safe container, drape loosely with microwave-safe plastic wrap, and cook at full power (100%) until steaming. *Note:* If your microwave accepts metal, you can also quick-thaw dishes frozen in foil pans; follow manufacturer's instructions.
- *Freezer to oven:* Remove foods in foil pans from the freezer and place directly in a hot oven. Note that reheating times may increase dramatically with this method (see recipe notes). ◆

The Low-Fat Cook

HEALTHY CHOICES FOR THE ACTIVE LIFESTYLE

BY ELAINE JOHNSON

APPETIZING BITES: Soft Medjools and cambozola cheese on crunchy baguette.

TUCKER & HOSSLER

One sweet date

■ By rights, Medjool dates—soft, sweet, and seemingly decadent—ought to be loaded with fat. They're not. They have none at all, in fact, and just 50 calories each. Those 50 calories go a long way in deliciously unusual starters, salads, and side dishes. To complement the dates' intense sweetness, we've added a splash of something tart, a hint of something salty, and a touch of something rich.

Medjool Cheese Toasts

PREP AND COOK TIME: About 15 minutes
MAKES: 12 pieces; 6 appetizer servings

1. Cut ¹/₂ a **baguette** (2¹/₂ in. wide; ¹/₂ lb. total) diagonally into 12 equal slices. Arrange slices in a single layer on a 12- by 15-inch baking sheet. Bake in a 450° oven until lightly toasted, about 5 minutes.
2. In a bowl, mix ¹/₂ teaspoon grated **lemon** peel with ¹/₃ cup **cambozola cheese**. Spread equally on 1 side of toast slices.
3. Cut 6 **Medjool dates** (2 in. long) in

half lengthwise; discard pits. Place 1 half, cut side down, on each toast.
4. Return pan to oven and bake until cheese is soft, 1 to 2 minutes. Top toast slices equally with 1¹/₂ teaspoons grated lemon peel.

Per serving: 182 cal., 16% (29 cal.) from fat; 5.1 g protein; 3.2 g fat (1.6 g sat.); 35 g carbo (2.1 g fiber); 317 mg sodium; 5.5 mg chol.

Date and Chicken Salad

PREP TIME: About 20 minutes
NOTES: Choose tangerines that have tight skins, such as Kinnow.
MAKES: 4 servings

> 1 head **fennel** (3¹/₂ to 4 in. wide)
> 2 cups shredded **boned, skinned cooked chicken breast**
> 10 **Medjool dates** (about 2 in. long)
> ¹/₂ pound **tangerines** (see notes)
> ¹/₃ cup **seasoned rice vinegar**
> 1 teaspoon **salad oil** (optional)
> ¹/₄ teaspoon **cayenne**
>   **Salt**

1. Trim stalks from fennel. Rinse feathery green leaves; chop enough to measure 2 to 3 tablespoons and save a few others for garnish. Discard remaining leaves and stalks. Trim root end, any bruised areas, and coarse fibers from fennel head. Rinse head and cut into paper-thin slices. In a bowl, combine chopped leaves, sliced fennel, and chicken.
2. Cut dates lengthwise into ¹/₂-inch-wide slices; discard pits. Add dates to bowl.
3. Rinse tangerines and cut in half crosswise. Ream juice from ¹/₂ the fruit and add to bowl. Cut remaining tangerines (including peel) vertically into paper-thin slices, discarding seeds; add to bowl, along with vinegar and oil. Sprinkle mixture with cayenne, mix gently, and spoon onto plates. Garnish with a few of the reserved green fennel leaves. Add salt to taste.

Per serving: 317 cal., 8.5% (27 cal.) from fat; 25 g protein; 3 g fat (0.7 g sat.); 51 g carbo (5.1 g fiber); 600 mg sodium; 60 mg chol.

Medjool Pilaf

PREP AND COOK TIME: About 45 minutes
MAKES: 4 servings

> ¹/₄ cup **sliced almonds**

> 1 tablespoon **butter** or margarine
> ¹/₂ cup chopped **onion**
> ³/₄ cup **Medjool dates** (about 5 oz.)
> 1 cup **basmati rice**
> ¹/₂ teaspoon **cumin seed**
> ¹/₂ teaspoon **ground ginger**
> ¹/₄ teaspoon **ground cardamom**
>   About ¹/₂ teaspoon **salt**
> 2 cups fat-skimmed **chicken broth**
> ¹/₂ cup **frozen petite peas**

1. In a 10- to 12-inch frying pan over medium heat, stir almonds often until golden, about 5 minutes. Pour from pan and reserve.
2. Add butter and onion to pan. Stir occasionally until onion is limp, about 5 minutes. Meanwhile, pit and chop ¹/₂ the dates. Cut remaining dates lengthwise into ¹/₂-inch-wide slices; discard pits.
3. Add rice to onion. Stir often until rice is opaque, about 4 minutes. Add cumin, ginger, and cardamom; stir 1 minute longer.
4. Add ¹/₂ teaspoon salt, broth, and chopped dates. Bring to a boil over high heat, then reduce heat, cover, and simmer, stirring occasionally, until rice is tender to bite, about 15 minutes.
5. Stir in peas and cook just until they're hot, 1 to 2 minutes. Pour pilaf into a bowl and top decoratively with sliced dates and almonds. Add more salt to taste.

Per serving: 356 cal., 18% (64 cal.) from fat; 12 g protein; 7.1 g fat (2.1 g sat.); 68 g carbo (4.2 g fiber); 411 mg sodium; 7.8 mg chol.

Date-Apricot Truffles

PREP TIME: About 20 minutes
MAKES: 12 pieces; 6 servings

1. Cut 8 **Medjool dates** (2 in. long) in half lengthwise and discard pits. Finely chop 4 date halves. In a bowl, mix chopped dates with ¹/₄ cup finely chopped **dried apricots**, 1¹/₂ teaspoons **honey,** and 1¹/₂ teaspoons **lemon juice.**
2. Spread ¹/₄ teaspoon **neufchâtel (light cream) cheese** (1 tablespoon total) in cut side of each date half. Mound apricot mixture equally onto cheese. Push 1 **roasted, salted almond** (12 total) into each mound.

Per serving: 112 cal., 14% (16 cal.) from fat; 1.4 g protein; 1.8 g fat (0.4 g sat.); 25 g carbo (2 g fiber); 27 mg sodium; 1.8 mg chol. ◆

foodguide

BY JERRY ANNE DI VECCHIO

PHOTOGRAPHS BY JAMES CARRIER

Shades of green

Muted colors, vibrant flavors in a fall salad

■ *Salad* is one of those words that get tossed around. It's applied to such a wide-ranging variety of presentations that one wonders, are there any limits? I'm certainly in no position to draw the line, as I consider even gazpacho a salad—a fluid one. Paul Bertolli of Oliveto Restaurant in Oakland, California, on the other hand, restricts his salad caprice to sounder turf with this lovely dish suited to the seasonal shift to cooler days. Sturdy flavors are cloaked in subtle colors—pale gold and faded greens, the reaction of artichokes, fennel, leeks, and celery to being poached, in this case in a flavorful broth. I use all the broth to make the dressing, a variation on Bertolli's creation. Offer the salad in small portions to start a meal, or in generous measure as a main dish.

Salad Capricciosa

PREP AND COOK TIME: About 2 hours and 20 minutes
NOTES: Up to 1 day ahead, cook vegetables; cover in liquid and chill. Garnish salads with frisée and red or white Belgian endive.
MAKES: 4 main-dish or 8 first-course servings

- 2 cups fat-skimmed **chicken broth**
- 1 cup **champagne vinegar** or white wine vinegar
- ½ cup **dry white wine**
- 2 **dried bay leaves**
- ½ teaspoon **dried thyme**
- ½ teaspoon **salt**
- 2 **artichokes** (each about 4 in. wide)
- 2 heads **fennel** (each 3 to 3½ in. wide)
- 4 **leeks** (each about ¾ in. thick)
- 1 head **celery** (about 2½ in. wide)
- ¼ cup **whipping cream**
- 1 can (2 oz.) **anchovy fillets,** drained
- 2 hard-cooked **large eggs,** shelled and mashed

1. In a 5- to 6-quart pan, combine broth, vinegar, wine, bay leaves, thyme, salt, and 1 cup water.

2. Break off artichoke leaves down to fleshy bottoms (save leaves to cook for other uses, if desired). With a vegetable peeler or knife, trim fibers from artichoke bottoms and trim stem ends; with a spoon, scrape out and discard fuzzy centers. Rinse artichoke bottoms and add to pan. Bring to a boil over high heat; reduce heat, cover, and simmer for 15 minutes.

3. As artichokes cook, rinse fennel and trim off stalks 1 to 2 inches above heads. Reserve feathery green leaves; discard stalks. Trim discolored spots, coarse fibers, and root ends from heads. Cut heads in half vertically.

4. Trim root ends and coarse tops from leeks; peel 1 layer off each leek. From green end, cut each leek in half lengthwise just down to white part. Rinse under running water, flipping green ends.

5. Trim tops off celery stalks to make head 8 to 9 inches long. Rinse.

6. Lay fennel, leeks, and celery over artichokes in pan (liquid does not cover). Cover pan and simmer until vegetables are just tender when pierced, 15 to 20 minutes longer. Let cool, covered, at least 1 hour. Lift out the vegetables.

7. Boil cooking liquid over high heat, uncovered, until reduced to ¾ cup, about 15 minutes. Pour through a strainer into a glass measure; discard residue. If needed, add water. Return liquid to pan, add cream, and bring to a boil over high heat. Remove from heat.

8. Slice vegetables vertically into 4 or 8 equal portions each (or cut thinner if desired). Arrange vegetables equally on plates, moisten with dressing, drape with anchovies, and sprinkle evenly with eggs. Chop some of the reserved green fennel leaves and use to garnish salads.

Per main-dish serving: 277 cal., 30% (82 cal.) from fat; 17 g protein; 9.1 g fat (4 g sat.); 35 g carbo (8 g fiber); 1,112 mg sodium; 129 mg chol.

A simple sole

■ After a day of touring beautiful, state-of-the-art tomato fields and high-tech greenhouses in Sinaloa, Mexico, I needed reassurance that delicious food has a simple side. I found it at Los Arcos Restaurant in Culiacán, close to the Sea of Cortez. This lively dish for a fragile fish is as easy as 1, 2, 3.

Green Chili Sole Casserole

PREP AND COOK TIME: About 45 minutes

MAKES: 4 servings

- 1 pound **mushrooms,** rinsed
- 2 tablespoons **butter** or olive oil
- 1/2 cup chopped **onion**
- 1 can (7 oz.) **diced green chilies**
- 2 tablespoons **all-purpose flour**
- 3/4 cup fat-skimmed **chicken broth**
- 1/2 cup **sour cream**
- 1 tablespoon **lime juice**
- 1 pound **sole fillets**
  Salt

1. Trim and discard discolored stem ends from mushrooms; thinly slice mushrooms. In a 10- to 12-inch frying pan over high heat, stir mushrooms in 1 tablespoon butter often until lightly browned, 12 to 15 minutes. Spoon into a shallow 1 1/2-quart casserole or divide equally among 4 shallow ramekins (about 1 1/2 cups each).

2. Add remaining butter and the onion and chilies to pan. Stir often until onion is limp, about 5 minutes. Add flour, mix well, and stir in broth. Purée mixture in a blender or food processor; return to pan. Add sour cream and stir over high heat until boiling. Remove from heat and add lime juice. Rinse fish, arrange in an even layer over mushrooms in casserole (or equally in ramekins), and cover with sauce.

3. Bake in a 400° oven until fish flakes when prodded, 12 to 15 minutes. Season with salt.

Per serving: 286 cal., 44% (126 cal.) from fat; 27 g protein; 14 g fat (7.7 g sat.); 14 g carbo (2.4 g fiber); 489 mg sodium; 83 mg chol.

Deconstruct a classic

■ The classics—literary and culinary—have much to offer if you don't take them too seriously. Case in point: macaroons. Made traditionally, they always strike me as overly complicated. All you need are three ingredients—nuts, sugar, and eggs. But the nuts don't have to be almonds, and the egg whites don't have to be whipped. Try shelled salted pistachios, which have a unique, subtle peachy fragrance. Just pop them into a food processor with sugar and an egg, then bake; in a few minutes, a new, chewy cookie classic is yours to savor.

Big Three Cookie

PREP AND COOK TIME: About 25 minutes

NOTES: If making up to 5 days ahead, cool and store airtight at room temperature; freeze to store longer. For an intriguing finish, before baking the cookies, sprinkle them lightly with salt as well as sugar.

MAKES: 18 cookies

- 1 cup **roasted, salted pistachios**
  About 3/4 cup **sugar**
- 1 **large egg**

1. In a food processor, whirl nuts, 3/4 cup sugar, and egg to a coarse paste.

2. Butter and flour a 12- by 15-inch baking sheet, plain or nonstick. Drop level tablespoons of pistachio mixture about 3 inches apart onto baking sheet. Sprinkle lightly with more sugar.

3. Bake cookies in a 325° oven until lightly browned, 14 to 18 minutes (10 to 12 minutes in a convection oven). Let cool on pan until firm, about 5 minutes. Slide a metal spatula under cookies to release; transfer to a rack. Serve warm or cool.

Per cookie: 86 cal., 47% (40 cal.) from fat; 1.5 g protein; 4.4 g fat (0.8 g sat.); 11 g carbo (0.8 g fiber); 63 mg sodium; 13 mg chol.

It's the pits

■ References to olive oil in Greek and Roman literature dating back 2,000 years set Roberto Crea to thinking. As a biochemist, he was intrigued by the descriptions of oils made by crushing the fruit without smashing the pit. By all accounts the result was a rich, full-flavored oil with a natural sweetness unobscured by bitter compounds from the pits. The scientific logic in this led Crea to pursue a new technology emulating the ancient process.

Simply put, Crea's Italian *integrale*-style olive oils are pressed from fruit that has been cut from the pit. And the results are as promised: richly fruited, delicately flavored oils that are, by technical measure, less acidic and therefore extra-virgin. They remind me of the first truly exquisite olive oil I ever tasted—handmade by Tio (Uncle) Giorgio from olives he grew and harvested on his farm in the hills east of Lucca in Tuscany.

As a California resident who grew up in Italy, Crea is producing integrale extra-virgin olive oils both here and there. CreAgri Supremo olive oils, in 500-ml. (16.9-oz.) bottles, are increasingly available in gourmet supermarkets and food shops. The price varies with the source: California oils cost about $21, Puglia oils (from Italy's east coast) about $23, and Tuscan oils about $25, plus shipping; to order, call (877) 787-7366 or visit www.SupremoOil.com.

THE LAZY COOK

Reformatting ravioli

■ Some years ago, *Sunset's* talented senior food writer Linda Anusasananan created a recipe for pumpkin ravioli that I loved. The creamy, golden filling melted in your mouth when released from its sheaths of tender pasta. But ravioli are a lot of work to make. More often than not, my Italian mother-in-law ordered them from her favorite shop in San Francisco's North Beach. The shop is gone, but a solution remains: layer the filling between sheets of lasagna, and spend more time enjoying than cooking the dish.

Golden Lasagna

PREP AND COOK TIME: About 1 hour, plus 15 minutes to stand

NOTES: If making lasagna up to 1 day ahead, assemble, cover, and chill. Bake, covered, for 30 minutes; uncover and bake until topping is lightly browned, 35 to 40 minutes.

MAKES: 8 servings

2 **onions** (1 lb. total), peeled and chopped

3 tablespoons **butter** or olive oil

2 tablespoons minced **fresh ginger**

1 tablespoon **curry powder**

2 packages (12 oz. each) thawed **frozen golden squash**

1 carton (15 oz.; 1¾ cups) **ricotta cheese**

Salt

1 **large egg**

¼ cup **all-purpose flour**

2 cups fat-skimmed **chicken broth**

1 cup **half-and-half** (light cream) or milk

About ½ teaspoon fresh-grated **nutmeg**

½ pound **dried lasagna**

½ cup **shredded parmesan cheese**

1. In a 10- to 12-inch frying pan over high heat, frequently stir onions with 2 tablespoons butter until limp, about 5 minutes. Scoop out ½ cup of the onion mixture and set aside. To frying pan, add ginger, curry powder, and squash; mix, then scrape into a bowl. Stir ricotta cheese into squash mixture and add salt to taste. Add egg and mix well.

2. Rinse and dry frying pan; return to high heat. Add remaining butter, the reserved onion mixture, and flour. Stir until flour is golden, about 3 minutes. Remove from heat; add broth and half-and-half. Mix until smooth. Stir over high heat until mixture boils; reduce heat and simmer, stirring often, about 5 minutes. Add ½ teaspoon nutmeg and salt to taste.

3. Meanwhile, in a 5- to 6-quart pan over high heat, bring about 3 quarts water to a boil. Add lasagna and cook, stirring occasionally, until tender to bite, 12 to 16 minutes. Drain, immerse in cold water, then drain again.

4. Spread about ½ cup of the onion sauce evenly over the bottom of a 9- by 13-inch casserole. Arrange ½ the lasagna neatly over sauce to cover. Spoon all the squash mixture onto pasta and spread level. Cover neatly with remaining pasta and coat completely with remaining onion sauce. Sprinkle with parmesan cheese and dust with more nutmeg.

5. Bake lasagna in a 375° oven until bubbling at edges and lightly browned on top, 35 to 40 minutes. Let stand 15 to 20 minutes; cut and serve with a wide spatula.

Per serving: 377 cal., 43% (162 cal.) from fat; 17 g protein; 18 g fat (11 g sat.); 38 g carbo (3.7 g fiber); 225 mg sodium; 80 mg chol. ◆

The Wine Guide

BY KAREN MacNEIL-FIFE

RICK MARIANI

Soft on red

■ It's time for a confession: I just don't get the superstar popularity of Merlot. Over and over I hear people say they prefer Merlot to other red wines. Why? "Because it's softer."

Softer than what?

Zinfandel? Well, Zinfandel can be as round and lush as red wine gets. Cabernet? The best Cabernets are as soft as cashmere pajamas. Pinot Noir? The top Pinots are downright sensual.

So where does this idea of Merlot being "softer" come from? Just what is softness in wine, anyway? And why is one wine soft and another not?

My theory is that the Merlot-softness connection began decades ago in Bordeaux, where Merlot (not Cabernet Sauvignon, as many assume) is the most widely planted grape. Most red wines from Bordeaux are blends primarily of Merlot, Cabernet Sauvignon, and Cabernet Franc. When asked what each of these grapes contributes, the Bordelais typically answer: "Merlot adds softness; Cabernet Sauvignon, structure; Cabernet Franc, aroma."

It's a tidy response—but a bit misleading. Recent advances in enology and viticulture paint a far more complex picture. Merlot, as it turns out, doesn't have a lock on softness. "Merlot is not a soft little feminine thing," says Robert Brittan, winemaker for Stags' Leap Winery in the Napa Valley. "We add Merlot to our Cabernet Sauvignon to give it structure and concentration. Great Merlot is not so much about softness as fullness."

"The word *soft* is overused, and wrongly used," agrees Richard Arrowood, wine master of Arrowood Vineyards & Winery in the Sonoma Valley. "Merlot is more a question of roundness. The tannin in Merlot gives the impression of roundness, while the tannin in Cabernet feels more sturdy on the palate."

Tannin. Now we're zeroing in. A compound that helps red wine age, tannin occurs naturally in grape skins. Red wines, which are always fermented with their skins, have a large amount as a result. "People talk about Cabernet having more tannin," says Arrowood, "and it's true. But what counts is not the total amount. It's the *character* of the tannin, the way it feels in the mouth." Tannin can feel dry and scratchy—or smooth and round. In the end, both Merlot and Cabernet can be soft—or not.

Which brings us to the question of why the tannins in some wines feel soft, while others don't. And the truth is, we know only part of the reason. "To get fullness, finesse, and what we call 'yummy Merlot flavors,' we have to get the grapes very, very ripe," says Brittan.

Elias Fernandez, winemaker for Napa's Shafer Vineyards, agrees. "Softness comes from ripeness," he says. "Really ripe grapes have tannin that coats your mouth in a silky, pleasant way. Unripe grapes make wine that feels hard and bitter."

You would think that picking grapes when they're perfectly ripe would be easy. But it's not. There is no mechanical instrument that can assess complete physiological maturity in a grape. Winemakers today must rely on what winemakers have relied on for millennia:

TOP FLIGHT

Truly soft wines tend to come from top vineyards, so are fairly expensive.

■ **Andrew Will "Klipsun Vineyards" Merlot 1997 (Washington)**, $40. Spicy and saturated with soft, syrupy black cherry flavors.

■ **Fetzer "Barrel Select" Merlot 1996 (North Coast, CA)**, $14. Not as rich as the others here, but the price is right. A soft, plummy wine for weeknight drinking.

■ **Livingston "Stanley's Selection" Cabernet Sauvignon 1995 (Napa Valley)**, $24. Sweetly ripe, super-soft blackberry fruit.

■ **Markham Merlot 199 (Napa Valley)**, $20. Fascinating flavors of menthol and tobacco around a soft core of cassis.

■ **Paradigm Merlot 1995 (Oakville, Napa Valley)**, $30. Mouthwatering blackberry flavors and lots of soft "baby fat."

■ **Shafer "Hillside Select" Cabernet Sauvignon 1994 (Stags Leap District, CA)**, $85. One of the great classics when it comes to softness. Totally hedonistic.

■ **Stags' Leap Winery Cabernet Sauvignon 1996 (Napa Valley)**, $32. Soft and concentrated, with delicious chocolate and blackberry flavors.

■ **Wente "Charles Wetmore Vineyard" Reserve Cabernet Sauvignon 1995 (Livermore Valley, CA)**, $21. Full of personality, with smoke, tar, and spicy mocha flavors, and a lovely soft texture.

instinct and past experience. Unfortunately, the window of opportunity is narrow. If the winemaker picks too early, the wine will taste hard. If he or she picks too late, the grapes will shrivel like raisins and the wine will taste like prune juice. The perfectly ripe grape is as elusive as the perfectly ripe peach.

In the end, Merlot is not necessarily softer than other red grapes. But when the winemaker does nail ripeness on the head, a round, full, and, yes, soft wine can emerge.

I like Merlot, by the way (though it may have seemed otherwise at first). But what I really love is softness—no matter what flavor it comes in. ◆

LAYERS OF APPLES and persimmons nestle beneath a spicy, crunchy topping.

Autumn fruit in a tart

Persimmons and apples nestle in a gingersnap crust

BY CHRISTINE WEBER HALE

Showy persimmons brighten the fall season, and if they are the crisp, flat-bottomed Fuyu, you can use them to make this streusel tart. It's an appealing dessert well suited to cooler days.

Persimmon-Apple Tart with Gingersnap Streusel

PREP AND COOK TIME: About 1 hour and 40 minutes

MAKES: 10 to 12 servings

Pastry for a single-crust 9-inch pie

1 cup crushed **gingersnap cookies**

⅓ cup firmly packed **brown sugar**

About 2 tablespoons **all-purpose flour**

3 tablespoons **butter** or margarine, melted

¼ cup **granulated sugar**

1 tablespoon **cornstarch**

2 **tart apples,** such as Newtown Pippin or Granny Smith (1 lb. total)

4 firm-ripe **Fuyu persimmons** (1½ lb. total)

2 tablespoons **lemon juice**

1. Roll pastry out on a floured board to fit a 9-inch tart pan with removable rim.

2. Lay pastry in pan, easing into corners. Fold excess pastry down and flush with pan rim, then press against pan side so pastry extends about ⅛ inch above rim.

3. Bake in a 350° oven until pastry is lightly browned, 10 to 15 minutes. Use hot or warm.

4. Meanwhile, in a bowl, stir together crushed gingersnaps, brown sugar, and 2 tablespoons flour. Mix in melted butter. Squeeze mixture to form lumps. Set aside.

5. In a large bowl, mix granulated sugar and cornstarch. Peel, core, and thinly slice apples. Stem, peel, and thinly slice persimmons. Add fruit to bowl along with lemon juice and mix well.

6. Pour mixture into pastry and shake pan to settle filling evenly, then crumble gingersnap mixture over it.

7. Bake tart on lowest rack of a 325° oven until pastry is browned and filling bubbles, 1 hour to 1 hour and 10 minutes. Lay a sheet of foil over streusel if it begins to darken before pastry is done. Let stand until warm or at room temperature; remove pan rim.

Per serving: 253 cal., 31% (79 cal.) from fat; 1.9 g protein; 8.8 g fat (3.1 g sat.); 44 g carbo (0.9 g fiber); 154 mg sodium; 7.8 mg chol. ◆

The Quick Cook

MEALS IN 30 MINUTES OR LESS

BY ANDREW BAKER AND CHRISTINE WEBER HALE

JENNIFER CHEUNG

MENU
Lamb Loin Roast
Chili Mascarpone Sauce
Roasted Tiny New Potato Halves
Tiny Green Beans
Lemon Cheesecake with
Raspberry Sauce

Petite roasts for special feasts

■ Party meals and elegant roasts go hand in hand. And for the occasion that's intimately scaled, there's a fine selection of diminutive roasts—with a big bonus: they can be table-ready in no more than half an hour.

Cuts that work include boned lamb loin (cut from the rack) and tenderloin of beef, pork, or venison. Because these roasts cook quickly, pan-brown them first, then finish in a hot oven; shorter times are for convection baking.

While the roast rests, use the pan with drippings to make a sauce. Five choices that go with every roast follow.

Lamb Loin Roast

PREP AND COOK TIME: About 30 minutes

MAKES: 6 servings

2 **boned lamb loins** (about $1\frac{1}{2}$ lb. total), fat-trimmed

Pan sauce (choices follow)

1. Rinse meat and pat dry. Place a 10- to 12-inch nonstick, ovenproof frying pan over high heat. When pan is hot, add lamb and brown well, 4 to 5 minutes.

2. Set frying pan in a 450° oven and bake until meat is medium-rare (pink in center of thickest part—cut to test—or 135° on a thermometer), 6 to 12 minutes, turning meat over once. Transfer to a platter; keep warm at least 5 minutes. Make sauce in frying pan.

3. Slice meat, adding juices to sauce. Serve sauce with meat.

Per serving: 192 cal., 47% (90 cal.) from fat; 23 g protein; 10 g fat (3.7 g sat.); 0 g carbo; 82 mg sodium; 75 mg chol.

Beef tenderloin. Use $1\frac{1}{2}$ pounds fat-trimmed **beef tenderloin.** With a sharp knife, cut lengthwise down center of meat and about $\frac{2}{3}$ of the way through it. Lay meat open and pat flat. Follow steps for lamb (above), cooking until meat is rare (red in center of thickest part—cut to test—or 125° on a thermometer), 7 to 12 minutes.

Per serving: 182 cal., 45% (81 cal.) from fat; 24 g protein; 9 g fat (3.3 g sat.); 0 g carbo; 61 mg sodium; 70 mg chol.

Pork tenderloins. Use 2 fat-trimmed **pork tenderloins** (about $1\frac{1}{2}$ lb. total). Follow steps for lamb (above), cooking until meat is no longer pink in center of thickest part (cut to test), or 150° on a thermometer, 9 to 15 minutes.

Per serving: 136 cal., 26% (35 cal.) from fat; 24 g protein; 3.9 g fat (1.3 g sat.); 0 g carbo; 57 mg sodium; 74 mg chol.

Venison tenderloins. Use 2 **venison tenderloins** (about $1\frac{1}{2}$ lb. total). Follow steps for lamb (above), cooking until meat is rare (red in center of thickest part—cut to test—or 125° on a thermometer), 6 to 12 minutes.

Per serving: 136 cal., 18% (24 cal.) from fat; 26 g protein; 2.7 g fat (1.1 g sat.); 0 g carbo; 58 mg sodium; 96 mg chol.

Pan sauces

Start with roast drippings, preceding.

Blackberry orange. Place frying pan with drippings over high heat. Add $1\frac{1}{2}$ cups fat-skimmed **beef broth,** 3 tablespoons **seedless blackberry jam,** 2 tablespoons **balsamic vinegar,** 1 tablespoon minced **orange** peel, and 2 teaspoons **prepared horseradish.** Boil, stirring, until $\frac{2}{3}$ cup, about 8 minutes.

Per tablespoon: 19 cal., 0% (0 cal.) from fat; 0.8 g protein; 0 g fat; 4.2 g carbo (0.1 g fiber); 14 mg sodium; 0 mg chol.

Brandy peppercorn. Place frying pan with drippings over high heat. Add 1 tablespoon **butter** or margarine, $\frac{3}{4}$ cup minced **shallots,** and 2 tablespoons drained **canned green peppercorns.** Stir over high heat until shallots are lightly browned, about 2 minutes. Add $\frac{3}{4}$ cup fat-skimmed **beef broth,** $\frac{1}{4}$ cup **brandy,** and 2 tablespoons **whipping cream.** Boil, stirring, until $\frac{2}{3}$ cup, about 3 minutes.

Per tablespoon: 36 cal., 53% (19 cal.) from fat; 0.7 g protein; 2.1 g fat (1.3 g sat.); 2.1 g carbo (0.1 g fiber); 79 mg sodium; 6.4 mg chol.

Chili mascarpone. Place frying pan with drippings over high heat. Add $\frac{1}{2}$ cup fat-skimmed **beef broth,** $\frac{1}{3}$ cup **tomato-based chili sauce,** $\frac{1}{3}$ cup **mascarpone** or whipping cream, and $\frac{1}{2}$ teaspoon **hot sauce.** Boil, stirring, until $\frac{2}{3}$ cup, about 4 minutes.

Per tablespoon: 45 cal., 69% (31 cal.) from fat; 1 g protein; 3.4 g fat (2.4 g sat.); 2.5 g carbo (0 g fiber); 135 mg sodium; 6.6 mg chol.

Paprika. In a blender or food processor, whirl 2 jars (4 oz. each) drained **pimientos** and 3 tablespoons fat-skimmed **chicken broth.** Place frying pan with drippings over high heat. Add pimiento mixture. Stir in $\frac{1}{4}$ cup **sour cream,** 1 teaspoon **lemon juice,** and $\frac{1}{2}$ teaspoon **hot paprika.** Boil, stirring, until $\frac{2}{3}$ cup, about 5 minutes.

Per tablespoon: 19 cal., 63% (12 cal.) from fat; 0.6 g protein; 1.3 g fat (0.8 g sat.); 1.5 g carbo (0 g fiber); 7.8 mg sodium; 2.5 mg chol.

Shiitake mushroom. Place frying pan with drippings over high heat. Add $\frac{1}{4}$ cup fat-skimmed **chicken broth** and 1 cup sliced **fresh shiitake mushroom caps.** Stir over high heat until mushrooms are browned, 2 to 3 minutes. Stir in 1 cup fat-skimmed chicken broth, 2 teaspoons **oyster sauce,** and 1 teaspoon **cornstarch** dissolved in 1 tablespoon **water.** Boil, stirring, until $\frac{2}{3}$ cup, about 5 minutes.

Per tablespoon: 8.3 cal., 0% (0 cal.) from fat; 1.3 g protein; 0 g fat ; 0.8 g carbo (0.1 g fiber); 57 mg sodium; 0 mg chol. ◆

Chimichanga mysteries

The origin of Tucson's deep-fried masterpiece
is an enigma wrapped in a tortilla

BY NORA BURBA TRULSSON

CHIMI CHAMP: In Tucson, Carlotta Flores's El Charro restaurants serve 10,000 chimichangas each week.

Once upon a time, somewhere in the Southwest, a clever cook dropped a burro into a deep-fat fryer, and the chimichanga, the savory staple of Arizona's Mexican restaurants, was born.

Just where and when this gastronomic event took place is the subject of much discussion among Tucsonans, who count the "chimi" as their own signature dish. Some claim to know the exact moment of creation, while others theorize that the crispy, golden brown delicacy evolved over the decades.

George Jacob, owner of Club 21 restaurant in Tucson, is a strict creationist. Not long after he opened his restaurant in 1946, he recalls serving an Easterner a plain burro—the meat-wrapped-in-flour-tortilla assemblage that's usually dubbed a burrito outside Arizona. The customer thought the burro looked raw. "I put some shortening on it and browned it on the grill," says Jacob, whose restaurant is still in its original location. "It looked pretty good, so we put it on the menu as a fried burro."

A few years later, a Mexican-born customer ordered a fried burro and called it *que chango,* which roughly translates to *how whimsical.* By 1954, Jacob's fried burro had morphed into *chimichanga* and earned a regular spot on his menu.

THE BIRTH OF A THINGAMAJIG

But does this make Jacob the chimichanga's founding father? Not according to Carlotta Flores, owner of Tucson's El Charro Café. Family legend says Flores's great-aunt, Monica Flin, who started the restaurant in 1922, cussed in the kitchen when a burro flipped into the deep fryer. As she was knee-deep in a gaggle of nieces and nephews, she changed the swear word to *chimichanga*—the Spanish equivalent of *thingamajig.*

Today Flores serves some 10,000 chimichangas a week at her two restaurant locations. She has expanded the chimichanga section of her menu to include both a vegetarian version and a *USA Today* version (rolled and fried, it's the size of the newspaper, folded). A while back, Flores switched the frying medium from the traditional lard to canola oil. About the same time, trying to be helpful, she printed a calorie count next to each chimi on the menu (starting at about 1,200 for a plain beef chimichanga). "Let's just say my customers didn't appreciate it," she says.

Frank Davis Jr., a third-generation Tucson restaurateur whose family started La Fuente in 1960, theorizes that geography influenced the development of the chimichanga. "I think it got started along the border, in Sonora, Mexico," he says. "Sonora is a

wheat capital of Mexico, and that's where they first started making the large, 16- to 18-inch flour tortillas that we use for chimichangas."

At La Fuente, customers order chimis with a variety of beef or chicken fillings, and get them either plain, enchilada-style (smothered in sauce, topped with melted cheese), or with sides of guacamole and sour cream.

Jim Griffith, a folklorist at the University of Arizona's Southwest Center, agrees with Davis on the chimi's Sonoran origins. "It probably developed somewhere in southern Arizona or northern Sonora where not only wheat but beef is grown," says Griffith. His first encounter with a chimichanga was during a mid-1950s Easter celebration at a Yaqui Indian village on the outskirts of Tucson. "I'm guessing, though, that they were around long before then," he says.

Whatever the place and year of its birth, the chimichanga has spread in popularity—you're almost as likely to find it on menus in Seattle as in Tucson. And as with any other ubiquitous dish, it has acquired permutations, including minichimis—smaller versions great as appetizers—and dessert chimichangas, filled with chocolate or fruit.

There is only one thing about chimichangas that everyone seems to agree upon. They are *muy* addicting.

A chimi tour of Tucson

Here are three classic Tucson venues for chimichangas. Area code is 520.
Club 21, 11–9 Tue-Sun, 11–10 Fri-Sat. 2920 N. Oracle Rd., 622-3092.
El Charro Café, 11–9 Sun-Thu, 11–10 Fri-Sat. 311 N. Court Ave., 622-1922, and 6310 E. Broadway, 745-1922.
La Fuente, 11–11 daily. 1749 N. Oracle, 623-8659.

These chimichanga recipes come from Carlotta Flores's cookbook, *El Charro Café: The Tastes and Traditions of Tucson* (Fisher Books, Tucson, 1998; $24.95; 520/744-6110).

Chimichangas El Charro

PREP AND COOK TIME: About 40 minutes, plus preparation of filling

NOTES: At El Charro Café, Carlotta Flores makes chimichangas with the overgrown, 16- or 18-inch flour tortillas renowned in the Sonoran region. But 12- to 14-inch tortillas (the fresher, the more flexible) make impressive chimis too—even 10-inchers will do—and they're easier to deep-fry at home. As a crisp alternative to frying, place rolled chimis in an oiled 10- by 15-inch pan and brush lightly with salad oil. Bake on the lowest rack in a 400° oven until golden, about 35 minutes. If desired, sprinkle with cheese and bake until cheese is melted, about 5 minutes longer.

Chimichangas can be filled with a variety of meats and vegetables; here are two of Flores's favorites. Fruit salsa is especially good with the pork filling.

MAKES: 6 servings

6 **flour tortillas** (12 to 14 in.)

Filling (choices follow)

About 1½ quarts **salad oil**

2 **firm-ripe avocados** (about ½ lb. each)

2 tablespoons **lime juice**

1 can (16 oz.) **red chili** or enchilada sauce

3 cups shredded **lettuce** (iceberg and/or romaine) and/or red cabbage

2 cups (about ½ lb.) **shredded jack** and/or cheddar cheese

Sour cream

Tomato or fruit **salsa**

1. Lay 1 tortilla flat. Fold ⅓ up over center. Spoon ⅙ of the filling across the doubled portion, leaving a 2-inch border at each end. Roll tortilla once, fold in ends, then roll snugly to enclose filling. Secure seam with toothpicks. Repeat to fill remaining tortillas.

2. In a 5- to 6-quart pan (at least 10 in. wide) or 14-inch wok over high heat,

CHIMI GOES VEGGIE: Squash updates the Southwestern classic.

JAMES CARRIER

bring about 1 inch oil to 360°; adjust heat to maintain temperature.

3. Using a wide metal spatula, lower 1 chimichanga at a time into hot oil, filling pan without crowding. Fry until golden on all sides, turning occasionally, 6 to 8 minutes total per chimi. Transfer to a towel-lined 10- by 15-inch pan. Keep warm in a 225° oven. Repeat to fry remaining chimichangas.

4. Meanwhile, peel, pit, and thinly slice avocados. Moisten slices with lime juice. In a 1- to 1½-quart pan over medium heat, warm chili sauce; pour into a small bowl.

5. Line a platter or plates with lettuce. Remove toothpicks from chimis and place, seam down, on lettuce. Sprinkle chimis evenly with 1 cup cheese and garnish with avocado. Serve with remaining cheese and the chili sauce, sour cream, and salsa, to taste.

Calabacitas Filling (Squash)

PREP AND COOK TIME: About 50 minutes

MAKES: About 8 cups

Rinse 2½ pounds **zucchini**, yellow crookneck, and/or pattypan **squash,** and trim ends. Cut squash into ½-inch chunks. In a 5- to 6-quart pan over medium-high heat, mix squash, 1 chopped **onion** (about ¾ lb.), 3 chopped **firm-ripe tomatoes** (about 1½ lb. total), ¼ cup minced garlic, and 2 tablespoons **salad oil**; stir occa-

sionally until onion is limp, about 8 minutes. Add 1 can (7 oz.) **diced green chilies** and 1 cup **frozen corn kernels.** Stir occasionally until squash is tender when pierced, about 10 minutes. Drain; reserve liquid for other uses. Season filling to taste with **salt** and **pepper.**

Per chimi with squash: 807 cal., 46% (369 cal.) from fat; 25 g protein; 41 g fat (11 g sat.); 94 g carbo (8.2 g fiber); 1,821 mg sodium; 40 mg chol.

Carnitas de Puerco Filling (Shredded Pork)

PREP AND COOK TIME: About 2¾ hours

MAKES: About 5½ cups

Rinse 2 pounds **boned pork loin** and put in a 5- to 6-quart pan. Add 1 peeled and quartered **onion** (about ¾ lb.), 2 peeled and diced **carrots** (about ½ lb. total), 10 to 12 peeled **garlic** cloves, and 1 teaspoon **salt.** Add water to barely cover meat (1½ to 2 qt.). Bring to a boil over high heat; reduce heat and simmer, covered, until pork is tender when pierced, 1¼ to 1½ hours. With a slotted spoon, transfer meat to a platter (reserve cooking liquid for other uses). When pork is cool enough to handle, in about 20 minutes, pull into shreds with 2 forks or your fingers.

Per chimi with pork: 927 cal., 50% (459 cal.) from fat; 50 g protein; 51 g fat (16 g sat.); 68 g carbo (3.8 g fiber); 1,654 mg sodium; 131 mg chol.

— *Sara Schneider* ◆

Kitchen Cabinet

READERS' RECIPES TESTED IN SUNSET'S KITCHENS

BY LINDA LAU ANUSASANANAN

IS IT A COOKIE OR A PIE? Chocolate and walnuts in a chewy filling.

Chocolate Chip Walnut Pie

Anne H. Beck, Arnold, California

Anne Beck made this customer-pleasing pie to sell in her former ice cream shop and deli. It tastes like a chocolate chip cookie, and is especially good warm.

PREP AND COOK TIME: 40 to 55 minutes

MAKES: 8 servings

- 1 **refrigerated pastry for a single-crust 9-inch pie** (½ of a 15-oz. package), at room temperature
- ½ cup (¼ lb.) melted **butter** or margarine
- 2 **large eggs**
- ½ cup **granulated sugar**
- ½ cup firmly packed **brown sugar**
- ½ cup **all-purpose flour**
- 1 cup (6 oz.) **semisweet chocolate chips**
- 1 cup chopped **walnuts**

  Vanilla ice cream (optional)

1. Unfold pastry round and ease evenly into a 9-inch pie pan.

2. In a bowl, beat butter, eggs, granulated sugar, and brown sugar until well blended. Add flour and mix well. Stir in chocolate chips and nuts.

3. Pour chocolate chip filling into pastry.

4. Bake on the lowest rack in a 325° oven until top is a rich golden brown, 40 to 45 minutes (about 30 minutes in a convection oven). Cool on rack at least 20 minutes. Serve warm or cool, cut into wedges, with ice cream.

Per serving: 563 cal., 56% (315 cal.) from fat; 6.4 g protein; 35 g fat (15 g sat.); 60 g carbo (0.9 g fiber); 274 mg sodium; 91 mg chol.

Macaroni with Anchovies and Arugula

Theresa Liu, Alameda, California

Even when Theresa Liu's refrigerator looks bare, she can find the makings for macaroni with anchovies. For freshness, she adds arugula, spinach leaves, frozen peas, or broccoli florets—depending on what the larder has to offer. Writes Liu, "Even proclaimed anchovy haters take to this dish."

PREP AND COOK TIME: About 25 minutes

MAKES: 3 or 4 servings

- 2½ cups (7 oz.) **dried macaroni**
- 9 cups **arugula leaves** (about 11 oz.), rinsed and drained
- 2 tablespoons **olive oil**
- 6 cloves **garlic,** peeled and chopped
- 1 can (2 oz.) **anchovy fillets,** drained and minced
- 1 can (2¼ oz.) **sliced black ripe olives,** drained
- ¼ teaspoon **pepper**
- ⅛ to ¼ teaspoon **hot chili flakes**

  About ½ cup **grated parmesan cheese**

1. In a covered 5- to 6-quart pan over high heat, bring 2 to 3 quarts water to a boil. Add macaroni and cook, uncovered, until barely tender to bite, about 6 minutes.

2. When macaroni is almost tender, add arugula; stir and cook just until leaves wilt, about 1 minute. Drain pasta and greens and put in a bowl. Quickly rinse and dry pan.

3. Add oil and garlic to pan over medium heat; stir until garlic is limp, about 1 minute. Add anchovies, olives, pepper, and chili flakes; stir and add pasta, greens, and ½ cup cheese. Mix well and pour back into bowl. Add more parmesan cheese to taste.

Per serving: 358 cal., 35% (126 cal.) from fat; 16 g protein; 14 g fat (3.5 g sat.); 43 g carbo (3 g fiber); 763 mg sodium; 14 mg chol.

Tofu Herb Dip

Maria Sandoval, Alameda, California

Searching for appealing foods for her daughter, who was on a low-fat diet,

Maria Sandoval came up with this nutritious and appealing appetizer dip. Most of our tasters never guessed that tofu was its base. Serve the herb dip with melba toast, crackers, thin baguette slices, or raw vegetables.

PREP AND COOK TIME: About 30 minutes

MAKES: 2⅛ cups; 18 servings

- 1 carton (12 to 14 oz.) **firm tofu**
- ¾ cup coarsely chopped **fresh cilantro**
- ¾ cup coarsely chopped **parsley**
- ¾ cup lightly packed **fresh mint** leaves, rinsed
- ½ cup sliced **green onions**
- ½ cup drained **canned roasted red peppers**
- 1 clove **garlic,** peeled
- 3 tablespoons **lemon juice**
- 2 tablespoons drained **capers**

   Salt and **pepper**

1. Rinse tofu and drain. Cut into ½-inch-thick slices and lay on several layers of towels. Cover with several layers of towels and press gently to remove excess liquid.

2. In a food processor, combine cilantro, parsley, mint, and green onions. Whirl until minced (or mince with a knife). Pour herbs into a small bowl.

3. Pat red peppers dry and put into a food processor or blender. Crumble tofu and add to red peppers along with garlic, lemon juice, and capers. Whirl until smooth. Add to herbs and stir to mix. Add salt and pepper to taste.

Per serving: 34 cal., 44% (15 cal.) from fat; 3.2 g protein; 1.7 g fat (0.2 g sat.); 2.2 g carbo (0.5 g fiber); 55 mg sodium; 0 mg chol.

Garam Masala Pork Chops

Joy Taylor, Grants Pass, Oregon

Intrigued, Joy Taylor bought garam masala, an aromatic Indian spice blend, and began to experiment. She particularly likes the mixture with fruit and pork, and serves it with hot cooked rice, drenched with the plentiful sauce. Look for garam masala in Indian markets and specialty food stores. Or use the spice alternatives.

PREP AND COOK TIME: About 30 minutes

MAKES: 4 servings

- 4 **center-cut loin pork chops** (each about 1 in. thick, 2⅓ lb. total)

SPINACH AND FRESH CHEESE on—or make that *in*—a savory roll.

- 4 teaspoons **salad oil**
- 2 tablespoons **garam masala** (or 1 tablespoon *each* ground coriander and ground cumin)
- 2 tablespoons **garlic powder**
- ¾ cup **cranberry-raspberry juice** blend
- ¼ cup fat-skimmed **chicken broth**
- 1 tablespoon **cornstarch**

   Salt and **pepper**

1. Trim and discard fat from chops. Rinse chops, pat dry, and rub with 1 teaspoon oil.

2. Mix garam masala and garlic powder. Rub spice mixture all over chops.

3. Place a 10- to 12-inch nonstick frying pan over medium-high heat. Add remaining 1 tablespoon oil and swirl to coat pan. Set chops in pan and brown well on each side, pressing meat flat with a spatula if needed to get even color, 2 to 3 minutes a side.

4. Stir cranberry-raspberry juice blend and broth into pan. Bring to a boil over high heat. Cover and simmer over low heat, turning once, until chops are no longer pink in center (cut to test), 15 to 18 minutes total. With a slotted spatula, transfer chops to a platter; keep warm.

5. Mix 2 tablespoons water with cornstarch; stir into pan, then stir over high heat until boiling, 2 minutes. Pour over chops. Add salt and pepper to taste.

Per serving: 337 cal., 37% (126 cal.) from fat; 39 g protein; 14 g fat (3.6 g sat.); 12 g carbo (0.2 g fiber); 124 mg sodium; 108 mg chol.

Hot Ricotta Spinach Loaf

Barbara R. Warner, Boise

When Barbara Warner moved from Southern California, her family missed the spinach bread they had enjoyed at their favorite Italian restaurant. Her solution was this quickly made loaf. Serve it as an appetizer or as a hot sandwich.

PREP AND COOK TIME: About 30 minutes

MAKES: 10 appetizer servings, or 5 sandwich servings

- 1 tube (10 oz., for 12-in. crust) **refrigerated pizza crust dough**
- 1 package (10 oz.) **frozen chopped spinach,** thawed
- 1 carton (8 oz.; 1 cup) **ricotta cheese**
- ½ cup grated **parmesan cheese**
- ¼ teaspoon **ground nutmeg**
- 1 clove **garlic,** peeled and minced or pressed
- 1 tablespoon **olive oil**
- 1 can (8 oz.; 1 cup) **marinara sauce**

1. On a 12- by 15-inch baking sheet, unroll pizza crust dough.

2. Squeeze excess moisture from spinach. Mix spinach, ricotta cheese, parmesan cheese, nutmeg, and garlic.

3. Spread mixture evenly over dough.

4. Starting at a long edge of dough, roll to enclose filling. Set the loaf, seam down, on baking sheet. Brush loaf top with olive oil.

5. Bake in a 425° oven until well browned, 12 to 15 minutes. Meanwhile, stir marinara sauce in a 1- to 1½-quart pan over medium heat until hot; or heat in a microwave-safe bowl in a microwave oven at full power (100%) until hot.

6. Slice loaf diagonally, making 10 equal portions. Offer 1 slice as an appetizer serving, or 2 slices as a main-dish sandwich. Spoon marinara sauce over slices to taste.

Per slice: 158 cal., 41% (64 cal.) from fat; 7.9 g protein; 7.1 g fat (2.9 g sat.); 17 g carbo (1.3 g fiber); 533 mg sodium; 15 mg chol. ◆

Our menu for a movable Thanksgiving feast (see page 260) includes this richly textured wild rice pilaf with kumquats.

November

PREPARED ON THE SPOT or transported, a magnificent roasted three-spice turkey is the Thanksgiving star.

To Grandma's house or a coastside cabin

Thanksgiving on the go

■ Thanksgiving means gathering. The pilgrims and Native Americans came together to share the bounty of their respective harvests. Following their lead, Americans are still carrying their turkeys to Grandmother's house—or the beach or the neighbors' garden. • Five groups of Westerners inspired our own movable feasts this year. Incorporating their favorite dishes, and a few of our own, we offer a mix-and-match folio of recipes—including make-ahead suggestions—for Thanksgiving dinner on the road. Karen MacNeil-Fife suggests great wines to take along. • Here are the pilgrims, their food, and our advice on transporting the feast.

BY ANDREW BAKER • PHOTOGRAPHS BY JAMES CARRIER
FOOD STYLING BY VALERIE AIKMAN-SMITH

GO FOR THE BOLD: Crispy focaccia topped with homemade tapenade, crumbled goat cheese, and roasted red peppers.

appetizers

Tapenade and Goat Cheese Bruschetta

Hamida Betty Rahman, Portland

PREP AND COOK TIME: About 20 minutes

NOTES: Instead of making the tapenade, you can use purchased tapenade, available at well-stocked supermarkets.

TO TRANSPORT: Seal the cooled toasted focaccia and the red peppers, goat cheese, tapenade, and parsley airtight in separate containers; carry the focaccia at room temperature, and keep red peppers, goat cheese, tapenade, and parsley cold. To serve, spread the tapenade and cheese onto focaccia pieces; top with red peppers and parsley.

MAKES: 8 to 10 servings

- 1 pound **plain** or herb **focaccia**
- ⅓ cup **canned roasted red peppers**
- 1½ cups **tapenade** (recipe follows; or see notes)
- 1 package (5 oz.) **fresh chèvre (goat) cheese**

  Parsley sprigs

1. Cut focaccia into 16 to 20 equal pieces. Arrange in a single layer on a 14-by 17-inch baking sheet.

2. Bake in a 375° oven until crisp, 7 to 10 minutes.

3. Meanwhile, cut red peppers into ¼-inch strips.

4. Spread all the tapenade evenly over top of focaccia pieces. Dot goat cheese evenly over tapenade, pressing lightly with your fingers so cheese adheres to surface.

5. Return focaccia to oven and bake until cheese is hot, about 5 minutes. Top equally with red peppers and parsley sprigs.

Per serving: 289 cal., 53% (153 cal.) from fat; 9.6 g protein; 17 g fat (4.4 g sat.); 25 g carbo (0.9 g fiber); 1,058 mg sodium; 11 mg chol.

Tapenade

Hamida Betty Rahman

PREP TIME: About 10 minutes

NOTES: If making tapenade up to 1 week ahead, chill airtight.

TO TRANSPORT: Put in a small bowl, cover, and keep cold.

MAKES: About 1½ cups

- 1 can (2 oz.) **anchovy fillets**

  Olive oil
- 2 cups pitted **calamata olives**
- 3 tablespoons drained **capers**
- 1 tablespoon chopped **garlic**

1. Drain oil from anchovies and measure; add enough olive oil to make 3 tablespoons total.

2. In a blender or food processor, combine oil, anchovies, olives, capers, and garlic.

3. Whirl until smooth, scraping container sides as needed.

Per tablespoon: 54 cal., 81% (44 cal.) from fat; 0.6 g protein; 4.9 g fat (0.6 g sat.); 1.8 g carbo (0 g fiber); 319 mg sodium; 1 mg chol.

Chili–Cream Cheese Quiche

PREP AND COOK TIME: About 1 hour

NOTES: If making crust up to 1 day before using, wrap airtight and let stand at room temperature; freeze to store longer. Thaw unwrapped. If making quiche up to 1 day ahead, let cool, cover, and chill.

TO TRANSPORT: Wrap quiche airtight and keep cold.

MAKES: 8 to 10 servings

1¼ cups **all-purpose flour**

¼ cup **cornmeal**

½ cup (¼ lb.) **butter** or margarine, in chunks

3 **large eggs**

⅓ cup **pine nuts**

About 1½ cups (one 3-oz. package and one 8-oz. package) **cream cheese**

1½ cups (6 oz.) **shredded sharp cheddar cheese**

1 can (4 oz.) **diced green chilies**

¼ cup chopped **canned roasted red peppers**

1. In a food processor or bowl, combine flour and cornmeal. Add butter; whirl or rub with your fingers until fine crumbs form. Add 1 egg; whirl or stir with a fork until dough holds together.

2. Spread and press dough evenly over bottom and up sides of a 10-inch tart pan with removable rim.

3. Bake in a 300° oven until pale gold, 25 to 30 minutes; use warm or cool.

4. Meanwhile, in an 8- to 10-inch frying pan over medium-high heat, stir or shake pine nuts until lightly browned, 3 to 4 minutes. Pour from pan.

5. In a large bowl with a mixer, beat cream cheese and remaining 2 eggs until well blended. Stir in cheddar cheese, green chilies, and red peppers. Pour cream cheese mixture evenly into crust. Sprinkle nuts on filling.

6. Bake quiche in a 350° oven just until center no longer jiggles when pan is gently shaken, about 25 minutes (about 18 minutes in a convection oven). Let cool at least 10 minutes.

7. Serve quiche warm or chilled. Cut into wedges.

Per serving: 379 cal., 71% (270 cal.) from fat; 12 g protein; 30 g fat (17 g sat.); 18 g carbo (1.3 g fiber); 387 mg sodium; 141 mg chol.

A THANKSGIVING PICNIC TAILORED FOR TRANSPORT

Hot Buttered Rum (pictured at left)

Beet Bisque with Apple-Herb Salsa

Hot Mushroom Salad

Confit Turkey Legs

Refrigerator Pickles

Roasted Onions, Yams, and Potatoes with Seasoned Butter

Wild Rice Pilaf

Refrigerator Rolls

Chocolate-Orange Hazelnut Pie

GAME PLAN

☐ **Up to 1 week ahead.** *Make* spiced sugar mixture for hot buttered rum, refrigerator pickles, and seasoned butter for roasted vegetables.

☐ **Up to 5 days ahead.** *Start* refrigerator rolls.

☐ **Up to 1 day ahead.** *Make* beet bisque with apple-herb salsa, and confit turkey legs. *Rinse* greens for hot mushroom salad. *Bake* refrigerator rolls and chocolate-orange hazelnut pie.

☐ **Up to 2 hours ahead.** *Finish* hot buttered rum. *Assemble* hot mushroom salad. *Roast* onions, yams, and potatoes. *Make* wild rice pilaf.

WINES

For this and the menu on page 268, go for expressive wines with bold, forward flavors rather than delicate wines. These dishes have dozens of dynamic ingredients. You need wines that won't be shy in that company.

■ **With the appetizers.** Cuvaison Chardonnay 1997 (Napa Valley), $19.95. Sassy and dramatic, with delicious apple and lemon flavors.

Why? Beets and apples are terrific with Chardonnay (and virtually anything flavored with tarragon is a Chardonnay home run), and the roundness of this particular one picks up on the creaminess of the soup. Chardonnay can also be very good with mushrooms, amplifying their earthiness and, in this case, offering a nice texture contrast to the chanterelles. *Note:* This beautifully balanced wine (not overly oaky or sweet) also pairs extremely well with the fruit- and nut-studded wild rice pilaf.

■ **With the main course.** Montevina "Terra d'Oro Deaver Old Vines" Zinfandel 1997 (Amador County, CA), $22. A ripe, rustic, and mouth-filling wine with big berry flavors.

Why? This rustic, slightly tannic Zin is just waiting for spicy dark meat. Its tannin is a perfect counterpoint to the black pepper and other spices in the confit turkey legs, yet it also has a lot of sweet ripe-berry fruit that is great with the roasted onions and yams. — *Karen MacNeil-Fife*

soups

Beet Bisque with Apple-Herb Salsa

PREP AND COOK TIME: About 1 hour

NOTES: Up to 1 day ahead, make soup and let cool; also make salsa. Cover soup and salsa separately, and chill.

TO TRANSPORT: Pour cold soup into a thermos; carry chilled apple salsa in a covered jar in an insulated container.

MAKES: About 10 cups; 8 to 10 servings

2½	pounds trimmed **golden** or red **beets**
1	pound **Granny Smith apples**
⅔	cup **lemon juice**
6	tablespoons minced **fresh mint** leaves
3	tablespoons minced **fresh tarragon** leaves
2½	cups fat-skimmed **chicken broth**
2	cups **half-and-half** (light cream)
	Fresh-ground **pepper**

1. Scrub beets. Put in a 5- to 6-quart pan with 2 quarts water. Bring to a boil over high heat; reduce heat, cover, and simmer until beets are tender when pierced, 30 to 40 minutes.

2. Drain beets and immerse in ice water until cool enough to handle, about 5 minutes. Pull or cut off skins and discard. Coarsely chop beets.

3. Meanwhile, rinse the apples; core them and cut into ½-inch chunks. In a small bowl, mix 1 cup of the apple chunks with 2 tablespoons lemon juice, 2 tablespoons mint, and 1 tablespoon tarragon.

4. Place remaining apple chunks in a 1- to 1½-quart pan. Add chicken broth and bring to a boil over high heat. Stir occasionally until apples are very tender when pierced, 2 to 3 minutes.

5. In a blender, whirl the apple-broth mixture, beets, remaining lemon juice, remaining mint, remaining tarragon, and the half-and-half, a portion at a time, until smooth. Cover and chill at least 1 hour.

6. Ladle soup into bowls. Add apple salsa and pepper to taste.

Per serving: 135 cal., 39% (53 cal.) from fat; 4.9 g protein; 5.9 g fat (3.5 g sat.); 18 g carbo (1.9 g fiber); 98 mg sodium; 18 mg chol.

LIQUID GOLD: Cool, creamy beet and apple soup with tangy apple-herb salsa.

Roasted Fennel and Potato Soup with Blue Cheese Croutons

PREP AND COOK TIME: About 50 minutes

NOTES: If making soup up to 1 day ahead, cool, cover, and chill. Let croutons cool, wrap airtight, and store at room temperature. To reheat soup, stir in a 3- to 4-quart pan over medium-high heat until steaming; or heat in a microwave-safe container in a microwave oven at full power (100%), stirring often, until steaming.

TO TRANSPORT: Put hot soup in a thermos. Seal fennel leaves in a heavy plastic food bag and keep cold. Seal cool croutons in another plastic bag and carry at room temperature.

MAKES: About 8 cups; 8 to 10 servings

2	heads **fennel** (3½ to 4 in. wide)
1	pound **russet potatoes,** peeled
2	tablespoons **olive** or salad **oil**
	About 6 cups fat-skimmed **chicken broth**
¼	pound **French bread**
¾	cup **crumbled blue cheese**
	Salt

1. Trim fennel stalks off heads. Rinse feathery green leaves and chop enough to make about ½ cup; discard remaining leaves and the stalks. Trim and discard root ends and bruised areas from fennel heads. Rinse heads and cut each crosswise into ½- to ¾-inch slices.

2. Cut potatoes into 1-inch chunks.

3. Put fennel slices and potatoes in a 10- by 15-inch pan and mix with oil.

4. Bake in a 450° oven until fennel is well browned, 30 to 35 minutes (20 to 25 minutes in a convection oven); turn as needed with a spatula to brown evenly.

5. In a blender or food processor, whirl vegetables, a portion at a time with enough broth to purée easily, until smooth. Pour purée into a 4- to 5-quart pan and add enough broth to make 8 cups. Stir often over medium heat until steaming.

6. Meanwhile, rinse and dry pan. Cut bread crosswise into 8 to 10 equal slices. Spread blue cheese equally onto 1 side of each piece and set bread, cheese side up, in pan.

7. Bake in a 350° oven until croutons are crisp and cheese is lightly browned, 15 to 20 minutes. Use hot, or cool on a rack.

8. Ladle soup into bowls, float 1 crouton in each, and sprinkle with chopped fennel leaves. Add salt to taste.

Per serving: 155 cal., 35% (55 cal.) from fat; 9.5 g protein; 6.1 g fat (2.3 g sat.); 15 g carbo (1.6 g fiber); 320 mg sodium; 7.6 mg chol.

Oyster Stew

Andrew Johnson, La Jolla, California

PREP AND COOK TIME: About 20 minutes

NOTES: For a leaner stew, use 2 cups whipping cream and 6 cups broth.

TO TRANSPORT: Put hot stew in a thermos.

MAKES: 10 cups; 8 to 10 servings

- 2 jars (10 to 12 oz. each) **shucked oysters**
- 6 tablespoons **butter** or margarine
- 4 cups **whipping cream**
- 4 cups fat-skimmed **chicken broth**
  About ¼ cup chopped **parsley**
  Salt and **pepper**

1. Pour oysters and juices into a 5- to 6-quart pan; with kitchen shears, snip oysters into 1-inch chunks. Add butter, cream, and broth. Stir often over medium-high heat until steaming, 10 to 15 minutes. Add parsley and salt and pepper to taste.

2. Ladle into bowls or cups.

Per serving: 394 cal., 87% (342 cal.) from fat; 9.4 g protein; 38 g fat (23 g sat.); 5.1 g carbo (0.1 g fiber); 197 mg sodium; 156 mg chol.

salads

Fall Salad

PREP AND COOK TIME: About 30 minutes

NOTES: Up to 1 day ahead, rinse arugula, radicchio, and frisée; wrap in towels, enclose in heavy plastic food bags, and chill. Toast and grind nuts, and mix oil and vinegar; cover airtight, separately, and keep at room temperature.

TO TRANSPORT: Carry leafy vegetables, ground hazelnuts, whole pear, slivered cheese, and dressing in separate containers; keep cold.

MAKES: 8 to 10 servings

- ⅓ cup **hazelnuts**
- 6 cups (5 to 6 oz.) **arugula**
- 1 head (10 to 12 oz.) **radicchio**
- 2 to 3 cups **frisée** or inner leaves of curly endive
- 1 **Asian pear** (about ¾ lb.)
- 2 ounces **parmesan cheese**
- ¼ cup **olive oil**
- ½ cup **red wine vinegar**
  Salt and **pepper**

1. In an 8- to 9-inch pan in a 350° oven, bake hazelnuts until dark gold under skins, 12 to 15 minutes. Pour onto a towel and let stand until cool enough to

FALL SALAD features Asian pear, parmesan cheese, and hazelnuts in spicy greens.

touch, about 5 minutes. Rub nuts in towel to remove loose skins. Lift nuts from towel; discard skins.

2. In a blender or food processor, whirl nuts until finely ground.

3. Meanwhile, discard any bruised leaves and tough stems from arugula, radicchio, and frisée. Separate radicchio and frisée leaves; discard cores. Rinse all the leaves and drain well.

4. Arrange radicchio leaves around the side of a wide, shallow bowl. Mound arugula and frisée in the center.

5. Rinse pear and cut into ¼-inch slices. Arrange slices on leaves and sprinkle with hazelnuts. With a vegetable peeler, shave parmesan into thin strips and scatter over salad.

6. In a small bowl, mix oil and vinegar. Pour over salad. Mix to serve, adding salt and pepper to taste.

Per serving: 124 cal., 70% (87 cal.) from fat; 3.9 g protein; 9.7 g fat (2 g sat.); 6.6 g carbo (2.1 g fiber); 118 mg sodium; 4.5 mg chol.

Hot Mushroom Salad

Patrice Benson, Seattle

PREP AND COOK TIME: About 30 minutes

NOTES: Up to 1 day ahead, rinse salad mix; wrap in towels, enclose in a heavy plastic food bag, and chill.

TO TRANSPORT: Put hot mushrooms (step 2) in a thermos. Seal salad mix in a heavy plastic food bag and keep cold.

MAKES: 8 to 10 servings

1¼ pounds **chanterelle** or common **mushrooms**

⅓ cup **olive oil**

1 tablespoon **Dijon mustard**

⅓ cup **sherry vinegar** or balsamic vinegar

3 quarts (about ¾ lb.) **salad mix,** rinsed and crisped

Salt and **pepper**

1. In a 12-inch frying pan or 3- to 4-quart pan over medium-high heat, stir mushrooms in 2 tablespoons oil until liquid evaporates and mushrooms are well browned, 15 to 20 minutes.

2. Add remaining oil, mustard, and vinegar. Stir until mixture boils.

3. Place salad mix in wide bowl. Spoon mushroom mixture onto greens and mix well. Add salt and pepper to taste.

Per serving: 89 cal., 75% (67 cal.) from fat; 1.6 g protein; 7.4 g fat (1 g sat.); 4.4 g carbo (1.1 g fiber); 46 mg sodium; 0 mg chol.

turkey

Three-Spice Turkey

PREP AND COOK TIME: About 6 hours

NOTES: Up to 1 day ahead, brine turkey and lift out; either cover and chill, or cook, cool, cover, and chill.

TO TRANSPORT: Carry hot, loosely wrapped, in a rimmed pan; or wrap chilled turkey and keep cold. Let turkey stand at room temperature no longer than 2 hours.

MAKES: Allow ¾ pound uncooked turkey per person, more for leftovers

1 **turkey** (15 to 20 lb.)

1 cup firmly packed **brown sugar**

¾ cup **salt**

3 tablespoons **ground cumin**

3 tablespoons **pepper**

1½ tablespoons **ground cinnamon**

1. Remove and discard leg truss from turkey. Pull off and discard lumps of fat. Remove giblets and neck (reserve for other uses). Rinse bird well and pierce all over with a fork.

2. In a bowl or pan (at least 12 qt.), combine 3 quarts water, brown sugar, salt, cumin, pepper, and cinnamon. Stir until sugar and salt are dissolved. Add turkey, cover, and chill for 4 hours, turning bird over occasionally.

3. Lift turkey from brine and rinse thoroughly under cold running water, rubbing gently to release salt; pat dry with towels. Discard brine. Insert a meat thermometer straight down through the thickest part of the turkey breast to the bone.

4. *On a charcoal barbecue* (20 to 22 in. wide) with a lid, mound and ignite 60 charcoal briquets on firegrate. When coals are spotted with gray ash, in about 20 minutes, push equal portions to opposite sides of firegrate. Place a foil drip pan between mounds of coals. To each mound, add 5 briquets now and every 30 minutes during cooking. Set grill in place. Set turkey, breast up, on grill over drip pan. Cover barbecue and open vents.

On a gas barbecue (with at least 11 in. between indirect-heat burners), turn heat to high, close lid, and heat for about 10 minutes. Adjust gas for indirect cooking (heat parallel to sides of bird and not beneath) and set a metal

Oven-roasted or barbecued whole turkey

See recipe for Three-Spice Turkey (above), step 4, for oven-roasting and barbecuing directions. Follow the chart below for oven temperatures and cooking times.

Turkey weight with giblets	Oven temp.	Internal temp.*	Cooking time**
10–13 lb.	350°	160°	1½–2¼ hr.
14–23 lb.	325°	160°	2–3 hr.
24–27 lb.	325°	160°	3–3¾ hr.
28–30 lb.	325°	160°	3½–4½ hr.

*To measure the internal temperature of the turkey, insert a thermometer through the thickest part of the breast to the bone.

**Times are for unstuffed birds. A stuffed bird may cook at the same rate as an unstuffed one; however, be prepared to allow 30 to 50 minutes more. (See page 294 for how to keep the bacteria levels in stuffed turkeys safe.) While turkeys take about the same time to roast in regular and convection heat, a convection oven does a better job of browning the bird beautifully all over.

When you remove the turkey legs, if you find that the meat around the thigh joint is still too pink, cut the drumsticks from the thighs and put the thighs in a shallow pan in a 450° oven until no longer pink, 10 to 15 minutes.

or foil drip pan in center (not over direct heat). Set grill in place. Set turkey, breast up, on grill over drip pan. Close barbecue lid. If edges of turkey close to heat begin to get too dark, slide folded strips of foil between bird and grill. Fat in drippings may flare when barbecue lid is opened; quench by pouring a little water into the pan.

In an oven, place turkey, breast up, on a V-shaped rack in a 12- by 17-inch roasting pan (or one that is at least 2 in. longer and wider than the bird). Roast in a 325° or 350° oven, depending on size of bird; see chart on page 266.

5. Cook turkey until thermometer reaches 160°, 2 to 3 hours; start checking after 1 hour.

6. Drain juices from cavity into drippings and reserve for gravy (recipes follow). Transfer turkey to a platter; let rest 15 to 30 minutes before carving.

Per ¼ pound boned cooked turkey with skin, based on percentages of white and dark meat in an average bird: 240 cal., 38% (90 cal.) from fat; 32 g protein; 10 g fat (3 g sat.); 2.9 g carbo (0 g fiber); 376 mg sodium; 93 mg chol.

Confit Turkey Legs

PREP AND COOK TIME: About 4 hours

NOTES: If making turkey legs up to 1 day ahead, cool, cover, and chill.

TO TRANSPORT: Wrap hot or chilled turkey legs and carry in an insulated bag.

MAKES: 8 to 10 servings

- 8 to 10 **turkey drumsticks** (6 to 6½ lb. total)
- 6 tablespoons **salt**
- ¼ cup firmly packed **brown sugar**
- 2 teaspoons **dried marjoram**
- 2 teaspoons **dried tarragon**
- 1 teaspoon **coarse-ground pepper**
- 1 tablespoon crushed **coriander seed**
- 1 tablespoon sliced **garlic**

1. Rinse turkey legs, pat dry, and lay in an 11- by 17-inch pan (or ½ each in 2 pans, 9 by 13 in.).

2. In a bowl, mix salt, brown sugar, marjoram, tarragon, pepper, coriander, and garlic. Rub mixture all over turkey legs. Cover and chill 1½ hours, turning several times.

3. Put turkey and spices in a fine-mesh colander and rinse meat well under cool running water, rubbing to release

BEACHSIDE BARBECUE

■ Every year, three generations of the Johnson family, and their friends, gather on the beach at La Jolla, California, for Thanksgiving. Judith Johnson makes a list of what everyone should bring: hot buttered rum (page 276) and her son Andrew's oyster stew (page 265) are perennial favorites. Her husband, Duke, barbecues a turkey, and while it cooks, he roasts foil-wrapped vegetables (potatoes, onions, and yams; page 271) in the coals, along with spiced apples for dessert.

The crowd changes from year to year, and guests are required to wear costumes: pilgrims, Indian scouts, rug weavers, fur traders. There are always games, from bocce to horseshoes. Having celebrated Thanksgiving outdoors for almost 20 years, the Johnsons know how to fit the feast to the setting—and get it there handily.

ACROSS TOWN TO GRANDMA'S HOUSE

■ Chet and Kristy Anderson of Longmont, Colorado, don't go far—just across town to Chet's mom's place. Still, there's a world to enjoy outside and a crowd to feed back home. They do a trail run in the morning. Then Chet and Kristy finish sautéing their signature brussels sprouts leaves with carrots, onions, celery, and pancetta (page 271) to go with two turkeys—theirs and the one Chet's mother supplies. Organic farmers by profession, Chet and Kristy often contribute a salad of arugula (from their greenhouse), gorgonzola, pears, and walnuts. And, if they have any pumpkins in their patch, a pie. Chet's sister, Dawn, makes frozen maple mousse (her grandmother's recipe; page 275) in an ice cream maker in the backyard under—you guessed it—twin maple trees.

as much salt as possible. Let drain.

4. Return meat and spices to pan. Add about ¼ inch water and cover pan tightly with foil.

5. Bake in a 325° oven until meat is very tender when pierced, about 1½ hours. Drain juices and skim off fat; taste juices and if not too salty, reserve for gravy (recipes follow).

6. Increase oven temperature to 450°. Return turkey to oven and bake, uncovered, until browned, 30 to 40 minutes, turning legs once. Serve hot or let cool to room temperature and chill.

Per serving: 273 cal., 43% (117 cal.) from fat; 36 g protein; 13 g fat (3.9 g sat.); 1.3 g carbo (0 g fiber); 566 mg sodium; 110 mg chol.

gravies

Golden Giblet Gravy

PREP AND COOK TIME: About 25 minutes

NOTES: If making gravy up to 1 day ahead, cool, cover, and chill. To reheat, stir over medium-high heat until steaming; or heat in a microwave-safe container in a microwave oven at full power (100%), stirring often, until steaming.

TO TRANSPORT: Carry hot gravy in a thermos.

MAKES: About 8 cups

Cooked turkey neck and giblets from giblet broth (recipe follows)

MENU

AN ELEGANT FEAST ON THE ROAD

Tapenade and Goat Cheese Bruschetta

Oyster Stew

Fall Salad

Three-Spice Turkey

Apricot Dressing (recipe on page 296)

Easy Wine Gravy

Cran-Apple Chutney

Sautéed Brussels Sprouts Leaves

Mashed Potato Fonduta

Rustic Red Onion–Herb Bread
(pictured at left)

Cranberry-Raspberry Charlotte
(recipe on page 287)

Chocolate Chestnut Torte
(recipe on page 288)

GAME PLAN

□ **Up to 1 week ahead.** *Make* tapenade for goat cheese bruschetta, and cran-apple chutney.

□ **Up to 3 days ahead.** *Thaw* turkey in refrigerator if frozen.

□ **Up to 2 days ahead.** *Make* chocolate chestnut torte.

□ **Up to 1 day ahead.** *Rinse* leafy vegetables for fall salad. *Brine* and *roast* turkey. *Make* apricot dressing and wine gravy. *Separate* brussels sprouts leaves. *Make* mashed potato fonduta, red onion–herb bread, and cranberry-raspberry charlotte.

□ **About ½ hour ahead.** *Assemble* bruschetta and salad. *Make* oyster stew. *Sauté* brussels sprouts leaves.

WINES

■ **With the appetizers.** Honig Sauvignon Blanc 1998 (Rutherford, CA), $13.50. Sassy, vibrant, and lemony, with great crispness.
Why? Goat cheese and tapenade are classic Old World mates for Sauvignon Blanc, especially a dramatic, linear Sauvignon like this one. The arugula and pears in the fall salad are also a downright winning match with Sauvignon Blanc—like on like.

■ **With the main course.** Saintsbury Pinot Noir 1997 (Carneros, CA), $22. A gorgeous, sweetly ripe Pinot Noir with lots of power (by Pinot standards). Berries, cherries, earth, smoke—they're all here.
Why? This is a very earthy, savory menu, with hints of spice and sweetness (the apricots). The musky sensuality of Pinot Noir is just the ticket—but it's important that the Pinot be on the powerful side; a frail one wouldn't stand up.

■ **With dessert.** *Cranberry-raspberry charlotte:* Chateau Ste. Michelle Late Harvest White Riesling Reserve 1997 (Columbia Valley, WA), $17. Beautiful spun honey and apricot flavors. Silky and very long in the mouth—a fabulous flavor and texture match. *Chocolate chestnut torte:* Schuetz Oles Port (Napa Valley), $22 (500-ml. bottle). This is a gorgeously crafted, utterly soft port made from Petite Syrah and Zinfandel grapes. It's one of the top ports being made in California. — *K.M.-F.*

1 tablespoon **butter** or margarine (optional)

½ cup **cornstarch**

8 cups **giblet broth** (recipe follows)

Fat-skimmed **drippings** from oven-roasted or barbecued turkey or confit turkey legs (recipes precede)

Salt and **pepper**

1. Pull meat off turkey neck; discard bones. Finely chop the neck meat, gizzard, and heart.

2. If desired, rinse liver, pat dry, and cut into 3 or 4 pieces. Melt butter in an 8- to 10-inch frying pan over medium-high heat. Add liver and turn occasionally until lightly browned, about 4 minutes. Let cool about 5 minutes; coarsely chop.

3. Place cornstarch in a 3- to 4-quart pan; stir in broth. Add turkey drippings. Frequently stir over high heat until mixture boils. Add giblets, including liver if using, and salt and pepper to taste.

Per ¼-cup serving: 39 cal., 21% (8.1 cal.) from fat; 5.3 g protein; 0.9 g fat (0.3 g sat.); 2 g carbo (0 g fiber); 33 mg sodium; 28 mg chol.

Giblet Broth

PREP AND COOK TIME: About 1¾ hours

NOTES: If making up to 1 day ahead, cool broth and giblets; cover separately and chill.

MAKES: About 8 cups

Giblets and neck from a 10- to 24-pound turkey

2 tablespoons **butter** or margarine

1 cup chopped **carrots**

1 cup chopped **celery**

1 cup chopped **onions**

About 10 cups fat-skimmed **chicken broth**

1. Rinse giblets and neck. Wrap liver airtight and chill to use in gravy (recipe precedes), or save for other uses.

2. In a 5- to 6-quart pan over high heat, melt butter; add gizzard, heart, and neck and turn often until well browned, about 5 minutes. Add carrots, celery, and onions and stir often until onions are lightly brown, about 5 minutes. Add broth and stir to release browned bits. Cover and bring to a boil. Reduce heat and simmer until gizzard is very tender when pierced, 1¼ to 1½ hours.

3. Pour the broth through a fine strainer into a 2-quart measure. Reserve neck and giblets; discard vegetables. If you have more than 8 cups of broth, boil to reduce; if you have less, add chicken broth.

Per cup: 71 cal., 37% (26 cal.) from fat; 10 g protein; 2.9 g fat (1.8 g sat.); 0.5 g carbo (0 g fiber); 125 mg sodium; 7.8 mg chol.

Easy Wine Gravy

PREP AND COOK TIME: About 25 minutes

NOTES: If serving a dry white wine with dinner, use the same wine in the gravy for a good flavor match. If making gravy up to 1 day ahead, cool, cover, and chill. To reheat, stir over medium-high heat until steaming; or heat in a microwave-safe container in a microwave oven at full power (100%), stirring often, until steaming.

TO TRANSPORT: Carry hot gravy in a thermos.

MAKES: About 8 cups

Follow directions for **easy gravy** (page 283), decreasing fat-skimmed **chicken broth** to 6 cups. Add 2 cups **Sauvignon Blanc** or other dry white wine to the onion mixture with the broth and turkey drippings in step 2.

Per ¼-cup serving: 35 cal., 23% (8.1 cal.) from fat; 1.8 g protein; 0.9 g fat (0.5 g sat.); 2.4 g carbo (0.1 g fiber); 22 mg sodium; 2.1 mg chol.

pickles and chutney

Refrigerator Pickles

PREP AND COOK TIME: About 30 minutes

NOTES: You can use canning jars, rings, and lids, which will seal, but remember that the pickles are not processed for storage. If making pickles up to 1 week ahead, chill.

TO TRANSPORT: Carry tightly covered in jars, cold or at room temperature.

MAKES: 2 pints; 8 to 10 servings

½ pound **mushrooms**

About ½ pound **zucchini** (green, yellow, or a mix)

1 **red bell pepper** (about ½ lb.)

4 **fresh red** or green **jalapeño** or Fresno **chilies**

2 teaspoons **whole allspice**

10 **thyme** sprigs (3 to 4 in.)

⅔ cup **sugar**

1½ cups **rice vinegar**

1. Rinse and drain mushrooms, zucchini, bell pepper, and chilies. Trim and discard discolored mushroom stem ends; cut mushrooms vertically into ¼-inch-thick slices. Trim and discard ends from zucchini; cut zucchini crosswise into ⅛-inch-thick slices. Stem and seed red bell pepper; cut into ¼-inch strips. Trim and discard chili stems; cut chilies crosswise into ¼-inch-thick slices.

2. Divide mushrooms, zucchini, bell pepper, chilies, and allspice equally between 2 jars (1 pt. each). Slide 5 thyme sprigs between vegetables and sides of each jar.

3. Combine sugar and vinegar in a 1- to 1½-quart pan. Bring to a boil over high heat, stirring until sugar dissolves. Carefully pour over vegetables in jars.

4. Put lids and rings on jars and close tightly. Chill at least 1 day and up to 1 week, occasionally turning jars over to keep vegetables evenly moistened.

Per serving: 69 cal., 2.6% (1.8 cal.) from fat; 1 g protein; 0.2 g fat (0 g sat.); 17 g carbo (0.8 g fiber); 2.8 mg sodium; 0 mg chol.

Cran-Apple Chutney
Hamida Betty Rahman

PREP AND COOK TIME: About 25 minutes

NOTES: If making chutney up to 1 week ahead, chill airtight.

TO TRANSPORT: Cover the chutney and

REFRIGERATOR PICKLES, cran-apple chutney, and cranberry relish (recipe page 283).

ROASTED ROOT VEGETABLES are dusted with toasted sesame seed; brussels sprouts leaves are sautéed with pancetta.

carry at room temperature.

MAKES: About 2 cups

- 1 **Granny Smith apple** (about ½ lb.), rinsed, cored, and chopped
- 1 cup **dried cranberries**
- ½ cup **golden raisins**
- ½ cup finely chopped **onion**
- ¾ cup firmly packed **brown sugar**
- ⅓ cup **cider vinegar**
- 1 tablespoon **mustard seed**
- 1 tablespoon minced **fresh ginger**
- 6 **whole cloves**
- 1 **cinnamon stick** (3 in.)
- ½ teaspoon **black peppercorns**
- ¼ teaspoon **hot chili flakes**

1. In a 3- to 4-quart pan, combine apple, cranberries, raisins, onion, brown sugar, vinegar, mustard seed, ginger, cloves, cinnamon stick, peppercorns, chili flakes, and 2 cups water.

2. Bring to a boil over high heat, stir-

ring often. Reduce heat and simmer, stirring often, until apple mashes easily when pressed and most of the liquid has evaporated, about 20 minutes. If desired, discard cinnamon stick and cloves. Serve warm, at room temperature, or chilled.

Per tablespoon: 45 cal., 4% (1.8 cal.) from fat; 0.2 g protein; 0.2 g fat (0 g sat.); 11 g carbo (0.6 g fiber); 2.5 mg sodium; 0 mg chol.

vegetables

Roasted Sesame Vegetables

PREP AND COOK TIME: About 1¼ hours

NOTES: If desired, use peeled and trimmed baby carrots instead of baby-cut carrots. Up to 1 day ahead, bake vegetables and add oil, vinegar, and soy sauce; cool, cover, and chill. Also toast sesame seed; cool, cover, and store at room temperature. Reheat vegetables, covered, in a 450° oven until hot in center, about 15 to 20 minutes.

TO TRANSPORT: Cover vegetables and carry in an insulated container. Carry toasted sesame seed separately at room temperature; sprinkle over vegetables just before serving.

MAKES: About 6 cups; 8 to 10 servings

- 1 pound **turnips**
- 1 pound **rutabagas**
- 1 pound **parsnips**
- 1 pound **red onions**
- 1 pound **baby-cut carrots**
- 3 tablespoons **Asian** (toasted) **sesame oil**
- 1 tablespoon **sesame seed**
- 3 tablespoons **rice vinegar**
- 1 tablespoon **soy sauce**

1. Peel turnips, rutabagas, and parsnips and cut into ½-inch chunks. Peel onions and cut into 1-inch chunks.

2. In a 10- by 15-inch pan, combine turnips, rutabagas, parsnips, onions, and carrots. Add 2 tablespoons oil and stir to coat vegetables.

3. Bake in a 450° oven until vegetables are tender when pierced, about 1 hour, turning often with a wide spatula to brown evenly.

4. Meanwhile, in a 6- to 8-inch frying pan over medium heat, stir or shake sesame seed until lightly browned, 2 to 4 minutes. Pour from pan into a small bowl.

5. Add remaining tablespoon oil and the vinegar and soy sauce to vegetables; mix well. Pour into a wide bowl. Sprinkle with sesame seed. Serve hot, warm, or at room temperature.

Per serving: 132 cal., 33% (44 cal.) from fat; 2.4 g protein; 4.9 g fat (0.7 g sat.); 21 g carbo (5.7 g fiber); 156 mg sodium; 0 mg chol.

Sautéed Brussels Sprouts Leaves

Chet and Kristy Anderson, Longmont, Colorado

PREP AND COOK TIME: About 45 minutes

NOTES: Up to 1 day ahead, separate brussels sprouts leaves (step 1); seal in a heavy plastic food bag and chill.

TO TRANSPORT: Complete step 2; cool vegetables, cover, and chill. Carry brussels sprouts leaves and sautéed vegetables separately in an insulated container. At the site, heat vegetable mixture in frying pan, and when it is sizzling, continue with step 3.

MAKES: 6 cups; 8 to 10 servings

2 pounds **brussels sprouts**

¾ cup finely chopped **carrot**

¾ cup finely chopped **celery**

¾ cup finely chopped **onion**

¾ cup finely chopped **pancetta** (about 5 oz.) or bacon

Salt and **pepper**

1. Rinse, drain, and core brussels sprouts. Separate leaves, discarding any that are bruised or discolored.

2. In a 14-inch frying pan or a 5- to 6-quart pan over high heat, stir carrot, celery, onion, and pancetta until vegetables are lightly browned, about 5 minutes. Add ⅔ cup water and stir to release any browned bits in pan.

3. Add brussels sprouts leaves and stir until slightly wilted, 10 to 14 minutes. Pour into a bowl; add salt and pepper to taste.

Per serving: 127 cal., 61% (77 cal.) from fat; 4.6 g protein; 8.5 g fat (3.1 g sat.); 10 g carbo (5.9 g fiber); 131 mg sodium; 9.5 mg chol.

Squash with Chilies and Ginger

Hamida Betty Rahman

PREP AND COOK TIME: About 1⅓ hours

NOTES: If making squash up to 1 day ahead, let cool, cover, and chill. To reheat, bake, covered, in a 400° oven until hot in center, 20 to 25 minutes.

TO TRANSPORT: Wrap hot squash and carry in an insulated container. Cover cilantro and keep cold. Garnish squash with cilantro before serving.

MAKES: About 9 cups; 8 to 10 servings

2 **onions** (about 1 lb. total)

2 tablespoons minced **fresh ginger**

2 tablespoons minced or pressed **garlic**

2 tablespoons minced **fresh jalapeño chilies**

2 teaspoons **olive** or salad **oil**

3½ pounds seeded **banana squash**

About 1 cup fat-skimmed **chicken broth**

Salt

¼ cup chopped **cilantro**

1. Peel onions and cut into ½-inch wedges. In a 10- to 12-inch frying pan over medium-high heat, frequently stir onions, ginger, garlic, and chilies in oil until vegetables are lightly browned, 15 to 20 minutes. Remove from heat.

2. Meanwhile, with a vegetable peeler, cut and discard skin from squash. Cut squash into 1-inch cubes.

3. In a shallow 3½- to 4-quart casserole, combine squash and onion mixture. Add ¼ inch broth. Cover casserole tightly with foil.

4. Bake in a 400° oven until squash is very tender when pierced, 40 to 50 minutes. Uncover, add salt to taste, and garnish with cilantro.

Per serving: 79 cal., 15% (12 cal.) from fat; 3.3 g protein; 1.3 g fat (0.2 g sat.); 16 g carbo (3 g fiber); 15 mg sodium; 0 mg chol.

potatoes and grains

Roasted Onions, Yams, and Potatoes with Seasoned Butter

Judith Johnson, La Jolla

PREP AND COOK TIME: About 1½ hours

NOTES: Instead of Italian seasoning mix, you can use ¾ teaspoon *each* dried oregano and dried rosemary. Up to 1 week ahead, season the butter (step 3); cover and chill.

TO TRANSPORT: Cover hot vegetables and carry in an insulated container. Wrap seasoned butter airtight in a small bowl and keep cold.

MAKES: 8 to 10 servings

4 **onions** (½ lb. each)

3 **yams** or sweet potatoes (½ lb. each)

3 **russet potatoes** (½ lb. each)

¾ cup (⅜ lb.) **butter** or margarine, at room temperature

1½ teaspoons **paprika**

1½ teaspoons **Italian seasoning mix**

Salt and fresh-ground **pepper**

1. Rinse onions and scrub yams and potatoes; set in a 10- by 15-inch pan.

2. Bake in a 450° oven until yams and potatoes give readily when gently pressed, about 1 hour (about 50 minutes in a convection oven).

3. Meanwhile, in a bowl, beat butter until fluffy. Stir in paprika and Italian seasoning mix.

4. Quarter vegetables, arrange on a platter, and dot with seasoned butter. Season to taste with salt and pepper.

Per serving: 284 cal., 44% (126 cal.) from fat; 3.4 g protein; 14 g fat (8.8 g sat.); 37 g carbo (5 g fiber); 158 mg sodium; 38 mg chol.

Two-Tone Potatoes Anna

PREP AND COOK TIME: About 1½ hours

NOTES: If making up to 1 day ahead, let cool, cover airtight, and chill. Reheat, covered, in a 425° oven until hot in the center, 25 to 30 minutes.

TO TRANSPORT: Cover hot potatoes and carry in an insulated container.

MAKES: 8 to 10 servings

1½ pounds **yams** or sweet potatoes

1½ pounds **russet potatoes**

10 tablespoons melted **butter** or margarine

½ cup **grated Parmesan cheese**

2 teaspoons crumbled **dried rosemary**

Salt and fresh-ground **pepper**

1. Peel yams and russet potatoes. Using a slicer, cut yams and potatoes into

uniformly thick $\frac{1}{16}$-inch slices. As cut, immerse russet potato slices in water to prevent browning.

2. Put 2 tablespoons butter in a 10-inch ovenproof nonstick frying pan and spread to cover bottom.

3. Drain russet potatoes and pat slices dry. Neatly overlap $\frac{1}{4}$ of the russet slices to cover pan bottom. Drizzle with 1 tablespoon butter and sprinkle with 1 tablespoon cheese and $\frac{1}{4}$ teaspoon rosemary. Neatly overlap $\frac{1}{4}$ of the yam slices over russets; drizzle with 1 tablespoon butter and sprinkle with 1 tablespoon cheese and $\frac{1}{4}$ teaspoon rosemary. Repeat layers, alternating russet potatoes and yams, until all the vegetables are in the pan. Drizzle with any remaining butter. Cover pan tightly with foil.

4. Bake on the lowest rack in a 425° oven for 30 minutes. Uncover and bake until vegetables are very tender when pierced and edges are brown and crisp, 35 to 45 minutes longer. Let stand 5 to 10 minutes.

5. Using a pan lid to hold potatoes in place, drain off any excess butter and save for other uses. Run a knife between pan sides and potatoes. Invert a platter over pan; holding together, invert both to release vegetables. Remove pan. Cut into wedges and serve, adding salt and pepper to taste.

Per serving: 219 cal., 45% (99 cal.) from fat; 3.8 g protein; 11 g fat (6.5 g sat.); 28 g carbo (3.5 g fiber); 178 mg sodium; 28 mg chol.

Mashed Potato Fonduta

PREP AND COOK TIME: About $1\frac{1}{4}$ hours

NOTES: White truffle oil is available in well-stocked supermarkets and specialty food stores. Up to 1 day ahead, assemble the potatoes through step 2; cool, cover, and chill. Reheat, covered, in a 350° oven until hot in the center, 35 to 45 minutes; then continue with step 3.

TO TRANSPORT: Cover hot potatoes and carry in an insulated container.

MAKES: 10 cups; 8 to 10 servings

- $4\frac{1}{2}$ pounds **russet potatoes**
- $1\frac{1}{2}$ cups **half-and-half** (light cream)
- 2 cups shredded **fontina cheese** (about $\frac{1}{2}$ lb.)
- 3 tablespoons **white truffle oil** (optional)

TART, VIBRANT kumquats sparkle in richly textured wild rice pilaf.

Fresh-grated **nutmeg**

Salt and fresh-ground **pepper**

1. Scrub potatoes, peel, and cut into 1-inch chunks. Put in a 5- to 6-quart pan with 3 quarts water. Bring to a boil over high heat; reduce heat, cover, and simmer until potatoes mash easily, about 25 minutes.

2. Drain potatoes and return to pan. Add half-and-half, $1\frac{1}{2}$ cups cheese, and $1\frac{1}{2}$ tablespoons truffle oil. Mash with a potato masher or beat with a mixer until smooth. Add nutmeg, salt, and pepper to taste. Spoon into a shallow 3-quart casserole and sprinkle with remaining cheese.

3. Broil potatoes 4 to 6 inches from heat until cheese is lightly browned, 5 to 6 minutes.

4. Drizzle remaining truffle oil over potatoes and dust with more nutmeg.

Per serving: 284 cal., 38% (108 cal.) from fat; 10 g protein; 12 g fat (6.9 g sat.); 35 g carbo (3.1 g fiber); 211 mg sodium; 40 mg chol.

Wild Rice Pilaf

PREP AND COOK TIME: About $1\frac{3}{4}$ hours

NOTES: If desired, save a few kumquat slices for garnish.

TO TRANSPORT: Cover hot pilaf and carry in an insulated container.

MAKES: About $8\frac{1}{2}$ cups; 8 to 10 servings

- $2\frac{1}{2}$ cups **wild rice**
- $\frac{1}{2}$ cup **slivered almonds**
- 1 cup finely chopped **onion**
- 1 cup finely chopped **celery**
- 2 tablespoons **butter** or margarine
- $2\frac{1}{2}$ cups fat-skimmed **chicken broth**
- $2\frac{1}{2}$ cups **apple cider** or juice
- $\frac{1}{4}$ cup chopped rinsed **kumquats** (about 8; $2\frac{1}{2}$ oz. total) or $\frac{1}{4}$ cup chopped dried apricots
- $\frac{1}{3}$ cup minced **parsley**

  Salt and fresh-ground **pepper**

1. Rinse wild rice well with cool water, and drain.

2. In a 12-inch frying pan or a 4- to 5-quart pan over medium-high heat, stir or shake almonds until golden, 3 to 4 minutes. Pour from pan.

3. Add onion, celery, and butter to pan. Stir often over medium-high heat until vegetables are lightly browned, about 10 minutes. Stir in wild rice, broth, and apple cider. Bring to a boil, cover, reduce heat, and simmer until grains begin to split and rice is tender to bite, 1¼ to 1½ hours. Drain any liquid.

4. Stir almonds, kumquats, and parsley into wild rice pilaf. Pour into a wide bowl. Add salt and pepper to taste.

Per serving: 254 cal., 22% (57 cal.) from fat; 9.6 g protein; 6.3 g fat (1.8 g sat.); 42 g carbo (3 g fiber); 60 mg sodium; 6.2 mg chol.

Thousand-Seed Pilaf

PREP AND COOK TIME: About 40 minutes

NOTES: Kalijira is a very small, basmati-type rice. If you can't find Kalijira, replace it with another ⅔ cup quinoa, couscous, or bulgur.

TO TRANSPORT: Cover hot or cool pilaf and carry in an insulated container. Seal lemon peel and parsley sprigs in separate heavy plastic food bags, and keep cold. Garnish just before serving.

MAKES: About 7 cups; 8 to 10 servings

 1 teaspoon *each* **cumin seed, mustard seed, dill seed,** and **coriander seed**

 ½ teaspoon *each* **celery seed** and **caraway seed**

 1 teaspoon **olive oil**

 ⅔ cup *each* **quinoa, couscous, bulgur wheat,** and **Kalijira rice** (see notes)

 6½ cups fat-skimmed **chicken broth**

 2 tablespoons **lemon juice**

 ⅓ cup **minced parsley**

　 About 1 tablespoon long, thin shreds **lemon** peel

　 Parsley sprigs, rinsed

　 Salt and fresh-ground **pepper**

1. Combine cumin, mustard, dill, coriander, celery, and caraway seed in a 12-inch frying pan or a 4- to 5-quart pan. Add oil. Stir often over high heat until seeds smell fragrant and begin to pop, about 2 minutes.

2. Meanwhile, rinse and drain quinoa.

COASTAL PILGRIMAGE

■ To escape big-city life, Penny and Paul Fredlund and Patrice and Ed Benson head to their "fabulous funky cabin," as Penny describes it, at Iron Springs Resort on a ridge overlooking the ocean near Copalis Beach, Washington. It's usually just the two couples and their families, but sometimes guests or relatives join them for a relaxed holiday—so relaxed, in fact, that they don't even have Thanksgiving dinner on Thursday. They start preparations that day and have the feast on Friday.

Patrice is a mycologist, so the group wanders into the forests of Sitka spruces and Douglas firs to gather wild porcini and chanterelle mushrooms, which they put in a dressing, or maybe soup, bruschetta, or salad

(page 266). They also dig for razor clams when they're available. They might pan-fry the clams for an easy appetizer or add them to a chowder. Ed's family recipe for refrigerator rolls (page 274) supplies the perfect accompaniment. Penny is in charge of desserts; a recent favorite is French custard apple pie (page 275).

NEIGHBORHOOD GET-TOGETHER

■ Sean Hogan and Parker Sanderson invite about 40 of their neighbors in Portland over for Thanksgiving dinner. In fact, the close-knit community is accustomed to pooling its efforts when it comes to foodstuffs: The neighborhood shares one garden, which spans the whole block. The house-wide porch on Hogan and Sanderson's turn-of-the-century home entices people to eat outdoors, but if the weather turns bad, indoor plans go into effect.

Frenzella Berry bakes pies or banana bread (page 274). Hamida Betty Rahman brings squash with fresh ginger, chilies, and garlic (page 271); a colorful chutney, either green apple (page 269) or cranberry-pear; and an appetizer of homemade tapenade and goat cheese spread on focaccia (page 262). Hogan is happy as long as no one brings creamed onions.

Add quinoa, couscous, bulgur, and rice to pan. Stir until grains are lightly toasted, 2 to 3 minutes.

3. Add broth; when it is boiling rapidly, cover pan, remove from heat, and let stand until liquid is absorbed, 15 to 20 minutes.

4. Stir in lemon juice and parsley; spoon pilaf into a bowl and garnish with lemon peel and parsley sprigs. Serve hot, warm, or at room temperature. Add salt and pepper to taste.

Per serving: 195 cal., 7.7% (15 cal.) from fat; 11 g protein; 1.7 g fat (0.2 g sat.); 35 g carbo (4 g fiber); 66 mg sodium; 0 mg chol.

breads

Rustic Tapenade Swirl Bread

PREP AND COOK TIME: About 3¼ hours

NOTES: You can make the tapenade (recipe on page 262) or buy it. If making bread up to 1 day ahead, wrap airtight and store at room temperature. To recrisp, set on a rack in a 350° oven for 5 to 7 minutes. (At mile-high altitude, dough rises in about ⅓ less time.)

TO TRANSPORT: Carry loaf, loosely

wrapped, at room temperature.

MAKES: 1 loaf (about 1 lb., 10 oz.); 8 to 10 servings

- 1 envelope **active dry yeast**

  About 3 cups **all-purpose flour**

- 1 teaspoon **sugar**

- 1 teaspoon **salt**

- ½ cup **tapenade** (see notes)

1. In a large bowl, sprinkle yeast over 1¼ cups warm (110°) water. Let stand until yeast is soft, about 5 minutes.

2. Mix 3 cups flour with the sugar and salt. Add to yeast mixture. Beat with a dough hook on medium speed, or with a heavy spoon, until dough is shiny and elastic (forms a thin, almost transparent skin when you stretch a piece with your fingers) but still slightly sticky, about 5 minutes with a mixer, 10 to 20 minutes by hand. If the dough is too stiff to beat, add more water, 1 to 2 teaspoons at a time, until it is easy to mix.

3. Cover bowl with plastic wrap and let dough rise in a warm place until doubled, about 1½ hours.

4. Scrape dough (it will collapse) onto a well-floured board, sprinkle evenly with about 2 tablespoons flour, and lightly pat into a 6- by 16-inch rectangle. Cover dough loosely with plastic wrap and let rest until puffy, about 30 minutes.

5. Spread tapenade evenly over dough. Beginning at a 16-inch edge, roll dough snugly into a log; pinch side seam to seal. Using your hand and a wide spatula, gently slide loaf, seam down, onto a buttered 14- by 17-inch baking sheet.

6. Place in a 475° oven and immediately reduce heat to 425°. Bake until bread is golden brown, 30 to 40 minutes. For a crisper crust, turn oven off, prop door slightly ajar, and leave loaf in oven about 10 minutes longer. Transfer loaf to a rack to cool. Serve warm or at room temperature.

Per serving: 191 cal., 21% (40 cal.) from fat; 4.4 g protein; 4.4 g fat (0.3 g sat.); 32 g carbo (1.2 g fiber); 550 mg sodium; 1 mg chol.

Rustic red onion–herb bread. Follow directions for **rustic tapenade swirl bread** (preceding), omitting tapenade. Instead, in a 10- to 12-inch frying pan, combine 1 cup finely chopped **red onion**, 1 teaspoon **sugar**, ⅓ cup **distilled white vinegar**, 1 cup **water**, and ½ teaspoon *each* **dried marjoram, dried basil, dried tarragon,** and **dried thyme.** Stir often over high heat until liquid is evaporated, 10 to 15 minutes. Let cool at least 10 minutes. Spread over dough as directed for tapenade in step 5.

Per serving: 165 cal., 4.4% (7.2 cal.) from fat; 4.7 g protein; 0.8 g fat (0.3 g sat.); 34 g carbo (1.5 g fiber); 240 mg sodium; 1 mg chol.

Banana Bread

Frenzella Berry, Portland

PREP AND COOK TIME: About 1½ hours

NOTES: If making bread up to 2 days ahead, cool, wrap airtight, and store at room temperature. (At mile-high altitude, reduce sugar to ¾ cup and baking powder to 1 teaspoon.)

TO TRANSPORT: Wrap bread airtight and carry at room temperature.

MAKES: 1 loaf (about 2½ lb.); 8 to 10 servings

- 2 **large eggs**

  About ½ cup (¼ lb.) melted **butter** or margarine, cooled

- 1 tablespoon **vanilla**

- 1 cup **sugar**

- 1 cup mashed **ripe banana** (about 1 lb. total)

- 2 cups **all-purpose flour**

- ½ teaspoon **salt**

- 1½ teaspoons **baking soda**

- 1½ teaspoons **baking powder**

- ¾ cup **buttermilk**

- ¾ cup **chopped pecans**

1. In a large bowl, beat eggs to blend. Add ½ cup butter, vanilla, sugar, and banana; mix well.

2. In another bowl, stir together flour, salt, baking soda, and baking powder.

3. Add dry ingredients to banana mixture, stir to moisten lightly, then add buttermilk and mix well. Stir in pecans. Scrape batter into a buttered 5- by 9-inch loaf pan.

4. Bake in a 325° oven until bread is well browned and begins to pull away from pan sides, 1 hour and 5 minutes to 1 hour and 10 minutes. Let cool in pan on a rack about 10 minutes; run a thin-bladed knife between bread and pan sides. Invert pan to remove bread; turn loaf rounded side up and let cool on rack. Serve warm or at room temperature.

Per serving: 354 cal., 43% (153 cal.) from fat; 5.4 g protein; 17 g fat (6.9 g sat.); 47 g carbo (1.6 g fiber); 508 mg sodium; 69 mg chol.

Refrigerator Rolls

Ed Benson, Seattle

PREP AND COOK TIME: About 1 hour, plus at least 4 hours to chill

NOTES: For a shiny crust, beat 1 large egg yolk to blend with 1 tablespoon water; brush mixture onto rolls just before baking. Up to 4 days before baking, complete recipe through step 2. Up to 1 day ahead, finish rolls; wrap airtight and store at room temperature. (At mile-high altitude, shaped rolls will rise in about ⅓ less time.)

TO TRANSPORT: Wrap rolls airtight and carry at room temperature.

MAKES: 2 dozen rolls

- 1 package **active dry yeast**

- ⅓ cup **sugar**

- 1 teaspoon **salt**

  About ½ cup (¼ lb.) melted **butter** or margarine, cooled

- 2 **large eggs**

  About 5 cups **all-purpose flour**

1. In a large bowl, sprinkle yeast over 1½ cups warm (110°) water. Let stand until yeast is soft, about 5 minutes.

2. Add sugar, salt, ½ cup butter, and eggs; beat to blend. Add 5 cups flour and stir until well moistened. Cover with plastic wrap and chill at least 4 hours and up to 4 days.

3. In bowl, punch down dough to expel air, then knead on a lightly floured board until smooth, about 1 minute.

4. Divide dough into 24 equal pieces. Form each into a smooth ball. Arrange equally in 2 buttered 9-inch round cake pans. Cover lightly with plastic wrap and let rise until puffy, about 40 minutes.

5. Bake in a 350° oven until golden brown, about 30 minutes (about 20 minutes in a convection oven).

6. Serve rolls hot, warm, or at room temperature.

Per roll: 149 cal., 29% (43 cal.) from fat; 3.4 g protein; 4.8 g fat (2.7 g sat.); 23 g carbo (0.8 g fiber); 145 mg sodium; 29 mg chol.

AUTUMN LEAVES ring a pair of Thanksgiving pies: Dense chocolate-hazelnut (foreground) and creamy French custard apple.

desserts

Frozen Maple Mousse

Dawn Anderson, Longmont

PREP AND COOK TIME: About 35 minutes, plus at least 25 minutes to freeze

TO TRANSPORT: Remove dasher from frozen mousse, cover canister, and carry on ice.

MAKES: About 6 cups; 8 to 10 servings

  9 **large egg** yolks

1½ cups **maple syrup**

  3 cups **whipping cream**

1. In the top of a double boiler, beat egg yolks to blend with maple syrup.

2. Nest in pan over simmering water and stir until mixture is thick enough to coat a metal spoon, about 10 minutes.

3. Immediately nest pan in ice water and stir mixture until cold, about 12 minutes.

4. Meanwhile, in a deep bowl with a mixer on high speed, whip cream until it holds soft peaks. Fold into maple mixture.

5. Pour into an ice cream maker (1½-qt. or larger capacity). Freeze as directed until mixture is firm enough to scoop, dasher is hard to turn, or machine stops.

Per serving: 387 cal., 63% (243 cal.) from fat; 4.1 g protein; 27 g fat (15 g sat.); 34 g carbo (0 g fiber); 35 mg sodium; 271 mg chol.

French Custard Apple Pie

Penny Fredlund, Seattle

PREP AND COOK TIME: About 1 hour, plus at least 30 minutes to cool

NOTES: If desired, use more pastry to make decorative cutouts for pie rim. If making up to 1 day ahead, cool, cover airtight, and chill.

TO TRANSPORT: Wrap chilled pie and carry in an insulated container.

MAKES: 8 to 10 servings

  1 **refrigerated pastry for single-crust 9-inch pie** (½ of a 15-oz. package)

1½ pounds **Golden Delicious apples**

  1 tablespoon **cornstarch**

  ½ cup **sugar**

  ¾ cup **whipping cream**

  3 **large egg** yolks

  1 tablespoon **vanilla**

  ⅛ teaspoon **ground cinnamon**

1. Gently fit pastry into a 9-inch pie pan. Fold under any excess pastry at rim and decoratively flute edge.

2. Peel apples, cut into quarters, and core. Arrange fruit in a single layer in pastry.

3. Bake on the bottom rack of a 350° oven for 30 minutes.

4. Meanwhile, in a bowl, mix cornstarch and sugar. Add cream, egg yolks, vanilla, and cinnamon. Whisk to blend.

5. Pour cream mixture over and around apples in pastry. Continue to bake until filling no longer jiggles in the center when pie is gently shaken,

40 to 45 minutes (about 35 minutes in a convection oven).

6. Let cool in pan on a rack at least 30 minutes. Serve warm or at room temperature.

Per serving: 244 cal., 48% (117 cal.) from fat; 2 g protein; 13 g fat (6.3 g sat.); 30 g carbo (1.1 g fiber); 115 mg sodium; 89 mg chol.

Chocolate-Orange Hazelnut Pie

PREP AND COOK TIME: About 1¼ hours, plus at least 30 minutes to cool

NOTES: Cocoa-hazelnut spread, such as Nutella, is sold in some well-stocked supermarkets and in specialty food stores. If desired, use more pastry to make decorative cutouts for the pie rim. If making up to 1 day ahead, cover pie airtight and store at room temperature.

TO TRANSPORT: Wrap cooled pie and carry at room temperature.

MAKES: 8 to 10 servings

- 1½ cups **hazelnuts**
- 1 **refrigerated pastry for single-crust 9-inch pie** (½ of a 15-oz. package)
- 1 jar (13 oz.; 1⅓ cups) **cocoa-flavor hazelnut spread** (see notes)
- 2 **large eggs**
- 3 tablespoons **orange-flavor liqueur**
- 2 tablespoons long, thin shreds **orange** peel

1. Bake hazelnuts in a 9- by 13-inch pan in a 350° oven until golden under skins, about 15 minutes. Pour onto a towel and let stand until cool enough to touch, about 5 minutes. Rub nuts in towel to remove loose skins. Lift nuts from towel; discard skins. Coarsely chop nuts.

2. Meanwhile, gently fit the pastry into a 9-inch pie pan. Fold under any excess pastry at rim and decoratively flute the edge.

3. In a bowl with a mixer, beat hazelnut spread, eggs, and liqueur until well blended. Stir in orange peel and toasted hazelnuts. Pour mixture into pastry.

4. Bake on the lowest rack of a 325° oven until filling is firm when pie is gently shaken, about 35 minutes (about 45 minutes in a 300° convection oven).

5. Cool pie on a rack at least 30 min-

utes. Serve warm or cool.

Per serving: 416 cal., 61% (252 cal.) from fat; 6.6 g protein; 28 g fat (4.7 g sat.); 36 g carbo (1.4 g fiber); 155 mg sodium; 48 mg chol.

beverage

Hot Buttered Rum

Judith Johnson

PREP AND COOK TIME: About 15 minutes

NOTES: To make hot spiced cider, omit rum. Up to 1 week ahead, make spiced butter-sugar mixture (step 1); cool, cover, and chill.

TO TRANSPORT: Put hot spiced cider in a thermos; carry rum separately at room temperature.

MAKES: 8 to 10 servings

- 2 tablespoons **butter** or margarine
- ¾ teaspoon **ground cinnamon**
- ½ teaspoon **ground nutmeg**
- ¼ teaspoon **ground cloves**
- ¼ teaspoon **ground allspice**
- ½ cup firmly packed **brown sugar**
- 8 to 10 cups **apple cider** or juice
- 1 to 2 cups **dark rum**
- 8 to 10 **cinnamon sticks** (about 3½ in. each; optional)

1. In a 1- to 1½-quart pan over medium heat, stir butter until melted. Add cinnamon, nutmeg, cloves, and allspice; stir, and add sugar. Remove from heat and mix well.

2. In a 4- to 5-quart pan over high heat, bring cider to a boil, about 15 minutes.

3. Combine butter mixture and hot cider in a pitcher or thermos. To serve, pour hot spiced cider into mugs (12 oz.) and to each add 2 to 3 tablespoons rum, to taste. Stir with cinnamon sticks or spoons.

Per serving: 208 cal., 11% (23 cal.) from fat; 0.1 g protein; 2.6 g fat (1.5 g sat.); 34 g carbo (0.2 g fiber); 34 mg sodium; 6.2 mg chol. ◆

Handy hampers and such

To enjoy a meal away from your home kitchen, you'll need to coordinate these factors: first, the last-minute cooking steps your dishes require and the equipment available at your destination; second, the number of foods on your menu that need to be carried hot or chilled and the equipment you have to do that job. Choose recipes that are big on make-ahead possibilities and small on last-minute cooking, and balance dishes that have hot or cold transport needs with foods that can be served at room temperature.

■ Build packing time into your schedule. There's always a final rush to get out the door; that's no time to start cooking.

■ Equip yourself with handy supplies for toting food.

Baskets and boxes. Go in style with the latest expensive picnic models or settle for basic transportation—cardboard. Anything works.

Ice chests and ice packs. The old-fashioned way to chill is still good. Best for foods in small and flexible containers.

Insulated bags and containers. They come in a variety of shapes and sizes, and keep hot foods hot and cold foods cold. Handy for casseroles. *Note: Foods transported hot or chilled can stand on the table up to two hours.*

Thermoses. Great not only for hot drinks but for soups and gravies as well.

Resealable heavy plastic food bags. They work well for lettuce, pilaf, even soup (seal one bag inside another).

The Quick Cook

MEALS IN 30 MINUTES OR LESS

BY BARBARA GOLDMAN

PENNE PASTA and cannellini beans pair up with sausage and fresh arugula in a hearty Italian-style soup.

JENNIFER CHEUNG

Pasta and beans

■ Dried pasta and canned beans are pantry partners without peer, ever ready to pair up in hearty, wholesome main dishes that satisfy in a hurry.

The potential combinations are staggering when you consider the innumerable pasta shapes and the expansive selection of canned beans that even a quick-stop market provides.

Pair a pasta shape that strikes your fancy (you don't even have to know how to pronounce it) with seasoned beans that seem like a good personality match in a soup or original *pasta e fagioli* (pasta and beans) dish. Just remember that both pasta and beans tend to absorb liquid as they stand, so be generous with the broth and ready to add more if it turns out the quick dinner you planned doesn't get eaten so quickly after all.

If you want to reduce the sodium in these dishes, rinse and drain canned beans before using.

Cannellini and Penne Soup

PREP AND COOK TIME: About 30 minutes
MAKES: 6 servings

1 pound **mild Italian sausage**

1 **onion** (½ lb.), chopped

4 cloves **garlic**, peeled and pressed

1 can (14½ oz.) fat-skimmed **chicken broth**

1 can (8 oz.) **tomato sauce**

½ cup **dry red wine**

1 teaspoon **dried oregano**

8 ounces **dried penne pasta**

¾ pound (about 10 cups) **arugula**

2 cans (15 oz. each) **cannellini** (white) **beans**

½ cup **shredded parmesan cheese**

Pepper

1. Discard sausage casings. In a **5-** to **6-quart pan** over high heat, break meat into chunks with a spoon. Add onion and garlic and stir often until onion is limp, about 5 minutes.

2. Add broth, tomato sauce, wine, oregano, pasta, and 2 cups water. Stirring often, bring to a boil and cook until pasta is just tender to bite, about 10 minutes.

3. Meanwhile, coarsely chop arugula. Add arugula and beans to pasta mixture. Stir occasionally, until soup is boiling, about 3 minutes.

4. Ladle into bowls and add cheese and pepper to taste.

Per serving: 609 cal., 40% (243 cal.) from fat; 29 g protein; 27 g fat (9.9 g sat.); 58 g carbo (8.5 g fiber); 1,242 mg sodium; 63 mg chol.

Black Beans and Fettuccine with Turkey

PREP AND COOK TIME: About 25 minutes
MAKES: 6 servings

1. In an **8-** to **10-quart pan** over high heat, stir 1 cup chopped **red bell pepper**, ½ cup chopped **onion**, 2 cloves minced **garlic**, and 1 tablespoon **olive oil** until onion is limp, about 5 minutes. Add 2 cups fat-skimmed **chicken broth**, 1 cup **water**, and 1 pound **dried fettuccine**. Stir often until pasta is just firm to bite, 8 to 10 minutes.

2. Add 1 package (10 oz.) **frozen corn kernels**, 2 cans (15 oz. each) **black beans**, 3 cups (¾ lb.) bite-size pieces **boned, skinned cooked turkey breast**, and 1 container (16 oz.) **fresh tomato salsa**. Stir until simmering, about 3 minutes. Mix in ½ cup *each* chopped **fresh cilantro, lime juice,** and **orange juice.** Ladle into bowls and add **salt** and **pepper** to taste.

Per serving: 587 cal., 8.3% (49 cal.) from fat; 41 g protein; 5.4 g fat (0.7 g sat.); 96 g carbo (11 g fiber); 914 mg sodium; 47 mg chol.

White Bean and Orzo Salad

PREP AND COOK TIME: About 25 minutes
MAKES: 4 servings

1. In a **6-** to **8-quart pan** over high heat, bring 2 quarts **water** to a boil. Add ½ pound (1¼ cups) **dried orzo pasta**; cook until tender to bite, 9 to 11 minutes. Drain; immerse in cold water. When cool, in about 3 minutes, drain pasta and pour into a large bowl.

2. Meanwhile, in a 10- to 12-inch frying pan over high heat, stir 1½ cups chopped **onions** and 1 tablespoon **olive oil** until onions are limp and slightly browned, about 5 minutes. Add to pasta.

3. Drain 1 can (15 oz.) **small white beans** and add to pasta along with 2 cups rinsed **cherry tomato** halves, ¼ cup fat-skimmed **chicken broth**, ⅓ cup **lemon juice**, ⅓ cup chopped **fresh mint** leaves, and ¼ cup chopped **parsley.** Mix and add **salt** to taste.

Per serving: 343 cal., 13% (46 cal.) from fat; 13 g protein; 5.1 g fat (0.7 g sat.); 62 g carbo (6.5 g fiber); 195 mg sodium; 0 mg chol. ◆

A Thanksgiving picnic

The high desert lures

one Tucson family

to share the

quintessential fall

meal alfresco

■ Every Thanksgiving, Tee Taylor and her family head to Sabino Canyon, about 15 miles from their home just outside Tucson. There, with the Santa Catalina Mountains as a backdrop and saguaro cactus as props, they feast on squash and peanut soup, chili- and sage-seasoned turkey, and whipped sweet potatoes. The food is cooked beforehand and carefully packed into baskets just before the trek. Taylor has perfected moving the feast over the past 10 years. (See how she and other Westerners transport Thanksgiving dinner with ease, starting on page 260.) The added advantage of the desert setting: equal encouragement for a hike or a nap.

BY ANDREW BAKER • PHOTOGRAPHS BY JUST LOOMIS • FOOD STYLING BY CHRISTINE MASTERSON

TEE TAYLOR (in orange shirt) joins family and friends (clockwise from left) Ken Hirschberg, Loy Brydon, Jill Merrick, Ty Brydon, David Brydon, and Heidi Kruse.

Layered Pâté

PREP TIME: About 20 minutes

NOTES: If making up to 1 day ahead, cover and chill. Spread pâté onto water crackers or small rounds of rye bread.

TO TRANSPORT: Cover chilled pâté in container and keep cold.

MAKES: 2 to 2½ cups; 8 to 10 servings

- ⅓ to ½ pound **liver pâté** such as braunschweiger or duck liver pâté
- ½ cup **chopped pecans**
- 2 tablespoons **brandy** (optional)
- ⅓ to ½ pound **cream cheese**, at room temperature
- ½ cup finely chopped **red onion**
- ¼ cup minced **fresh chives**

1. In a bowl, mash liver pâté until soft. Stir in pecans and brandy.

2. In another bowl, mix cream cheese and red onion until well blended.

3. Spread ½ the liver pâté mixture level in the bottom of a clear, straight-sided bowl (about 3-cup size). Spoon ½ the cream cheese mixture onto pâté mixture, and gently spread level. Repeat layers with remaining pâté mixture, then cream cheese mixture, gently spreading each level. Sprinkle with chives.

Per serving: 146 cal., 86% (126 cal.) from fat; 3.7 g protein; 14 g fat (5.2 g sat.); 2.6 g carbo (0.5 g fiber); 217 mg sodium; 40 mg chol.

Squash-Peanut Soup

PREP AND COOK TIME: About 25 minutes

NOTES: If making soup up to 1 day ahead, let cool, cover, and chill. To reheat, stir over medium-high heat until steaming; or heat in a microwave-safe container in a microwave oven at full power (100%), stirring often, until steaming.

TO TRANSPORT: Keep soup hot in a thermos. Seal slivered basil in a heavy plastic food bag and keep cool. Seal peanuts in another plastic bag and carry at room temperature.

MAKES: About 9 cups; 8 to 10 servings

- 4 packages (12 to 14 oz. each) **frozen puréed yellow squash**

  About 3 cups fat-skimmed **chicken broth**

- 1 cup **low-fat milk**
- ½ cup **chunky peanut butter**
- 1 teaspoon **ground cumin**
- ⅓ cup lightly packed **fresh basil** leaves, rinsed

Desert Feast

MENU

Layered Pâté

Squash-Peanut Soup

Chopped Salad

Turkey with Chili-Sage Glaze

Easy Gravy

Fresh Cranberry-Orange Relish

Green Beans with Sour Cream Onion Sauce

Cherry Tomatoes with Garlic

Whipped Sweet Potatoes with Marshmallow Crust

Crusty Rolls

Orange Pumpkins de Crème (page 289)

WINES

With the appetizers. Covey Run Riesling 1998 (Washington), $6. A fabulously fresh, fruity, zesty wine.

With the main course. Alban Estate Viognier 1998 (Edna Valley, CA), $28. Opulent, fruity, and floral, this elegant wine will stand up even to a turkey seasoned with chili and sage.

With dessert. Quady Elysium 1998 (California), $8.25 half-bottle (375 ml.). Made from Black Muscat grapes, with irresistible spicy, floral, honeyed flavors that aren't syrupy sweet.

— *Karen MacNeil-Fife*

TAYLOR SETS the table with dishes still warm from the oven. Her secret? She insulates them with thick towels.

thanksgiving **picnic**

$\frac{1}{3}$ cup **salted roasted peanuts**

Hot sauce

Salt

1. In a 5- to 6-quart pan, combine the squash with $2\frac{1}{2}$ cups broth and the milk, peanut butter, and cumin. Stir often over high heat until squash is thawed and mixture boils, 15 to 18 minutes. Add more broth to thin soup to desired consistency.

2. Meanwhile, stack basil leaves and cut crosswise into thin strips. Chop peanuts.

3. Ladle soup into individual bowls. Sprinkle with basil and chopped peanuts; add hot sauce and salt to taste.

Per serving: 152 cal., 55% (83 cal.) from fat; 9.5 g protein; 9.2 g fat (1.7 g sat.); 11 g carbo (1.4 g fiber); 120 mg sodium; 1 mg chol.

Chopped Salad

PREP TIME: About 15 minutes

NOTES: Up to 1 day ahead, combine vinegar and oil; cover and keep at room temperature. Rinse vegetables; wrap in towels, enclose separately in heavy plastic food bags, and chill.

TO TRANSPORT: Carry dressing at room temperature; keep combined salad ingredients cold.

MAKES: 10 cups; 8 to 10 servings

$\frac{1}{4}$ cup **seasoned rice vinegar**

2 tablespoons **garlic-flavor** or regular **olive oil**

3 cups lightly packed chopped **romaine lettuce hearts**

3 cups lightly packed chopped **red-leaf lettuce**

2 cups diced ($\frac{1}{2}$ in.) **cauliflower**

2 cups diced ($\frac{1}{2}$ in.) **zucchini**

Salt and fresh-ground **pepper**

1. In a large bowl, mix rice vinegar and oil.

2. Add romaine, red-leaf lettuce, cauliflower, and zucchini. Mix well and add salt and pepper to taste.

Per serving: 46 cal., 57% (26 cal.) from fat; 1.4 g protein; 2.9 g fat (0.4 g sat.); 4.4 g carbo (1.3 g fiber); 127 mg sodium; 0 mg chol.

Turkey with Chili-Sage Glaze

PREP AND COOK TIME: 2 to 3 hours

NOTES: If making up to 1 day ahead, cook turkey, cool, cover airtight, and chill.

TO TRANSPORT: Carry turkey hot, loosely wrapped, in a rimmed pan; or carry cold. Allow turkey to stand

COUNTDOWN

picnic game plan

☐ **UP TO 1 WEEK AHEAD.** *Make* cranberry-orange relish.

☐ **AT LEAST 3 DAYS AHEAD.** *Thaw* turkey in refrigerator if frozen.

☐ **UP TO 1 DAY AHEAD.** *Make* layered pâté, squash-peanut soup, and crusty rolls. *Prepare* dressing and *rinse* vegetables for chopped salad. *Roast* turkey. *Cook* green beans. *Prepare* sweet potatoes. *Bake* orange pumpkins de crème.

☐ **UP TO 4 HOURS AHEAD.** *Sauté* cherry tomatoes with garlic.

☐ **THE LAST HOUR.** *Make* sour cream onion sauce for beans. *Combine* vegetables for salad. *Bake* whipped sweet potatoes with marshmallow crust. *Reheat* soup and green beans.

CASUAL SURROUNDINGS call for casual foods (above). Accompany chili-glazed turkey with marshmallow-topped sweet potatoes, green beans with a creamy onion sauce, and garlic-rich cherry tomatoes, then spoon on gravy (right).

at room temperature no longer than 2 hours.

MAKES: Allow ¾ pound uncooked turkey per person, more for leftovers

- 1 **turkey** (15 to 20 lb.)
- 3 tablespoons **habanero** or Scotch bonnet **chili marmalade** or other hot red pepper or chili jelly
- 3 tablespoons **orange marmalade**
- 4 teaspoons **ground sage**

   Salt

1. Remove and discard leg truss from turkey. Pull off and discard lumps of fat. Remove giblets and neck (reserve for other uses). Rinse bird well. Insert a meat thermometer straight down through the thickest part of the turkey breast to the bone.

2. *On a charcoal barbecue* (20 to 22 in. wide) with a lid, mound and ignite 60 charcoal briquets on firegrate. When coals are spotted with gray ash, in about 20 minutes, push equal portions to opposite sides of firegrate. Place a foil drip pan between mounds of coals. To each mound, add 5 briquets now and every 30 minutes during cooking. Set grill in place. Set turkey, breast up, on grill over drip pan. Cover barbecue and open vents.

On a gas barbecue (with at least 11 in. between indirect-heat burners), turn heat to high, close lid, and heat for about 10 minutes. Adjust gas for indirect cooking (heat parallel to sides of bird and not beneath) and set a metal or foil drip pan in center (not over direct heat). Set grill in place. Set turkey, breast up, on grill over drip pan. Close barbecue lid. If edges of turkey near heat begin to get too dark, slide folded strips of foil between bird and grill. Fat in drippings may flare when barbecue lid is opened; quench by pouring a little water into the pan.

In an oven, place turkey, breast up, on a V-shaped rack in a 12- by 17-inch roasting pan (or one that is at least 2 in. longer and wider than the bird). Roast in a 325° or 350° oven, depending on size of bird; see chart on page 266.

3. In a glass bowl or measuring cup, mix habanero marmalade and orange marmalade. Heat in a microwave oven at full power (100%), stirring once, until soft, about 40 seconds. Stir in sage. When breast temperature is about 135° for birds up to 18 pounds and 145° for those over 18 pounds (about 45 minutes before turkey is done), spread marmalade glaze all over turkey. Continue to cook until thermometer reaches 160°. If wing and leg tips start to get too dark, cover with foil.

4. Drain juices from cavity into drippings and reserve for easy gravy (recipe follows). Transfer turkey to a large platter; let rest 15 to 30 minutes before carving. Add salt to taste.

Per ¼ pound boned cooked turkey with skin, based on percentages of white and dark meat in an average bird: 237 cal., 38% (90 cal.) from fat; 32 g protein; 10 g fat (3 g sat.); 2.1 g carbo (0 g fiber); 83 mg sodium; 93 mg chol.

Easy Gravy

PREP AND COOK TIME: About 25 minutes

NOTES: If making gravy up to 1 day ahead, cool, cover, and chill. To reheat, stir over medium-high heat until steaming; or heat in a microwave-safe container in a microwave oven at full power (100%), stirring often, until steaming.

TO TRANSPORT: Carry hot gravy in a thermos.

MAKES: About 8 cups

1   cup minced **onion**

1   teaspoon **fresh thyme** leaves or dried thyme

½   teaspoon chopped **fresh sage** leaves or dried rubbed sage

2   tablespoons **butter** or olive oil

2   quarts fat-skimmed **chicken** or giblet **broth** (recipe on page 268)

8   to 10 tablespoons **cornstarch**

    Fat-skimmed **drippings** from oven-roasted or barbecued turkey (recipe precedes)

    Salt and **pepper**

1. In a 3- to 4-quart pan, combine onion, thyme, sage, and butter. Stir often over high heat until onion is lightly browned, 3 to 4 minutes.

2. In a small bowl, blend about ½ cup broth with the cornstarch. Pour remaining broth and the turkey drippings into pan with the onion mixture. When it boils, add the cornstarch mixture, a portion at a time, until gravy

FALL-COLORED cherry tomatoes are sautéed with garlic and parsley.

is as thick as desired. Add salt and pepper to taste.

Per ¼-cup serving: 27 cal., 30% (8.1 cal.) from fat; 2.3 g protein; 0.9 g fat (0.5 g sat.); 2.3 g carbo (0.1 g fiber); 26 mg sodium; 2.1 mg chol.

Fresh Cranberry-Orange Relish

PREP AND COOK TIME: About 15 minutes

NOTES: If making up to 1 week ahead, cover and chill.

TO TRANSPORT: Cover and carry at room temperature.

MAKES: About 3 cups

5   cups (about 1¼ lb.) **fresh** or thawed frozen **cranberries**

1   **orange** (½ lb.)

¾   cup **sugar**

1. Sort cranberries, discarding any bruised or decayed fruit. Rinse berries.

2. Rinse orange and cut into 1-inch chunks; discard any seeds. In a blender or food processor, whirl orange, 2 cups cranberries, and sugar until puréed.

3. Pour purée into a 2- to 3-quart pan over high heat. Stir until mixture is boiling rapidly and begins to thicken, about 5 minutes. Add remaining cranberries and stir just until they begin to pop, about 5 minutes longer. Pour into a bowl. Serve warm or cool.

Per tablespoon: 20 cal., 0% (0 cal.) from fat; 0.1 g protein; 0 g fat; 5.3 g carbo (0.5 g fiber); 0.2 mg sodium; 0 mg chol.

Green Beans with Sour Cream Onion Sauce

PREP AND COOK TIME: About 40 minutes

NOTES: Up to 1 day ahead, cook beans, drain, immerse in ice water until cold, and drain again; cover and chill. Bring to room temperature to serve or immerse in hot water until warm, about 3 minutes.

TO TRANSPORT: Keep sauce hot in a thermos. Seal the beans in a heavy plastic food bag and carry at room temperature.

MAKES: 8 to 10 servings

1   cup thinly sliced **onions**

1¼   cups fat-skimmed **chicken broth**

¼   cup **dry** or cream **sherry**

1½   teaspoons **cornstarch**

1   cup **sour cream**

½   teaspoon **dried thyme**

2   pounds **green beans**, stem ends trimmed, rinsed

    Salt

1. In a 10- to 12-inch frying pan over high heat, frequently stir onions, 1 cup broth, and sherry until liquid is evaporated and onions begin to brown, 15 to 20 minutes.

2. In a bowl, mix cornstarch with remaining ¼ cup broth. Add sour cream and thyme; mix well. Add to onion mixture and scrape browned bits free from bottom of pan; stir until sauce boils. Keep warm.

3. Meanwhile, in a 5- to 6-quart pan over high heat, bring 2 quarts water to a boil. Add beans and cook until tender-crisp to bite, 5 to 10 minutes. Drain.

4. Put beans in a bowl and pour onion sauce over them. Add salt to taste.

Per serving: 87 cal., 51% (44 cal.) from fat; 3.4 g protein; 4.9 g fat (3 g sat.); 8.7 g carbo (1.7 g fiber); 27 mg sodium; 10 mg chol.

Cherry Tomatoes with Garlic

PREP AND COOK TIME: About 15 minutes

NOTES: Use a variety of tomatoes: round and pear-shaped; red, yellow, and orange.

TO TRANSPORT: Cover hot tomatoes and carry in an insulated bag; or let cool to room temperature, cover, and carry.

MAKES: 6 to 7 cups; 8 to 10 servings

2 pounds **cherry tomatoes** (about ³⁄₄ to 1 in., 6 to 7 cups; see notes)

4 teaspoons thinly sliced **garlic**

¹⁄₄ cup (¹⁄₈ lb.) **butter** or olive oil

¹⁄₄ cup minced **parsley**

Salt and **pepper**

1. Rinse tomatoes and discard any stems.

2. In a 10- to 12-inch frying pan over medium-high heat, stir garlic in butter until limp, about 2 minutes. Add tomatoes and parsley, and stir until tomatoes are hot, about 3 minutes. Add salt and pepper to taste. Pour into a bowl and serve hot, warm, or at room temperature.

Per serving: 64 cal., 72% (46 cal.) from fat; 0.9 g protein; 5.1 g fat (3 g sat.); 4.8 g carbo (1.3 g fiber); 58 mg sodium; 13 mg chol.

Whipped Sweet Potatoes with Marshmallow Crust

PREP AND COOK TIME: About 1¹⁄₂ hours

NOTES: If making up to 1 day ahead, complete recipe through step 3; cover and chill. Bake, covered, without marshmallow topping until warm in center, 20 to 30 minutes, then cover evenly with marshmallows and return to oven until topping is browned, about 10 minutes longer.

TO TRANSPORT: Cover hot casserole and carry in an insulated container.

MAKES: 8 to 10 servings

3 pounds **sweet potatoes** or yams

About 1¹⁄₂ cups **low-fat milk**

2 tablespoons minced **fresh ginger**

3 tablespoons **lime juice**

4 cups **miniature marshmallows**

2 tablespoons long, thin shreds **orange** peel

Salt

1. Scrub sweet potatoes, pierce in several places with a sharp knife, and place in a shallow pan (9 by 13 in. or 10 by 15 in.).

2. Bake in a 400° oven until sweet potatoes give readily when gently squeezed, about 1 hour, depending on size. Let stand until cool enough to handle, about 10 minutes.

3. Cut sweet potatoes in half and scoop flesh into a large bowl; discard peels. With a potato masher or a mixer, mash or beat sweet potatoes with milk. Stir in ginger, lime juice, and 2 cups marshmallows. Spread evenly in a shallow 3-quart casserole.

4. Cover sweet potatoes evenly with remaining marshmallows.

WELL-FED, the holiday celebrants rest after a postmeal hike.

5. Bake in a 400° oven until potatoes are hot in the center and marshmallow topping is richly browned, 15 to 20 minutes. Sprinkle with orange peel and serve, adding salt to taste.

Per serving: 180 cal., 3.5% (6.3 cal.) from fat; 3.2 g protein; 0.7 g fat (0.3 g sat.); 41 g carbo (3 g fiber); 41 mg sodium; 1.5 mg chol.

Crusty Rolls

PREP AND COOK TIME: About 2³⁄₄ hours

NOTES: If making up to 1 day ahead, cool, wrap airtight, and store at room temperature. The crust softens as rolls stand; to recrisp, heat on a rack in a 400° oven until crisp, about 5 minutes. (At mile-high altitude, shaped rolls rise in about ¹⁄₃ less time.)

TO TRANSPORT: Carry at room temperature.

MAKES: 20 rolls

1 tablespoon **sugar**

¹⁄₂ teaspoon **salt**

1 package **active dry yeast**

2 **large egg** whites

About 3¹⁄₂ cups **all-purpose flour**

About 2 tablespoons **olive** or salad **oil**

Cornmeal

1 **large egg** yolk

1. In a large bowl, combine 1 cup warm (about 110°) water, sugar, salt, and yeast; let stand until yeast is soft, about 5 minutes. Stir in egg whites, 1 cup flour, and 2 tablespoons oil.

2. Add 2¹⁄₂ more cups flour and stir until incorporated. Scrape dough (it is soft) onto a well-floured board and dust with more flour. Knead until smooth and elastic, about 10 minutes, adding flour as required to prevent sticking.

3. Place dough in an oiled bowl, and turn over to coat. Cover bowl with plastic wrap and let dough rise in a warm place until doubled, about 1 hour. Punch dough down, then knead briefly on a lightly floured board to expel air.

4. Divide dough into 20 equal pieces and shape each into a ball that is smooth on top. As you shape balls, dip bottoms in cornmeal. Set about 1¹⁄₂ inches apart on an oiled 12- by 15-inch baking sheet. Rub tops lightly with oil, drape with plastic wrap, and let rise until puffy, about 30 minutes.

5. In a small bowl, beat egg yolk with 1 tablespoon water to blend. Brush rolls lightly with egg yolk mixture.

6. Put a 10- by 15-inch pan on lowest rack of a 400° oven and pour in about ¹⁄₄ inch of boiling water. Put another oven rack just above bottom one. Bake rolls on this rack until richly browned, 25 to 30 minutes. Transfer rolls to a rack to cool. Serve warm or cool.

Per roll: 109 cal., 17% (19 cal.) from fat; 3.1 g protein; 2.1 g fat (0.3 g sat.); 19 g carbo (0.8 g fiber); 123 mg sodium; 11 mg chol. ◆

The Low-Fat Cook

HEALTHY CHOICES FOR THE ACTIVE LIFESTYLE

BY ELAINE JOHNSON

Is it a gift or dinner?

■ As a private chef—for notables such as George Lucas of *Star Wars* fame—Cheryl Forberg has earned a reputation for extravagant but light entrées.

One dish that she often chooses for her own parties is the Moroccan pie *bastilla*. She makes individual servings, easily packaged in purchased filo dough, exotically finished with a twist.

Traditionally, the heart of the pie is pigeon, eggs, nuts, a souk's worth of spices, and lots of butter. Forberg manages a lighter touch by using poached chicken breasts and egg whites in the filling. A fine mist of cooking oil, not butter, makes the pastry flaky and crisp. The lean, flavorful poaching broth becomes a smooth, sweet-hot sauce.

CHICKEN, ALMONDS, and spices are handsomely wrapped in filo.

ROBERT OLDING

Low-Fat Chicken Bastillas

PREP AND COOK TIME: About 1 hour
MAKES: 4 servings

  1 cup thickly sliced **onion**

  2 cloves **garlic,** minced

 1½ tablespoons minced **fresh ginger**

 1½ teaspoons **ground turmeric**

  1 teaspoon **ground coriander**

 ⅛ teaspoon **powdered saffron**

 ¾ teaspoon **hot chili flakes**

 1¼ teaspoons **ground cinnamon**

  3 cups fat-skimmed **unsalted** or reduced-sodium **chicken broth**

  1 pound **boned, skinned chicken breasts,** cut into ⅓- by 2-inch slices

  4 **large egg** whites

 ¼ cup chopped **fresh cilantro**

    Salt

 ⅓ cup finely chopped **almonds**

    About 1½ tablespoons **powdered sugar**

  6 sheets (12 by 17 in.) **filo dough**

    Cooking oil spray

  2 tablespoons **red jalapeño jelly**

  1 tablespoon **cornstarch**

1. In a 3- to 4-quart pan over high heat, bring onion, garlic, ginger, turmeric, coriander, saffron, chili flakes, ¼ teaspoon cinnamon, and broth to a rolling boil. Add chicken, cover, remove from heat, and let stand until chicken is no longer pink in center (cut to test), about 2 minutes. With a slotted spoon, transfer chicken, but not onion, to a bowl. Save the cooking broth.

2. Whisk ¼ cup of the cooking broth with egg whites just to blend. Place an 8- to 10-inch nonstick frying pan over medium heat. Pour egg mixture into pan and stir just until softly set, 3 to 5 minutes.

3. With a flexible spatula, gently combine egg mixture and cilantro with chicken. Season to taste with salt.

4. In another bowl, combine almonds, 1½ tablespoons sugar, and remaining 1 teaspoon cinnamon.

5. Working quickly so filo dough doesn't dry out, lightly spray each filo sheet with oil and make 3 stacks of 2 sheets each. From a 17-inch edge, cut each stack of filo dough into 3 equal parts; you'll have 9 stacks. Lay 1 stack of 2 strips at right angles across another. With 6 more stacks, make 3 more crosses; reserve remaining stack for other uses.

6. Using a slotted spoon, mound ¼ of the chicken mixture (add any accumulated liquid to the reserved cooking broth) onto center of each cross. Sprinkle mounds equally with almond mixture. For each bundle, gather filo strips up over filling and gently squeeze and twist to enclose. Set filo bundles well apart on an oiled 12- by 15-inch baking sheet.

7. Pull back tips of filo strips on each bundle to make "petals." Lightly spray bundles with oil.

8. Bake bastilla pastries in a 400° oven until golden brown, 15 to 18 minutes (10 to 12 minutes in a convection oven).

9. Meanwhile, boil reserved broth mixture over high heat until reduced to 2 cups, 5 to 10 minutes. Pour through a fine strainer into a bowl; discard residue. Rinse pan and return broth to it. Add jelly. Mix cornstarch with 1 tablespoon water and add to pan. Set pan over high heat and stir with a whisk until boiling.

10. With a wide spatula, transfer bastillas to plates. Dust with powdered sugar and accompany with sauce.

Per serving: 385 cal., 28% (108 cal.) from fat; 37 g protein; 12 g fat (1.7 g sat.); 33 g carbo (1.9 g fiber); 352 mg sodium; 69 mg chol. ◆

Save the last course for me

Creamy persimmon tart, cranberry charlotte, chestnut torte, and pumpkin pots de crème are worth the wait

BY LINDA LAU ANUSASANANAN

PHOTOGRAPHS BY JAMES CARRIER

■ Thanksgiving turkey with all the trimmings is a tough act to follow. Any dessert, after such a feast, has to have plenty of pizzazz to get attention. Plus, on this particular day, a dessert must also resonate with tradition. And in many households, it has to have the wherewithal to travel to family gatherings, indoors or out (see pages 260 and 278).

These four desserts, with their variations, fill the bill in every way. Each is notably handsome, but you don't have to be a pro to make them look good. Each takes a traditional flavor one step beyond expectation: cranberries in a light and luscious charlotte, golden persimmons in a gleaming tart, petite pumpkins filled with velvety custards (a fresh cross between pot de crème and pumpkin pie), and mellow chestnuts in a chocolate-cloaked torte. All can be made at least a day ahead and need only to be kept cool and secure to travel for hours at a time. Best of all, they can hold until "later," when the bird has settled and there's a little room for something special.

Persimmon Cream Tart

PREP AND COOK TIME: About 15 minutes

NOTES: If making up to 1 day ahead, invert a large bowl over tart on a plate to protect fruit and keep dessert airtight; chill.

MAKES: 8 to 10 servings

- 2 packages (8 oz. each) **neufchâtel** (light cream) or cream **cheese,** at room temperature
- ½ cup **orange marmalade**

  Butter crust (recipe follows)
- 3 **Fuyu persimmons** (about ¾ lb. total)

1. In a bowl with a mixer, beat cheese and 6 tablespoons marmalade until well blended. Spoon into cool baked butter crust and spread evenly.

2. Rinse, stem, and peel persimmons, then cut lengthwise into ¼-inch-thick wedges; discard any seeds. Lay fruit slices in concentric circles on cheese filling, slightly overlapping slices.

3. Put remaining marmalade in a glass measuring cup. Heat in a microwave oven on full power (100%) until melted, about 1 minute, stirring several times. Gently brush melted marmalade over persimmon slices.

4. Remove pan rim and cut tart into wedges.

Per serving: 360 cal., 53% (189 cal.) from fat; 6.8 g protein; 21 g fat (13 g sat.); 39 g carbo (0.4 g fiber); 285 mg sodium; 81 mg chol.

Butter Crust

PREP AND COOK TIME: About 35 minutes

NOTES: If making up to 1 day ahead, wrap cool crust airtight and let stand at

FUYU PERSIMMON slices form a radiant fan over creamy filling in a fall tart.

room temperature. Freeze to store longer; thaw unwrapped.

MAKES: 1 crust; 8 to 10 servings

- 1⅓ cups **all-purpose flour**
- ¼ cup **sugar**
- ½ cup (¼ lb.) **butter** or margarine, cut into chunks
- 1 **large egg** yolk

1. In a food processor or a bowl, combine flour and sugar. Add butter; whirl or rub with your fingers until fine crumbs form. Add egg yolk; whirl or mix with a fork until dough sticks together. Pat into a ball.

2. Press dough over bottom and up sides, flush with rim, of a 10- to 10½-inch tart pan with removable rim.

3. Bake in a 300° oven until golden brown, 35 to 40 minutes (25 to 30 minutes in a convection oven); let cool.

Per serving crust: 167 cal., 53% (89 cal.) from fat; 2.1 g protein; 9.9 g fat (5.9 g sat.); 18 g carbo (0.5 g fiber); 95 mg sodium; 46 mg chol.

Cranberry-Raspberry Charlotte

PREP AND COOK TIME: About 45 minutes, plus at least 4 hours to chill

NOTES: If making up to 1 day ahead, cover and chill. Garnish with fresh raspberries or cranberries, plain or sugared. To sugar, dip berries in beaten egg white, then sugar, and dry on a rack at least 15 minutes. If you're concerned about raw egg whites, use dried pasteurized egg whites, available in most supermarkets; reconstitute them according to package directions. Look

LADYFINGERS encase a refreshing cranberry-raspberry mousse.

for a charlotte mold in specialty cookware stores, or use a soufflé dish.

MAKES: 8 servings

12 to 14 double **ladyfingers** (about 3 oz. total)

¼ cup **kirsch** or other cherry-flavor liqueur, or orange juice

1¾ cups **cranberries,** fresh or frozen

1¾ cups **raspberries,** fresh or unsweetened frozen

1 cup **sugar**

1 envelope **unflavored gelatin**

2 **large egg** whites

¾ cup **whipping cream**

1. Smoothly line a 1½-quart charlotte mold (about 6 in. wide at top, 5 in. at bottom, 3½ in. tall) or 1½-quart soufflé dish with plastic wrap. Separate ladyfingers so each is flat on 1 side. Decoratively arrange a single layer of ladyfingers, rounded side down, in pan bottom; cut ladyfingers to a point at 1 end as needed to make them fit neatly into pan and to cover bottom completely. Stand remaining ladyfingers vertically, rounded side against pan, to cover sides of container. Lightly brush ladyfingers with 2 tablespoons kirsch.

2. Sort cranberries (thaw, if frozen) and discard bruised or decayed fruit. Rinse and drain cranberries and fresh raspberries (thaw frozen raspberries). In a blender, whirl cranberries, raspberries, and ¾ cup sugar until smooth. Rub purée through a fine strainer into a bowl.

3. In a 2- to 3-quart microwave-safe bowl, sprinkle gelatin over ¼ cup water.

Let soften about 5 minutes. Heat in a microwave oven at full power (100%) until mixture boils and is clear, 30 to 40 seconds. Add 1 cup berry purée and mix well. Nest bowl of berry-gelatin mixture in ice water and stir occasionally until it becomes very thick and syrupy, 5 to 10 minutes. If mixture gets firm, nest bowl in hot water and stir until syrupy.

4. Add 2 tablespoons kirsch to remaining purée; cover and chill up to 1 day.

5. In a deep bowl with a mixer on high speed, whip egg whites until foamy. Gradually add ¼ cup sugar, beating whites until they hold stiff, moist peaks. Stir about ⅓ of the whites into the syrupy berry-gelatin mixture, then gently fold in the remaining whites.

6. In the bowl used for beating whites (without washing beaters), whip cream until it holds soft peaks. Add to berry-gelatin mixture; gently fold together until well blended. Pour into ladyfinger-lined container. Cover airtight and chill until firm, at least 4 hours and up to 1 day.

7. Uncover charlotte. If filling is lower than rim of ladyfingers, carefully trim tips off ladyfingers so they are even with filling. Invert a flat plate over dessert. Holding containers together, invert. Lift off mold and gently remove plastic wrap. Cut dessert into wedges and serve with reserved cranberry-raspberry sauce.

Per serving: 254 cal., 29% (73 cal.) from fat; 3.6 g protein; 8.1 g fat (4.6 g sat.); 40 g carbo (2.1 g fiber); 39 mg sodium; 64 mg chol.

Chocolate Chestnut Torte

PREP AND COOK TIME: About 2¼ hours, plus 2 hours to chill

NOTES: If making dessert up to 2 days ahead, cover and chill.

MAKES: 12 servings

5 **large eggs,** separated

¼ teaspoon **cream of tartar**

¼ cup **sugar**

1 can (8¾ oz.; ¾ cup) **sweetened chestnut spread**

½ cup **fine dried bread crumbs**

⅔ cup coarsely chopped **bittersweet** or semisweet **chocolate**

6 tablespoons **orange-flavor liqueur**

1 cup **whipping cream**

Chestnut buttercream (recipe follows)

Chocolate ganache (recipe follows)

Glacéed chestnuts (optional) and/or raspberries

1. Butter bottom of a 9-inch cake or cheesecake pan (at least 3 in. tall) and line with baking parchment, microwave-safe cooking paper, or waxed paper cut to fit. Butter and flour pan.

2. In a deep bowl with a mixer on high speed, whip egg whites and cream of tartar until foamy. Gradually add sugar, beating until the whites hold stiff, moist peaks.

3. In another bowl with the mixer (without washing beaters), beat egg yolks and chestnut spread to blend well. Add the bread crumbs and chocolate; stir to blend.

4. Gently fold yolk mixture into whites until evenly blended. Scrape batter into prepared pan.

5. Bake in a 350° oven until cake top springs back when gently touched, 35 to 40 minutes (in a 325° convection oven, 40 to 45 minutes). Cool in pan on rack at least 45 minutes. Run a thin-bladed knife between cake and pan rim; remove rim. Invert cake onto a rack, remove pan bottom, and peel off paper.

6. With a serrated knife, cut the cake in half horizontally to make 2 layers. Gently brush off any crumbs. Carefully lift off top cake layer and set, cut side down, on a sheet of baking parchment or cooking or waxed paper. Cut a round of cardboard exactly the size of the cake. Set bottom half of cake, cut side up, on cardboard and drizzle it

CHESTNUT CREAM fills chocolate-flecked chestnut cake.

evenly with ½ the liqueur.

7. Wash and dry beaters and bowl used for whites. Whip cream in bowl just until it holds soft peaks. Add 1 cup chestnut buttercream and fold in to blend with cream.

8. Scoop chestnut–whipped cream mixture onto cake on cardboard; spread level. Set remaining cake layer, cut side down, on cream. Brush off crumbs. Drizzle cake top evenly with remaining liqueur.

9. With a thin spatula, spread remaining chestnut buttercream in a thin, smooth, even layer over top and sides of cake. Chill until firm, at least 1 hour, or cover with a large inverted bowl (to avoid marring cake) and chill up to 1 day.

10. Set cake on a rack in a 10- by 15-inch pan. Pour chocolate ganache in a steady, generous stream onto cake, starting in the center and quickly moving toward the edge, following a circular pattern so the chocolate flows evenly and smoothly over cake and down the sides. Use a small spatula to guide chocolate so it covers cake sides evenly. Let cake stand until ganache stops dripping, about 5 minutes. Lift rack with cake into another flat pan and put in the refrigerator to cool until ganache firms, at least 1 hour, or cover with a large inverted bowl and chill up to 1 day. Scrape remaining ganache into a bowl; see recipe for another use.

11. Lifting with cardboard base, set cake on a flat plate. Garnish with glacéed chestnuts. Cut cake into wedges.

Per serving: 377 cal., 62% (234 cal.) from fat; 5.2 g protein; 26 g fat (15 g sat.); 30 g carbo (2 g fiber); 157 mg sodium; 143 mg chol.

Chestnut buttercream. In a bowl with a mixer on high speed, whip ½ cup (¼ lb.) **butter** or margarine, at room temperature, with 1 can (8¾ oz.; ¾ cup) **sweetened chestnut spread** until blended well.

Chocolate ganache. In the top of a double boiler or a metal bowl set over simmering water, combine 1 pound (2¾ cups) chopped **bittersweet** or semisweet **chocolate** and 2 cups **whipping cream.** Stir often until chocolate is melted. Remove from heat and stir occasionally until a thermometer in center of mixture reads 98° to 100° (body temperature), 20 to 25 minutes. If too cool, gently stir mixture over simmering water to warm slightly. Makes 3½ cups, which is how much you need to get a smooth, thick coating on cake;

however, only about 1 cup sticks. Chill leftover ganache and use it to make truffles by scooping it into small balls and rolling them in **unsweetened cocoa.**

TINY, SWEET pumpkins make edible cups for a rich, delicate custard.

Orange Pumpkins de Crème

PREP AND COOK TIME: About 1¼ hours

NOTES: Filled pumpkins and lids can be cooked up to 1 day ahead; when cool, cover airtight and chill. Garnish with whipped cream, if desired.

MAKES: 8 servings

    8 **miniature pumpkins** (Jack Be Little or Munchkin; each 6 to 8 oz.) with stems

1¾ cups **half-and-half** (light cream)

    5 **large egg** yolks

 ⅓ cup **sugar**

    2 tablespoons **orange-flavor liqueur**

 ½ teaspoon **ground coriander**

       Finely shredded **orange** peel

1. Rinse pumpkins. Pierce each top deeply with a knife or sharp fork several times. Set pumpkins (a few at a time, if they don't all fit) on a rack at least 1 inch above 1½ inches of water in a 14-inch wok or a 5- to 6-quart pan. Cover pan and bring water to a boil over high heat. Keep water at a boil and steam pumpkins until tender when pierced, 15 to 20 minutes. If needed, add more boiling water to pan.

2. Let pumpkins cool until comfortable to touch, about 10 to 15 minutes. With

a small, sharp knife, cut down and around each stem to make an opening about 2 inches wide. Lift out stem end and reserve. With a small spoon, scoop seeds from pumpkins (without breaking through skin) and discard.

3. In a bowl, whisk together half-and-half, egg yolks, sugar, liqueur, and coriander.

4. Fill pumpkin shells equally with egg mixture.

5. Return filled pumpkins (a few at a time, if they don't all fit) and lids to a rack at least 1 inch above 1½ inches of water in the wok or pan. Drape foil over pumpkins to prevent condensation on the pan lid from dripping into filling. Cover pan and bring water to a boil over high heat. Keep water at a boil and steam until filling looks set in center and jiggles only slightly all over when gently shaken, 12 to 16 minutes.

6. Gently transfer pumpkins to plates or a dish and set lids alongside if desired. Serve warm or cool. Garnish each pumpkin with shredded orange peel.

Per serving: 185 cal., 46% (85 cal.) from fat; 4.7 g protein; 9.4 g fat (4.8 g sat.); 21 g carbo (0 g fiber); 28 mg sodium; 152 mg chol.

Ginger Pumpkins de Crème

Follow recipe for ***orange pumpkins de crème*** (preceding), but instead of orange-flavor liqueur, use **ginger-flavor liqueur,** or omit liqueur and use more half-and-half. Omit ground coriander and use **ground ginger,** and omit orange peel and garnish the filled pumpkins with **chopped ginger in syrup** or crystallized ginger.

Per serving: 197 cal., 43% (85 cal.) from fat; 4.7 g protein; 9.4 g fat (4.8 g sat.); 24 g carbo (0.1 g fiber); 31 mg sodium; 152 mg chol.

Coconut Pumpkins de Crème

Follow recipe for ***orange pumpkins de crème*** (preceding), but omit 1 cup of the half-and-half and add 1 cup **canned coconut milk,** omit orange liqueur and use **rum** or more half-and-half, and omit ground coriander and add ¼ teaspoon **ground cardamom.** In a 6- to 8-inch frying pan over medium-low heat, stir ¼ cup **dried sweetened shredded** or flaked **coconut** often until golden, 7 to 8 minutes. Pour from pan and let cool. Use instead of orange peel to garnish desserts.

Per serving: 209 cal., 56% (117 cal.) from fat; 4.4 g protein; 13 g fat (8.7 g sat.); 20 g carbo (0.2 g fiber); 25 mg sodium; 141 mg chol. ◆

foodguide

BY JERRY ANNE DI VECCHIO

PHOTOGRAPHS BY JAMES CARRIER

Crab with citrus sauce

Grapefruit gets its sea legs

■ The wild flavor pairings high-profile chefs once used to attract attention are losing steam as the popular palate warms to retro dishes like braised lamb shanks, beef Stroganoff, and chicken Kiev. However, those crazy, taste-expanding days deserve more praise than scorn, in my view, because new pleasures surfaced. One of the deserving survivors is grapefruit with fish. Citrus and seafood are no strangers to each other; lemon is indigenous in their long-standing partnership. But grapefruit requires a leap of faith, and some serious concentration—of the juice, that is. If you boil down grapefruit juice enough to concentrate its sweetness, taking the edge off its natural bitterness, the result is bright and refreshing.

Chef Katsuo "Naga" Nagasawa, of Cafe del Rey in Marina del Rey, California, surrounds his marvelous crab cakes (with so much sweet crab and so little else, they barely hang together) with a zesty grapefruit sauce, beurre blanc–style: with butter stirred in. For another exhilarating voyage, serve the sauce with grilled salmon (be sure to include the final swirl of butter).

Naga's Crab Cakes

PREP AND COOK TIME: 45 to 50 minutes

MAKES: 8 first-course, 4 main-dish servings

- 2 **pink** or ruby **grapefruit** (about 1 lb. each)
- $3/4$ pound **shelled cooked crab**
- 2 tablespoons diced ($1/4$ in.) **red bell pepper**
- 1 tablespoon diced ($1/4$ in.) **celery**
- 1 tablespoon diced ($1/4$ in.) **red onion**
- 2 tablespoons chopped **parsley**
- 1 **large egg**
- $1/2$ teaspoon **dry mustard**
- $1/4$ cup **mayonnaise**
- $1/8$ teaspoon fresh-ground **pepper**
- $1/8$ teaspoon **cayenne**

About 1 cup **panko** (Japanese-style coarse bread crumbs) or dried bread crumbs

- 6 to 7 tablespoons **butter** or margarine

Pink grapefruit sauce (recipe follows)

- 2 tablespoons minced **parsley**

1. With a knife, cut and discard peel and white membrane from grapefruit. Holding fruit over a strainer nested in a bowl, cut between inner membrane and segments to release; drop segments into strainer and collect juice to use for sauce. Discard membrane.

2. Sort through crab and discard any bits of shell.

3. In another bowl, combine red bell pepper, celery, onion, chopped parsley, egg, mustard, mayonnaise, pepper, and cayenne. Mix well with a fork. Add crab and stir just to mix.

4. Put panko in a shallow pan. Mound $1/8$ of the crab mixture on panko, and pat crumbs lightly on top. With a spatula, transfer cake (it's fragile) to a sheet of waxed paper. Repeat with remaining crab mixture to shape and coat remaining cakes. Set slightly apart on waxed paper.

5. In a 10- to 12-inch nonstick frying pan over medium heat, melt 2 tablespoons butter. When hot, set crab cakes slightly apart in pan. Cook, turning once, until browned on both sides, 5 to 8 minutes total. Add more butter if needed to brown evenly. As cooked, set cakes on warm plates and keep warm.

6. Set pan with pink grapefruit sauce over high heat, add 4 tablespoons butter, in chunks, and stir until melted, about $1 1/2$ minutes. Spoon warm sauce equally around crab cakes. Garnish with grapefruit segments and sprinkle with parsley.

Per first-course serving: 264 cal., 58% (153 cal.) from fat;

11 g protein; 17 g fat (7.3 g sat.); 16 g carbo (0.8 g fiber); 293 mg sodium; 100 mg chol.

Pink grapefruit sauce. In a 10- to 12-inch frying pan, combine 1 tablespoon **butter** or margarine, 1 tablespoon minced **onion,** and ¼ cup minced **mushrooms.** Stir often over high heat until mushrooms begin to brown, 2 to 3 minutes. Add ¼ teaspoon **dried thyme,** ½ cup **dry white wine,** and 2 cups **pink** or ruby **grapefruit juice** (include reserved juice from Naga's crab cakes, preceding). Boil over high heat, stirring occasionally, until mixture is reduced to ½ cup, about 15 minutes. Use in Naga's crab cakes, step 6 (preceding).

Barely time for barley

■ Soft, chewy barley is one of those rib-sticking ingredients common to long-simmered soups of yesteryear. I came across a memorable version one bitterly cold day in New York, in a little Hungarian restaurant. After lunching on big bowls of it, we begged the recipe from the owner-chef. But since then, I've barely had time to make the dish—until recently. What once took me several hours now takes a quarter of the time with quick-cook barley. The kernels are tender in just about 10 minutes; the soup's in the bowl in little more than half an hour.

Barley-Mushroom Soup

PREP AND COOK TIME: About 35 minutes
MAKES: About 9 cups; 6 servings

- ½ pound **Italian sausages**
- 1 **onion** (½ lb.), peeled and chopped
- 2 **carrots** (½ lb. total), peeled and chopped
- ½ pound **mushrooms,** rinsed, discolored stem ends trimmed, and thinly sliced
- 1 **Roma tomato** (3 to 4 oz.), rinsed, cored, and chopped
- 6 cups fat-skimmed **beef broth**
- ¾ cup **quick-cook barley**
- 1 package (10 oz.) **frozen chopped spinach**

  Sour cream or nonfat yogurt

  Salt and **pepper**

1. Remove and discard casings from sausages. Crumble meat into a 4- to 5-quart pan. Add onion, carrots, mushrooms, and tomato.

2. Stir often over high heat until meat begins to brown and vegetables are limp, 10 to 12 minutes.

3. Add broth and barley; scrape up browned bits. Add spinach. Bring to a boil over high heat, stirring occasionally. Cover, reduce heat, and simmer, stirring occasionally, until barley is tender to bite, about 10 minutes.

4. Ladle soup into bowls and add dollops of sour cream and salt and pepper to taste.

Per serving: 266 cal., 44% (117 cal.) from fat; 15 g protein; 13 g fat (4.3 g sat.); 25 g carbo (5.1 g fiber); 397 mg sodium; 29 mg chol.

Take aim and shoot

■ That's all there is to using the Raytek MiniTemp MT2 and MT4 infrared sensor thermometers: Point, pull the trigger, and a digital display shows the temperature at the spot sighted—0° to 500° Fahrenheit and -18° to 260° Celsius. MiniTemp MT4 also has a laser beam to confirm the accuracy of your aim; both thermometers are battery-powered. • Unlike probe thermometers, which must be immersed or inserted in foods, the MiniTemp MTs instantly read surface temperatures. Being limited to surfaces isn't the handicap you might think. The centers of soft mixtures can be swirled to the top, and with the laser beam to confirm your focus, you can even get a reading in the center of a piece of meat when you cut to test. The MT2 costs about $99, the MT4 about $139; call (800) 866-5478.

Masa master

■ At his signature restaurant in Denver, Kevin Taylor puts a delightful twist on polenta. It's made with ground corn, all right, but in the form of masa flour, with the distinctive flavor of corn tortillas. Taylor sometimes serves the crusty, moist wedges with tiny roasted chickens to soak up the juices. But they also go well with a Denver favorite, green chili stew with pork.

Polenta Gratin

PREP AND COOK TIME: About 50 minutes

MAKES: 18 triangles; 6 to 9 servings

1 cup **low-fat milk**

2 cups **dehydrated masa** (corn tortilla) **flour**

1½ cups fat-skimmed **chicken broth**

1 can (8 oz.) **tomato sauce**

1 tablespoon **butter** or margarine

Salt and **pepper**

About 1½ cups **salad oil**

¼ pound **gruyère** or Swiss **cheese,** shredded

¼ cup grated **parmesan cheese**

1. In a 4- to 5-quart pan, whisk milk into masa until smooth. Mix in broth and tomato sauce. Add butter.

2. Stir over medium-high heat until mixture is boiling, very thick, and slightly

darker, and holds its shape when mounded, 4 to 5 minutes. Add salt and pepper to taste.

3. Immediately spread the very stiff mixture evenly in an 8- or 9-inch square pan; it firms almost at once (if it doesn't, return mixture to pan and cook, stirring, until thick). Let cool at least 15 minutes. Invert polenta onto a counter. Cut into

9 equal squares, then cut each square in half diagonally.

4. Pour 1½ cups oil into a 14-inch wok or a deep 4- to 5-quart pan over high heat. When oil reaches 350°, fill pan with triangles without crowding; adjust heat to maintain temperature, and turn pieces as needed to brown on both sides, about 3 minutes per batch.

5. As browned, lay triangles side by side in a towel-lined 10- by 15-inch pan and keep warm in a 350° oven. Slip towel from under polenta, sprinkle with gruyère and parmesan cheeses, and bake until cheese is melted, 4 to 5 minutes.

Per triangle: 122 cal., 49% (60 cal.) from fat; 4.7 g protein; 6.7 g fat (2.3 g sat.); 12 g carbo (1.1 g fiber); 139 mg sodium; 10 mg chol.

STEP-BY-STEP

How to carve the Thanksgiving bird

■ There is no *one* way to cut a turkey down to size. But here are some tips that I find make the process less daunting.

TOOLS. Use **2 sharp knives:** a long, thin one for slicing and a short-bladed one (4 to 6 in.) for poking into joints. Use a **carving fork** to hold the bird in place or, for more control, grip the bird with your hand, using a **clean pot holder** or napkin to protect your fingers and the bird.

TURKEY. Let the cooked bird rest at least 20 minutes before carving to give juices time to settle and allow the meat to firm.

LEGS. With a long knife, make a cut parallel to the carcass at the base of the thigh on each side of the joint **(a).** Then press the turkey leg down to expose the hip joint, poke a short-bladed knife into the joint, and cut and twist to sever the tendon **(b).** Lay the leg on a plate and cut through the knee joint. Slice the meat off the thigh parallel to the bone.

WINGS. Use a long knife to cut under the wing parallel to the carcass on each side of the shoulder joint (tilt the knife at an angle). Push the wing down to expose the joint, poke a short-bladed knife tip into the joint, and cut and twist to sever the tendon. Cut wings apart at the joints.

BREAST. Use a long knife to make a horizontal cut along the bottom of the breast, starting at the wing joint **(c).** Then angle the blade upward, under the breast, parallel to the carcass, until you hit the vertical breastbone. Slice the breast parallel to the carcass **(d);** the base cut lets slices separate neatly. Or, to cut the breast free and carve it off the bird, make the same first cut along the base of the breast and upward. Then, from the top of the bird, cut between the breastbone and the meat along the length of the breast, angling the knife down, parallel to the carcass, to meet the first cut. Lift the breast half off, set it on a platter, and slice crosswise.

Still nervous about accomplishing all this in front of an audience? Retreat to the kitchen and whittle away in private. ◆

ILLUSTRATIONS: ERIC LARSEN

The Wine Guide

BY KAREN MacNEIL-FIFE

RICK MARIANI

Now we're cooking

■ Between Thanksgiving and New Year's, most of us think more about food, buy more groceries, and cook more than we do during the rest of the year, which makes it a good time to talk about wine, not as a beverage but as a flavor in cooking. When the recipe says "1 cup dry white wine," will anything costing from $3 to $30 do? Would an Australian Chardonnay and a French Muscadet work in the same recipe?

To begin with, it helps to know what happens to wine during cooking. Conventional wisdom has always been that the alcohol evaporates and is therefore eliminated. But that's not exactly the case. Recent U.S. Department of Agriculture research (as reported by the Mayo Clinic in 1997) shows that when you add wine to a boiling liquid, then immediately remove it from the heat, 85 percent of the alcohol remains. The longer you cook the mixture, however, the more alcohol is eliminated. After 15 minutes, 40 percent remains; after 1 hour, only 25 percent; and after 2½ hours, just 5 percent.

Clearly, people who must completely avoid alcohol shouldn't cook with wine. For most of us, however, a small amount presents no problem. The question is, how should the wine be used to take advantage of the flavors it can contribute?

Chefs are a good resource here. They use wine in two ways: First, as a basic building block to give stews, stocks, and marinades an extra dimension. Added early in the cooking process, wine marries with the other ingredients, so in the end you can't taste the wine itself, although it has added more layers of flavor and richness than water could have. Second, chefs often finish sauces, meats, and vegetable dishes with wine precisely so you *can* taste some of the actual wine.

Here are some guidelines.

1. Never use poor-quality wine. If you wouldn't drink it, don't pour it in the stew. A wine with sour or bitter flavors will contribute those flavors to the dish.

2. Never use cooking sherry or any other so-called cooking wines. These wretched liquids are horrible-tasting, cheap, thin base wines to which salt and food coloring have been added. They make foods taste worse, not better.

3. If a recipe calls for dry white wine, the best and easiest American choice is a quality Sauvignon Blanc, a wine that is completely dry and has a fresh, light herbal tilt. We've used it, for example, in our easy wine gravy for Thanksgiving on page 269. If the dish has bold or spicy flavors, however, try a Gewürztraminer, Riesling, or Viognier. They each have dynamic, exotic floral and fruity aromas and flavors, which create a fascinating counterbalance in a bold or spicy dish.

4. If the recipe calls for dry red wine, think about the heartiness of the dish. A rustic, long-cooked casserole of lamb shanks or a substantial beef stew needs a correspondingly robust wine. Use a big-bodied red Zinfandel or Petite Syrah. Less hearty dishes can take a less powerful red, such as a Merlot from Chile or a Chianti (Sangiovese grape) from Italy.

5. Match wine flavor to food flavor. Sometimes the flavor of the dish will suggest a desirable flavor in a wine. Every time I sauté mushrooms, for example, I can't help but add a little Pinot Noir, which, like mushrooms, is earthy.

6. Don't miss port, sherry, madeira, and marsala! I couldn't cook without these scrumptious wines. All four are fortified, which means they have slightly more alcohol than regular wines, but they pack a bigger wallop of flavor, too. And once opened, they last six months to a year. Get the real thing: port from Portugal, sherry from Spain, madeira from the island of Madeira, and marsala from Italy. California versions are very weak.

Port has a rich, sweet, deeply winey flavor—a must in meat casseroles. Use either ruby port or the style called late-bottled vintage port. Sherry's complex roasted, nutty flavors can transform just about any soup, stew, or sautéed dish. Two styles work best: amontillado and oloroso. Madeira, with its toffee-caramel flavors, can be mesmerizingly lush in sautéed vegetable dishes. Use the medium-rich style known as bual. And marsala's light, caramel-like fruitiness is incomparable in Mediterranean sautés. I like to use a dry one. ◆

WINE PANTRY

Here are some of my favorite versions of the absolutely staple wines for cooking. (And don't forget to sip a glass while you're stewing and sautéing.) Prices are approximate.

- **Sauvignon Blanc:** Callaway 1998 (Temecula, CA), $8
- **Gewürztraminer:** Louis M. Martini 1998 (Russian River Valley, CA), $12
- **Riesling:** Paul Thomas 1998 (Columbia Valley, WA), $6
- **Zinfandel:** Peachy Canyon Incredible Red Bin #106 1997 (California), $11
- **Petite Syrah:** Guenoc Petite Sirah 1996 (California), $16
- **Port:** Graham's Fine Ruby (Portugal), $14
- **Sherry:** Osborne Amontillado (Spain), $7
- **Madeira:** Blandy's 5-year-old Bual (Madeira), $17
- **Marsala:** Pellegrino Dry Superiore (Italy), $10

Kitchen Cabinet

READERS' RECIPES TESTED IN SUNSET'S KITCHENS

BY LINDA LAU ANUSASANANAN

PANCETTA, DRIED TOMATOES, and fresh herbs win the day in a cornbread dressing.

And the winners are:

■ Earlier this year, we invited you to send your favorite turkey dressing recipe to *Sunset's* Thanksgiving Kitchen Cabinet Contest. The entries poured in. After *Sunset's* food editors reviewed more than 400 recipes, then prepared and tasted a large number of finalists with a panel of judges, one grand-prize winner and four runners-up were selected. The competition was keen, and the winners outstanding. Here are the results.

Each recipe had a story, and one theme was prevalent, even among the winners: Favorite recipes grow out of family histories. Ingredients and mixtures that are considered traditional from past generations merge as inventive cooks blend them into dressings— or stuffing—to forge Thanksgiving classics of their own.

If you bake a casserole of dressing along with the turkey (see chart, page 266), the oven temperature you use depends on the size of the bird. If you need to reduce the oven to 325°, allow at least 10 additional minutes for dressings to reach the suggested temperature. If you are using a convection oven (at 325° to 350°), the dressing will be hot about 10 minutes earlier than times suggested for regular oven heat; a thermometer makes testing reliable.

If you prefer to stuff the turkey with dressing, follow these food safety steps: Fill the bird loosely with the dressing just before you put it in the oven. To be sure that dressing in the turkey is heated to a bacteria-safe 160° (hotter than dressing baked in a casserole), insert a thermometer into the center of the dressing when the bird is cooked. And as soon as the bird is removed from the oven, spoon the dressing into a bowl. If the dressing temperature is too low, use a microwave-safe bowl and heat dressing in a microwave oven at full power (100%), mixing often to distribute heat evenly until it is 160° throughout.

Grand-prize winner
Cornbread-Herb Dressing with Dried Tomatoes and Pancetta

Rita Ann Wilkins, La Verne, California

Rita Ann Wilkins's delicious culinary merger combines the American country cornbread used by her husband's grandmother with herbs, vegetables, and pancetta from her Italian grandmother's table. Wilkins uses her own herb cornbread recipe, but we've added those herbs to the dressing. You can either use a recipe for plain cornbread or make it from a mix.

PREP AND COOK TIME: About 1¼ hours

MAKES: About 14 cups; 14 to 16 servings

- 8 cups ½-inch cubes day-old **cornbread** (from scratch or a mix)
- ½ pound **thin-sliced pancetta,** chopped

  About 1 tablespoon **olive oil**
- 2 **onions** (¾ lb. total), peeled and chopped
- 3 tablespoons minced **garlic**
- 3 cups finely chopped **celery**
- 1 jar (about 12 oz.) **steamed chestnuts** or 1⅓ cups cooked and peeled, canned water-packed or vacuum-packed chestnuts, coarsely chopped
- 1 cup drained **oil-packed dried tomatoes,** chopped
- ½ cup chopped **Italian parsley**
- 3 tablespoons chopped **fresh sage** leaves or dried rubbed sage
- 3 tablespoons chopped **fresh basil** leaves or dried basil
- 2 teaspoons chopped **fresh rosemary** leaves or dried rosemary
- ½ cup (¼ lb.) melted **unsalted butter** or unsalted margarine

  Salt and **pepper**
- 1½ to 2 cups fat-skimmed **chicken broth**

1. In a 350° oven, bake cornbread cubes in a 12- by 17-inch roasting pan until edges begin to brown, 25 to 35 minutes; stir occasionally.

2. Meanwhile, in a 10- to 12-inch frying pan over medium-high heat, stir pancetta often until browned, about 8 minutes. With a slotted spoon, transfer pancetta to towels to drain. Pour out fat and measure; add enough olive oil to make ¼ cup total and return to the frying pan.

3. Place pan over medium-high heat. Add onions and stir often until limp, about 5 minutes. Add garlic and celery; stir often until celery is limp, 5 to 7 minutes.

4. To cornbread in roasting pan, add pancetta, onion mixture, chestnuts, tomatoes, parsley, sage, basil, rosemary, and butter. Mix well, adding salt and pepper to taste. Mix in broth, ½ cup at a time, until dressing is evenly moistened (for a crumbly dressing, use minimum amount). Spoon into a shallow 3-quart casserole and cover tightly. (If making up to 1 day ahead, chill.)

5. Bake in a 350° oven until hot (at least 150° in center), 35 to 40 minutes (50 to 65 minutes if chilled). For a crusty top, uncover the last 20 to 25 minutes.

Per serving: 299 cal., 51% (153 cal.) from fat; 7.4 g protein; 17 g fat (6.4 g sat.); 29 g carbo (3.2 g fiber); 544 mg sodium; 48 mg chol.

Runners-up

San Francisco–style Dressing

Doris Hussar, Salinas, California

This recipe was handed down to Doris Hussar from her German grandmother, a creative cook who worked, long ago, for families in San Francisco and put local ingredients to good use.

PREP AND COOK TIME: About 1¾ hours

MAKES: About 16 cups; 16 to 18 servings

- 1 loaf (1½ lb.) **sliced sourdough bread,** cut into ½-inch cubes
- ½ cup (¼ lb.) **butter** or margarine
- 2 **onions** (¾ lb. total), peeled and finely chopped
- 2 cups thinly sliced **celery,** including leaves
- ½ pound **mushrooms,** rinsed, discolored stem ends trimmed, and thinly sliced
- 1 **red bell pepper** (½ lb.), rinsed, stemmed, seeded, and cut into ¼-inch dice

SAN FRANCISCO–STYLE dressing is stuffed with flavorful ingredients. Add sourdough bread for the authentic touch.

- ½ cup finely chopped **Italian parsley**
- 5 **green onions,** ends trimmed, rinsed and thinly sliced
- 1 can (10½ oz.) **condensed chicken broth**
- 2 cans (6½ oz. each) **minced clams**
- 1 can (2¼ oz.) **sliced ripe black olives,** drained
- 2 teaspoons **Italian seasoning blend** or 1 teaspoon *each* dried oregano and dried basil

    Salt and coarse-ground **pepper**
- 2 **large eggs**

1. In a 325° oven, bake bread cubes in a 12- by 17-inch roasting pan until dry and firm to touch, 15 to 20 minutes; stir occasionally.

2. Meanwhile, in a 10- to 12-inch frying pan, combine butter, chopped onions, celery, mushrooms, and bell pepper; stir often over medium-high heat until vegetables are limp, 7 to 10 minutes.

3. Mix cooked vegetable mixture, parsley, green onions, broth, clams with juice, olives, and Italian seasonings with bread cubes in roasting pan. Add salt and pepper to taste. In a small bowl, beat eggs to blend, then stir into

bread mixture.

4. Spoon into a shallow 3-quart casserole and cover tightly. (If making up to 1 day ahead, chill.)

5. Bake in a 350° oven until hot (at least 150° in center), 35 to 40 minutes (50 to 65 minutes if chilled). For a crusty top, uncover the last 20 to 30 minutes.

Per serving: 199 cal., 34% (68 cal.) from fat; 8.3 g protein; 7.6 g fat (3.7 g sat.); 24 g carbo (2.1 g fiber); 452 mg sodium; 45 mg chol.

Chinese Sausage Rice Dressing

Jenny Gillette-Arroyo, Fremont, California

When she was a child, Jenny Gillette-Arroyo grew so attached to this dressing as part of Thanksgiving dinner, she still serves it annually. In fact, she makes twice as much as she needs, so there are extras to send home with guests. Look for Chinese sausage in the refrigerator section of Asian food markets and many well-stocked supermarkets.

PREP AND COOK TIME: About 1 hour and 5 minutes

MAKES: 9½ cups; 9 to 11 servings

- ¾ cup **long-grain white rice**
- ¾ cup **medium-grain white (pearl) rice**
- ¼ cup (⅛ lb.) **butter** or margarine
- 1 **onion** (6 oz.), peeled and chopped
- 1 cup chopped **celery**
- 1 pound **lop chong** (Chinese) **sausage,** cut into ¼-inch cubes
- 2 cans (8 oz. each) **sliced water chestnuts,** drained and chopped
- ½ cup chopped **fresh cilantro**
- 1 cup fat-skimmed **chicken broth**

    Salt and **pepper**

1. In a 2- to 3-quart pan, combine 2¼ cups water, long-grain rice, and medium-grain rice. Bring to a boil over high heat. Reduce heat to low, cover, and simmer until rice is tender to bite, about 20 minutes. Fluff with a fork.

2. Meanwhile, in a 10- to 12-inch frying pan over medium heat, stir butter, onion, and celery often until vegetables are limp, about 5 minutes.

3. In a large bowl, combine rice, onion mixture, sausage, water chestnuts, cilantro, and broth. Mix well and add salt and pepper to taste. Spoon into a shallow 2½- to 3-quart casserole and cover tightly. (If making up to 1 day ahead, chill.)

4. Bake in a 350° oven until hot (at least 150° in center), 35 to 40 minutes (50 to 55 minutes if chilled).

Per serving: 343 cal., 52% (180 cal.) from fat; 13 g protein; 20 g fat (8.7 g sat.); 26 g carbo (1.6 g fiber); 574 mg sodium; 48 mg chol.

Sausage-Nut Dressing

Sharon Lynch, Portola Valley, California

Sharon Lynch grew up in Texas with cornbread dressing. Her husband, from New York, grew up with bread dressing. When they married, her delicious solution for harmony was to bring the two together. "I've been making the same 'compromise dressing' for 16 years and get rave reviews," writes Lynch.

PREP AND COOK TIME: About 2½ hours (1½ hours if starting with cooked chestnuts)

MAKES: About 13 cups; 13 to 15 servings

- ½ pound **fresh chestnuts in the shell** or 1 cup cooked peeled chestnuts (water-packed canned, canned steamed, or vacuum-packed)
- 1 pound **hot Italian sausage**
- ½ pound **pork sausage links**
- ½ pound **mushrooms,** rinsed, discolored stem ends trimmed, and thinly sliced
- 1 cup chopped **onion**
- ½ cup chopped **celery**
- 1 clove **garlic,** peeled and minced
- ½ cup **pine nuts**
- 1 can (8 oz.) **oysters,** drained and chopped (optional)
- 3 cups ½-inch cubes **sourdough bread**
- 3 cups ½-inch chunks **cornbread** (from scratch or a mix)
- ½ cup **roasted pistachios,** chopped
- ¼ cup chopped **parsley**

- 1½ teaspoons **poultry seasoning**
- ½ teaspoon **dried thyme**
  Salt and **pepper**
- ½ cup **half-and-half** (light cream)

1. Discard any fresh chestnuts with mold. Cut an X about ½ inch long through flat side of the shell of each remaining chestnut. Place nuts in an 8- or 9-inch pan.

2. Bake in a 400° oven until nuts are no longer starchy-tasting, 20 to 30 minutes. Wrap hot nuts in a towel and enclose in a plastic bag; let stand about 10 minutes. With a short-bladed knife, pull shell and brown skin from 1 warm nut at a time.

3. Chop the cooked chestnuts and put in a large bowl.

4. Remove Italian and link sausages from casings and crumble meat into a 10- to 12-inch frying pan over high heat. Stir often until meat is browned and crumbly, about 12 minutes. With a slotted spoon, transfer sausages to bowl with chestnuts. Discard all fat from pan except 1 tablespoon.

5. To pan, add mushrooms, onion, celery, and garlic. Stir over high heat until most of the liquid is evaporated and the vegetables are limp, about 7 minutes. Add the pine nuts; stir until mixture is lightly browned, about 4 minutes longer.

6. To bowl with chestnuts and sausages, add the cooked vegetable mixture, oysters, sourdough bread, cornbread, pistachios, parsley, poultry seasoning, and thyme. Mix, and add salt and pepper to taste. Drizzle half-and-half over dressing; stir to moisten evenly. Spoon mixture into a shallow 3-quart casserole and cover tightly. (If making up to 1 day ahead, chill.)

7. Bake in a 350° oven until hot (at least 150° in center), 40 to 45 minutes (50 to 60 minutes if chilled).

Per serving: 267 cal., 54% (144 cal.) from fat; 10 g protein; 16 g fat (4.7 g sat.); 21 g carbo (2.9 g fiber); 475 mg sodium; 36 mg chol.

Apricot Dressing

Michelle Diez, Issaquah, Washington

According to Michelle Diez, this is the ultimate dressing. Her tangy secret is Chinese-style plum sauce; look for it in the Asian foods section of well-stocked supermarkets.

PREP AND COOK TIME: About 1½ hours

MAKES: About 12 cups; 12 to 14 servings

- 1 cup chopped **dried apricots**
- 1½ cups **orange juice**
- ¾ cup (⅜ lb.) **butter** or margarine
- 2 cups coarsely chopped **celery**
- 1 **onion** (½ lb.), peeled and chopped
- 1 cup **slivered almonds**
- 1 pound **bulk pork sausage**
- 1 bag (1 lb.) **herb stuffing mix**
- 1 jar (8 oz.) **plum sauce**
- ½ teaspoon **dried thyme**
- 1 to 2 cups fat-skimmed **chicken broth**
  Salt and **pepper**

1. In a 1- to 2-quart pan over high heat, bring apricots and orange juice to a boil. Remove from heat and let stand about 30 minutes.

2. Meanwhile, in a 10- to 12-inch frying pan over medium heat, frequently stir ½ cup butter, celery, and onion until vegetables are limp, about 15 minutes. Add almonds and stir until nuts are golden, 6 to 10 minutes longer. Scrape mixture into a large bowl.

3. In the same frying pan over medium-high heat, frequently stir sausage, crumbling with spoon, until browned, about 10 minutes. Drain and discard fat; add sausage to bowl. Add apricots with orange juice, stuffing mix, plum sauce, and thyme; mix well.

4. In the frying pan, combine ¼ cup butter and 1 cup broth; stir often over medium-high heat until butter is melted. Drizzle over mixture in bowl, mixing to moisten evenly; dressing will be crumbly. For a moister dressing, mix in up to 1 more cup broth. Add salt and pepper to taste. Spoon dressing into a shallow 3-quart casserole. (If making up to 1 day ahead, cover and chill.)

5. Bake in a 350° oven (uncovered for crusty dressing, covered tightly for moist dressing) until hot (at least 150° in center), 25 to 30 minutes (55 to 60 minutes if chilled).

Per serving: 398 cal., 47% (189 cal.) from fat; 10 g protein; 21 g fat (8.4 g sat.); 43 g carbo (4 g fiber); 863 mg sodium; 40 mg chol. ◆

Why?

BY LINDA LAU ANUSASANANAN

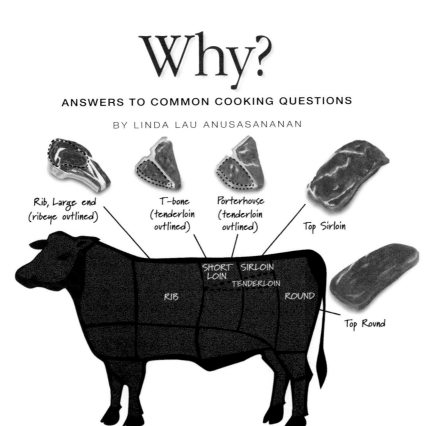

Rib, Large end (ribeye outlined)

T-bone (tenderloin outlined)

Porterhouse (tenderloin outlined)

Top Sirloin

SHORT LOIN SIRLOIN TENDERLOIN

RIB

ROUND

Top Round

MARINA THOMPSON

Prime-time beef

■ If your taste buds are set for a tender, juicy steak, it's the beef couch potato muscles that will deliver what you seek. Most steaks that come from these muscles have distinctive shapes and bones that make them easy to identify. Others fall far short in eating quality. So to help you avoid disappointment, here's a short lesson on steer anatomy.

WHAT MAKES STEAK TENDER?

The tenderest beef comes from muscles that do the least amount of work. A higher proportion of fat is marbled through these muscles, and it's the fat that contributes to their flavor and juiciness. These muscles are located along the animal's back in sections called primal cuts: the rib (rib and ribeye steak), short loin (top loin, T-bone, and porterhouse steak), and sirloin (top sirloin, sirloin, and tri-tip steak); see drawing above. The most tender muscle of all is the tenderloin, or beef fillet, which is in the center of the carcass under the bone in the short loin and sirloin sections.

Well-exercised muscles, the ones the animal uses most—such as the leg

(rump) and shoulder—can be tough and chewy if the meat is not properly cooked. But even though these cuts contain less fat marbling, they have great potential for flavor because the tough connective tissue breaks down and becomes delectably succulent when the meat is simmered. Only the eye-of-the-round from the leg (it looks like, and is similar in size to, the tenderloin) is very lean, firm, and usually dry-tasting—regardless of how it is cooked.

WHAT KEEPS A TENDER STEAK JUICY?

It's how, and how long, you cook a tender steak that affects its flavor and texture most.

Tender steaks do best with hot, dry heat: grilling, broiling, or pan-broiling. The high heat drives moisture from the surface of the meat fast enough for it to brown and develop rich flavors. This searing does not, as so often falsely advertised, "seal in juices." It just evaporates them. Juices continue to seep as long as the meat is cooking—and as it stands to cool. If enough of the juices are lost, as when cooked to well-done, the meat tastes dry, unless it's a tender cut marbled with fat. Some fat melts out

(and promotes browning), but enough remains to add to the eating quality of the meat.

If you like steaks with red to pink interiors, you can use less tender cuts—from the top sirloin and top round. Cooked rare, they are juicy and easy enough to chew to be very palatable. When cooked past the rare stage, lean

Mustard-Shallot Sauce

PREP AND COOK TIME: About 5 minutes

NOTES: Set any sautéed or grilled tender beef steak (³⁄₄ to 1 lb. total) from the rib, short loin, sirloin, or round in a platter with this sauce. Slice the meat and swirl the juices through the sauce. Serve meat with sauce, adding salt and pepper to taste.

MAKES: About ¹⁄₄ cup

In a 6- to 8-inch frying pan over medium heat, stir 2 tablespoons **olive oil** and ¹⁄₃ cup chopped **shallots** until shallots are limp, about 3 minutes. Add 1 tablespoon **Dijon mustard,** 3 tablespoons **dry vermouth,** and 1 teaspoon **balsamic vinegar** and stir until hot, about 30 seconds.

Per tablespoon: 87 cal., 70% (61 cal.) from fat; 0.3 g protein; 6.8 g fat (0.9 g sat.); 2.7 g carbo (0.1 g fiber); 93 mg sodium; 0 mg chol. ◆

A gift for a cook: Layer spices in a jar like a desert sand painting; shake or stir to use. For spice combinations, see page 310.

JAMES CARRIER

December

gifts from your kitchen

More than two dozen delicious ways to say, "Have a merry holiday"

BY LINDA LAU ANUSASANANAN AND ELAINE JOHNSON • PHOTOGRAPHS BY JAMES CARRIER

■ For gifts in good taste, what better place to start than where good tastes reign: the kitchen. In minutes or a few hours, your home-based Santa's factory can produce tender, flavorful cake and quick breads; beautiful fruit vinegars or liqueurs in glass; candies and confections with grown-up tastes and humorous shapes; gingerbread for cookies, thin and crisp,

and centerpieces that glow; and spice blends assembled into simple works of art.

So step away from the hurly-burly and spend a morning in a warm kitchen full of wonderful fragrances, with music to keep you company, and enjoy creating a steadily growing lineup of gifts you know won't have to be returned.

fruit under glass

Faz Poursohi, a Northern California restaurateur, displays dramatically scaled, bulbous jars filled with fruits in vinegars in many of his establishments. In clear jars, the beauty of the fruit is magnified by the liquid. And as it stands in the jars, the fruit becomes pickled and perfumes the liquid.

Poursohi's technique, which he brought from his homeland, Iran, works well with a wide variety of fruits and vinegars.

Recipients can use the flavored vinegars and chopped pickled fruit in salads and as seasonings. Or cook pickled fruit with some of the vinegar and sugar to make glistening sweet-sour relishes that complement meats and poultry. — *L.L.A.*

Citrus Vinegar and Pickled Fruit

PREP TIME: 5 to 10 minutes

NOTES: Lime and lemon vinegars develop a pleasant, slightly bitter flavor after a month or so. In addition to using the vinegar in salads, add a little of the chopped pickled fruit, peel and all.

MAKES: 2 to 6 cups vinegar and 4 to 7 cups fruit; jar sizes can vary, but liquid must cover fruit

1. Rinse 5 to 15 **limes** or lemons (2½ to 3 in. long), or 5 to 7 cups kumquats; if waxed, rub with a cloth under hot running water. Also rinse 3 to 6 fresh unsprayed **citrus leaves** (optional). In a 6- to 8-cup wide-mouth clear decorative jar with lid, tightly pack fruit, fitting leaves between fruit and jar.

2. Mix 4 cups **distilled white vinegar**

and ½ to ¾ cup **sugar** until clear. Pour into jar, filling to cover fruit. (If you need more liquid, blend each additional 1 cup vinegar with 2 to 3 tablespoons sugar.) If fruit floats above liquid, push a wad of clear plastic wrap (large enough to reach the rim of the jar) on top of it. Close jar airtight.

3. Let stand until vinegar is aromatic, at least 2 weeks or up to 3 months. (Limes and citrus leaves turn yellowish green as they stand.) Check occasionally to maintain liquid level; if it evaporates enough to expose fruit, the exposed parts discolor dramatically.

Per tablespoon vinegar: 7.8 cal., 0% (0 cal.) from fat; 0 g protein; 0 g fat; 2.3 g carbo (0 g fiber); 0.2 mg sodium; 0 mg chol.

Estimated per tablespoon chopped limes: 4 cal., 0% (0 cal.) from fat; 0.1 g protein; 0 g fat; 1.4 g carbo (0.7 g fiber); 0 mg sodium; 0 mg chol.

SWEETENED VINEGAR preserves fruit under glass. For months to come, use fruit and liquid in salads and more.

Cranberry Vinegar and Pickled Cranberries

Follow directions for **citrus vinegar and pickled fruit** (page 300), but instead of citrus, use 6 to 8 cups **fresh** or frozen **cranberries.** Sort, discarding bruised and decayed fruit. Rinse cranberries.

Per tablespoon vinegar: 7.8 cal., 0% (0 cal.) from fat; 0 g protein; 0 g fat; 2.3 g carbo (0 g fiber); 0.2 mg sodium; 0 mg chol.

Estimated per tablespoon chopped fruit: 3.4 cal., 0% (0 cal.) from fat; 0 g protein; 0 g fat; 0.9 g carbo (0.1 g fiber); 0 mg sodium; 0 mg chol.

Persimmon Vinegar and Pickled Persimmons

Follow directions for **citrus vinegar and pickled fruit** (page 300), but instead of citrus, use 6 **firm-ripe Fuyu persimmons** (2½ to 3 in. wide). Discard stems and leaves; rinse fruit. Persimmon skins stay firm, but interiors get very soft.

Per tablespoon vinegar: 7.8 cal., 0% (0 cal.) from fat; 0 g protein; 0 g fat; 2.3 g carbo (0 g fiber); 0.2 mg sodium; 0 mg chol.

Estimated per tablespoon chopped fruit: 24 cal., 3.8% (0.9 cal.) from fat; 0.2 g protein; 0.1 g fat (0 g sat.); 6.2 g carbo (0.5 g fiber); 0.6 mg sodium; 0 mg chol.

Pickled Fruit Relish

PREP AND COOK TIME: About 15 minutes

NOTES: Serve with roasted or grilled meats, poultry, seafood, or curries.

MAKES: About ⅓ cup

1. Use **pickled citrus,** cranberries, or persimmons (preceding). Chop limes or lemons, thinly slice kumquats (discard seeds), use cranberries whole, or scoop persimmon pulp from tough skin (discard skin and seeds).

2. In a 6- to 8-inch frying pan, mix ½ cup fruit with 2 to 4 tablespoons **sugar,** or to taste. Shake pan often over medium-high heat until mixture boils vigorously and fruit turns shiny and slightly translucent, 5 to 12 minutes. Serve warm or cool.

Per tablespoon with citrus: 27 cal., 0% (0 cal.) from fat; 0.1 g protein; 0 g fat; 7.6 g carbo (0 g fiber); 0.4 mg sodium; 0 mg chol.

Per tablespoon with cranberries: 28 cal., 0% (0 cal.) from fat; 0 g protein; 0 g fat; 7.3 g carbo (0.4 g fiber); 0.2 mg sodium; 0 mg chol.

Per tablespoon with persimmons: 43 cal., 2.1% (0.9 cal.) from fat; 0.1 g protein; 0.1 g fat (0 g sat.); 11 g carbo (0 g fiber); 0.3 mg sodium; 0 mg chol.

fruit with spirits

In these easy-to-make spirited infusions, fruit mellows alcohol with sweetness, fragrance, and personality. Dried fruit gives concentrated flavor, lemon brings freshness to vodka, and fresh pear smoothes the roughness out of young brandy. — *L.L.A.*

Peach-Ginger Liqueur

PREP AND COOK TIME: **20 minutes, plus 1 week to stand**

NOTES: Serve liqueur in small glasses to sip, or add to taste to chilled dry white wine, sparkling wine, or sparkling water. Also, you can drizzle liqueur over ice cream, pound cake, or sliced fruit. Use the liqueur-soaked fruit in fruitcakes; sprinkled on or swirled into ice cream; stirred into muffin batter, rice pudding, or tapioca; or mixed with cream cheese to spread on toast.

MAKES: About 5 cups liqueur, 4 cups fruit

- 4 cups (1 qt.) **vodka**
- 4 cups **sugar**
- 1 pound (3 cups) **dried peaches,** chopped
- ½ cup chopped **crystallized ginger**

1. In a 3- to 4-quart pan, combine vodka and sugar. Stir often over medium heat until mixture reaches 125° to 130° (hot to touch), about 5 minutes. Watch carefully; if overheated, fumes may ignite.

2. Place peaches and ginger in a wide-mouth glass jar (at least 2 qt.). Pour in hot vodka mixture. Seal airtight. (If seal is rubber or synthetic rubber, cover glass top with plastic wrap to protect seal; alcohol can soften it.) Let stand at least 1 week or up to 2 months.

3. Line a strainer with 4 layers of damp cheesecloth and set over an 8-cup glass measure or bowl with a pour spout. Pour liqueur and fruit, a portion at a time, through cloth. When fruit is no longer dripping, save for other uses; wrap airtight and refrigerate up to 3 months.

4. Pour liqueur into small bottles; seal airtight (if seals are rubber or synthetic rubber, see step 2). Serve liqueur, or store in a cool, dark place up to 1 year.

Per tablespoon: 64 cal., 0% (0 cal.) from fat; 0 g protein; 0 g fat; 8.1 g carbo (0.1 g fiber); 0.4 mg sodium; 0 mg chol.

Cranberry or Cherry Liqueur

Follow directions for **peach-ginger liqueur** (preceding), but instead of peaches and ginger, use 1 pound (4½ cups) **dried cranberries** or dried sweet cherries. Dried cranberries may contain a tiny amount of oil; use paper towels to gently blot off any oily film floating on the strained liqueur.

Per tablespoon: 63 cal., 0% (0 cal.) from fat; 0 g protein; 0 g fat; 8 g carbo (0 g fiber); 0.2 mg sodium; 0 mg chol.

Italian Lemon Aperitif

PREP AND COOK TIME: **35 minutes, plus 2 days to stand**

NOTES: Serve chilled or over ice, plain, or with sparkling water.

MAKES: 4½ cups

- 3 or 4 **lemons** (6 oz. each)
- 2 cups **sugar**
- 3 cups (750 ml.) **vodka**

1. Rinse 3 lemons; if waxed, rub with a cloth under hot running water. Dry with a cloth. Grate yellow part (white is bitter) from lemons to make 1 tablespoon.

2. In a 2- to 3-quart pan, combine peel, sugar, and vodka. Stir often over medium heat until mixture reaches 125° to 130° (hot to touch), about 5 minutes. Watch carefully; if overheated, fumes may ignite. Let cool.

3. Meanwhile, cut the 3 grated lemons in ½ and ream 8 to 10 tablespoons juice. Add juice to vodka mixture. Pour into bottles; seal airtight. (If seals are rubber or synthetic rubber, cover glass top with plastic wrap to protect seals; alcohol can soften them.) Store at least 2 days or up to 1 week in a cool, dark place. Pour through a strainer lined with 2 layers of damp cheesecloth into an 8-cup glass measure; return to bottles. If desired, pare fourth lemon to get long, thin strips of peel and drop into bottles. Serve or seal airtight and store up to 1 year in a cool, dark place.

Per tablespoon: 43 cal., 0% (0 cal.) from fat; 0 g protein; 0 g fat; 5.7 g carbo (0 g fiber); 0.2 mg sodium; 0 mg chol.

Pear Brandy

PREP TIME: **2 to 3 minutes, plus 1 week standing**

NOTES: Start with an inexpensive brandy. The pear mellows the liquor.

MAKES: 3 cups

1 **firm-ripe pear**

3 cups (750 ml.) **brandy**

Rinse pear, dry, and place in a wide-mouth decorative glass jar (at least 1 qt.). Pour brandy over pear (pear must be covered). Seal airtight. (If seal is rubber or synthetic rubber, cover glass top with plastic wrap to protect seal from alcohol, which can soften it.)

Store at least 1 week or up to 1 year at room temperature.

Per tablespoon: 37 cal., 0% (0 cal.) from fat; 0 g protein; 0 g fat; 0.1 g carbo (0 g fiber); 0 mg sodium; 0 mg chol.

love 'em from the oven

This golden cake and two spicy breads have in common a sweet tenderness—in taste, texture, and thoughtfulness. For a busy host or hostess, they provide at-the-ready refreshment to share with guests.

The fruit cake, although laden with chunks of dried tropical fruit and crunchy macadamias, bears no resemblance to its denser, traditional namesake; it's a fine dessert topped with scoops of intensely vanilla ice cream or warm caramel sauce. The pumpkin bread and its applesauce variation, full of plump raisins and walnuts, make delightful offerings for breakfast or brunch.

Bake these gifts in sizes to suit the recipients: one large cake or bread in a tube pan, or multiple loaves, big or small. For built-in gift packaging, use paper baking molds available in specialty cookware stores or by mail from Sur La Table; (800) 243-0852. — *L.L.A.*

Golden Fruit Cake

PREP AND COOK TIME: 2 to 2¼ hours

NOTES: Mile-high bakers need to increase flour to 4½ cups, reduce sugar to 2 cups, and increase applesauce to 2 cups; baking time may be about 10 minutes less.

MAKES: 1 tube cake (12-cup size), 2 loaf cakes (about 4½ by 8½ in.), or 6 loaf cakes (about 3 by 5½ in.)

About ⅔ cup (⅓ lb.) **butter** or margarine, at room temperature

About 3⅓ cups **all-purpose flour**

3⅓ cups **sugar**

4 **large eggs**

1 jar (15 oz.; about 1⅔ cups) **applesauce**

1½ teaspoons grated **lemon** peel

2 teaspoons **baking soda**

1½ teaspoons **ground ginger**

½ teaspoon **ground coriander**

½ teaspoon **baking powder**

¾ cup coarsely chopped **dried mangoes** or dried apricots

¾ cup coarsely chopped **dried sweetened pineapple**

⅔ cup coarsely chopped **salted roasted macadamia nuts**

1. Butter and flour baking pans (choices follow).

2. In a large bowl with mixer, beat ⅔ cup butter and the sugar until well mixed. Beat in eggs until blended. Stir in applesauce and lemon peel.

3. In another bowl, mix 3⅓ cups flour with baking soda, ginger, coriander, and baking powder. Add to egg mixture and beat until blended. Stir in mangoes, pineapple, and nuts.

4. Fill pan (or pans; see following) as directed.

5. Bake in a 325° oven (300° in a convection oven) until cake is browned, pulling from pan sides, and a toothpick

TENDER GOLDEN FRUIT CAKES, studded with chunks of dried mangoes, dried pineapple, and macadamia nuts, bake in small or large pans.

inserted in center comes out clean (for time, see following).

6. Set cake (or cakes) in pan on a rack to cool 15 to 20 minutes. To remove cake from metal pans, run a thin-bladed knife between cake and pan, then invert onto a rack. Or leave in pans or paper baking molds. Let cake stand until cool. Serve or wrap airtight and chill up to 2 weeks; freeze to store longer.

Per 2-oz. piece: 195 cal., 28% (55 cal.) from fat; 2.3 g protein; 6.1 g fat (2.7 g sat.); 34 g carbo (0.7 g fiber); 134 mg sodium; 33 mg chol.

To make 1 tube cake (4¼ to 4½ lb.): Follow directions for **golden fruit cake** (preceding), using a nonstick 10-inch-wide (12-cup) tube pan. Scrape all the cake batter into pan. Bake as directed, about 1½ hours.

To make 2 loaf cakes (2⅛ to 2¼ lb. each): Follow directions for **golden fruit cake** (preceding), using 2 loaf pans (metal or paper baking molds), each about 4½ by 8½ inches. Divide cake batter equally between pans. Bake as directed, about 1½ hours.

To make 6 loaf cakes (about ¾ lb. each): Follow directions for **golden fruit cake** (preceding), using 6 loaf pans, each about 3 by 5½ inches (metal or paper baking molds). Divide cake batter equally among pans. Bake as directed, about 50 minutes.

Pumpkin Bread

PREP AND COOK TIME: 2 to 2¼ hours

NOTES: Mile-high bakers need to increase flour in bread to 4½ cups, reduce sugar to 2⅔ cups, and increase pumpkin to 2 cups. Baking time may be about 10 minutes less. Bake as directed for **golden fruit cake** (page 303), in pan sizes desired.

MAKES: 1 tube bread (12-cup size), 2 loaves (about 4½ by 8½ in.), or 6 loaves (about 3 by 5½ in.)

> About ⅔ cup (⅓ lb.) **butter** or margarine, at room temperature
>
> About 3⅓ cups **all-purpose flour**

3⅓ cups **sugar**

4 **large eggs**

1 can (15 oz.; about 1¾ cups) **pumpkin**

2 teaspoons **baking soda**

1 teaspoon **ground cinnamon**

½ teaspoon **ground nutmeg**

½ teaspoon **baking powder**

1½ cups **raisins**

⅔ cup coarsely chopped **walnuts**

1. Butter and flour baking pans (for sizes, see preceding recipe).

2. In a large bowl with a mixer, beat ⅔ cup butter and the sugar until well mixed. Beat in eggs until well blended. Stir in pumpkin.

3. In another bowl, mix 3⅓ cups flour, baking soda, cinnamon, nutmeg, and baking powder. Add to egg mixture and beat until blended. Stir in raisins and chopped walnuts.

4. To bake, serve, and store, follow steps 4 through 6 (page 303).

Per 2-oz. piece: 192 cal., 27% (51 cal.) from fat; 2.6 g protein; 5.7 g fat (2.5 g sat.); 34 g carbo (1 g fiber); 122 mg sodium; 33 mg chol.

Spicy Applesauce Bread

Follow recipe for **golden fruit cake** (page 303), but omit ginger, coriander, dried mangoes, dried pineapple, and macadamia nuts. Instead, use 1 teaspoon **ground cloves**, 1½ cups **raisins**, and ⅔ cup coarsely chopped **pecans**.

Per 2-oz. piece: 196 cal., 26% (50 cal.) from fat; 2.3 g protein; 5.6 g fat (2.5 g sat.); 35 g carbo (0.9 g fiber); 122 mg sodium; 33 mg chol.

gumdrops for grown-ups

The secret to the vibrant, chewy character of these fresh candies is real fruit: pure peach, mingled berries, and pineapple with a ginger kick. Simmer the puréed fruit with sugar and gelatin until it's concentrated into a thick paste. Let the paste cool long enough for the surface to feel only slightly tacky to touch; gelatin helps the mixture hold its shape. Coat the cut candies with sugar for sparkle and to keep the pieces from sticking together.

The concept may be adult, but the results suit all who are young of heart.

— E.J.

Peach Jelly Chews

PREP AND COOK TIME: 1¼ to 1½ hours, plus up to 24 hours to firm

NOTES: If pan is narrower than suggested, mixture cooks longer and is darker in color. Use a pan with a light interior so you can see color changes that indicate doneness.

MAKES: 49 pieces

THESE SUGAR-COATED jelly chews explode with intense fruit flavor.

2 packages (1 lb. each) **frozen unsweetened sliced peaches**

About 3¾ cups **sugar**

3 envelopes (2 tablespoons total) **unflavored gelatin**

2 teaspoons grated **lemon** peel

1 tablespoon **lemon juice**

1. In a 6- to 8-quart pan, preferably 11 inches wide, combine peaches and ⅓ cup water. Bring to a boil over high heat, stirring. Reduce heat and simmer, covered, stirring occasionally, until fruit mashes easily, 10 to 12 minutes.

2. Whirl fruit mixture in a blender or food processor, a portion at a time, until smoothly puréed. Return to pan.

3. In a bowl, mix 3½ cups sugar with the gelatin. Add to fruit mixture.

4. Bring to a boil over high heat, stirring often. Stir and boil 5 minutes. Reduce heat to medium and stir often until mixture is thick enough to leave a trail when the spoon is drawn across the pan bottom and juices in the trail are just beginning to turn a darker gold, 25 to 35 minutes. At once, remove from heat.

5. Stir lemon peel and lemon juice into peach mixture, then scrape mixture into an oiled 8- or 9-inch square pan. Let candy dry, uncovered, for 16 to 24 hours; it should feel firm and not sticky when touched.

6. On a board, coat a 10-inch square area with about ¼ cup sugar. Invert pan to release candy onto sugar; if it sticks, use a metal spatula, dipped in sugar, to ease from pan. With a long, sharp knife, dipped in sugar to prevent sticking, cut candy into 49 equal pieces (make 6 cuts lengthwise and 6 crosswise). Coat each piece with sugar.

7. Serve candies, or arrange in a container with plastic wrap between layers and seal airtight. Store up to 1 month at room temperature.

Per piece: 70 cal., 1.3% (0.9 cal.) from fat; 0.5 g protein; 0.1 g fat (0 g sat.); 17 g carbo (0.3 g fiber); 1.1 mg sodium; 0 mg chol.

Apple-Cranberry Jelly Chews

Rinse 1¾ pounds **Granny Smith apples** and cut into wedges; discard stems; don't core or peel.

Sort 2 cups (½ lb.) **fresh** or frozen **cranberries,** discarding bruised and decayed fruit. Rinse and drain cranberries.

Follow directions for **peach jelly chews** (preceding), but instead of peaches, use apples and cranberries. Rub puréed fruit (step 2) through a fine strainer back into pan, pressing firmly to extract liquid; discard residue.

Reduce sugar in fruit mixture (step 3) to 3 cups.

The cooking time (step 4) is 15 to 25 minutes.

Per piece: 72 cal., 1.3% (0.9 cal.) from fat; 0.4 g protein; 0.1 g fat (0 g sat.); 18 g carbo (0 g fiber); 1.1 mg sodium; 0 mg chol.

Pineapple Jelly Chews

Cut 2 **peeled cored pineapples** (3 lb. total) into 2-inch chunks (7 cups total). Rinse and coarsely chop ½ pound **fresh ginger** (1½ cups).

Follow directions for **peach jelly chews** (page 304), but instead of peaches, use the pineapple and ginger. Omit lemon peel.

Simmer (step 1) until pineapple breaks easily with a spoon, 20 to 25 minutes.

Rub purée (step 2) through a fine strainer back into pan, pressing firmly to extract liquid; discard residue.

Reduce sugar in fruit mixture (step 3) to 3 cups, and increase unflavored gelatin to 6 envelopes (4⅔ tablespoons).

Increase lemon juice to ⅓ cup and stir into uncooked puréed mixture (step 3).

The cooking time (step 4) is 20 to 30 minutes.

Per piece: 78 cal., 2.3% (1.8 cal.) from fat; 0.5 g protein; 0.2 g fat (0 g sat.); 19 g carbo (0 g fiber); 1.9 mg sodium; 0 mg chol.

Raspberry-Cranberry Jelly Chews

In a bowl, thaw 6 cups **frozen sweetened raspberries,** saving juice. Rub raspberries and juice through a fine strainer into another bowl; discard residue.

Sort 2 cups (½ lb.) **fresh** or frozen **cranberries,** discarding bruised and decayed fruit. Rinse and drain cranberries.

Follow directions for **peach jelly chews** (page 304), but instead of peaches, use strained raspberries and whole cranberries. Simmer (step 1) until cranberries are soft when pressed, 3 to 5 minutes. Omit lemon peel and lemon juice.

Reduce sugar in fruit mixture (step 3) to 3 cups and increase unflavored gelatin to 5 envelopes (3⅔ tablespoons total).

The cooking time (step 4) is 15 to 20 minutes.

Per piece: 84 cal., 1.1% (0.9 cal.) from fat; 0.8 g protein; 0.1 g fat (0 g sat.); 21 g carbo (0.2 g fiber); 1.9 mg sodium; 0 mg chol.

candy-clad whimsies

At Napa Valley Chocolates in St. Helena, California, Candy Dreyer delights in creating special sweets, often with a touch of humor that brings out the smiles. Favorites with her customers are marshmallow snowmen, candy twist elves, and chocolate-dipped peppermint canes. — L.L.A.

Marshmallow Snowmen

PREP AND COOK TIME: 30 minutes

NOTES: Buy candy designed to melt for coating or dipping; it's usually found beside cooking chocolates at the supermarket. For easy dipping, you melt more than needed to coat the marshmallows; save the extra for other uses. Candies suited for decorations (whole or cut in pieces) include orange, green, or red gumdrops, black licorice sticks or thin black licorice whips (or strings), small colored candies, miniature chocolate chips, and colored sugars.

To make a drying rack for snowmen, cut top flaps from a corrugated cardboard box, leaving a neat edge. Make holes in the corrugated edge by pushing a craft or lollipop stick into the edge at 4-inch intervals. Place a couple of food cans (3 to 4 lb. total) in the box so it will sit steady. Push snowman-filled sticks into prepared holes to hold confections vertically while candy firms.

MAKES: 6 marshmallow snowmen

Candies for decorating (see notes) or dried currants

1 cup (6 oz.) chopped **red**, green, or brown **candy chips** or chunks made for melted coatings (see notes)

18 **marshmallows** (1 in. wide)

6 **wood craft sticks** (3½ in.) or cardboard lollipop sticks (8 in.)

2 cups (12 oz.) chopped **white candy chips** or chunks made for melted coatings (see notes)

1 to 2 teaspoons **solid shortening** (optional)

6 **cellophane bags** (4 by 8 in.)

Red or green **ribbons** (¼ in. wide)

TOP-HATTED SNOWMEN are marshmallows in sweet disguise.

5. In a 2-cup glass measure or small, deep microwave-safe bowl, heat chopped white candy chips in a microwave oven at 50% power until chips are soft, about 2 minutes. Stir candy until smooth; if lumpy, heat in microwave oven for 20-second intervals, stirring frequently. If mixture is too thick for dipping (it varies with brands), stir in shortening; heat at 20-second intervals and stir often.

6. One stick at a time, quickly dip marshmallows into white candy to coat, using a spoon to pour candy over uncovered spots. Lift stick, letting excess candy drip back into cup. Lay marshmallow men at least 3 inches apart on paper-lined pan.

7. While candy coating is still soft, but not runny, make a face on the side of the top marshmallow of each stick. Use gumdrop wedge (see notes) for the nose, and chocolate chips, currants, or other small candies for eyes. On bottom marshmallow, press tiny candies down center for buttons; use thin licorice strips for twiggy arms or scarves. Pick up a stick and set hat on the snowman's head. If marshmallow coating firms before decorating is complete, glue with more melted candy (reheat in microwave, as needed). Stand snowman upright (see notes for rack). Repeat to make other snowmen.

8. When coating is firm to touch, 5 to 10 minutes, slip a cellophane bag over each snowman. Tie ribbons around bottom to close bag.

Per snowman: 431 cal., 40% (171 cal.) from fat; 0.4 g protein; 19 g fat (17 g sat.); 65 g carbo (0 g fiber); 81 mg sodium; 0 mg chol.

Chocolate Candy-Cane Stirrers

PREP AND COOK TIME: About 12 minutes

NOTES: To avoid a white "bloom" on cooling chocolate, be careful not to overheat it. If you need to remelt chocolate, add a little fresh chopped chocolate. About ½ the chocolate or candy coating will be left after dipping canes, but you need the volume to get a smooth finish. Use leftovers to make another simple confection: Dunk dried apricots into the extra and lay fruit on waxed paper. Chill until firm. Package airtight; keep cool.

MAKES: 50 coated canes

> About 1 cup finely chopped
> **semisweet chocolate**

50 **peppermint candy canes** or sticks
   (2½ in. long)

   Cellophane or clear plastic wrap

1. Assemble candies for decorating by colors. If desired, cut orange gumdrops into slender wedges for carrot-shaped noses, green gumdrops into leaves, red gumdrops into berries, licorice sticks into twiglike arms.

2. *To make hats,* heat chopped red (or green or brown) candy chips in a 1-cup glass measure or small, deep microwave-safe bowl in a microwave oven at 50% power until chips are soft, 2 to 2½ minutes. Stir candy until smooth; if lumpy, heat in a microwave oven for 20-second intervals, stirring frequently.

3. Line a 12- by 15-inch baking sheet with nonstick cooking paper, cooking parchment, or waxed paper. Set 6 marshmallows, flat side down, at least 2 inches apart on paper. Spoon about 1 tablespoon melted red (or color of choice) candy onto the center of 1 marshmallow

top and quickly, using a small metal spatula or dinner knife, spread candy over top and around side of marshmallow; spread excess that flows onto paper into a ½-inch-wide rim for the hat. Add more melted candy, as needed, to make brim even. If desired, while candy is still soft, decorate hat with gumdrops cut to resemble leaves and berries (see notes). Repeat to make remaining hats. Chill hats, uncovered, until firm to touch, about 10 minutes.

4. *To make snowmen,* line another 12- by 15-inch baking sheet with nonstick cooking paper, baking parchment, or waxed paper. Dip 1 craft stick about 3 inches into water. Slide through the center of a flat end of 1 marshmallow, then into, but not through, a second marshmallow, pushing them together. Repeat to make remaining snowmen;

lay on the baking sheet.

1. In a 1-cup glass measure or small, deep microwave-safe bowl, heat ¾ cup chocolate in a microwave oven at 50% power until chocolate is soft, about 1½ minutes. Stir chocolate until smooth. If needed, return to microwave and heat for 20-second intervals, stirring often. Add ¼ cup chocolate and stir until smooth. Set container in a small bowl of hot water (water should come halfway up sides of cup) to keep chocolate soft; *don't get water in chocolate or it will harden.*

2. Cover a 12- by 15-inch baking sheet with nonstick cooking paper, baking parchment, or waxed paper. Dip straight ends of candy canes into chocolate, coating ½ to ¾ of the canes; use a spoon to pour chocolate over canes if needed. Lift out canes and lay slightly apart on the baking sheet.

3. If desired, drizzle a ribbon of chocolate from spoon over coated sections of the candy canes. Chill 3 to 4 minutes, then return canes to room temperature until chocolate is firm, about 15 minutes. Wrap each cane in cellophane or clear plastic wrap.

Per cane: 39 cal., 14% (5.4 cal.) from fat; 0.1 g protein; 0.6 g fat (0.4 g sat.); 8.6 g carbo (0 g fiber); 4.8 mg sodium; 0 mg chol.

Red Twist Elves

PREP AND COOK TIME: About 15 minutes, plus 10 minutes to firm

NOTES: For a quick and amusing gift, dip the ends of candy twists into melted white candy chips, then stud white candy with cut pieces of other candies to make arms and faces for the elves. For bright hats, dip white end of twists into melted colored candy chips. For candies for decorating, use cut pieces of orange, red, or dark-colored gumdrops for facial details, and whole miniature chocolate chips and other tiny candies or cake decors for mouths, eyes, buttons, and other finishing touches.

MAKES: 6 to 8 pieces

1 to 2 **black licorice** or red candy **laces** or strands (about 36 in. total)

6 to 8 **red candy twists** (also called red licorice; 6 in. long)

Candies for decorating (see notes)

1 cup (6 oz.) chopped **white candy chips** or chunks made for melted coatings

1 to 2 teaspoons **solid shortening** (optional)

5 tablespoons finely chopped **red** or green **candy chips** or chunks made for melted coatings

6 to 8 **cellophane bags** or pieces of cellophane (4 by 8 in.)

Red or green **ribbon** (¼ in. wide)

1. Cut licorice laces into 1½- to 2-inch lengths to make arms for candy twists. If desired, cut tiny pieces of laces to make eyes or mouths. Cut gumdrop wedges to make noses.

2. In a 2-cup glass measure or small, deep microwave-safe bowl, heat white candy chips in a microwave oven at 50% power until soft, about 1½ minutes. Stir until candy is smooth. If needed, return to microwave and heat for 20-second intervals, stirring occasionally. If mixture is too thick for dipping (it varies with brands), stir in solid shortening; heat at 20-second intervals until more fluid.

3. Cover a 12- by 15-inch baking sheet with nonstick cooking paper, cooking parchment, or waxed paper. One at a time, dip ¾ of a red candy twist into white candy, coating 1 end evenly; if needed, spoon candy onto twist to coat. Lift out; let excess drip into the cup. Lay twists slightly apart on baking sheet. While coating is soft, press candies into it to make a face about 1 inch from candy-coated end of twist. Press black licorice strands in coating to make arms. Don't move until firm, about 10 minutes.

4. In a 1-cup glass measure or small, deep microwave-safe bowl, heat ¼ cup chopped red or green candy in a microwave oven at 50% power until soft, about 1 minute. Stir until smooth. If needed, return to microwave and heat for 20-second intervals and stir often until smooth. Add remaining chopped candy and stir until smooth. (This cools

CHOCOLATE-DIPPED CANDY CANES are designed for flavor meltdown. Hang chocolate tips of the canes inside cups and fill with hot cocoa.

colored coating enough to avoid melting white coating on twist.)

5. To make a cap, dip white end of twist about ½ inch into colored candy coating. Lift out, drain briefly into bowl, and lay on baking sheet. Let cool until firm, at least 10 minutes.

6. Enclose each elf in a cellophane bag or wrap; tie with a ribbon at neck.

Per piece: 204 cal., 41% (84 cal.) from fat; 0.5 g protein; 9.3 g fat (7.3 g sat.); 30 g carbo (0 g fiber); 69 mg sodium; 0 mg chol.

gingerbread enlightenment

Cast a colorful glow on holiday tables with light that shines through the shimmering candy windows of gingerbread votives. These durable gifts are easily assembled. And the same spicy dough, rolled thin, makes very crisp, traditional gingerbread cookies. You might want to fill the box-shaped votive with cookies as part of your gift. When the candle is inside and aglow, set a plate of cookies alongside for nibblers who might otherwise be tempted to break off votive corners. — *E.J.*

Gingerbread Votives

PREP AND COOK TIME: Starting with prepared dough, about 4 hours, plus 3½ hours for candy and icing to harden

NOTES: You'll need sturdy cardboard for patterns; dowels for rolling dough so cookies will be evenly thick; hard, transparent candies to melt for windows (such as red or green fruit-flavor balls or Jolly Ranchers); and 2 votive candles, each in a 2- to 3-inch-wide holder. Do not use larger candles; they can melt or scorch candy or gingerbread.

For the votive base pattern, cut a 5½-inch cardboard square. For the wall frame pattern, cut a 5-inch square, then cut out the center to make a ½-inch-wide border. For gingerbread shapes to center in the wall frames, use a 3-inch-wide star (or other holiday shape) cookie cutter. If you want an open-center star, use a similar cutter that is no more than 1¾ inches wide. Or cut cardboard stars to use as patterns.

The votives retain their shape and color for up to 2 weeks if stored airtight (in a large plastic bag); unwrapped, the candy windows are inclined to get sticky or drip if weather is damp. Although edible, the votives are very hard.

MAKES: 2 votives; use extra dough for gingerbread people (recipe follows)

Butter or salad oil

All-purpose flour

1 recipe's worth of **gingerbread dough** (recipe follows)

2 **dowels** (each ¼ in. thick and about 12 in. long; see notes)

Cardboard patterns (see notes)

2 cups (1 lb.) **transparent red** or green **hard candies** (see notes)

1 recipe's worth of **cement icing** (recipe follows)

1. Butter and flour 3 baking sheets, each 12 by 15 to 17 inches.

2. For each votive, make a base, 4 wall frames, and 4 stars, using a total of about ½ the dough: Place ¾ cup dough on a baking sheet. With a flour-dusted rolling pin supported on each end by dowels, roll dough into a square. Lay flour-dusted 5½-inch square cardboard base pattern on dough and neatly cut around it with a long, flour-dusted knife. Lift off scraps and save to reroll with remaining dough.

3. Near the end of another baking sheet, repeat to roll another ¾ cup dough into a square. Lay flour-dusted wall frame pattern on dough. Neatly cut around inside and outside edges; lift off and save dough outside the frame. Then, with a flour-dusted 3-inch star cookie cutter (see notes), cut a star in the center of the frame. Lift out dough around the star; save scraps. If desired, use a flour-dusted smaller cutter (see notes) to cut out the center of the cookie; lift out center and save. Repeat to make another frame on the other end of baking sheet.

4. Repeat step 3 to make 2 more wall frames, each with a star in the center.

5. As pans are filled, bake cookies in a 275° oven for 5 minutes. Remove from oven, let cookies firm for 3 minutes, then place patterns and cutters on cookies, and, with a sharp knife, neatly trim all edges; discard scraps. Return to oven and bake until cookies are slightly darker at edges and give only slightly when lightly pressed, 16 to 20 minutes more for frames and stars, 22 to 28 minutes more for base. When more than 1 pan is in the oven, switch positions about every 10 minutes for even browning.

6. Remove cookies from oven and slide a long, slender spatula under them to release. Let stand about 5 minutes, then transfer to racks to cool.

7. Wash, dry, butter, and flour baking sheets. Repeat steps 2 through 6 to make base, frames, and stars for second votive.

8. To make colored windows, lay all the cookie wall frames in a single layer, slightly apart, on lightly buttered foil. Center a star cookie in each frame.

9. Place 1 cup candies (1 color) in a 2-cup glass measure. Heat in a microwave oven on full power (100%) for 2 minutes; stir. Heat on full power until candy is melted and bubbling, 10 to 15 seconds more; watch to avoid scorching. Quickly pour candy into openings around stars in frames (take care—it's very hot), filling frames to about ½ their thickness. As candy in cup hardens, reheat it in the microwave for a few seconds to soften. Add remaining 1 cup candies (don't mix colors), melt, and use to fill remaining frames. Let cookies stand until candy is cool and hard, about 30 minutes.

10. Gently lift wall frames from foil.

11. To assemble each votive, pipe cement icing through a pastry bag fitted with a plain or star ¼-inch tip, or spread with a small spatula. Pipe (or spread) a ¼-inch-wide strip of cement icing along the top or side of 1 edge of a cookie base. Set an edge of a wall frame in icing and hold in place until icing firms a little, about 1 minute. Pipe icing along the edge of the base adjacent to the mounted wall. Also pipe icing onto 1 edge of a second wall. Press iced edge of second wall against the mounted wall, and a plain edge into the icing on the base. Repeat to mount and join remaining walls.

12. If desired, use the edge of a knife to trim icing flush with walls and base. Or decorate votives with more icing. Let stand until icing is hard, about 3 hours. Use, or wrap airtight, but loosely (to avoid touching candy windows) and store up to 2 weeks.

Because of variables, nutrition information cannot be accurately calculated.

Gingerbread Dough

PREP TIME: About 15 minutes

NOTES: If making up to 4 days ahead, cover and chill.

MAKES: About 4½ cups

1¼ cups firmly packed **brown sugar**

1 tablespoon **baking soda**

1½ teaspoons **ground ginger**

1 teaspoon **ground cinnamon**

¾ cup **whipping cream**

CANDLES GLOW through shiny candy windows in gingerbread-framed votives.

¾ cup **light molasses**

1 teaspoon **vanilla**

4½ cups **all-purpose flour**

In large bowl, mix sugar, baking soda, ginger, and cinnamon. Add cream, molasses, and vanilla. Beat with a mixer on low speed until blended. Add 2 cups flour and beat slowly until well mixed. Add remaining flour; mix well or squeeze dough with your hands until thoroughly blended.

Cement Icing

PREP TIME: About 15 minutes

NOTES: If you are concerned about egg safety, rehydrate dried egg white as the package directs and use instead of the raw egg white.

MAKES: About 1 cup

1 **large egg** white

⅛ teaspoon **cream of tartar**

1½ cups **powdered sugar**

In a deep bowl with a mixer on high speed, whip egg white, cream of tartar, and 1 teaspoon water until frothy. Add powdered sugar, mix, then beat on high

speed until mixture is very stiff but still spreadable, 5 to 8 minutes. Use, or cover airtight and store at room temperature up to 8 hours; to prevent drying, keep covered except when using.

Per tablespoon: 45 cal., 0% (0 cal.) from fat; 0.2 g protein; 0 g fat; 11 g carbo (0 g fiber); 3.5 mg sodium; 0 mg chol.

Gingerbread People

PREP AND COOK TIME: Starting with prepared dough, about 2 hours for ⅛-inch-thick cookies

MAKES: 4½ dozen ⅛-inch-thick, 7 dozen ¹⁄₁₆-inch-thick people-shaped cookies (5 in. tall, 3½ in. wide)

Butter or salad oil

All-purpose flour

2 **dowels** (each ⅛ to ¹⁄₁₆ in. thick and about 12 in. long)

1 recipe's worth of **gingerbread dough** (page 308)

1 recipe's worth of **cement icing** (optional; recipe precedes)

1. Butter and flour 2 or 3 baking sheets, each 12 by 15 to 17 inches.

2. With a flour-dusted rolling pin sup-

ported on each end by equal-size dowels, roll dough a portion at a time on a floured board.

3. Cut dough with flour-dusted cookie cutters (any shape you like). With a wide spatula, transfer cookies to baking sheets, spacing about ¼ inch apart. Add scraps to remaining dough and repeat to roll dough and cut remaining cookies.

4. As pans are filled, bake cookies in a 275° oven until they give a little when pressed in center and are slightly but evenly browned, 15 to 18 minutes for ¹⁄₁₆-inch-thick cookies, 20 to 25 minutes for ⅛-inch-thick cookies. Let cool on pans 5 minutes. With spatula, transfer to racks to cool. If needed, wash, dry, butter, and flour baking sheets to fill again.

5. If desired, decorate cookies with icing piped through a pastry bag fitted with a plain ¼-inch tip; let stand until icing is dry and hard, about 30 minutes.

6. Serve cookies, or wrap airtight and store at room temperature up to 2 weeks; freeze to store longer.

Per ⅛-inch-thick cookie: 82 cal., 15% (12 cal.) from fat; 1.2 g protein; 1.3 g fat (0.7 g sat.); 16 g carbo (0.3 g fiber); 76 mg sodium; 4.1 mg chol.

LAYER SPICES in a jar like a desert sand painting. Shake or stir to use.

stratified spices

Like a geologic slice of time, these seasoning blends are layered in clear jars to show off the natural hues of the ingredients. Bands of colors range from the stark white of salt and sugar to the rusty reds of paprika or chilies and the bright green of dried parsley, with many subtler shades in between. Each layer of flavor, however, has a purpose. Tie on a tag or glue on a label with suggestions for how to use each seasoning mixture, as noted with the recipe. All the cook needs to do is give the bottle a shake or stir. If you want to make larger amounts, simply multiply the ingredients. — *L.L.A*

Indian Masala

PREP TIME: About 5 minutes

NOTES: Rub onto poultry, vegetables, pork, or beef, and roast or barbecue.

MAKES: About 6 tablespoons

In a $\frac{1}{3}$- to $\frac{1}{2}$-cup tall, narrow clear jar, layer the following, contrasting light layers with dark: $2\frac{1}{2}$ tablespoons **paprika**, 1 tablespoon **ground coriander**, 1 tablespoon **ground cumin**, $\frac{3}{4}$ teaspoon **pepper**, $\frac{1}{2}$ teaspoon **ground cinnamon**, $\frac{1}{2}$ teaspoon **ground ginger**, $\frac{1}{2}$ teaspoon **ground turmeric**, and $\frac{1}{4}$ teaspoon **cayenne**. To use, shake jar or stir spices until blended.

Per teaspoon: 5 cal., 36% (1.8 cal.) from fat; 0.2 g protein; 0.2 g fat (0 g sat.); 0.9 g carbo (0.1 g fiber); 1.1 mg sodium; 0 mg chol.

California Chili Powder

PREP TIME: About 5 minutes

NOTES: Use to season cooked dried beans (home-cooked or canned), soups, and stews; or rub onto meats, seafood, or poultry to pan-fry, roast, or barbecue.

MAKES: About 7 tablespoons

In a $\frac{1}{3}$- to $\frac{1}{2}$-cup tall, narrow clear jar, layer the following, contrasting light layers with dark: $\frac{1}{4}$ cup **ground California** or New Mexico **chilies** (also called California or New Mexico chili powder), 1 tablespoon **ground cumin**, 1 to 2 teaspoons **cayenne**, 2 teaspoons **dried oregano**, 2 teaspoons **onion salt**, 1 teaspoon **garlic powder**. To use, shake jar or stir spices until blended.

Per teaspoon: 6.7 cal., 40% (2.7 cal.) from fat; 0.3 g protein; 0.3 g fat (0 g sat.); 1.1 g carbo (0.5 g fiber); 129 mg sodium; 0 mg chol.

Mediterranean Herb Salad Mix

PREP TIME: About 5 minutes

NOTES: Sprinkle over green salads as you mix or, to make a dressing, combine 2 tablespoons of this herb blend with $\frac{1}{4}$ cup wine vinegar and $\frac{1}{2}$ cup olive oil.

MAKES: About 5 tablespoons

In a $\frac{1}{3}$- to $\frac{1}{2}$-cup tall, narrow clear jar, layer the following, contrasting light layers with dark: 1 tablespoon **dried parsley**, 1 tablespoon **dried onion flakes**, 2 tablespoons **dried basil**, $1\frac{1}{2}$ teaspoons **garlic salt**, $1\frac{1}{2}$ teaspoons **lemon-pepper**. To use, shake jar or stir spices until blended.

Per tablespoon: 7 cal., 13% (0.9 cal.) from fat; 0.3 g protein; 0.1 g fat (0 g sat.); 1.7 g carbo (0 g fiber); 559 mg sodium; 0 mg chol.

Five-Spice Sugar

PREP TIME: About 5 minutes

NOTES: Sprinkle liberally onto buttered toast, sliced fruit, or tapioca pudding. Or sprinkle the sugar onto muffin batter in pans before baking.

MAKES: About 5 tablespoons

In a $\frac{1}{3}$- to $\frac{1}{2}$-cup tall, narrow clear jar, layer the following, contrasting light layers with dark: 5 tablespoons **sugar**, $\frac{1}{2}$ teaspoon **ground cinnamon**, $\frac{1}{2}$ teaspoon **ground nutmeg**, $\frac{1}{2}$ teaspoon **ground ginger**, $\frac{1}{2}$ teaspoon **ground cardamom**, $\frac{1}{2}$ teaspoon **ground coriander**. To use, shake jar or stir spices until blended.

Per teaspoon: 17 cal., 0% (0 cal.) from fat; 0 g protein; 0 g fat; 4.3 g carbo (0 g fiber); 0.1 mg sodium; 0 mg chol. ◆

The Quick Cook

BY ANDREW BAKER

MICHAEL LAMOTTE

SPICE-COATED SALMON, quickly seared, nestles on tender-crisp braised bok choy.

Braisingly fresh

■ Like many cooks, Sam Gugino favors meals that come together quickly. But as a food editor and writer, he's not willing to sacrifice flavor to speed. Armed with the conviction that the two goals aren't diametrically opposed, he wrote *Cooking to Beat the Clock: Delicious, Inspired Meals in 15 Minutes* (Chronicle Books, San Francisco, 1999; $16.95; 800/722-6657 or www.chroniclebooks.com).

Gugino lets big flavors speak in his Asian-spiced salmon with braised bok choy. We liked the results so much that we've added variations on pan-browned, spice-rubbed fish to go with briefly braised greens. Gugino uses two frying pans; the greens get started in one while the fish cooks in the other. If you cook the greens first, then keep them warm while you brown the fish in the same pan, you add about 10 minutes to the cooking process but cut back on cleanup.

Asian-spiced Salmon with Braised Bok Choy

PREP AND COOK TIME: About 15 minutes
NOTES: To make a blend similar to five spice, use equal parts ground cinnamon, ground cloves, ground ginger, and finely crushed anise seed.
MAKES: 4 servings

1½	pounds **bok choy**
2	teaspoons minced **garlic**
4	teaspoons **salad oil**
¾	cup fat-skimmed **chicken broth**
1½	pounds **boned salmon fillet with skin** (maximum 1 in. thick)
2	tablespoons **Chinese five spice** (see notes)
	Salt and **pepper**

1. Rinse bok choy; trim off and discard tough stem ends and any bruised parts. Cut leafy tops crosswise into 2-inch strips; cut stems crosswise into 1-inch pieces.
2. In a 10- to 12-inch frying pan over high heat, stir garlic in 2 teaspoons oil until sizzling, 1 to 2 minutes. Add bok choy and broth, cover, and cook until thickest stems are just tender when pierced, 4 to 5 minutes; keep warm.
3. Meanwhile, rinse salmon, pat dry, and cut into 4 equal pieces. Rub fish evenly with five spice. Pour remaining 2 teaspoons oil into a 10- to 12-inch frying pan over high heat. When oil is hot, in about 1 minute, lay salmon, skin down, in pan; cook 3 minutes. With a wide spatula, turn fish and cook until it is opaque but still moist-looking in center of thickest part (cut to test), about 3 minutes more.
4. Place salmon in wide bowls and spoon bok choy and broth equally around fish. Season to taste with salt and pepper.

Per serving: 394 cal., 55% (216 cal.) from fat; 38 g protein; 24 g fat (4.3 g sat.); 6.7 g carbo (2.3 g fiber); 215 mg sodium; 100 mg chol.

Sesame-Ginger Salmon with Braised Bok Choy

PREP AND COOK TIME: About 15 minutes
MAKES: 4 servings

Follow directions for **Asian-spiced salmon with braised bok choy** (preceding), but omit Chinese five spice and use 4 teaspoons **sesame seed** mixed with 1½ teaspoons **ground ginger** to coat fish.

Per serving: 400 cal., 56% (225 cal.) from fat; 38 g protein; 25 g fat (4.5 g sat.); 5 g carbo (1.9 g fiber); 213 mg sodium; 100 mg chol.

Salt and Pepper Bass with Braised Spinach

PREP AND COOK TIME: About 15 minutes
MAKES: 4 servings

Follow directions for **Asian-spiced salmon with braised bok choy** (at left), but instead of bok choy use 2 packages (10 oz. each) **washed spinach leaves** (add in batches) and decrease chicken broth to ¼ cup. Instead of the salmon, use 1½ pounds **boned, skinned bass** (white seabass or grouper bass), cut into 4 equal portions. Instead of Chinese five spice, use 1½ teaspoons **kosher salt** mixed with 2 teaspoons **pepper**. Rub salt mixture on fish.

Per serving: 245 cal., 31% (77 cal.) from fat; 36 g protein; 8.5 g fat (1.5 g sat.); 6.5 g carbo (4.1 g fiber); 1,337 mg sodium; 70 mg chol. ◆

LINDA AND JIM DeMARTINI of Hillsborough, California, raise a glass with friends Karen Michel and Bill Austin. Festive flavors on the menu (below): Pisco sours and sweet-spiced nuts, Western caviars and sparkling wines, foie gras in lobster broth with porcini-parmesan breadsticks, and a stunning croquembouche.

Party on!

Set the stage for the next millennium with an elegant feast of Western flavors

BY ANDREW BAKER • PHOTOGRAPHS BY JUST LOOMIS
FOOD STYLING BY VALERIE AIKMAN-SMITH

■ NEW YEAR'S EVE 1899 PASSED QUIETLY IN THE PAGES OF *SUNSET*. WRITERS FOUND MORE SIGNIFICANCE IN THE booming Western frontier, from gold mining in Oregon to leisure travel in Mexico, than in the turning of the century, while advertisements extolled expanding railroads and grand hotels. • But this New Year's Eve cannot slip by unnoticed. It's a new *millennium* we're celebrating, after all. • Such a milestone calls for a menu of the most elegant foods the West has to offer, many of which were in vogue 100 years ago: sparkling wine, nuts, oysters, caviar, beef tenderloin, cheese. While such heady foodstuffs never go out of style, the mode of the party is by necessity—and choice—different. Then, dinner party hosts usually had a cadre of domestic help. Now, budgets and voluntary informality steer most of us to assemble galas ourselves. This one comes together easily with a make-ahead game plan (page 314). • And in modern Western fashion, revelers can be dressed to the nines as befits the year—black tie de rigueur—while plates can be optional. The entire menu is finger-friendly (except for a steaming lobster broth, which requires small cups or bowls and spoons), so just about all you need is napkins. • Your guests can progress in stages from table to table through the courses of this stand-up feast or, more likely, backtrack and mingle to savor the best flavors of the century.

COUNTDOWN

game *plan*

up to 2 weeks ahead:
Bake, fill, and *freeze* cream puffs.

up to 1 week ahead:
Make sweet-spiced nuts.

up to 2 days ahead:
Roast potato slices.
Assemble croquembouche.

up to 1 day ahead:
Mix base for pisco sours. *Make* lobster broth, porcini-parmesan breadsticks, pesto for oysters, chive sour cream sauce for caviar, wasabi mustard sauce for roast beef, and tequila–wheat berry salad. *Assemble* brie with fennel and mushrooms. *Roast* beef tenderloin. *Bake* chicken wings.

FRUITY PISCO SOURS (above left) kick off the celebration on an old-fashioned note. Chris DeMartini (right) keeps the sparkling wine flowing all evening.

STAGE 1:

Warm-ups

When guests arrive, toast the evening with a drink that was popular in the West at the turn of the last century—the pisco sour. Span the years by nibbling nuts flavored with contemporary Southeast Asian seasonings.

Pisco Sours

PREP TIME: About 5 minutes

NOTES: Pisco is a South American brandy made from Muscat grapes; for less intensity, use a Muscat wine such as Essensia or Beaumes-de-Venise instead. To serve in a salt-rimmed glass, rub a lime wedge around rim, dip in salt, then add ice and pisco mixture. If making up to 1 day ahead, mix pisco, lime juice, and tangerine juice; cover and chill. Add club soda just before serving.

MAKES: 12 cups; 12 servings

- 1½ cups **pisco** (Muscat brandy)
- ¾ cup **lime juice**
- 5 cups **tangerine juice** or orange-tangerine juice blend
- 4¾ cups **club soda**

    About 6 cups **ice cubes**

    Lime slices

1. In a pitcher, combine pisco, lime juice, tangerine juice, and club soda.

2. Put ½ cup ice cubes in each glass (12- to 14-oz. size) and fill with pisco mixture. Garnish with lime slices.

Per serving: 120 cal., 1.5% (1.8 cal.) from fat; 0.5 g protein; 0.2 g fat (0 g sat.); 11 g carbo (0 g fiber); 23 mg sodium; 0 mg chol.

Pisco sour slushes. Use all ingredients for **pisco sours** (preceding) except ice. Pour **tangerine juice** into ice cube trays and freeze until solid, about 2 hours; release cubes and use, or seal in a plastic freezer bag and freeze up to 1 week. In a blender, combine ½ the **pisco** and ½ the **lime juice.** Cover, turn to high, and drop ½ the frozen tangerine juice cubes through opening in lid. Whirl until mixture is slushy; pour into a pitcher. Repeat to whirl remaining pisco, lime juice, and tangerine cubes; add to pitcher. Add chilled **club soda.** Pour into glasses (8 to 10 oz.); garnish with **lime** slices.

Per serving: 120 cal., 1.5% (1.8 cal.) from fat; 0.5 g protein; 0.2 g fat (0 g sat.); 11 g carbo (0 g fiber); 23 mg sodium; 0 mg chol.

Tangerine sours. Follow directions for **pisco sours** (at left), but omit pisco and increase lime juice to 2¼ cups.

Per serving: 59 cal., 4.6% (2.7 cal.) from fat; 0.7 g protein; 0.3 g fat (0 g sat.); 14 g carbo (0 g fiber); 25 mg sodium; 0 mg chol.

Sweet-Spiced Nuts

PREP AND COOK TIME: About 40 minutes

NOTES: If making nuts up to 1 week ahead, cool, package airtight, and chill.

MAKES: About 4 cups; 12 servings

- ¼ cup **honey**
- 4 teaspoons **Thai green curry paste** or hot curry powder
- 2 teaspoons **olive** or salad **oil**
- 1¼ teaspoons **salt**
- 1 cup **cashews**
- 1 cup **macadamias**
- 1 cup **almonds**
- 1 cup **pecan halves**
- ⅓ cup **sweetened shredded dried coconut**

1. In a bowl, mix honey, curry paste, oil, and salt. Add all the nuts and the coconut; mix well. Spread in a single layer in a 10- by 15-inch pan.

2. Bake in a 300° oven, turning often with a wide spatula, until nuts are dark gold, about 30 minutes.

3. Turn nuts often with spatula as they cool. Serve warm or cool.

Per serving: 315 cal., 80% (252 cal.) from fat; 5.7 g protein; 28 g fat (4 g sat.); 16 g carbo (2.4 g fiber); 315 mg sodium; 0.3 mg chol.

STAGE 2:

From the sea

The sea teems with New Year's metaphors—change and regeneration with each tide—and elegant party foods. Begin with lobster broth with foie gras, to sip from tiny cups. Then move to a briny bounty of seafoods: oysters on the half-shell; bites of salmon, trout, crab, and caviar on crisp potato slices, topped with dabs of chive-studded sour cream. *To serve 12,* you'll need 1 to 1½ pounds thin-sliced smoked salmon, about 1 pound whole smoked trout, ¾ to 1 pound shelled cooked crab (plus cracked crab legs, if desired), and about 12 ounces assorted caviars (see caviar bar, page 317). Nest crab and caviar containers in ice. Note: Foie gras and caviars are sold in specialty food shops. Or order from Seattle Caviar Company (888/323-3005 or www.caviar.com) or Caviarteria (800/422-8427 or www.caviarteria.com).

Foie Gras in Lobster Broth

PREP AND COOK TIME: About 1 hour

NOTES: If making up to 1 day ahead, chill broth and lobster meat separately.

MAKES: About 6 cups broth; 12 servings

- 2 **fresh** or thawed frozen **lobster tails** (about 1 lb. total)
- 2 tablespoons **butter** or margarine
- 1 cup chopped **onion**
- 1 cup chopped **carrots**
- 1 cup chopped **celery**
- 1 cup **dry white wine**
- **Salt**
- ¼ pound **fresh** or canned **foie gras** or duck liver pâté
- ¾ cup thinly sliced **green onions** (including tops)

1. With kitchen shears, cut through top of lobster shells lengthwise down the center. Set tails, cut sides up, on a board. With a heavy knife, slice tails in half lengthwise through cuts. Rinse.

2. Put lobster in shells and 8 cups water in a 4- to 5-quart pan over high heat. When just beginning to boil, turn heat to low and cook until lobster meat is barely opaque but still moist-looking in center of thickest part (cut to test), about 10 minutes. With a slotted spoon, lift lobster tails from pan and let cool. Pour liquid from pan and reserve.

3. When lobster is cool enough to touch, in about 5 minutes, pull meat from shells; break shells into about

TIERED CENTERPIECE: Turn a brass planter (6-inch diameter) upside down in position on table. Secure a gold-framed square mirror to base of planter with double-sided picture-mounting tape. Place a smaller planter or gold-sprayed vase upside down in center of mirror; secure a gold charger to top. Repeat with another planter or vase and smaller mirror; place a gold vase filled with flowers on top. Place brass or glass votives filled with flowers and greenery around layers; fill in with fruit. Note: If using candles, make sure flames are not under layer above. Design: Jill Slater.

AN ARRAY OF SEAFOOD (from left): Smoked salmon topped with fresh salmon roe (ikura), surrounded by caviar-crowned cucumber slices; toasted baguette slices and chive sour cream; cooked shelled crab and cracked crab legs; shucked oysters on the half-shell with cilantro-ginger pesto; and a trio of caviars (clockwise from top: orange ikura, green wasabi-flavor tobiko, and red lumpfish). Replenish seafood every two hours with chilled backups, or nest the oysters and bowls of crab and caviar in ice. At right: A cup of steaming lobster broth with slices of truffle-studded foie gras and porcini-parmesan breadsticks.

2-inch pieces and return to pan. Chop ¼ of the lobster meat and add to pan along with butter, onion, carrots, and celery. Stir over medium-high heat until vegetables are limp but not browned, about 7 minutes.

4. Add reserved cooking liquid and wine. Boil over high heat until liquid is reduced to 6 cups, about 25 minutes. Pour through a fine strainer into a pitcher; discard residue. Season broth to taste with salt, and keep hot.

5. Meanwhile, cut remaining lobster meat into ½-inch chunks. Cut foie gras into ¼- to ½-inch chunks. Place lobster, foie gras, and green onions in separate small bowls.

6. To eat, spoon a piece of lobster and a chunk of foie gras into each small cup (demitasse); or use 3- to 4-ounce bowls. Pour hot broth into cup; add green onions to taste. Sip broth and use a small spoon to eat lobster and foie gras.

Per serving: 115 cal., 50% (57 cal.) from fat; 10 g protein; 6.3 g fat (2.6 g sat.); 4 g carbo (0.8 g fiber); 258 mg sodium; 49 mg chol.

Porcini-Parmesan Breadsticks

PREP AND COOK TIME: About 2¼ hours

NOTES: If the dried mushrooms are not crisp enough to snap when you bend them, pour into an 8- or 9-inch pan and bake in a 350° oven until brittle, about 5 minutes. If making breadsticks up to 1 day ahead, wrap airtight when cool and store at room temperature; freeze to store longer. To crisp, return to baking sheets and heat in a 350° oven until warm, about 5 minutes.

MAKES: 24 breadsticks; 12 servings

1 ounce (about 1 cup) **dried porcini mushrooms**

1 package **active dry yeast**

1 teaspoon **sugar**

About 1½ teaspoons **kosher salt**

About 2 tablespoons **olive** or salad **oil**

About 2¾ cups **all-purpose flour**

½ cup **grated parmesan cheese**

1 **large egg** yolk

1. In a blender or food processor, whirl dried mushrooms to a fine powder. Let powder settle before removing lid. Pour powder through a fine strainer into a small bowl; reserve any mushroom grinds remaining in strainer for other uses.

2. In a large bowl, combine yeast, sugar, and 1 cup warm (110°) water. Let stand until yeast is dissolved, about 5 minutes. Add porcini powder, ½ teaspoon salt, 2 tablespoons olive oil, 1½ cups flour, and ¼ cup parmesan cheese. Beat with a heavy spoon or a mixer until dough is stretchy, 1 to 2 minutes.

the half-shell in crushed ice on a rimmed tray. Spoon sauce equally onto the oysters.

Per piece: 19 cal., 63% (12 cal.) from fat; 1.1 g protein; 1.3 g fat (0.2 g sat.); 0.8 g carbo (0 g fiber); 59 mg sodium; 7.8 mg chol.

Caviar Bar

Once caviar from Western sturgeon was so abundant that it was commonplace fare in San Francisco pubs. Most of us, however, know caviar as an extravagance imported from the Caspian Sea. Now a small amount is available from locally farmed sturgeon as an alternative. But costly sturgeon caviar is only one of many choices. Others—moderately expensive to bargain-priced—include roe from salmon, whitefish, flying fish, and lumpfish. Choose an assortment to fit your budget, allowing at least 1 ounce per person (see "From the sea," page 315).

Arrange **caviar** in dishes on ice and serve with **roasted potato slices** and **chive sour cream sauce** (recipes follow).

Roasted Potato Slices

PREP AND COOK TIME: About 1 hour

NOTES: The sliced potatoes darken slightly before they're baked, but this doesn't affect their final color. If making up to 2 days ahead, cool and store airtight at room temperature.

MAKES: About 120 pieces; 12 servings

    About 3 tablespoons melted **butter** or margarine

2 **russet potatoes** (about 2½ in. wide and 4½ in. long; about 14 oz. total), scrubbed

    Salt

1. Butter 2 nonstick baking sheets (about 13 by 15 in.).

2. With a slicer or a knife, cut the potatoes crosswise into uniformly thick ¹⁄₁₆-inch slices.

3. Lay ½ the slices about ½ inch apart on prepared baking sheets. Brush with butter and sprinkle lightly with salt.

4. Bake in a 350° oven until slices are golden and crisp, 10 to 15 minutes; switch pan positions halfway through cooking.

5. Transfer potato slices to a towel-covered rack. Repeat from step 3 to bake remaining slices. When cool, serve or package airtight.

Per serving: 52 cal., 50% (26 cal.) from fat; 0.7 g protein; 2.9 g fat (1.8 g sat.); 5.9 g carbo (0.6 g fiber); 32 mg sodium; 7.8 mg chol.

---

5. Oil 2 baking sheets (14 by 17 in.). With a sharp knife, cut dough lengthwise into 24 equal strips. Pick up a dough strip, holding both ends, and let strip stretch until it's as long as the baking sheet; lay strip on sheet. Repeat to shape remaining strips and space at least ½ inch apart on sheet.

6. In a small bowl, beat egg yolk to blend with 1 tablespoon water. Brush onto dough strips, sprinkle evenly with remaining parmesan cheese, then sprinkle with 1 to 2 teaspoons salt (most falls off).

7. Bake in a 350° oven until breadsticks are golden, 22 to 25 minutes (12 to 15 minutes in a convection oven); switch pan positions halfway through baking. With a wide spatula, transfer breadsticks to a rack. Serve hot, warm, or at room temperature.

Per breadstick: 84 cal., 27% (23 cal.) from fat; 2.9 g protein; 2.5 g fat (0.7 g sat.); 12 g carbo (0.8 g fiber); 131 mg sodium; 10 mg chol.

Oysters on the Half-Shell with Cilantro-Ginger Pesto

PREP TIME: About 12 minutes

NOTES: If making pesto up to 1 day ahead, cover and chill. Have oysters shucked at the market up to 1 day ahead; set, cup side up, on a rimmed tray; cover and chill.

MAKES: 24 oysters and ⅔ cup sauce; 12 servings

1. In a blender, purée 1 tablespoon **soy sauce** or Asian fish sauce (*nuoc mam* or *nam pla*), 5 teaspoons **lemon juice,** 5 teaspoons **olive oil,** 5 teaspoons minced **fresh ginger,** and 1½ cups coarsely chopped **fresh cilantro.**

2. Nest 2 dozen **shucked oysters on**

---

3. *To knead dough by hand,* stir in 1 cup flour. Scrape dough onto a lightly floured board and knead until smooth and elastic, about 10 minutes; add flour as required to prevent sticking.

To knead with a dough hook, mix in 1 cup flour. Beat until dough pulls from sides of bowl and no longer feels sticky, about 3 minutes; if required, beat in more flour, 1 tablespoon at a time.

4. On a lightly floured board, pat dough into a 6- by 12-inch rectangle. Brush with about ½ teaspoon oil, lightly cover with plastic wrap, and let stand until puffy, about 45 minutes.

Chive Sour Cream Sauce

PREP TIME: About 8 minutes

NOTES: If making up to 1 day ahead, chill airtight. For even color, use a blender; otherwise, you can mince all the chives and mix with sour cream.

MAKES: About ¾ cup

In a blender, purée ¾ cup **sour cream** and ¼ cup chopped **fresh chives** until pale green. Scrape into a bowl and stir in 2 tablespoons minced fresh chives and **salt** to taste.

Per teaspoon: 10 cal., 90% (9 cal.) from fat; 0.2 g protein; 1 g fat (0.6 g sat.); 0.2 g carbo (0 g fiber); 2.6 mg sodium; 2.1 mg chol.

STAGE 3:

From the land

A scoop of warm brie and wild mushrooms on a toasted baguette slice makes the transition to earthier flavors. Tequila-flavor wheat berry salad, cupped in small lettuce leaves, adds a bright note. Tuck slices of perfectly roasted beef tenderloin into miniature pocket breads for petite sandwiches pungent with mustard. And give humble chicken wings first-class treatment with a lemon-pepper glaze. Add variety and color with a kaleidoscope of cherry tomatoes and olives, such as calamata, cracked green, and almond-stuffed.

Baked Brie with Fennel and Mushrooms

PREP AND COOK TIME: About 50 minutes

NOTES: Use whole brie cheese (1 large or 2 small); cut pieces will ooze. Along with baguette slices, offer Belgian endive leaves to hold spoonfuls of cheese: rinse 2 heads (about 10 oz. total) and separate leaves. If starting brie up to 1 day ahead, prepare ingredients through step 6; chill cheese and reserved fennel greens separately airtight, and store cooled toast airtight at room temperature.

MAKES: 12 servings

- 1 head **fennel** (about 3½ in. wide)
- 1 pound **chanterelle** or common **mushrooms**
- 2 tablespoons **butter** or margarine
- 1 cup **brandy,** white wine, or fat-skimmed chicken broth
- ¾ to 1 pound **brie cheese** (see notes)
- 2 **slender baguettes** (1 lb. total)

WELL-GROUNDED

MAIN COURSE (clockwise from front): Tequila-spiked wheat berry salad in lettuce cups, lemon- and pepper-coated chicken wings, warm brie cheese with wild mushrooms and fennel, roast beef with wasabi mustard sauce in pocket breads, olives, and cherry tomatoes.

1. Rinse and drain fennel. Cut off stalks; chop enough of the feathery green leaves to make about ¼ cup, and reserve (discard stalks with remaining greens). Trim root ends, bruised areas, and coarse fibers from fennel head; cut head into ¼-inch chunks.

2. Rinse mushrooms, drain, and trim off discolored stem ends and any bruises. Thinly slice mushrooms.

3. In a 10- to 12-inch frying pan over high heat, frequently stir chopped fennel head, mushrooms, and butter until liquid is evaporated and mixture begins to brown, 10 to 15 minutes.

4. Add brandy; stir until almost all the liquid is evaporated, 3 to 6 minutes.

5. Spoon ½ the fennel mixture into a shallow casserole about 3 inches wider than the brie (or ¼ of the fennel mixture into each of 2 shallow casseroles if using small cheeses). Set brie in casserole (or casseroles) and spoon remaining fennel mixture evenly over and around cheese.

6. Cut baguettes diagonally crosswise into ¼-inch slices. Lay slices on 2 baking sheets (14 by 17 in.). Bake in a 350° oven until lightly toasted, 10 to 13 minutes. Transfer slices to a rack to cool.

7. Bake cheese in a 350° oven until runny in the center (cut to test), 10 to 15 minutes, 25 to 35 minutes if chilled.

8. Sprinkle reserved chopped fennel leaves over cheese. To serve, set casserole with cheese on an electric warming tray or over a candle to keep warm. Spoon cheese and fennel mixture onto toasted baguette slices.

Per serving: 253 cal., 39% (99 cal.) from fat; 10 g protein; 11 g fat (1.5 g sat.); 22 g carbo (1.8 g fiber); 455 mg sodium; 34 mg chol.

Tequila–Wheat Berry Salad

PREP AND COOK TIME: About 1¼ hours

NOTES: If making up to 1 day ahead, chill salad and lettuce leaves separately airtight.

MAKES: 4 cups; 12 servings

- 2 cups **tequila**
- 2 cups fat-skimmed **chicken broth**
- 2 cups **wheat berries**
- 2 tablespoons minced **fresh red** or green **jalapeño chilies**
- 5 tablespoons **lime juice**
- ¼ cup minced **fresh cilantro**
- 2 tablespoons finely chopped **green onions**

  Salt
- 24 to 36 **butter lettuce** leaves, rinsed and crisped

  Ice cubes

MAKE THE PARTY SPARKLE: Group martini glasses of different sizes together and fill bottoms of glasses with clear or colored glass marbles. Nest tealights or small votive candles in the marbles. Design: Ann Bertelsen.

MARTINI VOTIVES

a *toast* to the *millennium*

BY KAREN MacNEIL-FIFE

WESTERN SPARKLING WINES

Korbel Brut nonvintage (California), $10. Light, simple, and frothy.

Gruet Brut nonvintage (New Mexico), $13. A delightful surprise from a state not hitherto known for wine. Crisp and clean, with light appley notes.

Mumm Cuvée Napa "Brut Prestige" nonvintage (Napa Valley), $15. Sleek on the palate, with fresh, lively flavors.

Gloria Ferrer Royal Cuvée 1991 (Carneros, CA), $20. Creamy yet racy, with subtle nutty overtones.

Schramsberg Blanc de Blancs 1996 (Napa Valley), $27. A classic made primarily from Chardonnay grapes. Sophisticated and creamy, with rich brioche flavors.

Roederer Estate "L'Ermitage" 1993 (Mendocino), $38. Complex and nuanced, with elegant creamy, yeasty flavors.

WHITE WINES

Amity Vineyards Pinot Blanc 1997 (Willamette Valley), $12. A slew of delicious Pinot Blancs are coming out of Oregon, and most of them are a steal. This one, with its snappy lime flavors, is built for seafood. Also try the Pinot Blancs from Bethel Heights and Willakenzie Estate.

Zaca Mesa "Zaca Vineyards" Roussanne 1997 (Santa Barbara County), $17. Exudes elegance, with fascinating floral, lime, and peach blossom flavors.

St. Supéry "White Meritage" 1997 (Napa Valley), $20. This fabulous creamy blend of Sauvignon Blanc and Sémillon is fresh and lively, yet complex.

RED WINES

Hedges Cabernet/Merlot 1997 (Washington), $10. Amazing for the price. Lovely notes of vanilla and cassis.

Geyser Peak Cabernet Sauvignon 1996 (Sonoma County), $16. Rugged and powerful, with delicious laurel, cassis, and leathery notes.

Lolonis Zinfandel 1997 (Mendocino), $17. Juicy and intense, with wonderful spiced boysenberry flavors.

Lambert Bridge Merlot 1996 (Sonoma County), $20. Big and soft with deep, briary chocolate and espresso flavors.

Edmunds St. John "Durell Vineyard" Syrah 1997 (Carneros, CA), $30. Somewhat hard to find, but a classic that shouldn't be missed. One of the deepest, most primordial, brooding Syrahs made in California.

Shafer "Hillside Select" Cabernet Sauvignon 1995 (Stags Leap District, CA), $110. Super-concentrated and utterly gorgeous, with a texture that approaches cashmere. Expensive—but the millennium comes only once in a lifetime.

AFTER-DINNER WINES, EAUX DE VIE, AND BRANDY

Quady Elysium 1998 (California), $14 (750 ml.). A sensational light-bodied dessert wine with absolutely delicious spun honey and spice flavors. Made from Black Muscat grapes.

Bonny Doon Muscat Vin de Glacière 1997 (Monterey), $15 (375 ml.). Modeled after the great eisweins of Germany,

WRAP CHAMPAGNE FLUTES with removable, adhesive-backed silver foil tape (available at stained-glass supply stores) to just above the middle; cut off diagonally. Attach a colored glass stone (available at craft stores) over end with clear-drying liquid glue. — A.B.

Bonny Doon's vin de glacière (*wine of the icebox*) detonates in the mouth with a profusion of sweet apricot, peach, and orange blossom flavors.

Clear Creek Distillery Pear Brandy, $20 (375 ml.). This Oregon distillery makes what many consider the best clear brandies (eaux de vie) in America. Made from whole Oregon Bartlett pears that have been crushed, fermented, and distilled, this one is pure essence of fruit.

Germain-Robin Select XO, $100. In numerous blind tastings, this stunning, utterly smooth brandy from Mendocino County has bested some of the top Cognacs from France. Germain-Robin is double-distilled in a traditional alembic apparatus.

NOTE: Prices are approximate and, especially this year, subject to fluctuation.

---

1. In a 3- to 4-quart pan over high heat, frequently stir tequila, broth, and wheat berries until boiling. Cover pan, reduce heat, and simmer until wheat berries are tender to bite, 45 to 50 minutes.

2. Drain wheat berries, reserving liquid. Put grain in a wide bowl and return liquid to pan. Boil liquid over high heat, stirring occasionally, until reduced to about 2 tablespoons, about 5 minutes.

Add liquid to wheat berries; stir occasionally until cooled to room temperature, about 15 minutes. Stir in chilies, lime juice, cilantro, and green onions, and add salt to taste.

3. Mound lettuce leaves in a bowl and nest in larger bowl filled with ice. To eat, spoon a little wheat berry salad onto a lettuce leaf and fold leaf over salad to enclose.

Per serving: 117 cal., 5.4% (6.3 cal.) from fat; 5.6 g protein; 0.7 g fat (0 g sat.); 24 g carbo (4.9 g fiber); 15 mg sodium; 0 mg chol.

Roast Beef Tenderloin with Wasabi Mustard Sauce

PREP AND COOK TIME: About **55 minutes**

NOTES: If roasting beef up to 1 day ahead, cool, cover, and chill. Instead of roasting the tenderloin, you can buy 2 pounds of thin-sliced roast beef. Offer miniature pocket bread halves to hold slices of beef with sauce. You will need about 18 rounds (4 in.). If desired, substitute 1 tablespoon prepared horseradish for wasabi paste. Accompany with fresh greens such as watercress, sprouts, or cilantro to tuck into pockets.

MAKES: About 1 cup sauce; 12 servings

1. In a 9- by 13-inch pan, roast a 3-pound piece of **beef tenderloin** in a 400° oven until thermometer inserted in center of thickest part reaches 135° for medium-rare, about 50 minutes. Cool beef and thinly slice. Arrange slices, overlapping, on a platter.

2. In a bowl, stir together ¾ cup **coarse-grain mustard,** 3 tablespoons **honey,** and 2 teaspoons **wasabi paste.**

3. Tuck slices of beef into pocket bread halves (see notes) and add mustard sauce to taste.

Per serving beef: 274 cal., 69% (189 cal.) from fat; 19 g protein; 21 g fat (8.4 g sat.); 0 g carbo; 46 mg sodium; 71 mg chol.

Per tablespoon mustard sauce: 32 cal., 0% (0 cal.) from fat; 0.1 g protein; 0 g fat; 4.6 g carbo; 180 mg sodium; 0 mg chol.

Lemon-Pepper Chicken Wings

PREP AND COOK TIME: About 1¼ hours

NOTES: If making up to 1 day ahead, cool, cover pan, and chill; reheat, covered, in a 300° oven about 25 minutes.

MAKES: 12 servings

 5 pounds **chicken wings** or about 4¼ pounds chicken drumettes

 ⅓ cup **lemon juice**

 3 tablespoons **honey**

 ¾ teaspoon **dried thyme**

 1¼ teaspoons grated **lemon** peel

 2½ teaspoons **dried peppercorns** (black, green, pink, or a combination), coarsely ground

 Salt

1. Cut chicken wings apart at joints; reserve tips for other uses. Rinse wings (or drumettes) and place in a single layer in 2 pans, each 10 by 15 inches.

2. Bake in a 400° oven until well browned, about 1 hour and 10 minutes (about 50 minutes in a convection oven); turn pieces occasionally with a wide spatula, and switch pan positions halfway through cooking.

3. Meanwhile, in a bowl, stir together

TEST YOUR LUCK for the new millennium with a decadent croquembouche: Will your cream puff be filled with coffee- or gianduia-flavor pastry cream?

lemon juice, honey, thyme, lemon peel, and ground peppercorns.

4. Drain and discard fat from chicken wings. Consolidate the wings in 1 pan. Pour the lemon juice mixture over wings and turn pieces with spatula to mix well.

5. Return chicken to oven and bake until sauce thickens and sticks to wings, 12 to 15 minutes, turning pieces often and scraping pan to release any browned bits.

6. Place wings in a chafing dish or on a platter. Add salt to taste. Keep chafing dish warm over a flame, or put platter on an electric warming tray.

Per serving: 227 cal., 56% (126 cal.) from fat; 19 g protein; 14 g fat (3.9 g sat.); 5.2 g carbo (0.1 g fiber); 61 mg sodium; 60 mg chol.

STAGE 4:

A sweet finale

Midnight, December 31, 1999, deserves a grand finale—to the party and the century. This *croquembouche* (French for *crunch in the mouth*), a lavish tower of caramel-drizzled cream puffs filled with gianduia- and coffee-flavor pastry creams, fills the bill. It looks elaborate, but the recipe has many make-ahead steps.

Celebrate the innovation of the 1900s with fresh cherries on the stem from Chile (it's summer there). Then linger through the first hours of the year 2000 over coffee, a chocolate truffle or two, and cordials made here in the West.

Croquembouche

ASSEMBLY TIME: About 45 minutes

NOTES: Up to 2 weeks ahead, bake cream puffs; store airtight at room temperature up to 1 day. Make fillings and fill puffs. Set on baking sheets and freeze; when hard, transfer to plastic freezer bags, seal airtight, and return to freezer. Up to 2 days before the party, assemble croquembouche (no need to thaw puffs) and refreeze (serve frozen).

MAKES: 12 servings

> **Gianduia pastry cream** (recipe follows)
>
> **Cream puffs** (recipe follows)
>
> **Coffee pastry cream** (recipe follows)
>
> ¾ cup **sugar**

1. Spoon gianduia pastry cream into a pastry bag fitted with a plain ⅛- to ¼-inch-wide tip. Push pastry tip into the X-shaped cut in the bottom of 1 cream puff. Squeeze bag to fill the puff as full as possible. Repeat to fill ½ the cream puffs. Scoop any extra pastry cream into a bowl, cover, and chill for other uses.

2. Rinse and dry pastry bag. Spoon coffee pastry cream into bag. Repeat step 1 to fill remaining cream puffs.

3. Put sugar in a 10- to 12-inch nonstick frying pan over high heat; frequently shake and tilt pan to mix until sugar is melted and amber, 3 to 4 minutes. Remove from heat.

4. Working quickly (be careful, melted sugar is hot), dip bottoms of cream puffs, 1 at a time, into caramelized sugar and set 10, caramel sides down and edges touching, in a ring on a flat plate. Make a second, slightly smaller, ring of cream puffs on the first. Repeat, with each ring slightly smaller than the last, forming a cone-shaped tower. Attach any extra cream puffs around base of cone.

5. Place pan with remaining caramelized sugar over heat until melted again. Drizzle over croquembouche. Keep assembled croquembouche in freezer until ready to serve.

6. Use 2 forks to break off cream puffs, 1 at a time; hold in napkins to eat.

Per serving: 380 cal., 47% (180 cal.) from fat; 5.8 g protein; 20 g fat (10 g sat.); 43 g carbo (1 g fiber); 120 mg sodium; 145 mg chol.

Cream Puffs

PREP AND COOK TIME: About 50 minutes

MAKES: About 60 cream puffs, each 1½ inches wide

> About ½ cup (¼ lb.) **butter** or margarine, in chunks
>
> 2 teaspoons **sugar**
>
> 1 cup **all-purpose flour**
>
> 4 **large eggs**

1. In a 2- to 3-quart pan over high heat, stir 1 cup water, ½ cup butter, and sugar until butter is melted and mixture boils, about 3 minutes.

2. Add flour, remove from heat, and stir until dough holds together. Add eggs, 1 at a time, beating vigorously after each addition until smooth. Let cool to room temperature, 10 to 15 minutes.

3. Spoon dough in 2-teaspoon portions 1 inch apart on 2 buttered baking sheets, each 12 by 15 inches.

4. Bake in a 375° oven until puffs are well browned and firm to touch, 25 to 30 minutes; switch pans halfway through baking.

5. Cut an X-shaped slit in the bottom of each puff and set on racks to cool.

Per cream puff: 27 cal., 63% (17 cal.) from fat; 0.6 g protein; 1.9 g fat (1.1 g sat.); 1.8 g carbo (0.1 g fiber); 20 mg sodium; 18 mg chol.

Gianduia Pastry Cream

PREP AND COOK TIME: About 35 minutes

MAKES: About 1½ cups

> ½ cup **hazelnuts**
>
> 3 tablespoons **hazelnut-flavor liqueur**
>
> ⅓ cup **sugar**
>
> 1 tablespoon **cornstarch**
>
> ⅔ cup **milk**
>
> 1 **large egg** yolk
>
> 3 ounces **semisweet chocolate**, chopped (about ½ cup)
>
> ⅓ cup **whipping cream**

1. Bake hazelnuts in an 8- to 9-inch pan in a 350° oven until dark gold under skins, about 15 minutes. Pour onto a towel and let stand until cool enough to touch, about 5 minutes. Rub nuts in towel to remove loose skins. Lift nuts from towel; discard skins.

2. In a blender or food processor, whirl nuts and liqueur to a smooth paste, scraping container sides often. Make sure all chunks are ground; they clog the pastry bag tip.

3. In a 1½- to 2-quart pan, mix sugar with cornstarch. Add milk and stir over high heat until boiling. Remove from heat, add egg yolk, and stir to blend. Rub mixture through a fine strainer into a bowl; discard residue. Add chocolate to bowl and stir until melted. Add hazelnut mixture and stir to blend. Nest bowl in ice water and stir often until pastry cream is cool, about 12 minutes.

4. In a bowl with a mixer on high speed, whip cream until it holds soft peaks. Fold into pastry cream.

Per tablespoon: 65 cal., 55% (36 cal.) from fat; 0.9 g protein; 4 g fat (1.6 g sat.); 6.6 g carbo (0.4 g fiber); 5.2 mg sodium; 13 mg chol.

Coffee pastry cream. Follow directions for **gianduia pastry cream** (preceding), but omit hazelnuts, hazelnut-flavor liqueur, and chocolate. Increase cornstarch to 2 tablespoons and stir in 2 tablespoons **coffee-flavor liqueur** and ¼ cup **instant espresso powder** with egg yolk in step 3.

Per tablespoon: 34 cal., 38% (13 cal.) from fat; 0.5 g protein; 1.4 g fat (0.8 g sat.); 4.3 g carbo (0 g fiber); 5 mg sodium; 13 mg chol. ◆

CHICKEN, OLIVES, and corn peek from under masa in a scoop from a party-size pie.

JAMES CARRIER

A great big tamale pie

Wrapped in banana leaves, it's a crowd-dazzler

BY LINDA LAU ANUSASANANAN

In the northern part of the Huasteca region of Veracruz, Mexico, they like their tamales *big*. Crusty, yard-long banana leaf bundles filled with chicken, chili sauce, and masa bake slowly in an adobe oven, emerging as a cross between a steamed tamale and a tamale pie. A simplified crowd-size version makes a magnificent centerpiece for a fiesta of your own. Just add a spinach salad with avocado and oranges.

Giant Chicken Tamale Pie

PREP AND COOK TIME: About 2 hours to assemble, 2¾ hours to bake

NOTES: Look for frozen banana leaves in Asian markets, and dehydrated masa flour in well-stocked supermarkets and Latino grocery stores. Assemble casserole up to 1 day ahead.

MAKES: 12 to 15 servings

- 5 pounds **boned, skinned chicken thighs**
  Chipotle sauce (recipe follows)
- 1 jar (5 oz.) **Spanish-style olives,** drained
- 2 cups **frozen corn kernels**
- 3 to 4 thawed **frozen banana leaves** (15 by 24 in. each; optional)
  About 3 tablespoons **salad oil**
- 8 cups **dehydrated masa flour** (corn tortilla flour)

- 2½ tablespoons **baking powder**
  About ½ teaspoon **salt**
- 7½ cups fat-skimmed **chicken broth**
  Sour cream

1. Rinse chicken and pat dry; trim off and discard excess fat. Cut thighs in half. In a large bowl, mix chicken, 4 cups chipotle sauce, olives, and corn.

2. Rinse banana leaves and pat dry. Line a 12- by 17-inch roasting pan with 2 or 3 banana leaves so they extend above entire pan rim by 2 to 3 inches (if leaves aren't large enough, or if they split, overlap smaller pieces). Or omit leaves and rub pan with 1 tablespoon oil.

3. In another large bowl, mix masa flour with baking powder and ½ teaspoon salt. Add broth and mix until evenly moistened. Spread a ¼-inch-thick layer of masa dough over bottom and up sides of pan (using about 5 cups).

4. Arrange chicken mixture evenly in pan and spread level.

5. Drop remaining masa dough in small dollops evenly over chicken mixture; gently spread to cover filling, sealing masa at pan rim. Drizzle top with 3 tablespoons oil, and with your fingertips, spread to coat surface. Fold leaf edges over masa and cover top with another banana leaf. If making up to 1 day ahead, seal pan with foil and chill. Also cover and chill remaining chili sauce.

6. Bake, covered with foil, in a 350° oven for 2 hours (2½ hours if chilled).

Remove foil; leave banana leaf in place (if used). Continue baking until masa is firm when pressed and a thermometer inserted in center of casserole registers 180° to 185°, about 45 minutes longer. Let stand at least 20 minutes.

7. Heat remaining chili sauce in a microwave-safe bowl in a microwave oven at full power (100%) until steaming, about 3 minutes, or stir in a 2- to 3-quart pan over low heat until hot, about 5 minutes. Pour into a serving bowl.

8. Lift banana leaf off top of casserole. Cut into portions and lift out with a wide spatula or use a large spoon to scoop to bottom of casserole. Add sour cream, salt, and extra chili sauce to taste.

Per serving: 623 cal., 20% (126 cal.) from fat; 44 g protein; 14 g fat (2.4 g sat.); 86 g carbo (6.5 g fiber); 2,351 mg sodium; 126 mg chol.

Chipotle Sauce

PREP AND COOK TIME: About 30 minutes

NOTES: If making sauce up to 3 days ahead, cover and chill. Look for canned chipotle chilies in Mexican markets and well-stocked supermarkets.

MAKES: About 5½ cups

- 2 teaspoons **salad oil**
- 1 **onion** (½ lb. total), peeled and chopped
- 4 cloves **garlic,** peeled and minced
- 1 tablespoon **dried oregano**
- 1½ teaspoons **cumin seed**
- ¼ teaspoon **ground allspice**
- 4 to 6 **canned chipotle chilies in sauce**
- 2 cans (28-oz. size and 10-oz. size; 4¾ cups total) **red chili** or enchilada **sauce**
- 2 cans (6 oz. each) **tomato paste**
  Salt

1. In a 3- to 4-quart pan over medium-high heat, frequently stir oil, onion, and garlic until onion is lightly browned, 8 to 10 minutes. Add oregano, cumin, and allspice and stir until fragrant, about 30 seconds. Remove from heat.

2. Meanwhile, in a blender, purée chipotles (for less heat, remove seeds), small can (10 oz.) chili sauce, and tomato paste until smooth. Add to onion mixture.

3. Add remaining can (28 oz.) chili sauce to onion-chipotle mixture and stir to blend well. Season to taste with salt.

Per ¼ cup: 100 cal., 8.1% (8.1 cal.) from fat; 2.6 g protein; 0.9 g fat (0.1 g sat.); 22 g carbo (0.9 g fiber); 1,111 mg sodium; 0 mg chol. ◆

Celebration roasts

Two classics accommodate an elegant dinner for 4 or a feast for 18

BY ELAINE JOHNSON
PHOTOGRAPHS BY CARIN KRASNER

■ A beautiful roast is pure tabletop drama. Two of the grandest of all, the Wellington and the crown—both retro icons of dinner-party chic—are back in vogue. For a contemporary twist, scale them to an intimate group instead of a crowd: Wellington done with a petite pork tenderloin, or a crown of lamb ribs, makes an elegant centerpiece for a small party. However, the traditional beef Wellington and crown roast of pork are still absolute showstoppers for a throng.

The good news is that these roasts couldn't be easier to prepare. In the case of the Wellingtons, all assembly can be done ahead so the roasts stand ready to bake and serve. The crowns only need to be popped into the oven.

Beauty has its price, of course—typically $50 to $75 for the large roasts. Protect your investment with a reliable thermometer; cook the meat just to the recommended temperature.

Moroccan Crown Lamb Roast

PREP AND COOK TIME: About 1 hour, plus 3 hours to marinate

NOTES: Order 2 fat-trimmed lamb rib roasts, 9 bones each. Have the backbones cut off for easy carving, roasts joined to make a crown, and, if desired, ends of rib bones trimmed. If starting up to 1 day ahead, chill meat in marinade (step 2).

MAKES: 6 to 9 servings

- 1 **crown lamb roast** (18 ribs total, about 3½ lb.; see notes)
- 1 tablespoon grated **tangerine** peel (orange part only)
- ½ cup **tangerine juice**
- ⅓ cup chopped **fresh cilantro**
- 3 tablespoons **lemon juice**
- 2 tablespoons minced **fresh ginger**
- 1 tablespoon **ground cumin**
- 1 tablespoon **paprika**
- 1 tablespoon minced **garlic**
- 1 teaspoon **salt**
- **Tangerine rice** (recipe follows)

1. Rinse meat and pat dry.

2. In a deep bowl, combine tangerine peel, tangerine juice, cilantro, lemon juice, ginger, cumin, paprika, garlic, and salt. Add meat; turn to coat. Cover and chill at least 3 hours or up to 1 day, basting meat occasionally.

3. Lift meat from bowl; reserve marinade. Set roast, bone tips up, in a shallow 10- by 15-inch pan.

4. Bake in a 450° oven until a thermometer inserted horizontally through roast into center of thickest part reads 150° for rare, 35 to 40 minutes, or 155° for medium-rare, 40 to 45 minutes; if areas of the roast begin to get too dark, drape with foil.

5. With 2 wide spatulas, transfer roast to a platter and let rest 15 to 20 minutes. Mound some of the tangerine rice in center of roast; put remainder in a bowl. Cut between ribs to serve.

Per serving lamb: 233 cal., 50% (117 cal.) from fat; 26 g protein; 13 g fat (4.7 g sat.); 0.8 g carbo (0 g fiber); 144 mg sodium; 87 mg chol.

Tangerine rice. Measure reserved **lamb marinade** (step 3, preceding) and add enough fat-skimmed **chicken broth** (about 2¼ cups) to make 3 cups total. Rinse 1½ cups **basmati rice** in cool water, changing frequently, until water is clear; drain rice. Put rice in a 4- to 5-quart pan and add marinade mixture. Bring to a boil over high heat. Cover, reduce heat, and simmer until rice is tender to bite, 15 to 20 minutes, stirring occasionally. Whack 1 package

CROWN ROAST OF LAMB—two rib sections, trimmed and tied—takes little effort to cook and provides a royal spectacle. Tangerine rice is the jewel in the crown.

(10 oz.) **frozen petite peas** on a counter to break apart. Stir peas and ½ cup thinly sliced **green onions,** including tops, into rice. Cook until peas are hot, about 1 minute.

Per serving rice: 252 cal., 5.2% (13 cal.) from fat; 11 g protein; 1.4 g fat (0 g sat.); 55 g carbo (2.7 g fiber); 285 mg sodium; 0 mg chol.

Tangerine Crown Pork Roast

PREP AND COOK TIME: About 2½ hours, plus 3 hours to marinate

NOTES: Order 2 pork loins, 9 bones each. Have the backbones cut off for easy carving, and the roasts tied together to make a crown.

MAKES: 18 servings

Follow directions for **Moroccan crown lamb roast** (page 324), but instead of the crown lamb roast, use 1 **crown pork loin roast** (18 ribs total, about 10 lb.; see notes), fat-trimmed. In marinade (step 2), omit the cilantro, lemon juice, cumin, paprika, garlic, and salt. Add ½ cup **soy sauce** and ¼ cup **honey** to the tangerine peel, tangerine juice, and ginger.

Bake (step 4) in a 350° oven until a thermometer inserted horizontally through the middle of the roast into the center of the thickest part reads 155°, 2 to 2¼ hours.

Meanwhile, use reserved marinade to make **tangerine rice** (preceding), but add enough fat-skimmed **chicken broth** (about 4½ cups) to make 6 cups total liquid, and use 3 cups **basmati rice.** Cook in a 5- to 6-quart pan, and increase **green onions** to 1 cup.

Per serving pork: 295 cal., 40% (117 cal.) from fat; 40 g protein; 13 g fat (4.9 g sat.); 1.4 g carbo (0 g fiber); 187 mg sodium; 112 mg chol.

Cabernet Beef Wellington

PREP AND COOK TIME: About 1¾ hours, plus 4 hours to chill

NOTES: Up to 1 day ahead, roast meat and cook mushrooms; chill separately, airtight. Up to 4 hours ahead, wrap meat in pastry; cover and chill. Bake just before serving; meat reheats but doesn't cook further. To serve sauce hot, make while the roast rests; otherwise, make up to 2 hours ahead and let stand at room temperature.

MAKES: 12 servings

- 1 **beef tenderloin** (about 4 lb.), fat-trimmed

  About 1 tablespoon **olive oil**

  Salt and **pepper**
- 1 pound **mushrooms**
- ¼ cup **Cabernet Sauvignon** or other dry red wine
- 2 tablespoons **butter** or margarine
- 2 tablespoons minced **shallots**
- ¼ teaspoon **ground nutmeg**
- 1 package (14- or 17.3-oz. size) thawed **frozen puff pastry**
- 1 **large egg** yolk

  Watercress sprigs, rinsed and crisped

  Cabernet béarnaise sauce (recipe follows)

1. Rinse beef and pat dry. If tenderloin tapers, fold tip under to make roast uniformly thick. Tie crosswise at 2-inch intervals with cotton string to form a compact roll. Rub meat with oil and sprinkle with salt and pepper. Set on a rack in a shallow 10- by 15-inch pan.

2. Roast meat in a 425° oven until a thermometer inserted in center of thickest part reaches 120° (very rare), about 40 minutes, or to your taste.

3. Transfer meat to a rimmed plate and let cool 20 minutes. Add meat juices and ¼ cup water to roasting pan and scrape drippings free; pour into a small container, cover, and chill. Cover roast and chill until cold, at least 4 hours.

4. Meanwhile, rinse mushrooms, trim off and discard discolored stem ends, and mince. In a 10- to 12-inch frying pan over medium-high heat, frequently stir mushrooms, wine, butter, shallots, and nutmeg until liquid is evaporated and mushrooms are browned, 20 to 25 minutes. Let cool, about 15 minutes.

5. Unfold pastry on a lightly floured

PUFF PASTRY blanket around beef Wellington encloses a succulent layer of sautéed mushrooms—a double match for Cabernet béarnaise sauce.

3. Turn heat under butter to high and heat to 230° (foam begins to brown), about 5 minutes.

4. Put egg yolks in a blender and whirl at high speed; add shallot mixture, then gradually pour in butter, adding it all in about 10 seconds. Stir in lemon juice to taste. Serve hot or at room temperature.

Per tablespoon: 95 cal., 92% (87 cal.) from fat; 0.7 g protein; 9.7 g fat (5.7 g sat.); 0.5 g carbo (0 g fiber); 91 mg sodium; 63 mg chol.

Sake-Shiitake Pork Wellington

PREP AND COOK TIME: About 1¼ hours, plus 1 hour to chill

NOTES: Make up to 1 day ahead, as directed for beef Wellington (page 325).

MAKES: 4 servings

1. Trim fat from 1 **pork tenderloin** (about 1 lb.). Rinse meat, pat dry, and fold tip under to make roast evenly thick. Tie at 2-inch intervals with cotton string. Rub with 1 teaspoon **olive oil** and sprinkle with **salt** and **pepper.**

2. In a 10- to 12-inch ovenproof nonstick frying pan over high heat, turn meat to brown all sides, about 4 minutes total.

3. Put pan with meat in a 450° oven. Bake until a thermometer inserted into center of thickest part reads 150°, 5 to 8 minutes. Let cool 20 minutes; cover and chill until cold, at least 1 hour.

4. Trim and discard tough stems from ¼ pound **fresh shiitake mushrooms;** rinse caps and finely chop. In a 10- to 12-inch frying pan over medium-high heat, frequently stir mushrooms, 2 tablespoons **sake,** 1 tablespoon minced **shallots,** and 1 tablespoon **butter** or olive oil until mushrooms are lightly browned, about 10 minutes. Let cool, about 20 minutes.

5. Unfold ½ package (14- or 17.3-oz. size) thawed **frozen puff pastry.** Cut a ½-inch-wide strip off 1 edge and reserve. Roll pastry into a neat rectangle 1½ inches longer than the roast and 1½ inches wider than its circumference.

6. Follow directions for **Cabernet beef Wellington,** steps 6 through 9, to wrap, decorate, egg-glaze, and bake pork.

7. As meat bakes, make sauce: In a 10- to 12-inch frying pan, combine 1 tablespoon minced **shallots,** 3 tablespoons **seasoned rice vinegar,** ¼ cup **sake,** and ½ cup **whipping cream.** Boil over high heat, stirring often, until reduced to ½ cup, 8 to 10 minutes. Serve hot.

Per serving: 578 cal., 56% (324 cal.) from fat; 29 g protein; 36 g fat (12 g sat.); 30 g carbo (1.1 g fiber); 445 mg sodium; 115 mg chol. ◆

board; if there are 2 sheets, stack them. Cut a ½-inch-wide strip off 1 edge and reserve. Roll pastry into a neat rectangle 2 inches longer than the roast and 2 inches wider than its circumference.

6. Gently pat mushroom mixture over pastry up to 1 inch from edges. Pat beef dry and remove string. Center roast lengthwise on pastry. Brush pastry edges with water. Using both hands, quickly lift 1 long side over meat. Repeat to lift opposite side over meat; press edges together to seal. Fold in pastry ends, overlapping to cover ends of roast; press firmly to seal. Set roast seam down in an oiled rimmed 10- by 15-inch pan.

7. On floured board, roll reserved pastry strip ⅛ inch thick. With the tip of a sharp knife or flour-dusted cookie cutters, cut out decorative shapes, such as leaves. Brush a little water onto 1 side and arrange on roast, moistened sides down; press gently to hold in place.

8. In a small bowl, beat egg yolk to blend with 1 tablespoon water. Brush mixture over pastry.

9. Bake Wellington in a 400° oven until pastry is richly browned, 25 to 30 minutes. With 2 wide spatulas, transfer roast to a platter. Let rest 15 to 20 minutes. Garnish with watercress. Cut roast crosswise into 1-inch-wide slices.

10. Serve with Cabernet béarnaise sauce and salt and pepper to taste.

Per serving beef: 472 cal., 53% (252 cal.) from fat; 35 g protein; 28 g fat (7.8 g sat.); 18 g carbo (1 g fiber); 186 mg sodium; 117 mg chol.

Cabernet Béarnaise Sauce

PREP AND COOK TIME: About 10 minutes

NOTES: This method gets the sauce hot enough to be bacteria-safe. The mixture should be smooth. If it curdles, to reconstruct, put 1 tablespoon hot water in a bowl and, whisking, pour curdled sauce into water.

MAKES: 1 cup

- ¾ cup (⅜ lb.) **butter** or margarine
- 2 tablespoons minced **shallots**
- 2 teaspoons minced **fresh tarragon** leaves or ¾ teaspoon dried tarragon
- ½ cup **Cabernet Sauvignon** or other dry red wine

  Roast drippings, fat-skimmed (preceding, step 3)

- 3 **large egg** yolks
- 1 to 2 tablespoons **lemon juice**

1. In a 1- to 1½-quart pan over low heat, melt butter and keep hot.

2. Meanwhile, in a 10- to 12-inch frying pan over high heat, boil shallots, tarragon, wine, and roast drippings, stirring often, until liquid is reduced to about ¼ cup, 5 to 7 minutes. Keep hot.

The Low-Fat Cook

HEALTHY CHOICES FOR THE ACTIVE LIFESTYLE

BY ELAINE JOHNSON

ELEGANT MERINGUE SWIRLS add peak flavor but very little fat to holiday get-togethers.

Mad about meringues

■ Ethereally crisp, meltingly sweet, and gracefully shaped—petite meringues are perfect for holiday cookie trays for these qualities alone. But the slow-baked, crunchy confections have a secret weapon that makes them invaluable during this season of overindulgence: They have almost zero fat content. You can afford to dress them up with bits of toffee or peppermint candies, almonds and bright cherry bits, coffee beans, or dots of chocolate.

With a pastry bag and tip, you can unleash your creativity as you put the squeeze on the meringue and make squiggles, swirls, poufs, wreaths, or even bulbous Michelin Man rings. Or shape the cookies with a spoon.

Marvelous Meringues

PREP AND COOK TIME: About 1¾ hours

MAKES: About 40 (1½-in.) mounds or 14 (6-in.) sticks

3 **large egg** whites

½ teaspoon **cream of tartar**

¾ cup **sugar**

½ teaspoon **vanilla**

¼ cup **toffee candy bits** or coarsely crushed peppermint candies

1. Line 2 baking sheets (each 14 by 17 in.) with cooking parchment, or butter and flour sheets.

2. In a deep bowl with mixer at high speed, whip egg whites and cream of tartar until foamy. Whip in sugar, 1 tablespoon every 30 seconds, then continue to beat until meringue holds very stiff peaks.

3. Beat in vanilla, then fold in candy. If using parchment, smear a little meringue on the underside of each corner to make it stick to baking sheets.

4. Spoon meringue into a pastry bag fitted with a ½-inch plain tip, or use a spoon to shape the mixture. Pipe or spoon 1½- to 2-inch mounds of meringue about 1 inch apart on baking sheets. Or shape meringue into straight or zigzag sticks 1 to 1½ inches wide and about 6 inches long.

5. Bake in a 200° oven until meringues are white to ivory-colored and give slightly when gently pressed, 1¼ to 1½ hours (1 to 1¼ hours in a convection oven); switch pan positions halfway through baking. Turn off heat and leave meringues in closed oven for 1 hour.

6. Slide a spatula under meringues to release. Serve, or if making ahead, store airtight up to 1 week.

Per mound: 24 cal., 19% (4.5 cal.) from fat; 0.3 g protein; 0.5 g fat (0.2 g sat.); 4.7 g carbo (0 g fiber); 13 mg sodium; 0.5 mg chol.

Spumoni Wreaths

Follow directions for **marvelous meringues** (preceding), omitting toffee. Add ½ teaspoon **almond extract.** In step 4, use a pastry bag fitted with a ½-inch fluted tip, and pipe 2½-inch-wide rings of meringue onto baking sheets.

On towels, pat dry 3 tablespoons coarsely chopped **maraschino cherries.** Arrange 3 cherry pieces in a cluster on each meringue ring. Push 2 **sliced almond** pieces (1½ tablespoons total) next to cherries, like leaves. Then continue as directed. Makes 36.

Per wreath: 21 cal., 4.3% (0.9 cal.) from fat; 0.3 g protein; 0.1 g fat (0 g sat.); 4.6 g carbo (0 g fiber); 4.7 mg sodium; 0 mg chol.

Coffee Meringues

Follow directions for **marvelous meringues**, omitting toffee. In step 3, fold 1½ tablespoons **dried instant espresso** into meringue. Shape meringue into mounds as directed, then gently press 1 **roasted coffee bean** (1 tablespoon total) onto the top of each mound. Continue as directed.

Per mound: 16 cal., 0% (0 cal.) from fat; 0.3 g protein; 0 g fat; 3.8 g carbo (0 g fiber); 4.2 mg sodium; 0 mg chol.

Chocolate Meringues

Follow directions for **marvelous meringues,** omitting toffee. In step 3, fold 3 tablespoons **unsweetened cocoa** into meringue. Shape meringue into mounds as directed, then gently press ½ teaspoon **miniature chocolate chips** (6½ tablespoons total) onto the top of each mound. Continue as directed.

Per mound: 25 cal., 18% (4.5 cal.) from fat; 0.4 g protein; 0.5 g fat (0.3 g sat.); 5.1 g carbo (0.1 g fiber); 4.3 mg sodium; 0 mg chol. ◆

TUCKER & HOSSLER

foodguide

BY JERRY ANNE DI VECCHIO

PHOTOGRAPHS BY JAMES CARRIER

Royal treat

A cake at home on a pedestal

■ When my friend Danielle entertains, she's apt to offer one of her two favorite things for dessert: chocolate—in any form—or a princess cake, an old Swedish classic. The name is fitting; that's precisely how you feel when dessert is served. And this royal cake can pull rank during the holidays. Santa would swoon if he found a wedge waiting with his glass of milk.

The smooth mantle of marzipan that wraps a princess cake like a gift is probably what makes most cooks assume it's difficult to make. Nothing could be further from the delicious truth. This very manageable dessert is assembled like building blocks. And it has the potential for a wide variety of flavor shifts. Bake one cake, split it, moisten the layers with a light syrup (any flavor you like, with or without liqueur), and fill them generously with a fluffy cream (good enough for dessert on its own, flavored as you like). The easiest part looks the hardest: the marzipan wrap (the Swedes like to tint it pale green). Just roll out the marzipan like a pie crust and fit it onto the cake like a second skin—with that spandex cling.

Princess Gâteau

PREP AND CHILL TIME: With all the ingredients ready to use, about 1½ hours

NOTES: You can assemble the cake up to 2 days ahead. The cake and syrup can be made 1 day before assembling; cover separately and store at room temperature. Prepare filling just before you put the cake together.

MAKES: 8 to 10 servings

- **Sponge cake** (recipe follows)
- **Orange syrup** (recipe follows)
- **Cream filling** (recipe follows)
- 2 packages (7 oz. each) **marzipan**

1. With a long, serrated knife, slice cake in half horizontally. Place bottom half, cut side up, on a wide plate. Moisten evenly with ⅔ of the orange syrup.

2. Spoon all the cream filling onto bottom cake half; if it flows over the sides, set cake in the refrigerator for a few minutes until filling is firm enough to stay in place, then scrape it back on top.

3. Set remaining cake half, cut side down, on filling, aligning neatly with bottom half. With a short spatula held upright against cake sides, smooth filling into crevices between the layers. Cover airtight with a large inverted bowl and chill at least 1 hour.

4. With a thin skewer, pierce top of cake (but not filling) at ½-inch intervals, then slowly spoon remaining orange syrup over cake, letting it soak in. Cover cake with bowl again and chill while you roll out marzipan.

5. With your hands, knead marzipan into a single lump, then pat into a ¼- to ½-inch-thick round, pressing edges to keep them smooth. With a rolling pin, roll marzipan between 2 sheets of plastic wrap (keep smooth) to make a neat round 14 to 15 inches wide (lift plastic occasionally to press cracking edges together, then lay plastic back on top).

6. Pull off top piece of plastic wrap. Supporting marzipan with bottom piece of plastic wrap, invert it over cake, center, lay it on cake, and peel off wrap. Gently press marzipan neatly against sides of cake and plate rim around cake. With a knife or fluted ravioli cutter, trim marzipan flush with cake base on plate. Remove scraps and shape into decorations, such as the ribbon shown above (see box at right); arrange on cake. Serve cake, or cover with inverted bowl and chill.

Per serving: 338 cal., 32% (108 cal.) from fat; 6 g protein; 12 g fat (7 g sat.); 47 g carbo (0.3 g fiber); 130 mg sodium; 99 mg chol.

What is marzipan?

Marzipan is a confection made with blanched almonds, ground into a fine paste, and blended with sugar syrup and, maybe, egg whites. As malleable as clay, it's often modeled into little animals and vegetables. They're so cute, you usually don't want to eat them until they're dried out—and then you won't want to. When fresh, however, marzipan is tasty and easy to handle. • For smooth, flat pieces, roll marzipan between sheets of plastic wrap (keep them smooth). Some cooks use powdered sugar instead of plastic wrap to prevent sticking, but plastic achieves a cleaner look.

Sponge Cake

PREP AND COOK TIME: About 35 minutes

MAKES: A 9-inch cake; 8 to 10 servings

> About 2 tablespoons **butter** or margarine
>
> 1 cup **all-purpose flour**
>
> 1 teaspoon **baking powder**
>
> $\frac{1}{2}$ cup **low-fat milk**
>
> 2 **large eggs**
>
> 1 cup **sugar**
>
> 1 teaspoon **vanilla**

1. Lightly butter a 9-inch round cake pan with removable rim.

2. In a bowl, mix flour and baking powder.

3. In a 1- or 2-cup glass measure in a microwave oven at full power (100%), or in a 1- to $1\frac{1}{2}$-quart pan over medium heat, warm milk with 2 tablespoons butter until butter is melted, stirring occasionally, 1 to 2 minutes.

4. In another bowl with a mixer on high speed, whip eggs, sugar, and vanilla until foamy. Add flour and milk mixtures. Stir to mix, then beat until well blended. Scrape batter into buttered pan.

5. Bake in a 350° oven until cake edge just begins to pull from pan sides and top springs back when lightly pressed in the center, 20 to 25 minutes. Invert cake onto a rack and turn rounded side up. Let cool 20 minutes. Use, or cover when cool and store at room temperature up to 1 day.

Per serving: 168 cal., 21% (35 cal.) from fat; 3 g protein; 3.9 g fat (2.1 g sat.); 30 g carbo (0.3 g fiber); 95 mg sodium; 50 mg chol.

Orange Syrup

PREP AND COOK TIME: About 25 minutes

MAKES: About 1 cup

In a $1\frac{1}{2}$- to 2-quart pan over high heat, bring to a boil $1\frac{1}{4}$ cups **orange juice**, $\frac{1}{4}$ cup **sugar**, $\frac{1}{4}$ cup **water**, 2 tablespoons **lemon juice**, 1 teaspoon **coriander seed**, and 1 teaspoon grated **orange** peel. Boil until reduced to $\frac{3}{4}$ cup, 10 to 15 minutes. Let cool at least 10 minutes. Pour through a fine strainer into a bowl; discard residue. Add $\frac{1}{4}$ cup **rum**, orange-flavor liqueur, or more orange juice.

TINT AND SHAPE IT

Add food coloring, a few drops at a time, to a lump of the naturally ivory-color marzipan; knead in your hands or on a board until the color is evenly distributed. For contoured ribbons, gently bend marzipan strips with your fingers into desired shapes. For figures, shape small pieces and press together.

Per tablespoon: 29 cal., 0% (0 cal.) from fat; 0.1 g protein; 0 g fat; 5.4 g carbo (0 g fiber); 0.7 mg sodium; 0 mg chol.

Cream Filling

PREP AND COOK TIME: About 15 minutes

MAKES: About 4 cups

1. In a $1\frac{1}{2}$- to 2-quart pan, combine $\frac{1}{4}$ cup **sugar**, $1\frac{1}{2}$ teaspoons **cornstarch**, 1 envelope **unflavored gelatin**, $1\frac{1}{2}$ cups **low-fat milk**, and 1 teaspoon grated **orange** peel.

2. In a small bowl, beat 1 **large egg** to blend; stir into milk mixture. Whisk over high heat until mixture boils, 3 to 4 minutes.

3. Immediately nest pan in ice water. Add 2 tablespoons **rum**, orange-flavor liqueur, or orange juice and stir often until mixture is cool and holds soft mounds when spooned, but is not firm, 6 to 8 minutes.

4. In a deep bowl with a mixer on high speed, beat 1 cup **whipping cream** until it holds distinct peaks. Fold cooked mixture into cream. Nest bowl in ice water and stir occasionally until mixture holds soft mounds, 3 to 5 minutes.

Per tablespoon: 19 cal., 63% (12 cal.) from fat; 0.4 g protein; 1.3 g fat (0.8 g sat.); 1.2 g carbo (0 g fiber); 5.3 mg sodium; 7.7 mg chol.

Little squirts

■ Handling a pastry bag is easy, provided you tend to a few details. Most important, keep the flow going in the right direction by twisting the top of the bag snugly down to the contents, then squeezing with steady pressure. This is no problem if you're using both hands, as is typical when decorating a cake. But when applying decorations to tiny bases, as for these classic savory cheese appetizers, you need one hand to hold the base down so the piped mixture detaches from the bag instead of lifting up the base.

The secret is to fold the twisted top down against the side of the bag, place your palm against it, then, surrounding the bag with your hand, pinch the base of the twist shut with your thumb and index finger (see

photo, near right). When you're working with one hand, the bag should not be more than half full; otherwise, the top can pop loose.

Pastry bags vary in convenience. Canvas ones need to be laundered; those with plasticized finishes can be hand-washed. Inexpensive (40 to 60 cents each) heavy-duty clear plastic bags are disposable. But with all, you can change tips midstream. Before filling the bag, insert a screw-based neck (sold in cookware stores) into the hole, fit the decorative tip over its narrow end, and secure.

Liptauer Appetizers

PREP TIME: About 25 minutes
NOTES: For the smoothest flow, liptauer mixture should contain no particles.
MAKES: 48 pieces; 8 servings
1. In a bowl, beat 1 package (8 oz.) **cream cheese** to blend with 2 tablespoons

low-fat milk, 2 teaspoons **anchovy paste**, and 1 teaspoon **paprika**. Grate 1 tablespoon **onion** and rub through a fine strainer into cheese mixture. Stir to blend. Put cheese mixture in a pastry bag with a star tip.
2. Cut ¼ pound **thin-sliced firm-textured, dense pumpernickel**, rye, or other dark **bread** into 48 equal pieces. Arrange on a platter.
3. Twist bag top tightly down to filling, fold top down against bag, and grasp bag in one hand to hold top in place (see instructions pre-

ceding). Squeeze to press about 1 teaspoon of the cheese mixture onto each square of bread, holding bread with the other hand. Release pressure on bag slightly and lift straight up to detach bag from cheese.
4. Sprinkle appetizers lightly with **caraway seed** (about 1 teaspoon total), dot each with a drained **caper,** and sprinkle with chopped **fresh chives.**

Per piece: 24 cal., 67% (16 cal.) from fat; 0.6 g protein; 1.8 g fat (1 g sat.); 1.3 g carbo (0.1 g fiber); 47 mg sodium; 5.3 mg chol.

Emergency fare

EASY SUPPER

■ This savory pie—which looks impressive with very little effort on the cook's part—is one of my hip-pocket solutions when an unpremeditated urge to invite guests for dinner strikes. Except for the sausages, the ingredients are kitchen staples.

Sausage Pie

PREP AND COOK TIME: 45 minutes
NOTES: If you don't have green onions, sprinkle the pie with a couple of tablespoons of chopped parsley, watercress, fresh basil leaves—even lettuce—to give the dish a fresh-looking finish. Serve with Dijon mustard and sour cream or plain yogurt.
MAKES: 6 servings

1 **onion** (½ lb.), peeled and diced
1 tablespoon **butter** or olive oil
¾ cup **low-fat milk**
¾ cup **all-purpose flour**
3 **large eggs**
1 to 1¼ pounds cooked **kielbasa** (Polish) **sausages,** cut into 3-inch chunks
½ cup chopped **green onions** (including tops)
Salt

1. In a shallow 2-quart pan or a 10-inch frying pan over medium-high heat, frequently stir diced onion and butter until onion is limp, about 5 minutes.

2. Meanwhile, in a bowl with a whisk, or in a blender, mix milk, flour, and eggs until smooth.

3. Lay sausages in center of pan with onions. Pour milk mixture evenly over meat.

4. Bake in a 425° oven until egg mixture is puffed, very crisp, and richly browned, 35 to 40 minutes (25 to 30 minutes in a 400° convection oven). Remove sausage pie from oven and sprinkle with green onions. Scoop portions onto plates and add salt to taste.

Per serving: 374 cal., 60% (225 cal.) from fat; 16 g protein; 25 g fat (9.7 g sat.); 19 g carbo (1.1 g fiber); 883 mg sodium; 163 mg chol. ◆

Mashed potatoes, please

The ultimate comfort food takes well to lively seasonings

BY LINDA LAU ANUSASANANAN

Like so many other comfort foods, mashed potatoes need to be *just so* to do their job—to make you feel good, inside and out. But, chameleon-like, they can conform to any taste or mood.

Like yours fluffy? Choose brown, rough-skinned russets, which can take a beating. The starch in potatoes is contained in tiny packets called potato buds. When the packets are broken, the starch oozes out and the potatoes become gluey. Russets have tough packets that resist breaking.

Prefer the flavor and denser texture of thin-skinned (white or red) or golden-fleshed varieties? Although they have more delicate potato buds, they can be mashed, if you're gentle.

Use a potato masher or a ricer (it looks like a giant garlic press) for the best results with any potato. An electric mixer also works well, but avoid overbeating thin-skinned varieties. And don't use a food processor on any potato unless you want glue.

Add liquid and fat for a soft, creamy texture; the kinds and amounts you use determine how rich the dish is. Then rev it up with seasonings to fit your whim.

Mashed Potatoes, As You Like Them

PREP AND COOK TIME: About 45 minutes

NOTES: Other liquids you can use: half-and-half (light cream), buttermilk (be careful—it curdles if boiled), vegetable broth, or the potato cooking water. Other fats and cheeses: extra-virgin olive oil, margarine, or herb-flavor Boursin or Rondelé cheese.

MAKES: 7 to 8 cups; 7 or 8 servings

- 3 pounds **russet**, Yukon Gold, or thin-skinned red or white **potatoes**
- 1¼ to 1¾ cups **milk** or fat-skimmed chicken broth (see notes)
- 2 to 8 tablespoons (¹⁄₁₆ to ¼ lb.) **butter,** regular or nonfat sour cream, cream cheese, or neufchâtel (light cream) cheese, at room temperature (see notes)

  Seasoning choices (optional; suggestions follow)

  Salt and **pepper**

1. In a covered 5- to 6-quart pan over high heat, bring 1 quart water to a boil.

2. Peel and rinse potatoes (or if desired, scrub potatoes and leave skin on). Cut potatoes into 1-inch chunks.

3. Add potatoes to boiling water, cover, and return to a boil, 3 to 4 minutes. Reduce heat to medium and simmer until potatoes mash easily, 8 to 10 minutes.

4. Meanwhile, heat milk or other liquid in a microwave-safe container in a microwave oven at full power (100%) just until steaming (don't boil). Or warm in a 1- to 1½-quart pan over medium heat.

5. Drain liquid from potatoes (save liquid if using instead of milk). Mash potatoes with a potato masher or a mixer; or press (peeled only), a portion at a time, through a ricer into another pan. Add butter or other fat, seasoning choices, and hot milk, a little at a time, and mix or beat until potatoes have desired consistency. Season to taste with salt and pepper. If potatoes have cooled, stir occasionally over low heat until hot; or warm in a microwave oven.

Per serving: 172 cal., 23% (40 cal.) from fat; 4.2 g protein; 4.4 g fat (2.6 g sat.); 29 g carbo (2.6 g fiber); 60 mg sodium; 13 mg chol.

Seasoning choices

Roasted garlic. Cut 2 heads **garlic** (3 oz. each) in half crosswise. Brush cut sides generously with **olive oil** and set, cut side down, in an 8- to 9-inch square pan. Bake in a 350° oven until garlic is golden brown on bottom and oozing sticky juices, about 35 minutes (about 30 minutes in a convection oven). Slip a thin spatula under garlic to release from pan. Pluck or squeeze cloves from peel and add to potatoes in step 5 (above).

Per serving of potatoes: 210 cal., 24% (50 cal.) from fat; 5.4 g protein; 5.6 g fat (2.7 g sat.); 35 g carbo (2.9 g fiber); 63 mg sodium; 13 mg chol.

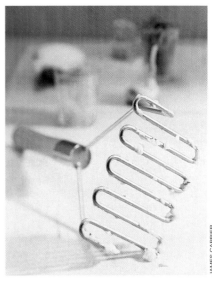

MANUAL OR MECHANICAL, the best way to mash potatoes is with flavor.

Green onion. Add 1 cup minced **green onions** (including tops) to milk in step 4, and heat, stirring occasionally, until onions are wilted, about 5 minutes. Add to potatoes in step 5.

Per serving of potatoes: 176 cal., 23% (41 cal.) from fat; 4.4 g protein; 4.5 g fat (2.6 g sat.); 30 g carbo (2.9 g fiber); 62 mg sodium; 13 mg chol.

Cheese. Add 2 cups (½ lb.) **shredded sharp cheddar cheese** or 1 cup (¼ lb.) crumbled gorgonzola or grated parmesan cheese to potatoes in step 5.

Per serving of potatoes: 287 cal., 44% (126 cal.) from fat; 11 g protein; 14 g fat (8.6 g sat.); 30 g carbo (2.6 g fiber); 236 mg sodium; 43 mg chol.

Provençal. Add ¼ cup chopped **parsley,** 1 or 2 cloves **garlic** (peeled and pressed or minced), 1 teaspoon minced **fresh thyme** leaves or dried thyme, and 1 teaspoon grated **lemon** peel to potatoes in step 5.

Per serving of potatoes: 174 cal., 23% (40 cal.) from fat; 4.3 g protein; 4.4 g fat (2.6 g sat.); 30 g carbo (2.6 g fiber); 61 mg sodium; 13 mg chol.

Chipotle chili. Add 2 or 3 finely minced **canned chipotle chilies in sauce** (wearing rubber gloves, remove seeds for less heat) to potatoes in step 5.

Per serving of potatoes: 176 cal., 23% (41 cal.) from fat; 4.2 g protein; 4.6 g fat (2.6 g sat.); 30 g carbo (2.6 g fiber); 91 mg sodium; 13 mg chol.

Wasabi. Add 2 to 3 teaspoons **prepared wasabi** to potatoes in step 5.

Per serving of potatoes: 173 cal., 23% (40 cal.) from fat; 4.3 g protein; 4.4 g fat (2.6 g sat.); 29 g carbo (2.6 g fiber); 60 mg sodium; 13 mg chol. ◆

Kitchen Cabinet

READERS' RECIPES TESTED IN SUNSET'S KITCHENS

BY LINDA LAU ANUSASANANAN

HOLIDAY COLORS revel in a radicchio and spinach salad.

Spinach and Radicchio Salad with Grapefruit

Barbara Diamond, Portland, Oregon

Although Barbara Diamond originally created this salad to pack for a ready-to-eat dinner exchange program her family shares with their neighbors, the Sugerman/Byrds, it's too colorful to keep under wraps. Consider serving the salad as the opening course for a holiday meal.

PREP AND COOK TIME: About 45 minutes

MAKES: About 6 servings

- ¼ cup **pine nuts**
- 2 **ruby** or pink **grapefruit** (1½ lb. total)
- ¼ cup **olive oil**
- 2 tablespoons **balsamic vinegar**
- 4 cups (4 to 5 oz.) **baby spinach leaves,** rinsed and crisped
- 4 cups (5 to 6 oz.) bite-size pieces **radicchio leaves,** rinsed and crisped
- ½ cup **pitted prunes,** cut into thin slivers
- 3 tablespoons thinly sliced **green onions** (including tops)
- **Salt** and **pepper**

1. In a 6- to 8-inch frying pan over medium heat, stir or shake pine nuts until golden, about 5 minutes. Cool.

2. With a small, sharp knife, cut peel and white membrane from grapefruit. Over a bowl, cut between inner membranes and fruit, lifting out segments; reserve juice for another use.

3. In a wide bowl, whisk oil with vinegar. Add spinach, radicchio, prunes, and green onions; arrange grapefruit and nuts on salad. Mix, adding salt and pepper to taste.

Per serving: 171 cal., 63% (108 cal.) from fat; 3 g protein; 12 g fat (1.7 g sat.); 16 g carbo (2.7 g fiber); 22 mg sodium; 0 mg chol.

Ginger Carrot Soup

Ruth P. Kurisu, Laguna Niguel, California

"My neighbors have three bunnies that eat carrot tops, but not carrots," writes Ruth Kurisu. As a result, she is constantly inventing recipes to keep the carrot inventory in check.

PREP AND COOK TIME: About 1 hour

MAKES: 8 to 10 servings

- 2 tablespoons **butter** or margarine
- 2 **onions** (¾ lb. total), peeled and chopped
- 6 cups fat-skimmed **chicken broth**
- 2 pounds **carrots,** peeled and sliced
- 2 tablespoons grated **fresh ginger**
- 1 cup **whipping cream**
- ½ cup **cognac** (optional)
  Salt and **white pepper**
  Sour cream and **parsley sprigs**

1. In a 5- to 6-quart pan over medium-high heat, stir butter and onions often until onions are limp, about 3 minutes. Add broth, carrots, and ginger. Cover and bring to a boil. Reduce heat and simmer until carrots are tender when pierced, 15 to 20 minutes.

2. In a blender, whirl mixture a portion at a time until smooth. Return to pan and add cream. Stir over high heat until hot. Mix in cognac. For a smoother flavor, bring soup to a boil. Add salt and pepper to taste.

3. Ladle into bowls. Garnish with dollops of sour cream and parsley sprigs.

Per serving: 158 cal., 56% (89 cal.) from fat; 6.5 g protein; 9.9 g fat (6.1 g sat.); 12 g carbo (3.1 g fiber); 106 mg sodium; 33 mg chol.

Chocolate Pancakes

Laura Yeager, Lacey, Washington

In her worldwide travels as an army officer and military spouse, Laura Yeager reports no sightings of chocolate pancakes like the ones she makes. Her kids love them topped with whipped cream plus berry syrup and fresh fruit.

PREP AND COOK TIME: About 30 minutes

MAKES: 8 pancakes; 4 servings

- ¼ cup **sugar**
- ¼ cup **unsweetened cocoa**
- 2 teaspoons **baking powder**
- ¼ teaspoon **salt**
- 1 cup **all-purpose flour**
- 1 **large egg**
- 1 cup **milk**
  About 3 tablespoons melted **butter** or margarine

½ teaspoon **vanilla**

½ cup **miniature semisweet chocolate chips**

Raspberry syrup

Raspberries, rinsed, or sliced bananas

Sweetened **whipped cream**

1. In a bowl, stir sugar, cocoa, baking powder, and salt until well blended. Add flour and mix.

2. In a small bowl, beat egg to blend with milk, 3 tablespoons butter, and vanilla.

3. Add egg mixture and chocolate chips to flour mixture; stir just until evenly moistened.

4. Place a nonstick griddle or 10- to 12-inch nonstick frying pan over medium heat. When hot, lightly butter if desired. Spoon ¼-cup portions of batter onto griddle, about ½ inch apart. Cook pancakes until edges look dry and bubbles on surface begin to pop, about 3 minutes each. Turn pancakes over and lightly brown other side. Transfer to a plate and keep warm; repeat to cook remaining pancakes.

5. Serve pancakes with syrup, berries or bananas, and whipped cream to taste.

Per serving: 327 cal., 41% (135 cal.) from fat; 7 g protein; 15 g fat (8.7 g sat.); 46 g carbo (2 g fiber); 418 mg sodium; 68 mg chol.

Cal-Mex Chicken Soufflé Casserole

Chuck Allen, Cathedral City, California

Don't let the word *soufflé* give you a sinking feeling about this hearty main-dish casserole. Chuck Allen cloaks a flavorful blend of chicken, chilies, and cheese with a fluffy mantle of whipped eggs that are reminiscent of the coating on chiles rellenos.

PREP AND COOK TIME: About 1 hour

MAKES: 6 to 8 servings

4 cups bite-size pieces **boned, skinned cooked chicken** or turkey

1 cup (¼ lb.) **shredded cheddar cheese**

1 cup (¼ lb.) **shredded jack cheese**

1 can (4 oz.) **diced green chilies**

1 jar (4 oz.) **diced pimientos,** drained

¼ cup **all-purpose flour**

1 can (12 oz.) **evaporated milk**

4 **large eggs,** separated

CHICKEN, CHILIES, and cheese merge under a soufflé-like blanket.

JAMES CARRIER

About ¼ teaspoon **salt**

Green chili salsa

1. Evenly distribute chicken pieces in a buttered 9- by 13-inch casserole.

2. In a bowl, mix cheddar cheese, jack cheese, green chilies, and pimientos. Reserve ¼ cup of the mixture; sprinkle remainder evenly over chicken.

3. In small bowl, mix flour and ½ cup evaporated milk until smooth, then stir in remaining milk. Add egg yolks and ¼ teaspoon salt; mix to blend.

4. In a deep bowl with a mixer on high speed, whip egg whites until they hold stiff peaks. Add whites to yolk mixture; fold to blend well. Spread mixture evenly over chicken. Sprinkle evenly with remaining cheese mixture.

5. Bake casserole in a 325° oven until well browned, 40 to 45 minutes. Let stand 5 to 10 minutes. Scoop out portions; add salt and salsa to taste.

Per serving: 364 cal., 52% (189 cal.) from fat; 34 g protein; 21 g fat (9.9 g sat.); 9.4 g carbo (0.3 g fiber); 467 mg sodium; 213 mg chol.

Apple-Almond Tart

Karen Callaghan, Sonoita, Arizona

While she was in the restaurant business, Karen Callaghan developed this jam-glazed apple tart. Now she serves it to complement one of her son's wines, Callaghan Vineyards Riesling.

PREP AND COOK TIME: About 1¾ hours

MAKES: 8 or 9 servings

½ cup **slivered almonds**

1¼ cups **all-purpose flour**

1 cup plus 1 tablespoon **sugar**

¾ cup (⅜ lb.) **butter** or margarine

1 **large egg** yolk

3 **large eggs**

2 **Granny Smith apples** (1 lb. total)

3 tablespoons **apricot jam**

2 tablespoons **orange-flavor liqueur**

1. In a 325° oven in an 8- to 9-inch-wide pan, bake almonds until golden, 8 to 10 minutes; shaking the pan or stirring the nuts occasionally. Pour from pan and let cool.

2. Meanwhile, in a food processor or bowl, mix flour and 1 tablespoon sugar. Add ½ cup butter, cut into small pieces. Whirl or rub with your fingers until mixture forms fine crumbs. Add 1 egg yolk; whirl or mix with a fork until dough holds together. Pat into a smooth ball, then firmly press dough over bottom and up sides of a 9-inch tart pan with removable rim.

3. In food processor (unwashed), whirl almonds and 1 cup sugar until nuts are finely ground. Add remaining butter and whole eggs; whirl until smooth.

4. Peel and core apples; slice ⅛ inch thick. Overlap slices neatly in dough-lined pan. Pour nut mixture over fruit.

5. Bake in a 325° oven until crust is well browned and apples are tender when pierced, 50 to 60 minutes (1¼ hours in a 300° convection oven). Filling puffs, then settles around apples.

6. As tart bakes, in a 6- to 8-inch frying pan over medium heat, stir jam until melted; add liqueur. Spoon warm jam evenly over hot tart. Return to oven and bake until jam bubbles slightly, 3 to 5 minutes.

7. Let tart cool on a rack at least 30 minutes; remove pan rim. Serve warm or cool, cut into wedges.

Per serving: 417 cal., 47% (198 cal.) from fat; 5.9 g protein; 22 g fat (11 g sat.); 50 g carbo (1.7 g fiber); 184 mg sodium; 136 mg chol. ◆

Stretched Strudel, Sweet or Savory

PREP AND COOK TIME: About 1 hour and 10 minutes

NOTES: For a head start and a crisp crust, fill strudel 3 to 4 hours ahead; cover and chill. Uncover and bake to serve. Cover and chill any leftovers; reheat, uncovered, in a 350° oven until warm.

MAKES: 1 strudel; 12 to 18 servings

> **All-purpose flour**
>
> **Strudel dough** (recipe follows)
>
> About ½ cup (¼ lb.) melted **butter** or margarine
>
> ¼ cup **granulated sugar** or fine dried bread crumbs
>
> ⅓ cup finely chopped **roasted, salted pistachios** (optional)
>
> **Filling** (recipes follow)
>
> **Powdered sugar** (optional)

1. Cover a table (at least 3 feet wide) with a clean, smooth tablecloth. Dust the cloth lightly with flour. Dust strudel dough oval with flour and place in center of cloth. Roll dough into an 18- by 28-inch oval. It should be thin enough to almost see through.

2. Gather 2 to 4 people. Remove any sharp rings from fingers. Close your hands to form fists and, with knuckles up, slip hands under dough, meeting in the center. Working from the center out, gently and slowly ease your fists to the edge of the oval, stretching the dough as it slides over the backs of your hands. If dough tears, lay it on the table, moisten the torn edges, overlap

The art of strudel

A forgiving dough for the traditionalist to stretch, a fast filo shortcut for the harried cook—and five fine fillings

BY LINDA LAU ANUSASANANAN • PHOTOGRAPHS BY KEVIN CANDLAND

Stretching strudel dough paper-thin looks hard to do. Fortunately, things are not always as they seem. It takes only a little help (at least one extra pair of hands), time, and patience to shape traditional dough. And for those with less of all three to give, a simple filo-dough strudel is an effective alternative.

The traditional dough must be slapped around a little to make it stretchy. Paper-thin sheets of filo, on the other hand, need to be brushed with butter. Both pastries get crisp and golden when they're baked. Filled with something sweet—dried fruit and chocolate or nuts, for instance—they're lovely for dessert and wonderful for brunch. And a savory strudel, like the caraway-cheese, crab-artichoke, or curried onion version here, is an excellent offering for a special lunch or a buffet supper.

It does take time to stretch and roll, but you can do these steps ahead, then pull the strudel from the oven, warm and flaky, just before serving.

them, and press to seal. In unison, return your hands under dough to center and repeat, stretching dough evenly and smoothly as often as required to form a 24- by 36-inch oval. At the center it will be about as thin as the membrane inside an eggshell (thin enough to see through clearly—see photo on page 334); the edges will be thicker. Lay dough on table and, if needed, stretch dough gently to even out any thick spots; trim off and discard thick rim.

3. Gently brush dough with 6 tablespoons melted butter. Sprinkle 3 tablespoons sugar (for sweet filling) or bread crumbs (for savory filling) and the pistachios evenly over dough.

4. Spread filling in a 3-inch band across 1 long side of dough, about 2 inches in from the edge and the short sides. Fold short sides over ends of filling. Gently lift cloth under the filled end of dough (see photo below), guiding it forward to form a compact roll, ending seam down.

5. Carefully curve roll into a horseshoe shape and transfer it to a buttered 14- by 17-inch baking sheet. Brush roll with about 2 tablespoons butter and sprinkle with remaining sugar or crumbs.

6. Bake strudel on center rack in a 375° oven until browned and crisp, 35 to 45 minutes (30 to 40 minutes in a convection oven); a little filling may ooze out. Let cool on pan about 5 minutes, then slide onto a rack until warm or cool. If filling is sweet, sprinkle strudel with powdered sugar just before serving. With a thin, sharp knife, cut strudel into 1½-inch-wide slices.

Strudel Dough

PREP TIME: About 15 minutes, plus 20 to 40 minutes to rest

NOTES: A soft, supple dough is crucial. If it's too hard and dry, it won't stretch. Add only enough flour to keep dough from sticking to your hands. To make dough in a food processor, mix dry ingredients in the processor bowl. With motor running, pour in egg mixture and pulse just to moisten dry ingredients. Then whirl dough until it's smooth, soft, and slightly tacky when touched, about 30 seconds; add a little flour if needed.

MAKES: 14 ounces

1. In a large bowl, mix 1⅔ cups **all-purpose flour** and ¼ teaspoon **salt.**

2. In another bowl, beat 1 **large egg,** 2 tablespoons melted **butter** or margarine, and ½ cup **warm water** to blend. Make a well in the center of the dry ingredients and pour egg mixture into it.

3. Stir liquid with a fork, gradually drawing in dry ingredients to moisten and make a soft dough.

4. Knead dough in bowl or on a lightly floured board (using just enough flour to prevent sticking) until dough feels smooth, supple, and slightly tacky when touched, about 5 minutes.

5. Pick up dough and slam down onto an unfloured board repeatedly until it feels very smooth and is not sticky, about 5 minutes.

6. Shape dough into a smooth oval and brush lightly with melted butter or margarine. Cover with plastic wrap and let rest at room temperature 20 to 40 minutes.

Filo Strudel

PREP AND COOK TIME: About 35 minutes

NOTES: If filo dough is frozen, thaw in the refrigerator at least 8 hours or overnight. For a head start and a crisp crust, up to 4 hours ahead, fill strudel, cover airtight, and chill. Uncover and bake to serve.

MAKES: 2 strudels; 12 to 18 servings total

> 12 sheets **filo dough** (about 12 by 18 in.)
>
> About ⅔ cup (⅓ lb.) melted **butter** or margarine
>
> **Filling** (recipes follow)
>
> **Powdered sugar** (optional)

LIFT CLOTH to roll delicate strudel dough, topped with a sweet or savory filling, into a compact roll.

1. On a 12- by 24-inch piece of plastic wrap, lay 1 filo sheet flat (cover remaining filo with plastic wrap to prevent drying) and brush lightly with melted butter. Top with another filo sheet and brush lightly with more butter. Repeat to stack a total of 6 sheets.

2. Spread ½ the filling in a 3-inch band across 1 long side of dough, 2 inches in from the edge and the sides. Fold long edge and the ends of dough over filling. Gently lift plastic wrap under filled side of dough, guiding it forward to form a compact roll, ending seam down. Repeat steps 1 and 2 with remaining filo and filling to roll second strudel.

3. Gently transfer strudel rolls, seams down, to a buttered baking sheet (14 by 17 in., preferably without a rim). Brush strudel tops with remaining melted butter.

4. Bake on the center rack in a 375° oven until golden brown all over, about 25 minutes (about 20 minutes in a convection oven).

5. Using 2 wide spatulas, slide strudels, 1 at a time, onto a platter. If filling is sweet, sprinkle lightly with powdered sugar. Cut into 1½-inch-wide slices.

Fruit-Chocolate Filling

PREP TIME: 20 minutes

NOTES: If making filling up to 2 days ahead, cover and chill.

MAKES: 4 cups

1. In a small bowl, mix ½ cup chopped **dried apricots,** ⅓ cup chopped **dried cranberries,** and 3 tablespoons **orange-flavor liqueur** or orange juice. Let stand 5 to 10 minutes, stirring several times.

2. In another bowl, beat 2 packages (8 oz. each) **neufchâtel** (light cream) **cheese** and ⅔ cup **sugar** until blended. Add 1 **large egg,** ¾ teaspoon grated **orange** peel, and ¼ teaspoon **ground cardamom;** beat until blended. Stir in dried fruit–liqueur mixture and ⅓ cup chopped **semi-sweet chocolate.**

Per serving with strudel dough: 253 cal., 50% (126 cal.) from fat; 4.9 g protein; 14 g fat (8.6 g sat.); 28 g carbo (0.9 g fiber); 208 mg sodium; 61 mg chol.

Per serving with filo dough: 229 cal., 59% (135 cal.) from fat; 4.1 g protein; 15 g fat (8.7 g sat.); 21 g carbo (0.6 g fiber); 235 mg sodium; 49 mg chol.

Prune-Almond Filling

PREP AND COOK TIME: About 20 minutes

NOTES: If making filling up to 2 days ahead, cover and chill.

MAKES: 4 cups

1. In a small bowl, mix ⅔ cup chopped **pitted prunes** and 3 tablespoons **rum** or brandy. Let stand 5 to 10 minutes, stirring several times.

2. In a 6- to 8-inch frying pan over medium heat, stir or shake ½ cup chopped **almonds** until golden, about 3 minutes. Pour from pan.

3. In a bowl, beat 2 packages (8 oz. each) **neufchâtel** (light cream) **cheese** until smooth. Add 1 **large egg**, ⅔ cup **sugar**, 1 teaspoon grated **lemon** peel, and 1 teaspoon **anise seed**; beat until blended. Stir in prune mixture and almonds.

Per serving with strudel dough: 256 cal., 53% (135 cal.) from fat; 5.5 g protein; 15 g fat (8.2 g sat.); 26 g carbo (1.2 g fiber); 208 mg sodium; 61 mg chol.

Per serving with filo dough: 232 cal., 62% (144 cal.) from fat; 4.7 g protein; 16 g fat (8.3 g sat.); 19 g carbo (0.8 g fiber); 235 mg sodium; 49 mg chol.

Caraway-Cheese Filling

PREP AND COOK TIME: About 40 minutes

NOTES: If making filling up to 2 days ahead, cover and chill.

MAKES: 4 cups

1. Peel and thinly slice 2 **onions** (1 lb. total). In a 5- to 6-quart pan, combine onions, ½ cup **vegetable broth** or fat-skimmed chicken broth, and 2 teaspoons **caraway seed**. Cover and cook over medium-high heat, stirring occasionally, until most of the liquid is evaporated, 15 to 20 minutes. Uncover pan and turn heat to high; stir often, scraping up brown film that forms on pan bottom, until onions are lightly browned, 8 to 10 minutes. Let cool.

2. In a bowl, beat 2 packages (8 oz. each) **neufchâtel** (light cream) **cheese** until smooth. Add 1 **large egg**; beat until blended. Stir in 2 cups (8 oz.) shredded **Swiss cheese** and onion mixture.

Per serving with strudel dough: 249 cal., 61% (153 cal.) from fat; 8.6 g protein; 17 g fat (10 g sat.); 16 g carbo (0.8 g fiber); 242 mg sodium; 72 mg chol.

Per serving with filo dough: 225 cal., 68% (153 cal.) from fat; 7.7 g protein; 17 g fat (10 g sat.); 10 g carbo (0.5 g fiber); 269 mg sodium; 61 mg chol.

Crab-Artichoke Filling

PREP TIME: About 20 minutes

NOTES: If making filling up to 1 day ahead, cover and chill.

MAKES: 4 cups

1. Drain and chop 1 can (14 oz.) **artichoke bottoms.**

2. In a bowl, beat 2 packages (8 oz.) **neufchâtel** (light cream) **cheese** until smooth. Add 1 **large egg**; beat until blended. Add ½ cup chopped **green onions**, 1 teaspoon chopped **fresh** or dried **tarragon leaves**, ¼ teaspoon **salt**, 2 cloves **garlic** (peeled and pressed or minced). Stir in artichokes and ½ pound **shelled cooked crab.**

Per serving with strudel dough: 214 cal., 55% (117 cal.) from fat; 7.8 g protein; 13 g fat (8.1 g sat.); 16 g carbo (0.8 g fiber); 337 mg sodium; 73 mg chol.

Per serving with filo dough: 190 cal., 66% (126 cal.) from fat; 7 g protein; 14 g fat (8.2 g sat.); 9.3 g carbo (0.4 g fiber); 364 mg sodium; 62 mg chol.

Curried Onion Filling

PREP AND COOK TIME: About 45 minutes

NOTES: If making up to 2 days ahead, cover and chill.

MAKES: 4 cups

1. Peel and thinly slice 3 **onions** (1½ lb. total).

2. In a 10- to 12-inch frying pan over medium-high heat, cook onions and ½ cup **vegetable broth**, covered, stirring occasionally, until most of the liquid is evaporated, 20 to 25 minutes. Uncover pan and turn heat to high; stir often, scraping up brown film that forms on pan bottom, until onions are lightly browned, 10 to 15 minutes.

3. Add 1 tablespoon **curry powder** and 1 teaspoon **ground coriander;** stir until fragrant, about 1 minute. Remove from heat, stir in ¼ cup chopped **Major Grey chutney** and ¼ cup **golden raisins**. Add **salt and pepper** to taste.

4. In a bowl, beat 2 packages (8 oz. each) **neufchâtel** (light cream) **cheese** until smooth. Add 1 **large egg**; beat until blended. Stir in onion mixture.

Per serving with strudel dough: 226 cal., 52% (117 cal.) from fat; 5.2 g protein; 13 g fat (8 g sat.); 22 g carbo (1.1 g fiber); 248 mg sodium; 61 mg chol.

Per serving with filo dough: 202 cal., 62% (126 cal.) from fat; 4.4 g protein; 14 g fat (8.1 g sat.); 15 g carbo (0.8 g fiber); 275 mg sodium; 49 mg chol. ◆

TO USE OUR NUTRITIONAL INFORMATION

The most current data from the USDA is used for our recipes: calorie count; fat calories; grams of protein, total and saturated fat, and carbohydrates; and milligrams of sodium and cholesterol.

This analysis is usually given for a single serving, based on the largest number of servings listed. Or it's for a specific amount, such as per tablespoon (for sauces); or by unit, as per cookie.

Optional ingredients are not included, nor are those for which no specific amount is stated (salt added to taste, for example). If an ingredient is listed with an alternative, calculations are based on the first choice listed. Likewise, if a range is given for the amount of an ingredient (such as ½ to 1 cup milk), values are figured on the first, lower amount.

Recipes using broth are calculated on the sodium content of salt-free broth, homemade or canned. If you use canned salted chicken broth, the sodium content will be higher.

Articles Index

Index of Recipe Titles

Low-Fat Recipes *(30 percent or less calories from fat)*

General Index

Sauce(s) (cont'd.)
crisp jicama guacamole, 188
Faz's herb, 188
for fish, 188
Grandma's tomato, 240
grapefruit beurre blanc, 189
grilled two-chili salsa, 189
hollandaise, 109
kiwi fruit salsa verde, 189
lime, 164
macadamia pesto, 189
mango-masala, 189
mustard-shallot, 297
mustard-tarragon, 140
paprika, 253
pickled cabbage relish, 189
pimiento, 217
pink grapefruit, 291
roasted tomato-caper, 189
romesco, with grilled lamb chops, 217
rosemary cream, with pork tenderloin, 119
sherry-almond, 189
shiitake mushroom, 253
sour cream onion, with green beans, 283
spicy peanut, 128
sweet plum, 165
wasabi mustard, with roast beef tenderloin, 320
wasabi, with salmon fettuccine, 16
Sauces for fish, 188
Sausage(s)
apricot dressing, 298
barley-mushroom soup, 291
chicken, linguisa, and vegetable soup, 43
Chinese, rice dressing, 295
Italian oven-fried meatballs, 233
-nut dressing, 298
chutney mustard for, 220
pie, 330
pilaf, 141
potato, fennel, and salami casserole, 40
potato "risotto" with broccoli and, 10
sloppy lasagna, 18
and spinach manicotti, 242
Savory rice with peas and cashews, 35
Savory squash and leek casserole, 45
Scallop and shrimp salad, grilled, 190
Scallops, poached, with dried-tomato orzo, 18
Scone secrets, 60
Scones, Jammer cream, 60
Scrambled eggs with asparagus, 92
Seabass, Chilean, with Thai-spiced mashed yams, 17
Senegalese apple soup, 63
Sesame dressing with beans, 198

Sesame-ginger salmon with braised bok choy, 311
Sesame teriyaki seasoning, for corn, 140
Sesame vegetables, roasted, 270
Shallot(s)
and caramelized onion cream soup, 63
fried, 115
-mustard sauce, 297
sherried, with gnocchi, 18
Shellfish. See also specific shell-fish
Basque steamed mussels, 30
Cambodian steamed mussels, 17
Dungeness crab risotto, 43
garlic butterflied shrimp, 149
grilled grapefruit-rosemary shrimp, 72
grilled scallop and shrimp salad, 190
marinated clams, 218
Mexican crab and corn soup, 30
Naga's crab cakes, 290
orange-fennel cioppino, 29
oysters on the half-shell with cilantro-ginger pesto, 317
poached scallops with dried-tomato orzo, 18
Portuguese clam and cilantro soup, 31
shrimp provençal, 116
shrimp with dried tomatoes and linguine, 116
Vietnamese sweet-sour shrimp soup, 31
Shepherd's pie, 19
Sherry-almond sauce, for fish, 189
Sherry and onions with lamb shanks, 244
Shiitake mushroom pan sauce, 253
Shortcake, English, 186
Shrimp
with black bean sauce, 117
cocktail sauce for, 221
with dried tomatoes and linguine, 116
egg drop soup with mustard greens, 14
with fettuccine, 44
garlic butterflied, 149
grape and pear salad cups, 230
grilled grapefruit-rosemary, 72
and grilled scallop salad, 190
kung pao risotto, 16
lemon-basil, with rice, 117
-mango tostadas, 11
with peanut-coconut soup, 90
provençal, 116
satay, 127
tumble with lettuce, 141
Vietnamese sweet-sour soup, 31

Shrimp chips, 125
Shrimp-flavor crackers, 126
Skirt steaks, orange-soy, 148
Slaw
apple, 19
green papaya and carrot, 106
the other, 138
radish, 66
Slush, peach-orange, 92
Smelt and fennel in prosciutto, 187
Smoked salmon sushi salad, 81
Smoothie, berry rice, 87
Smoothie, oat breakfast, 87
Snowmen, marshmallow, 305
Sole casserole, green chili, 249
Sole with creamed mushrooms, 189
Sorbet, papaya, 107
Soto ayam, 114
Soto resah, 115
Soufflé, raspberry-macaroon, 130
Soufflés, cheddar-garlic porta-bella, 99
Soup. See also Chowder; Stew
barley-mushroom, 291
Basque steamed mussels, 30
beet bisque with apple-herb salsa, 264
beggar's bundle, 14
black and gold, 11
cannellini and penne, 277
caramelized onion and shallot cream, 63
chard, bean, and pancetta, 244
chicken, linguisa, and vegetable, 43
cream of mushroom, 87
French onion, 243
ginger carrot, 332
lamb, 141
Mexican crab and corn, 30
orange-fennel cioppino, 29
oyster stew, 265
papaya gazpacho, 105
pasta and fresh bean, 200
peanut-coconut, with shrimp, 90
Portuguese clam and cilantro, 31
potato-fennel, 62
roasted fennel and potato with blue cheese croutons, 264
Senegalese apple, 63
soto ayam, 114
soto resah, 115
squash-peanut, 280
tarragon pea, 63
tortilla, 13
Vietnamese sweet-sour shrimp, 31
white chicken chili, 12
wild rice and mushroom, 62
Sour cream cucumber salad, 78
Southwest orzo and bean salad, 211

Soy and ginger flank steak, 246
Soy-orange skirt steaks, 148
Soy sauce, sweet, 126
Spaghetti and meatballs, 18
Spanish herbed fries, 217
Spiced nuts, sweet-, 315
Spice-dusted papaya, 106
Spice mixtures for gifts, 310
Spice paste, Balinese, 125
Spicy applesauce bread, 304
Spiedini di mozzarella, 98
Spinach
braised, with salt and pepper bass, 311
creamed, with pernod, 132
loaf, hot ricotta, 257
noodles provençal, 162
-parmesan dip, baked, 93
and plum salad, hot, 165
and radicchio salad with grapefruit, 332
with refried beans, 151
salad, 221
salad, purple flash, 135
salad, warm, 10
and sausage manicotti, 242
Sponge cake, 329
Spread, blue cheese with spiced walnuts, 65
Spring vegetable tart, Lavande, 109
Spumoni wreaths, 327
Squash
banana, with chilies and ginger, 271
black and gold soup, 11
filling for chimichangas, 255
golden lasagna, 250
-peanut soup, 280
savory, and leek casserole, 44
Star fruit, wands with vanilla-rum syrup, 56
Steak, garlic flank, 210
Steak sandwich platter, teriyaki, 222
Steaks, orange-soy skirt, 148
Steak with apricots, 138
Stew. See also Chowder; Soup
lamb and mushroom, 43
lentil-barley, 245
oyster, 265
turkey chipotle masa, 13
Stir-fry, lemon-chicken, 15
St. Paddy's potatoes with green sauce, 59
Strawberries, fruit wands with vanilla-rum syrup, 56
Strawberries, marinated, with mint, 51
Strawberry and chocolate pavlovas, 19
Strawberry-begonia salad, 136
Strudel, 334–336
Sugar, five-spice, 310
Sugar-glazed blueberries, 155
Sunchoke dip, 55
Sundaes, cream puff, 53
Sundaes, papaya–kiwi fruit, 107
Sushi rice salad, 81